A GUIDE TO DOING STATISTICS IN SECOND LANGUAGE RESEARCH USING SPSS AND R

This valuable book shows second language researchers how to use the statistical program SPSS to conduct statistical tests frequently done in second language acquisition (SLA) research. This second edition has additional information on how to use the statistical program R, which is free and strongly supported by statisticians. Using data sets from real SLA studies, this book shows newcomers to both statistics and SPSS or R how to generate descriptive statistics, choose a statistical test, and conduct and interpret a variety of basic statistical tests including *t*-tests, correlation, multiple regression and analysis of variance (ANOVA). In addition, this book represents an excellent way for readers already familiar with the SPSS program to cross a bridge into using the more versatile R program. It will gently bring readers along step by step, first with a graphical user interface for R, and slowly into understanding and using R code directly. Robust tests, including bootstrapping, that help researchers avoid problems with violating assumptions about the shape of their data are included. The text is abundantly illustrated with graphs and tables depicting actual data sets, and exercises throughout the book help readers understand concepts (such as the difference between independent and dependent variables) and work out statistical analyses.

Jenifer Larson-Hall is a Second Language Acquisition researcher and Lecturer of English as a Second Language at Fukuoka JoGakuin University, Japan.

Second Language Acquisition Research Series

Susan M. Gass and Alison Mackey, Series Editors

Monographs on Theoretical Issues:

Schachter/Gass Second Language Classroom Research: Issues and Opportunities (1996)
Birdsong Second Language Acquisition and the Critical Period Hypotheses (1999)
Ohta Second Language Acquisition Processes in the Classroom: Learning Japanese (2001)
Major Foreign Accent: Ontogeny and Phylogeny of Second Language Phonology (2001)
VanPatten Processing Instruction: Theory, Research, and Commentary (2003)
VanPatten/Williams/Rott/Overstreet Form–Meaning Connections in Second Language Acquisition (2004)
Bardovi-Harlig/Hartford Interlanguage Pragmatics: Exploring Institutional Talk (2005)
Dörnyei The Psychology of the Language Learner: Individual Differences in Second Language Acquisition (2005)
Long Problems in SLA (2007)
VanPatten/Williams Theories in Second Language Acquisition (2007)
Ortega/Byrnes The Longitudinal Study of Advanced L2 Capacities (2008)
Liceras/Zobl/Goodluck The Role of Formal Features in Second Language Acquisition (2008)
Philp/Adams/Iwashita Peer Interaction and Second Language Learning (2013)
VanPatten/Williams Theories in Second Language Acquisition, Second Edition (2014)
Leow Explicit Learning in the L2 Classroom (2015)
Dörnyei/Ryan The Psychology of the Language Learner – Revisited (2015)

Monographs on Research Methodology:

Tarone/Gass/Cohen Research Methodology in Second Language Acquisition (1994)
Yule Referential Communication Tasks (1997)
Gass/Mackey Stimulated Recall Methodology in Second Language Research (2000)
Markee Conversation Analysis (2000)
Gass/Mackey Data Elicitation for Second and Foreign Language Research (2007)
Duff Case Study Research in Applied Linguistics (2007)
McDonough/Trofimovich Using Priming Methods in Second Language Research (2008)
Larson-Hall A Guide to Doing Statistics in Second Language Research Using SPSS (2009)
Dörnyei /Taguchi Questionnaires in Second Language Research: Construction, Administration, and Processing, Second Edition (2009)
Bowles The Think-Aloud Controversy in Second Language Research (2010)
Jiang Conducting Reaction Time Research for Second Language Studies (2011)
Barkhuizen/Benson/Chik Narrative Inquiry in Language Teaching and Learning Research (2013)
Jegerski/VanPatten Research Methods in Second Language Psycholinguistics (2013)
Larson-Hall A Guide to Doing Statistics in Second Language Research Using SPSS and R, Second Edition (2015)
Plonsky Advancing Quantitative Methods in Second Language Research (2015)

Of Related Interest:

Gass Input, Interaction, and the Second Language Learner (1997)
Gass/Sorace/Selinker Second Language Learning Data Analysis, Second Edition (1998)
Mackey/Gass Second Language Research: Methodology and Design (2005)
Gass/Selinker Second Language Acquisition: An Introductory Course, Third Edition (2008)

A GUIDE TO DOING STATISTICS IN SECOND LANGUAGE RESEARCH USING SPSS AND R

Second Edition

Jenifer Larson-Hall
Fukuoka JoGakuin University

Routledge
Taylor & Francis Group
LONDON AND NEW YORK

First published 2016
by Routledge
711 Third Avenue, New York, NY 10017

and by Routledge
2 Park Square, Milton Park, Abingdon, Oxon, OX14 4RN

Routledge is an imprint of the Taylor & Francis Group, an informa business

Library of Congress Cataloging in Publication Data
A catalog record for this book has been requested

ISBN: 978-1-138-02456-4 (hbk)
ISBN: 978-1-138-02457-1 (pbk)
ISBN: 978-1-315-77566-1 (ebk)

Typeset in Goudy
by Swales & Willis Ltd, Exeter, Devon, UK

For Andrew, who doesn't care much about numbers, but who has made my life quantitatively better

CONTENTS

PREFACE

I wrote this book for myself. I remember being a graduate student, working on my dissertation and struggling to make sense of the statistics I needed to analyze my dissertation. I wanted a book to help me understand SPSS that would use examples from my field, but none existed. This book was born of that longing. This book is written to help those new to the field of statistics feel they have some idea of what they are doing when they analyze their own data, and how to do it using a statistical program.

In the first edition of the book only SPSS was included. In this edition, the statistical programs SPSS and R are illustrated side by side so that those who want to use SPSS can continue to do so, those who know SPSS but want to learn R can do so more easily, and those who want to start learning statistics with R can also do so. I originally wrote the book that way, and I am pleased to have that format now, although it makes the book quite a bit larger. Including R increased the size enough that I needed to cut down the finished product in my revised edition. I have thus cut out most of the sections that were formerly labeled "Advanced Topic," as well as the three chapters on chi-square, analysis of covariance (ANCOVA) and non-parametric statistics. In my experience, chi-square and ANCOVA are not used as frequently in second language acquisition (SLA) as the other statistical tests that remain in the second edition. Nevertheless, they are good and useful chapters, so if you need information on them, please look at them online! I was especially pleased with the many interesting graphics that are available for the categorical variables that are found in the Chi-Square chapter, so if you need any of those, take a look online. I cut out the Non-Parametric Statistics (i.e. the classical types of non-parametric statistics, such as the Kruskal–Wallis or Mann–Whitney U tests). I judged that robust statistics, which are mostly non-parametric, would be better substitutes than these tests, but the chapter is still available online, if readers would prefer these traditional tests. There are also alternative ways of conducting tests (usually in R), such as the sections cut from Chapter 11 on RM-ANOVA, which tell how to use mixed-effect models instead of the least-squares approach.

I have included a graphical user interface to R called R Commander. I think this program makes it easier to work into R, but there are many places in the book where you will need to go to the R Console (the command-line interface) to do things in the book, so I have tried to ease the reader into the R code by showing the code from any R Commander menu choices, and explaining the parts of these. There are quite a number of advantages, as I see it, to learning R instead of SPSS if you are just learning about statistics:

- It is free.
- It is supported by the statistical community and, as such, continues to be updated with new packages that can do different things.
- R has more sophisticated analyses and is extremely strong in the area of graphics.
- Using command syntax for statistics helps users understand better what they are doing in the statistical analysis.

Some users may be concerned that because R is free, that means it is of low quality. Muenchen (2008) noted that, at the time, comparisons of R with SPSS found that the quality of R was just as high as SPSS, and that the R base packages were reviewed and revised just as carefully as SPSS. (This is not necessarily true for all the R packages, however, and Muenchen noted that you can find reviews of individual packages at http://crantastic.org/.)

Muenchen also noted that R could do everything that SPSS could do and more, and if you bought a commercial copy of SPSS with all of the functionality of R, it would cost tens of thousands of dollars. In Japan, where I am currently working at a university, access to SPSS is not automatic and requires purchase of an individual site license. Perhaps your institution does not mind spending over USD100,000 for licenses for multiple users. However, as more institutions seek to pare down expenses, learning R (which can do everything that SPSS can do) makes more and more sense.

Now that I can use R, I have included information about how to conduct various kinds of robust statistics in the book, although some of the sections on robust analyses in R have had to be moved online. For more information on how to do robust analyses in different ways, see those online sections. Currently, SPSS can perform bootstrapping, and I have shown how to do that in this book, but there are several other robust tests that can only be performed in R. It is true that SPSS has a way to run R, but one must use scripts to do so, and I have not felt moved to try to figure this system out, feeling that if one is going to learn scripts, one might just as well start using R. In addition, SPSS cannot run the current version of R and is instead using R from a number of versions back. (R releases come out twice a year.)

I am a strong advocate for using robust statistics, which basically rely on the techniques of parametric statistics but use computer-intensive techniques that eliminate the requirement that data be normally distributed (an assumption that probably is often not true in our field; see Larson-Hall & Herrington, 2009).

Almost all of the data sets analyzed in the book and the application activities are real data, gathered from recently published articles or theses. I am deeply grateful to these authors for allowing me to use their data, and I feel strongly that those who publish work based on a statistical analysis of the data should make that data available to others. The statistical analysis one does can affect the types of hypotheses and theories that go forward in our field, but we can all recognize that most of us are not statistical experts and we may make some mistakes in our analyses. Providing the raw data serves as a way to check that analyses are done properly, and, if provided at the submission stage, errors can be caught early. I do want to note, however, that authors who have made their data sets available for this book have done so in order for readers to follow along with the analyses in the book and do application activities. If you wanted to do any other kind of analysis on your own that would be published using these data, you should contact the authors and ask for permission to either coauthor or use their data (depending on your purposes).

This book was updated with the most recent version of IBM SPSS Statistics available at the time of writing, and I was working on a PC. As of this writing, the most recent version of SPSS was 22.0 (2013). SPSS 22 is quite different in some ways from previous versions, and for those who may be working with an older version I have tried to provide some guidance about possible differences. I have used small capitals to distinguish commands in SPSS and R and make them stand out on the page. For example, if you need to first open the File menu and then choose the Print option, I would write FILE > PRINT.

I also used the most recent version of R, which was version 3.1.3 (released 9 March 2015) and R Commander version 2.1–7 (released 19 February 2015). I used R on both a PC and a Mac. Because these programs are updated frequently, there may be some times especially when certain packages do not work. I urge you at those times to google the package and see what might have replaced it.

I have written this book mainly as a way for those totally new to statistics to understand some of the most basic statistical tests that are widely used in the field of SLA and applied linguistics. I suggest that the best way to read most chapters is to open the data sets that are included with the book and work along with me in SPSS or R. You can learn a lot just by recreating what you see me do in the text. The application activities will then help you move on to try the analysis by yourself, but I have included detailed answers to all activities so you can check what you are doing. My ultimate goal, of course, is that eventually you will be able to apply the techniques to your own data. I assume that readers of this book will be familiar with how to use Microsoft Windows or Mac OS X and pull-down menus, and how to open and close files. These data files will be available on the website that accompanies this book. SPSS files have the .sav extension, while most R files are .csv, which are comma-delimited text files.

Some sections in the chapters are labeled "Advanced Topic." These sections can be skipped by novices who are already feeling overwhelmed by the regular statistics, but they provide additional information or justifications for choices I have made to the more statistically knowledgeable readers.

For the novice to statistics, the book is meant to be read in chronological order for both parts of the book. Part I introduces the fundamental concepts in statistics that are necessary to beginning a statistical analysis. Part II then provides information in individual chapters about basic statistical procedures that are commonly used in second language research. In some cases these chapters also build upon one another, although users who are familiar with statistics and just looking up information on one specific technique can skip directly to the relevant chapter.

Part I consists of four chapters. In Chapter 1, I start things off by telling you how to set yourself up with SPSS or R and how to start entering data and manipulating it. One important point here is how to deal with missing data. It seems most researchers believe they need to throw out incomplete data but I find many statisticians enthusiastic about the use of missing-data imputation, and there are sophisticated statistical methods to do so. If your data are missing at random, this is a better choice than eliminating partial data entries that researchers have worked hard to gather, so if you do not know about imputation, be sure to take a look at Chapter 1. Throughout the book important terms are highlighted in bold, and summaries of their meanings are found in the glossary. In Chapter 2, I discuss some essential ideas that are necessary to understanding further chapters, such as identifying whether variables are independent or dependent and what null hypothesis testing is. Hidden statistical assumptions authors have are revealed in this chapter and can help those new to statistics to better understand the statistical jargon that they will often see. In Chapter 3, I show how to produce numerical summaries of data, such as means, medians and standard deviations, and how to check for measures that might indicate problems with standard statistical assumptions, such as a normal distribution and equal variances for all groups. Graphic ways of evaluating the same types of information have been intentionally placed in the same chapter, for I feel that graphic summaries are just as informative as, if not more so, numerical summaries, and I argue strongly for more use of graphic summaries in our research. Chapter 4 is the result of my first reading many papers that argue that we are often on the wrong track with our statistical analyses when we rely on a single dichotomous measure such as a *p* value (less or greater than 0.05) to tell us whether our results are important, and then reading Geoff Cumming's recent (2012) book called *Understanding the New Statistics*. Cumming is persuasive and clear in his argument that we need to bring better ways of measuring and hypothesizing about our data into use, and this includes mostly confidence intervals and effect sizes. In the first edition, I did urge readers to use confidence intervals, but I did not understand then as well as I do now, thanks to Cumming, how to do so in a way that actually used the confidence intervals differently from *p* values. I hope the information in this chapter conveys the beauty of confidence intervals, the problems with *p* values and the excitement I feel about the "new statistics" to you as well as Cumming did to me (and I do urge you to read Cumming for more information!).

In Chapter 5, I lay out the different statistical tests that will be covered in Part II. I provide information about how to choose a test, depending on the questions and the types of data you have. I illustrate how these statistical tests are used in actual studies in second language research. I hope this will help you understand the differences between the tests, although you should know that figuring out statistics does take some time and you should not expect to be an expert after reading Chapter 5! But maybe you will have a small inkling of how the various tests are used. In the remaining six chapters of

Part II, I go over various types of statistical analyses that are common in the field of second language research. In Chapter 6, I cover correlation; in Chapter 7, I introduce the reader to multiple regression; in Chapter 8, I look at *t*-tests; in Chapter 9, I look at the one-way analysis of variance (ANOVA); and in Chapter 10, I extend ANOVA to the case where there is more than one independent variable (factorial ANOVA). In Chapter 11, I extend ANOVA even further to the case where there are repeated measures. Three more chapters are available online: Chi-Square, ANCOVA (an ANOVA analysis with covariates) and Non-Parametric Tests. In general, the chapters go from conceptually easier tests to more difficult ones, although this is not true for regression analysis.

Writing this book has given me a great appreciation for the vast world of statistics, which I do not pretend to be a master of. Like our own field of second language research, the field of statistics is always evolving and progressing, and there are controversies throughout it as well. If I have advocated an approach that is not embraced by the statistical community wholeheartedly, I have tried to provide reasons for my choice and additional reading that can be done on the topic. Although I have tried my hardest to make this book accessible and helpful for readers, I would appreciate being informed of any typos or errors in this book or answers to application activities, or any areas where my explanations have not been clear enough. Because of the watchful eye of many readers, I am convinced that this edition would be error-free if I were simply updating the SPSS version. But because I have added in a whole new statistical program, there are bound to be places where I have again made mistakes. I understand that this is frustrating, especially when you are trying to learn a new topic, and I apologize in advance. I cannot give you a free copy of the book if you catch things, but I hope you will feel the satisfaction of helping others if you do find something and pass it along. Please check the website for errata as I will post these as readers send them to me.

ACKNOWLEDGMENTS

I would like to thank the many individuals who have helped me to write this book. First is Richard Herrington, who guided and helped me discover many treasures of statistics, including R. He provided many articles, many answers and just fun philosophizing along the way. Susan Gass and Alison Mackey were instrumental in helping me get this book accepted into the Second Language Acquisition Research Series and providing encouragement. Elysse Preposi and Leah Babb-Rosenfeld, editors at Routledge, were very helpful in the laborious process of getting the book into its best form possible and I appreciate their warm help. Many thanks to the students in my Research Methods courses who provided feedback on the book in its various stages. I also thank the reviewers of the book for their careful work in reading the manuscript and providing useful feedback. A number of readers of the first edition helpfully sent me corrections, the most thorough and enthusiastic being Gabriele Pallotti from Italy, whose notes of a careful reading of the entire book were quite helpful. Other readers who have written more recently and whose names are thus not lost to the mists of time include Yves Bestgen, Tuan Phu, Matthias Raess and Lawrence Cheung. I sincerely appreciate their help, and the only reason I am sorry to be expanding this book and including R is that there will most likely be a number more mistakes that will occur. I welcome input on this and apologize in advance. I again want to profusely thank the authors who have given permission for the reproduction of their data in the examples presented in the book. They are cited individually in their respective chapters, but I feel this book is much more relevant and interesting to readers because of the data that they provided me with. Last but not least is my family who did not see much of me in the final stages of finishing this revision, and were very patient in giving me the time to get it finished. A special thank you to my son, Lachlan, who graphed out the data for the small multiples figure in the online chapter on ANCOVA.

Part I

Statistical Ideas

Chapter 1

Getting Started with the Software and Using the Computer for Experimental Details

> In my view R is such a versatile tool for scientific computing that anyone contemplating a career in science, and who expects to [do] their own computations that have a substantial data analysis component, should learn R.
>
> John Maindonald (R Help thread, 5 January 2006)

In this chapter I will provide instructions for getting started with both SPSS and R. SPSS—now owned by the IBM corporation and called IBM SPSS Statistics—is probably the most commonly used statistical program in the field of social sciences for which it was originally developed, and is used by many researchers working in the field of second language research. It uses a graphical user interface (GUI) with drop-down menus that should be familiar to those who use programs such as Microsoft Word or Excel. I will also explain how to get started with R, which is the programming language and software environment most statisticians use and has grown greatly in popularity in the last decade, including with linguists. (See an R-lang mailing list created by Roger Levy in 2007, which also contains an archive of all prior messages.) By itself R does not have an intuitive GUI, but in this book I will show you how to use a GUI called R Commander that will help simplify the use of R for beginners.

In this chapter I will first explain how to physically get started by opening the software and either importing or entering your own **data** into a spreadsheet. (Data are the information you have.) Another important part of getting started is being able to save data. Once you have some data to work with, this chapter then goes on to explain ways you might like to manipulate your data, such as combining columns or calculating percentages, filtering out some cases of participants that you do not want to include in the analysis, or creating new groups from existing columns of data. I will also give you some help as to what to do if you have missing data, and finally, some resources for getting more help with these programs. The SPSS instructions throughout have been tested only with a PC (not Mac) with SPSS. The R instructions have been tested on both a PC and a Mac and any differences between these platforms will be noted in the text or on the website.

1.1 Getting Started with SPSS

First, open SPSS by either clicking on the SPSS icon IBM SPSS Statistics 22 or going through the Programs menu from Windows. When you open SPSS you will see an "SPSS Data Editor" as in Figure 1.1, which looks like a spreadsheet for entering data. In SPSS version 10.0 and later, before you get to the **Data Editor** you will have a pop-up window which tries to help you get started. Usually you will choose either to type in new data or to open up an existing data set, like the ones provided for this book. Data files saved using SPSS have the extension .sav.

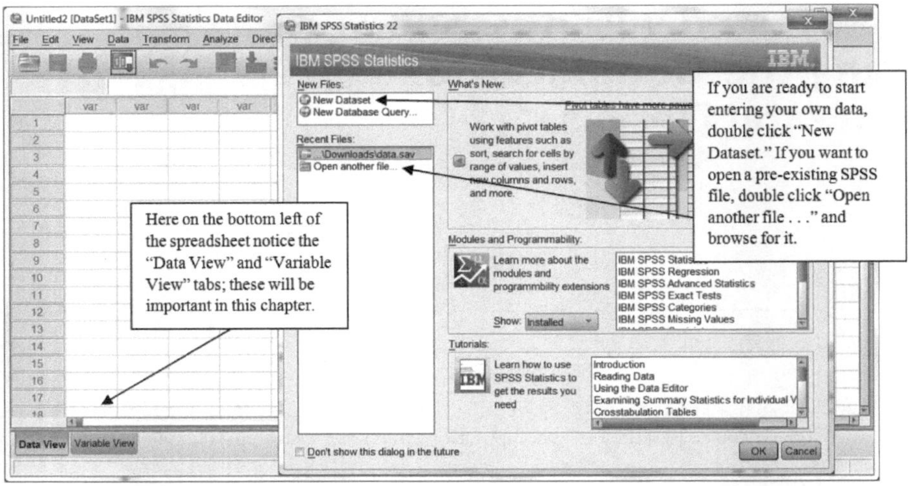

Figure 1.1 What you'll see when starting up SPSS.

Note that there are two tabs in the Data Editor at the bottom of the spreadsheet. One is the "**Data View**," which is the default view. The other is the "**Variable View**." If you click on this tab, you will see a different spreadsheet that is used to enter specific information about your variables, such as their names, type and number of decimal points you want to see, among others.

SPSS has two different types of windows. One is the Data Editor, which looks like a spreadsheet and is where you enter your data. The other type of window is where any output appears. This window is called the "Statistics Viewer." In SPSS, any calls to perform data analysis, such as creating a graph, doing a statistical test or creating a table result in objects automatically appearing in the Statistics Viewer (see Figure 1.2). If you save data from the Statistics Viewer, these files have a .spv extension.

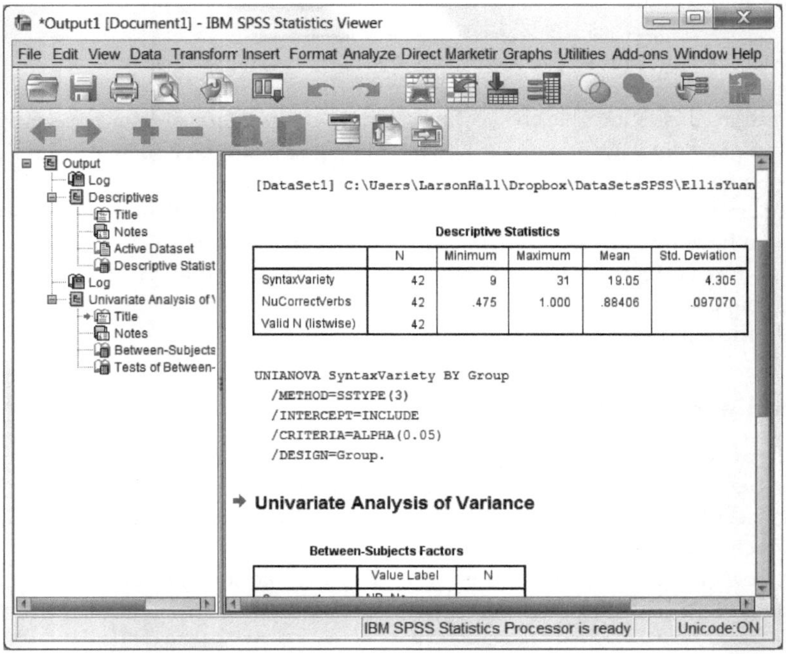

Figure 1.2 The Statistics Viewer window.

(Versions of SPSS older than 16.0 created .spo files as the output files, and these cannot be opened in SPSS 16 unless you install the SPSS 15.0 Smart Viewer, available on the installation CD, according to the SPSS help files.)

Section 1.1 deals with entering and importing data into SPSS as well as saving files. If you want information about and practice with manipulating variables in SPSS, such as moving columns or rows or simply deleting them, combining two or more variables into one variable, recoding groups or excluding cases from your data, see the online section titled "Manipulating variables in SPSS."

1.1.1 Opening a Data File

Once you have SPSS open, I am sure you will want to get started trying to do things! If you have not used the initial pop-up menu shown in Figure 1.1 to open a file that has already been created, you can also do this through the menus using the sequence FILE > OPEN > DATA and then navigating to the .sav file you want. If you do this, you will see that the spreadsheet in the SPSS Data Editor becomes filled with data, as shown in Figure 1.3.

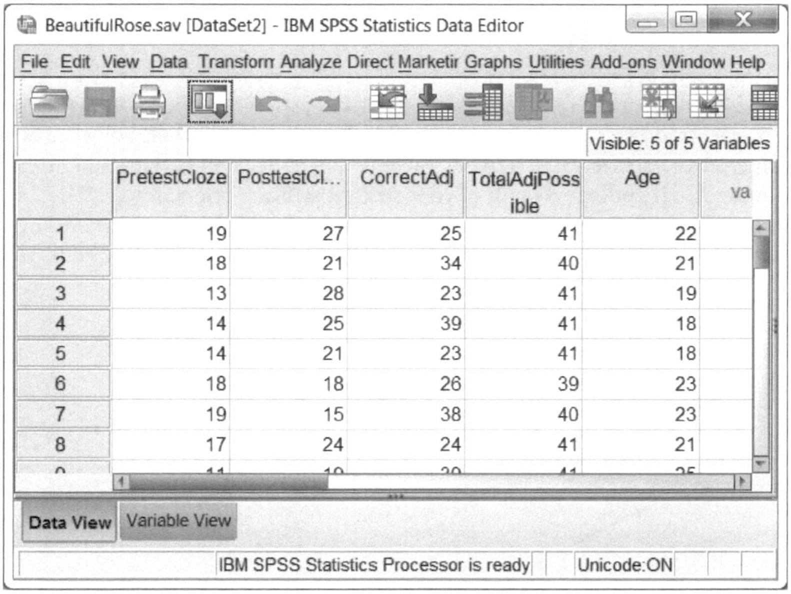

Figure 1.3 The Data Editor in "Data View" ("Data View" tab is highlighted at bottom) with data in it.

1.1.2 Entering Your Own Data

If you are going to create your own data file and would like to open a new spreadsheet through the menu system then you would go to FILE > NEW > DATA, which opens a blank spreadsheet. Since SPSS version 16.0, whenever you carry out any command through the menu system, the SPSS syntax for that command is documented in the Statistics Viewer. For example, Figure 1.4 shows the Viewer after opening up a new file.

There are a few things you need to know about data entry before you start inputting your numbers:

- Rows in SPSS are cases. This means that each participant should occupy one row.
- Columns in SPSS are separate variables, such as ID number, score on a test or category in a certain group.
- You can name each case (participant) by making your first column the ID number of each participant.

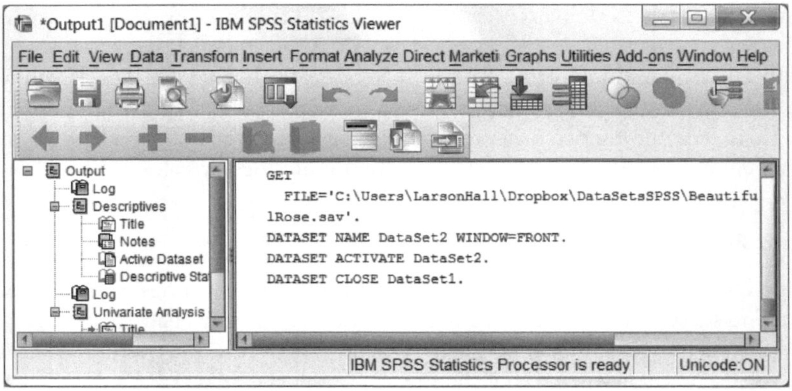

Figure 1.4 Command syntax appears in the Statistics Viewer whenever you use a menu sequence, even just opening a blank spreadsheet, as shown here.

Your first step in entering data is to define the columns, which are your variables. To do this, go to the "Variable View" tab in the lower left-hand corner of the spreadsheet, shown in Figure 1.5 (the format of the spreadsheet will change, and the tab that says "Variable View" will turn yellow). As I will be talking about variables a lot, let me define them here. A **variable** is a collection of data that all belong to the same sort. For example, the ID numbers of all of your participants are one variable. Their scores on a certain test will be another variable. If the participants belonged to a certain experimental group, that group will be another variable. You can see that a variable, then, can consist of a collection of numbers, non-numeric labels (such as "control" or "group 1"), or just a string of information (such as MQ433 in a participant label).

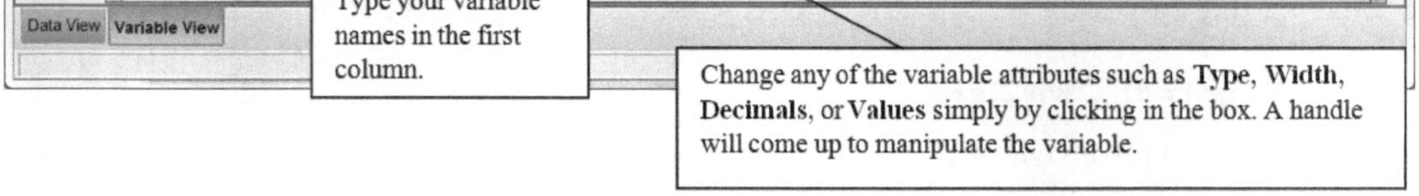

Figure 1.5 Variable view in SPSS (click the "Variable View" tab at the bottom left corner).

In the Data Editor, when you are looking at the Variable View, you will see the following columns:

Name

When you are naming your variables, you want to give them informative names to make it easier to remember what information is contained in each column. Here are a few things to remember about naming your variables:

- Names can be up to 64 bytes long, resulting in 64 characters for most languages or 32 characters for languages like Japanese, Chinese or Korean (previous versions of SPSS, up to version 12.0, allowed only eight characters).
- Names cannot start with a number.
- Names cannot contain certain characters that are used in SPSS syntax, such as a slash "/", question mark "?", exclamation point "!" or quantity sign ">" or "<"). On the other hand, the underscore sign (_), periods and the number sign (#) are fine.
- Names cannot contain blank spaces, such as "My Data File."

When trying to give your variables informative names it is probably a good idea to use the "every word capitalized" convention, for example, "EnglishSpeakingTest." This convention makes it easy to read the words. Current versions of SPSS are case-sensitive and will preserve capitalization.

Type

The Type column defines your type of variable. The default choice is Numeric, which means your variable will be a number and can be used in statistical calculations. If you want to make your variable a different type, click on the right side of the cell and a small gray box like the following will appear: Numeric ... . If you click on the box you will see a choice of many different types of variables, as shown in Figure 1.6.

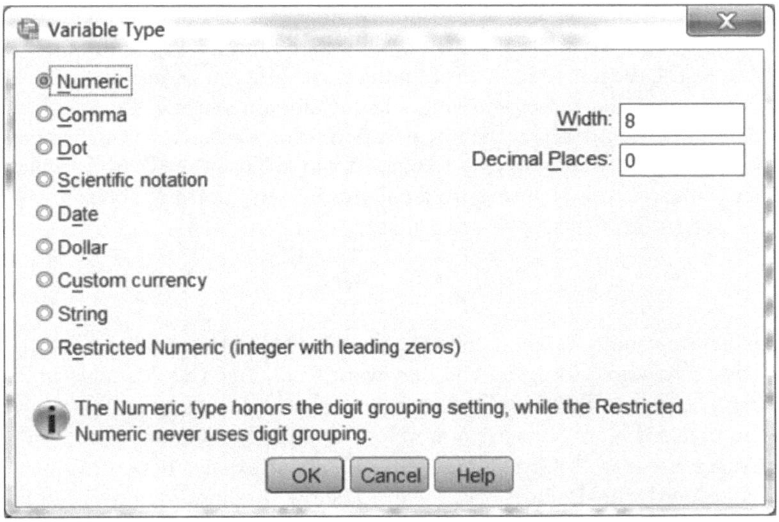

Figure 1.6 Variable type choices in the "Variable View" tab of the Data Editor.

I have never actually used any other types besides Numeric and String. The Restricted Numeric choice is not one you will probably want (this choice was not available in SPSS version 16). It adds zeros to fill out the width of the variable, values are restricted to non-negative integers and you can enter values using scientific notation. So, whereas the number 19 might appear when using the Numeric choice, in Restricted Numeric it would look like 00000019, if your column width was set to the default of eight digits.

In SPSS, **string variables** are used for non-quantitative information you want to enter, such as names or comments. Your alphanumeric ID number might also be a string. Be careful, because string variables can generally not be used in statistical analyses. To make a categorical factor that you can use in statistical analyses, choose a numeric variable that you make categorical by labeling your participants' groups with a number (e.g. 1 = male and 2 = female) and then defining what each number means in the Values column.

Width

The Width column specifies how many characters should be displayed in the column. For most numbers you will not need anything wider than the default eight characters (see Figure 1.7).

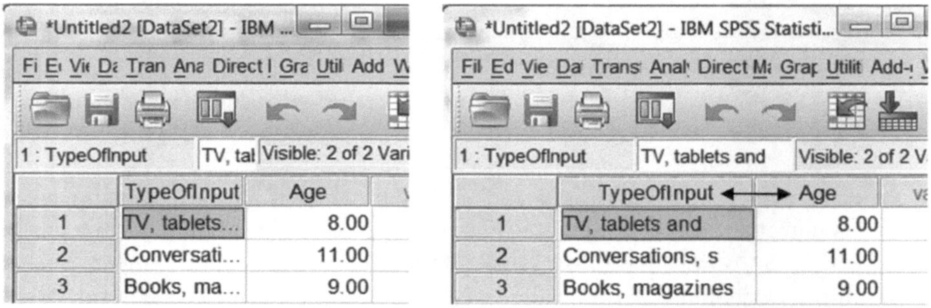

Figure 1.7 **How the width of the column limits the number of characters.**

However, if you have a string (treated as just words, not numbers, by SPSS) you might want to increase the width of the column. For example, Figure 1.7 shows a column, "TypeOfInput," which has a width of 16 characters. In the default size of the column on the left you cannot actually see all 16 characters, but the "..." indicates that more data is included than you can see. To see all of the characters that are entered, just put the mouse on the line between columns—an arrow will appear (as shown in Figure 1.7) and you can pull the column over to make it wider. Thus the Width specification limits how many characters you can actually enter into a column but says nothing about how many you can actually see.

Decimals

The Decimals column specifies how many decimal points to show for Numeric variables. The default is two decimal points. If you have whole integers, you may want to change the decimals to 0. You can change the default to 0 by going to Edit > Options and then select the Data tab. Under the area labeled "Display Format for New Numeric Variables" change the decimal place to 0. You can change the default width here as well. One potential problem with 0 as a default, however, is that, if you enter in data that has decimal places, SPSS cannot show that, and will round numbers up or down, so that 1.5 becomes 2 and 1.1 becomes 1. Do not worry! The actual number you entered is still there; you just need to see it by telling SPSS to show you more decimal places.

Label

The fifth column in the Variable View, the Label column, is for giving a variable a more detailed name. This column is pretty much a holdover from the days when SPSS only let variable names be eight characters long, and you may have wanted to type in something more descriptive so when you came back to your data set after a long absence you would know what the variable was. At this point, you should consider whether you want a label with extra information that is not contained in your variable name. On the one hand, this might be useful later on if your variable name is abbreviated or shortened. On the other hand, labels can sometimes be distracting. This is because in current versions of SPSS the label, and not the variable name, will appear in various places, such as the name of the variable when you are conducting your analysis, or on output printouts and may prove cumbersome for interpreting data if you type a name that is too long, although you can change whether the label is seen at all by going to the EDIT > OPTIONS, and in the GENERAL tab choosing to "Display names."

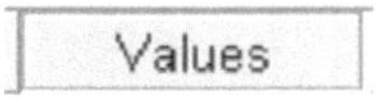

I have already told you that if you have a category like group membership or gender, you will need to enter this as numbers, so that all females might be labeled 1 and all the males 2. But how will you remember which is which? If you enter this information as a string, say by using "M" and "F," you will not be able to use the variable to conduct statistical analyses, so you definitely want to enter the information by labeling each category with a number as a Numeric variable. However, these numbers will not be very informative to you later, especially if you come back to your data file years later. The thing to do in SPSS is to give your variable Values. Click on the cell under the Values column that you want to define, and a gray handle will appear on the right-hand side of the box like this: None ... . Click the gray handle once to open it, and you will see a box as in Figure 1.8. Enter the value and the label, and then click on ADD. Go back to the "Value" and "Label" boxes to add more definitions as needed. The CHANGE and REMOVE buttons below ADD can be useful if, at a later time, you want to edit your definitions or remove some categories.

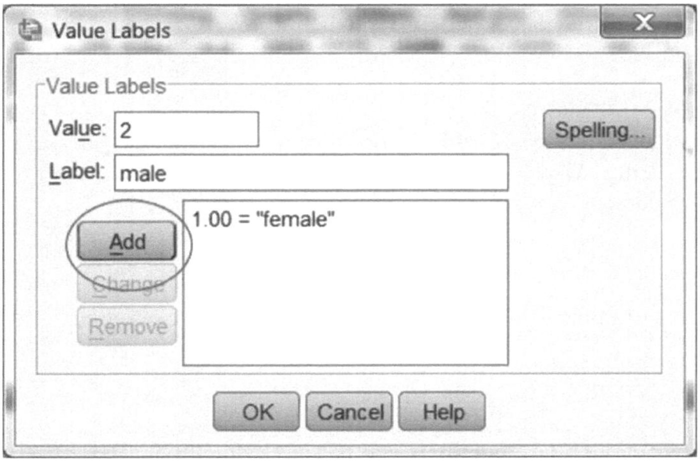

Figure 1.8 Defining values for variables in SPSS.

Tip 1: If you are going to be setting up the same values for more than one row of data in the Variable View it is easy to copy the values from one variable to another. In Variable View, first set up the values for one variable. Right-click on that box with the values (like this box: {1.00, Under...) and a menu will come up (don't right-click on the grey handle; instead, click anywhere else in the white cell). The menu has the choice of COPY or PASTE. Copy the variable values you want, then go to the cell under the Values column where you want to apply the same values, right-click on the white cell, and choose PASTE.

> **Tip:** There is a way to customize many aspects of SPSS. For example, let us say that you do not expect most of your variables to need any decimal points, but the default for SPSS is two decimal places. Use the EDIT > OPTIONS menu choice. In the OPTIONS box you will see lots of places where you can customize the way SPSS looks, including:
>
> - whether names or labels are displayed in the output (GENERAL tab);
> - the language used (LANGUAGE tab);
> - the fonts used in titles and output (VIEWER tab);
> - display format for new variables—width and number of decimals (DATA tab);
> - which columns are displayed in the "VARIABLE VIEW" tab (the "CUSTOMIZE VARIABLE VIEW" button in the DATA tab);
> - the look of output in tables (in the PIVOT TABLES tab);
> - whether you want syntax printed to the Viewer window and where to save it (the FILE LOCATIONS tab).
>
> . . . and many more. Check it out for yourself!

Missing

This column lets you specify which value you want to give to data that is missing. For example, some people like to label all missing data as "999" instead of just having an empty space. (Although I do not recommend this! See Section 1.5 for my recommendations for fixing missing data.)

Columns

Use this column to define how wide a column you will see, not how many characters you can put in it, which is what the confusingly named Width column does. You can also manipulate the width of columns manually with a mouse by dragging.

Align

This specifies whether data in the Data Editor are aligned to the left or right of the column.

Measure

In this column you can label your variables as Nominal, Ordinal or Scale (Interval). I have never found a reason to do this, however!

1.1.3 Application Activity for Getting Started with SPSS

1 Open up an existing SPSS file. If you have downloaded the data for this book, open up the DeKeyser2000.sav file. What are the names of the variables? What do the numbers "1" and "2" refer to in the group membership variable "Status"?

2 Open a new file in SPSS and name it "Trial." Create three variables entitled "Group," "Results," and "Gender." Fill the columns with data for three groups of 10 participants each. Define each group however you want and give the groups variable labels. Give the Gender column variable labels also.

3 Change the default setting in SPSS for which columns to display in the Variable View. You will have to decide for yourself which columns you would like to keep and which you will get rid of.

1.1.4 Importing Data into SPSS

You may want to use SPSS with files that have previously been saved in another format. SPSS can convert data that are saved in Microsoft Excel, Notepad or WordPad (.txt files), SAS, Lotus, dBase or Microsoft Access.

To import Excel, dBase or Microsoft Access files, open the "Database Wizard." You can choose this as an option when you first start up SPSS (see Figure 1.1; under "New Database," which you would use to open a blank database, choose "New Database Query" instead) or start it manually by going to File > Open Database > New Query. The wizard will pop up and guide you through the process of importing Excel, dBase or Microsoft Access files, giving a preview of the data along the way so you can see how the data will be arranged when they are imported into SPSS.

To import Notepad or WordPad (.txt) files, go to File > Read Text Data. You can open other types of files that SPSS can read, such as SAS or Lotus files, this way also; just click on the "Files of type" drop-down menu and you will be able to choose the type of file you want (see Figure 1.9).

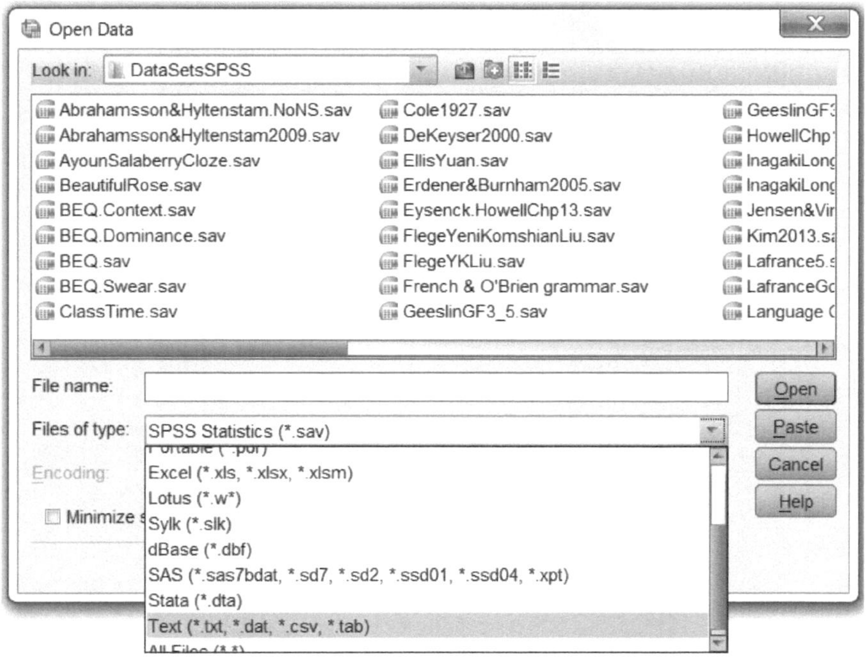

Figure 1.9 Types of files you can import into SPSS.

1.1.5 Saving Your Work in SPSS

Once you have created your data set or imported it into SPSS, you will want to save it as an SPSS file so you can easily open it again. Do this by going to File > Save. It is also possible to save SPSS files in other formats by using the File > Save As option. In previous versions of SPSS the program would not allow you to have more than one Data Editor open, but SPSS version 16 onwards allows this (and also adds the Viewer as a separate page). You can also click on the icon that looks like a floppy disk to save your data ( ). SPSS does not automatically back up your files, so if you are entering data you should save often.

In older versions of SPSS, it was not possible to have more than one Data Editor spreadsheet file open at a time. Now you can have multiple Data Editors open, but be aware that, if you have only one Data Editor open and then close it, you will leave SPSS. (The system will give you warning and ask you if you want to save it before you exit, though.) To open another file SPSS will need to start up all over again. (This principle holds true for Microsoft Word and also other Windows software.) If you want to close one file and open another, open your next file before closing the previous one and you will not have to open the SPSS program again.

In older versions of SPSS if you tried to open another file before closing the previous one, a dialog box would appear to ask if you wanted to save the file before closing it. If you said no, all of your data would be lost. Ouch! If you are working with an older version of SPSS (e.g. version 12.0), be careful of this point and always save your data before opening a new file.

Another type of object that you might want to save is your output. This is what appears in the Statistics Viewer window (see Figure 1.10). If you want to save only parts of the output, you can just click on certain parts and delete them before saving the file. This file is saved as a .spv file (this extension is new to SPSS 16.0; older versions used .spo instead) and can be opened later as "Output" (FILE > OPEN > OUTPUT). As you can see in Figure 1.10, there are two parts to this window. On the left side of this window there is an outline view of all of the parts of the output, while on the right is the actual output.

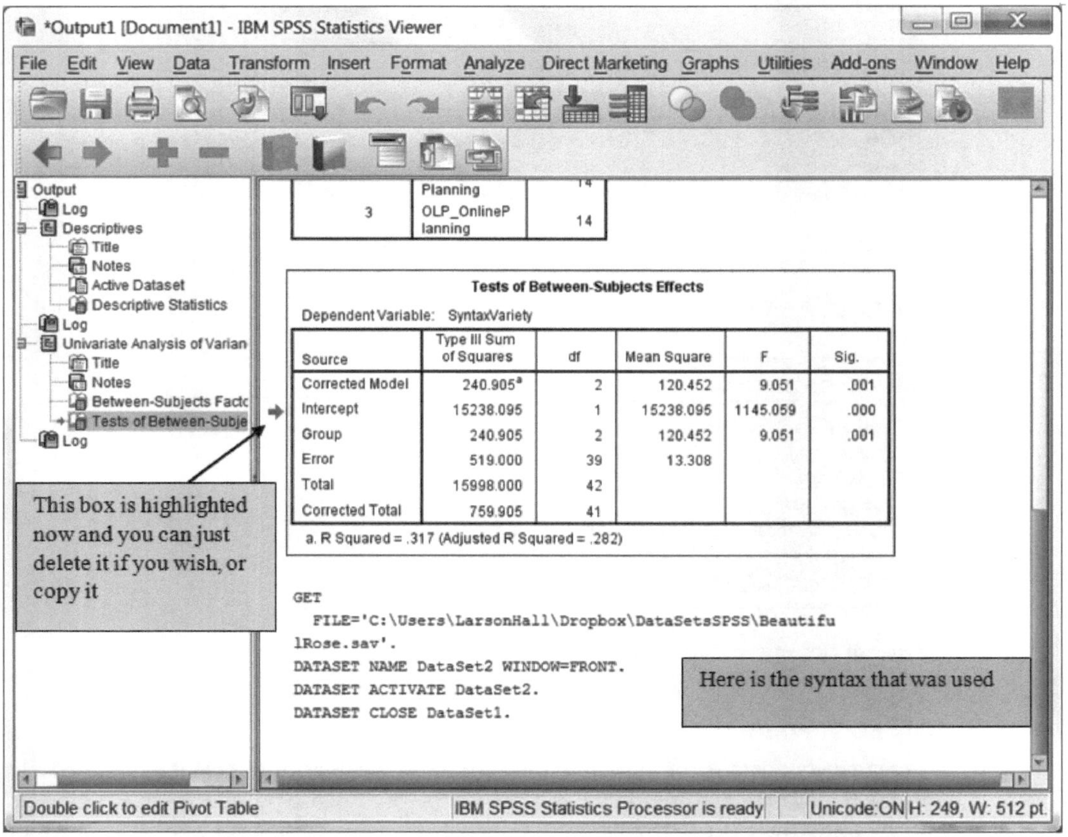

Figure 1.10 Output in the Statistics Viewer window.

New with version 16.0, any time you make a choice from a menu, the SPSS syntax for that choice is recorded into the output file. (If you do not like this, you can change it in the EDIT > OPTIONS box, VIEWER tab, click off the "Display commands in the log" box.) If you save the output associated with your file, save your entire session and you can recreate your choices by running the syntax.

> **Tip:** To run syntax from your output, click on the syntax commands you want, and copy them using the Ctrl + C button sequence (or EDIT > COPY). To open up a syntax window, choose FILE > NEW > SYNTAX. Paste in the commands; then in the Syntax Editor choose RUN > CURRENT. Also, using syntax in SPSS can be helpful if you have to run the same analysis many times and just need to modify one part of it (say, the variable name).

1.1.6 Application Activities for Importing and Saving Files

1. Either find the file for this book called "read.txt" or find/create your own text file (using Windows Notepad). The read.txt file has data separated by a space. Import these data into SPSS. You may have to try to experiment with the Text Import Wizard to get the SPSS file to come out looking good.
2. Create a simple output for any file by going to ANALYZE > DESCRIPTIVE STATISTICS > FREQUENCIES and moving one variable to the "Variable(s)" box. Click on OK to continue. Now you have both a Data Editor and an **SPSS Viewer** open. Save both of them.

1.2 Getting Started with R

In this book I will work with the most recent version of R at the time of writing, version 3.1.1, released on 10 July 2014 (R Core Team, 2014). Two major versions of R are released every year, so by the time you read this there will doubtless be a more up-to-date version of R to download, but new versions of R mainly deal with fixing bugs and I have found as I have used R over the years that almost all of the same commands still work even with newer versions of R. If you find that a command listed in this book does not work, your first thoughts should be to check that the syntax is exactly as I have given it. However, occasionally commands are "deprecated" or packages removed, and R will tell you that too. Try searching the Web for information about what command or package people are using now. The R programming language was first created by Robert Gentleman and Ross Ihaka at the University of Auckland, New Zealand, but now is developed by the R Development Core Team (2013).

The R Console is command line driven, and few of its functions are found in the drop-down menus of the R Console. I have found it helpful to work with a GUI created for R called R Commander. In this chapter I will show you how to get started using both of these. R Commander is highly useful for those new to R, but once you understand R better you will want to use the R Console to customize commands and also to use commands that are not available in R Commander.

Sections 1.2 and 1.3 will deal with setting up R, entering and importing data, and saving files. If you want information about and practice with manipulating variables in R, such as moving columns or rows or simply deleting them, combining two or more variables into one variable, recoding groups or excluding cases from your data, see the online section: "Manipulating variables in R."

1.2.1 Downloading and Installing R

You must have access to the Internet to download R. Navigate your Internet browser to the R Project for Statistical Computing home page: www.r-project.org/. Under "Getting Started," note the "download R" hyperlink (Step 1 in Figure 1.11). Click on this link and select a suitable CRAN mirror (i.e. a download site) (Step 2 in Figure 1.11). (For example, if you are based in Australia, you have two download sites to choose from.) You should choose a download site near you. I have once in a while found some CRAN mirrors to be faulty, so if you find you are using a mirror location that does not seem to work, try a different one. It is worth emphasizing here that you must *always* choose a CRAN mirror site whenever you download anything into R. This applies to your first download but also after you have R running but you later want to add additional R packages.

Once you have navigated to your chosen CRAN mirror download site, you will see a box titled "Download and Install R" (Step 3 in Figure 1.11). Choose the version that matches the computing environment you use (Linux, Mac OS X and Windows are available).

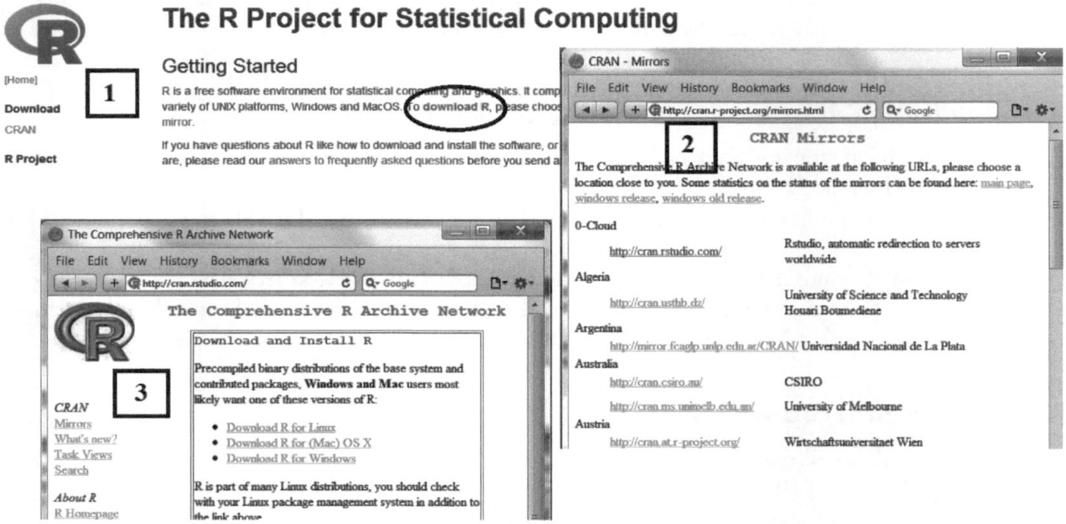

Figure 1.11 Downloading R from the Internet (first steps).

For Windows, this choice will take you to a place where you will see the "base," "contrib" and "Rtools" hyperlinks (see Figure 1.12). Click the bold link that says "install R for the first time" or the "base" hyperlink (both lead to the same page). On the next page click on "Download R 3.2.0 for Windows." (This version of R will change by the time you read this book.)

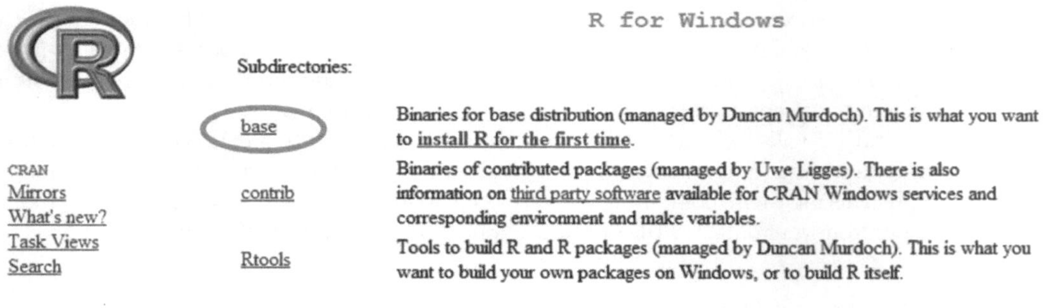

Figure 1.12 Downloading the correct file for R.

For the Mac version, after you have chosen the CRAN mirror, the link you want to click is "R-3.2.0.pkg" (or the latest version).

Follow the normal protocol for downloading and installing executable files on your computer. Once the executable file is downloaded onto your computer, double-click on it, then click on Run (or it may run automatically), and a Setup Wizard will appear, after you have chosen a language. You can either follow the defaults in the wizard or customize your version of R, which is explained in the following section.

1.2.2 Customizing R in Windows

In Windows, when you run the Setup Wizard, you will click a series of buttons and eventually come to the "Startup options." You have the option to customize, as shown in Figure 1.13. I recommend clicking on Yes.

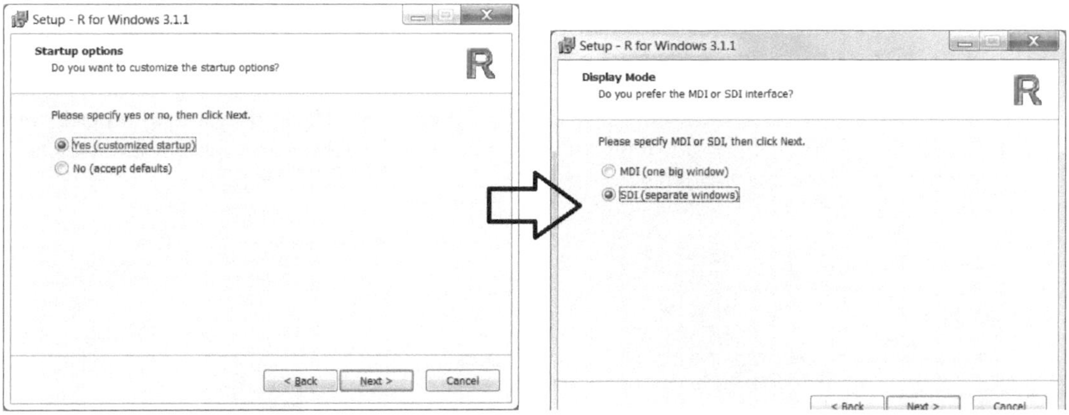

Figure 1.13 Windows Startup options in R (for customizing display).

On the next screen (shown on the right in Figure 1.13), the Display Mode option, I recommend that you choose the SDI option. R's default is MDI, meaning that there is one big window, but I find it much easier to use R when graphics and the help menu pop up in separate windows (as they do for the SDI choice, shown in Figure 1.14). Once you have chosen SDI, I have no other recommendations about further customization and I just keep the default choices in subsequent windows.

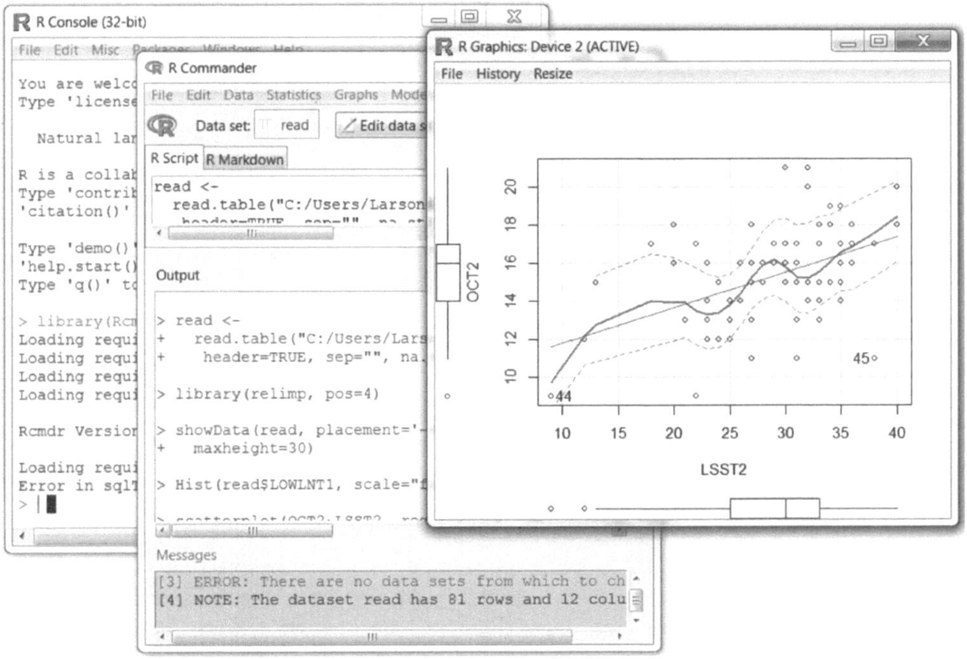

Figure 1.14 Single window interface in R (with several windows open).

If, after having installed R, you find you want to further customize R by changing font sizes, font colors, etc., or that you later want to change to SDI if you did not do so in the install, navigate in the R Console, using the drop-down menus, to EDIT > GUI PREFERENCES. Figure 1.15 shows the Rgui Configuration Editor. If you have not done so before, you could change options to set the style to single windows (SDI). I also like to change the settings here to allocate more memory so that I can see all of my R commands in one session (I have put in "999999" in the "buffer chars" box, and '9999' in the "lines" box). You might also want to change the default colors of the text commands here as well.

In order to change these values permanently, you will need to save them. Click on "Save ..." and navigate to PROGRAM FILES > R > (R-3.2.0). (The step in parentheses may not be necessary.) Choose the R Console file and click on "Save." A dialog box will ask if you want to replace the previous file. Click on "Yes." Close down all windows and restart R to see the changes. (You do not need to save the workspace image when you exit.)

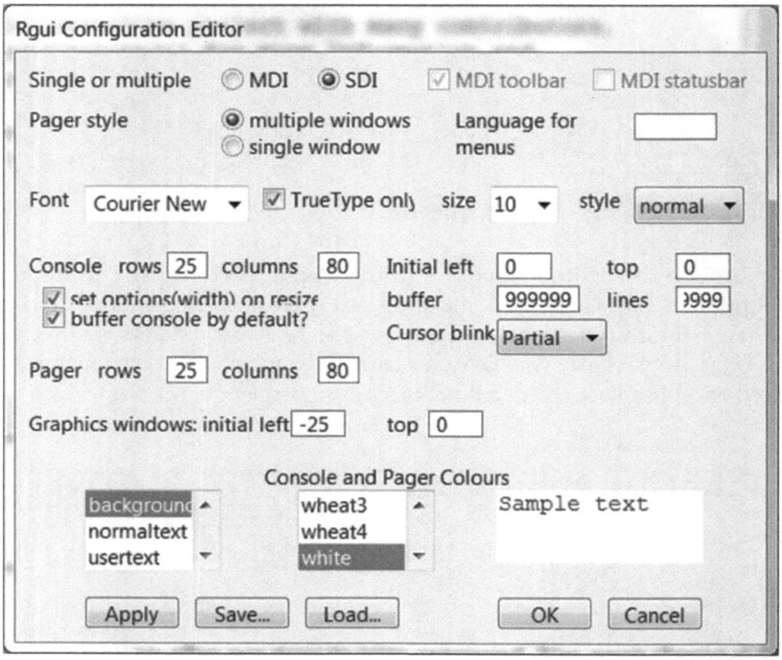

Figure 1.15 Customizing R with the Rgui Configuration Editor.

Mac Tip: The R GUI for the Mac is not configurable in this way. Basically, it will be set up with the single display interface (SDI) without any extra work. If you push the pretty color wheel button you will have the option to change some of the colors and other options for R on the Mac.

At this point, you will still be wondering what you should do! The next step that I recommend is to download a more user-friendly graphical interface that works in concert with R called *R Commander* created by John Fox (2005). Readers familiar with SPSS and other drop-down-menu-type programs will initially feel more comfortable using R Commander than R. (Some R enthusiasts prefer other R GUIs, such as RStudio or JGR, but I find R Commander the most intuitive.) The R environment is run with scripts, and in the long run it can be much more advantageous to have scripts that you can easily bring back up as you perform multiple calculations. But to get started, in this book I will be walking the reader through the use of R Commander as much as possible.

> **Tip:** When you want to open R again, you may find that there are two R shortcuts on your desktop. If you have a 64-bit system, use the Ri386 one. The Rx64 one will not work properly with R Commander. You can find out whether your computer runs a 32-bit, 64-bit, 86-bit or higher operating system by navigating to CONTROL PANEL > SYSTEM AND SECURITY > SYSTEM, then checking in the area that says "System Type."

1.2.3 Loading Packages and R Commander

Before you start installing packages, you should set your working directory because this is where all of your packages will download to. Follow the menu sequence in the R Console FILE > CHANGE DIR … and then choose the file that you want. Once this is done, navigate to the menu PACKAGES > INSTALL PACKAGE(S). You will need to select your CRAN mirror site first to continue with the installation. Once you have made your choice for a CRAN mirror site, a list of packages will pop up. For now, just scroll down alphabetically to the "r" section of the list and choose Rcmdr (Fox, 2005). Click on OK and the package will load. Instead of doing the menu route, you can also type the following command in the R Console:

```
install.packages("Rcmdr")
```

(Remember, in this book commands in the R Console will be written in the Arial font, and should be typed *exactly* as they are shown, here with a period between "install" and "packages," and also parentheses and quotation marks around the word "Rcmdr".) On a Mac, you can change the working directory by going to MISC > CHANGE WORKING DIRECTORY or you can also use FILE > CHANGE working directory in R Commander. To install packages for Mac, go to the R Console and choose PACKAGES & DATA > PACKAGE INSTALLER and click on the "Get List" button.

> **Mac Tip:** Before installation, for a Mac it is important to check that your operating system (OS) is up to date. If not, R and R Commander may not run properly. Check this by running the software update from the Apple menu at the top left of your screen. Next, check to see whether the X windowing system is correctly installed on your Mac. You will need this for R Commander to run. Before OS X 10.8, this system was called X11 but now it is called XQuartz and does not automatically get installed with R. As systems are likely to change, please see the more detailed instructions at this website: http://faculty.umf.maine.edu/sarah.hardy/public.www/. Then click on "Mac Instructions."

If you have not picked a CRAN mirror during your session, this window will automatically pop up after you type in your command. You must choose a CRAN mirror in a specific physical location to download from before you can continue with your installation.

You will use a number of packages in this book, but you might like to explore other packages on your own. There are hundreds of packages available, some for very specific purposes, such as one for dealing with magnetic resonance imaging (MRI) and functional MRI (fMRI) data. One good way to explore these is to use the RGui drop-down menu to go to HELP > HTML HELP. This opens a separate window in your Internet browser, although you do not need to be connected to the Internet for it to work. Click on the Packages link, and you will see a package index that gives a brief description of each package. Further clicking on specific packages will take you to pages that give you documentation for each command. At this point, most of this documentation will be cryptic and frustrating, so I do not recommend browsing this area just yet. As you become more familiar with R, however, this may be a helpful site.

Once R Commander has been downloaded, start it by typing the following line in the R Console window:

```
library(Rcmdr)
```

This must be typed exactly as given above; there is no menu command to obtain it. Notice that because R is a scripted environment (like UNIX), spelling and punctuation matter. The "R" of R Commander must be capitalized, and the rest of the letters ("cmdr") must be lowercase.

The first time you try to open R Commander, if you have not done a complete download of all CRAN files, it will tell you that you need to download some additional files; just follow the directions for this, and install from the CRAN site, not a local directory. Once those files are downloaded, use the library() command again (or type the up ↑ arrow until you come back to your previous command), and the library will open. The R Commander window is shown in Figure 1.16.

After loading R Commander, it can be a good idea to perform a complete install of all of the CRAN packages. You have already chosen your CRAN mirror site, so if you click on PACKAGES > INSTALL PACKAGE(S) in the R Console menu, the entire list of packages available in R will pop up. To do a complete install you would just highlight every single package and click on OK to download all of them. This will take about four hours, so you could let it run on your computer overnight or during a time when you are in meetings or classes. If you do not have time now to do this, or do not think you have enough room on your computer, or your computer freezes up when you try to download them all at once (as mine did!), I will also give a list of the packages that I actually use in this book in the next section and just these can be downloaded separately in much less time than a total install of all the packages.

Figure 1.16 The R Commander graphical user interface (GUI).

1.2.4 A list of all the R Packages Used in this Book

Chapter 1	Amelia, mice, Rcmdr
Chapter 2	—
Chapter 3	boot, fBasics, lattice, mice, nortest, Rcmdr
Chapter 4	multcomp, pwr
Chapter 5	—
Chapter 6	boot, Hmisc, mvoutlier, TeachingDemos, Rcmdr, WRS and its dependent packages: MASS, akima, robustbasem cobs, robust, mgcv, scatterplot3d, quantreg, rrcov, lars, pwr, trimcluster, multicore, mc2d, psych, Rfit
Chapter 7	MASS, mice, relaimpo, Rcmdr, tree, WRS
Chapter 8	boot, ggplot2, Rcmdr, WRS and its dependent packages
Chapter 9	boot, bootES, HH, ggplot2, HH, multcomp, Rcmdr, WRS
Chapter 10	epitools, HH, mice, multcomp, phia, plyr, Rcmdr, WRS
Chapter 11	ez, HH, lattice, reshape2, WRS

And here is a list of all of the packages in alphabetical order:

akima	MASS	Rcmdr
Amelia	mc2d	relaimpo
boot	mgcv	reshape2
bootES	mice	Rfit
cobs	multcomp	robust
epitools	multicore	robustbase
ez	mvoutlier	rrcov
fBasics	nortest	scatterplot3d
ggplot2	phia	TeachingDemos
HH	plyr	tree
Hmisc	psych	trimcluster
lars	pwr	WRS
lattice	quantreg	

Tip: To keep your R packages up to date, every so often you should run the menu sequence PACKAGES > UPDATE PACKAGES. Perhaps it would be a good idea to run this every time you open your R Console. While writing this book, I spent several wasted hours trying to get a very simple command to run, and it would not because I did not have the updated version of the package that would work with my updated version of R.

1.3 Working with Data in R and R Commander

While you can certainly learn something about R without any data entered, my first inclination is to get my own data into the program so that I can start working with it. This section will explain how to do that.

1.3.1 Entering Your Own Data

In R Commander (remember, to open R Commander from the R Console, type library(Rcmdr) first!), enter data by navigating to the DATA > NEW DATA SET window, as shown in Figure 1.17. Replace the default title "Data set" and enter a name for your data set. I named mine "LarsonHall". Remember that whether you capitalize or not, you will need to enter the name for your data set in exactly the same way when you call it up again, so for my name I will have to remember that the initial "L" as well as the "H" is capitalized. If you enter an illegal character in the name, the "New Data Set" dialog box will reset itself. The restrictions are similar to those for other types of programs like SPSS (no numbers initially, certain kinds of punctuation like a slash "/" not allowed, etc.).

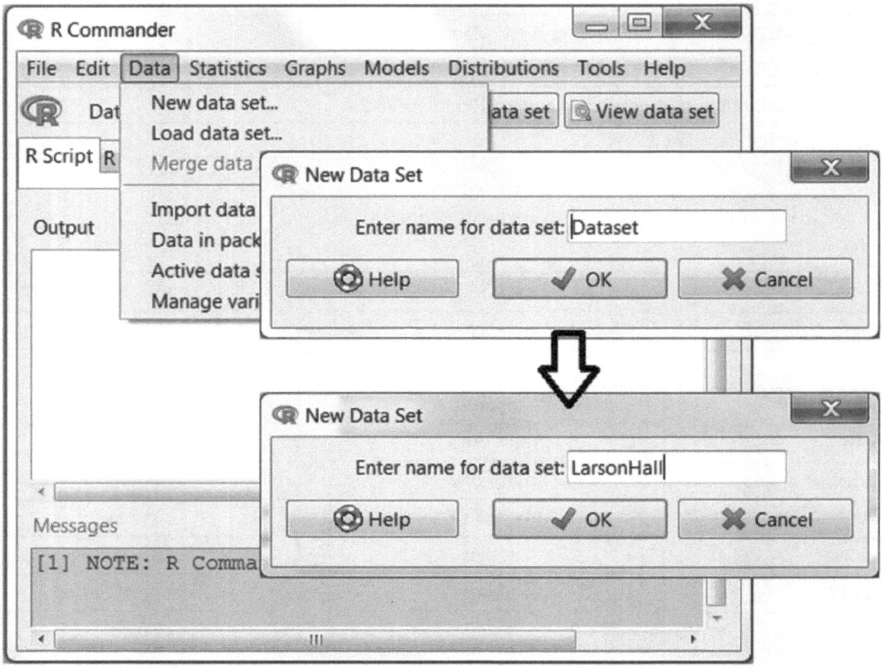

Figure 1.17 Setting up a new spreadsheet for data in R Commander.

After you enter the name and click OK, a spreadsheet automatically appears. Click on buttons to add more rows and columns, as many as you need, then manually enter your data. You can also click on the existing column names and give them more informative names. You can close this spreadsheet and the data frame will still be available as long as the same session of R is open. However, you will need to save the data before you exit from R if you want it to be available to you at a later time.

You can also use the R Console to enter data. First create a data frame, giving it whatever name you want. Here I name it "Experiment1".

```
Experiment1=data.frame()
```

Now give a command that lets you enter data into your newly created data frame:

```
fix(Experiment1)
```

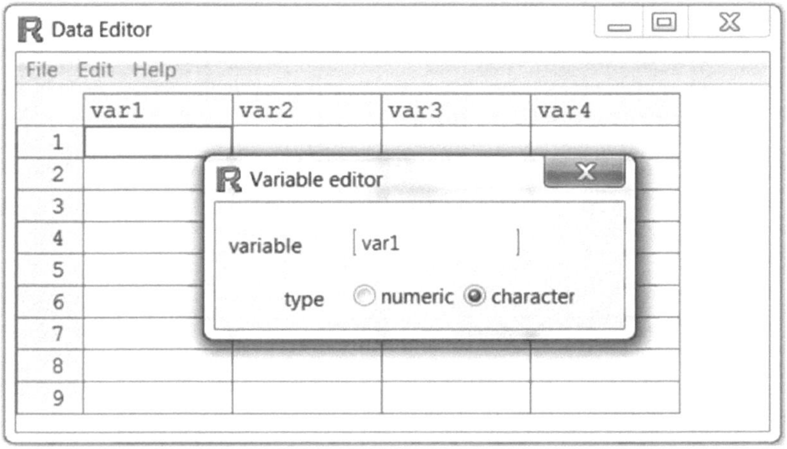

Figure 1.18 Entering data directly into R through the data editor.

When you type this, at least on a Windows machine, you will get the spreadsheet shown in Figure 1.18. In this spreadsheet you simply type in your data, and as you move the cursor down farther more rows are added, or if you move the cursor to the right more variables are added. When you click on the column heading, "var1", you will get a pop-up window asking you to choose what type of variable you want. A **variable** is a collection of data that are all of the same sort. There are two major types of variables in R: **character** and **numerical variables**. Character variables are non-numerical strings. You can make your categorical variables into "character" variables in R. Be careful with your variable names. You want them to be descriptive, but if you use commands in R you will also need to type them a lot, so you don't want them to be too long.

You can also enter data (or any commands) into R by just copying and pasting them in. You can do this from a pdf copy of a book or any online content. For example, say you wanted to paste in a line of scores for an experiment that you found online where the scores were separated by white space:

22 25 35 22 31 30 18 30 24 28 22 28 30 19 20 21 26 24

You could copy this line and paste it in to the **scan( )** command:

```
> onlineExp<-scan(text="22 25 35 22 31 30 18 30 24 28 22 28 30 19 20 21 26 24")#Scores
Read 18 items
> onlineExp
 [1] 22 25 35 22 31 30 18 30 24 28 22 28 30 19 20 21 26 24
```

This results in a list of numbers. Note that the hash mark "#" is used to make commentary on R code (here it notes what the numbers refer to) and will not affect the code that R reads.

Tip: If you do enter your data directly into R or R Commander it might be worth making a simple .txt file that will explain your variable names more descriptively. Then save that file wherever you store your data files. Sometimes when you come back to your data years later, you cannot remember what your variable names meant, so the .txt file can help you remember.

Actually, anything that can be done through a drop-down menu in R Commander can also be done by means of commands in R. R Commander puts the command it used in the top "Script Window."

1.3.2 Importing Files into R through R Commander

Importing files into R can be most easily done by using R Commander. Click on DATA > IMPORT DATA. A list of data types that can be imported will be shown, as in Figure 1.19.

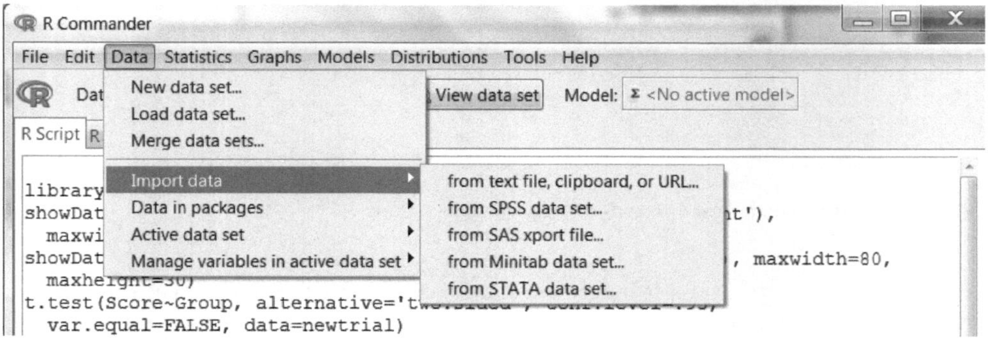

Figure 1.19 Importing data through R Commander.

R Commander has commands to import text files (including .txt, .csv, .dif and .sylk), SPSS, Minitab and STATA files. These will be imported as data frames. (This information will be more important later on when we are working with commands that need data to be arranged in certain ways.) Data from Excel, SAS, Systat and S-PLUS can also be imported. (See the R Data ImportExport Manual.pdf under the HELP > MANUALS (IN PDF) menu in the R Console for more information.)

This method of importing is fairly straightforward, but especially for comma- or tab-delimited text files you may need to experiment a couple of times to get your data to line up the way you want. Most of the data for this book are SPSS files, and Figure 1.20 shows the import dialog box for SPSS files after you choose DATA > IMPORT DATA > FROM SPSS DATA SET in R Commander.

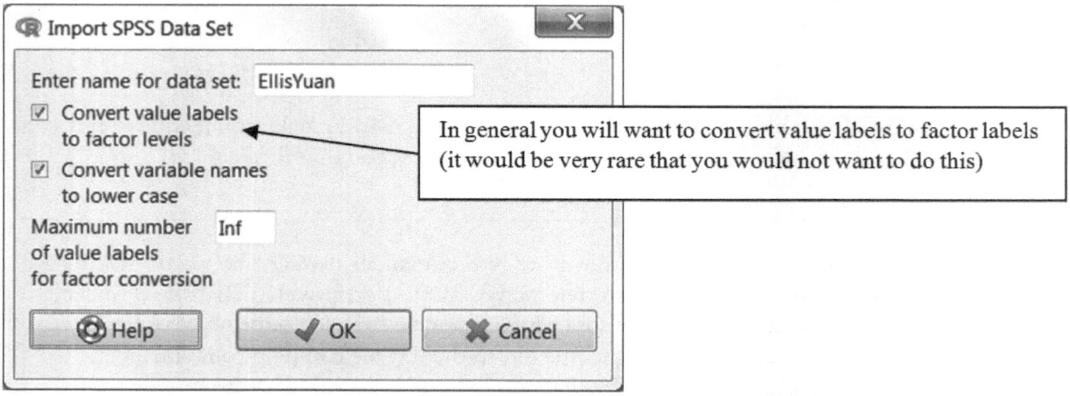

Figure 1.20 Importing SPSS files into R through R Commander.

Once you have chosen the correct settings, R Commander lets you browse to where the files are on your computer (if you are uploading from your local file system). After using this command, you will want to be sure to look at your file that just loaded. I imported the EllisYuan SPSS file in, and when I click on the "View data set" button on R Commander I can see that everything looks good and lines up nicely (see Figure 1.21).

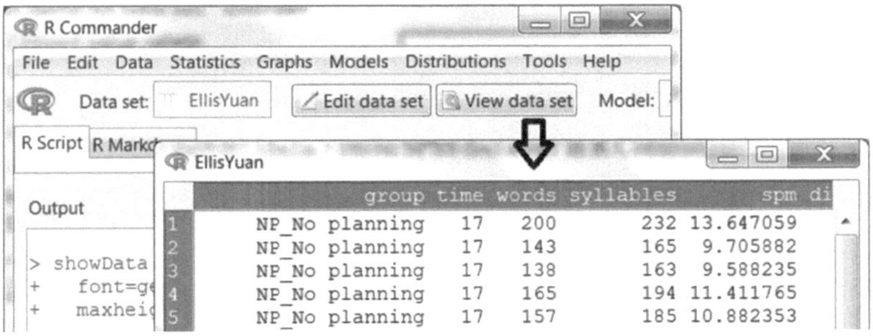

Figure 1.21 Verifying that data set has imported properly by opening the "View data set" button.

Some data for this book are text files, such as Read.txt. I will demonstrate how to open a .txt file. The box in Figure 1.22 will appear after I have made the choice DATA > IMPORT DATA > FROM TEXT FILE, CLIPBOARD, OR URL. I think the .txt file is tab-delimited, so when I open up the dialog box for text files, I need to make the appropriate choices, as shown in Figure 1.22.

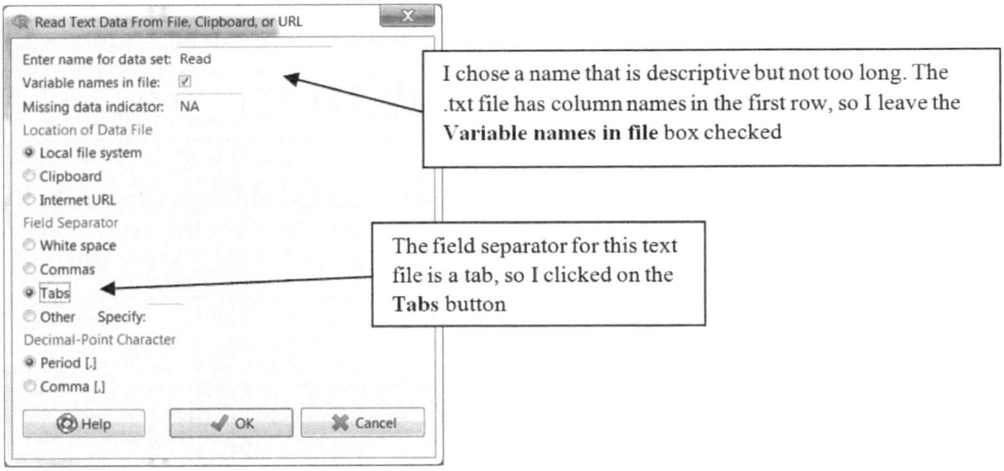

Figure 1.22 Importing text files into R through R Commander.

When I check on this file, however (note that once you have multiple data sets open, you will need to choose the correct one with the "Data set" button in R Commander), it does not line up right (see Figure 1.23)!

Going back and opening up the Read.txt file, I see that it is not tab-delimited. Instead, headings are separated by two spaces, but the columns of numbers are separated by spaces of varying lengths—some are just one space, some are three, others are four, etc.! However, this is not a problem, because everything is separated by white space, no matter how many spaces are between it. Going back to the dialog box in Figure 1.22, you can see that one of the choices for importing a text file is "White space." When I choose this, the file will then import correctly.

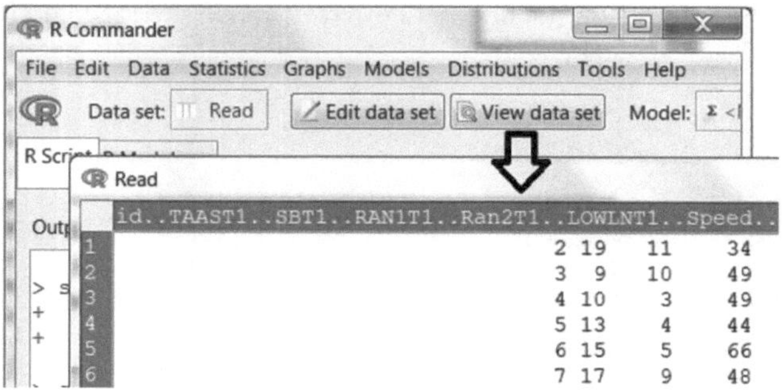

Figure 1.23 There is a problem after importing a text file into R.

Getting Data into R

Using the R Commander menu commands:

DATA > NEW DATA SET	Opens a new spreadsheet you can fill in.
DATA > IMPORT DATA >	Imports data from a variety of sources you can choose from.

Using the R line command for a new data set:

<u>Exp1</u>=data.frame()	#create a data frame and name it (replace underline)
fix(<u>Exp1</u>)	#enter data in your new data set

Using the R line command for an existing data set:

Consult the R Data Import/Export manual in R Console at HELP > MANUALS (IN PDF).

Getting data into R using line commands is more complicated and something I never do without R Commander. You can consult the R Data Import/Export manual for more information if you would like to learn how to do this. Find this manual from the R Console by going to HELP > MANUALS (IN PDF).

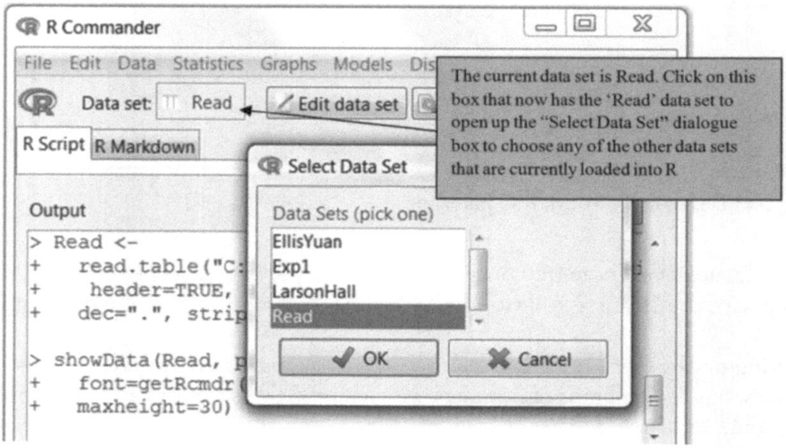

Figure 1.24 Selecting a data set in R Commander.

1.3.3 Viewing Entered Data

Once you have entered your data into R, you can look at it by clicking on the "View data set" button along the top of the R Commander box (see Figure 1.21). To make sure that the data set you want is the active data set, make sure it is listed in the "Data set" box along the top of R Commander (Figure 1.24). If the data you want is not currently active, just click in the box to select the correct data set.

You can also get a printout of any data set in the R Console by simply typing the name of the data set:

```
> EllisYuan
                    group time words syllables
1        NP_No planning   17   200       232
2        NP_No planning   17   143       165
3        NP_No planning   17   138       163
4        NP_No planning   17   165       194
5        NP_No planning   17   157       185
```

You can see any one of these variables (which are in columns) by typing the name of the data set followed by the "$" symbol and the name of the variable, like this:

```
> EllisYuan$words
 [1] 200 143 138 165 157 194 158 164 204 225 161 194 196 240 240 208
[17] 285 240 240 197 240 256 253 168 242 212 200 255 240 206 313 217
[33] 157 224 232 168 193 180 206 169 194 198
```

If you have forgotten the names of the variables, in R Console you can call them up with the names() command.

```
> names(EllisYuan)
 [1] "group"                "time"
 [3] "words"                "syllables"
 [5] "spm"                  "disfluencies"
```

Note that any line with the command prompt ">" showing indicates that I have typed the part that follows the command prompt into R. Throughout this book I have chosen not to type in the prompt when I myself type commands; however, when I copy what appears in R you will see the command prompt. If you copy that command, do **not** put in the command prompt sign!

1.3.4 Saving Data and Reading It Back In

Once you have created your own data set or imported a data set into R, you can save it. There are various ways of doing this, but the one I prefer is to save data as a .csv file. This is a comma-delimited file, and is saved as an Excel file. The easiest way of doing this is in R Commander. Go to DATA > ACTIVE DATA SET > EXPORT ACTIVE DATA SET, and you will see the dialog box in Figure 1.25.

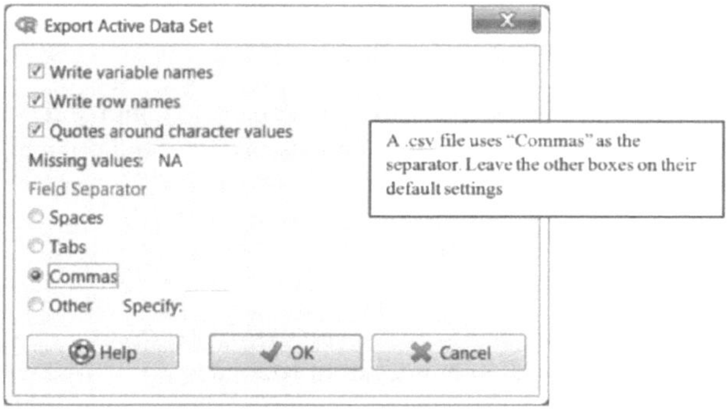

Figure 1.25 Saving data files (as Excel files) in R Commander.

Once you click on OK, you will see a dialog box that lets you save your data in the usual way. Remember that the data you want to save should be the currently active data. (You will see the name in the "File name" line, so if it is wrong, you will know!) Now you can navigate to wherever you want to save the file. Pull down the menu for file type ("Save as type") and choose "Text files." It will be marked as an Excel (.csv) file. To read it back into R, use the **read()** command below with the saved file in the working directory.

Instead of saving your file you could just save your R workspace when you exit, and when you open it back up again your file will still be loaded into R, but I have found that this may be dangerous and you may lose your work. (This may be more a function of my computer having problems than R, I don't know!) In any case, it is a good idea to have a backup of your data, so it is a good idea to save your files somewhere. When leaving R Commander, you will be asked a series of questions (Save script file? Save output file?). You do not need to save anything in R Commander to keep all of your files loaded up into R—just make sure to say "Yes" to "Save workspace image?" when you exit R.

You can also save files with the R Console, but it is a little more complicated. Here is the syntax for how to do it:

```
write.csv(EllisYuan, file="EllisYuan.csv", row.names=FALSE)
```

write.csv( )	Writes a comma-delimited file in Excel format; by default it will keep column names; it saves the data as a data frame (unless it is a matrix).
file="EllisYuan.csv"	Names file; do not forget the quotation marks around it!
row.names=FALSE	If set to FALSE, names for rows are not expected. If you do want row names, just do not include this argument.

The object will be saved in R's working directory. You can find out where the working directory is by typing the command **getwd()** like this:

```
getwd()
[1] "C:/Users/LarsonHall/Documents"
```

You can see that my working directory is in the Documents folder. If you would like to reset this, you can do this by using the **setwd()** command or, as mentioned in Section 1.2.3, you can use the menu sequence in the R Console File > Change Dir and then choose the file that you want. Here I have reset my working directory to a file I created on the desktop, called "R Files":

```
setwd("C:/Users/LarsonHall/Desktop/R Files")
```

By the way, to find out what the directory of the file is where you want to save it, just right click on your folder and open the Properties. In this box you will see the location of your file. Note, however, that this location is written with the slashes going the opposite way (mine says C:\Users\LarsonHall\Desktop) from the way you need to type them in R!

If the file you saved is in the working directory, you can open it with the **read.csv( )** command. (Note that the blank parentheses mean you will put something inside of it! In this case, it is a filename.) To make this file part of the objects on the R workspace, type:

```
dekeyser=read.csv("dekeyser.csv")
```

This will put the data set **dekeyser** on your workspace as an object you can manipulate. You can verify which objects you have on your workspace by using the **ls( )** command. In this case, you will leave the parentheses empty.

```
ls()
[1] "EllisYuan" "Exp1" "LarsonHall"      "Read"
```

1.3.5 Saving Graphics Files

Graphics are one of the strong points of R. You will want to be able to cut and paste graphics from the **"R Graphics: Device."** This is a separate window from the R Console and R Commander, which will pop up whenever you call for a graphic. The Graphics window has a pull-down menu. Pull down the File menu, and you have the choice to Save as a Metafile, Postscript, PDF, PNG, BMP, TIFF or JPEG file. What I usually do, however, is to take the Copy to Clipboard choice, and then choose As a metafile. The file is then available on the clipboard and can be pasted and resized anywhere you like. These two ways of saving graphics, by either converting directly into a separate file, or by copying on to the clipboard, are shown in Figure 1.26.

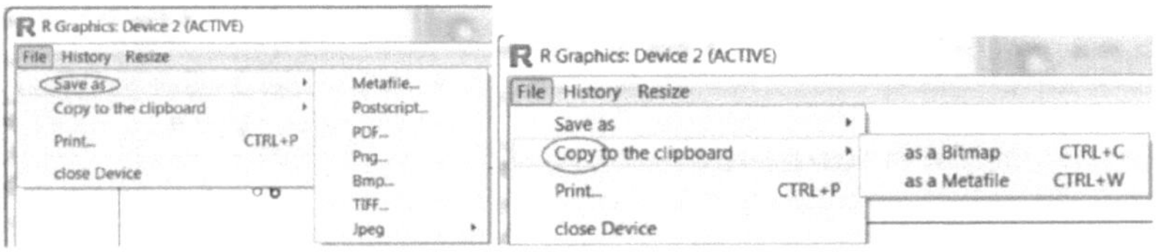

Figure 1.26 Choices for saving graphics or copying them to the clipboard.

1.3.6 Closing R and R Commander

When you close R and R Commander, they will ask you various questions about whether you want to save information. One question is "Save workspace image?" If you say Yes, all of the objects and command lines you used in your session will be available to you when you open up R again. For example, in this session I had the object EllisYuan open, and if I save the workspace, that object will be automatically available when I open up R again, as will all of the commands I used, such as write.csv(EllisYuan, file="EllisYuan.csv", row.names=F). Once reloaded, I can access these commands by simply clicking on the up ↑ and down ↓ arrows.

Thus, one of the advantages of R is that by saving your workspace with your other data and files you will have easy access to all of your data files and commands for future reference. However, R does not automatically let you give the workspace a special name and save it in a place different from the working directory if you just shut down your windows. Therefore, you should use the R Console menu to save your workspace before you close the windows. Choose File > Save Workspace from the drop-down menu in R Console. You will be able to navigate to the folder of your choice and give the .RData file a unique name. When you start R again, you can load this workspace by using the drop-down menu in the R Console, going to File and then Load Workspace. In the past, however, I have found that these workspaces are easily corrupted, so I would also recommend saving your data files as explained in Section 1.3.4.

If you have saved a particular workspace and this comes up every time you start R but you want to start with a fresh workspace, you can find the .RData file in your working directory and simply delete it. The next time you open up R there will be no objects and no commands saved. (You can verify this by using the command ls( ) to list all objects.)

Another exit question is "Save script file?". If you say yes, all of your command lines will be saved in a file called .Rhistory wherever your working directory is. If you start R again by clicking on this icon, all of your previous commands will be available. This command is also available in the R Console by using the File menu and choosing Save History. Again, this feature can be quite useful for referencing your analysis in the future.

1.3.7 Application Activities Practicing Entering Data into R

1. Create a new data set called Count. Assume it has two variables, Score and Group, where Score is numeric and Group is a character variable. Randomly enter the numbers 1–9 for the score (create 10 entries). For Group label the first five entries "C" for the control group and the next five entries "T" for the treatment group. Click on OK to close the spreadsheet. When you are finished, type Count in the R Console to make sure your data frame looks good.
2. There is a .txt file that you will use later in this book called read.txt. (Download it onto your computer from the Routledge website.) Import this file into R, and call it read. These data have variable names in the file and the numbers are separated by spaces, so in the dialog box for importing, choose the "Field Separator" called "White space." Use the button along the top of the R Commander GUI that says "View data set" to make sure the data frame looks appropriate.
3. There are many SPSS files that you will need to import into R. Let us try importing the one called DeKeyser2000.sav. (Files labeled .sav are from SPSS; again, you will need to download this onto your computer from the Routledge website.) Name the file dekeyser and keep the other defaults for importing the same. After it is imported, either use the "View data set" button in R Commander, or type the name of the file in the R Console to see the data frame.

1.4 Understanding the R Environment

There are many excellent books you may want to read to help you learn more about R. I have read several of them (Crawley, 2007; Dalgaard, 2002; Verzani, 2004), and what helped me most was following along on my computer, doing in R what they showed on the page. These books all started with the process of helping the reader understand how R works by beginning to use R as a calculator. I will follow their example. In fact, if you should do nothing more than learn how to use R as a calculator, you will be happy you did. I do not use a calculator anymore for my monthly budget; I use R, and after learning R I hope you will see why! But my main point here is that in trying to understand how R actually works, you really need to dig in and copy what I am doing. Section 1.2 helped you get R and R Commander set up on your computer. You now need to continue being active by replicating on your version of R what I do in this book. To help you learn to manipulate variables in R the same way that they can be manipulated in SPSS, you will need to learn more about the basic nature of R and how it works, so this section starts by having you use R as a calculator and understand how data is arranged in R. Once you have understood the basics, it will become easier to see how to manipulate variables within your data set.

This section will not be very useful to you unless you actually work along with the book on a computer by yourself. But you can take this exercise a step further if you not only copy what I do, but if you also intentionally make mistakes and see what happens when you do so. Working this way you will learn a lot about R and how it works.

1.4.1 Using R as a Calculator

R can add up numbers. Type the following sequence and see what happens:

```
67+35+99+10308
```

R will follow your input line with an output line that looks like this:

```
[1] 10509
```

This is the sum of the numbers you just added up. The symbols for other basic mathematical functions are a dash for a minus sign (-), a star for multiplication (*) and a slash for division (/). A decimal point is represented by a period (.). Use parentheses to perform mathematical functions in a preferred order. Thus:

```
(240+50*10)/2 #240 plus 50 times 10 divided by 2
```

will be a different result from

```
240+(50*10)/2
```

because the parentheses group the numbers differently.

> **Tip:** You can scroll through previous commands by hitting the arrow up button. Once you have a previous command in the input line, you cannot use your mouse to move to different parts of the command to edit, but you can use the arrow forward or arrow back keys to edit your command (on a Mac you can though!). Try this with the parentheses for the two numbers above; bring up the previous command with the parentheses around (240 + 50 * 10) and delete the first parentheses to put it in front of the 50 now. You will want this skill for when you do the application activity. You can use the escape button (ESC) to get back to a blank prompt.

This is a traditional way to add commentary after the command line in R. If you could copy and paste this command into R, the hash mark would tell R to ignore anything after it, and it would not try to compute anything. Notice that I added a commentary after a hash mark (#) in one of the command lines above. If you did not enter the hash mark, like this:

```
(240+50*10)/2 #240 plus 50 times 10 divided by 2
```

and then entered this line into R, you would see the following error message:

```
Error: unexpected numeric constant in "(240+50*10)/2 240"
```

When working with R, you are sure to receive lots of error messages. It is useful to pay attention to these, as they can help you figure out what you did wrong.

One more useful set of functions is raising a number to a power and taking its square root. Take the square root by using the command sqrt( ). The parentheses indicate that you need to put the number you are calculating into the parentheses after that command, like this:

```
> sqrt(16)
[1] 4
```

Remember that if you are using one of R's built-in functions, like the square root calculation, it will require that the arguments to the command be found in parentheses. You will get an error message if you forget to put the parentheses in. The error message will depend on which mistake you made. Look at the following examples:

```
> sqrt32
Error: object 'sqrt32' not found
```

Here, R thinks you are calling an object that has the name 'sqrt32', but it does not have that object in its memory.

```
> sqrt 32
Error: unexpected numeric constant in "sqrt 32"
```

Here the error message is different because I put a space between the command and the number, so now R does not think it is an object, but it cannot evaluate the function without the parentheses.

```
> sqrt(32
+
```

Here I put the first parenthesis in but forgot the second one so R writes a plus sign to give me a chance to continue and finish my command. If I typed an ending parentheses R would carry out the calculation. However, if you want to get out of a command without finishing the calculation, click on the ESC button.

> **Mac Tip**: The Mac GUI automatically includes both the beginning and ending parentheses when you put in the first parentheses, so on a Mac you cannot make this last mistake of just including one side of the parentheses.

You might also want to raise a number to a power, and you can do this by adding the caret (^) mark after the base number and before the number you want to raise it to. Therefore, the number 105 would be represented in R as 10^5. Notice the result you get when you try to calculate 10^5.

```
> 10^5
[1] 1e+05
```

R does not think you need to see the number 100,000. But if it has been a while since you have done math, remember that here the "e" means you take the number that is in front of it and move the decimal point to the right for the number of spaces indicated by the number after the plus sign. In this case, that number is simple (a 1 with 5 zeros after it), but in other cases it would not be:

```
> 93754683^9
[1] 5.596761e+71
```

R as a Calculator

To use R as a calculator, enter numbers and numerical function symbols after the command prompt.

+	= add
-	= subtract
*	= multiply
/	= divide
sqrt()	= square root function
^	= raise a number before the caret symbol to a power given after symbol

Use parentheses to group your mathematical operations, if needed.

1.4.2 Using R as a Calculator Practice Activities

Perform the mathematical functions described below using R.

1 Add the numbers 88, 2689, 331, 389, and 2.
2 Subtract 89.32 from 25338
3 Multiply 59 and 26. Divide by the square root of 24.
4 Let us pretend you make USD2500 a month. Subtract out your rent (800), money for food (500), health care costs (150), car payment (136), car insurance (55), car gas (260), gym membership (35), and entertainment expenses (225). How much do you have left to save?
5 Add 275 and 38 together then raise that to the third power and divide everything by 6.
6 Divide 258367 by 268. Add 245 and 897 to that number. Multiply the result by 4 raised to the 20th power.

7 Whoops! You forgot to add in a couple of bills this month, so go back to your calculations in item #4 and subtract your cell phone bill ($63.24), your cable bill ($35.10) and a new pair of glasses this month ($180). And your rent just went up to $850 a month, so change that. Now how much can you save?
8 Multiply 42 by 84, divide that by the sum of 90, 266, and 35, then raise that whole result to the third power.

1.4.3 Objects in R

So there you have it—you have seen how R can be your calculator! Actually, the reason I like R better than a calculator is that I have all the numbers printed out in front of me so I can check my math, but I can also go back and change numbers or add more later, just like in the application activity. But we will now move on to looking at R as more than a calculator. Any command that we tell R to do can be put into an object. We name the object ourselves. The command line below shows how I take all my budget calculations from the application activity and put them into an object I will call Savings:

```
Savings <-2500-(850+500+150+136+55+260+35+225+63.24+35.10+180)
```

Notice that I use the sequence of two symbols, the less than sign (<) and the dash (-) (together called the assignment operator), to show that whatever is on the right side is going into the object on the left side of the symbols. You can also use an equal sign here (=), which is of course easier to type, but the assignment operator may be helpful because it shows which way the assignment is going. (The part on the right is assigned into the object named on the left.) Venables and Smith (2005) noted that the equal sign (=) is an equivalent to the assignment operator (<-) in most cases, but there are some exceptions. You will see me use both the equal sign and the alternate assignment operator throughout the book.

Notice that when you type the command line that calculates my savings for the month of March into R, you will not see anything. R will not return any answer until you ask it to. When you type in the name of the object, then you get the results of the calculation:

```
> Savings
[1] 10.66
```

This type of object has only one entry. But let us create another object that has several entries. I cannot just enter the name of an object that is not defined though, so I will first make a couple more objects for my budget:

```
Salary<-2500
Fixed.Expenses<-c(850,500,150,136,55,260,35,225)
Bills<-c(63.24,35.10)
Additional.Expenses<-180
```

Notice in every case where I am entering more than one number, I have used a "c" before the parentheses. The "c" stands for "concatenation" and is a built-in, primitive function of R. For more information about primitive functions of R, type library(help="base"). This is a function that combines its arguments to make a **vector**, which is basically a column of data if you think of the data set up in a spreadsheet. Now I will create a formula to calculate my savings every month without having to type in my fixed numbers every time:

```
Savings=Salary-(sum(Fixed.Expenses) + sum(Bills) + Additional.Expenses)
```

Notice that I had to use a function, sum(), that sums up the numbers, for every object with more than one entry. If I had not done this, R would have returned a collection of numbers as an answer, not just one number. (Try it yourself; write the equation without the command sum() and see what the object summary returns.)

Now R has stored that number in the object called **Savings**. If I want to see it, I have to ask R to show me what is in the object, by just typing its name:

```
> Savings
[1] 10.66
```

Obviously, this is what we calculated before, but the point is that now each month I could, for example, just redefine my "Bills" category and my "Additional Expenses" category and then run the equation again to see how much I can save that month.

At this point, you can now understand how you could create a vector of numbers. You would simply use the c() command and enter a series of numbers separated by commas. Vectors can also consist of character strings, as well as numbers. To tell R that these are not numbers, you need to insert double or single quotation marks around the character strings, like this:

```
MyFamily<-c('Andrea','Mark','Annette','Caroline')
```

```
> MyFamily
[1] "Andrea"   "Mark"     "Annette"  "Caroline"
```

If you forget the quotation marks, R thinks you are looking for previously defined objects (like those I defined in my budget calculation), and gives you an error message:

```
> MyFamily<-c(Andrea,Mark,Annette,Caroline)
Error: object 'Andrea' not found
```

You cannot combine numbers and character strings in the same vector. If you put numbers and character strings into the same object, R will coerce everything to be of the same type, which here is a character. (We can tell because the quotation marks are around the numbers as well as the names.)

```
MyFamily<-c('Andrea',23,'Mark',15, 'Annette',45, 'Caroline', 18)
```

```
> MyFamily
[1] "Andrea"   "23"       "Mark"     "15"       "Annette"  "45"
[7] "Caroline" "18"
```

In R you will create objects. A vector is one column of data, consisting of numbers or character strings. A vector can have only one type or the other, not both in the same vector. Create a vector by naming the vector on the left side of the equation and then specifying on the right the content:

```
FavoriteAmericanIdols<-c('Constantine', 'Clay Aiken', 'Kelly Clarkson')
FavoriteNumbers<-c(25,8,17,22)
```

Use the c() concatenation function to combine the elements of the vector together. A vector may also consist of mathematical operations on previously defined objects:

```
LuckyNumber=sum(FavoriteNumbers)
LuckyNumber
[1] 72
```

1.4.4 Creating Objects in R Practice Activities

1. Create a numeric vector of the following numbers and call it "Years": 1976, 2003, 2009, 1900. Look at the vector you just made. Did it rearrange the order of the numbers?
2. Create a character vector with your own family's names in it and call it "MyFamily". Look at the vector you just made. Are the names listed with a single quotation mark, double quotation mark, or no quotation mark?

3 Create a numeric vector that lists your monthly income called "Salary". Create another numeric vector that lists your monthly expenses called "Expenses". Create one more vector called "Budget" that subtracts the sum of your monthly expenses from your salary. Show your vectors.

1.4.5 Types of Data in R

This section looks at the different types, or classes, of data in R. This is not just an academic exercise; the class of data in R will often determine how graphics will be displayed in the **plot()** command, how generic functions such as **summary()** treat the data, and whether you can use specific types of commands that may require the data to be in a certain format to work. It is thus important to understand some of the types of data that you will meet most frequently when using R.

If you import data, you create an object that R labels a data frame. A data frame is a collection of columns and rows of data, and the data can be numeric or character. (Remember that characters in R are symbols that have no numerical value.) It only has two dimensions, that of rows and columns. All of the columns must have the same length. Most of the data you will work with are in data frames, and you can think of it as a traditional table. You can see an example of a data frame in Table 1.1. To create the data frame in Table 1.1, I simply asked R to give me just the first few rows of data by using the **head()** command with the **mcguireSR** data set. This data set comes from work by McGuire (2009) on how fluency of English as a second language learner is affected by a focus on language chunking. If you want to follow along, import this text file and call it mcguireSR. (It is comma-delimited, so read it in using the R Console as outlined on p. 26.

```
head(mcguireSR) #gives first few rows of the data frame
```

An object with just one column of numbers (if you think of the numbers arranged in a spreadsheet) creates a vector. Some commands for robust statistics that you will see later in the book require arguments that are vectors. If you take just one column out of a data frame and turn it into an object with a new name, this is a vector. For example, one column of posttest data is taken out of the imported data set called **mcguireSR**:

```
mcguireSR$Post.test
```

```
 [1] 140.5 134.0 143.3 156.3 162.0 141.3 134.2 160.0 134.2 137.2 168.9 128.5
[13] 145.9 147.5 127.7 174.8 165.5 151.8 179.4
```

I then put these numbers into an object I name **MPT** (for McGuire posttest):

```
MPT=mcguireSR$Post.test
```

```
> is.vector(MPT)
[1] TRUE
> class(MPT)
[1] "numeric"
```

A command that asks if an object is a vector (**is.vector( )**) verifies that it is. A more general command **class()** tells you what type of data you have, but if it is a vector, it will be classified as numeric or character. You can see a vector of data in Table 1.1. For the vector in Table 1.1, I just typed the data from the posttest into a vector by hand:

```
mcguireVector=c(140.5, 134, 143.3, 156.3, 162.0, 141.3)
class(mcguireVector)
[1] "numeric"
```

Another object in R that you may need for doing robust statistics is a list. A list is just a collection of vectors, which may be of different lengths and different types. (This is different from a data frame, where all of the columns must be the same length.) You can see an example of the **mcguireSR** data turned into a list in Table 1.1. The syntax for massaging the data into a list is a little complicated. Do not worry too much about it here; I will give you another example when you need to turn your data into a list; it is more important to just understand now how a list differs from a data frame or a vector:

```
mcguirelist=list() #this creates an empty list
mcguirelist[[1]]<-c('Control', 'Control', 'Experimental', 'Experimental', 'Experimental', 'Experimental')
#the designation [[1]] says that this is the first column of data. I wanted this column to
#consist of characters, not numbers, so I had to put quotation marks around each word


mcguirelist[[2]]<-c(140.5,134.0,143.3,156.3,162.0,141.3)
mcguirelist[[3]]<-c(126.60,140.38,103.80, 135,60,133.66,146.10)
class(mcguirelist)

[1] "list"
```

Table 1.1 Illustrations of R Data Types: Data Frames, Vectors and Lists

Data frame (all columns same length)

	Group	Posttest	Pretest
1	Control	140.5	126.60
2	Control	134.0	140.38
3	Experimental	143.3	103.80
4	Experimental	156.3	135.60
5	Experimental	162.0	133.66
6	Experimental	141.3	146.10

Vector (just the posttest data)

[1] 140.5 134.0 143.3 156.3 162.0 141.3

List (columns can be different lengths)

```
[[1]]
[1] "Control"   "Control"   "Experimental"   "Experimental"   "Experimental"
[6] "Experimental"

[[2]]
[1] 140.5  134.0  143.3  156.3  162.0  141.3

[[3]]
[1] 126.60  140.38  103.80  135.00  60.00  133.66  146.10
```

There are a number of other types of data in R, namely matrices, arrays and factors. A **matrix** is similar to a data frame, but all the data must be either numeric or character. An **array** can have more than two dimensions, and looks like a list of tables. It is often used with categorical data. These first two data types are not used much in this book so I will not explain them further. More information can be found in Appendix A, however.

The last additional type of data is the factor. A factor is a vector that is a categorical variable and it contains a vector of integers as well as a vector of character strings that characterize those integers. This is a very useful data type to use with statistical procedures, but in most cases, if you import your data and your categorical variables as strings, R will automatically classify them as factors, so no further attention to this is needed on your part. For example, the imported **mcguireSR** data set has an independent variable (IV) **Group**, which contains character strings. If these data are summarized, because they are a factor, R can count how many people belong to each group.

```
summary(mcguireSR$Group)
Control Experimental
      8           11

class(mcguireSR$Group)
[1] "factor"
```

You can find out what type of data you have by using the class() command. Here is a brief summary of the types of data in R:

data frame:	a traditional table with columns and rows
vector:	one column of a traditional table, where items are numeric or character strings
matrix:	a table where all variables are numeric or all variables are character
list:	a collection of vectors; it differs from a table because the vectors can have different lengths.
array:	a collection of data; a one-dimensional array is a vector; a two-dimensional array is a matrix; arrays can be larger than two dimensions as well.
factor:	a vector that has character strings which can be counted

1.4.6 Types of Data Practice Activities

1. Import and open the BEQ.Dominance data set. (It is an SPSS .sav file.) It has 1578 rows and 4 columns. (You can see this in a note in the messages window at the bottom of R Commander.) Find out what type of data this is (use the **class()** command).
2. There are four variables in this beq data. Find out their names by typing **names(beq)**. The variable CatDominance in the beq data set is a categorical variable. Find out if it is indeed a factor. (Remember that you can pick this variable out of the set by writing the name of the data set followed by a dollar symbol ($) and the name of the variable.)
3. How many levels are there in the CatDominance variable? How many people in each level? Use the **summary()** command.
4. Referring back to the vectors you created in the application activity 1.4.4, find out what class of data your objects MyFamily and Salary are. What is the difference between these two types of vectors?

1.4.7 Functions in R

There are many built-in functions of R that we will use in future sections. Here, I will start with a few simple and basic ones so that you can see how functions work in R. They will not necessarily be useful later, as there are more complex functions that will include the simple functions we look at here, but they will serve as a basic introduction to functions. We will start with the function **sum()**. The arguments of **sum()** are numbers that are listed inside the parentheses, with each number followed by a comma.

```
sum(34,10,26)
[1] 70
```

The function **mean()** will return the average of any numbers included in its arguments.

```
mean(34,10,26)
[1] 34
```

If you have imported a data set, such as the data frame **mcguireSR**, you can find the mean score of the entire numeric vector with this function as well. In other words, you can put any numeric object inside the **mean()** function, not just single numbers.

```
mean(mcguireSR$Pre.test)
[1] 137.7547
```

However, if you put in a non-numeric vector, such as the factor **Group** in the **mcguireSR** data frame, you will get an error message.

```
mean(mcguireSR$Group)
Warning in mean.default(mcguireSR$Group) :
  argument is not numeric or logical: returning NA
[1] NA
```

Several other short and simple functions could be used on a numeric vector:

```
length(mcguireSR$Post.test) #gives N
[1] 19

min(mcguireSR$Post.test) #minimum score
[1] 127.7

max(mcguireSR$Post.test) #maximum
[1] 179.4

range(mcguireSR$Post.test) #minimum and maximum score=range
[1] 127.7 179.4

sd(mcguireSR$Post.test) #standard deviation
[1] 15.74295

var(mcguireSR$Post.test) #variance (=sd^2)
[1] 247.8405
```

There are many built-in functions in R. Here is a summary of some very simple ones.

sum( )	adds arguments together
mean( )	gives average of arguments
length( )	returns *N* of vector
min( )	minimum score
max( )	maximum score
range( )	gives minimum and maximum
sd( )	standard deviation
var( )	variance

1.4.8 Functions in R Practice Activities

1 Import the SPSS data set DeKeyser2000.sav. Call it dekeyser. Verify that the variance of the GJTScore is just the standard deviation squared using the **var( )** and **sd( )** functions.

2 Calculate the average age of the participants in the dekeyser data frame (use the names( ) command to help you get the right name for this column of data). Use the function mean( ).
3 Which is the oldest age in the deKeyser data set? Use the function max( ).
4 Import the SPSS data set LarsonHallPartial.sav. Call it partial. How many participants were there in this study? (Count the number of participants using the length( ) function.) What were the mean and standard deviation of their accuracy on words beginning in R/L?

1.4.9 The R Workspace

In section 1.3.4 I mentioned the command ls( ), which lists the names of objects that are in the R workspace. These are the data sets the user has imported into R, and the functions the user has defined. R Commander's "Data set" button will list the imported data sets, but not the functions that the user has defined. (You will understand better how you yourself might define a function when you work through the next chapter.)

If you want to clean this workspace up, you can remove data sets or functions with the rm( ) command:

```
rm(partial) #remove the data set partial
```

This can be useful if you have defined something you want to redefine, or just want to clear things off your workspace.

1.4.10 Specifying Variables within a Data Set, and Attaching and Detaching Data Sets

As you are working with a specific data set in R, it can be highly useful to attach your data set to the R search path. By attaching your data set, you can change the way you call for arguments, and thus save yourself some time in typing. When you attach a data frame, you can refer to variables by their names alone without having to call them up as components of the larger data frame. For example, in the data frame called dekeyser there are three variables, as can be seen in this R printout:

```
names(dekeyser)
[1] "age"      "gjtscore" "status"
age
Error: object 'age' not found
dekeyser$age
 [1]  8 11  9 11 13  4  1 12  3 10  6 11  5  9
[26] 26 21 23 17 25 20 34 25 22 33 35 29 28 26 (data cut)
```

Note that if I try to call up the variable age from the DeKeyser data frame, it tells me it cannot be found. That is because to call up a variable, I need to first specify the data set that the variable comes from, as in the command to print the variable age with dekeyser$age.

If, however, I attach the data frame first, I can legitimately call up just the variable age.

```
attach(dekeyser)
age
[1]  8 11  9 11 13  4  1 12  3 10  6 11 (data cut)
```

The command **search( )** will tell me which objects are attached most highly in R's search path. (It always starts with ".GlobalEnv", so do not try to remove that one.)

```
search()
[1] ".GlobalEnv"          "dekeyser"            "package:markdown"
[4] "package:knitr"       "package:foreign"     "package:car"        (data cut)
```

After you are done working with a particular data set, it is always a good idea to take it off of the search path so that you can later attach other data sets.

```
detach(dekeyser)
```

You can also remove the data set by using the command rm(), but this will completely delete the data from R.

1.5 Missing Data

It is a very common occurrence, especially in a research design where data are collected at different time periods, to be missing data for some participants. The question of what to do with missing data is a rich one and cannot be fully explored here, but there are many articles that deal with missing data imputation if you are interested in reading further about it, such as Allison (2002), Little and Rubin (1987) and McKnight, McKnight, Sidani and Figueredo (2007). I will merely give a short summary of what can be done when the missing data points do not follow any kind of pattern. An example of a pattern of missing data would be that in administering a questionnaire you found that all respondents from a particular first language background would not answer a certain question. If this whole group is left out of a summary of the data, this distorts the findings. In this case, it may be best to delete the entire question or variable.

It is up to the user to explicitly specify what to do with missing values. I would like to point out, however, that Wilkinson (1999) suggested that the worst way to deal with missing data is listwise and pairwise deletion. These are the easiest ways to deal with missing data, but not the best ways. If you delete an entire case because a value in one variable is missing (listwise deletion), this of course means that all the work you went to in obtaining data from that participant is wasted, and of course with a smaller sample size your power to find results is reduced. Pairwise deletion is when you omit data for those cases where the variable(s) you are examining do not have data, but you do not omit the whole case from your data set. Doing this results in different *N*s for different comparisons in the data set, and means that the parameters of the model are biased.

Howell (2012) suggested that two methods have become widely recognized as the best solutions to the problem of missing data, now that we have computer programs which can easily run them. These are the expectation/maximization algorithm (EM) and multiple imputation. The details of how these methods work are beyond the scope of this book, but Howell provides a comprehensive summary at his Treatment of Missing Data Web page (www.uvm.edu/~dhowell/StatPages/More_Stuff/Missing_Data/Missing.html). In this book, I will use programs to impute the data that use multiple imputation methods. Non-technically, imputation will examine the values in your file and fill in values that are predicted to occur, but it will also add some randomness to these data so as not to bias the statistical parameters. **Multiple imputation (MI)** will perform a number of different imputations (and create a number of files, usually five) that are then pooled when you do your statistical analysis, resulting in more accuracy than if just one imputation were used.

1.5.1 Missing Data and Multiple Imputation in SPSS

Missing data in an SPSS file are indicated by an incomplete pattern of results in the SPSS spreadsheet. If you do not have some parts of data for a particular participant (a row in an SPSS spreadsheet), then there will simply be a blank space in the spreadsheet, as in Figure 1.27.

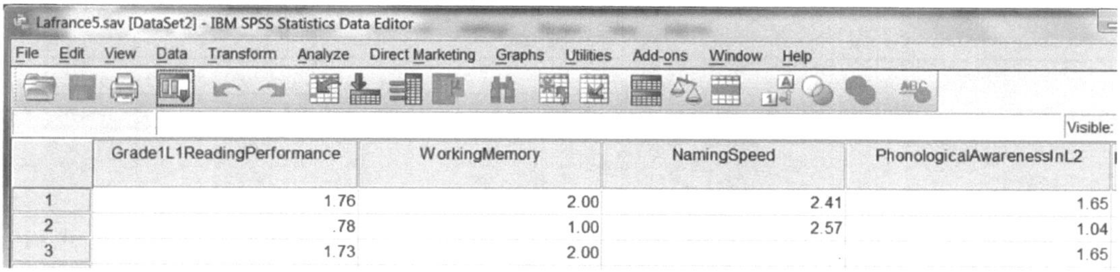

Figure 1.27 Missing data in an SPSS spreadsheet, indicated by a blank cell (under "NamingSpeed").

Some researchers like to fill in a number for missing values, such as 999 or -9, but if you do not already do this, I would not recommend it. Simply leave the cell blank, and we will perform a procedure to fill in the missing cells.

If you do not do anything to address the issue of missing data in your data file, then when you perform analyses in SPSS, SPSS will use listwise or pairwise deletion as a default. Since I have already noted that listwise or pairwise deletion are the worst ways to deal with missing data in your files, if your data are in fact missing at random, and not a pattern that should in fact be taken into account in your analysis, then you should correct the situation by using MI. So start the process by going to ANALYZE > MISSING VALUE ANALYSIS. A dialog box will pop up and give you options for exploring the missingness in your data file. This dialog box would allow you to impute missing data using EM methods, but generally imputation is considered to be the best alternative (Howell, 2008) so do not impute from this dialog box. You can see from Figure 1.28 that I have moved all of the variables over to the "Quantitative Variables" box because the Lafrance5 data set does not have any categorical variables. I then pushed the button labeled "Patterns", and chose the second choice, "Cases with missing values, sorted by missing value patterns".

The output in Table 1.2 shows counts and what percentage of the data is missing. For the Lafrance5 data set, three cases are missing data for the NamingSpeed variable, which is 7.5% of the data set.

A further piece of output (not shown) gives the actual row numbers that are missing data, which could be useful to researchers to check to make sure they have not simply forgotten to type in the data or have made some other type of mistake. Looking at the data we can decide these data are missing completely at random, and thus we can feel justified in imputing the data.

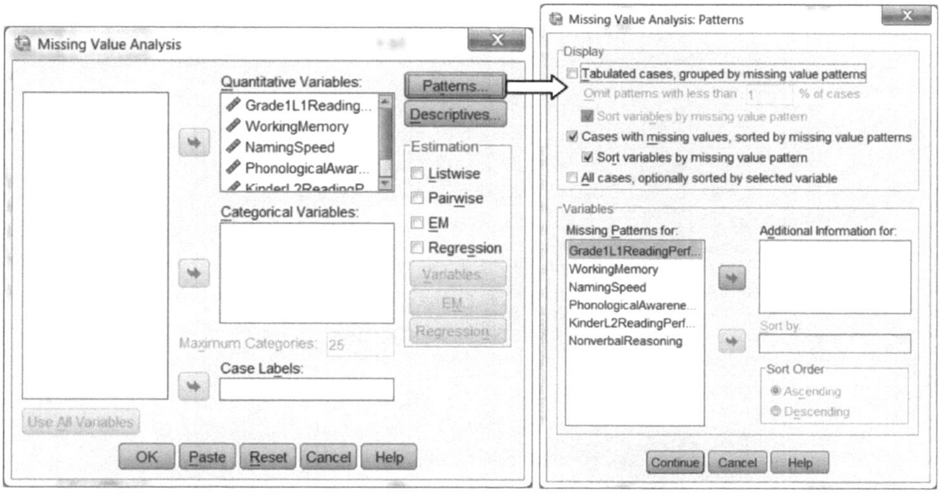

Figure 1.28 Looking for patterns in missing data.

Table 1.2 Missing Value Analysis Output from SPSS

Univariate Statistics

	N	Mean	Std. Deviation	Missing		No. of Extremes[a]	
				Count	Percent	Low	High
Grade1L1ReadingPerformance	40	1.3713	.44937	0	.0	1	0
WorkingMemory	40	2.5750	1.25856	0	.0	3	1
NamingSpeed	37	2.2414	.12846	3	7.5	0	1
PhonologicalAwarenessInL2	40	1.4854	.20789	0	.0	0	0
KinderL2ReadingPerformance	40	.5173	.57666	0	.0	0	0
NonverbalReasoning	40	48.6000	7.19972	0	.0	0	0

a. Number of cases outside the range (Q1 - 1.5*IQR, Q3 + 1.5*IQR).

To do the imputation, choose Analyze > Multiple Imputation > Impute Missing Data Values. The multiple imputation procedure will create a set of new data that can be used in further analysis within SPSS, so it is a good idea to move over all of the variables that you think you will use in your analysis, even if, as in this case, only one variable has missing data. I decided to move over all of the variables into the box that says "Variables in Model" (see Figure 1.29). The number of imputation iterations is set at five, and this is a fine default level. Give a name to your new imputed data set at the bottom of the dialog box.

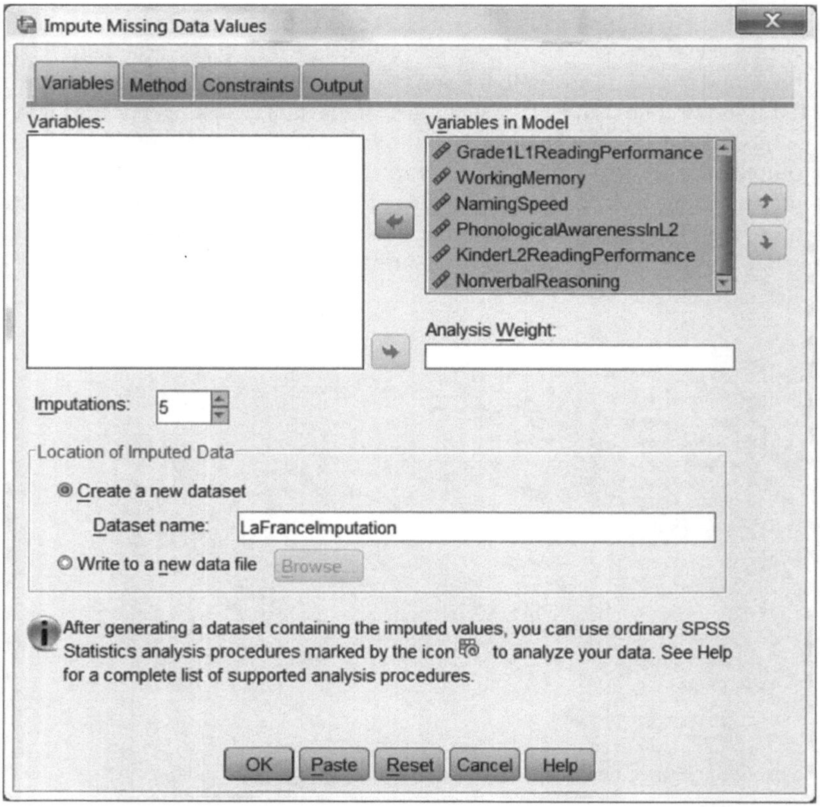

Figure 1.29 Multiple imputation in SPSS.

The output of this procedure is not really what you are interested in. Instead, if you go to the menus at the top of the SPSS window and pull down the Window menu, you will see the file that contains your newly imputed data (here, I named it "LaFranceImputation"), as shown in Figure 1.30.

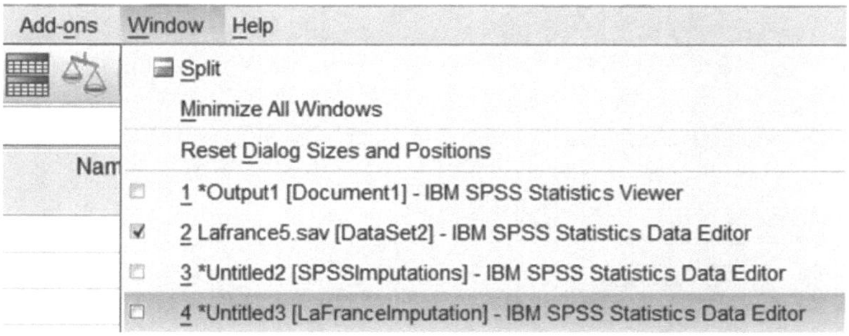

Figure 1.30 Finding your imputed file in SPSS.

Check that file and it will open. Note that the first column is titled "Imputation_". This gives the imputation iteration. In the first iteration, labeled "0," the missing data are still missing, but in every run after that (1 through 5) the missing data are filled in and marked by a highlighted cell in the spreadsheet (as in Figure 1.31).

	Imputation_	Grade1L1ReadingPerformance	WorkingMemory	NamingSpeed
37	0	1.82	3.00	2.03
38	0	1.83	6.00	2.14
39	0	1.40	2.00	2.22
40	0	1.69	2.00	2.16
41	1	1.76	2.00	2.41
42	1	.78	1.00	2.57
43	1	1.73	2.00	2.31
44	1	1.51	2.00	2.18
45	1	1.51	4.00	2.01

Figure 1.31 Imputed cells are highlighted in every imputation run (after the original data file, labeled as "0" in the "Imputation_" column).

You are now ready to use the imputed data file in various analyses in SPSS. If you have the imputed data set open and you pull down the ANALYSIS menu, you will now see this icon (noted in the bottom of the dialog window shown in Figure 1.29) that means you can use your imputed data with this analysis. Figure 1.32 shows that the imputed Lafrance5 file can be used in a Linear regression model, Binary Logistic regression model, Multinomial Logistic regression model or Ordinal model. We will use a linear regression model on this later, and the only thing that will change compared to an ordinary regression is that you put the "Imputation_" variable into the box called "Selection variable", then open the "Rule" button and choose to use all five imputations (Figure 1.33). The printout will contain data for all five imputations separately, but there will also be a result for "Pooled" data, which uses all five iterations of the imputations. These are the data you should look for. You might also want to look at David Howell's explanation of this process (www.uvm.edu/~dhowell/StatPages/More_Stuff/Missing_Data/MissingDataSPSS.html).

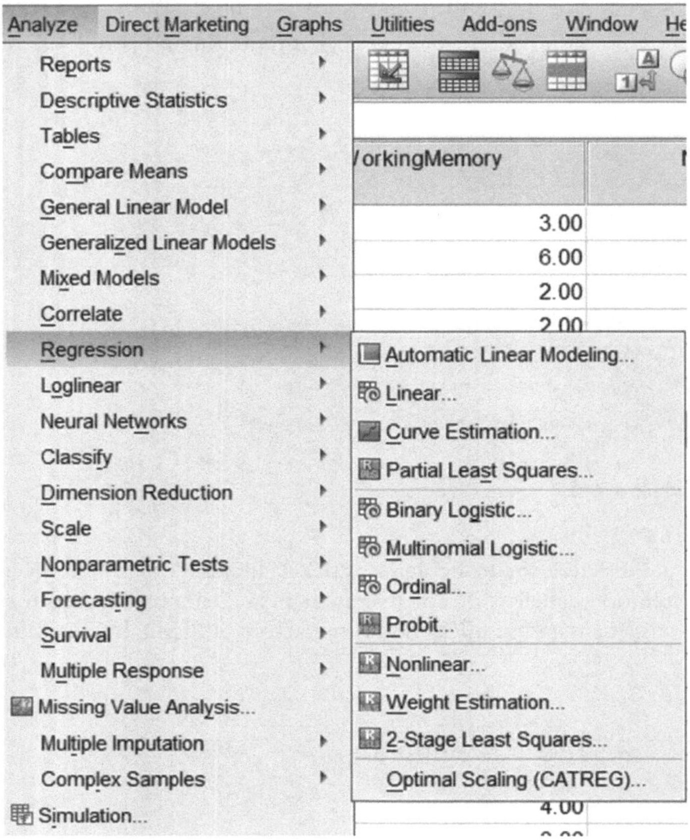

Figure 1.32 SPSS regression analyses, with those procedures which can use multiply imputed data marked with an icon.

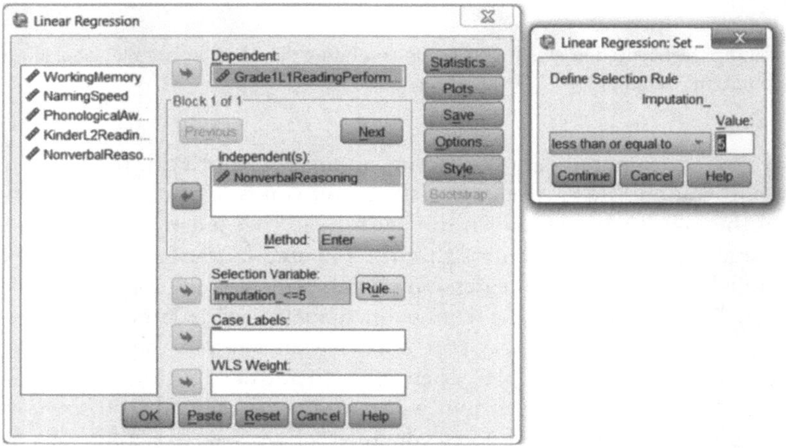

Figure 1.33 Performing a linear regression using multiple imputation data in SPSS.

1.5.2 Missing Data Application Activity in SPSS

1 Create a new file called "ClassTest"

Pretest	*Posttest*	*Delayed posttest*
22	87	91
4	56	68
75	77	75
36	59	64
25	42	76
48		79
51	48	

You are entering in missing data (leaving some cells blank). Save the data set you created as an SPSS file.

2 Do a missing value analysis on the data set. What percentage of the data is missing in each variable? Look at your imputed files and verify that there are now no missing data, and look at how the missing data value varies from file to file.

1.5.3 Missing Data and Multiple Imputation in R

R will import an empty cell by filling in with the letters "NA" for "not available." If you enter data and are missing a piece, you can simply type in NA yourself. However, R commands differ as to how they deal with NA data. Some commands do not have a problem with it, other commands will automatically deal with missing data, and for other commands they will not work if any data are missing. However, for commands that automatically deal with missing data, it is likely that they will perform listwise or pairwise deletion, which we noted was the easiest but least wise way to deal with missing data. Therefore, this section addresses how to perform MI on data sets that are missing data.

One way to check if you have any missing data is by using the command is.na( ).This command will return a "FALSE" if the value is present and a "TRUE" if the value is missing. Here I try it for the extremely large data set, beq.

```
is.na(beq)
 catdominance numberoflang sex age
[1,] FALSE  FALSE FALSE FALSE
[2,] FALSE  FALSE FALSE FALSE
[3,] FALSE  FALSE FALSE FALSE
[4,] TRUE   FALSE FALSE FALSE
[5,] TRUE   FALSE FALSE FALSE
```

The results return what are called "logical" answers in R. R has queried about whether each piece of data is missing, and is told that it is false that the data are missing. If you found the answer "TRUE" that would mean data were missing. Of course, if your data set is small enough, just glancing through it without any special commands can give you the same type of information! However, for larger data sets this is impractical. This command is much more economical and summarizes whether you have NAs in each variable:

```
sapply(beq, function(x)(sum(is.na(x)))) #NA counts
```

If you have missing values missing at random, you can easily impute variables with the "mice" package (van Buuren & Groothuis-Oudshoorn, 2011). The default method of imputation depends on the measurement level of the column, according to the mice help file, but for an interval level variable, the default will be predictive mean matching. According to Kabacoff (2011), the mice( ) function imputes missing values by Gibbs sampling: "By default, each variable containing missing values is predicted from all other variables in the data set. These prediction equations are used to impute plausible values for the missing data. The process iterates until convergence over the missing values is achieved" (p. 366).

Multiple imputation will produce several different complete data sets where the missing values have been imputed, and since each imputation is random, each completed data set is slightly different. Thus, we will want to create this set of imputed data sets, but then use our statistical model on all of the imputed data sets. (If you do not specify any number, the mice package will automatically create five data sets.) We will create an object we call fit, and then pool the data from all of the imputed data sets. Although you have not yet read about regression in Chapter 7, in that chapter I use the Lafrance and Gottardo (2005) data (the SPSS file is Lafrance5.sav, imported as lafrance) to run a regression. The regression is fairly complicated, so I will simplify for the sake of example. Let us say we decide to model the variance in First Grade L1 reading performance (grade1l1readingperformance) by just one IV of phonological awareness in L2 (phonologicalawarenessinl2). Then the regression model is written in R like this: lm(grade1l1readingperformance~ phonologicalawarenessinl2, data=lafrance). Thus, I will put this model inside the imputation commands:

```
install.packages("mice")
library(mice)
imp<-mice(lafrance, 5) #5 is the default number of imputed data sets
fit<-with(imp, lm(grade1l1readingperformance~ phonologicalawarenessinl2, data=lafrance))
pooled<-pool(fit)
summary(pooled)
```

Optionally, if the format of having multiple files does not work for the statistical test that you are doing, you do have the option to have mice return just one imputed object to you that you can name differently from the original and then work with. In this case, open the mice package and complete() the first line above where you impute the file. Next:

```
complete(imp) #shows the completed data matrix
implafrance<-complete(imp) #name the new file to work with
```

Another package that performs imputations is the Amelia package (named after Amelia Earhart) (Honaker & Blackwell, 2011). Although I found this package harder to work with than the mice package, I liked the missing values map that this package produced, so I will show you how to obtain this. It is not something I would publish, but you can examine it to see if you find any patterns of missingness in your data. Open this package, then open the Amelia GUI. The window on the left in Figure 1.34 shows where you can load your data set. The window on the right in Figure 1.34 shows what the lafrance data set looks like loaded up into Amelia.

```
library(Amelia)
AmeliaView()
```

You can see from Figure 1.34 that all six variables for the lafrance data are listed with their mean scores, standard deviations and missing data already listed. If you push the button for the "Missingness Map" you will see a visual representation of your missing data (Figure 1.35).

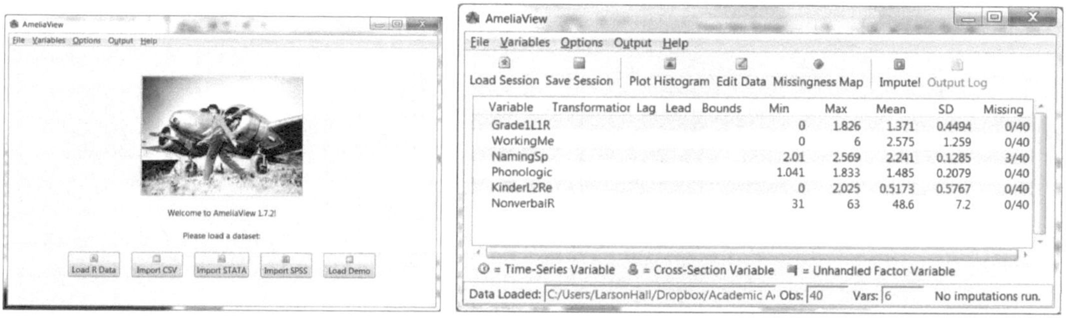

Figure 1.34 The Amelia GUI for visualizing and imputing data.

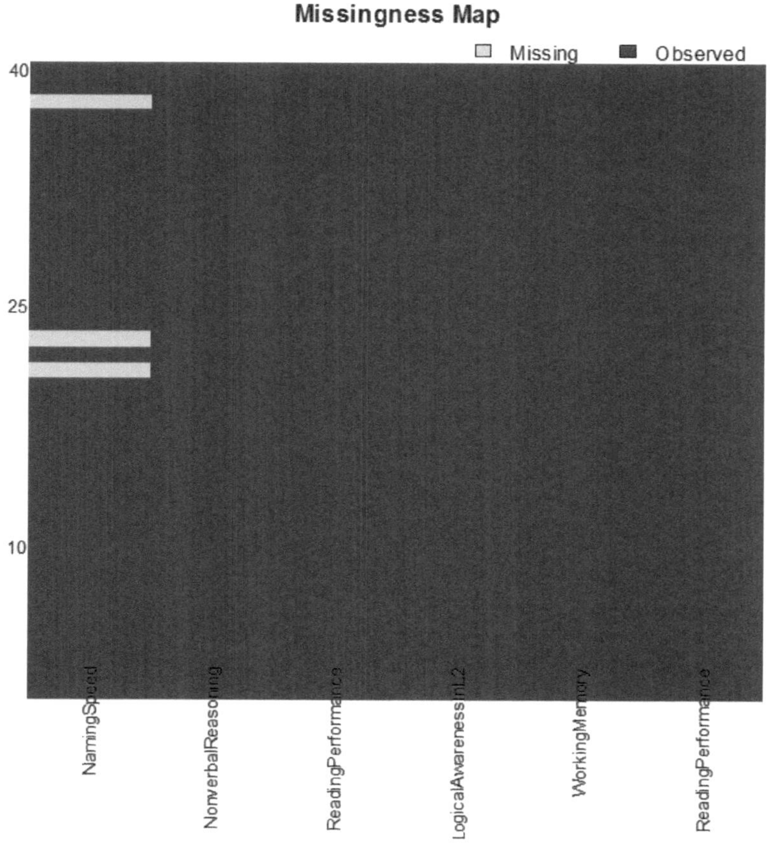

Figure 1.35 Missing data map from Amelia package.

Once you are done with this map, you will need to quit AmeliaView to use the R Console again. Although some researchers seem resistant to the idea of imputing data, from all that I have read it is a much better way to deal with data missing at random than to simply eliminate entire rows of data, so I highly recommend it in these circumstances.

1.5.4 Missing Data Application Activity in R

1 Create a new file called "ClassTest."

Pretest	*Posttest*	*Delayed posttest*
22	87	91
4	56	68
75	77	75
36	59	64
25	42	76
48	NA	79
51	48	NA

You are entering missing data (using the NA designation). After you have created the file, go ahead and check to see if you have any missing data (of course you do!). Save the data set you created as a .csv file.

2 Using AmeliaView, look at a Missingness Map of the data set. Then use the **mice** package to impute the file. Go ahead and use the **complete( )** command and give your imputed data set a new name. Look at the new data set with AmeliaView's Missingness Map. Is anything missing anymore? Which values did the missing values receive? (These will vary because of the random nature of the imputation, but say what yours is anyway.)

1.6 Getting Help

1.6.1 Getting Help with SPSS

Within the SPSS program there are a lot of options for help. If you go to the menu sequence HELP > TOPICS, you will be directed to a Web page that has an extensive list of topics you can search. These help topics are also available from within whichever command you are currently running. For example, if you feel like you need help understanding something about correlations better, if you click on the "Help" button within the correlation command, you will be taken straight to the Web page that concerns correlation.

1.6.2 Getting Help with R

R is an extremely versatile tool, but if you are a novice user, you will find that you will often run into glitches. A command will not work the way I have described, and you will not know why. So to help you out, I would like to introduce you to ways of getting more help in R.

First, if one of the steps I have outlined in the book does not work, try going through the following troubleshooting checklist. I assume that your problem arises when using the R Console, not when using R Commander.

Troubleshooting checklist for novices to R:

- Have you typed the command exactly as shown in the book? Are the capitalized letters capital and the non-capitalized letters non-capital? Since R records what you do, you can go back and look at your command to check this.

- Have you used the appropriate punctuation? Have you closed the parentheses on the command? If you typed the command in Microsoft Word first, you might have a problem with smart quotes. An error message like this

  Error: unexpected input in "hist(norm.x, xlab=""

  shows there is a problem with the quotation marks.
- Do you have any missing data (marked with NA)? If so, can the command you are trying to use deal with NAs? Read the help file to see what is said about missing data there. You may need to delete the row that contains missing data; try imputing the data so that you will not have any NAs.
- What is the structure of your file? Is your file in the correct format for the command? Use the str( ) command to see whether your variables are numerical, character or factors.

Next, there are help files available in R. If the command you want to use does not seem to be working correctly, you can call for further help. For example, if you wanted more information about how to set the working directory with the setwd( ) command, you would type:

```
help(setwd)
```

If you do not know the name of a command that you would like to use, you can use the help function to try to find the default command for that test in R. For example, if you want to use a ***t*-test** but do not know the command name, you can use the help.search( ) function, and put in the name you think it might be. You should put quotation marks around the thing you are searching for, like this:

```
help.search("ttest")
```

This command will bring up a list of lots of tests, none looking very helpful. A revision of the search to:

```
help.search("t-test")
```

brings up more promising results. However, you can actually find the *t*-test command more easily if you run a *t*-test in R Commander from the pull-down menu, and look at the function that is used, and as a novice that is the way that I recommend going first. However, later in your career with R, you may want help with functions that are not in R Commander, and you can use this command to help search for help files.

Help files in R are extremely helpful, but they can be confusing at first. I was first thrown by the expression "foo". This means to substitute in whatever the name of your file is. For example, write.csv (foo, file="foo.csv") means to just put in the name of your file wherever "foo" is. Thus, if my file is dekeyser, I would read the help files as telling me to use the command write.csv(dekeyser, file="dekeyser.csv").

There is more information in Appendix A on how to understand the R help files, but here are a couple of tips. Let us say you wanted to figure out how *t*-tests work, and you have discovered the command is t.test(). The last section, the Example section, may be the most useful for you at first. You can type:

```
example(t.test)
```

Some commands and results will appear in the R Console, and if there are any graphics they will pop up in the R Graphics Device. Here is some output from the *t*-test:

```
t.test> ## Classical example: Student's sleep data
t.test> plot(extra ~ group, data = sleep)
Waiting to confirm page change...

t.test> ## Traditional interface
t.test> with(sleep, t.test(extra[group == 1], extra[group == 2]))

        Welch Two Sample t-test

data:  extra[group == 1] and extra[group == 2]
t = -1.8608, df = 17.776, p-value = 0.0794
alternative hypothesis: true difference in means is not equal to 0
95 percent confidence interval:
 -3.3654832  0.2054832
sample estimates:
mean of x mean of y
     0.75      2.33
```

Remember, the hash mark ('#') means commentary, so the beginning of this example tells you it is a Classical example. The next line calls for a plot, and here is where the Graphics Device popped up. When I clicked on it, it outputted a box plot. The fifth line down shows me one way of calling for a *t*-test, by using the with() command, where the data are called sleep. I see that the *t*-test on that line must have two arguments, but in this case it looks like the data are all found in the same column called "extra", but are split into two groups, labeled simply as 1 and 2. After that the results for this test are printed out. Since you probably do not know the with() command yet this example may not be clear, but the "Usage" and "Arguments" sections of the help file will tell you what types of arguments you need to put in the command. For *t*-tests, you will see in the "Usage" section that the syntax is:

```
t.test(x, . . .)
```

This means that you must have an argument "x" in the syntax. The "Arguments" section tells you that x is "a (non-empty) numeric vector of data values." In other words, you must have at least one vector (one column) of data as an argument. One vector would be fine for a one-way *t*-test, but most *t*-tests will include two vectors of data, and the "Arguments" section tells you that another argument "y" can be included, which is another numeric vector. (Also, the dots in the syntax show that other things, including those things that are listed in the Arguments section, can be inserted into the command.)

The third entry in the "Arguments" section is shown below.

`alternative` a character string specifying the alternative hypothesis, must be one of `"two.sided"` (default), `"greater"` or `"less"`. You can specify just the initial letter.

This means that you can insert a command "alternative" into the syntax, like this:

```
t.test(x,y, alternative="two.sided")
```

The entry does note, however, that "two.sided" is the default, so it does not have to actually be inserted (as can be seen in the two-tailed *t*-test found in the example data above). However, if you want to have a one-tailed *t*-test, you can use the alternative="greater" or alternative="less" argument to call for this.

If you keep trying to understand the help files, eventually they will provide help! There are also some useful FAQs and manuals found under menu choice under Help in the R Console.

Another excellent place to try to find help is an online search. I have found that answers from the Stack Overflow (http://stackoverflow.com/) website tend to be quite helpful. You can post questions there, but be sure to follow the protocols and search the archives first so you will not be asking a question that has already been asked. This is also true for the http://finzi.psych.upenn.edu/search.html website. I have found that if you submit a legitimate question, people there can get you answers quite quickly! If you go to the R Project for Statistical Computing website (www.r-project.org/) and click on "FAQs" on the left-hand menu, you can find answers to common questions. The "Search" link on the left-hand menu takes you to a list of places to search for archived answers to R questions.

1.7 Summary

In this chapter you have become familiar with the SPSS and R environments. For SPSS, when you open up the program, two basic windows will launch. One is the Data Editor, where we enter data in the "Data View" tab and define variables in the "Variable View" tab. The other window is the SPSS Viewer, where we can see the output we requested. Both windows contain all of the menu options available in SPSS.

For R, you have downloaded the free program which shows the R Console, and also the R GUI I use in this book, R Commander, which recreates a menu-type environment for R. R Commander is an easy way of launching yourself into R, but in some cases we have been forced to use the R Console as well, and both programs will be used integratively through the rest of the book.

You have tried your hand at both importing data into the programs and creating new data files. You also know how to save both your data files and your output files once you are finished. Once you have data in your program, you can start working with it and manipulating it. This chapter did not incorporate the sections on manipulating data in R and SPSS because these are shown for each case that needs it in the following chapters; for general practice, see the online sections called "Manipulating Variables in SPSS" and "Manipulating Variables in R." Useful techniques covered in those sections include: calculating new variables, recoding old variables into new variables, excluding cases from a data set and sorting variables.

Another important aspect of this chapter was learning how to deal with missing data by imputing values that are missing at random. This results in multiple files that have different values for the missing data, and there are special techniques or programs for pooling these data together in your analysis. If you need to generate random numbers, Excel and R both have programs for doing so. For help with this, see the online section on "Random Number Generation."

Lastly, I have listed some sources of help, most extensively for the R program, since in the R Console commands there is more room for errors than in the menu-driven SPSS and R Commander programs.

Chapter 2

Some Preliminaries to Understanding Statistics

> To steal a line from Winer (1971, p. 442), "Statistical elegance does not necessarily imply scientifically meaningful inferences." Common sense is at least as important as statistical manipulations.
>
> David C. Howell (2002, p. 463)

Since becoming interested in statistics, I have had my colleagues occasionally send me their students who are working on an experiment for their thesis. "Help them with their statistics!" my colleagues plead. These novice researchers know conceptually what they want to test, but empirically are not sure how to go about designing an experiment that involves statistical analysis. For example, the student may know they want to test whether listeners will rate some accents as more desirable than others, but they do not know where to go from there. This chapter contains information that is essential to understand how to do an experimental project. This chapter does not explain which test you will want to use to evaluate your data statistically (that will come later), but it covers the basic concepts that are necessary to understand which test you will need. This will give those who are new to experimental design and statistics a brief overview of some of the basic issues that must be understood to carry out a statistical analysis. These concepts may not seem like "common sense" (a reference to the quotation at the beginning of the chapter) yet, but doing statistics should not be mysterious handwaving that results in a "**statistically significant**" finding. You need to understand your numbers and understand what you are testing when you use statistics. This chapter is a start to that understanding.

In the first chapter I defined a variable as a collection of data that are all of the same kind. We saw in Chapter 1 that variables are shown as columns in a spreadsheet. The first part of this chapter will help you to understand more about the characteristics of your variables, because these characteristics will, to a large part, determine what types of statistical tests you can use. If you can, you should try to understand *before* you start your data collection what types of variables you are going to be collecting and recording. The second part of the chapter will describe some rather abstract ideas that you will nevertheless need to be aware of as you undertake statistical tests. I have set this up as a discussion of the hidden assumptions underlying statistical testing because most of the time you will not openly read of these ideas in a journal article or a report on research, but they are ideas that are understood by those who do statistics (or, at least, they *should* be understood!).

These include understanding the difference between the sample of people that you collect data from and the wider population of people you hope to generalize your results to. Statistics that can be generalized to a population wider than your sample are called inferential statistics. In this section, I will also introduce (but will revisit in Chapter 4) the concept of hypothesis testing in statistics, which rather perversely is set up to test hypotheses that you hardly ever believe in! In the latter part of the hidden assumptions section, I will explain some of the parts of the statistical result that are common to every test and that you will often see reported in research articles, including *p*-values, degrees of freedom (df) and effect sizes. I will also try to demystify how statistical testing works. Having a basic understanding of these concepts will help you start with your own research project or just help you understand more when you read statistical results in a journal article. The last section of the chapter deals with an emerging type of statistics called "robust statistics" and recommends their use in the future.

2.1 Variables

My first question to the novice researcher is "What is your **research question**?" I cannot help you formulate this—you will have to do this on your own! Your research question can be informal at first, but it will contain the seeds to beginning a formal statistical investigation. Here are some of the questions my recent graduate students have had:

- Would playing an online role-playing game in another language help students learn Spanish better?
- Will providing different types of targeted feedback on written work help students improve in their ability to use grammar accurately?
- Are people who are good at music better at detecting Chinese tone than people who are not?
- Will students learn vocabulary better if they are able to associate them through multiword expressions rather than just singly?
- What kinds of phonological problems will Koreans and Japanese learners of English have?

Once I know what your research question is, my next question is "What are your variables?" In other words, before we can proceed with any kind of statistical analysis we need to know what kinds of measurements will be done. For this question we need to think about how we can **operationalize** the research question or, in other words, take an abstract idea and make it measurable. For example, in the first question, my student wanted to know if students would get better at Spanish. How will we measure their Spanish? Are we interested in their speaking ability, their listening ability, their reading ability or all of these? Say we are interested in their speaking ability. Then how will we measure it? Will we give them a standardized Spanish oral proficiency interview (OPI) test? Will we just have an informal interview? Will we use grades from their last Spanish class? All of these are ways to operationalize the variable of "speaking proficiency in Spanish," although some may be better than others.

Think about what needs to be measured to operationalize the research question in each of the questions listed earlier. Here are the ideas I can see that need to be measured:

1 How will we measure Spanish proficiency? What group will participants be in? (We need at least two groups to show that it is the role-playing game that helps participants improve.)
2 What types of feedback will be provided and to how many groups? How will we measure grammatical accuracy and on what forms? How will we measure improvement in accuracy?
3 How do we measure how good people are at music? How do we measure how well they perceive Chinese tones?
4 How will we measure vocabulary knowledge? What group will participants be in? (Will there be a control group that does not try to learn any vocabulary at all?)
5 How will we measure phonological problems (will we target contrasts or specific sounds?) and how many will we test?

2.1.1 Levels of Measurement of Variables

Answering these questions and thus operationalizing your research question will result in measuring variables. These variables may differ substantially from one another. For example, measuring Spanish speaking proficiency will probably be done through some kind of test where participants will receive a variety of scores. This type of variable is called a **continuous variable**. The values of a continuous variable consist of numbers that represent a measurement and involve a large range of possible answers.

Table 2.1 Continuous vs. Categorical Variable Practice

1	Spanish proficiency will be measured with an OPI.	continuous or categorical
	There will be three groups: those who play games, those who speak with a conversation partner and those who do not do anything special.	continuous or categorical
2	There will be three types of feedback given to students on article usage: direct correction, indirect correction by circling and no feedback.	continuous or categorical
	Grammatical accuracy will be measured by the number of accurate article usages out of all obligatory contexts. This will be measured on four different essays.	continuous or categorical
3	Facility with music will be measured through a perfect pitch test, with a maximum possible score of 20 points.	continuous or categorical
	Chinese tone perception will be measured through an identification test of four tones, with 30 items in total.	continuous or categorical
4	Vocabulary knowledge will be measured by having students put a check by the words they know and then totaling this number out of ten words.	continuous or categorical
	There will be three groups: those who learn multiword expressions, those who focus on single words, and those who are not specifically asked to memorize any words at all.	continuous or categorical
5	Five contrasts in English with ten items each will be played for the listeners, resulting in a test with a maximum possible score of 50 points.	continuous or categorical
	There are two groups of people with different first language (L1) backgrounds: Korean and Japanese.	continuous or categorical

A continuous variable contrasts with a **categorical variable**, where the values of the variable basically do not have any inherent numerical value and consist of categories where one category is not rated any higher than any other. Categorical variables often have a very restricted range of possible values.

In the earlier examples, the number of groups that will be tested is a categorical variable, while scores on tests or measurements, such as grammatical accuracy or perception of Chinese tones, are continuous variables. In Table 2.1, I have listed the variables that will be needed for each of the operationalized variables in the five research questions my students asked, and a possible way of operationalizing the variable. Decide if each one is a continuous or categorical variable.

Here are the answers: (1) continuous, categorical; (2) categorical, continuous; (3) continuous, continuous; (4) continuous, categorical; (5) continuous, categorical. It should be clear now that any type of grouping of participants will result in a categorical variable. In addition, whenever you give someone a test with a large number of items, this will result in a continuous variable.

I have started out with this broad division of measurements into continuous and categorical variables. The skill of identifying whether your variables are continuous or categorical is absolutely essential for deciding what statistical test to use. In general, the division between continuous and categorical is the most important division to know when it comes to performing statistical tests, as some tests can be used only when all variables are continuous, while other tests can be used only when there is at least one categorical and one continuous variable. However, many authors make a more detailed division of variable measurement into three or even four different types of measurement. For example, Mackey and Gass (2005) have discussed three levels of measurement: nominal, ordinal and interval scales. **Nominal scales**, which measure **categorical variables**, do not have any inherent numerical value. They are used to group people or data, and include measurements like gender, group membership in an experiment, first or second language background, or presence/absence of a linguistic feature. **Ordinal scales** are rank-ordered and do have some inherent numerical value. For example, we might have first-, second- and third-year students of French. If we assigned the students a number based on their number of years of study, we would expect this to be reflected in their knowledge of French, with students with a higher number having a greater knowledge of French. We might not expect, however, that the difference between third- and second-year students would be the same as between second- and first-year students. In other words, there is no guarantee that there are equal intervals of measurement between the participants. In an **interval scale**, which measures **continuous variables**, however, we would like to say that the difference between getting a 9 and a 10 on a 10-point test is the same as the difference between getting a 3 and a 4 on the test. In other words, the intervals are assumed to be equal. Some authors will also distinguish a **ratio scale** (Howell, 2002), which has all the properties of an interval scale plus a true zero point. An example Howell (2002) gives is that of weight. A 40-lb rock is twice as heavy as a 20-lb rock, and something that weighed 0 lb means that the thing that is being measured is absent, so the scale truly has a zero point. The more advanced reader may want to be aware of several other types of measurements. Within the category of interval scale that I have outlined here, Crawley (2007) distinguishes several more levels that can affect the choice of statistical test. Thus, for a **dependent variable** (DV) that a beginner might treat as an interval scale, we can distinguish between those measurements that are proportions or counts. If the measurement is a proportion, such as the number of mistakes out of every 100 words, then a logistic model would provide a better fit than a normal regression or analysis of variance (ANOVA) model. If the measurement is a count (such as the number of mistakes on a writing assignment) then a log linear model provides a better fit. And if a DV that is nominal has only two choices and is thus a binary scale, a binary logistic model provides a better fit. These types of statistical tests are not treated in this book, however, and the interested reader is advised to consult Crawley (2007) or Tabachnick and Fidell (2001).

Why do you need to know about nominal, ordinal and interval scales? The truth is that you probably do not, but it is good to be familiar with the terms. (Howell (2002) agrees with me on this!) As I noted earlier, the division between categorical and continuous variables—which is the same as the division between nominal and interval scales—is in practice the division that is important in deciding which statistical test to choose. Researchers who use a measurement that is ordinal end up classifying it as either categorical or continuous, often depending on how many points there are in the scale. For example, if you have recorded the years of study of college learners of French and you have three levels, you will most likely call this a categorical variable with no inherent numerical value, even though you do realize that most learners in their third year of French study will perform better than learners in their first year. On the other hand, if you have a seven-point Likert scale measuring the amount of language anxiety, you will be likely to call this a continuous measurement, even though you may acknowledge that a score of 4 on the scale (= moderate anxiety) may not be exactly twice of what the score of 2 is (= little anxiety).

In truth, it is not the measurement itself but how the researcher chooses to look at it that is the deciding factor in whether you will call a measurement continuous or categorical. For example, you may ask people their age, which is certainly an interval scale (in fact, it is a ratio scale, because it has a true zero point), but then classify them as young versus old, making your measurement into a nominal scale. This example shows what Howell (2002) stated, which is that the researcher must remember that the event itself and the numbers that we measure are different things, and that "the validity of statements about the objects or events that we think we are measuring hinges primarily on our knowledge of those objects or events, not on the measurement scale" (p. 9).

2.1.2 Application Activity: Practice in Identifying Levels of Measurement

Look at the following studies. The variables measured in the study to answer the research question are listed in the tables. Look at each variable and decide whether it is categorical or continuous.

Kondo-Brown (2006): Does accuracy in guessing the meaning of unfamiliar Japanese words differ depending on proficiency level?

1	Proficiency level (Participants are divided into high and low proficiency on the basis of reading comprehension tests, with a maximum possible score of 20 points.)	continuous or categorical
	Accuracy level measured on a series of different tests, but generally most of the tests had about 16 points or more.	continuous or categorical

Boers, Eyckmans, Kappel, Stengers, and Demecheleer (2006): Will explicit instruction in noticing formulaic sequences help one group speak more fluently than another group that does not get this instruction?

2	Two experimental groups, one that was led to notice formulaic sequences and another that was not.	continuous or categorical
	Fluency ratings done by judges who listened to taped conversations and rated them for fluency on a 20-point scale.	continuous or categorical

Paavola, Kunnari, and Moilanen (2005): Does the number of times a mother changes her behavior because of a child's action affect the number of phrases an infant understands?

3	Number of times mother modifies behavior contingent on child's action counted in two separate sessions of 20 minutes each. (These are all added up together.)	continuous or categorical
	Number of phrases the child knows based on the MacArthur Inventory parental report	continuous or categorical

Erdener and Burnham (2005): Does first language orthography affect how well participants can produce non-words in a language that has an orthography similar or different to their L1?

4	Two groups of participants with different orthographies (L1 = Australian English or L1 = Turkish).	continuous or categorical
	Two groups of target languages with different orthographies (L2 = Irish English or L2 = Spanish).	continuous or categorical
	Number of phoneme errors on 96 non-words.	continuous or categorical

Bialystok, Craik, Klein, and Viswanathan (2004): Do age and being bilingual affect the accuracy with which participants perform on the Simon test (a test that measures whether participants can ignore irrelevant information)?

5	Score on the 28-item Simon test.	continuous or categorical
	Age, divided into two groups (young: 30–54; older: 60–88).	continuous or categorical
	Status as bilingual or monolingual.	continuous or categorical

2.1.3 Dependent and Independent Variables

Another important dichotomy between variables is whether they are considered independent or dependent. Both independent and DVs can be measured as nominal, ordinal or interval, so this division is independent of the measurement scale. This dichotomy relates to *the way the variables function in the experiment.*

Independent variables are those that we think may have an effect on the DV. Often the researcher controls these variables. For example, an independent variable (IV) would be membership in one of three experimental conditions for learning vocabulary: mnemonic memorization, rote memorization and exposure to context-laden sentences. The researcher randomly assigns participants to the groups, and suspects that the group the participant is in will affect their scores on a vocabulary test administered later. Independent variables are not always variables that the researcher manipulates, however.

If you think that amount of motivation and presence at a weekly French conversation chat group influence fluency in French, you will simply try to measure motivation and chat group attendance. In this case your measure of motivation and a count of number of French club meetings attended are your IVs. You have not fixed them in the way you might assign students to a certain group, but you are still interested in how these variables influence fluency.

Here are some common IVs in second language research studies:

- experimental group membership;
- L1 background;
- proficiency level;
- age;
- status as monolingual or bilingual;
- type of phonemic contrast;
- amount of motivation or language anxiety;
- amount of language use.

The variable that you are interested in seeing affected is the DV or **response variable**. For our French example, the DV is a "fluency in French" measure. If the IVs have been fixed, then the DV is beyond the experimenter's control. For example, the researcher may fix which experimental group the participants belong to, and then measure their scores after the treatment on a vocabulary test. Assignment to a group has been fixed, but then scores on the vocabulary test are out of the control of the researcher. Of course, the researcher is hoping (betting? guessing?) that the scores *will* be affected by the experimental group. In this sense, the DV "depends" on the IV.

Here are some common dependent (response) variables in second language research studies:

- fluency ratings;
- score on discrete-point tests;
- number of accurate grammatical forms out of all instances of that grammatical form used;
- electrocardiogram or magnetic resonance imaging (MRI) brain response patterns;
- pronunciation rating;
- reaction time;
- holistic writing score;
- number and length of *t*-units.

As Howell (2002, p. 4) said, "Basically, the study is about the IVs, and the results of the study (the data) are the dependent variables." I remember first encountering the idea of dependent and IVs, and it took a little while before I got them straight, but maybe it will help if you look at a variable and think, "Do I think these data will be influenced by some other variables?" If so, it is a DV. If you think the data will be an explanatory factor for some other results, then it is an IV. While DVs may be categorical or continuous, IVs are generally categorical. It is extremely important to understand the difference between independent and DVs correctly because this classification will affect what test you will choose to analyze your data with.

Now I hate to tell you this, but actually the difference between independent and DVs is not always clear-cut, and in some cases this traditional dichotomy may not really be applicable. In this discussion I have been assuming that you will have a variable that depends for its outcome on some other variables (the IVs). In such a case the researcher is clearly trying to establish some kind of causal relationship. For example, I cause outcomes to differ because I put the participants in different experimental groups, or I cause reaction times to differ because some participants had to answer questions with syntactical violations.

However, sometimes you will not find a cause-and-effect relationship. You will only be looking at the relationship between two variables and you would not be able to say which one depends on the other. For example, if you wanted to know how time spent in the classroom per day and time spent speaking to native speakers are related, you would be interested in the relationship between these two variables, but you could not say that time spent in the classroom necessarily affected the time students spent speaking to native speakers of the language, or vice versa. In this case, correlation is the type of test you would look at to examine whether there are important relationships between the variables. Robinson (2005) had a research question where he was not looking for a cause-and-effect relationship between the variables. His question was whether there was a relationship between measured intelligence scores and the ability to abstract rules of language implicitly (i.e. without conscious awareness). He thus used a correlation to examine the possible relationship between intelligence and implicit induction ability.

The next section provides some practice in identifying dependent and IVs in experimental studies. All of the research questions given here are from real studies, but for the sake of simplicity sometimes they have been modified so that they focus on one specific aspect of the entire study. But be careful—there may be some questions here where the answer is that there *is* no dependent or Independent Variable!

2.1.4 Application Activities: Practice in Identifying Variables

Write the independent and DVs in the tables. In some cases, there may be more than one IV, but there is never more than one DV.

1 Wharton (2000): Do high-proficiency learners use more language learning strategies than low-proficiency learners?

Independent:	Dependent:

2 Munro, Derwing, and Morton (2006): Does L1 background influence the way that English learners rate the speech of other English learners for comprehensibility?

Independent:	Dependent:

3 Hirata (2004): Does pronunciation training with visual feedback help learners improve their perception of phonemically contrastive pairs of words more than training without visual feedback?

Independent:	Dependent:

4 Proctor, August, Carlo, and Snow (2006): What kind of relationship exists among an oral language measure and a reading comprehension measure in English for Fourth Grade bilinguals?

Independent:	Dependent:

5 Bialystok, Craik, Klein, and Viswanathan (2004): Do age and being bilingual affect the accuracy with which participants perform on the Simon test (a test that measures whether participants can ignore irrelevant information)?

Independent:	Dependent:

6 Wartenburger et al. (2003): Do age of acquisition (AOA) and proficiency level affect what neural substrates are activated in the brain among different types of Italian–German bilinguals?

Independent:	Dependent:

7 Mizuno (1998) hypothesized that there would be a relationship between the amount of cultural exposure students had before they went overseas and the amount of cultural exposure they would obtain once they were living in the country.

Independent:	Dependent:

8 Larson-Hall (2004): Do learners perform differently in their ability to perceive phonemic contrasts in non-words in the second language depending on their proficiency level and on the sounds that are contrasted?

Independent:	Dependent:

9 Poehner and Lantolf (2013): Will computer-mediated training on a listening comprehension task help learners to perform better on similar tasks (transfer items) in the same test which do not have any hints (mediation)?

Independent:	Dependent:

10 Sasaki (2004): Do Japanese users of English improve in their English writing fluency over time (measured at four different intervals and specifically number of words written per minute), and do the students in this group who studied abroad improve more than those who never left Japan?

Independent:	Dependent:

2.1.5 Summary of Variables

You should now be able to take a research question and decide what the variables are, whether they are categorical or continuous variables, and whether they are dependent or IVs. Once you can take this step, you will be very far along on the path toward deciding what type of statistical test you will need to analyze your data.

2.1.6 Fixed versus Random Effects (Advanced Topic)

Recently, the usefulness of mixed-effect models, which contain both fixed and random effects, has been pointed out in various publications (Baayen, Davidson, & Bates, 2008; Cunnings, 2012; Quené & van den Bergh, 2008). Throughout most of this book I will not generally distinguish between fixed and random effects. I essentially treat all IVs as fixed effects in regression and ANOVA models. However, to conduct a repeated measures test in R, a mixed-effect model that distinguishes between fixed and random effects can be used. It is possible that advanced statistics users will also want to conduct other types of regression and ANOVA models using random effects as well, so I provide a discussion here of this dichotomy.

Fixed effects are those whose parameters are fixed and are the only ones we want to consider. **Random effects** are those effects where we want to generalize beyond the parameters that make up the variable. A "subject" term is clearly a random effect, because we want to generalize the results of our study beyond those particular individuals who took the test. If "subject" were a fixed effect, that would mean we were truly only interested in the behavior of those particular people in our study, and no one else. On the other hand, if we had two treatment conditions and we were only interested in the effects of those conditions compared against each other, the variable of condition would be a fixed effect.

In 1999, Raaijmakers, Schrijnemakers, and Gremmen noted that most language stimuli that are used within an experiment should also be considered random effects, because we are not really interested in how the experimental participants deal with the exact stimuli that they are presented with in our experiment, but in those stimuli representing a larger class of type of language. For example, we do not really want to know if our participants can judge only the exact 100 sentences in our grammaticality judgment task as correct or incorrect, but any type of sentence with that basic grammar that they should encounter. So language stimuli may also be treated as random effects.

Note that the difference between fixed and random factors is *not* the same as between-subject and within-subject factors.

Table 2.2 contains a list of attributes of fixed and random effects, and gives possible examples of each for second language research studies, although classification always depends on the intent of the researcher. This table draws on information from Crawley (2007), Galwey (2006) and Pinheiro and Bates (2000).

Table 2.2 Characteristics of Fixed and Random Effects

Fixed effects	
Fixed effects have informative labels for factor levels.	Examples of fixed effects:
If one of the levels of a variable were replaced by another level, the study would be radically altered.	treatment type male or female
Fixed effects have factor levels that exhaust the possibilities.	native speaker or not
We are only interested in the levels that are in our study, and we don't want to generalize further.	child versus adult first language (L1)
Fixed effects are associated with an entire population or certain repeatable levels of experimental factors.	target language
Random effects	
Random effects have uninformative factor levels.	Examples of random
If one of the levels of a variable were replaced by another level, the study would be essentially unchanged.	effects: subjects
Random effects have factor levels that do not exhaust the possibilities.	words or sentences used
We want to generalize beyond the levels that we currently have.	classroom
Random effects are associated with individual experimental units drawn at random from a population.	school

2.2 Understanding Hidden Assumptions about How Statistical Testing Works

If you are a beginner to statistics and have done some reading in the literature that contains statistical results, here is how you might think statistical testing works:

The researcher lays out a research **hypothesis** that seems plausible given previous research and logical reasoning.

I hypothesize that the more frequently the participants study with their vocabulary flash cards, the better they will score on a vocabulary cloze test.

This sounds like a very plausible hypothesis!

The researcher presents basic information about the participants, such as their age, gender, first language and proficiency level in a second language, and then gives mean scores on whatever test was used.

SD means standard deviation, a measure of variability in the mean score

I tested 50 English-speaking learners of Russian (27 were women, 23 were men, mean age = 22.6). They were all studying Russian at a large university on the west coast of the USA. They were enrolled in Russian classes ranging from first- to fourth-year. The students reported spending,

on average, 13.4 minutes per day (SD = 25.6) studying their flash cards, and their score on the vocabulary cloze test was 36.2 (SD = 11.0).

The researcher then reports something called a "**p-value**" and proclaims whether the results are statistically significant or not.

There was a statistically significant relationship between the amount of time spent studying the flash cards and the scores on the test, $r = 0.20$, $p = 0.03$.

> Here is the p-value: 0.03. It is less than 0.05, so the researcher says the result is "statistically significant."

If the results are statistically significant, the researcher assumes the hypothesis was correct and goes on to list the implications from this finding. If the results are not statistically significant, the researcher tries to explain what other factors might need to be investigated next time.

This study has shown that individualized vocabulary flash card study can help students learn the vocabulary, and that those who spend more time with their flash cards will remember the vocabulary better. Another good feature of the system is that the flash cards can be used outside of class. Teachers might thus be interested in instituting this vocabulary flash card system as homework for their students.

This impression of how statistical testing works is not mistaken on the surface (this is indeed what you often read in research papers), but there are a variety of issues that lie beneath the surface that the researcher understands but does not communicate directly to you. It is to these hidden assumptions that we will turn our attention in the following section.

2.2.1 Hypothesis Testing

In a research paper, the author usually provides a research question, either directly or indirectly. As a novice reader, you will think that this hypothesis, based on previous research and logical reasoning, is what is tested statistically. You are wrong.

It turns out that a statistical test will not test the logical, intuitively understandable hypothesis that you see in the paper but, instead, it will test a **null hypothesis**, which is rarely one the researcher believes is true. This topic will be treated in more detail in Chapter 4, but it is very confusing to new researchers, so I will introduce it briefly in this chapter.

To conduct null hypothesis testing, we will set up a null hypothesis (H_0) that says that there is no difference between groups or that there is no relationship between variables. It may seem strange to set up a hypothesis that we may not really believe, but the idea is that "we can never prove something to be true, but we can prove something to be false" (Howell, 2002, p. 98). Actually, this is a good point to remember for the whole enterprise of scientific hypothesis testing in a **quantitative approach** (i.e. one that deals with numbers, thinks that truth can be ascertained objectively and seeks to have replicable and verifiable results). You should be careful when you make claims that a study has "proved" a point, because we cannot prove something to be true! Instead, say that a study supports a certain hypothesis or provides more evidence that an idea is plausible. The old chestnut says that you cannot prove that unicorns do not exist; you can only gather data that show it is likely that they do not. On the other hand, it will only take one unicorn to prove the hypothesis false. For advanced readers, it turns out that there are ways to prove the null hypothesis (H_0), although they are statistically more complicated. See Streiner (2003) for more information.

So the statistically savvy researcher does indeed list the plausible, logical hypothesis in the research paper, but also knows that, when they perform a statistical test, they are testing the null hypothesis. Let us walk through the steps of this with our researcher. Let us say our researcher believes that pre-class massages will decrease language learning anxiety. (A unique idea that I have not seen in the literature, but I am sure I would like to be a participant in the study!) In the research report, the researcher lays out the logical hypothesis:

$H_{logical}$: Pre-class massages will decrease language learning anxiety, so that a class that gets pre-class massages will have less anxiety than a class that does not.

However, the researcher has also somewhere, perhaps only in their head, laid out a null hypothesis:

H_0: There is no difference in language learning anxiety between the class that gets pre-class massages and the class that does not.

Now suppose that we indeed find that the amount of language learning anxiety is lower, on average, in the class that gets massages. This is our one unicorn we needed to prove the hypothesis false! Now, just because we have proved the hypothesis false does not mean that we have proved that the opposite (or the logical) hypothesis is true. But what we saw is that we can **reject the null hypothesis**. Now, if we reject the null hypothesis, this means we reject the idea that there is no difference between groups or no relationship among variables. Once we reject the null hypothesis we will be able to accept the **alternative hypothesis**, which in this case would be:

H_a: There is a difference in language learning anxiety between the class that gets pre-class massages and the class that does not.

If we consider an extremely simplified example relating to groups we can see that, mathematically, it is easier to prove the null hypothesis false than to prove it true:

H_0: The difference between the groups is 0 (no difference between groups).
H_a: The difference between the groups is not 0 (a difference between groups).

Let us say that we then calculated the average score for each group and found that the difference between groups was only 0.0003. Although this seems like a very small difference, it would refute the null hypothesis that the difference was 0 (it would be our unicorn). On the other hand, to prove the alternative hypothesis, we could gather lots of examples of times when the difference between groups was not 0, but this would not prove that the difference was 0 (in the same way that collecting lots of evidence that horses but not unicorns exist would not prove that unicorns do not exist).

Although I hope I have convinced you here that a null hypothesis is much easier to prove than the logically reasoned hypothesis you might really set out to investigate, there are problems with using this system of null hypothesis testing. We will examine the problems with this approach and how to best remedy them in more detail in Chapter 4.

2.2.2 Application Activities: Creating Null Hypotheses

Look at the research questions given here and create a null hypothesis:

1. Boers, Eyckmans, Kappel, Stengers, and Demecheleer (2006): Will explicit instruction in noticing formulaic sequences help one group speak more fluently than another group that does not get this instruction?
2. Proctor, August, Carlo, and Snow (2006): What kind of relationship exists between an oral language measure and a reading comprehension measure in English for Fourth Grade bilinguals?
3. Wartenburger et al. (2003): Do AOA and proficiency level affect what neural substrates are activated in the brain among different types of Italian–German bilinguals?
4. van Compernolle (2012): Can conceptual explanations and schema for orienting basis of action (SCOBA) help English-speaking learners of French improve their performance on an appropriate judgment questionnaire (AJQ) regarding the use of the tu/vous pronoun distinction?
5. Granena (2013): To what extent is sequence learning ability related to morphosyntactic abilities in an L2?

2.2.3 Who Gets Tested? Populations versus Samples and Inferential Statistics

The next assumption you may have about how statistics works is that a researcher tests a group of people and these are the people that the researcher wants to comment about. You may think this because the researcher presents summary information about the participants, such as their mean age, the number of men and women tested, their L1 backgrounds, and so on. In most cases, you are wrong.

The researcher must indeed test a certain selection of people, called a **sample**. But the researcher in fact does not want to comment just about these people, but instead wants to make a generalization to a wider group of people. If the researcher were really going to comment only on whether brain activation patterns from a functional MRI differentiated eight bilingual participants from eight monolingual participants in Dresden, Germany, you probably would not care much. Usually, you will care because of what you think the research study says about differences between bilinguals and monolinguals in general and in a variety of languages. What you care about is the wider population of people that the sample was drawn from. The population is the group of people (or collection of texts or test scores) in which you are interested.

Many second language research studies test a sample of only 10 or 15 participants in each group, but they are of interest to the wider research community because of the population that readers suppose the findings apply to. The population may be assumed to be all English as second language learners in the United States, or all French as foreign language learners in England, or all immigrants of all language backgrounds to any country. Put this way, it may sound a little grandiose to think that our studies, done with a very small sample, apply to such large populations!

The reason why we may be able to make the leap from conclusions drawn on a sample to conclusions drawn to the wider population is because of **inferential statistics**. Inferential statistics are those that can be used to make inferences to the population that the sample is assumed to come from. Inferential statistics can be contrasted with **descriptive statistics**, which are measures that are derived from the sample. So, when you read a research report and see the number of men and women who participated, their mean ages and their mean scores on a test, these numbers are all descriptive statistics. Descriptive statistics may include counts of how many times some feature is found in a piece of writing, or graphs such as histograms that graphically show such counts. Descriptive statistics are very appropriate in situations where you want to numerically describe some kind of phenomenon. More information about how to calculate descriptive statistics is found in Chapter 3. You will definitely want to include descriptive statistics in your research report; conversely, if you are reading a research report you should understand what an average score means.

But usually a research report will not stop with descriptive statistics. If a statistical test is conducted, then the researcher assumes that the results of that test can be applied to the wider population from which the sample was selected (unless they explicitly note some reservations). One of the problems with making this kind of inference, however, is that, for inferential statistics to be applicable, the sample should be a **random sample**. This means that each person (or each item or thing) in the population is equally likely to be picked. When a second language research study is conducted with intact classrooms, although this is convenient for the researcher, the sampling is not random. Maybe students have heard about the teachers and some have deliberately chosen a teacher they think they will like; maybe most of the students who are taking the 8 a.m. Spanish class are business majors who all have required classes at the other times that Spanish is offered. There are any number of factors that may make the intact classroom less than a random sampling of students. An experiment that uses volunteers is also not a random sampling because those who volunteer to do something are often different from those who would never voluntarily include themselves in a study. Hatch and Lazaraton (1991) noted that a pool of volunteers is a group from which a random sample might be drawn, although the volunteers still may not be representative of the population.

To imagine a truly random sample, think of a political survey you might hear about on the news that says how many people will vote for the Republican candidate this election year and how many are voting for the Democratic candidate. Such surveys do not sample every registered voter in the country; however, they do identify registered voters in a certain area as their population and then contact a random sampling of those voters until they reach a certain number of participants that has been decided on beforehand. (They test about 1000, I heard John Zogby, a pollster, say on the *Diane Rehm Show* on 3 September 2008.) With such a random sampling, pollsters can then perform inferential statistics on the data and say that they would expect the same kinds of results even with different samples of people (within certain boundaries of error). They thus try to generalize the results from a particular sample of people to a wider population. Inferential statistics try to say something about the overall population of people or data that they describe, without sampling every piece of data or every person in that set.

As you read this, you may be getting worried. You have never heard of a study in second language research that collected data from a truly random sampling of people! Does that mean that we cannot make any inferences from these studies to a wider population? Come to think of it, you may have noticed that most researchers do not identify the wider population that their sample comes from. If they tested English as a second language (ESL) learners at a certain university, is their sample representative of all ESL learners at that university, or all ESL learners in the entire country, or maybe the entire world? It seems to me that most people who write reports and most people who read them are content to let this issue be fairly vague. Although not having random samples may compromise the external validity of a study, probably the best we can hope for in our field is that both readers and researchers will try to be careful in the limits of the generalizations they make and only draw those that are truly justified. Generalizing to wider populations would also be supported by replication studies, which are not widely seen but have been called for in the field (Porte, 2012). If you are creating your own research project, you should consult a book such as Mackey and Gass (2005), which gives more detail on research methodology as you decide how to sample your population.

2.2.4 What Does a P-Value Mean?

When you read a research report, you will have noticed lots of mind-numbing mathematical symbols in the Results section. If you are like most novices to statistics, you probably just skip over this entire section and go to the Discussion section, where the author interprets all that gobbledygook for you. That can be OK in some cases but in other cases the author may not be completely accurate in interpreting the results or may overstate their case. If you think the only thing you need to glean from the results section is the *p*-value, then you are wrong.

You will not be able to be a savvy consumer of research (let alone carry out your own analyses) unless you can understand more about all those symbols in the Results section of a paper. So in this section I will try to introduce you to the reasoning behind a statistical test and what things get reported.

At this point we have seen that the descriptive statistics about the sample that was tested should be reported, things like which first language background the participants have and their mean scores on a test. The next step the researcher will take is to perform a statistical test with the data, which means using inferential statistics. To this point, in our field, the main results that the researcher will report are the statistic, the df, the ***p*-value** and possibly an effect size. (In Chapter 4, I will argue that we should instead focus our attention mainly on confidence intervals and effect sizes, but that is a discussion for later on.) Here is an example from Munro and Derwing (2006, p. 526):

> To compare the accentedness scores across the seven error conditions, we first submitted the listeners' ratings to a one-way repeated measures analysis of variance, with seven levels of the repeated measure. A significant effect of error condition was observed, $F(6, 72) = 76.22$, $p < .001$, η^2p (partial eta-squared) = .864.

Munro and Derwing reported an *F* statistic of 76.22, the df (the total df split into two numbers that reflect the allocation to variability between groups first and variability within groups second), which were 6 and 72, and a *p*-value of < 0.001. They additionally reported an **effect size** (partial eta-squared) of 0.864. (An effect size measures how much effect can be attributed to the influence of an IV on a DV, or to the relationship between variables; effect sizes will be discussed further in Chapter 4.) I will give a brief explanation here of what these numbers mean.

First of all, even if the researcher does not explicitly state what kind of statistical test was used, you can tell what kind of test was used by the **statistic** that is reported. Each statistical test has a certain mathematical symbol associated with it. For example:

- A chi-square test has a chi (χ).
- A correlation has a Pearson's *r*.
- A *t*-test has a *t*.
- An ANOVA has an *F*.

This statistic is calculated and its result is a number. In general, the higher this number is and the greater it is than 1, the more likely it is that the *p*-value is going to be very small. Munro and Derwing (2006) reported a very large *F*-value of 76.22, and you can notice that their *p*-value is very small. The *F*-value means their results come from an ANOVA statistical test. At this point, you can think of it as the result of a calculation involving mostly mean scores and standard deviations. I assume that you are familiar with what means or averages are, but I will elaborate on standard deviations in Chapter 3. For now, think of **standard deviations** as measuring how much people vary from the mean.

The next number you should see is something that represents the df. The **df** basically counts how many free components you have in your data set. To understand what that means, let us imagine we have four contestants on a game show, and each gets to pick one of four doors, behind which there is either a great prize, such as a car or a boat, or a booby prize. How many of the contestants have any freedom to choose a door? Figure 2.1 shows visually what I describe in words here.

Contestant 1, Alice, can choose door 1, 2, 3 or 4. She chooses door 2. Contestant 2, Gary, can choose door 1, 3 or 4. He chooses door 4. Now, contestant 3, K'Lynne, can choose either door 1 or door 3. It is not as much choice as Alice had, but it is still a choice. She chooses door 3. Now the last contestant, contestant 4, Eric, has no choice. He is left with door 1. In this case, we would say there were three df, because three of the four people have a choice, but the last person's choice is fixed. We have only three choices that include some variation and this means we have three df.

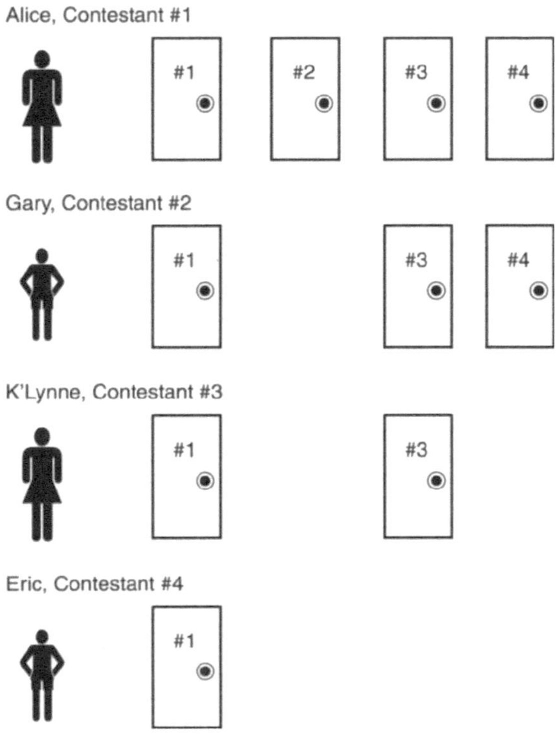

Figure 2.1 Degrees of freedom as the number of people who can make a choice (=3 here).

When you perform a test that has group variation as well as individual variation, as shown in the quotation by Munro and Derwing (2006), you will need to report two numbers for the df. The first one deals with the amount of variation due to groups. Thus, even if Munro and Derwing had not told you, you would know that there were seven groups in the ANOVA test because the first number, for group df, is 6, and that means there were seven groups.

The second number is reported as the "error" df in an ANOVA table, and this is the total df, which is always $N-1$, where N is the **sample size** or number of participants in the study, minus the variation for number of groups or variables (k, or the between-group variation). This does not hold true if the test has repeated measures, however. The second degree of freedom (df) reported is equal to $k(n-1)$, where n = the number of observations per group or variable. We can therefore figure out how many observations are in each group in the Munro and Derwing report: $72 = k(n-1) = 7(n-1)$, therefore $7n = 72 + 7 = 79$, so $n = 79/7 = 11.3$. (This is not quite equal to the 13 listeners in each group reported in Munro and Derwing, but possibly they used a correction, which can affect the df.)

You may wonder why you need to know what df are anyway. When researchers had to look up information for their statistical tests in tables, the df was a piece of information that was necessary to determine the **critical value** for finding statistical significance or not (i.e. the number above which the statistical test would be considered "significant"). Nowadays, if you use a computer to calculate your statistics (which is what I am assuming you will do!), you will not personally need to take note of your df. However, you should still report it. Table 2.2 gives you an idea of how this worked. For example, if you had a *t*-test, you would look up the alpha level you were interested in and find the df. (Table 2.2 includes only $\alpha = 0.05$, but a real table would include many choices.) That would tell you the critical value for a one-tailed test, but I have doubled it so that the critical value given here is for a two-tailed test. As an example, if you calculated a *t*-value of 2.05 when you had 14 df, and your $\alpha = 0.05$, then you would find that your critical value was 2.14, and thus you would not be able to reject the null hypothesis because your **calculated *t*-value** was less than the critical value. In other words, the probability of finding a value of 2.05 or larger if the null hypothesis were true is greater than 0.05.

Table 2.2 Selected Critical Values of the *T*-Distribution

df =	1	2	3	4	5	6	7	8	9	10
p = 0.05	12.71	4.30	3.18	2.78	2.57	2.45	2.36	2.31	2.26	2.23
df =	11	12	13	14	15	16	17	18	19	20
p = 0.05	2.20	2.18	2.16	2.14	2.13	2.12	2.11	2.10	2.09	2.09

Next we want to understand what a *p*-value is. The *p*-value is the probability that we would find a statistic as large as the one we found if the null hypothesis were true. In other words, the *p*-value represents the probability of the data given the hypothesis, which we could write as $p(D \mid H_0)$. Remember that our hypothesis is the null hypothesis, which says there is no relationship between variables or no difference between groups. So, in Munro and Derwing's results, the *p*-value of less than 0.001 says that the chance that we would find an *F* statistic of 76.22 if there were really no difference between groups is less than 1 in 1000. This is a pretty small chance, and we decide we are safe in rejecting the null hypothesis and in assuming there are some differences among the groups. In general, in the field of second language research we use a cutoff point of 0.05 when we decide whether to reject null hypotheses, although I will argue in Chapter 4 that it would be a good idea to set this higher to 0.10.

In Chapter 4, I will also talk more about understanding *p*-values. But, for now, just memorize this phrase to understand *p*-values the correct way: The probability of finding a [insert statistic name here] this large or larger if the null hypothesis were true is [insert *p*-value].

For example, in section 2.2 where I presented the made-up example of the vocabulary flash cards experiment, we could say that "the probability of finding an *r* [correlation coefficient] this large or larger if the null hypothesis were true is 0.03 [3%]." Let us say for the example of pre-class massage and anxiety I made up in section 2.2.1 that the result was $t = 9.6$, $p = 0.002$. We could then say that "the probability of finding a *t* [*t*-test statistic] this large or larger if the null hypothesis were true is 0.002 [0.2%]."

In sum, the researcher will not just proclaim the *p*-value and declare their hypothesis to be statistically significant or not. They will in fact tell you, overtly or not, what kind of statistical test they used and report the value of that statistic, they will report the df associated with the test (which can tell you something about the number of participants or groups if this was not mentioned) and they will report a *p*-value. I will argue in Chapter 4 that these three data points are not nearly as useful for both understanding results as well as progressing in our knowledge of the field as information about effect sizes and confidence intervals of point estimates. However, these are the pieces of information that have been seen as important up until now, so you will need to understand them.

2.2.5 Effect Sizes

In this book I plan to begin implementing Cumming's "New Statistics" (2012), by which is meant that effect sizes and confidence intervals get more attention and interpretation than *p*-values and test statistics. In Chapter 4, I present arguments for implementing such a change in our field. But since this revolution in statistical thinking is just beginning to take hold, I feel that I do have to help my reader understand the previous type of statistical thinking. That is what I am trying to do in this chapter, but it is time to get started with the new statistics as best we can. Thus, in this section I present findings from actual research studies, and I only use examples from studies that give effect sizes, since a number of editors in journals in the SLA field have been requiring effect sizes for a while (e.g. Ellis, 2000, for *Language Learning*, and Chapelle & Duff, 2003, for *TESOL Quarterly*). Let us get started right from the beginning in trying to understand effect sizes right along with the old-style statistics.

An effect size is a measure of how important the result is. In essence, it is the difference between the mean scores of the groups, but standardized so it is comparable across studies, and also it takes into account the amount of variation across groups as well by using the standard deviation. In the old statistics, researchers would often state that a result was "significant," meaning statistically significant, meaning that the *p*-value was below 0.05, meaning only that the probability of getting a test statistic that big or bigger if the null hypothesis were true was such and such a number. That did not really mean that the result was *important*. For example, remember when I discussed how a null hypothesis could be invalidated even if the difference between groups were only 0.0003 in section 2.2.1? In this case we could say the results were "statistically significant" but the actual and practical difference between groups would be so small that most people would say the results were equal.

An effect size tells us what we really want to know, which is:

- How strong is the correlation between two variables?
- How big is the difference between two groups?

There are two main types of effect sizes, one having to do with the strength of correlations and the other with the difference between groups. As you get more experience with a certain subfield in SLA you may have a more specifically honed idea of how to interpret effect sizes, but for now, let us use Oswald and Plonsky's (2010) rule of thumb for interpretation of effect sizes in the SLA field. They suggest Cohen's $d = 0.40$ is a small effect, $d = 0.70$ a medium effect and $d = 1.00$ a large effect. For *r* correlation coefficients, they suggest $r = 0.25$ is a small effect, $r = 0.40$ is a medium effect and $r = 0.60$ is a large effect.

2.2.6 Understanding Statistical Reporting

The previous sections explained briefly how to interpret four numbers you will often see reported in experimental results—the test statistic, the df, the *p*-value and the effect size. Let us practice using results from real journal articles and see if you can begin to understand what those mysterious statistical reports mean. In this section, I will walk you through the answers; then I will ask you in the next section to do it on your own.

1 Larson-Hall (2008, p. 49):

> "In fact, the correlation [with amount of input] is not statistical for the phonemic discrimination task among the earlier starters ($r = -0.07$, $n = 61$, $p = 0.57$, power = 0.08), but it is statistical for the GJT ($r = 0.27$, $n = 61$, $p = 0.035$, power = 0.56)."

a What does the *r* reported here refer to?
The statistic r *is used to give the results for a correlation.*

b This report does not give the df. Why not?
The total number of participants is given instead of the df (n = 61). *Correlations do not report df; they report total sample size.*

c What does $p = 0.57$ mean? (Spell out the meaning of a *p*-value in words; also make the inference as to what it means for the null hypothesis that there is no relationship between the variables.)
P = 0.57 *means "the probability of finding an* r *this large or larger if the null hypothesis were true is* 57%." *This is quite likely, so we cannot reject the null hypothesis and we conclude that there is no relationship between amount of input and scores on the phonemic discrimination task.*

d The second reported correlation has a *p*-value less than 0.05, making it a statistical correlation. What do you notice about the relative sizes of the *r*-values of the non-statistical versus the statistical results? (Note that for a correlation, the *r*-value is the test statistic as well as the effect size.)
The r *of the first correlation is negative, but this does not make any difference to its absolute size. In size, it is quite small and in practical consideration unimportant. However, the second* r*-value is* 0.27, *which is much larger than the first* r*-value of* 0.07. *The larger a statistic is, the more likely it will have a small* p*-value. A correlation can only range from* 0 *to* 1, *so you can see that, relatively, the* 0.27 *is not huge but it is not so small either. As an effect size, we can say that it is a small effect size, but big enough that we notice it. Oswald and Plonsky's* (2010) *guidelines would suggest that we call it a small effect size.*

2 Granena (2013, p. 685):

> "Regarding LLAMA D [a language aptitude test], the three groups did not score comparably on the test, according to a one-way ANOVA ($F(2,117) = 5.051$, $p = 0.008$, $\eta_p^2 = 0.079$)."

a What does the F reported here refer to?
The F*-value reports the results of an ANOVA test.*

b Using the df, calculate how many groups or variables were tested. How many participants were in each partition?
The first df (1) *refers to the number of groups or variables. Of course, the author tells us how many groups there were, but we can verify since the number of groups equals df* + 1, *so the first degree of freedom correctly shows there were three groups tested. The second degree of freedom* (117) *refers to the number of participants, and the formula is* df = k(n–1) *where* n = *number in each group and* k = *number of groups. We know there were three groups, so* 117 = 3(n–1). *Solving the equation,* n = 40. *If group numbers were equally distributed, there were* 40 *participants in each of the three groups, or* 120 *participants overall tested in this test, whatever their distribution into the groups. (Actually there was a group of NS controls with only* 20 *participants, and then there were* 50 *participants each in two larger groups.)*

c What does $p = 0.008$ mean? (Spell out the meaning of a *p*-value in words; also make the inference as to what it means for the null hypothesis that the groups do not differ.)
P = 0.036 *means that "the probability of finding an* F *this large or larger if the null hypothesis were true is* 8 *in* 1000." *This probability is small and much less than the traditional cutoff point of* 0.05,

so the author rejects the null hypothesis that all of the groups performed similarly on the aptitude test and accepts the alternative hypothesis that different groups performed differently on the test.

d What does $\eta_p^2 = 0.079$ mean?
Here the Greek letter eta (η) is used, and the p *means that it is a partial eta-squared statistic. This effect size is used to give a measure of the effect when there is more than one factor in the ANOVA, giving an effect size while controlling for the effect of the other variables. Actually, in this ANOVA test there is only one variable, but SPSS always gives partial eta-squared, not eta-squared, even for one-way ANOVAs, so I assume that is why Granena gave this effect size measure. This number is a strength of association number ranging from 0 to 1, meant to describe how much of the total variation can be attributed to this factor, controlling for the other factors (Pierce, Block, & Aguinis, 2004).*

More information can be found in Chapter 4, but for now, let us note that Cohen's (1988) guidelines for interpreting the size of effect sizes says that a small eta-squared would be 0.01, a medium 0.06 and a large 0.14. Therefore, we could say that the effect size for this comparison is a medium effect size. That means that there was a fair amount of difference in how the participants performed on this aptitude test.

3 Abrahamsson (2012, p. 200):

> "post-hoc test confirmed that the differences between adjacent groups—that is, between the NSs and the early learners and between the early and late L2 learners—were statistically significant, $t = 7.33$ and 7.81, respectively, $p < .01$ . . . The effect size of the NS and early L2 group difference was very large (Cohen's $d = 1.65$), whereas the effect size of the difference between the two L2 groups was large ($d = -1.10$)."

a What does the *t* reported here refer to? *The* t*-value reports the results of a* t*-test. Here, there are two* t*-tests because two pairs of comparisons were done, one with native speakers against early L2 learners, and another with early L2 learners versus late L2 learners.*

b Knowing that the df associated with a *t*-statistic equal the number of participants minus 2 (one for each of the groups), how many total participants were there? *We do not know from this excerpt because the df were not given.*

c What does $p < 0.01$ mean? (Spell out the meaning of a *p*-value in words; also make the inference as to what it means for the null hypothesis that the groups differ.) P < 0.01 *means that "the probability of finding a* t *this large or larger if the null hypothesis were true is 1%." This means we can reject the null hypothesis that there is no difference between either pair of groups and conclude that there are indeed differences between the NS and early L2 learners group, and between the two L2 learners groups.*

d What do you notice about the size of the *t*-statistic in this study compared to, say, the *F* statistic in question 2? *The* t*-statistics here are quite large, as both are over 7. In Question 2,* F *was only 5.051, which was still much larger than 1, and in both cases the results are statistically significant, and large as we will see from the effect size for the present study. In fact, as a rule of thumb, if a* t *or* F *or* χ^2 *is larger than 2, the* p*-value will probably be lower than 0.05.*

e Do you accept the author's interpretation about the size of the effect size? *An effect size of* $d = 1.10$ *(being negative makes no difference to our conclusions) is indeed large given Oswald and Plonsky's (2010) guidelines, where they spelled out a* $d = 0.4$ *as being a small effect size, a* $d = 0.7$ *as a medium effect size and* $d = 1.00$ *as being a large effect size. The guidelines make no mention of effect sizes larger than 1.00, but generally we agree with the author that an effect size of* $d = 1.65$ *is very large indeed.*

4 Mackey (2006, p. 421):

> "learners who noticed questions being significantly more likely to develop in terms of higher-level questions (83% of those who noticed questions developed): $\chi^2(1, 23) = 7.326$, $p = 0.007$."

a What does the χ^2 reported here refer to? *The χ^2 reports the results of a chi-square test.*

b Normally only one df is reported for this test, and that is the first number in parentheses given here after the statistic. (The second number in parentheses is the number of participants tested in this test, $N = 23$). The df is equal to the number of rows in the table (R) minus 1 multiplied by the number of columns in the table (C) minus 1. Knowing that df = (R−1)(C−1), how many rows and columns were involved in this test? *There are two rows and two columns: df = (2-1) (2-1).*

c What does $p = 0.007$ mean (spell out the meaning of a *p*-value in words; also make the inference as to what it means for the null hypothesis that there is no relationship between the variables)? P = 0.007 *means that "the probability of finding a χ^2 this large or larger if the null hypothesis were true is 7 in 1000." This is a very small probability thus we reject the null hypothesis that there is no difference between learners who noticed and their question development, and conclude that there is a relationship between noticing questions and progressing to higher-level questions.*

d What do you notice about the size of the statistic? *It is 7, which is quite a bit larger than 2 (and thus the* p-*value is quite low).*

5 Fordyce (2014, pp. 20–21):

> "To investigate the Time variable in more detail, post hoc repeated measures analysis of variance was carried out for each group [explicit vs. implicit instruction in epistemic verbs] independently. There were significant effects for both treatment groups: explicit group, $F(2,72)$, $p < .001$, eta-squared = .42; implicit group, $F(1.76, 75.48)$, $p < 0.5$, eta-squared = .07. This shows a large effect size for the explicit group compared with a small effect size for the implicit group."

a What does the F reported here refer to? *The* F*-value reports the results of an ANOVA test, and specifically the author has told us it was a repeated measures ANOVA.*

b To test whether the variable of Time (participants were tested at different time periods) resulted in different results for the same group of people, Fordyce tells us here he did two repeated measures ANOVAs, one with just the explicit group, and one with just the implicit group. Using the df for the explicit group (the implicit group's df are not whole integers because Fordyce used a Greenhouse–Geisser correction for this ANOVA since it did not meet the sphericity assumption), calculate how many time periods were tested. (The variable in this ANOVA is Time, not a number of different groups.) Let's not worry about the second df as the calculation of this for a repeated measures design is more complicated than for the normal ANOVA. *The first degree of freedom (2) refers to the number of groups or variables, which in this case we understand refers to time periods. The number of time periods equals df + 1, so there were three time periods tested (pretest, posttest, and delayed posttest).*

c What does $p < 0.001$ for the explicit group mean? (Spell out the meaning of a *p*-value in words; also make the inference as to what it means for the null hypothesis that the groups do not differ.) P < 0.001 *means "the probability of finding an F this large or larger if the null hypothesis were true is less than 1 in 1000." For the explicit group, this means that we reject the null hypothesis that the participants performed in the same way at each time period, and accept the null hypothesis that the participants performed in a different way across all the time periods. (Further investigation will be necessarily to pinpoint where the differences were since there are three different time periods.)*

d What does $p < 0.5$ for the implicit group mean? *Normally it would mean "the probability of finding an F this large or larger if the null hypothesis were true is 50%" and thus we would accept the null hypothesis that for the implicit group, performance did not differ across the time periods, but since the sentence following the one I quoted here says "the epistemic type score of both treatment groups developed significantly during the experimental period" (p. 21), I assume that "p < 0.5" was a typo and the author meant to say "p < 0.05." In this case, it would be nice to know* *the exact number since p = 0.043 would not be very different from p = 0.057, again pointing out the arbitrary convention of rejecting as unimportant any p-value over 0.05 and celebrating as important any p-value under 0.05. More on this in Chapter 4, but the take-away message is that we need to look at the effect sizes to get a better idea of what is important. Anyway, the inference is that we can reject the null hypothesis and conclude that the groups do differ.*

e Do you accept the author's guidelines about the size of the effect size? *Use Cohen's (1988) guidelines as a rough guide to interpret the eta-squared effect sizes, the same as we did for the partial eta-squared effect sizes (they will be the same when there is only one factor in the ANOVA): a small eta-squared would be 0.01, a medium 0.06 and a large 0.14. In this case we could agree that an eta-squared of 0.42 for the explicit group was quite large, explaining 42% of the variance in the data, but the eta-squared of 0.07 for the implicit group would be considered a medium effect size by Cohen's standards, not a small effect size. However, Cohen's guidelines are just that, guidelines, and the impact that time has on the variation in the implicit group, explaining just 7% of the variance, is definitely smaller than that of the explicit group.*

2.2.7 Application Activities: Understanding Statistical Reporting

Now that you have worked through the examples in the previous section, try a few more on your own:

1 Gurzynski-Weiss and Baralt (2013, p. 23)

> "There were no statistical differences between how learners perceived morphological feedback in FTF [face-to-face] mode (M = 0.67 feedback episodes correctly perceived as targeting morphosyntax, SD = 0.64) compared to CMC [computer-mediated communication] (M = 0.63, SD = 0.82), $t(23) = -0.20$, $p = 0.85$, $d = 0.05$."

a What does the *t* reported here refer to?
b How many people participated in this test?
c What does $p = 0.85$ mean? (Spell out the meaning of a *p*-value in words; also make the inference as to what it means for the null hypothesis that there is no difference between perception of morphological feedback in face-to-face mode versus computer-mediated chat mode)?
d What do you notice about the size of the *t*-statistic?
e $d = 0.05$ refers to the effect size. Comment on the size, referring back to the Abrahamsson (#3d) example in the text.

2 Polio, Fleck, and Leder (1998, Table 6, p. 54):

Results of ANOVA for EFT/TT

Source of variance	*SS*	*DF*	*MS*	*F*	*Sig.*
Between-subject					
E/C	0.00	1	0.00	0.01	0.935
within-group	3.51	63	0.06		

This one is a little different! Polio, Fleck, and Leder did not report statistical results in words; they reported them in a table and then interpreted the inferences for their hypotheses. This part of the statistics tested whether there were differences in groups that received error correction or not.

a What does the *F* reported here refer to?
b What do you notice about the size of *F*?

c How many people in total participated in this test? (Remember that there were two groups; also remember the formula df = $k(n-1)$, where n = number in each group or variable and k = number of groups/variables.)

d What does sig = 0.935 mean? (Sig refers to the *p*-value; spell out the meaning of a *p*-value in words; also make the inference as to what it means for the null hypothesis that there is no difference between groups.)

e This paper was published before most people were reporting effect sizes. Let us pretend that the authors noted that the effect size was eta-squared = 0.003. Comment on the effect size, referring back to the Granena (#2d) example in the text.

3 Rosa and O'Neill (1999): Rosa and O'Neill also reported their results in a table, but I am going to interweave those results with their prose:

> "Frequency counts of the number of individuals that produced each type of verbal report were performed . . . Results revealed a significant relationship between formal instruction and type of verbal report [p. 536] . . . df = 4, $\chi^2 = 16.454$, $p < 0.05$ [p. 537]."

a What does the χ^2 reported here refer to?

b How many rows and columns were involved in this test, if I tell you the number of rows = the number of columns?

c What does $p < 0.05$ mean? (Spell out the meaning of a *p*-value in words; also make the inference as to what it means for the null hypothesis that there is no relationship between the variables.)

4 Williams (2005, p. 287):

> "Next, correlations between mean phase 1 generalization performance and the following factors were calculated: performance on the PSTM test, $r = .01$, the number of L2s spoken to an intermediate level or better, $r = .263$, and the number of gender languages spoken to an intermediate level or better, including L1, $r = 0.357$, $p < .05$."

a What do the *r*-values reported here refer to?

b How many people's results were tested in this statistical test?

c What does $p < 0.05$ mean? (Spell out the meaning of a *p*-value in words; also make the inference as to what it means for the null hypothesis that there is no relationship between the variables; lastly remark on the fact that there are three tests but only one *p*-value.)

d Comment on the effect size of the three correlations listed, referring back to the Larson-Hall (#1d) example.

2.2.8 The Inner Workings of Statistical Testing

As a novice to statistics, when you read a research report it may seem that finding "statistically significant" results is the holy grail of research. If a *p*-value of less than 0.05 is found, the author seems to assume that their (logical and plausible) hypothesis was correct and moves ahead assuming that the hypothesis is now established. It is much rarer to find in the published literature results that do not establish the hypothesis that the author was hoping for. Russell and Spada (2006) have suggested that a publication bias against studies which do not find "significant" results for treatments is an established fact. When a study gets published where a treatment did not result in a positive result, the author will often try to explain the problem by referring to another explanation that could be plausible. (Instead of just thinking that, especially in the case of studies with small sample sizes, the lack of an effect may be due to too little power; I argue this case in the last section of Chapter 4.) In this section I want to explain how hypothesis testing works so that it will seem less mysterious and you will be able to be more critical of the process.

You already know from previous sections that the result of a statistical test is a statistic such as *t* or *F*, and there is an associated probability for that statistic. But how is that probability calculated? Let us start from the beginning thinking about what a statistical test tests. To illustrate this process, let us take the question proposed by one of my students and listed earlier in the chapter. We want to know whether students of Spanish who play an online role-playing game will learn Spanish faster than students who meet with a conversation partner for the same amount of time every day. So let us say we set it up so both groups do this extra work in Spanish for 30 minutes a day, three times a week. After a semester, we test our students using a 50-item cloze test. We tested both groups at the beginning of the semester too, and we find that the game group on average gained 10 points on the test over the semester while the conversation group gained 7 points. There is thus a mean difference between the groups of three points.

Now, there is always variability in measurement. For example, if the same Spanish student took the cloze test one day and then again a day later, that student might receive different test scores. (You might rightly argue that the increase was because the student had learned from the test, but let us suppose we had two different but equal versions and the student took a different one each time.) The same kind of variability happens on a group level as well. The group who played online games might have had a gain score of 12 if they were tested on another day (with a different but equivalent version of the test). Since fluctuation is normal, we want to know what amount of fluctuation is not just due to chance alone. That is, if the groups differ by three points only, this amount of variation may just be due to random fluctuations in scores. However, if the groups differ by 10 points, it will become unlikely that this much variation is due simply to chance. As Crawley (2005, p. 2) has suggested, "We need a way of discriminating between variation that is scientifically interesting, and variation that just reflects background heterogeneity. That is why we need statistics."

This part is where common sense can come in too. Statistically, it may be possible to find a difference between our groups when there are only 3 points difference in gain scores, but you yourself should realize that a gain of 3 points on a 50-point test is not very much. Now this may be good news—if students could use the role-playing game and get the benefits of talking to native speakers without having to actually seek out native speakers to talk to, then even if online game playing is not spectacularly better than talking to native speakers it may be a much easier choice with pretty much the same results. Do you see in this case that it really does not matter whether your statistics say the difference between the groups is "significant" or not? Even if the statistics say that the game-playing group is statistically better than the conversation group, the size of the difference is not huge (as measured by an effect size, which I discuss in detail in Chapter 4). And if the statistics say there is no difference between the groups, that does not matter, because playing an online game may logistically be easier than finding native speakers.

Now we return to how statistical testing works. In this case we would use a *t*-test to find out whether the difference between two mean scores is statistically significant. The *t*-test is not mysterious—it calculates a number based on subtracting the mean score of one group from that of the other group and then dividing this by a measure of the variation in scores that involves the standard deviation and the sample size. This calculation results in a number. This number is a point on the x-axis of a ***t*-distribution**. The *t*-distribution looks a lot like a **normal distribution** (what you might think of as a bell-shaped curve) but is slightly different, and its shape has been calculated by previous statisticians depending on the df it has. For example, the left panel of Figure 2.2 compares the *t*-distribution for two df to a normal distribution. The two distributions are similar, but you can see that the normal distribution (black line) is more concentrated around the mean than the *t*-distribution (gray dotted line). The right panel of Figure 2.2 shows how the shape of the *t*-distribution changes as more df are used. (The more df, the more the center peaks and gets sharper, the more the tails get lower and the more it looks like a normal curve!)

Let us say the value of the *t*-statistic is somewhere around 3.5 with two df. The probability that we would find a number this large or larger will be the area under the curve from the point of that

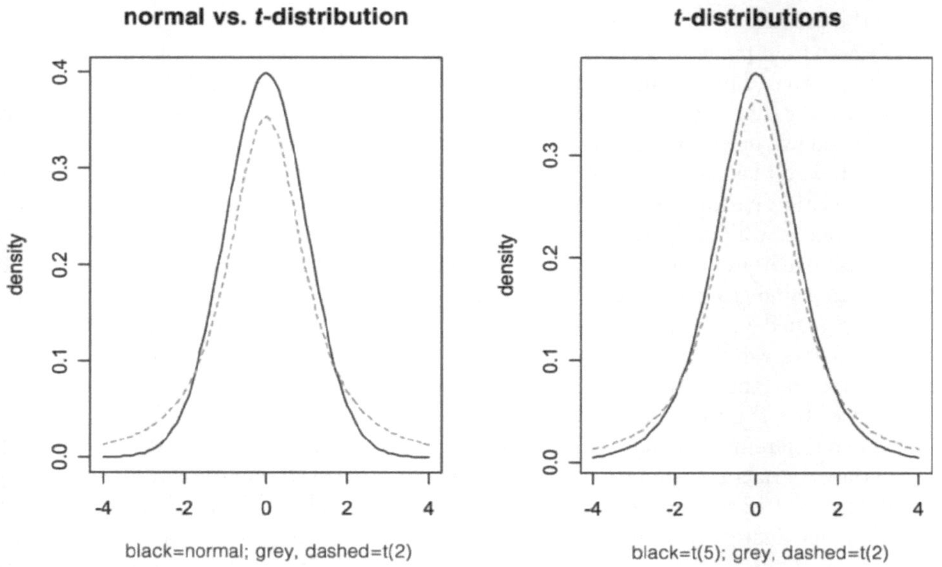

Figure 2.2 Probability density functions. On the left, the normal distribution (the black line) has less data in the tails (the extreme ends) than the *t*-distribution with 2 df. On the right, the *t*-distribution at *df*=2 (dashed line) and *df*=5 (black line) are compared.

t-statistic number to the end of the curve. Actually, the area calculated will be from both sides of the curve, the extreme right and extreme left, if you are testing the hypothesis that the difference between groups could go either way; this is called **two-tailed testing**, and I will explain it further in Chapter 4. So Figure 2.3 shows that, if you run a line up from + 3.5 on the x-axis to the density probability curve,

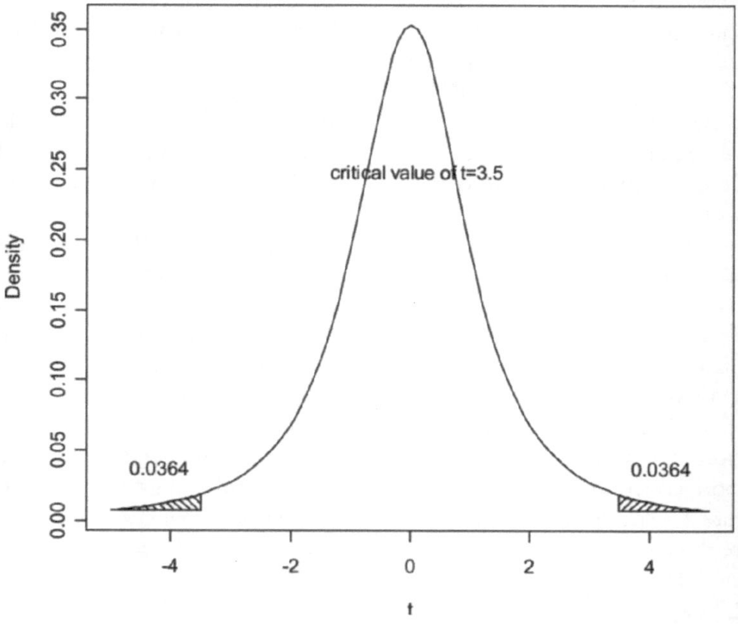

Figure 2.3 A *t*-distribution with *df*=2 evaluated at a critical value of 3.5. The area shaded under the curve is the probability that we will find a critical value this large or larger

all of the area to the right under the curve is 0.0364. Add to that the area under the curve on the left tail, and the *p*-value is 0.0364 + 0.0364 = 0.0728. This area is the *p*-value that the computer will calculate for you!

Now you already know what the *p*-value means. It is the probability of finding a statistic that large or larger if the null hypothesis is true. (But now you know why we say "or larger," since the probability is counting the area under the curve for larger numbers as well.) If the probability of finding such a number is large, that means that it is quite likely we would find a variation this large in the sample just from random chance, and thus we could not reject the null hypothesis. Just because we cannot reject the null hypothesis does not mean, however, that we must accept it. (In other words, we do not have to conclude that our treatment had no effect.). Some authors, including Wilkinson (1999), believe that the phrase "accept the null hypothesis" is unfortunate and should never be used. Instead, we should say "fail to reject the null hypothesis." Howell (2002) states that there is still much debate in this area and that some traditions encourage the idea of either rejecting or accepting the null hypothesis. In order not to confuse novice readers further in this confusing area, I will use the term "accept the null hypothesis" instead of "fail to reject."One reason for not accepting the null hypothesis might be because we did not have enough **power** to find differences when there actually were differences—perhaps the sample sizes were too small or the measurement error was too large to find real differences. (Power is the probability of detecting a statistical result when there are in fact differences between groups or relationships between variables. You might think of the analogy of a microscope, which needs sufficient power to see sufficient detail.) In this case we might conclude that no conclusion could be made! Further testing with more participants would be necessary.

Now, in this example I demonstrated how the *p*-value would be calculated for a *t*-test using a *t*-distribution, but the other types of statistical tests also use their own distributions. For example, there is a chi-square distribution and an *F*-distribution. Just like the *t*-distribution, these tests change shape depending on the number of df. The details of this do not matter to you, but what I do want you to understand is that there is no mystery to the entire process.

2.2.9 Application Activity: The Inner Workings of Statistical Testing

1 In your own words, explain what a statistic such as a *t*-value is.
2 In your own words, explain how a *p*-value is associated with a statistic such as a *t*-value.

2.2.10 Summary of Hidden Assumptions

Hopefully, after going through this section of the book you have realized that there is more to the Results section to think about than just a *p*-value. First, you need to realize that the researcher has had to set up a null hypothesis to test their real and plausible hypothesis. Second, you should realize that, if the researcher uses inferential statistics such as a correlation or an ANOVA, they are hoping that the results of their research will apply to a wider population than just those sampled in the study. Third, you have learned how to interpret what a statistic means, what df are and how a *p*-value is calculated. We have also focused on effect sizes, which are increasingly being reported and which should be crucial to your consideration of whether research findings are more important or interesting than *p*-values. This is the state of how research findings are reported in our field currently, but in Chapter 4 I will argue that we need to finally implement the new statistics. As you do so, you will increasingly notice the way that just *p*-values do not give you enough information.

2.3 Parametric and Non-Parametric Statistics

I said earlier that statistics that make inferences about the population are called inferential statistics. One common type of inferential statistics is **parametric statistics**. Parametric statistics try to determine, from the statistics calculated from an actual sample, what the parameters of the population are.

In other words, it uses what can actually be measured (the statistics) to estimate what the thing of interest that we cannot actually measure is (the parameter). Parametric statistics are based on assuming a certain type of distribution of the data, which is why there are many assumptions about data distribution that need to be met to legitimately use parametric statistics.

Parametric statistics are not the only kind of statistics available, however. Many people have also heard about **non-parametric statistics**. Non-parametric statistics do not rely on the data having a normal distribution, although they may have other assumptions that parametric tests have, such as data that are independent. There are older types of non-parametric tests that have been available as counterparts to the parametric tests for years. Some non-parametric tests you may have seen reported in the literature include the **Mann–Whitney U test** for two independent samples and the Kruskal–Wallis one-way ANOVA.

These older types of non-parametric tests do not require that data be normally distributed, but they still impose assumptions on data distribution, such as the requirement that **variances** be equal across groups or across the data set. (The variance is a measure of how tightly or loosely bunched up scores are around the mean.) Maxwell and Delaney (2004, p. 113) noted that a non-parametric **Kruskal–Wallis test** requires variances to be equal and, if they are not, this non-parametric test will perform just as badly as the parametric one-way ANOVA when variances are not equal. Rank-based methods such as the Kruskal–Wallis test can provide some protection against the effects of **outliers** (data that are markedly different from the rest of the data), whereas parametric methods cannot.

However, a newer type of non-parametric statistics has gained favor recently among statisticians, one that has been known about for many years but whose computing requirements were too large before the widespread advent of computers. These type of statistics are called **robust statistics**, and I believe that these type of non-parametric statistics should be the ones that researchers use if they want to use non-parametric statistics. (See Larson-Hall & Herrington, 2009, for more information about why robust statistics are desirable in applied linguistics.) In fact, Howell (2007) stated that such types of robust statistics, which include resampling procedures, will in the end certainly replace the parametric statistics whose assumptions are too strict and often not met (p. 680). Wilcox (2001) lamented that, although modern statistics has made great strides in improving methodology and practical applications for quantitative methods, the average researcher in an applied field generally has no knowledge of these modern advances. Introductory statistics textbooks cover the classic statistics methods that were formulated prior to 1960 and, most tellingly, before modern computing was available. Robust methods were developed in response to the realization that even small deviations from a normal distribution could cause the "classical" parametric statistics to fail (Jurečková & Picek, 2006; Wilcox, 2001). In other words, "classical" procedures were not robust (did not perform well) in the face of some kinds of violations of assumptions.

For this reason, each chapter includes information about how to perform some kind of robust statistical test. There are many methods and many different types of robust tests. In SPSS, there will generally only be one choice for a robust test, so I will detail that. For R, the choices are unlimited but I will generally try to implement both bootstrapping and means trimming, both inferential, following Wilcox's (2012a, 2012b) recommendations on the best type of robust test to use for each type of statistical procedure.

2.3.1 Why Robust Statistics?

Many textbooks will claim that parametric statistics are robust to violations of assumptions. For example, you may have heard that the Student's *t*-distribution (the *t*-test) is rather robust to violations of assumptions. According to Wilcox (2003), the Student's *t*-distribution on which the *t*-test is based can perform accurately if both groups have identical distributions, equal variances and equal sample sizes. The Student's *t*-test is not very robust to even slight departures from a normal distribution. Even just one outlier in a group can change our conclusion from rejecting the null hypothesis to one where we would have to accept it. This is because an outlier will inflate the group variance, and having a larger

Table 2.3 Scores on an Imaginary Vocabulary Test

Group 1:	4	5	6	7	8	9	10	11	12	13
Group 2:	1	2	3	4	5	6	7	8	9	10

variance in the denominator will decrease the *t*-statistic. The smaller the *t*-statistic is, the more likely we will reject.

Wilcox (2003, p. 242) gives a striking example of the influence of just one outlier. Suppose that we had two groups who received the scores shown in Table 2.3 on a vocabulary test.

In Table 2.3, the sample mean for group 1 is $X_1 = 8.5$, the mean for group 2 is $X_2 = 5.5$ and the value of a *t*-test comparing the two groups is $t = 2.22$. The critical value for *t* is 2.1, so, since *t* is higher than the critical value, the probability that the two groups come from the same population, given the results we found, is less than 5%, and so we would reject the null hypothesis that the groups have equal means. We would say that group 1 performed better than group 2, because their mean score is higher, and the *t*-test tells us it is statistically different from that of group 1. Now consider what would happen if we increased the largest score in group 1 from 13 to 23. Clearly 23 would be an outlier to the data point in this distribution. This would make the sample mean $X_1 = 9.5$. It would seem then that we would have even more reason to find the groups to be different from one another. However, the increase in this one score means that the sample variance (s^2) has also increased, from $s_1^2 = 9.17$ to 29.17. As a result, *t* now decreases to $t = 2.04$ and we can no longer reject the null hypothesis! This example illustrates how even one outlier can have a large effect on the conclusions we draw when we use theoretical assumptions about our distributions.

It is true that most second language researchers, when faced with an obvious outlier like this, would probably just remove it, apparently removing the problem. However, taking away outliers in this fashion is not objective and not replicable (Wilcox, 1998). It results in a violation of the assumption of independence (Huber, 1981). Sometimes, in a large data set, when one outlier is removed, other points that previously did not seem like outliers then become so. Robust statistics provides objective and replicable ways to remove outliers, such as using a trimmed mean.

The problem with the mean is that it is unduly influenced by outliers and is not robust to small deviations from normality in the sample distribution. The median is useful when the distribution is skewed or non-normal, but it discards all of the information in the sample except for one or two numbers. Modern statistical estimators of location, such as the trimmed mean, have been formulated to be more robust to violations in normality and to outliers than the mean, but include more information than the median. Although it may seem counterintuitive to "throw away" information from the sample by using trimmed means or M-estimators, Wilcox (2001) asserted that, when there are outliers in the data (which results in a distribution with heavy tails), the 20% trimmed mean gives higher power, shorter confidence intervals and a variance that is smaller, and thus closer to the population means. Even when the distribution does not have heavy tails, Wilcox suggested that for skewed curves the trimmed mean will be a more accurate measure than the untrimmed mean, again providing an advantage when hypothesis testing or computing confidence intervals. And when distributions are completely normal (as I suspect they almost never are in our field), trimmed means are only slightly less accurate than the sample mean, so almost all the evidence is in favor of consistently using robust measures of location.

According to Herrington (2001), robust estimation "involves calculating estimators that are relatively insensitive to the tails of a data distribution, but which conform to a normal theory approximation at the center of the data distribution" (p. 2). Robust estimators thus use principled ways of eliminating data points that can be considered outliers (Wilcox, 2012a). Robust statistics will be nearly as powerful as parametric statistics if data are completely normally distributed, but they will be more powerful (meaning they will be more likely to find differences if any exist) and more accurate (meaning they will estimate more precise confidence intervals) than parametric statistics if the data are not normally distributed (Westfall & Young, 1993; Wilcox, 2001). There are thus very good reasons for preferring robust statistics over parametric or classical non-parametric statistics. Robust statistics are different from both parametric and non-parametric statistics, not just a way of cleaning up the data before using parametric statistics. However, in kind, robust statistics are more similar to parametric statistics than non-parametric statistics.

One type of robust statistic available in both SPSS and R is the bootstrap. In this type of approach:

> the observed data are used repeatedly, in a computer-intensive simulation analysis, to provide inferences. In simple terms, resampling does with a computer what the experimenter would do in practice, if it were possible: he or she would repeat the experiment. (Westfall & Young, 1993, p. 12)

One of the choices that will have to be made while doing bootstrapping is how many bootstrap samples to take. Although it is possible, using modern computing power, to generate even 100,000 samples (Chernick, 2007), a number of investigators, including Wasserman & Bockenholt (1989) and Manly (1997) have asserted that 1000 or so samples should suffice. A recent paper about bootstrapping and SLA by LaFlair, Egbert, and Plonsky (2015) followed Chernick's (1999) suggestion to use 10,000 samples, but sometimes this can result in long processing times. So you will find me in this book at times trying 10,000 samples, but sometimes cutting down if I have found that 10,000 creates a long wait time.

It is exciting to be able to introduce a few types of robust statistics in this book, but keep in mind that this is an active area of research in statistics and changes and updates will probably continue to be made to best practices.

2.4 Summary

In this chapter, I have laid out the basic foundations for understanding statistics as they are reported in most research reports in the field. I explained the issue of what a variable is, whether it can be classified as dependent or independent, and what level of measurement it has. I then talked about the hidden assumptions behind how the traditional parametric statistics approaches hypothesis testing, including null and alternative hypotheses, *p*-values, df and statistical significance. Many journals now require effect sizes to be reported as well, and I explained these in this chapter. With the information in this chapter, you should begin to understand some of the statistical underpinnings of the numbers you see reported in research papers, but the approach detailed in this chapter can be considered the "old" statistics and as we move forth in the book I hope to bring you along with me to move to the "new" statistics approach to data.

Chapter 3

Describing Data Numerically and Graphically and Assessing Assumptions for Parametric Tests

> The business of the statistician is to catalyze the scientific learning process.
>
> George E. P. Box

Science often consists of taking objects and putting them in some kind of arrangement to see a pattern that we could not previously see. In this chapter I will describe different ways to order your data to find patterns. Although numerical summaries can be helpful in finding patterns, human beings often find that graphics are even more helpful in achieving this goal. In general, at the beginning of each chapter I will provide information and examples of graphics that are most suited to each statistical test treated in the chapter. However, this chapter provides information that is common and necessary for every statistical test treated in this book.

First, I will talk about measures of location that try to give a sense of the typical score of a data set. The number we will be most interested in is the mean, but I will also discuss the median and the mode. Next, I will talk about measures of variability in the data, such as the **standard deviation (SD)** and the variance. These measures give a sense of how far scores deviate from the average. Our statistical software has tests that can call for a variety of measures of location and variability at the same time.

A second focus of the chapter is to look at both numerical and graphical summaries of data that help explore whether data fit the assumptions that are necessary to perform parametric statistics. It may seem strange to talk about satisfying assumptions for statistical tests before we have even begun to talk about the statistical tests themselves, but the assumption that your sampled data come from a normal distribution of data holds for every test in parametric statistics. I will demonstrate a variety of graphic and numerical ways to test this assumption. The assumption of equal variances (called the **homogeneity of variances assumption**) if there are different groups of data is one that applies in every case where groups are found. The main ways to test this assumption are to look at the SD and graphically at box plots.

3.1 Numerical Summaries of Data

The more data that are given in a research paper the better. I personally think it would be very valuable if the data sets research studies are based on were widely available, either in databases, as online appendices to journals, or published in their entirety along with submitted articles (and I do again thank those researchers who have allowed me to use their data in this book). At the very least, researchers can mention that data sets are available on request. Many readers follow the American Psychological Association (APA) format when writing papers, but they may not realize that the APA's Ethics Code requires that authors share their data for the sake of reanalysis. Clay (2009) lists as advantages of data sharing the ability to put all of your data into circulation (not just what fits into the journal article) and the ability to use the data to answer research questions the original researcher did not think of. Anyone who has done a statistical analysis on their data realizes that not every question that could be asked has been asked. Not every piece of information about the data has been inserted into the article.

(I know, I have tried to and reviewers have found it very tedious!) Having this information available could help future researchers who want to ask different questions than the ones the author did.

Other advantages to data sharing include cost savings for those who can use data in different ways, for quality control and as a teaching tool. For the example of cost savings, Clay (2009) cites bilingualism researcher Judith Kroll, who said she uses databases for comparing research with bilinguals to data from monolinguals. As for quality control, I personally have had reviewers find some errors in my data set by noticing some anomalous entries in the data tables I submitted along with my articles. When I have gone back to check, I have found mistakes in data entry. I am getting personal here because I want to show that everyone can make mistakes with statistics and it is perhaps to be expected. When authors do not provide a way for others to check on their numbers and calculations, we are left to trust that an expert in linguistics has done all of their statistics in a reasonable way, and this may not be a reasonable assumption.

Larson-Hall and Plonsky (2015), who have tried to establish some standards for the reporting of quantitative research in the second language acquisition (SLA) field, suggested that every original research paper should include both a numeric and a graphic summary of the data set. Descriptive statistics include mean scores and SDs, which are described in this chapter, as well as effect sizes and **confidence intervals (CIs)**, which will be addressed in Chapter 4. Graphic summaries are helpful both as a way to examine your data before any statistics are run, and also as a way to make your findings more intuitively accessible to readers in your report.

One of the goals when doing a numerical summary is for you to become familiar with trends in your data, such as the "typical" score (which you will often measure with the mean), how spread out your data are (which you can measure with the SD and the range), and, if you have groups, how they differ from one another. Another goal should be to screen your data. Sometimes errors will enter your data set during data entry, and numerical summaries can help you look for anomalies in your data. For example, if you look at the minimum and maximum scores on a 200-point test, a maximum score of 300 would alert you to a problem. If you found that the mean and SD of one group were wildly divergent from those of another group, you may also have reason to suspect there is some problem with your data entry. In these cases, using graphic summaries (described in Section 3.5) can also help you quickly identify points in your data set that may be implausible. If you have entered data correctly but think you have found outliers, then you will have to decide what to do with these. Section 3.9.1 deals with this issue.

3.1.1 The Mean, Median and Mode

The **mean** of a variable is what most people think of as the average. Let us take for an example made-up scores on a hearing test from a group of 10 older people:

Table 3.1 Fictional Hearing Test Data

Hearing test:	354	289	580	446	268	575	425	739	518	483

There are 10 scores in Table 3.1, and the mean involves adding all of them together and dividing by 10 to get $\overline{X} = 467.7$. ($\overline{X}$, pronounced "x bar," is the way statisticians represent the mean, but when it is difficult to find this symbol on your computer you can use the symbol M instead to designate the mean; the bar on top symbolizes the fact that these are data from the sample, meaning the actual people we tested, and not the population, which is the whole group of people we would like to generalize to, but do not directly test.) The mean is represented mathematically as $\overline{X} = \frac{\sum X}{n}$ where $\sum X =$ the sum of all of the numbers in the set and n = the number of items in the set. The idea is then that we could ask what score would be typical of the 10 participants. Of course, some participants scored higher than this number and some scored lower. In fact, no one actually scored 467.7. However, this is the number that results in the smallest amount of distance between the mean score and the amount that each actual score differs from the mean.

The following example shows that the mean is the line that minimizes the distance to all the data points in the set. If we want to know how far it is from the mean to each point, we might think we should just subtract each point from the mean, and add up all those distances, like this: (467.7 − 354) + (467.7 − 289) + . . . + (467.7 − 483). The problem is that because the distances are both positive and negative (see Figure 3.1), the distances will cancel each other out and become zero. So one way to get around this is to do the exact same thing, except just square each distance and then take the square root of the whole thing, like this:

$$\sqrt{((467.7-354)^2+(467.7-289)^2+\ldots+(467.7-483)^2)}$$

This procedure is called the **sum of squares** because it squares all of the differences and then sums them. It turns out that the sum of squares always minimizes the distance to all the data points in the set, and this is called the **least-squares principle**. The sum of squares for the mean in this case is 187,528.1.

If we picked a different number that was not the mean, for example 483, the sum of squares would be 189,869. If we picked 466, the sum of squares would be 187,557. We could continue to test this out with other numbers, and find that the smallest number is the one calculated when we use the mean. The mean thus uses all of the numbers in a data set and is the number that, in the sense of minimizing the distance from itself to all other points, best represents a typical score.

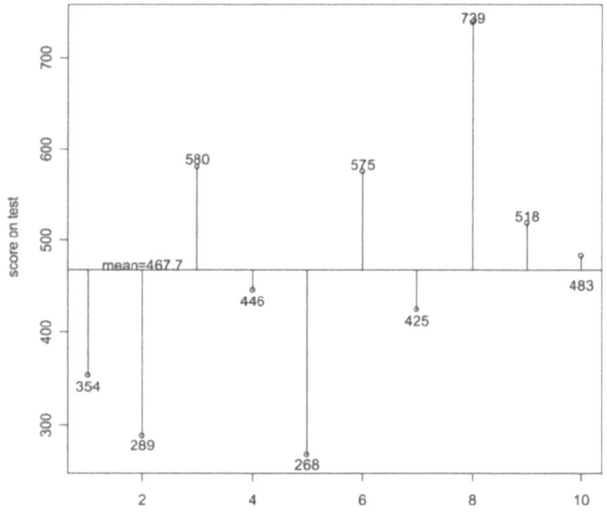

Figure 3.1 The mean line (at 467.7) is the one that minimizes the distance from all 10 points to the line. Any other line would result in larger absolute distances from the points to the line.

The mean is fundamental in statistics and is used in almost every kind of statistical test discussed in this book. There is one large problem with the mean, though, as a summary of data. This problem is that extreme values, called outliers, can have a disproportional influence on the mean score. Because the mean takes every point into account, if an extreme score is included in the data set the mean can change drastically. For example, if the person recording the data made a mistake in data entry and changed the last value from 483 to 4833, the mean score would become 902.7. Although this number still minimizes the sum of squares, you can see that it now does not seem very representative of the group, since 9 out of the 10 participants scored much lower than this point.

The median and mode are not nearly as important to statistical calculations as the mean. The **median** is the point at which 50% of the scores are higher and 50% of the scores are lower. In our hearing test example, there are 10 scores, so no single one can be the median. If we order the numbers from

Table 3.2 Ordered Hearing Test Data

Hearing test:	268	289	354	425	446	↕ 483	518	575	580	739

lowest to highest as in Table 3.2, we see that the point where half of the numbers are below and half are above lies between 446 and 483. In fact, the median is calculated as half of the distance between these two points, which would be 464.5.

When a distribution of data is **symmetric**, meaning that both halves of the distribution curve around the midpoint are mirror images of each other, the mean and the median will be at approximately the same point. Here we see the median of 464.5 is quite close to the mean of 467.7. In the case where we mistakenly typed 4833 instead of 483, however, the median would be 464.5 while the mean became 902.7. These two numbers are not very close together, and illustrate how one advantage of the median is that it is resistant to extreme values. One drawback of the median is that it essentially throws away all information about the data set except for the middle score. Another problem that Howell (2002) pointed out is that the median cannot readily enter into statistical calculations, and this is the major advantage that the mean has over both the median and the mode.

The **mode** is the most frequently occurring score in the data set. In the hearing test data set, no score occurs more than once, so there are multiple modes. Although the mode may be an appropriate estimator of location for some data sets, I have never seen it used in second language research data. However, in graphic representations we sometimes see reference to more than one "mode" in the distribution. This means there is more than one peak of data in the distribution.

3.1.2 Standard Deviation, Variance and Standard Error

It is not just enough to have a measurement of the typical score or the middle of the distribution. We also want to know something more about the spread or dispersion of the data. We might find all of the observations tightly clustered around the typical score, or we may find them extremely spread out from that typical score.

The SD, variance and standard error are measurements of the spread of the data. They are very important concepts in statistics but may be less familiar and less intuitive initially to the beginner than mean and median.

The variance is the average squared distance from the mean to any point. This is not an intuitive idea, but the idea of the sum of squares explained above showed that the sum of squares seeks to minimize the distance from the mean to any point. We want an average of this number, so we divide by $N - 1$. (The reason why we divide by $N - 1$ instead of just N is that $N - 1$ is a better estimate of the population variance and is used for inferential statistics, while dividing by N is a better estimate of the actual data set variance, which is not usually what we are interested in.) Thus, we can say that the variance is the expected squared distance of a point from the mean value of the data set (Wilcox, 2003, p. 96). As an intuitive idea, if the mean is the horizontal line that minimizes the distance to all of the points (as in Figure 3.1), the variance is the average of those distances or, from Figure 3.1, the average of the length of those lines from the mean to every point. Mathematically, this looks like:

$$s_x^2 = \frac{\Sigma(X - \overline{X})^2}{N - 1}$$

For the hearing test data,

$$s^2 = \frac{187{,}528.1}{(10 - 1)} = 20{,}836$$

so $s = 144.3$. This means that the average length of those bars from the horizontal mean bar to the actual point in Figure 3.1 is 144.3 units. Just like the mean, this is probably not the real length of any of those bars, but it does a good job representing the average length of those bars.

You will also see the Greek symbol sigma squared (σ^2) used to represent the variance. This is the population variance; in other words, this is the variance of all the people which we would like to generalize our results to, which is what we actually want to estimate and which, in real life, we pretty much never know, so we just use s^2 to give us the best estimate of σ^2.

The SD (also written as s or s.d.) is just the positive square root of the variance. For the hearing test data, the square root of s^2 was 144.3. Basically what we are doing is taking an average of the amount each observation varies from the mean score, although we have to square and then take the square root of it not to end up with zero.

It is clear that, if the scores are more tightly clustered around the mean, the SD will be smaller, while, if they are spread out further from the mean, the SD will be larger. Figure 3.2 tries to graphically illustrate this difference. The two sets of data have the same mean (5.6), but the data on the left are much more spread out from the mean and thus have a much larger SD (3.6). In contrast, the data on the right are tightly bunched near the mean and thus the SD is much smaller (0.9).

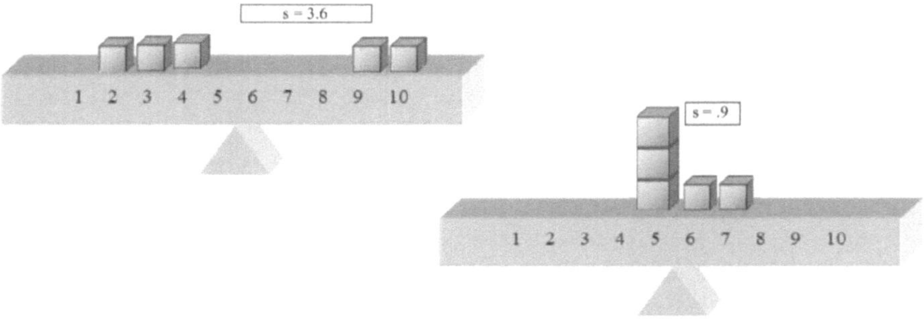

Figure 3.2 Smaller standard deviations are closer to the mean and larger ones are more spread out.

Figure 3.3 shows graphically what different normal distributions look like when their SDs differ. A standard normal distribution has a mean of 0 and a SD of 1. (There is an interactive normal probability distribution graph at www.intmath.com/counting-probability/normal-distribution-graph-interactive.php where you can change the SD of a normal distribution and see how it affects the shape of the curve.)

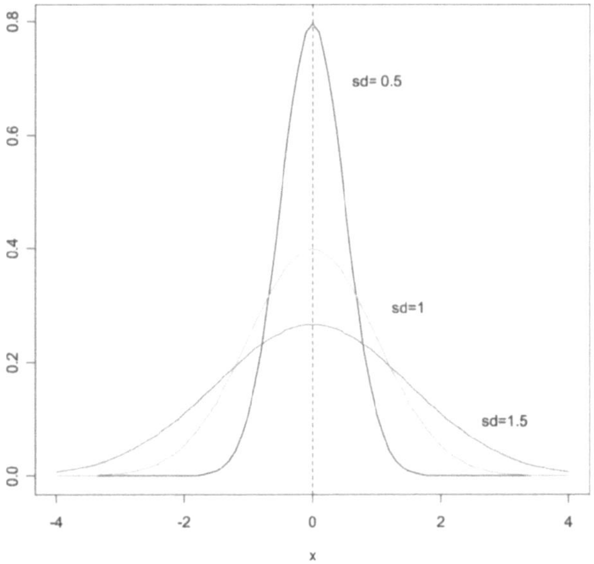

Figure 3.3 Varying standard deviations for a normal distribution with mean zero. Notice that the distribution spreads out further from the center as the standard deviation gets larger.

Whatever the size of the SD, if the data come from a normal distribution there is a rule for determining what percentage of the data fall within each SD. Approximately 68% of the data will fall within ±1 SD of the mean (34% on each side of the mean; this is illustrated graphically in Figure 3.4). Two SDs from the mean will encompass 95% of the data (34 + 34 + 13.5 + 13.5) and three SDs will cover 99.7% of all data. Flege, Yeni-Komshian, and Liu (1999) used this fact to label any data from non-native speakers that fell within two SDs of the mean of native speakers as "native-like." For example, if native speakers got a mean of 9.3 on a 10-point test, with a SD of 0.4, then if a non-native speaker scored 8.5 or higher on the test they would be considered to be within the "native speaker range" of scores. This seems a legitimate and objective way to classify a native speaker range of performance, although for judgment of pronunciation I think I prefer the method used in Abrahamsson and Hyltenstam (2009) where native speakers had to simply decide if the speaker they were listening to was a native speaker or not, and this score (either 0 or 1) got aggregated over 10 different judges. It seems to me this makes the judge's task a lot more straightforward, which would add to the validity and **reliability** of the test.

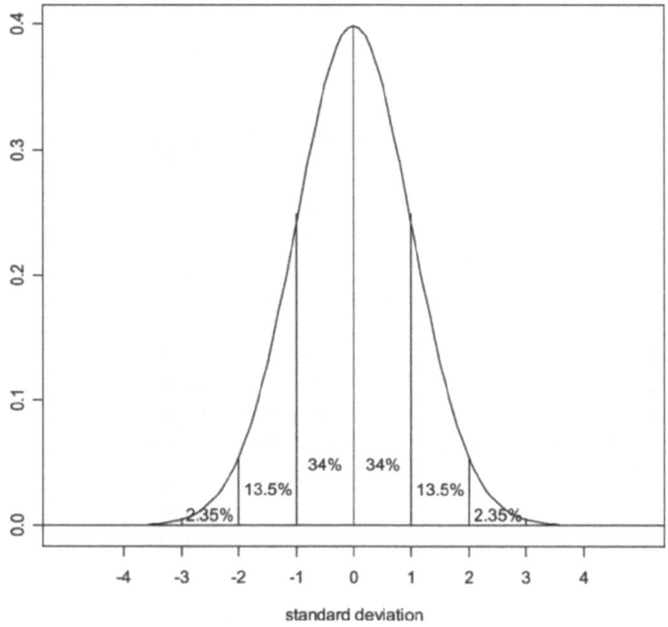

Figure 3.4 How much of the data of a normal curve is found in each standard deviation away from the mean.

In summary, both the SD and the variance measure the same thing, which is the average amount of distance from the mean to any point. The variance is just the square of the SD. Sometimes you will hear the term "standard error" used as well, and you may wonder how that relates to the variance and the SD. The **standard error of the mean (SEM)** is *not* the same as the SD, and it is worth trying to better understand what the SEM is. A brilliant book on statistics called *Understanding the New Statistics: Effect Sizes, Confidence Intervals, and Meta-Analysis* by Geoff Cumming (2012) was published since the first edition of this book. I will call on help from Cumming to better explain this important idea.

First, Cumming (2012) suggests you learn a mnemonic that explains the SEM: "The standard error is the SD of the sampling distribution of the sample mean" (p. 59). The formula for the SEM is: $SE = \frac{\sigma}{\sqrt{N}}$. It is calculated by dividing the SD of the population distribution (σ, but usually estimated by the sample SD, s) by the square root of the number of observations (N). That is the words, but what helped me to understand this concept better was to look at a simulation that Cumming devised called ESCI. You can run it yourself on Microsoft Excel, after you download it for free from www.latrobe.edu.au/psy/research/cognitive-and-developmental-psychology/esci. To download, open this Web page, scroll down to the third tab (The software) and click on it. Download the correct file for Windows or Mac, according to the Excel version you have. Go ahead and open it up. Inside the folder that you have downloaded, open up the file that is called "ESCI Chapters 1–4." When I opened this up, it opened up in Excel but with a front page that looked similar to a Web page (see Figure 3.5). On this page there was a security warning that macros had been disabled. You want to disable them. If you get a warning, you can click on the "OPTIONS. . ." button and enable the content. If you cannot find that, go to the Review menu and click on "Unprotect sheet." You want the "CIjumping" tab from chapter 3 of ESCI (circled in Figure 3.5). Go to that tab in the Excel file.

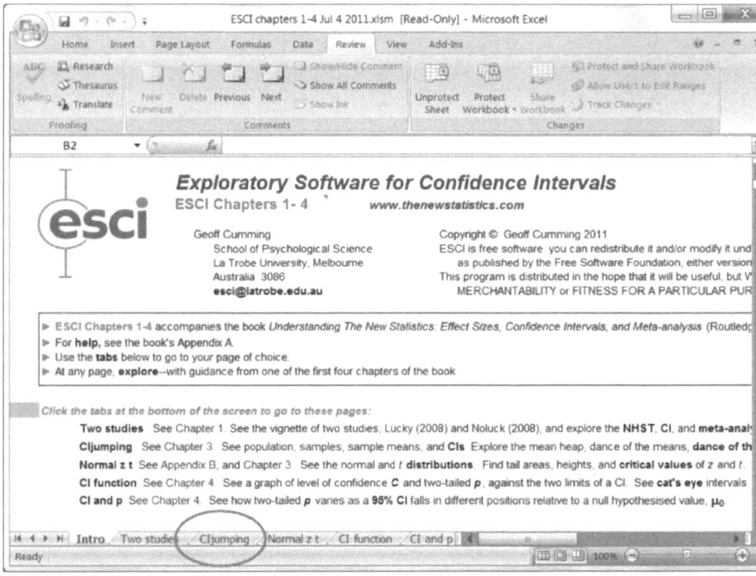

Figure 3.5 Excel file containing ESCI program. Navigate to the CIjumping tab at the bottom.

Now we play with the simulation! The first thing is to push the clear button, which is circled in Figure 3.6. Then click on the box to the left of the "Clear" button in the orange bar (if you can see color; if not, Cumming calls this the area "near red 3," meaning anywhere in the colored area that has red 3 in its top left corner) that says "Display means." (It is checked already in Figure 3.6.) This will put one (green) dot on the graph. Next, go to the blue bar (near red 4) and check the box that says "Display data points", then press the gray "Take sample" button to the right of the "Clear" button. This will put $N = 20$ (as default specified in the orange bar/near red 3) points that made up that first mean dot on the graph as well. These first two steps are already done and shown in Figure 3.6. Notice that the default mean is $\mu = 50$ and the default SD is $\sigma = 20$ (shown in the yellow band/near red 2).

Continue to press the "Take sample" button and you will see the mean dot travel down the page. Compare the sample mean value with the population mean value. (Remember, it is set at 50 by default.) Cumming says each new click of the "Take Sample" button is like running your experiment again, so you can check how the sample mean and SD compare to the population mean and SD, which are set by default. You can keep clicking the "Take Sample" button or use the button to the right of that, "Run-Stop", to take samples quickly, and watch the mean dots falling down the page. Cumming calls it the "dance of the means" (see Figure 3.7) and suggests you might want to play your choice of backing music for the dance.

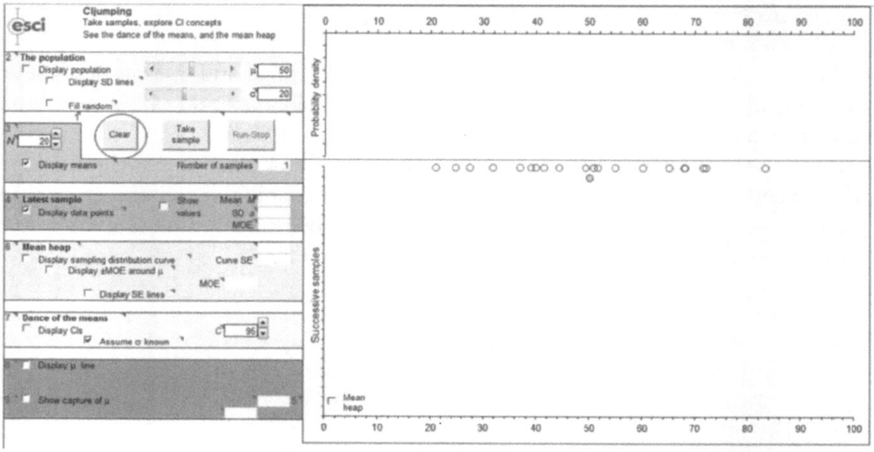

Figure 3.6 Cumming's (2012) ESCI simulation program for SEM demonstration: first step.

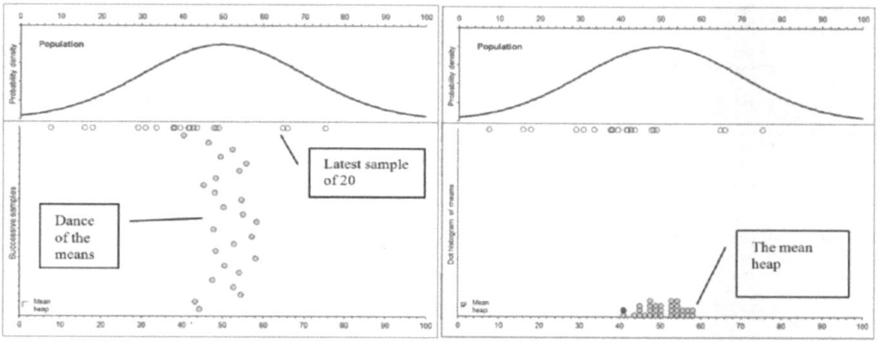

Figure 3.7 Cumming's (2012) ESCI simulation program for SEM demonstration: dance of the means and mean heap.

If you click the box in the bottom left side of the graph called "Mean heap," the dots all fall down to the bottom, as in the right-hand window of Figure 3.7. This shows the sampling distribution of the mean. In other words, it is all of the mean scores of all of the repeated "experiments" we did. Clearly, even if the population mean is the same, the sample mean will not be the same every time. Remember the chant for the SE? "The standard error is the SD of the sampling distribution of the sample mean." The mean heap is the sampling distribution of the sample mean. So the SE is the SD of this collection of sample means! I continue to take samples with the same values, and also click the "Display sampling distribution curve" box, which is in the light blue band/near red 6, and "Display SD lines" in the first yellow band/near red 2. This gives me the display in Figure 3.8, which shows the graph after 150 samples. Compare the SD lines of the population density curve at the top of the graph, where we know the population mean is 50 and the SD is 20, to the SE bars around the mean heap, which are the SDs of the sampling distribution of the sample mean. So the SE is really just a particular kind of SD, and after seeing the dance of the means, you can better understand what this SE is. The smaller the SE is, the more precise the estimate, therefore, we want SEs to be as small as possible, but remember that the equation is $SE = \frac{\sigma}{\sqrt{N}}$, so to get the variation to be smaller we need to increase the N quite a bit since we are taking the square root of it. For example, Cumming (2012) suggests that to halve the amount of variation we need to increase the N by four times.

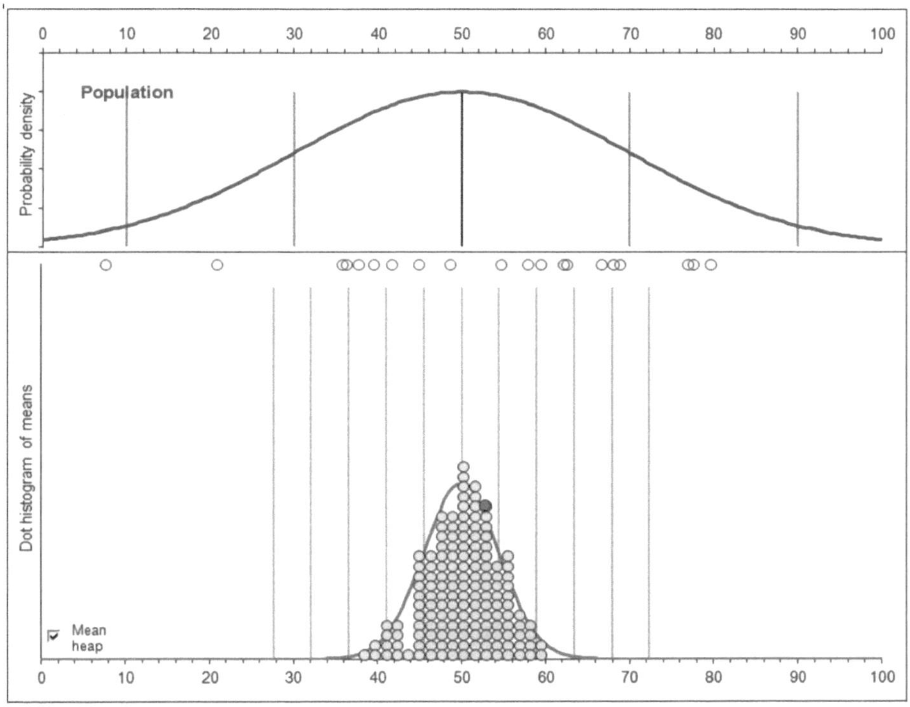

Figure 3.8 Cumming's (2012) ESCI simulation program for SEM demonstration: standard deviation of the population density curve versus standard error of the sample mean density curve.

If you have downloaded ESCI and followed along with me (and I hope you have), I urge you to play with other factors, such as increasing or decreasing the *N* and seeing how the dance of the means changes. (Does the SE get wider or narrower with a larger *N*? If you click on the light blue band/near red 6 in the box that says "Display sampling distribution curve" you will see a number for the curve SE; it will not change no matter how many samples you take. For $N = 20$ it was 4.4721.) Try increasing and decreasing the SD. (Does the SE get wider or narrower as you increase the SD?)

You can see that most of the dots in the mean heap fall near the center of the heap, and in fact, we can think of this heap as being part of a normal curve, where we can use our rule of thumb to realize that about 95% of the data will fall within + 2 SDs of the mean. We understand that there is some variability and error to our estimate of the mean in this heap of means, and this estimate of variability around the SE is called the **margin of error (MOE)**, which you can read as M-O-E or "MOW-ee"). So MOE = approximately 2 SEs (exactly, MOE = 1.96 SE). Figure 3.9 shows the MOE on a new sampling where I kept the mean at 50 but increased the SD to 30, and decreased the *N* to 15. The MOE will be important for calculating the CI, which is the topic of the next section.

3.1.3 Confidence Intervals

I want to help bring about a change in the way we think about and present our statistical data in the field. I do so because researchers who do work in psychology, education, sociology and other social science disciplines who are also statistical experts have been urging applied practitioners for years to change the way they do statistics. For example, a book published in 1997 was called *What If There Were No Significance Tests?* (Harlow, Mulaik, & Steiger, 1997). Another book I consulted extensively for the first edition of this book was called *Beyond Significance Testing: Reforming Data Analysis Methods in Behavioral Research* (Kline, 2004) and was published by the APA. For years such persons have been

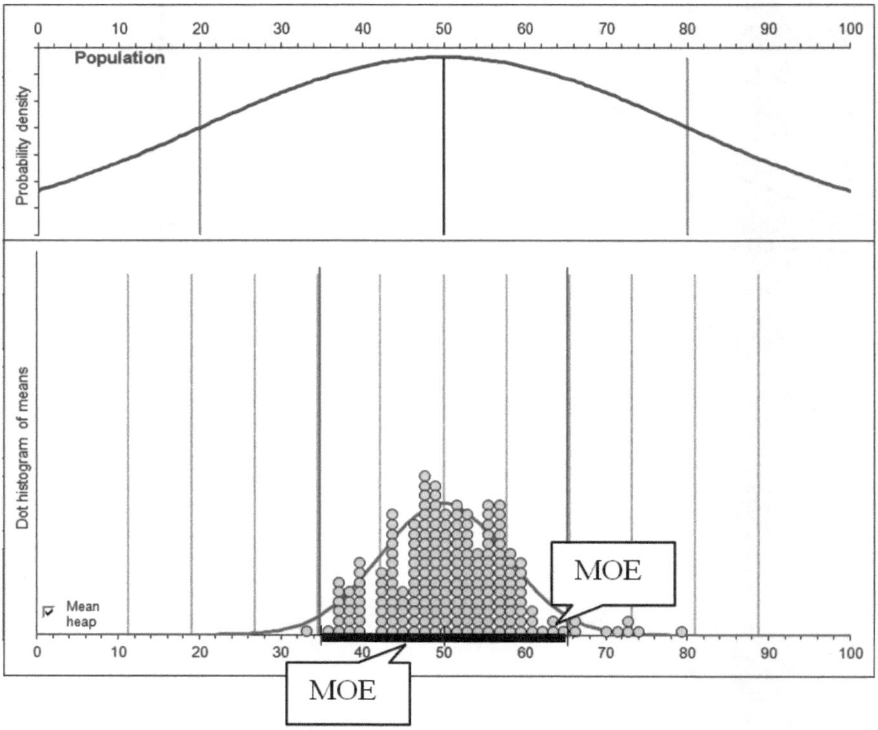

Figure 3.9 **The margin of error (MOE) is approximately 2 standard errors wide.**

urging reform, but it has been slow in coming. However, now appears to be the time that things are beginning to change in psychology, and it is also happening in our field of SLA. Heidi Byrnes, editor of *The Modern Language Journal*, remarked in an editor's note in 2013 that there is a "methodological turn" (p. 825) happening in our field.

I am mentioning this idea in the section about CIs because CIs are one of the main changes in the "new statistics." (This is the name of a 2012 book by Geoff Cumming that I have been greatly inspired by.) In an article that Luke Plonsky and I coauthored (Larson-Hall & Plonsky, 2015) where we gave some recommendations for the SLA field regarding statistical reporting, we urged researchers to report CIs in addition to, or perhaps even as an alternative to, statistical tests. This is because CIs can give you all of the information that the results of a statistical test, such as a *t*-test or an analysis of variance (ANOVA), does, but gives you even more information beyond that. However, the most important part of a CI is that it starts researchers thinking in a more "synthetic" way about their research. Instead of seeing one research article as the answer to a question, it views one report as a building block in the database of research that we are building up to answer a question, as one part of a whole where the question is not whether this or that treatment had an effect or showed a relationship with some other variable, but *how big* of an effect the treatment had, or *how strong* the relationship was. This is thinking in terms of estimating the effect of an experiment, not dichotomous thinking about whether there was an effect or not.

The CI will give a range of numbers around a point interval, like a mean score, or a difference in mean scores between groups, where, with a certain prespecified amount of confidence (usually 95%), we believe that the true parameter lies. So for a mean score, we have sampled a certain group and found the sample mean, but the **95% CI** will tell us a range of plausible values where we could expect to find the true mean of the population, with 95% confidence. Our CIs vary and 95% of the time our generated CIs will capture the true mean, but 5% of the time the CI will not contain the true mean. You can see that this would be important to people who are working in the same subdiscipline and trying to zero in on the effects of the same type of treatment.

In the first edition I said that a 95% CI represented an interval where, if the study were replicated 100 times, 95% of the time the parameter would be found within this confidence interval range. However, this statement is mistaken, and Cumming (2012) has corrected my thinking on this. If we look at the situation as trying to predict whether the next replication of the study will have a mean score that falls within the same CI, the probability that the CI generated in the first study will contain the mean of the next replication experiment is only 83%. Cumming (2012) suggested that "On average, a 95% CI is an 83% prediction interval. There's a .83 chance it will capture the mean of a single replication experiment" (p. 129).

Reporting of CIs is not common in our field yet. Larson-Hall and Plonsky (2015) reviewed six meta-analyses that examined the percentage of studies containing CIs; three of the meta-analyses reported that no studies had CIs, while the other three reported that 3, 3 and 5% of their surveyed studies contained CIs. Until CIs become commonplace in our field, they should be explained when reported. Even after they become commonplace, when reporting CIs, you should remark on them as well as report them.

We can use CIs instead of *p*-values for inferential purposes. In this chapter, I will be examining descriptive statistics; our statistical programs give us CIs for the point estimate of the mean score of a group. (In fact, we could get a CI for the SD, or for the skewness as well.) One of the big ideas we should take away from CIs is that *any* point estimate that we hope represents an entire population is only an approximation and can vary widely. In other words, yes, there is only one mean score for a sample of people who take your test. But if you want to generalize the results to a population of people who could take your test (say, all of the English as a second language students at your university, or all of the French learners in the USA or all of the bilinguals in the world), then you will have to accept that there will be a range of variation in that estimate, which you can calculate statistically with a certain amount of confidence.

When we get into using a CI in the place of a *p*-value to examine the results of a study, we will generally be looking at a difference in mean scores between groups or at the relationship between two variables. In this chapter, the descriptive statistics I will ask you to look at will just be giving us a CI around the point estimate of the mean score of a group. We can make some inferential conclusions with those CIs too, because of course the difference is based on the same information about variability between groups that is contained in each separate group, but we have to be careful. For example, we cannot just say that if the CIs of the mean scores of two groups overlap that there is no difference between the groups. It is useful to understand the relationship between overlap of CIs and how it relates to the *p*-value for the difference. For two independent means, Cumming (2012, p. 158) says the following rules hold if the sample sizes are at least 10 and the SDs are moderately similar (so that the arms of the CIs are not too different in length):

1 If there is no overlap but if the ends of the CIs of two independent means just touch, then the *p*-value for null hypothesis testing is $p = 0.01$.
2 If there is no overlap and the ends of the CIs have a gap between them, then $p < 0.01$.
3 If the CIs overlap by about half of the average length of the arm of the interval, then p is approximately 0.05. Only a small amount of overlap (less than half of the average age) means $p < 0.05$.

In other words, the difference between two groups could still be statistically significant even if the CIs overlap by a moderate amount. You can play around with the amount of the overlap of CIs for two independent means in Cumming's ESCI program, "Compare A and B", found in the file "ESCI chapters 5–6." I will reproduce some figures from that ESCI program here to illustrate the rules given earlier on. In each case, N also affects the results, and I used $N = 100$ for group A and $N = 88$ for group B. Means and SDs are noted for each figure on the figure itself.

Figure 3.10A shows the situation where the tips of the CIs just touch. Here the difference between groups is statistically significant, and you can see from the *p*-value at the bottom of the graph that the *p*-value is quite small. If the CIs do not overlap at all, and there is a gap between them (as seen in Figure 3.10B), then there is definitely a statistically significant difference between the groups. In the last situation, where the CIs overlap, it is still possible that the groups are statistically different. Here I have set the SDs to be similar so the arms of the CI are basically the same size, and the overlap of the arms is actually more than half (0.57 of the average arm length), but the *p*-value is still less than 0.05. You can see that there can be a good amount of overlap of the CIs and still have statistical difference between the groups.

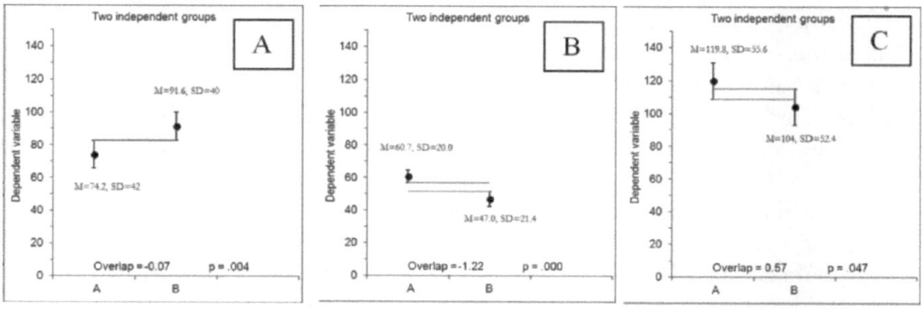

Figure 3.10 Confidence intervals on two independent means (ESCI Compare A B figures).

The situation changes for paired data, of course, such as the Kim (2013) data which tests the same participants at different time periods. Actually, Cumming (2012) says that no overlap rule is possible for this type of design. You cannot make any inferences about the differences between groups from the overlap of CIs in a repeated measures design where the same participants are tested at different time intervals or on different measures, such as different phonemic contrasts or a grammar test vs. a vocabulary test.

One more thing to mention in connection with descriptive CIs (that we can use for inferential purposes too) is that there are several different types of CIs that we can generate. The calculation for a 95% CI is [M − MOE, M + MOE], where MOE is about 2 SEs. In more detail, the 95% CI is $[M - 1.96 \times SD/\sqrt{N}, M + 1.96 \times SD/\sqrt{N}]$. The basic CI uses the sample mean, the sample SD (as an approximation to the population SD, σ), and *N* in its calculations. Both SPSS and R give basic and bootstrapped CIs.

To find out more about what **bootstrapping** is as applied to SLA data, see LaFlair, Egbert, and Plonsky (2015) and Larson-Hall and Herrington (2009). Very briefly, bootstrapping is a procedure where values are randomly resampled from the original sample of data to form new samples. These samples generate an empirical distribution of data that can be examined for statistical significance in the same way that a normal distribution can be, and 95% CIs can also be calculated from this empirical distribution in the same way as they are for the original sample distribution; however, if you use a non-parametric bootstrap, you do not have to assume that the data are normally distributed. We argued in Larson-Hall and Herrington (2009) that this method is preferable to assuming a normal distribution for most SLA data sets, which are too small to ever really know if they are normally distributed or not. Plonsky, Egbert, and LaFlair (2014) found that bootstrapping may not always be advisable, but do recommend it in situations of obvious violations of normality assumptions as well as times when a study has very low or very high power (to avoid finding spurious results due to the small or large sample size).

The procedures in both SPSS and R provide several types of bootstrapped CIs. In this book, I recommend you choose the non-parametric **bias-corrected and accelerated (BCa)** bootstrap. This is the type recommended by Plonsky, Egbert, and LaFlair (2014), as well as other statisticians (Crawley, 2007; Efron and Tibshirani, 1993). Manly (1997) explains that the BCa adjusts for the median not being equal to the mean as well as the "standard deviation varying with the mean of the distribution" (p. 68). By using a non-parametric approach, we avoid having to make the restrictive assumptions about the data that parametric statistics use. Efron and Tibshirani (1993) noted that the main reason for presupposing a parametric assumption is not because this is the best way to do things, but simply because it made it much easier for statisticians, before computers, to make the calculations necessary to obtain the SE. The non-parametric assumption frees us from many constraints about the shape of the data. Chernick (2007) warns, however, that sample size still matters. He says that $n < 10$ is probably still too small to be able to trust results, and that a minimum rule of thumb for sample size is $n = 30$, although he recommends "that in most cases it would be wise to take $n \geq 50$ observations (p. 174).

3.1.4 The Number of Observations and Other Numerical Summaries You Might Want to Report

Besides reporting the mean and SD, you will want to be sure to report the number of participants in your study. Since not all studies consist of those done with participants, we can say that you also want to report the number of observations in the study. Two other numerical summaries of data that you might want to include or that are good to understand are the **range** and the **interquartile range**.

The range is simply a single number that is the maximum data point minus the minimum data point. The range can be used to get a sense of how far apart the ends of the data points are spread. You might decide instead to just report the minimum and maximum points of a data set as well.

It is possible to divide the data into four parts, or quartiles. The part of the data from the 25th to the 75th percentile is also the area from the first to the third quartile (often called Q1 and Q3), and is called the **interquartile range (IQR)**. This is another way of looking at the central part of the distribution. It is probably wiser to report the IQR by visually displaying a box plot than by giving the actual numbers. The hinges of the box plot are not exactly the same as the IQR, but according to Howell (2002, p. 58) they are "closely related to the first and third quartiles."

Two other numbers you will get in the descriptive statistics are **skewness** and **kurtosis**. These are terms that refer to the shape of the curve that makes up the data—whether it is symmetric around the mean (skewness) or pointy versus flat (kurtosis). I will discuss these concepts in more detail in Section 3.5.2, where we will see that the concepts may be more easily understood visually, but numerically some sources give as a rule of thumb that the skewness should be less than 2 or even 1. These data are usually not reported in research reports, but should be examined when looking at whether your data are normally distributed.

3.1.5 Reporting Numerical Summaries

It is a simple matter to obtain numerical summaries with SPSS or R. What may be more perplexing is deciding how to report them. I have had reviewers of my articles object to including both a numerical summary and a graphic summary. However, I argue in this book that both are necessary, so I would urge you to include numerical summaries, either through including summary tables or through inserting means, SDs and counts when statistical tests are reported. As an example of reporting summaries along with statistical test results, I give the following report of a *t*-test conducted with the fictional hearing test group data shown in Section 3.1:

> An independent samples *t*-test was conducted with a group of older participants who took the L2 phoneme discrimination task (M = 467.7, $s = 144.3$, $N = 10$) and young participants in their 30s (M = 709.6, $s = 106.8$, $N = 10$) and found to be statistical ($t_{16.5} = -4.26$, 95%CI [−361.9, −121.9], $d = 1.9$). The effect size (**Cohen's *d***, which says that the difference between groups is 1.9 SDs) for these groups was extremely large, which leads us to believe that age plays a large role in the ability to hear second language phonemes accurately.

I would also include what I call a data-accountable graphic (Larson-Hall, in preparation), one that lets the reader see all of the data from the experiment, so they can perceive the overall trends and get the big picture, but also notice the variability in the data that comes from the individual data points. I used a box plot overlaid with dots here and created it as the Dot Plot Maker website (http://data.vanderbilt.edu/~graywh/dotplot/). This way you see all of the data points, as well as the median line in the box plot, the first and third quartiles (the ends of the box), and the minimum and maximum points of the data set (the ends of the whiskers).

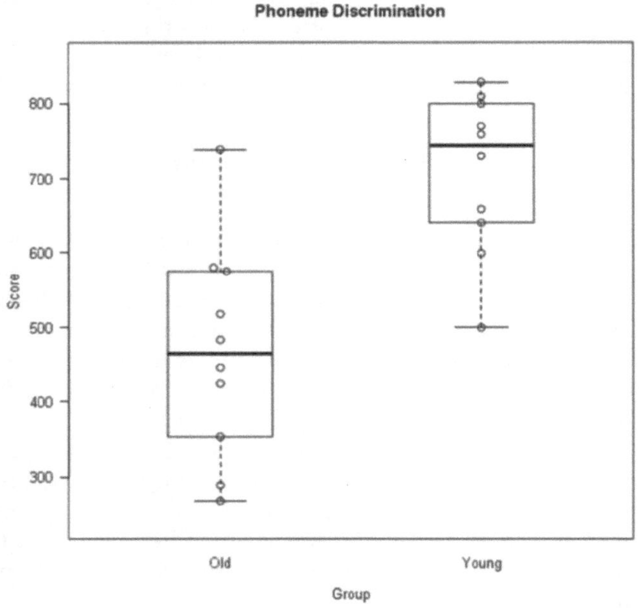

Figure 3.11 Box plot with overlaid dots of fictional phoneme discrimination test.

3.1.6 Data for this Chapter

In order to illustrate how the software performs numerical summaries, I will use data from two studies. One was gathered in an experiment on teaching L1 Korean learners of L2 English how to understand sarcasm using concept-based instruction (Kim, 2013). This is a study that used both qualitative measures (interviews, essay writing and Schema for the Orienting Basis of Action) and quantitative measures to study how well mediation would help second language learners detect and understand sarcasm. We will look only at the quantitative measure in this section, which included a pretest, posttest and delayed posttest. Three points were possible for each test item, which scored whether the learner identified the sarcastic utterance and then three cues that indicated it was a sarcastic comment (1 point was given to the first cue in conjunction with identifying the utterance), and there were 10 items, for a possible total of 30 points maximum. The Kim study is thus a study that sampled the same learners at more than one time period.

The other study uses data from Part I of Abrahamsson and Hyltenstam (2009), which looks at participants from different ages of onset and their scores on a test of perceived nativeness from a spontaneous monologue on the subject of Astrid Lindgren, author of the famous children's book, *Pippi Longstocking*. The participants were Spanish/Swedish bilinguals who arrived in Sweden at different ages of acquisition. The learners were split by the authors of the study into a group of those who arrived in Sweden at age 11 or younger, and those who arrived at age 12 or older, and various tests were done to compare these groups. These groups were also compared to monolingual native speakers of Swedish. The Abrahamsson and Hyltenstam study is thus a study that samples data at one time period, but splits the participants up into groups.

The following sections will show you how to obtain the mean scores for each group, the SD, the range and the minimum and maximum points, and a count of how many participants are in each group. In addition, we will look at skewness and kurtosis numbers.

3.2 Using SPSS to Get Numerical Summaries

3.2.1 Obtaining Numerical Summaries with SPSS and Splitting Groups

There are several ways to get numerical summaries with SPSS. One of the easiest is when you actually run your statistical test. However, even without running the test there are several ways of obtaining numerical summaries. One is ANALYZE > DESCRIPTIVE STATISTICS > DESCRIPTIVES. If you choose this way and you have groups whose descriptive statistics you would like to see separately, you will need to tell SPSS to first split up the data based on these groups. If you do not have separate groups, there would be no need to perform this step. To split data into groups, choose DATA > SPLIT FILE. (I am using the Abrahamsson and Hyltenstam 2009.sav file to demonstrate this, and the split file dialog box is shown in Figure 3.12.)

Tip: When splitting the data, both the "Compare groups" choice and the "Organize output by groups" will provide separate group analysis. The former will provide the output in one table while the latter will provide separate tables. I find the "Compare groups" side-by-side option visually more useful.

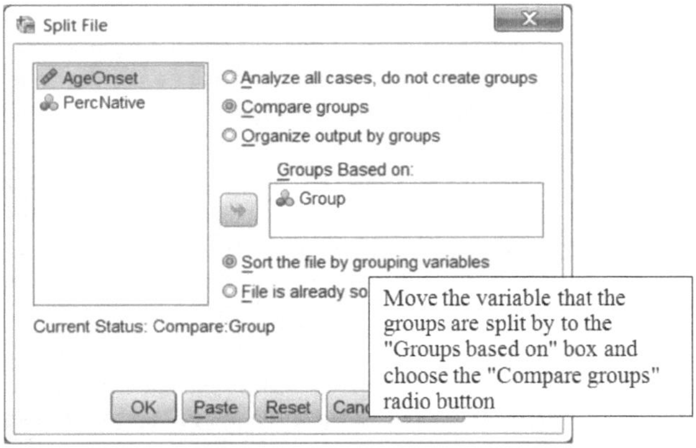

Figure 3.12 Splitting files into groups for data analysis.

Tip: You may enter up to eight variables to split your group by. Each one is nested within the previous variable. Therefore, if I had a variable called "Sex" that split men and women, and I entered "Group" first and then "Sex", I would receive summaries where each group was separately summarized for males and females.

Now that the data are ready to be analyzed, we can proceed to obtain various descriptive statistics for the data using ANALYZE > DESCRIPTIVE STATISTICS > DESCRIPTIVES (Figure 3.13). To pick which statistical measures you want, open the "OPTIONS" button from the DESCRIPTIVES box, shown to the right in Figure 3.13. As a default, you will find the descriptive statistics for mean, SD, and minimum and maximum scores already ticked. I also asked for the kurtosis and skewness numbers.

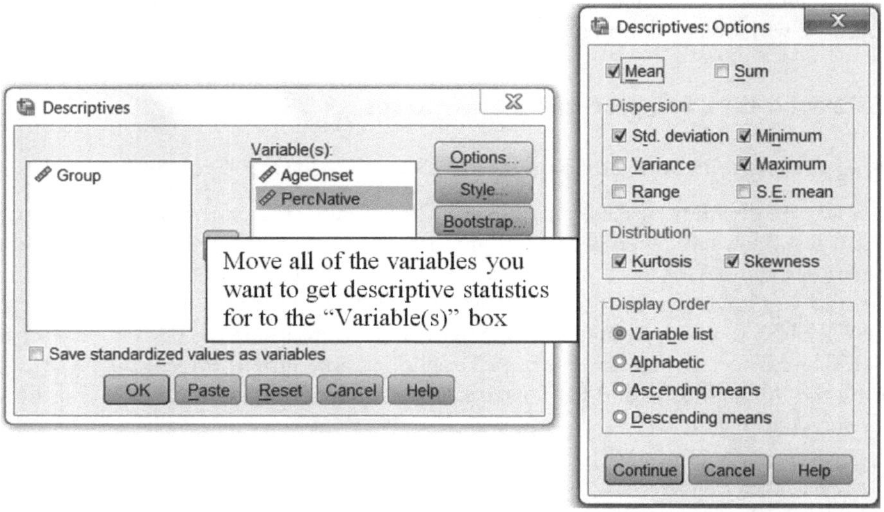

Figure 3.13 Using the ANALYZE > DESCRIPTIVE STATISTICS > DESCRIPTIVES option to get numerical summaries.

The box that says "Save standardized values as variables" on the DESCRIPTIVES box (on the left side in Figure 3.13) will create a column of ***z*-scores**, which are the scores adjusted so that they reflect how many SDs the score is away from the mean. I have never had to use this function myself so I do not recommend doing this, but I just wanted to point out what this box meant. The button that says "Style" lets you create a certain style to format your tables but I recommend typing your data into a table yourself, not using SPSS's tables when you put data into a research paper, so I would not use this button. Last, there is a button that says "Bootstrap" and you can use this button to generate bootstrapped 95% CIs of your data. Let us ask for these. Within this dialog box, first click on the "Perform bootstrapping" box. Then you can choose whether to use percentile or BCa bootstrapping for the CIs. The SPSS help files state that the BCa is more accurate but takes longer to compute, but I recommend the BCa. Leave the other defaults alone.

Table 3.3 shows the output of the call from Figure 3.13 for the variable of PERCEIVED NATIVELIKENESS (PERCNATIVE). The data have been split into the three groups in the GROUP variable. The first column shows how many participants there are in each group. The actual minimum and maximum scores on the test are shown in the next two columns, and we see that the range of scores is quite small among the monolingual native speakers (NS), but is large for both age of onset groups. Even in the lowest age bilingual group there are participants who score a zero (meaning that no judges thought they were NS of Swedish), and even in the older bilingual group there are participants who score a 10 (meaning that all 10 judges thought they were NS of Swedish). The data in the mean column show that although both bilingual groups have large ranges (the difference between the minimum and maximum score), their means are quite different. Both groups have similarly large SDs, however, while the NS group has a very small SD.

The skewness and kurtosis numbers for the monolinguals are quite large, if we use the rule of thumb that any number over 1 or 2 is problematic. The data for the monolinguals are definitely not normally distributed! The skewness for those with age of onset 11 or younger is over 1 but not 2, so this group may also not be normally distributed. We will look in more detail at these issues of normality in the next section.

Finally, the bootstrapped CI shows the plausible range of values where, with 95% confidence, you could expect the mean score for this population of participants to fall. Thus, for example, for the age

Table 3.3 Descriptive Statistics for the Variable "Perceived Nativelikeness" in the Abrahamsson and Hyltenstam 2009 Data Set, with the Data Split by the GROUP Variable

Descriptive Statistics Group	*N*	*Min*	*Max*	*Mean*	*SD*	*Skewness*	*Kurtosis*	*BCa bootstrapped 95% CI of mean*
Monolingual Native Speakers	20	9	10	9.9	0.3	−2.9	7.0	[9.8, 10]
Age of Onset ≤ 11	107	0	10	7.9	2.9	−1.4	0.9	[7.4, 8.5]
Age of Onset > 12	88	0	10	2.5	3.0	0.9	−0.4	[1.9, 3.1]

SD = standard deviation; CI = confidence interval

of onset 12 and over group, the point estimate for the mean is quite low at 2.5 points out of 10, but the CI shows that it might be as low as 1.9 or as high as 3.1. (This is still fairly low, though, for participants who self-identified as bilinguals whose Swedish accent was usually not noticed as being non-native-like.) Note that none of the CIs overlap, meaning we already know that statistically all three of the groups are different from each other.

At this point, if you have split your data you might want to go back to DATA > SPLIT FILE and reset the choice to "Analyze all cases, do not create groups." If you do not do this, when you later perform statistical analyses you will receive a warning like "There are fewer than two groups for the dependent variable."

Another way to obtain a numerical summary with SPSS is to use the ANALYZE > DESCRIPTIVE STATISTICS > EXPLORE choice on the menu. With this choice, you will not need to split your file because you can put the splitting variable (if you have groups) in the "Factor List" box. (See Figure 3.14, although in the Kim2013.sav file I am using here there is no group variable so nothing is in this box in this figure.)

If you open the "Statistics" button on the EXPLORE box you will not find the same detailed options for descriptive statistics as were available in the DESCRIPTIVES option, but the statistics that will

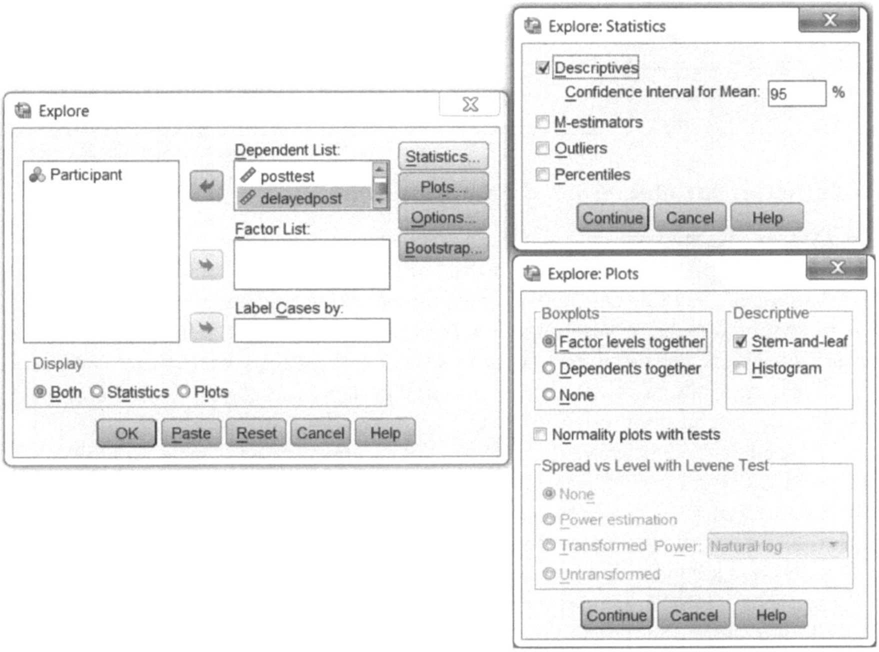

Figure 3.14 Using the ANALYZE > DESCRIPTIVE STATISTICS > EXPLORE option to get numerical summaries.

appear are the mean, the 95% CI for the mean, the 5% trimmed mean, the median, the variance, the SD, the minimum and maximum points, the range, the IQR, skewness and kurtosis. Also, by default the EXPLORE option will give you a box plot and a stem and leaf plot. (This can be adjusted with the "Plots" button, which you can also see open in Figure 3.14.) The choice for the "Bootstrap" button is the same as for the ANALYZE > DESCRIPTIVE STATISTICS > DESCRIPTIVES choice explained earlier.

Here is what I would say in prose about the descriptive statistics for the Kim 2013 data:

> For the pretest, the nine participants scored low on the test (M = 7.4, 95% BCa boostrap CI [4.6, 10.8], SD = 5.2). Scores improved in the posttest with concurrent reduction in their SD (M=16.6, CI [14.9, 18.4], SD=3.0). Scores on the delayed posttest, given five weeks after the posttest, improved even more (M = 19.4, CI [17.9, 21.6], SD = 3.0).

I will not show the output for the EXPLORE option, but it is similar to the DESCRIPTIVES option in the variety of statistical measures available, and provides more in the way of graphs. However, for descriptive statistics I prefer the DESCRIPTIVES option because the data are more compactly provided in the output. You should experiment to see which choice you like best.

Obtaining the Mean, SD, Quartiles and CIs with SPSS

There are two major ways to do this if you are not also running a statistical test:

1 Use the ANALYZE > DESCRIPTIVE STATISTICS > DESCRIPTIVES option. If you have groups, first separate them by going to DATA > SPLIT FILE, choosing the "Compare groups" option, and moving the group variable into the right-hand box. Click on the "Options" button to choose the descriptive statistics you want. Also, to obtain CIs, open the "Bootstrap" button and click the box to "Perform bootstrapping." Change the "Confidence Intervals" choice to "Bias corrected accelerated" but do not change any of the other defaults.
2 Use the ANALYZE > DESCRIPTIVE STATISTICS > EXPLORE option. If you have groups, put the splitting variable into the "Factor List" box. Choose whether to receive just numerical statistics, plots or both from the "Display" area of the dialog box. To get CIs, follow the directions given for the DESCRIPTIVES choice in the previous item

3.2.2 Application Activities for Numerical Summaries in SPSS

1 Use the DeKeyser2000.sav file. Split the data by the STATUS variable and examine the GJT scores. Make sure you have data for the number of participants, the minimum and maximum scores, the mean and 95% bootstrapped BCa CI, and the SD. By just eyeballing the statistics, does it look as though the groups have similar mean scores (maximum possible score was 200)? What about the SD?
2 Use the Obarow.sav file. Look at the numerical summaries for the gain score in the immediate posttest (GNSC1.1) split according to the four experimental groups (TRTMNT1). Each group was tested on 20 vocabulary words, but most knew at least 15 of the words in the pretest. Obtain summaries for the number of participants, mean scores and 95% bootstrapped BCa CI, SDs, and minimum and maximum scores. Do the groups appear to have similar mean scores (and CIs) and SDs?
3 Use the LarsonHall.Forgotten.sav file. The main result of interest is scores on the R/L/W listening test, which is reported by percentage correct. Split by experimental group (STATUS, where Non = never studied English outside Japan; Early = had lived in the USA as children; Late = were studying in the USA as adults). Obtain summaries for the number of participants, mean scores and 95% bootstrapped BCa CI, SDs, and minimum and maximum scores. The groups are all Japanese learners of English. Which groups are similar in their mean scores and SDs? Which group performed the best?

3.3 Using R to get Numerical Summaries

Follow along with me in this section by importing the SPSS files Abrahamsson&Hyltenstam 2009.sav and Kim2013.sav. Name the first file **ah2009** and the second **kim2013** when you import them into R Commander. If you are restarting R, remember to type in **library(Rcmdr)** in the R Console to open up the R Commander program. In R Commander, use the DATA > IMPORT DATA > FROM SPSS DATA SET menu choice to import the files.

3.3.1 Basic Descriptive Statistics in R

With the **ah2009** data set active, in R Commander, choose STATISTICS > SUMMARIES > NUMERICAL SUMMARIES (see the dialog box in Figure 3.15). This will let you make a summary of one variable with all cases lumped together, or you can also summarize the variable by groups. There is another command in R Commander for descriptives (STATISTICS > SUMMARIES > TABLE OF STATISTICS), but it only gives one type of statistic at a time and does not give any statistic that the NUMERICAL SUMMARIES command does not give, except for a trimmed mean, which could be entered into the "Other" box as mean, tr = 0.2, where the amount you want to trim can be set to anything. Additionally, it can only be used when you are splitting the data by a factor, so it is not as useful in my opinion as the NUMERICAL SUMMARIES command.

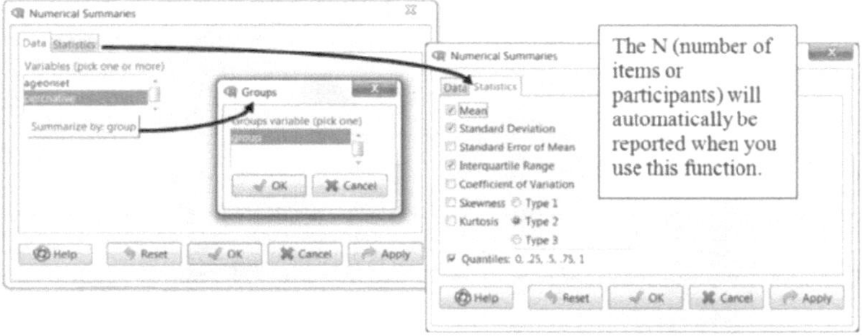

Figure 3.15 Inside the "Numerical Summaries" box in R Commander.

For this particular data set, I want to see summaries of the variable **Percnative** (perceived nativeness) divided into three groups by the variable **Group**. When you open up this command in R Commander, if your group variable is a factor, you may not see it listed, **Group**. That is because this is a character variable, so it is automatically categorized differently from the numerical variables of **ageonset** and **percnative**, and it is ready to choose when I open the "Summarize by groups" button on the "Data" tab. If you choose the "Statistics" tab on this command, you can choose what types of descriptive statistics you would like to receive. Mean, SD and IQR are chosen by default as is quantiles. You can also choose the standard error (SE), the coefficient of variation (this is the SD/mean and is a normalized measure of dispersion of the data, but we will not be using it), skewness and kurtosis. Skewness and kurtosis can be calculated by different formulas, and the program automatically picks formula 2. Click on the "Help" button if you want more information about these statistics.

By the way, if you find that a variable you want to be a factor is not, you will need to change its status in the R Console. Check the status as a factor by typing **class(ah2009$group)**. If it is not a factor, make it a factor by typing **ah2009$group<-as.factor (ah2009$group)**.

R Commander uses the **numSummary** command to produce the summary.

In order to help you understand the syntax of this command, I have devised a table that walks you through each part of the syntax one block at a time. It should enable you to change and configure the syntax to your own data set and your own statistical needs. It is not that interesting to read, but use it when you want to walk through the syntax of the commands in R. I recommend trying to copy these commands with first my data and then your own data as you go along so that when we need to leave R Commander in future chapters, you will understand the basics of how the R syntax works.

```
numSummary(ah2009[,"percnative"], groups=ah2009$group, statistics=c("mean",
"sd", "IQR", "quantiles", "cv", "skewness", "kurtosis"), quantiles=c(0,.25,.5,.75,1), type="2")
```

numSummary( )	The numSummary() command was created for the Rcmdr package. It gives neatly formatted basic descriptive statistic summaries.
ah2009[,"percnative"],	The first argument that the numSummary( ) command needs is the name of the data file (mine is ah2009), followed by square brackets, then a comma (indicating that we should use all of the rows); after the comma, the column (which is the variable) is named.
groups=ah2009$group	If you want the data to be split by groups, include this argument. My group variable is named group, but it must be specified as the variable from the data set, so it is written ah2009$group. This variable must be a factor (you can check whether it is a factor by using the class() command, described in Section 1.4.5).
statistics=c(. . .)	Descriptive statistics functions are specified inside the c( ) or concatenation command. This is a built-in, primitive R command that combines its arguments.
"mean" "sd" "IQR" "quantiles" "cv" "skewness" "kurtosis"	These are the descriptive statistics you can call for in this function. Any or all of them can be included, but must be put into parentheses and separated by commas.
quantiles=c(0,.25,.5,.75,1),	This lists which quantiles to report. By default it lists all five.
type="2"	Use this as one definition in computing skewness and kurtosis.

The output is nicely formatted in a very compact table:

```
                    mean        sd IQR   skewness   kurtosis 0% 25% 50% 75% 100% data:n
NativeSpeaker   9.900000 0.3077935   0 -2.8879391  7.0370370  9  10  10  10   10     20
AOA 11 or under 7.934579 2.9050088   3 -1.4232519  0.8503498  0   7   9  10   10    107
AOA over 11     2.522727 3.0018281   5  0.9383579 -0.4478808  0   0   1   5   10     88
```

First we see the mean, then the SD, then the IQR (the difference between the 25th and 75th percentile of scores), the skewness, kurtosis, and then the individual quartile numbers (the 5-number summary of quartiles equals: the minimum, Q1 = 25%, the median (also called Q2), Q3 = 75%, and the maximum), and finally the number (*N*) of items evaluated. If there are missing values they will also be counted in a column at the end of the output as well.

From the IQR statistic and the 5-number summary for percentiles, we see that the range of scores is quite small among the monolingual NS, but is larger for both age of onset groups. Although there are zeros (meaning that no judges thought they were NS of Swedish) in the lowest age bilingual group (age of acquisition (AOA) ≤ 11), the fact that the median score for the younger group is 9 while it is 1 for the older group shows the groups are quite different. The data in the mean column show that although both bilingual groups have large ranges (the difference between the 0% and 100% quantiles), their means are quite different. Both groups have similarly large SDs, however, while the NS group has a very small SD.

We can see that if numbers over 1 or 2 are problematic for skewness, there is skewness in the NS group and at least the AOA ≤ 11 groups.

Another quick way to get basic descriptive statistics in one fell swoop is found in the fBasics package (Wuertz & R Metrics Core Team, 2014) using the basicStats( ) command (remember that you can obtain a package in the R Console by typing install.packages("basicStats")). If you want to analyze the entire data set, all of the variables must be numerical. (You will get an error message if any of the variables are character.) I will show you the results of this for the Kim (2013) data set.

Set off command with a space: library (fBasics)
basic stats (Kim 2013)

```
             participant   pretest    posttest delayedpost
nobs            9.000000  9.000000    9.000000    9.000000
NAs             0.000000  0.000000    0.000000    0.000000
Minimum         1.000000  1.000000   13.000000   16.000000
Maximum         9.000000 18.000000   20.000000   24.000000
1. Quartile     3.000000  4.000000   14.000000   17.000000
3. Quartile     7.000000 10.000000   19.000000   23.000000
Mean            5.000000  7.444444   16.555556   19.666667
Median          5.000000  6.000000   16.000000   19.000000
Sum            45.000000 67.000000  149.000000  177.000000
SE Mean         0.912871  1.748897    0.987577    1.000000
```

To get these same data with this command split by groups, which means you would have a character (not numerical) variable in your data set, you would have to choose a specific variable (column), and then specific rows that your groups are found in. For example, in the ah2009 data set, for our main variable of interest, percnative, the NS group is found in rows 1 through 20, so to get the data for this group I would type the following into the R Console:

```
basicStats(ah2009$percnative[1:20]) #chooses just rows 1–20 which are the NS group
```

The commands given to this point would give you all of the data you can get from the SPSS commands for descriptive statistics seen in Section 3.2.1, except for the bootstrapped CIs. The boot.ci command in the boot package (Canty, Davison, & Hinkley, 2015) will give five different types of CIs for any parameter. My output only has four because one cannot be calculated.) Let us try it for the mean of the pretest variable in the kim2013 data set:

```
library(boot)
samplemean<-function(x,d){
   return(mean(x[d]))
   } #write a function that gets the mean score of the data set x
b=boot(kim2013$pretest, samplemean, R=1000) #sample a bootstrap with R=1000 replicates
#and put it into an object "b"
plot(b) #check that the bootstrap makes sense before carrying on;
#you should see a fairly normally distributed histogram of t, but if the histogram and Q-Q plot
#don't seem normal, you can try a larger bootstrap sample (i.e. more replicates)
#(see Chp. 4 for more info on CIs)
boot.ci(b)
```

```
Intervals :
Level      Normal              Basic
95%   ( 4.087, 10.672 )   ( 4.000, 10.442 )

Level     Percentile            BCa
95%   ( 4.447, 10.889 )   ( 4.667, 11.394 )
```

To find out more about what bootstrapping is, see LaFlair, Egbert, and Plonsky (2015) and Larson-Hall and Herrington (2009). Very briefly, bootstrapping is a procedure where values are randomly resampled from the original sample of data to form new samples. In this case, since we specified R = 1000, 1000 of these samples were taken. These samples generate an empirical distribution of data that can be examined for statistical significance in the same way that a normal distribution can be, and 95% CIs can also be calculated from this empirical distribution in the same way as they are for the original sample distribution. As I mentioned in Section 3.1.3, the most accurate bootstrap method for the CI of the mean is the BCa, so I recommend choosing that CI whenever possible.

Obtaining the Mean, SD and Quartiles with R

1 For R Commander:

Import your data set and make sure it is the active data set in R Commander.

Choose STATISTICS > SUMMARIES > NUMERICAL SUMMARIES

Click on the "Summarize by groups . . ." button if you have categorical groups.

2 For R:

The basic R code for the R Commander command is:

```
numSummary(ah2009[,"percnative"], groups= ah2009$group, statistics=c("mean", "sd", "IQR", "quantiles")
quantiles=c(0.25, .5, .75, 1))
```

*Change the underlined parts for your own data

Another method that produces a large number of summary items is to use the basicStats( ) command from the fBasics library.

Put in the whole data set if all variables are numerical: basicStats(kim2013)

Specify one variable and further split by rows if trying to get summaries for different groups: basicStats(ah2009$percnative[1:20])

Obtaining 95% CIs of the Mean with R

Open the boot library:

```
library(boot)
```

Write a function that returns the mean:

```
samplemean<-function(x,d){
return(mean(x[d]))
}
```

Take a bootstrap sample with 1000 replicates:

```
b=boot(kim2013$pretest, samplemean, R=1000)
```

*Remember to add row numbers to the data set if you are splitting by groups!

Check the bootstrap to make sure it looks like a normal distribution (otherwise, try more samples or give up on the bootstrapping) and then call for the CIs:

```
plot(b)
boot.ci(b)
```

3.3.2 Application Activities for Numerical Summaries in R

1 Import the SPSS file DeKeyser2000.sav and name it **dekeyser**. Summarize the scores for the GJT grouped by the **Status** variable. Make sure you have data for the number of participants, the mean and the SD. Also list the 95% BCa boostrapped CI for the mean scores for each group. By just eye-balling the statistics, does it look as though the groups have similar mean scores and CIs around the mean (maximum possible score was 200)? What about the SD?
2 Import the SPSS file Obarow.sav and call it **obarow**. (It has 81 rows and 35 columns.) Summarize the scores for the gain score in the immediate posttest (**gnsc1.1**) grouped according to the four experimental groups (**trtmnt1**). Each group was tested on 20 vocabulary words, but most knew at least 15 of the words in the pretest. Obtain summaries for the number of participants, mean scores and SDs. Find the 95% BCa bootstrapped CI for the means of each group. Do the groups appear to have similar mean scores, CIs and SDs? There is some missing data in this file so use the **mice( )** package and impute the data first (as explained in Section 1.5.3).
3 Use the LarsonHall.Forgotten.sav file, and name it **forget**. The main result of interest is scores on the R/L/W listening test, which is reported by percentage correct. Split by experimental group (Status: Non = never studied English outside Japan; Early = had lived in the USA as children; Late = were studying in the USA as adults). Obtain summaries for the number of participants, mean scores and 95% bootstrapped BCa CI, SDs, and minimum and maximum scores. The groups are all Japanese learners of English. Which groups are similar in their mean scores and SDs? Which group performed best?

3.4 Satisfying Assumptions for Parametric Tests

In the field of second language research, very few researchers actually say anything about whether they have satisfied the **assumptions** underlying parametric statistical tests when they report the results of their experiments. It always seemed to me, on reading books of the kind that you are now holding, that the authors made statements about how important satisfying the assumptions was, but then in practice either used made-up data sets that were constructed to satisfy the requirements, or paid little attention to deciding whether the data did indeed satisfy the requirements. One of my goals when I approached writing this book was to pay more attention to these assumptions and help you understand how to do this too.

I soon found that answers in this area are not easy. Take, for example, the assumption of a normal distribution of the data. Probably most people have heard of a normal curve and a normal distribution of data, and understand that with respect to grades, for example, a normal distribution would mean that most people in a class would receive Cs, a lesser number Bs and Ds, and then the smallest number would receive As and Fs. An assumption underlying every kind of "classic" statistical procedure that will be reviewed in this book, from correlation to multiple regression, is that the data are normally distributed. Yet how do we know if our own data are normally distributed? As we will see in the next section, there are no clear rules about a cutoff level for "normal" and "non-normal" distributions. Sometimes writers in this area like to make pronouncements, such as "A non-normal distribution is one in which the skewness level is over 1." However, such pronouncements are essentially arbitrary. I understand that, for those who do not know statistics well, absolute rules and pronouncements are quite attractive. Yet I will assure you that such pronouncements have no standing in the statistical field.

As we shall see in this chapter, unless a data set is quite large it can be impossible to tell whether the data are normally distributed or not. Visually looking for normality by examining graphics such as the **histogram** or a **Quantile-Quantile plot (Q-Q plot)** (both explained later in this chapter) can help, but such methods are not always conclusive. Furthermore, there are numerical ways of assessing normality, such as the **Kolmogorov–Smirnov** goodness-of-fit test, but these formal kinds of tests often suffer from low power, which means they cannot always accurately detect whether data are normally distributed or not (Wilcox, 2003). Staudte and Sheather (1990) suggested that, generally, such tests will not reject data unless they are grossly non-normal, and so they are usually not sensitive enough for small samples. It seems we are in a pickle—we do not have any fail-safe way to determine whether our data are normally distributed, but our tests require it. If we continue to use the "classical" types of statistical tests, our only solution appears to be the same one as has been used for so long—soldier on pretty much just assuming that our data are normally distributed unless we find strong and clear evidence to the contrary. However, throughout this book I present robust tests that can deal with the fact that data are not normally distributed or have unequal variances. These tests can deal with data which fit the assumptions of parametric statistics just as well as parametric tests, but deal with data that violate those assumptions better than parametric tests (Wilcox, 2012a, 2012b), so I believe they should be our main tool in doing statistical work.

One common problem for the assumption of a normal distribution in real data sets is finding outliers in the data, points that stand out as not fitting with the rest of the data set. The presence of outliers means there is more data in the extreme ends (the tails) of a distribution curve than there should be. Maronna, Martin, and Yohai (2006) noted that these tails are the crucial point in determining whether one has an exactly normal distribution, but these are also the places where you have the least data. The way you deal with outliers is very important and I will discuss possible treatments later in this chapter.

Another common problem with real data sets in second language research is that they often do not satisfy the other foundational assumption of classic statistics, which is that group variances should be equal (the homogeneity of variances assumption). This assumption says that the mean scores of the groups may differ but their variances should be the same. If groups that we assume are going to differ, such as native vs. non-native speakers of a language, are paired in an experiment, it is likely that the variances will be quite different, usually with non-native speakers having a much larger variance than NS. For some tests (like the *t*-test), there are ways to adjust for violations of this assumption, but for others (such as ANOVA) there are no handy corrections. The problem is not that the violation of these assumptions offends a "god of statistics" who exists in the ether, but rather that with violations of the assumptions one might not be able to find differences that do exist between groups of participants (or relationships that do exist between variables).

In Sections 3.2 and 3.3 we saw that in both statistical programs that we are using it has become a fairly simple matter to call for robust statistics such as bootstrapping, which do not depend on the assumption of a normal distribution. Throughout this book, therefore, I will show ways of working with statistics that depend on the assumption of normality, but also show other, more robust methods of statistical analysis.

3.5 Graphic Summaries of Data: Examining the Shape of Distributions for Normality

Applied researchers should always look at the shape of their data before conducting statistical tests. Looking at data can give you some idea about whether your data are normally distributed. Although there are authors, such as Weinberg and Abramowitz (2002, p. 276), who say that sample sizes larger than 30 eliminate the need to check data for normality, researchers using simulation studies have found that, depending on the kinds of deviations from normality, even sample sizes of 160 may not be robust enough to overcome problems when distributions are skewed (Wilcox, 1998). What this means is that, even though you may be comparing two groups with 150 participants each, if your data are highly skewed, even with no outliers, you may not be able to find group differences that really do exist.

Another reason to look at your data visually is that it will give you a means of verifying what is happening. For example, if you have examined histograms of your two groups and found their distributions are quite similar and centered at the same basic mean, you would then be surprised to numerically find a large difference between groups. Graphics give you a way to look at your data that can replicate and even go beyond what you see in the numbers when you are doing your statistics. A wise report by the APA statistical task force strongly urges all researchers to look at their data before undertaking any statistical analysis (Wilkinson, 1999). This is not a "fishing expedition" to look for statistical relationships, but rather a sound practice that can save grief later by catching anomalies in the data.

Table 3.4 Anscombe's (1973) Data Showing a Need for Visual Examination

X(1–3)	Y1	Y2	Y3	X4	Y4
10	8.04	9.14	7.46	8	6.58
8	6.95	8.14	6.77	8	5.76
13	7.58	8.74	12.74	8	7.71
9	8.81	8.77	7.11	8	8.84
11	8.33	9.26	7.81	8	8.47
14	9.96	8.10	8.84	8	7.04
6	7.24	6.13	6.08	8	5.25
4	4.26	3.10	5.39	19	12.50
12	10.84	9.13	8.15	8	5.56
7	4.82	7.26	6.42	8	7.91
5	5.68	4.74	5.73	8	6.89

Statisticians have long been emphasizing the need to see graphical summaries of data as just as essential as numerical summaries. Anscombe (1973) noted that there is a feeling that numerical summaries are precise while graphs are rough, and that looking at the data is cheating. However, he produced an example that showed the absolute necessity of looking at graphs. The data he used were those in Table 3.4. In each case, the X variable will be matched with the corresponding Y variable, so X1 will be correlated with Y1, X2 with Y2, and so on.

Numerically, all of these data sets look the same; they share the same mean of the *xs* ($\overline{X} = 9$) and *ys* ($\overline{Y} = 7.5$), the straight line that can be drawn through the data is the same ($y = 3 + 0.5x$), their R^2 effect sizes are the same ($R^2 = 0.667$), and so on. However, when we take a look at the graphs that are generated by **scatterplots** of the data (the X column crossed with the Y column and each point plotted on the graph), we see that not all of the data sets are appropriate for running correlations (regressions) because they are not all linear.

For graph 1 in Figure 3.16 the assumption of linearity is met, and this is what we think the data are like when we are doing a correlation. Graph 2 has a curvature to the data set. Anscombe (1973) suggested that it would possibly fit a quadratic distribution. Graph 3 has one outlier, which means a regression line drawn here would not be the best fit for the rest of the points, and Graph 4 seems to be described very unsatisfactorily by assuming a linear fit! The point of this illustration is to help you realize that graphs are just as necessary and useful as numerical summaries.

3.5.1 Histograms

One way to look at the distribution of data is to look at a graph called a histogram. A histogram divides data up into partitions and, in the usual case, gives a frequency distribution of the number of scores contained in each partition (called a bin). If, instead of a **frequency count**, we use proportions, the overall area of the graph will equal 1, and we can overlay the histogram with a normal curve to judge whether our data seem to follow a normal distribution. Notice that a histogram is *not* a **bar graph**. A bar graph is a common plot in the field, but this kind of graph summarizes the scores of groups rather than the distribution of the data. The left panel of Figure 3.17 shows a histogram of a variable from Ellis and Yuan (2004) that measured the number of words participants produced in a written essay. The histogram divides the result up into bins that measure the frequency of certain numbers of words, so that we see that the most frequent number of words produced in the essays was about 185 words (the bin just below the 200) and 230 words (both happened nine times). In contrast, the right panel of Figure 3.17 shows a bar graph of the average score of the number of words produced by each of the

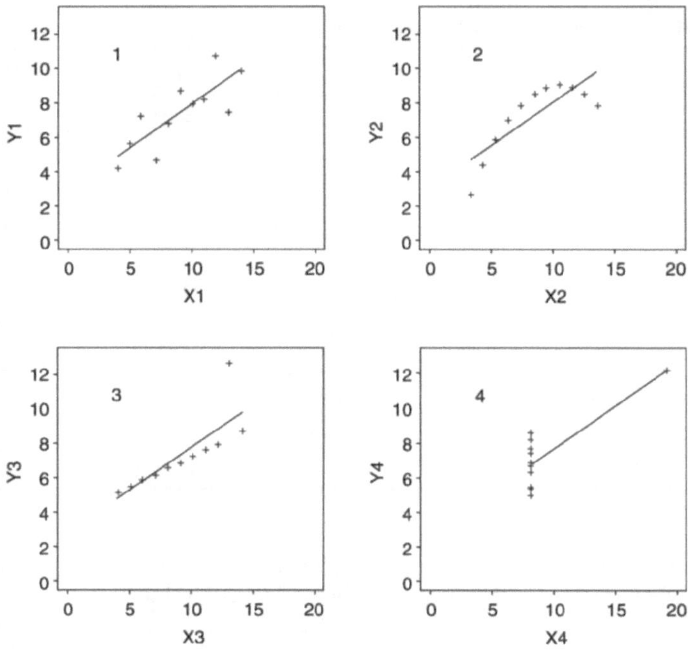

Figure 3.16 Anscombe's (1973) data examined visually with scatterplots.

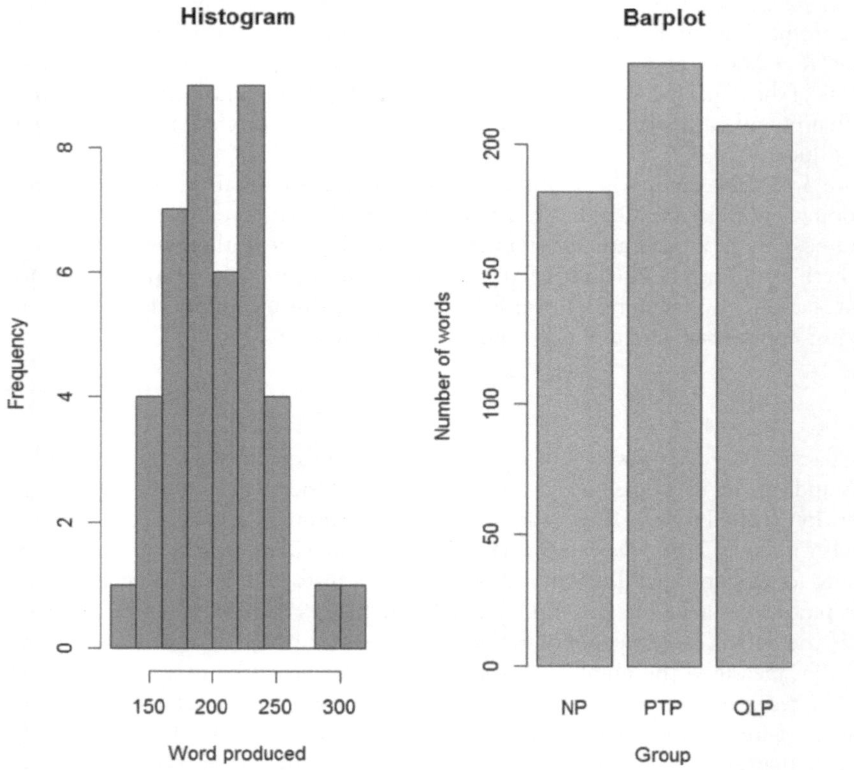

Figure 3.17 A comparison of a histogram to a barplot for the Ellis and Yuan (2004) data.

three groups. The PTP group produced the most words, at somewhere over 200 on average. Although in both cases the graphics produce bars, they answer very different questions and only the histogram is appropriate for looking at the distribution of scores.

Histograms can give information about whether distributions are symmetrically distributed or skewed, and whether they have one mode (peak) or several, and a histogram with an overlaid normal curve can be evaluated to see whether the data should be considered normally distributed. I should note here, though, that the shape of a histogram does depend on how the data are binned, or split into groups. There are different algorithms for doing this, and histograms can only be a general, not exact, measure of the normality of a distribution. They should be used in conjunction with other graphics and with numerical measures of normality.

In Figure 3.18, I show the normal distributions that I generated, all with zero as their mean and a SD of 1. The histograms in Figure 3.18 differ in the *N* (number of sampled points) they contain, starting with 20 points, then going to 50 and then 500. There are two reasons for examining these graphs. The first is to see visually how a larger number of samples, even though all are generated from a normal distribution, will conform more to a normal distribution. The second reason is to show that, because of inherent variability, even samples taken from a *known* normal distribution will not follow the density curve of a normal distribution exactly. In other words, I want to show a range of what could be considered "normally distributed" samples.

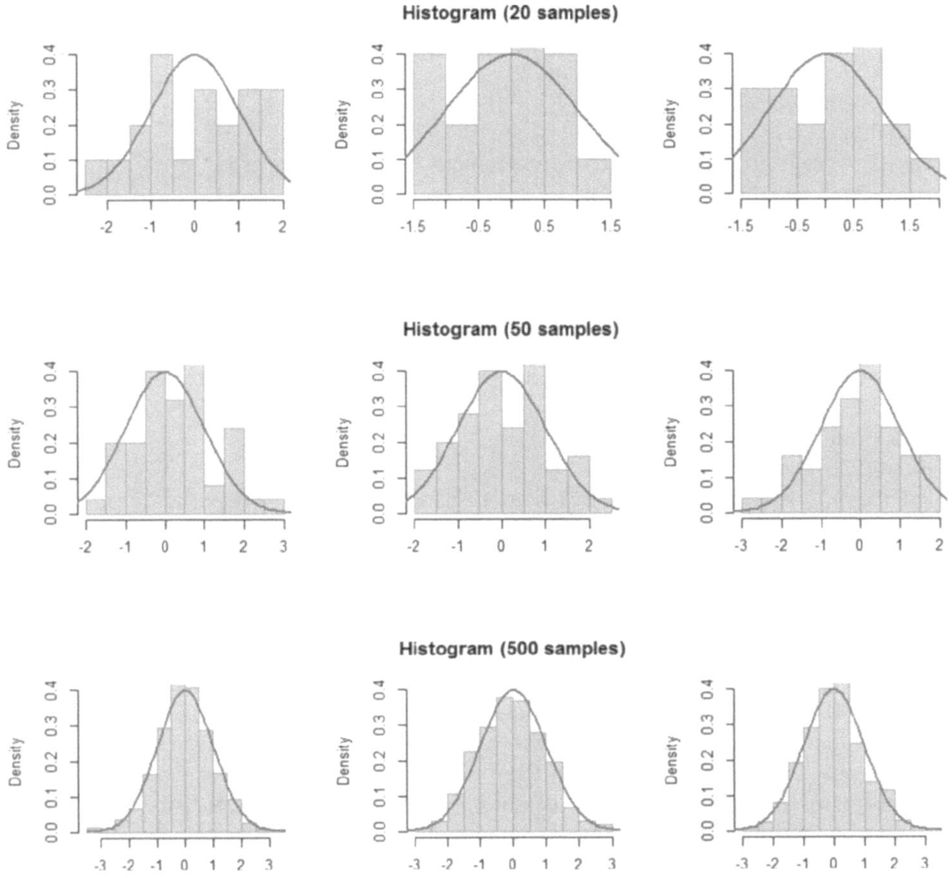

Figure 3.18 Distribution of various sample sizes generated from a normal distribution.

Here is the R code if you want to make more examples of your own:

```
par(mfrow=c(3,3))
x=seq(-3.5, 3.5, .1)
dn=dnorm(x)

twenty=rnorm(20,0,1)
hist(twenty, main="", xlab="", col="lightgray", border="darkgray", ylim=c(0,.4), prob=T)
lines(x, dn, col="red", lwd=2)
twenty=rnorm(20,0,1)
hist(twenty, xlab="", main="Histogram (20 samples)", col="lightgray", border="darkgray",
ylim=c(0,.4), prob=T)
lines(x, dn, col="red", lwd=2)

twenty=rnorm(20,0,1)
hist(twenty, main="", xlab="", col="lightgray", border="darkgray", ylim=c(0,.4), prob=T)
lines(x, dn, col="red", lwd=2)
fifty=rnorm(50,0,1)
hist(fifty, main="", xlab="", col="lightgray", border="darkgray", ylim=c(0,.4), prob=T)
lines(x, dn, col="red", lwd=2)

fifty=rnorm(50,0,1)
hist(fifty, xlab="", col="lightgray", border="darkgray", ylim=c(0,.4), prob=T, , main="Histogram
(50 samples)")
lines(x, dn, col="red", lwd=2)
fifty=rnorm(50,0,1)
hist(fifty, main="", xlab="", col="lightgray", border="darkgray", ylim=c(0,.4), prob=T)
lines(x, dn, col="red", lwd=2)

fivehund=rnorm(500,0,1)
hist(fivehund, main="", xlab="", col="lightgray", border="darkgray", ylim=c(0,.4), prob=T)
lines(x, dn, col="red", lwd=2)
fivehund=rnorm(500,0,1)
hist(fivehund, xlab="", col="lightgray", border="darkgray", ylim=c(0,.4), prob=T, , main="Histogram
(500 samples)")
lines(x, dn, col="red", lwd=2)
fivehund=rnorm(500,0,1)
hist(fivehund, main="", xlab="", col="lightgray", border="darkgray", ylim=c(0,.4), prob=T)
lines(x, dn, col="red", lwd=2)
```

3.5.2 Skewness and Kurtosis

Skewness and kurtosis are two ways to describe deviations in the shape of distributions. If a **sampling distribution** (in other words, the actual distribution we obtain through our experimentation) is skewed, that means it is not symmetric around the mean. A distribution can be **positively skewed**, which means that scores are bunched up toward the left side of the graph, or **negatively skewed**, which means that scores are bunched up toward the right side of the graph. Both of these situations are shown in Figure 3.19. This nomenclature has always seemed non-intuitive to me, but I remember it by thinking of the position of the tail (the end of the distribution where there are fewer data points). If the tail of the distribution goes to the right and toward larger numbers, it is positive, while if the tail of the distribution goes to the left and toward smaller numbers and negative numbers, it is negative.

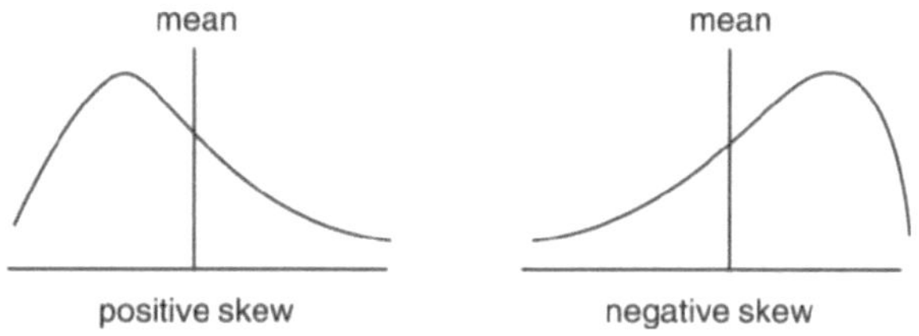

Figure 3.19 Non-normal distributions (skewed and bimodal).

As was seen previously, there are numerical measurements of skewness that can be obtained. Howell (2002) stated that these are not used in the social sciences, and they do not seem to be used in second language research either. We can find some statements giving us some rules of thumb for using the skewness number to evaluate the normality of the data. The SPSS help files say a skewness level over 1 indicates a significant departure from normality. Porte (2002) stated that if the skewness level is under 1 there is no cause for concern.

However, these statements seem to be some of those rules we would like to have but which we should be cautious about trusting. In fact, Westfall and Young (1993) performed a simulation study that found that, even with $N = 160$, a skewed distribution could change the conclusions that should have been drawn from the data. This means that, if our data are skewed, group differences (or relationships among variables) that do exist may not be found. What can be done if your data are skewed? Transformations (treated later in this chapter) can help reduce the skewness of data. You can also change from using parametric statistics to bootstrapped statistics, which do not require a normal distribution.

As Figure 3.18 with multiple samples from a normal distribution should have hinted, with smaller sample sizes there will be an immense amount of variation in the distribution of data, even if we know it is taken from a normal distribution. At the level of 10 or 15 samples per group, it is extremely unlikely that even samples generated from a normal distribution will follow the smooth line of a normal distribution. However, none of these small samples showed the amount of skewness that is seen in Figure 3.19. So while it may be impossible to say that one's data come from an exactly normal distribution, it is possible to visually note whether there is extreme skewness by looking at a histogram of the distribution.

If skewness describes the shape of the distribution as far as symmetry along a vertical line through the mean goes, kurtosis describes the shape of the distribution as far as the concentration of scores around the mean goes. Howell (2002, p. 30) gives the clearest explanation I have encountered: "basically [kurtosis] refers to the relative concentration of scores in the center, the upper and lower ends (tails), and the shoulders (between the center and the tails) of a distribution." A distribution that is too flat at the peak of the normal curve is called **platykurtic** (it is like a plateau), and a curve that has too many scores collected in the center of the distribution is called **leptokurtic**. Figure 3.20 (taken from Wikipedia) demonstrates distributions with kurtosis. The graph on the left shows leptokurtic distributions and the graph on the right shows platykurtic distributions.

As with skewness, kurtosis is, in my experience, never remarked upon in the literature in our field. Nevertheless, it is important to understand that there are many ways distributions could differ from a normal distribution.

As an example of visually looking at histograms to check for skewness, let us look at histograms of the R/L/W listening test variable from the Larson-Hall and Connell (2005) data in Figure 3.21. The data are separated into groups of non-immersionists (those who never lived abroad), late immersionists (those who went to live in the USA as adults) and early immersionists (those who lived in the USA as children).

Figure 3.21 shows a range of distributions. In each group there were about 15 participants. Although the non-immersionists' distribution looks fairly symmetrical, the distribution of the early immersionists

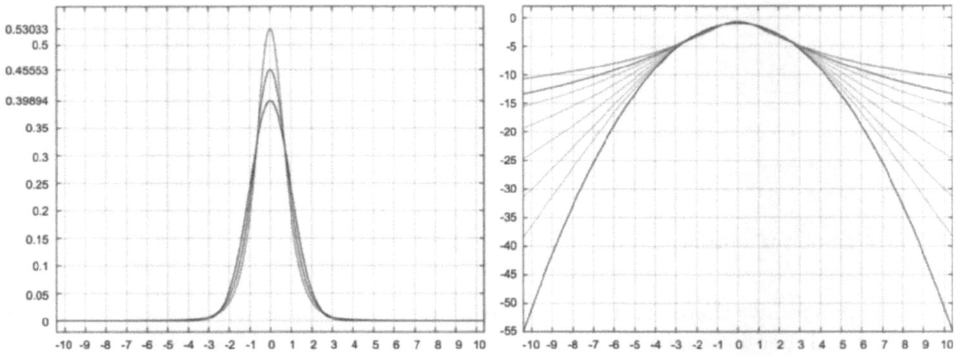

Figure 3.20 Leptokurtic (left panel) and platykurtic (right panel) distributions.

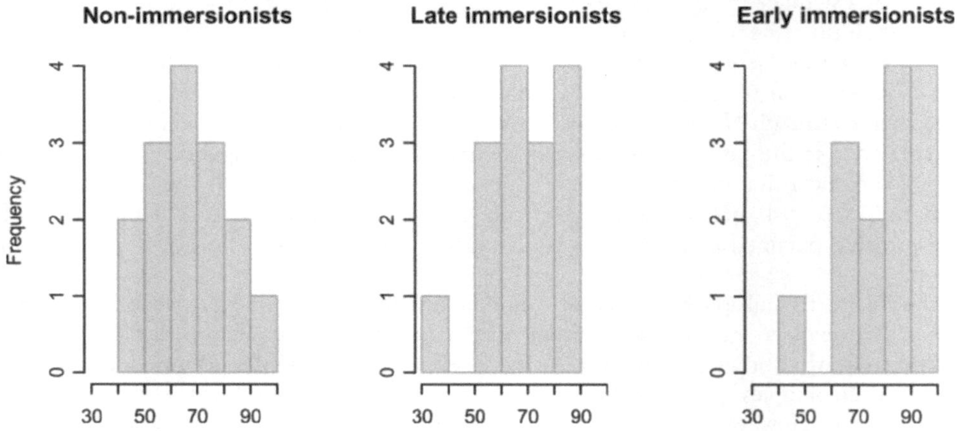

Figure 3.21 Histograms of the Larson-Hall and Connell (2005) data.

seems markedly negatively skewed. For the late immersionists the distribution seems to be **bimodal**, meaning there are two prominent peaks of data. In the case of the late immersionists, these peaks are of the same height (but that is not necessary to call a distribution a bimodal or multimodal one). This means that both "late" and "early" groups received higher scores on the measure than one would expect if the data were normally distributed. A bimodal distribution might be a sign that your data should be divided into two different groups, although that does not seem like the right solution to me for this data set.

3.5.3 Stem and Leaf Plots

Histograms display data using somewhat arbitrarily defined slices of the data to create the bins of the plot. Individual data points cannot clearly be seen. **Stem and leaf plots** basically display the same kind of information as a histogram that uses frequency counts, but use the data itself to show the distribution, and thus retain all of the data points. An example of a stem and leaf plot using the Larson-Hall and Connell (2005) data from the R/L/W listening test is shown in Table 3.5, divided up by the three Japanese groups.

The results are for a test that had a maximum of 96 points. Looking at the data from the non-immersionist group (those who had never lived abroad), the scores are divided into their tens values to the left of the bar, and their ones value to the right of the bar. Thus the lowest score was 47. There

Table 3.5 A Stem and Leaf Plot of the Larson-Hall and Connell (2005) Data

Non-immersionists (N=15)	*Late immersionists (N=15)*	*Early immersionists (N=14)*
4 | 7	2 | 6	4 | 7
5 | 0167	4 | 278	5 |
6 | 377	6 | 3456357	6 | 48
7 | 018	8 | 4990	7 | 068
8 | 026		8 | 799
9 | 1		9 | 01355

were four scores in the 50s, all of them different. However, two people in the 60s score 67, so the 7 is repeated twice after the 6. Thus, every individual point is clearly represented.

However, we can also look at the shape of the distribution. Although there is some clustering of scores in the middle for the non- and late immersionists, the early immersionists' scores are clearly skewed negatively. (Think of turning the numbers on their side so that the tens column is horizontal; then the cluster of numbers is on the right, and the tail extends to the left, or toward smaller and negative numbers.)

3.5.4 Quantile-Quantile Plots

The Q-Q plot plots the quantiles of the data under consideration against the quantiles of the normal distribution. If a median divides the distribution up at its halfway point, a quantile divides the data up the same way at every point that is a quarter of a whole. For example, the 25th quantile notes the point at which 25% of the data are below it and 75% are above it. The Q-Q plot uses points at many different quantiles. If the sampling distribution and the normal distribution are similar, the points should fall in a straight line. If the Q-Q plot shows that there is not a straight line, this tells us it departs from a normal distribution, and can also give us some information about what kind of distribution it is. Verzani (2004) suggested that if the right tail is short the quantile line will curve down, while if the right tail is long the quantile line will curve up.

Figure 3.22 provides a series of Q-Q plots where samples were drawn from a normal distribution. The reference line passes through the first (25th) and third (75th) quantiles. It can be seen that as sample size increases the points conform more closely to the reference line, but the figure is meant to show the type of variation that may occur even with samples from normal distributions.

Figure 3.23 shows Q-Q plots for the Larson-Hall and Connell (2005) data we have been examining. The Q-Q plot for the early immersionists shows a clear departure from a straight line, with the top of the line bending down because the right tail is short. The late immersionist Q-Q plot shows more departure from the reference line than that of the non-immersionists. This command uses the lattice package (Sarkar, 2008) and is given on p. 119.

3.6 Obtaining Exploratory Visual Summaries in SPSS

One easy way to obtain many exploratory graphs in one fell swoop is to "Explore" the data. (This was noted earlier in the chapter as one way to also obtain numerical summaries.) Using the Larson-Hall and Connell (2005) data set we were examining in Section 3.5 (LarsonHall.Forgotten.sav), I choose ANALYZE > DESCRIPTIVE STATISTICS > EXPLORE from the menu. I put the RLW TEST variable in the "Dependent List" and the categorical variable STATUS in the "Factor List" box (see Figure 3.14 for the dialog box). To see what graphics are available, open the "Plots" button.

Figure 3.24 shows what plots are available. I have asked for stem and leaf plots, histograms and normality plots with tests. The box plots provided by this option are not very informative. (Chapter 9 gives information on how to obtain better box plots.)

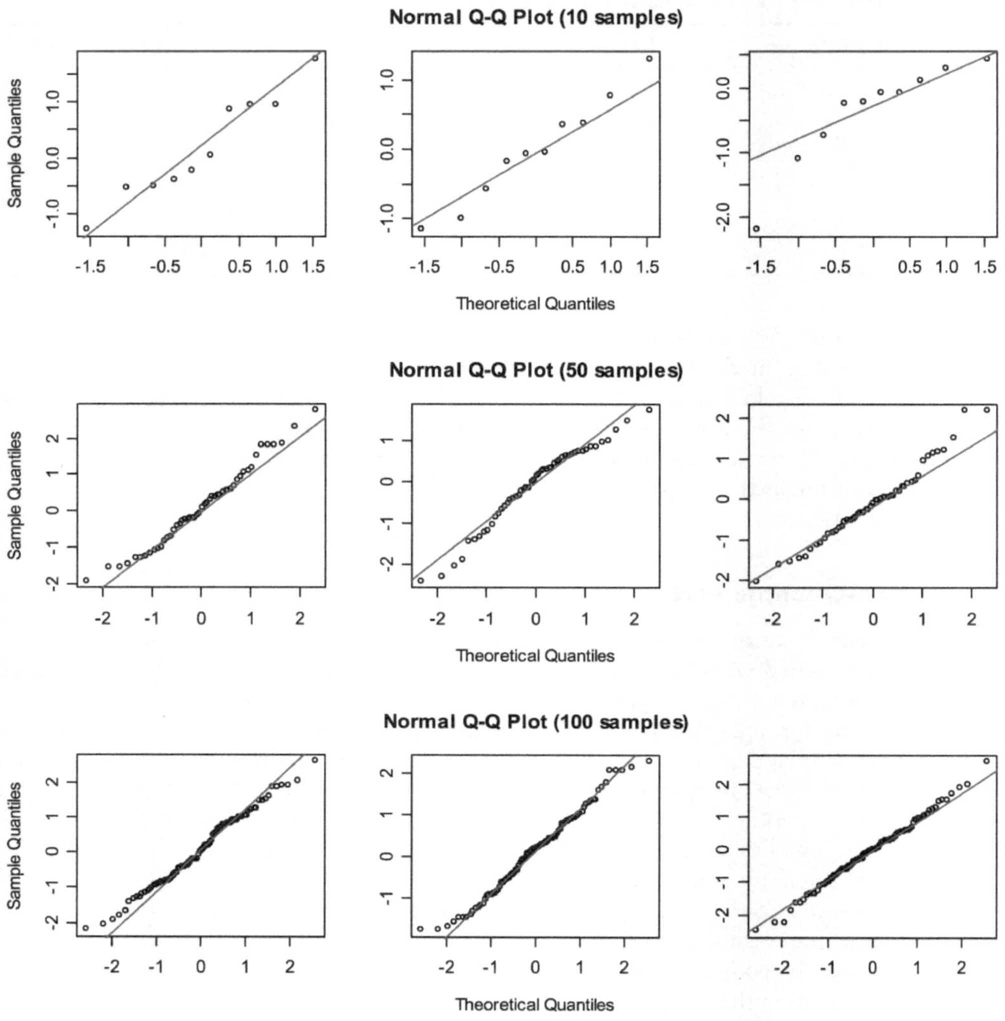

Figure 3.22 Q-Q plots of various sample sizes generated from a normal distribution.

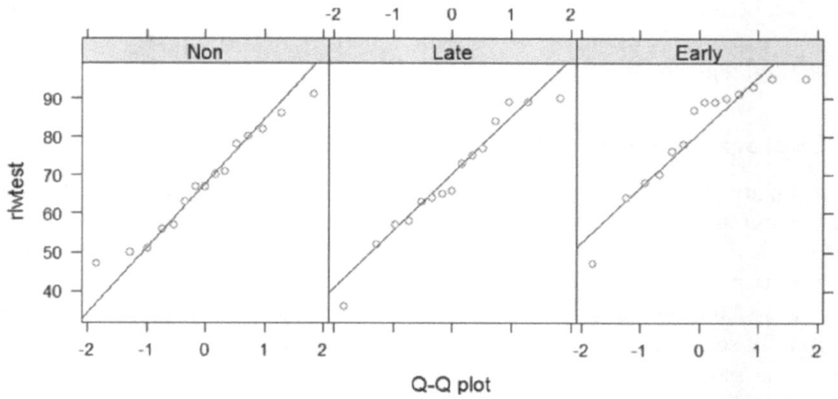

Figure 3.23 Q-Q plots for the Larson-Hall and Connell (2005) data.

Figure 3.24 Plots available in the ANALYZE > DESCRIPTIVE STATISTICS > EXPLORE (then "Plots" button) option.

If you continue with the Explore option and leave the default for both statistics and plots, the output produces a large amount of descriptive statistics. After these numerical summaries you will see the results of tests for normality. (N.B. if you have left your data in a split-group format, the output will be considerably less compact than what I am showing here.) These tests give formal tests of the hypothesis that the distribution of the variable (or group) follows a normal distribution. Because the null hypothesis is that the sampling distribution comes from the same distribution as the normal distribution, if the *p*-value (Sig. column) is less than 0.05 you would reject the null hypothesis and accept the alternative hypothesis that the data are not normally distributed.

The output shown in Table 3.6 gives the results of both the Kolmogorov–Smirnov (with the Lilliefors test) goodness-of-fit and the Shapiro–Wilk normality test. Ricci (2005) suggested that the Shapiro–Wilk test is the most powerful test for small sample sizes (under 50). Notice that both tests indicate that the early immersionist data set differs statistically from a normal distribution. That is what we have also deduced from looking at histograms, stem and leaf plots, and Q-Q plots in Section 3.5.

If the *p*-value is greater than 0.05, we do not reject the null hypothesis, but we also cannot conclusively say that our distribution is normal. This is because these kinds of formal tests of assumptions often suffer from low power, which means they do not have enough power to detect violations of the null hypothesis (Wilcox, 2003). Thus, we cannot be any surer that a distribution is exactly normal by looking at the numerical results of these tests than we can of looking at a histogram. For this reason, it is important not just to rely on a formal test of normality but to examine graphics as well (Wilkinson, 1999).

Table 3.6 Output from ANALYZE > DESCRIPTIVES > EXPLORE concerning Tests of Normality

Tests of Normality

		Kolmogorov–Smirnov[a]			*Shapiro–Wilk*		
	Status	*Statistic*	*df*	*Sig.*	*Statistic*	*df*	*Sig.*
Score on the R/L/W Listening test	Non	.116	15	.200*	.961	15	.714
	Late	.116	15	.200*	.951	15	.545
	Early	.238	14	.031	.870	14	.042

[a]Lilliefors Significance Correction
*This is a lower bound of the true significance

The next part of the output provides a wealth of graphs. There are histograms, stem and leaf plots, normal Q-Q plots and detrended normal Q-Q plots. A detrended Q-Q plot plots the deviation of the points away from the diagonal in a Q-Q plot. There should be no specific pattern of points, and points should be found both above and below the line.All of these graphs provide slightly different ways of visualizing your data. Most of these graphs can also be called for separately by going to the GRAPHS drop-down menu. In Sections 3.2 and 3.3 we looked at the Abrahamsson and Hyltenstam (2009) data numerically, so let us look now and comment on the data as seen visually. I put the variable PERCNATIVE in the "Dependent List," and GROUP in the "Factor List." The numerical tests of normality (Kolmogorov–Smirnov and Shapiro–Wilk) all show that all three groups are non-normally distributed (the *p*-value is 0.000 for all the tests). Figure 3.25 shows histograms for all three groups.

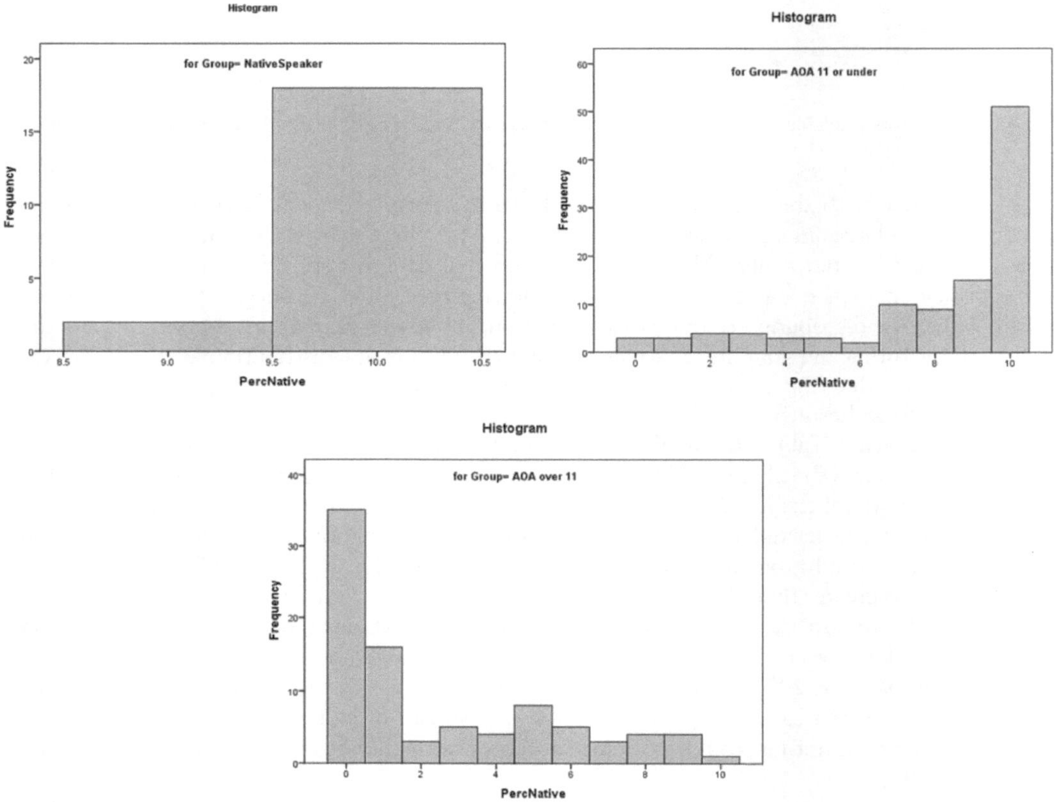

Figure 3.25 Histograms for the three groups in the Abrahamsson and Hyltenstam (2009) data.

The histogram for the NS is highly non-normal and negatively skewed, since most NS received a 10 on this task. The histogram for the groups who started learning Swedish at age 11 or younger is also highly negatively skewed, as the highest number of participants in this group scored a 10. On the other hand, the histogram for the groups who started learning Swedish at age 12 or older is skewed positively, with the highest number of scores being those at the lower levels. (Remember that 0 means that none of these speakers was judged to be a native speaker by any of the 10 judges.)

The stem and leaf plots generated by SPSS in the Explore option are not very compact so I will not show them here, but they show the same kind of non-normality seen in the histograms. Lastly, the

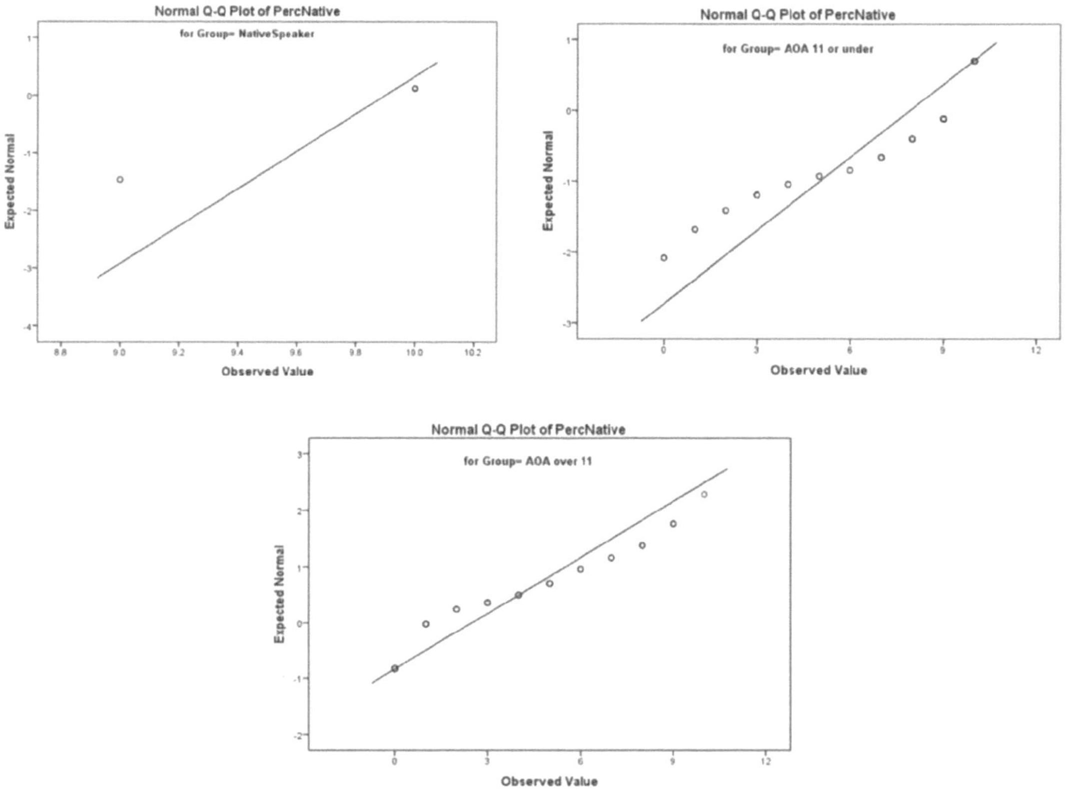

Figure 3.26 Q-Q plots for the Abrahamsson and Hyltenstam (2009) data.

Q-Q plots also look distinctly non-normal, with the points waving all around the line and not on it in a straight line as they should be (see Figure 3.26).

Tip: Another way to explore your data is through ANALYZE > DESCRIPTIVE STATISTICS > FREQUENCIES. Although it provides the same kind of information as the Explore option does, it can be a better format when you are looking at variables for correlation or multiple regression because it puts the variables side by side in columns instead of on top of each other, like this:

Statistics

		SK.NR.raw	SK.L1.WR. logged	SK.L2. WM.raw	SK.L2.NS. logged	SK.L2.PA. logged
N	Valid	40	40	40	37	40
	Missing	0	0	0	3	0
Mean		48.6000	.6015	2.5750	2.2414	1.4854

In addition, you can call for histograms with normal curves imposed in the "Charts" button, like those seen in Figure 3.18. This can be a useful feature.

Obtaining Graphics to Assess Normality in SPSS

There are two main ways of doing this through the DESCRIPTIVE STATISTICS menu (individual graphs can be called through the GRAPHS menu):

1 Use the ANALYZE > DESCRIPTIVE STATISTICS > EXPLORE option and pick graphs in the "Plots" button.
2 Use ANALYZE > DESCRIPTIVE STATISTICS > FREQUENCIES. This can call up histograms with overlaid normal distribution curves. If you use this option you will need to use DATA > SPLIT FILES to split up groups first.

3.6.1 Application Activities: Looking at Normality Assumptions

Keep your output from these activities open, as you will use some of the same output for the application activity in Section 3.8.1:

1 Chapter 6 on correlation will feature data from Flege, Yeni-Komshian, and Liu (1999). Use the FlegeYKLiu.sav file and use one or both of the two options from the DESCRIPTIVE STATISTICS menu to examine the data for pronunciation divided according to groups. From the available evidence, do the data appear to be normally distributed?
2 Look at a histogram with the GJT variable for each of the two groups in the DeKeyser2000.sav file. Use the ANALYZE > DESCRIPTIVE STATISTICS > FREQUENCIES option and put a normal curve on the histogram. (You will need to split the file first.) What is the shape of the histograms?
3 Chapter 11 on repeated-measures ANOVA will feature data from Lyster (2004). Use the Lyster.written.sav file and use one or both of the two options from the DESCRIPTIVE STATISTICS menu to examine the gain scores for the comprehension task (COMPGAIN1, COMPGAIN2) divided according to groups (called COND for condition). From the available evidence, do the data appear to be normally distributed?
4 Leow (1997) is a study that published its data in the research report. This study was the first to use think-aloud procedures to explore the role of language awareness in SLA (Sanz & Leow, 2011). In the study, Leow had participants fill in a crossword puzzle that targeted stem-changing vowels in Spanish verbs, all the while reporting what they were thinking. The data are in the comma-delimited leow1997.csv file, so first import it into SPSS. Look at the data for the "Production" variable, divided by groups (those who had awareness of a rule vs. those who did not). Are these data normally distributed?

My point in looking at assumptions in all of these studies is that there are some places in almost every study where the data are not exactly normally distributed (outliers or some kind of clear skewness). My advice is to generally replace parametric statistics with more robust measures, such as non-parametric bootstrapping, and I will illustrate how to do that in Part II of this book. These tests are conducted and reported in almost exactly the same way as parametric tests so making a change to more robust tests is in practice not any harder than conducting parametric tests, but gives added assurance to the researcher that the results are more accurate.

3.7 Obtaining Exploratory Visual Summaries in R

There is no analog in R to the SPSS version of getting a large number of exploratory visual summaries with one command. Therefore, this section simply shows how to get histograms, stem and leaf plots, and Q-Q plots with R.

3.7.1 Creating Histograms with R

If you want a histogram of an entire variable (not split by groups), it is easy to use R Commander to do this. Go to GRAPHS > HISTOGRAM (see Figure 3.27). I will use the Kim (2013) data to illustrate this, and examine the POSTTEST variable.

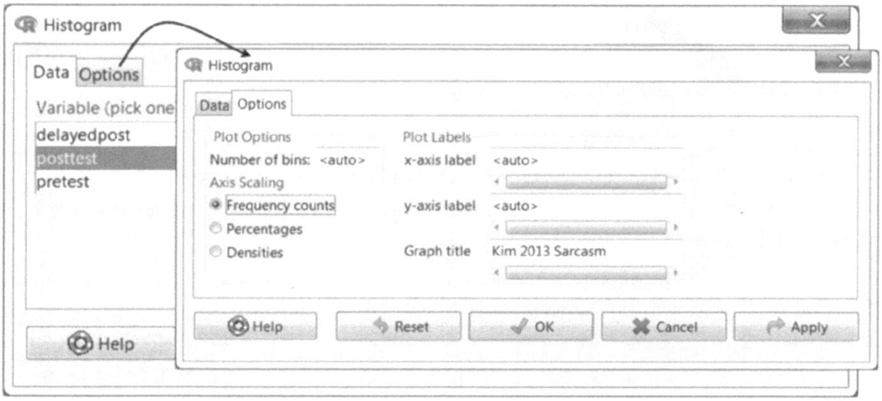

Figure 3.27 Obtaining a histogram in R Commander.

Figure 3.28 is the histogram as R Commander originally prints it out. You can see that the data seem positively skewed, with the most frequent score being 13. There are only nine participants so it would be hard to know if the data were from a normal distribution or not.

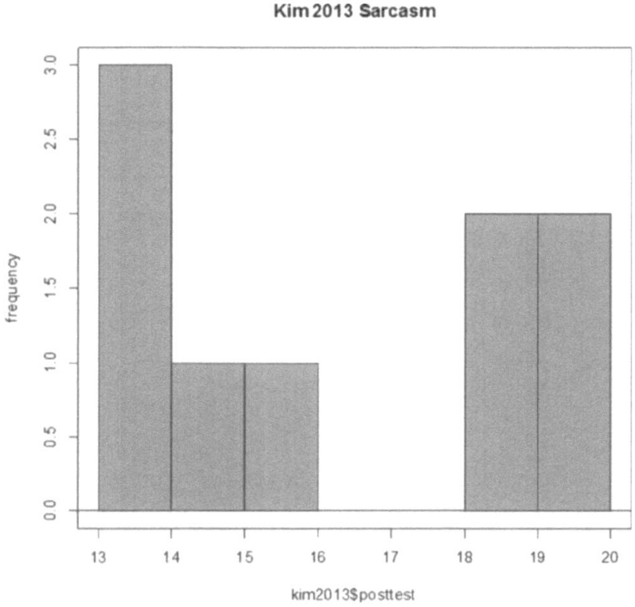

Figure 3.28 Histogram of the Kim (2013) posttest variable.

There are many ways you might want to change the histogram that R Commander generates, the most important one being how to create separate histograms for separate groups. You can easily do this in the R Console by specifying which rows to use in the histogram command. For example, in the

Abrahamsson and Hyltenstam (2009) data set, to make a histogram for only the group of AOA 11 or younger, which are found in rows 21 through to 127, add brackets with the row numbers to the variable to the Hist() command that R Commander uses:

```
Hist(ah2009$percnative[21:127])
```

Everything else for this command is a default, so nothing else is necessary. But there are many parameters you might *like* to change to make a prettier histogram. You can use R Commander to see the code that generates a histogram, then take that code and play with it in R Console until you get the look you like.

The commands used to generate the three histograms with the Larson-Hall and Connell (2005) data in Figure 3.21 are given below (importing the LarsonHall.Forgotten.sav data as **forget**). Note that the first histogram leaves the y-axis label in but the second and third histograms get rid of the y-axis label by putting nothing between the parentheses.

```
par(mfrow=c(1,3)) #sets the graphics display to 1 row, 3 columns
Hist(forget$rlwtest[1:15], col="gray", border="darkgray", xlab="", main="Non-immersionists")
Hist(forget$ rlwtest[16:30], col="gray", border="darkgray", xlab="", ylab="", main="Late immersionists")
Hist(forget$ rlwtest[31:44], col="gray", border="darkgray", xlab="", ylab="", main="Early immersionists")
```

The code below makes a histogram by taking 50 samples from the normal distribution. I used this code repeatedly, just changing the number of samples, to make the graphic in Figure 3.18 with different numbers of samples of the normal distribution.

```
hist(rnorm(50,0,1),xlab="", main="", col="lightgray", border="black",prob=T)
```

hist(x, . . .)	The command for a histogram; many other general graphics parameters can be added.
rnorm(50,0,1)	Generates 50 samples of a normal distribution with mean=0 and s=1.
xlab="", main=""	Deletes the generic x label and main title that R would automatically print.
col="lightgray"	Colors the inside of the histogram bins.
border="black"	Changes the color of the bin borders.
prob=T	Changes the scaling to density; can also use scale="density" (also "percent" or "frequency").

To overlay the histogram with a density plot of the normal distribution (Figure 3.29), I used the following code:

```
par(mfrow=c(1,1))
norm.x=rnorm(50,0,1)
x=seq(-3.5, 3.5, .1)
dn=dnorm(x)
hist(norm.x, xlab="", main="50 samples", col="lightgray", border="darkgray", prob=T)
lines(x, dn, col="red", lwd=2)
```

Note that in R you could use the command **Hist( )** or **hist( )**. **Hist( )** is specific to R Commander and is set up to call the **hist( )** command, but adds a couple of default arguments that **hist( )** does not have.

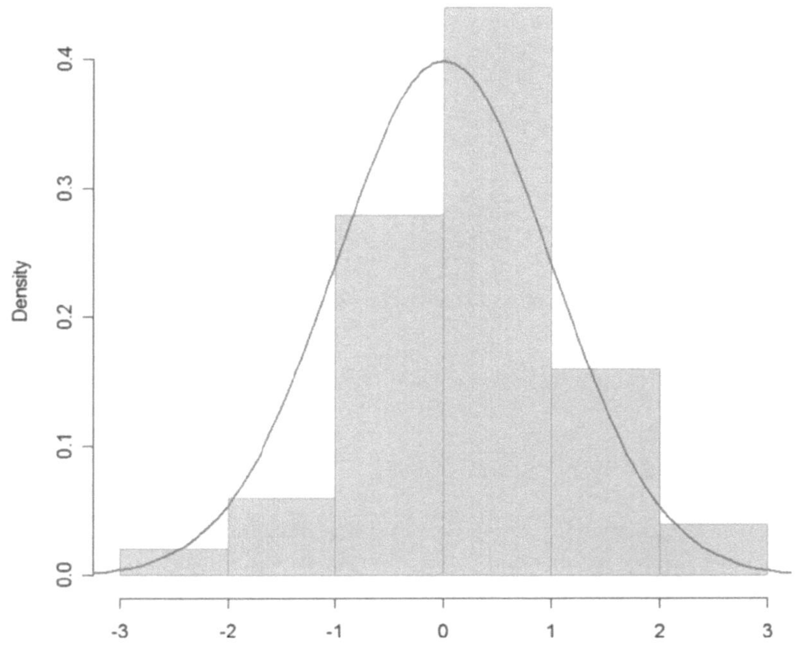

Figure 3.29 Histogram with overlaid normal distribution.

Obtaining Histograms in R

1 Use the hist command:
Hist(kim2013$pretest) OR hist(kim2013$pretest)

2 To get histograms split by groups, specify the row numbers of the group, like this:
Hist(ah2009$percnative[21:127]) #AOA 11 and under group

3.7.2 Creating Stem and Leaf Plots with R

R Commander provides a direct command to obtain a stem and leaf plot: GRAPHS > STEM AND LEAF DISPLAY. If you open this you will see an "OPTIONS" tab, where the first choice is number of "Parts per stem." This refers to how many lines you will have for each beginning number. Left on "Automatic" for the Abrahamsson and Hyltenstam (2009) data set, it gives two parts per stem as shown on the left in Figure 3.30, but I prefer the compact picture given by just one part per stem as on the right in Figure 3.30.

The R code for the plot on the right of Figure 3.30 is:

```
stem.leaf(ah2009$percnative, m=1, na.rm=TRUE) #m refers to number of parts per stem
```

If you want to have a stem and leaf plot divided up by groups, the easiest way to do it is to use the R code and use specific row numbers. For the Abrahamsson and Hyltenstam (2009) data set, to make a histogram for only the group of AOA 12 or older, which are found in rows 128 through

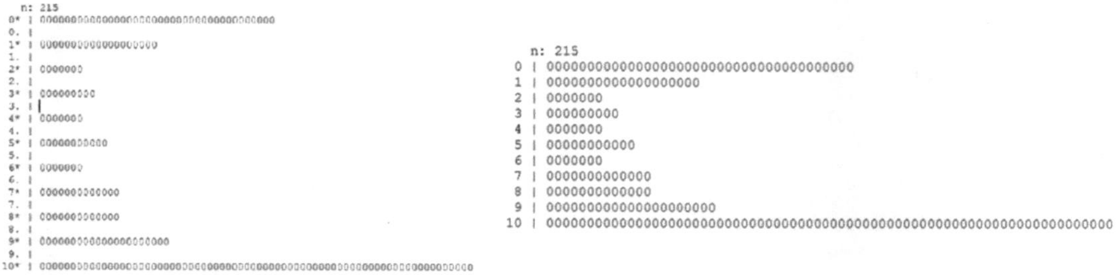

Figure 3.30 Stem and leaf plots from the Abrahamsson and Hyltenstam (2009) data set (PERCNATIVE variable).

to 215, add brackets with the row numbers to the variable to the **stem.leaf()** command that R Commander uses:

```
stem.leaf(ah2009$percnative[128:215], m=1, na.rm=TRUE)
```

There are other options in the R Commander dialog box, and one of them is "Trim outliers." This option is self-explanatory, but I do not recommend this option for most data sets, as when you are exploring your data you *want* to see everything in it, not exclude points that look like outliers. Uncheck this box but leave the others checked. The option "Show depths" prints counts of each line. The option "Reverse negative leaves" applies when you might have values that are negative and positive.

One more nifty stem and leaf plot that you can only call up in the R Console is a back-to-back stem and leaf plot. You can only put in two variables, but let us say I wanted to compare some pretest data with posttest data. Figure 3.31 shows what I get when I compare them back-to-back.

The numbers in the middle of Figure 3.31 (from 6 to 20) are the actual values on the test, and the zeros represent one case of each. The numbers on the far left and far right are the counts of how

```
________________________________________________
  1 | 2: represents 1.2, leaf unit: 0.1
   back$preobjectid          back$postobjectid
________________________________________________
                    |  6 |0                1
  2               00|  7 |00               3
 10        000000000|  8 |0000             7
 17         0000000|  9 |0                8
 26       000000000| 10 |000             11
 29             000| 11 |0000            15
 (8)       00000000| 12 |00              17
 27              00| 13 |000             20
 25            0000| 14 |0000000         27
 21           00000| 15 |0000            31
 16            0000| 16 |00000           (5)
 12           00000| 17 |0000            28
  7              00| 18 |000000          24
  5           00000| 19 |00000000        18
                   | 20 |0000000000      10
________________________________________________
n:                 64      64
________________________________________________
```

Figure 3.31 A back-to-back stem and leaf plot of two variables.

many cases are included; however, they are cumulative counts going down only until the number in parentheses, which is the median of that side's cases, and below that point the count is reversed from the bottom up. Total *N* is printed at the bottom. That count can be turned off by changing the default value of depth=TRUE to depth=FALSE. Here is the R command for the back-to-back stem and leaf plot:

```
stem.leaf.backback(example$pretest, example$posttest)
```

Creating a Stem and Leaf Plot

From the R Commander menu, choose GRAPHS > STEM AND LEAF DISPLAY. Pick the variable you want to graph. On the "Options" tab, uncheck the "Trim outliers" box. Possibly change "Parts per stem" to 1.

1. **The basic R code for the stem and leaf plot is:**
   stem.leaf(ah2009$percnative, m=1) #m is the number of parts per stem
2. **To graph stem and leaf plots for different groups, add row numbers to the variable:**
   stem.leaf(ah2009$percnative[1:20], m=1) #graphs the NS group

3.7.3 Creating Q-Q Plots with R

Using R Commander, go to GRAPHS > QUANTILE-COMPARISON PLOT. Pick your variable, then go to the OPTIONS tab, as shown in Figure 3.32. If you want to be able to manually identify the row number of points that are far away from the normal distribution, click on the "Interactively with mouse" button under "Identify points."

In the Q-Q plot in Figure 3.33, the dotted lines contain a simulated 95% CI envelope. Maronna, Martin, and Yohai (2006, p. 10) stated that if no points fall outside the CI we may be "moderately sure that the data are normally distributed." For this data set, however, we do have one point that falls outside the envelope (top right-hand side), and several points that are right on the border. Thus it would be hard to conclude that these data are exactly normally distributed.

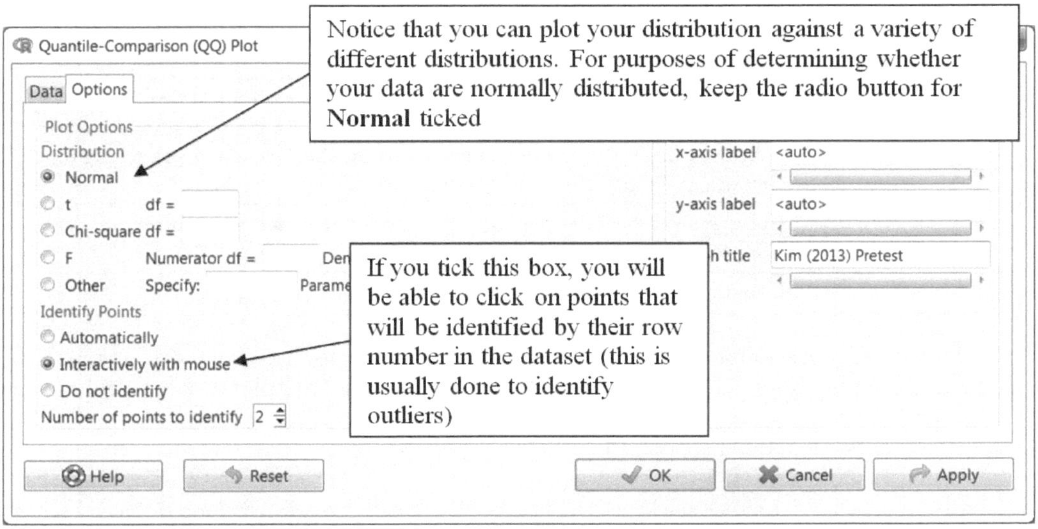

Figure 3.32 Dialog box for a Q-Q plot in R Commander.

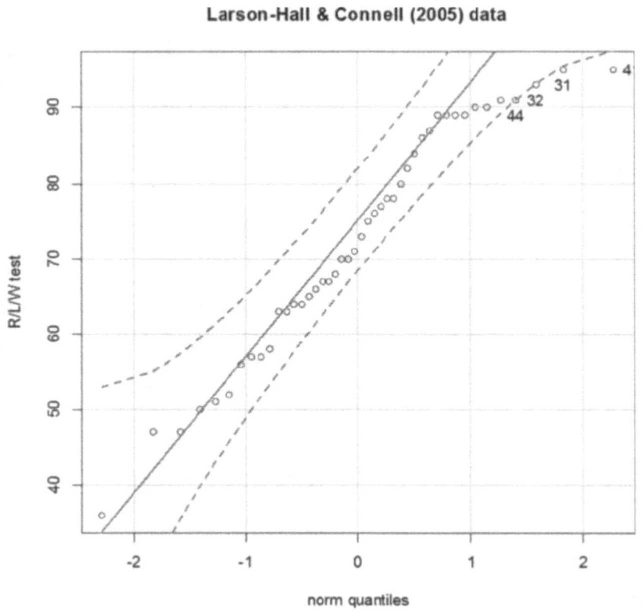

Figure 3.33 A Q-Q plot with 95% confidence intervals.

Here is the R code for the Q-Q plot shown in Figure 3.33 (called up through R Commander):

```
qqPlot(forget$rlwtest, dist="norm", id.method="identify", id.n=2, labels=rownames(forget), ylab=
"R/L/W test", main="Larson-Hall & Connell (2005) data")
```

qqPlot (x, . . .)	Performs the quantile-comparisons plot.
dist="norm"	qqPlot can plot data against several different distributions, "t", "f", and "chisq", but the default is the normal distribution.
id.method="identify"	The default setting is id.method="y", which will identify the id.n points (however many you specify in the next setting) with the largest value of the absolute value of y-mean(y). Here, set to "identify", it allows you to use the mouse to choose the points you want to identify.
id.n=2	Lets you set the number of points you want identified automatically, if previous setting set to identify automatically.
. . .	The other parameters are for specifying labels on the graph.

To analyze a Q-Q plot for different groups, just specify the specific row numbers of the group in the command. In the **forget** data set, rows 1–15 are the Non group, so this Q-Q plot is only for that group:

```
qqPlot(forget$rlwtest[1:15], dist="norm")
```

Additionally, the **Lattice** graphics package can produce nice side-by-side versions of the Q-Q test (and many other graphics) split by groups. The following commands produced Figure 3.23, which was shown earlier in this chapter:

```
library(lattice)
qqmath(~rlwtest|status,aspect="xy", data=forget,layout=c(3,1),xlab="Q-Q plot", prepanel =
prepanel.qqmathline,
panel = function(x, ...) {
panel.qqmathline(x, ...)
panel.qqmath(x, ...)
})
```

The commands following the command in bold are used to insert the reference line into the graphic and were taken from the example found in the help(qqmath) page. (If you had any trouble with this part you could just copy these lines from the help page; examples are found at the very bottom of the help page.) If the command in bold is used by itself, it will produce the three Q-Q plots without the reference line. This command in bold is analyzed here:

```
qqmath(~rlwtest|status, aspect="xy", data=forget, layout=c(3,1), xlab="Q-Q plot")
```

qqmath (~rlwtest|status, . . .)	Performs a Q-Q plot on the data split by the second argument (status).
aspect="xy"	This argument controls the physical aspect ratio of the panels; "xy" keeps a certain aspect ratio; alternatively, aspect="fill" makes the panels as large as possible.
data=forget	Specifies the data set.
layout=c(3,1)	Specifies that there should be three columns and one row; if not specified, the layout will be automatically plotted.
xlab="Q-Q plot"	Gives the x label.

To learn more about both traditional graphics and lattice graphics in R, see the indispensable book by Paul Murrell (2006).

Creating Q-Q Plots with R

From the R Commander menu, choose GRAPHS > QUANTILE-COMPARISON PLOT. Pick the variable you want to graph. On the "OPTIONS" tab decide how you want to identify outliers.

1 The basic R code for this Q-Q plot is:
qqPlot(forget$rlwtest, dist="norm")

2 To graph Q-Q plots for different groups, add row numbers to the variable:
qqPlot(forget$rlwtest[1:15], dist="norm") #graphs the Non group

3 The lattice library also has a nice Q-Q plot that will split data into groups in a side-by-side layout. After opening the lattice library, use the following basic command:
qqmath(~rlwtest|status, aspect="xy", data=forget)

3.7.4 Testing for Normality with R

In the SPSS output, along with graphical tests for normality, numerical tests were also included. So, to parallel the output of SPSS, this section includes information about how to get numerical tests of normality in R. A number of tests are available, including the Shapiro–Wilk and Kolmogorov–Smirnov tests. The Shapiro–Wilk test essentially only needs one argument. This test for normality is appropriately used with group sizes under 50. To call for the Shapiro–Wilk test in R Commander, use this path: STATISTICS > SUMMARIES > SHAPIRO–WILK TEST OF NORMALITY. If your data is split by groups, however, this will not be a useful test since you cannot split the groups. To look at data split by groups you will need to use the R code, and the easiest way to split it by groups is to put in your row numbers for each group:

```
shapiro.test(forget$rlwtest[1:15]) #rows 1–15 are the non group
```

```
      Shapiro-Wilk normality test

data:  forget$rlwtest[1:15]
W = 0.9613, p-value = 0.7142
```

If the p-value is above 0.05, the data are considered to be normally distributed, so the result here says that the non-immersionists data are normally distributed.

The Kolmogorov–Smirnov test is only available using R code. The command for this test needs two arguments. Most commonly, you would use a one-sided test to assess whether the data come from a normal distribution, in which case the second argument needs to be specified as the pnorm distribution (the normal distribution).

```
ks.test(forget$rlwtest[1:15],"pnorm")
```

```
      One-sample Kolmogorov-Smirnov test

data:  forget$rlwtest[1:15]
D = 1, p-value = 1.872e-13
alternative hypothesis: two-sided
```

The results give a very small p-value (1.872e-13 means you would move the decimal point 13 places to the left of where it is), indicating that the non-immersionists' data are not normally distributed. Note that this conflicts with the results of the Shapiro–Wilk test for normality.

The nortest package (Gross & Ligges, 2012) provides five more tests of normality. Ricci (2005) stated that the Lilliefors test is especially useful with small group sizes, and is an adjustment of the Kolmogorov–Smirnov test.

```
library(nortest)
lillie.test(forget$rlwtest[1:15])
```

```
      Lilliefors (Kolmogorov-Smirnov) normality test

data:  forget$rlwtest[1:15]
D = 0.1156, p-value = 0.8512
```

Here the Lilliefors test agrees with the results of the Shapiro–Wilk test in concluding that the data for the non-immersionists are normally distributed. I want to warn readers here that just because a numerical normality test does not find a p-value less than 0.05 does not necessarily mean your distribution is normal though. If your data set is small, these kinds of tests often do not have enough power to find deviations from the normal distribution. Graphical tools are just as important as these numerical tests and should be considered in addition to numerical tests.

3.7.5 Application Activities: Looking at Normality Assumptions with R

Keep your output from the activities in Checking Normality as you will use some of the same output for the application activity on homogeneity of variances as well.

1 Create a histogram with the GJT variable **gjtscore** for each of the two **status** groups in the SPSS file DeKeyser2000.sav file (imported as **dekeyser**; it has 57 rows and 3 columns). What is the shape of the histograms? Describe them in terms of skewness and normality. Next, look at Q-Q plots for the same groups. Using R Commander, you will get a Q-Q plot for the whole group, so to look at the results by the two different groups, take the R code from the output and copy it into the R Console with square brackets after the variable, containing the row numbers. The "Under 15 group" is found in rows 1–15 and the "Over 15" group is found in rows 16–57. Do you see the same trends in the Q-Q plots as in the histograms?
2 Chapter 6 on correlation will feature data from Flege, Yeni-Komshian, and Liu (1999). Import the SPSS file FlegeYKLiu.sav file and name it **fyl**. (It has 264 rows and 3 columns.) Examine the data for pronunciation divided according to groups by using Q-Q plots. These data should be divided into eight different groups, so use the **lattice** package Q-Q plots which split the data automatically. From the available evidence, do the data appear to be normally distributed?
3 Chapter 11 on repeated-measures ANOVA will feature data from Lyster (2004). Import the SPSS file Lyster.written.sav and name it **lyster**. (It has 180 rows and 12 columns.) Examine the gain scores for the comprehension task (**compgain1,compgain2**) divided according to groups (**cond** for condition). From the available evidence, do the data appear to be normally distributed? Look at Q-Q plots and histograms. Check the Shapiro–Wilk normality numbers as well.
4 Leow (1997) is a study that published its data in the research report. This study was the first to use think-aloud procedures to explore the role of language awareness in SLA (Sanz & Leow, 2011). In the study, Leow had participants fill in a crossword puzzle that targeted stem-changing vowels in Spanish verbs, all the while reporting what they were thinking. The data are in the comma-delimited leow1997.csv file, so first import it into R as **leow**. Look at the data for the "Production" variable, divided by groups (those who had awareness of a rule vs. those who did not). Are these data normally distributed?

My point in looking at assumptions in all of these studies is that there are some places in almost every study where the data are not exactly normally distributed (outliers or some kind of clear skewness). My advice is to generally replace parametric statistics with more robust measures, such as non-parametric bootstrapping, and I will illustrate how to do that in Part II of this book. These tests are conducted and reported in almost exactly the same way as parametric tests, so making a change to more robust tests is practically not any harder than conducting parametric tests, but gives added assurance to the researcher that the results are more accurate.

3.8 Examining the Shape of Distributions: The Assumption of Homogeneity

Another important assumption when parametric statistics are applied to group data is that the variances of the groups are equal (the homogeneity of variances assumption). Remember that the variance is a number that measures the average squared distance from the mean to any point, so it measures dispersion around the mean, and the SD is just the square root of this number. The idea of a statistical test of two groups is that, if we look at two groups whose distributions are equal and whose variances are equal, all we then need to do is to check whether their mean scores differ enough to consider the groups part of the same distribution or in fact as two separate distributions.

Graphics that illustrate this idea will be helpful. The left panel of Figure 3.34 shows density plots of non-overlapping distributions that have equal SDs ($s = 0.25$), but whose means are at different points. (The means are −3, 0 and 3.) The second graph shows density plots of distributions that do overlap. They have the same means as the first figure. Their SDs are all equal at 1.

The distributions of the left panel of Figure 3.34 would certainly be considered as statistically different, while for those of the right panel this is not a certainty. One can infer from these figures

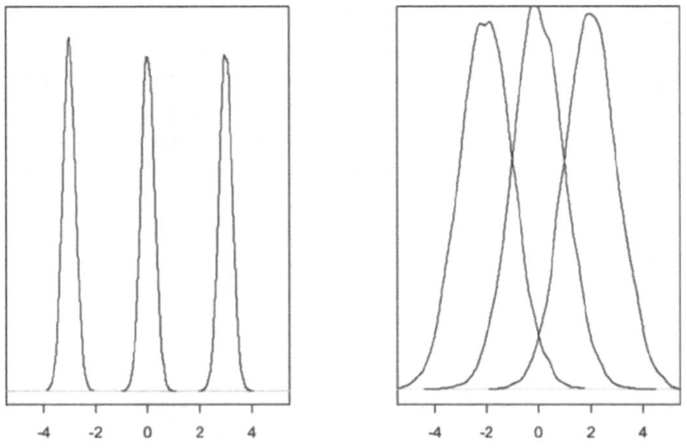

Figure 3.34 Density plots of three groups whose means differ.

that, if the SDs (and thus the variances) of all the groups were of different sizes, then a test that assumed they were the same and was only looking for differences in the means might easily run into problems.

Just as with the assumption of normality, there are different ways of examining the homogeneity of variances in one's own data. First, and simplest, is to look at the numerical output for the SD. One can eyeball these numbers in relation to the scale that they were measured on and get a sense of whether variances are in fact equal. A second way of checking variances is to look at side-by-side box plots of groups. (See Chapter 7 for more information about making and interpreting box plots.) Although the box in the box plot is not the SD (it is the area from the 25th to 75th quantile), it is showing the amount of variability in the central part of the distribution and thus can be examined for a rough sense of variance. The box plots in the first graph (a) of Figure 3.35 for the R/L/W test variable show that variances are not substantially different among the three Japanese groups, as the lengths of their boxes are not markedly different. (However, the early immersionists' distribution is quite skewed, as shown by the fact that the median line is not in the middle of the shaded box.)

However, in a different test of accentedness, where NS of English were also tested (graph (b) in Figure 3.35), there are clear differences in variances. The native speaker group has a shorter box (and less variance) than any of the non-native groups, and the "non" group also has a much longer box than any of the three other groups.

A third way to test for homogeneity of variances is to use **Levene's test** of homogeneity of variances. Tabachnick and Fidell (2001) stated that, while most formal tests of homogeneity of variances also measure normality, Levene's test does not.

In SPSS, Levene's test can be called for when doing the actual statistical test. For example, when you call for a *t*-test to see if two groups are statistically different, a test for homogeneity of differences will also be run at the same time.

In R Commander, choose STATISTICS > VARIANCES > LEVENE'S TEST to call for this test. One or more factors can be chosen to split the data. The help files for this test state that using the median, not the mean (you can choose which to use in the dialog box), results in a more robust test, so do not change the default on this unless you have a good reason to choose the mean.

As with the formal tests of normality seen in previous sections of this chapter, if the probability is *over* 0.05 for Levene's test, variances are considered to be homogeneous. This is because Levene's test checks the null hypothesis that variances are equal, so, if the probability is less than $p = 0.05$, we will reject the null hypothesis and conclude that variances are *not* equal. As with many other formal tests

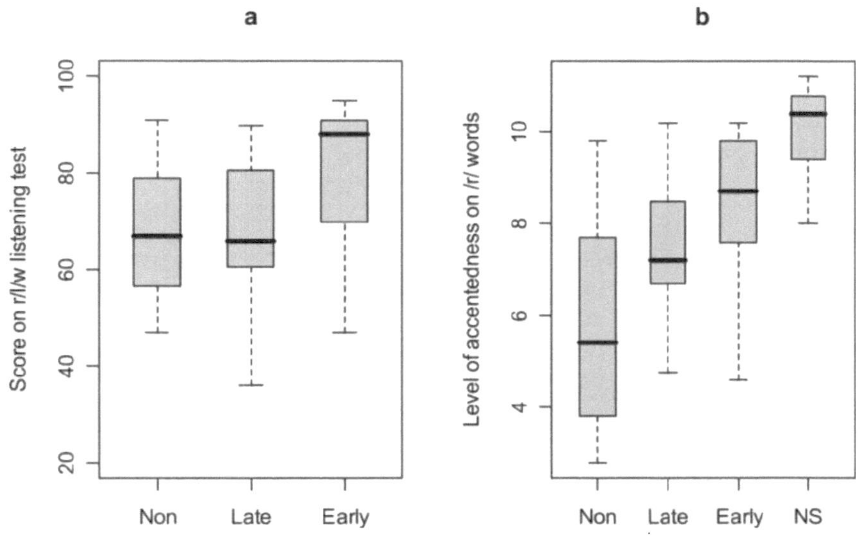

Figure 3.35 Box plots can be examined for homogeneity of variances; in graph (a) the lengths of the boxes are all roughly equal, meaning variances are approximately equal, while in graph (b) the boxes have markedly different lengths, violating the homogeneity of variance assumption.

of assumptions, however, with small sample sizes this test may not have enough power to detect violations of assumptions (Dalgaard, 2002; Wilcox, 2003).

What recourse do we have if our groups do not have homogeneous variances? If we stick to parametric statistics, when we use a *t*-test, there is a correction that is performed for groups whose variances are not the same. If we use an ANOVA there is no such correction, but we could choose not to compare groups that have non-homogeneous variances or combine certain groups to achieve a better effect. Again, the main effect of not having homogeneous variances is that, although group differences may actually exist, we might not be able to find them. Thus, if you perform a statistical test and find that the group differences you thought would be there are not found, you might consider that this result is due to non-homogeneous variances.

Another possibility to avoid problems with non-homogeneous groups is to use robust statistical procedures, such as bootstrapping and means trimming. These robust methods deal with problems due to both violations of normal distributions and homogeneity of variances in a manner that is objective and more robust to violations than parametric statistics. (See Larson-Hall & Herrington, 2009, for more detailed explanations with examples from the SLA field, or other non-technical and readable summaries, such as Erceg-Hurn & Mirosevich, 2008, and Wilcox, 1992, 1995, 1998.) These robust techniques will be demonstrated throughout the chapters for each type of test.

3.8.1 Checking Homogeneity of Variance (with SPSS or R)

1 Check the homogeneity of variances assumption for pronunciation for the groups in the Flege, Yeni-Komshian, and Liu (1999) study by looking at the SDs for each group. (Use the FlegeYKLiu.sav file and refer back to exercises 3.6.1 for SPSS or 3.7.5 for R.) The maximum number of points on this test was nine. If using R, also run Levene's test. What do you conclude about the equality of variances?

2 Check the homogeneity of variances assumption for the **GJTScore** variable for the two groups in the DeKeyser (2000) study by looking at the SDs for each group. (Use the DeKeyser2000.sav file.) The maximum number of points on this test was 200. If using R, also run Levene's test. What do you conclude about the equality of variances?

3 Check the homogeneity of variances assumption for the **CompGain2** variable for the four groups in the Lyster (2004) study by looking at the SDs for each group. (Use the Lyster.Written.sav file.) The maximum number of points any person gained was 21. If using R, also run Levene's test. What do you conclude about the equality of variances?

3.9 Dealing with Departures from Expectations

3.9.1 Outliers

Sometimes, in your data you will find points that stand out as being different from the bulk of the data. We saw in earlier sections of this chapter that, if we are using the mean, one outlier can have a large effect on describing the typical value of a data set. Outliers are very problematic for "classic" statistics (and by this I mean parametric statistical methods that do not use robust methods of estimation) because data are assumed to follow a normal distribution *exactly*. If you have a distribution that is *approximately* normal, this unfortunately does not result in *approximately* the correct conclusions, as Maronna, Martin, and Yohai (2006) have pointed out. If you are doing a complex math problem and you forget to carry a one to the tens position when adding numbers together, this will result in a *completely* wrong conclusion, not an *approximately* wrong conclusion. The presence of an outlier means that the distribution is not exactly a normal distribution.

Many texts that talk only about classic statistics advise you to use graphic summaries to identify outliers, and then remove them or run the analysis both with and without them. This chapter has explored many graphic approaches that can identify univariate outliers (outliers in a single variable), such as histograms, Q-Q plots, or stem and leaf plots. Tabachnick and Fidell (2001, p. 71) have argued that deletion is a good solution if the point is "highly correlated with others or is not critical to the analysis."

There are, however, several problems with simply manually deleting outliers. The first is that it is not objective, and completely up to the discretion of the individual researcher (Huber, 1981; Maronna, Martin, & Yohai, 2006). In addition, sometimes one outlier may mask another, so that when you throw away one data point you then find another that stands out, and where do you stop? Another objection is that the data may have come from a genuinely non-normal distribution, but you are ignoring that by cleaning up the data (Huber, 1981). A third problem is that, after removing an outlier, the data are not independent anymore, which is one of the assumptions of all statistical tests (Huber, 1981; Wilcox, 1998).

The problem becomes even more complex when you have more than one variable, such as in regression analysis, and you need to examine whether there are multivariate outliers. This is again one of those difficult areas where "classic" statistics really does not have a better answer than that of manually deleting outliers and reporting the results both with and without what you consider to be outliers.

Researchers in the field of statistics have found that there are better methods of analysis that are more robust to departures from the classical assumptions of normality of distributions and homogeneity of variances. These are called robust methods, and throughout the book I will demonstrate how to use some of these methods in both SPSS and R. Robust methods will result in the objective elimination of outliers and will perform better than if data had been simply cleaned up. Robust methods are a more principled and powerful way to both identify and eliminate outliers. SPSS version 22.0 (which I have used for this edition) has implemented bootstrapping in all of the procedures that will be demonstrated in this book. R, being an open platform, is more updated in being able to perform other kinds of robust procedures, such as means trimming or Winsorizing, but one may have to use different libraries to access all of the procedures.

3.9.2 Transforming Data

Another procedure that is commonly advised in books that treat "classic" statistics is to **transform** your data when you find it does not fit the parameters of a normal distribution, such as being skewed or having outliers. Transforming your variables can also result in more homogeneous variances. Most authors also caution, however, that interpreting the transformed values may be difficult. Tabachnick and Fidell (2001) note that if you are using a scale that has little intrinsic meaning, however, transformation does not seriously hinder later interpretation.

I have very rarely seen researchers in second language research report transforming variables. I suspect that many feel as I did, which is that this is a complicated area that I did not understand well enough to actually use in my work. Either that or researchers may have tried transformations and found that it did not make much difference to the normality of their distributions or the size of the variances. Tabachnick and Fidell (2001) have reported that they have had good success with improving distributional assumptions using transformations when variables are skewed in different directions, or some variables are skewed while others are not. However, when all the variables are skewed to about the same level, the authors suggested that in such a case transformations do not seem to make much difference.

Tabachnick and Fidell (2001) have a very useful table that gives recommendations for what kinds of transformations to use when data appear in various shapes. These transformations are simple to do. If you do decide to transform your data, you should check all of the indicators of normality and homogeneity of variances (as well as other assumptions that apply only in certain tests, such as the linearity assumption in correlation) with the transformed data to see whether any improvement has been achieved. Tabachnick and Fidell's recommendations are summarized in Table 3.7.

Table 3.7 Recommended Transformations for Data Problems

Distributed shape	*Recommended transformation (X = column you want to transform)*	*Transformation if any zeros found in data*
Moderate positive skewness	sqrt(X)	
Substantial positive skewness	log10(X)	log10(X + C*)
Severe positive skewness	1/X	1/(X + C)
Moderate negative skewness	sqrt(Z**–X)	
Substantial negative skewness	log10(Z**–X)	
Severe negative skewness	log10(Z**–X)	

*C is a constant that is added so that the smallest value will equal 1
**Z is a constant that is added such that (Z–X) does not equal 0

To perform transformations of the data in SPSS, go to TRANSFORM > COMPUTE VARIABLE. Choose the appropriate function you want to use. In SPSS 12.0 you could choose these directly from the list under the "Function" box, but in SPSS 15.0 and higher there is a box of "Function groups." Most of the functions you will want can be found in the "Arithmetic" group, such as the log function and the square root. Double-click on the function you want and it will appear in the "Numeric Expression" box with a question mark. Put the column you want to transform into that question mark area (see Figure 3.36). A new column appears and you can use this to perform statistical calculations (after checking to see if your transformed variable is better than the original one!).

Throughout the exercises in this chapter we have seen that the "GJTScore" variable in DeKeyser (2000) is negatively skewed. I will walk you through an example of transforming these data. Tabachnick and Fidell (2001) recommended using a reflect and square root transformation for moderately negatively skewed data. To determine the Z constant, we first find that the largest value in the data set is 199. We will add 1, so that Z = 200. For SPSS then, the expression I write in the box (see Figure 3.36) is SQRT(200-GJTSCORE). After obtaining this new column, I need to check on the distribution of this new variable, which I do by looking at a histogram (GRAPHS > LEGACY DIALOGS > HISTOGRAM).

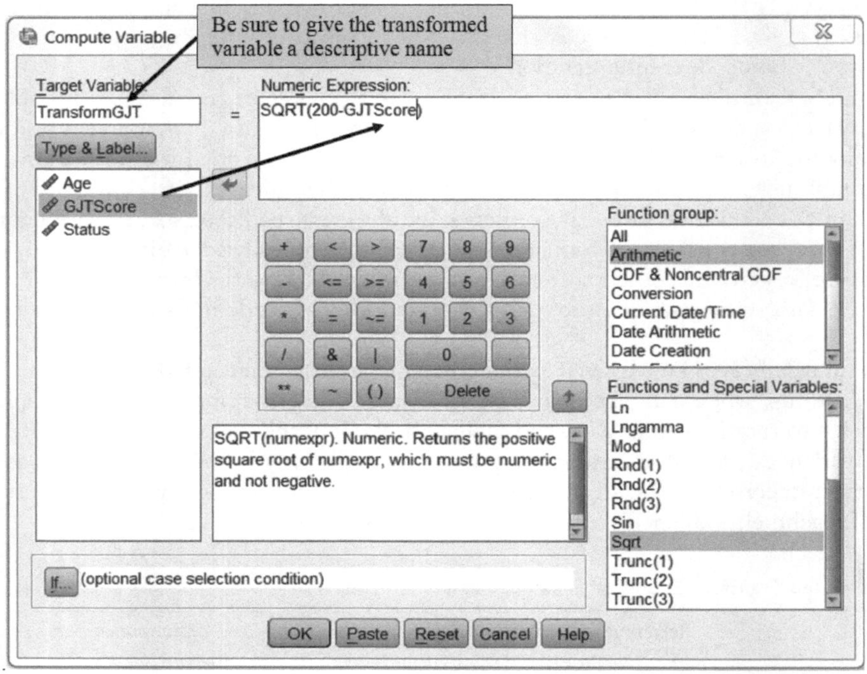

Figure 3.36 Performing a transformation in SPSS.

There is no way to transform data in R Commander, so you will need to use the R Console to transform data. Fortunately, it is quite easy to do so and not very different from what you need to do in SPSS. You simply choose which transformation you want to use (you basically choose the syntax shown in Table 3.7) and apply it to the right side of an equation. For example, I assume that you read the previous paragraph about transforming the DeKeyser (2000) data. Use this equation that I gave for SPSS and put the transformed variable back into the original data file with a new name, like this (assuming you imported the file DeKeyser2000 as **dekeyser** into R):

```
dekeyser$gjtscoreTransform<-sqrt(200-dekeyser$gjtscore)
```

Create a histogram of this variable in R with this command:

```
hist(dekeyser$gjtscoreTransform)
```

Although the histogram in Figure 3.37 seems to show less skewness in the transformed variable, the skewness value of the non-transformed variable is −0.3 while the skewness of the transformed variable is −0.4, a little worse but really not much of a difference. It is probably not worthwhile to transform this variable, given there is little improvement. A check of the more extreme transformation using the LG10 function does not reveal a more normal distribution either.

3.10 Summary

There are many ways your data may not fit the standard assumptions for parametric statistical tests. Two of the assumptions about your data that can be examined through both numerical and graphical

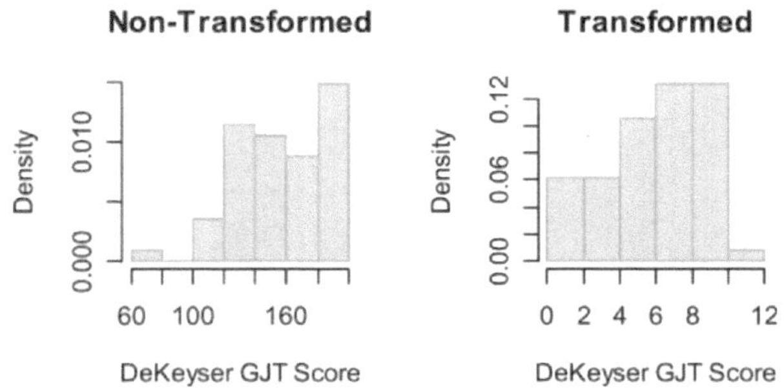

Figure 3.37 Checking the "GJTScore" variable with and without transformation for skewness.

means are that your data are normally distributed and that, if there are groups, their variances are equal.

The first assumption of a normal distribution is an exact one, but with small sample sizes it is impossible to tell whether your data come from an exactly normal distribution or not. You can numerically examine the assumption of normality by using formal tests such as the Shapiro–Wilk test (the best one for sample sizes under 50). You can graphically examine the assumption of normality by looking at graphs such as histograms (with normal curves superimposed), stem and leaf plots, and Q-Q plots. With sample sizes under 30, the best you can hope for in these examinations is to see whether the data are skewed or not. You may also be able to tell if there are outliers in your distribution. I have argued that the best remedy for dealing with departures from expectations of parametric statistics is to use robust statistics, which will be illustrated throughout the chapters. These robust statistics function in the same way as parametric statistics and can be interpreted in the same ways as well.

The second assumption explored in this chapter is that, if you have groups of data, they will have approximately equal variances (this assumption is not exact). This assumption can be explored numerically by comparing the SDs of your groups and considering the scale used. This assumption can be explored visually by looking at box plots and examining the length of the boxes. Levene's test is a numerical test of the homogeneity of variances assumption. If this assumption is not met, a *t*-test can correct for the problem. For other tests, you might want to consider not including a group with a highly different variance. Robust methods and transformations can also help with this problem, even though they may *not* always solve it.

Chapter 4

Changing the Way We Do Statistics

The New Statistics

> To the [researcher] who practices this religion, Statistics refers to the seeking out and interpretation of *p*-values. Like any good religion, it involves vague mysteries capable of contradictory and irrational interpretation . . . And it provides Salvation: Proper invocation of the religious dogmas of Statistics will result in publication in prestigious journals. This form of Salvation yields fruit in this world (increases in salary, prestige, invitations to speak at meetings) and beyond this life (continual reference in the citation indexes).
>
> David S. Salsburg (1985, p. 220)

As a writer of a textbook on statistics, I feel an obligation to introduce advances in statistics into our own field. Second language acquisition (SLA) practitioners do not want those reporting on SLA to confine themselves to research done in the 1970s at the beginning of our discipline's history, important as those first steps may have been. SLA has made advances in knowledge since then and anyone who references SLA findings should keep abreast of current research findings. In turn we should pay the same courtesy to the field of statistics by incorporating advances in that field into our work too, in spite of the fact that none of us are statistical experts. In the first edition of this book I argued for a few first steps toward newer statistical practices, but in the second edition I feel I must reach even further to try to argue for more significant steps toward "The New Statistics". *Understanding the New Statistics: Effect Sizes, Confidence Intervals, and Meta-Analysis* is the title of a book published by Geoff Cumming in 2012, from which I will derive the majority of my recommendations in this chapter. (See also Larson-Hall & Plonsky, 2015, which aims to be a guideline as to methodological reporting for the field of SLA.) The main difference in these new statistics is an emphasis on the size of effects, measured through effect sizes and confidence intervals (CIs), over dichotomous "significant vs. non-significant" *p*-value decisions and a view toward meta-analysis, which emphasizes the collective results of various studies over the findings of just one study. This way of thinking has apparently been used for decades in physics, chemistry and biology. Cumming argues for a shift in fields that are still using the "old" statistics, such as psychology, education and medicine, and I see evidence that such a shift is beginning, and I believe the SLA field would also benefit from it.

One problem with such an approach in a textbook is that readers new to the whole idea of statistics basically need to know something about what went before, so they can understand the new direction and still be able to read and understand research done using the "old" statistics. By the way, the "new statistics" are not very new at all; such ideas have been around for 50 years or more, but as Cumming (2012) points out, actually adopting these ways of thinking about and reporting on statistics would definitely be a new direction. Because I believe we are at a turning point where the new statistics can really take hold and begin to make a difference in how we think about our own data and our research findings, this book will, of a necessity, make a clear departure from the conventional ways of doing statistics that we have used until now, but I will also have to explain the "old" statistics. I will start with the "new" statistics at the beginning of the chapter, and add in sections about the "old" statistics later, making comments in those sections about why the "new" way of doing things is preferable.

I have stated my belief that we should adopt the "new statistics," but you may wonder why any change needs to happen. The main reason is that the way we do statistics influences how we think about our results, and an approach focused on a simple dichotomy such as that of null hypothesis significance testing (NHST) provides us with a too simple and uninformative way of thinking about our research. Statistical thinkers have long railed against the practice of making dichotomous decisions based on a p-value. (In Chapter 2 you were given a preliminary introduction to NHST; you may then remember that basically if the p-value is less than or equal to $p = 0.05$, you reject the null hypothesis that there is no difference between groups or no relationship between variables, and if the p-value is greater than 0.05, then you accept the null hypothesis and conclude that there is no difference between groups or relationship between variables.)

The quotation at the beginning of the chapter compares the use of NHST to a religion, where followers blindly and almost uncomprehendingly invoke their rituals to understand the world. This may seem a harsh comparison, but the criticisms against the NHST are indeed harsh, as evidenced by this sampling of quotes about the use of NHST (emphasis added):

- "Null hypotheses of no difference are usually known to be false before the data are collected . . . when they are, their rejection or acceptance simply reflects the size of the sample and the power of the test, and is ***not a contribution to science***." (Savage, 1957, pp. 332–333)
- "The idea that one should proceed no further with an analysis, once a non-significant F-value for treatments is found, has led many experimenters to ***overlook important information*** in the interpretation of their data." (Little, 1981)
- "Statistical 'recipes' are followed blindly, and ***ritual has taken over from scientific thinking***." (Preece, 1984, p. 519)
- "[T]he grotesque emphasis on significance tests in statistics courses of all kinds . . . is taught to people, who if they come away with no other notion, will remember that statistics is about tests for significant differences. . . . The apparatus on which their statistics course has been constructed is often ***worse than irrelevant, it is misleading*** about what is important in examining data and making inferences." (Nelder, in discussion of Chatfield, 1985)
- "I suggest to you that Sir Ronald [Fisher] has befuddled us, mesmerized us, and led us down the primrose path. I believe that the almost universal reliance on merely refuting the null hypothesis as the standard method for corroborating substantive theories in the soft areas is a terrible mistake, is basically unsound, poor scientific strategy, and ***one of the worst things that ever happened*** in the history of psychology." (Meehl, 1978, p. 817)
- "I'm not making some nit-picking statistician's correction. I am saying that the whole business [NHST] is so radically defective as to be ***scientifically almost pointless***." (Meehl, 1978, p. 823)
- "It is remarkable that despite two decades of . . . attacks, the ***mystifying doctrine*** of null hypothesis testing is still today the Bible from which our future research generation is taught." (Gigerenzer & Murray, 1987, p. 27)
- "It is difficult to estimate the ***handicap*** that widespread, incorrect, and intractable use of a primary data analytic method [NHST] has on a scientific discipline, but the deleterious effects are doubtless substantial." (Tryon, 1998, p. 796)
- "[NHST] is ***not only useless, it is also harmful*** because it is interpreted to mean something it is not." (Carver, 1978, p. 392)
- "It is time for researchers to avail themselves of the full arsenal of quantitative and qualitative statistical tools. . . . The current practice of focusing exclusively on a dichotomous reject-nonreject decision strategy of null hypothesis testing can ***actually impede scientific progress***. . . . The focus of research should be on . . . what data tell us about the magnitude of effects, the practical significance of effects, and the steady accumulation of knowledge." (Kirk, 2003, p. 100)

After even a quick perusal of these quotes you can see that a large number of scholars feel that it is not a good idea to continue to perpetuate NHST as a legitimate way of doing statistics. But what can be put in its place? The answer is CIs and effect sizes, so let us then begin with the heart of the chapter by focusing on these two ideas.

4.1 Introduction to Confidence Intervals

What do researchers want to know about the results of a study? Faulkner, Fidler and Cumming (2008) contacted the authors of 193 published works and asked them this question. They found that when researchers read about the results of a randomized, controlled study they wanted to know whether there was an effect, how large the effect was and to what extent it was practically important. A dichotomous NHST conclusion tells us whether there was an effect, but does not address any of the other questions. (An effect is "statistically significant" because the *p*-value is below 0.05, or "statistically non-significant" because the *p*-value is above 0.05.) Reporting a CI, which is "a range of plausible values for the corresponding parameter" (Kline, 2004, p. 27), whether that parameter be the true mean, the difference in scores, a correlation coefficient or something else, tells us whether there was an effect, how large that effect was, and shows us how much confidence we can have that a point estimate, such as a mean score, is a good estimate of the effect. With this information, the researcher is more easily able to understand and explain to readers how practically important the result is as well.

Cumming (2012) states that there are a number of ways to interpret CIs, but that the one that is agreed on by everyone is that a CI calculated from the sample data is "one from the potentially infinite sequence of intervals that we'd obtain if the experiment were repeated indefinitely" (p. 78). If our parameter is the mean of a group, for example, we would hope that the CI from our sample contains the true mean of the population we are trying to describe, and if we have a 95% CI, we can say that "we are 95% confident that our interval includes μ [the true mean]" (Cumming, 2012, p. 79).

To understand CIs more intuitively, Cumming uses his ESCI program to show the "dance of the CIs." In Chapter 3, we used Cumming's ESCI program to help you understand the standard error (SE) (Section 3.1.2), and we saw that the margin of error (the MOE) was one half of the CI and about two times the SE. I invite you to download ESCI for free from www.latrobe.edu.au/psy/research/cognitive-and-developmental-psychology/esci (see instructions in the following application activity, Section 4.1.1) if you have not done so before now, and follow along with me as I try to demonstrate how to understand CIs. I know it is easier to just read it, but you definitely will get a much more intuitive sense of how CIs work if you actually do it yourself!

In ESCI chapters 1–4, in the "CIjumping tab", we were able to take repeated samples of a population where we knew the population mean (μ) and the population standard deviation (SD; σ). We saw in Figure 3.8 that if we took repeated samples from that population and collapsed all the mean scores into a pile (the "mean heap") that they formed a sampling distribution curve. But in reality, when we perform an experiment, we do not sample from a known population; instead, we take one sample that we hope is representative of the population. A sample of 15 data points is shown in Figure 4.1. You can get a sample like this in the ESCI file "CIjumping tab" by clicking on the "Display means" box in the band near red 3 (and choosing an *N*; I had 15 data points), and then clicking on "Display data points" in the band near red 4. Click on the gray "Take sample" button to take a sample. To see the 95% CI of the mean for this

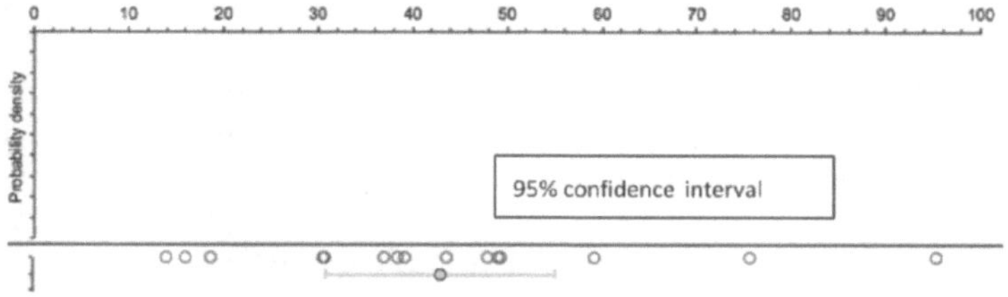

Figure 4.1 A sample of $N=15$ data points from an experiment. The mean is shown as the filled-in (green) dot, and the line around the filled-in dot shows the 95% confidence interval.

sample, click on the "Display CIs" box in the band near red 7. You could use the spinner here to see what a 99% CI or a 90% CI looked like too, but we will assume that 95% CIs are the norm.

The CI in Figure 4.1 is calculated from the SDs of the 15 data points. If we repeatedly sampled the same population we would get a "dance of the CIs," as seen in Figure 4.2. (We are assuming that we know the true population mean and SD but pretending to take a sample from it without knowing the true mean or SD.) The dots in the middle of the CI are the mean scores of the sample, and the 95% CI bars are calculated using the sample SD. The green (lighter) vertical lines are the MOE around the true population mean, which is set at 50 (the darker vertical line). To recreate this yourself in ESCI, in the "CIjumping tab", click "Display + MOE around μ" in the band near red 6, and the "Display μ line" near red 8.

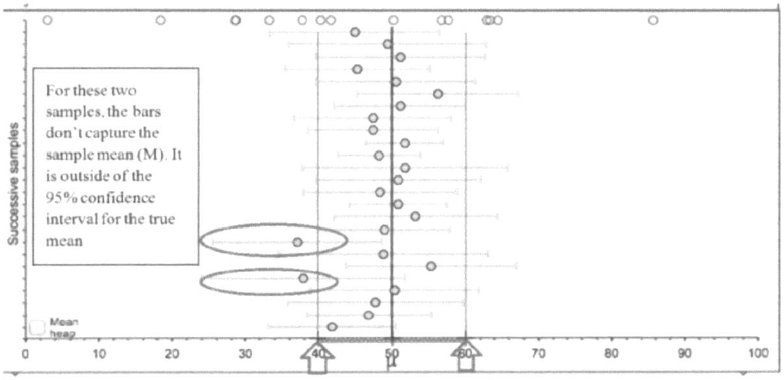

Figure 4.2 "Dance of the confidence intervals" of repeated samplings from a population with mean=50 and standard deviation=20.

> *Interpretation of a Confidence Interval*
>
> **One of an infinite number of intervals, some percentage of which will capture the population parameter. In other words, think of Figure 4.2 and imagine that your CI is just one of these intervals, 95% of which will capture the true mean (or whatever your parameter is).**

What we see then is that if we repeatedly sampled this population (push "Run-Stop" button), most of the time the CI that we calculated would contain a mean that was found within the 95% CI calculated with the known population mean and SD. In fact, if we have calculated a 95% CI, then in 95% of the cases, the interval we calculate from our sample data will include the (unknown in real life) population mean (which in Figure 4.2 is $\mu = 50$). Unfortunately, this does *not* mean the opposite—it does *not* mean that if we replicated the study 100 times, 95% of the time the mean score from our own data would be found in the CI of the true mean. The 95% CI is a parameter, and it makes predictions about the population mean (μ), not the mean of the study we have just conducted. So we can be pretty sure that the CI generated from our sample contains the true mean of the population, but we cannot be sure that the mean score found in our particular sample is necessarily close to the true mean and would be contained in most CIs. In other words, what we see is that it is the CI that we can have faith in, much more than one specific mean score.

4.1.1 Application Activity for ESCI and Confidence Intervals

To understand CIs better, these activities ask you to use Cumming's ESCI program and generate an image with specific parameters. It is helpful to do ALL of the activities in this section.

First download ESCI (at least chapters 1–4) from www.latrobe.edu.au/psy/research/cognitive-and-developmental-psychology/esci. (Scroll down the page and find "The Software" button then scroll down to find the correct version for your operating system.) After it is downloaded, click to open the Excel file. (For Windows, ESCI runs under Excel 2003, 2007 and 2010. For Mac, ESCI runs under Excel 2011 but not Excel 2008.) If you are asked, you should "Enable Macros" to get the program to work correctly. (See the ESCI Readme file for more advice for different versions of Excel.) Go to the "CIjumping tab". You will see red numbers and triangles near them. When your mouse hovers on the red triangles, you should get pop-up comments. If you do not, consult the ESCI Readme file for more help.

1 Under the top yellow bar, click the gray "Clear" button. In the first yellow bar, you will see a red 2 and also a red 1. If you hover over the pop-up for red 1 you will see that it suggests you click all three buttons in the yellow bar ("Display population," "Display SD lines," and "Fill random"). Notice that the population mean (μ) is set to 50, and the population SD (σ) to 20. Click on all the buttons in the yellow bar. Let us say our population is all of the French-speaking English learners in the world. We are going to sample from this population when we do an experiment. Let us recreate that in ESCI by clicking near red 4 (in the blue bar) on "Display data points," changing the *N* near red 3 (in the orange bar) to 15, and pressing the gray "Take sample" button. You will see 15 dots underneath the population curve that represent one sample from the population. This is all that I want you to do for exercise #1, but if you need to show your work, probably the easiest way is to take a screenshot. (Cumming suggests clicking on the figure, very close to its edge to select it, copy it and paste it using Paste Special/Picture (Enhanced metafile) but when I did this the picture came apart into different areas, not just one picture.) On a Windows computer, press the PRNT SCRN (or PRINT SCREEN) key, paste it into the PAINT PROGRAM, then select the part you need and copy and paste it into a Word document. On a Mac, open the LAUNCHPAD, then under UTILITIES find the "Grab" program. Open it and choose the menu sequence CAPTURE > SELECTION. Drag the mouse over the area you want to copy and when you let go what you have copied will appear in its own separate window. Copy and paste it into a new file.

2 Press the "Clear" button and do what you did in exercise #1 again, but this time with $\mu = 30$, and $\sigma = 10$ (slide the sliders to the right number). Keep $N = 15$ (a typical sample in our field) and now press the "Take sample" button many times. If the "Mean heap" button at the bottom of the figure is clicked (which it is by default), you will see the mean of those samples piling up as little green dots at the bottom of the figure. Cumming (2012) calls this the "mean heap," and there is a green line showing the distribution of these mean scores. As you take each sample, look at the points on the sample to help you deduce the randomness of the distribution of samples out of a population. You know the true (population) mean and SD, but you can see how the sample mean differs. If you are satisfied that you have deduced some of the randomness of sampling, go ahead and click on the gray "Run-Stop" button which will take samples continuously, and watch the mean heap pile up. Underneath the "Run-Stop" button is a box that tells you the number of samples you have taken. Take at least 100 samples. That is all you should do for this exercise.

3 Press the "Clear" button. (If you ever want to get back to the ESCI defaults, just exit the Excel file but do not save it. When you open it again, you will have all the defaults back.) This time, let us set $\mu = 45$ and $\sigma = 22$. Choose $N = 30$. Make sure "Display data points" near red 4 is ticked. Click off the "Mean heap" button at the bottom of the figure, and "Take sample." Now you will see the mean dot surrounded by a 95% CI. Take more samples or click the "Run-Stop" button to get more samples, but try to notice each time whether the CI from each sample contains what we know is the true (population) mean of 45. If your image contains at least 20 CI bars, chances are good that at least one of them will not go through the mean line. To help you see this more clearly, click on "Show capture of μ" in the purple band near red 9. Any CIs that do not contain the population mean will be shown in red. Take a screenshot of your picture; state how many CIs are visible in your image and how many do not contain the population mean.

4 Repeat exercise #3, but this time set $\sigma = 40$. (Keep the mean as $\mu = 45$). What do you notice about how this changes your CIs? Take a screenshot of your picture; state how many CIs are visible in your image and how many do not contain the population mean.

5 Play around with changing the CI level in the lower yellow band around red 7. For example, you could change it from the default 95% to 99% or 90%. What happens when you make the CIs larger (99%)? What happens when you make the CIs smaller (90%)? Answer this just in words.

4.1.2 Interpreting Confidence Intervals

We can use a CI in the same way as a *p*-value: if the CI goes through 0, it is similar to the *p*-value being above 0.05, and we conclude that there was not an effect for a treatment or a relationship among the variables. But if the CI does not go through zero, this is similar to the *p*-value being below 0.05, and we conclude that there was an effect for a treatment or a relationship among variables. However, the value of a CI lies in not just using it like a *p*-value or merely in answering the question of whether there was an effect or not; it also adds to the information by telling us more about the size of the effect. The CI shows how far from zero the difference lies, giving an intuitively understandable measure of effect size.

In addition, the CI tells us about how much faith we can have in our point estimates, like mean scores or differences between means or correlation coefficients. If there is a lot of **sampling error** in a study, then CIs will be wide, which means that our sampling error is large, and we must say that our point results may not be very good estimates. You can see that we want to have small CIs, and if we do, this means we have more precision in estimating correlations or mean differences in samples or whatever we are measuring. However, CIs may still be unsettling to those who are used to the dichotomous, black-and-white nature of the NHST process. The fact is that the uncertainty was always there, but the NHST results were hiding the uncertainty, while CIs not only show the uncertainty but make that uncertainty crystal clear!

For example, let us say we spent five hours teaching French language students the rules about how to determine grammatical gender in French words and then practicing doing so, and then looked at how much they improved from a pretest to a posttest on gender markers, where the maximum score on the test was 100 points. A successful NHST result would tell us that students improved "statistically significantly" from pretest to posttest, $p = 0.02$. All we know from this NHST result is that the students improved, which does tell us whether there was a result of our teaching, but it does not tell us how much the students improved. Of course, we could look at the mean of the difference between the pretest and posttest, and let us say it was M = 30. On a 100-point test, that seems to be a fairly large difference, so although the NHST did not tell us how big an effect the teaching and practicing had, we know there was an effect, and we get the impression from the mean score that the result is quite large. Now, let us say that instead of the NHST, instead we reported a CI around the difference in the pretest and posttest mean: M = 30, 95% CI [10, 50]. Here we have results in the original measurement scale, which makes it very easy to understand exactly how much possible improvement took place. The mean score (M) is a point estimate, but the CI shows us that we would expect to find the true parameter (the true difference in mean scores) somewhere between 10 points of difference and 50 points of difference, with 95% confidence. (Remember the dance of the CIs in Figure 4.2 and how we would expect different CIs with each sampling of the population, but that 95% of the time the true population parameter would be contained in those different CIs.) This interval is quite wide! It shows that although the mean difference as a point estimate is 30, it could be as small as only 10 points of difference, or it could be as large as 50 points of difference. So now we know that there was an effect of our teaching, and we get a sense of how large the effect was from the range of numbers in the CI, and we also see how precise our estimate for the mean score. This CI shows us that the point estimate of M = 30 is not a very precise measurement. We do not really understand exactly how much effect the teaching had. If the true mean difference were only 10 points, we might think our five hours of teaching and practicing time was not very effective. So instead of hiding that lack of precision under one number (a mean score of 30), the CI lets us know that we should not have too much faith in it. However, we can be fairly confident that our teaching had some good effect, because we are 95% confident that our students will gain 10 points of improvement, at the very least.

Interpretation of a Confidence Interval

A plausible range of values for whatever parameter is being estimated, be it a mean score, a difference in mean scores, a correlation coefficient, or whatever. It is therefore an inferential statistic: it makes predictions about the entire population, based on the sample.

A visual representation of CIs can be helpful for readers to understand the results of a study. Below I contrast *p*-value information with CI information for data from a study by Lyster (2004). Lyster tested four groups that differed in the type of feedback they received on French grammatical errors. In one written test, he looked at what articles they assigned to nouns in a text. We want to know which groups did better than which other groups. We can first look at the results of **pairwise comparisons** between each group. A pairwise comparison is simply a statistical comparison between two groups. These comparisons are found in Table 4.1.

Table 4.1 Pairwise Comparisons between Four Conditions in Lyster (2004) on a Written Completion Task for Articles. (Score is Gain Score between Pretest and First Posttest, with 40 Points Possible on Test.)

Comparison	*Estimate of mean difference*	*Standard error*	*t-value*	*p-value*
FFIprompt–FFIrecast	5.20	1.06	4.91	<0.001
FFIonly–FFIrecast	−2.20	1.10	−2.01	0.19
Comparison–FFIrecast	−4.30	1.05	−4.10	<0.001
FFIonly–FFIprompt	−7.40	1.03	−7.19	<0.001
Comparison–FFIprompt	−9.50	0.98	−9.70	<0.001
Comparison–FFIonly	−2.10	1.02	−2.06	0.17

Table 4.1 shows that there were statistical differences (in other words, *p*-values below 0.05) for all pairs except for those between the "form-focused input (FFI) only" and the "FFI recast" group and also between the "FFI only" group and the control group (who did not receive any feedback). The same information, plus more, can be gleaned by looking at the 95% CIs of each of the comparisons in Figure 4.3.

In Figure 4.3, the comparisons where the line goes through zero are the non-statistical comparisons. Whether the difference is positive or negative does not matter much, as this just depends on which group gets subtracted from the other. However, all of the intervals are medium-sized, covering about five points each. This shows how much precision the estimates of mean differences given in Table 4.1 have. In other words, there is some wiggle room around those estimates. Also, the pairwise comparison between the "FFI prompt" and "Comparison" groups is farthest from zero, meaning it has the biggest effect size. (The estimate is nearly 10 points of difference, which may range from as little as 7 points of difference to as large as 12 points of difference.) Thus, statistical significance, estimate precision and effect size can all be gleaned quite quickly from CIs, especially if they are visually presented, as they are here. I used the plot(confint()) command associated with the glht procedure and the multcomp package (Hothorn, Bretz, & Westfall, 2008) from R to create the graphic. Remember that you can obtain a package in the R Console by typing install.packages("multcomp")).

Cumming (2012) also provides another view of CIs which he calls the "cat's eye picture." It shows the "plausibility for μ . . . for values within and beyond the CI" (p. 98). It is really just the sampling distribution of the mean scores (M) from a dance of the means. Figure 4.4 shows a dance of the CIs that we obtain for this distribution. I have set it up so that the samples are from a population with a mean $\mu = 50$ and SD $\sigma = 50$. I used Cumming's ESCI program, chapters 5–6, "CIs and replication" tab to obtain this picture.

The curve at the right-hand side of Figure 4.4 shows the relative likelihood that we would find a sample mean (M) at that point in the distribution. Thus, it shows that mean values closer to the

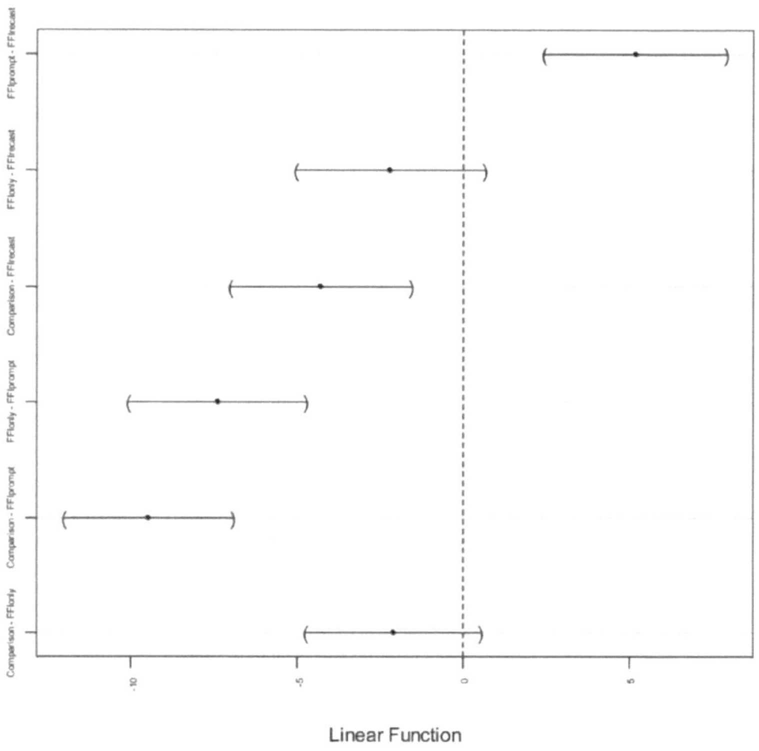

Figure 4.3 Visually representing 95% confidence intervals in pairwise comparisons on the Lyster (2004) data.

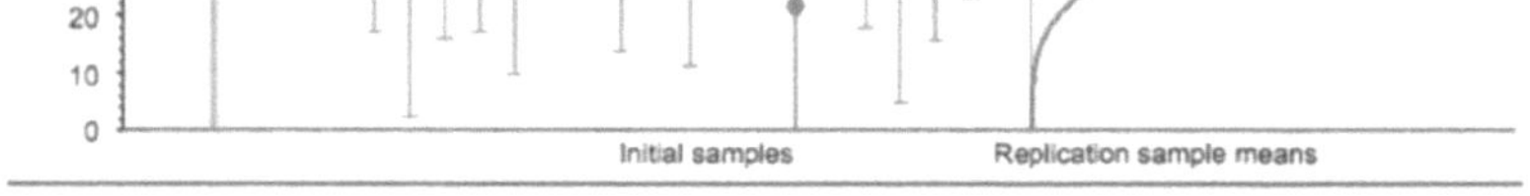

Figure 4.4 A dance of confidence intervals from a population with known μ =50 and σ =50. There is one interval outside the 95% confidence interval dotted lines (in red). The curve on the right is the normally distributed sampling distribution of M, shaded to include 95% of the sample means.

population mean μ (set at $\mu = 50$ in this simulation but in real life unknown) are more likely than those farther away from μ. The cat's eye picture simply takes this curve, creates a mirror image of it and centers it on M (the mean we get in our actual sampling). Figure 4.5 shows CIs of one specific sample taken from two independent groups and the corresponding cat's eye picture of each CI. (I made this image with Cumming's ESCI program, Windows version, chapters 5–6, "Compare A B" tab).

The fatness of the cat's eye shows the likelihood of values at that point. This means that values along the CI that are closer to M are more likely to be the true mean than values farther away from M. In other words, values for M that are closer to M are more plausible as the true mean than values which

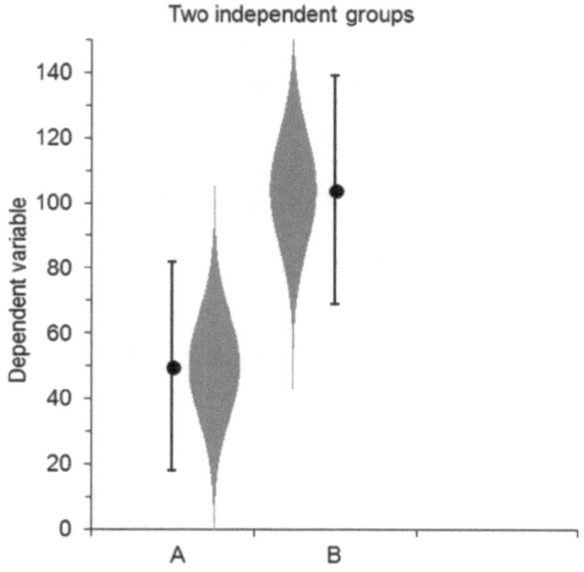

Figure 4.5 Confidence intervals of two groups and their corresponding cat's eye picture, with the fatness of the cat's eye showing the plausibility of values at each point on the confidence interval.

are farther away. Thus, when we are thinking about how to interpret confidence levels, we should keep the cat's eye picture in mind as it tells us that values close to the mean are more likely than those toward the farther end of the CI.

Beyond giving us inferential data about a sample we have collected, CIs are also a tool we can use as we think about studies as being part of a collection of knowledge about a topic. In other words, CIs nudge us to think about replication and meta-analysis of studies. This is because CIs can tell us something about what the likely result will be if a study is replicated. Remembering Figure 4.2, we understand that there is some relationship between all of the CIs that are generated from sampling the same population, even though the samples differ in their mean scores and CIs. In fact, there is an 83% chance that a mean score from a replication will fall within the 95% CI found in the original study (Cumming, 2012). To illustrate concretely, if someone replicated the Lyster (2004) study I have just looked at, there is an 83% chance that the mean difference they will find between the FFI prompt and Comparison groups will lie within the 95% CI generated from Lyster's same, which was [−5.4, −0.6]. And if we had a number of studies gathered into a meta-analysis, we can imagine that we could view a collection of CIs, as in Figure 4.2, helping us to more accurately pinpoint the true parameter value of the population (which, in that figure, we know, but in real life we do not!).

To summarize, CIs provide all of the information that can be gleaned from a *p*-value, plus several additional pieces of information: (1) an understanding of effect size in the original measurement; (2) an understanding of the precision of the estimate and how much confidence can be placed in the point estimate; (3) a range of values that is predictive (an 83% chance) of where the estimate, such as the mean, of subsequent replications of the study will lie. A CI can answer the real questions that we have as consumers of research, the questions mentioned at the beginning of this section—Was there was an effect? How large was the effect? To what extent is it practically important? Confidence intervals will get us closer to knowing what we want to know than *p*-values will.

I have argued in this section that CIs are much more informative than *p*-values. I have presented evidence that many experts think NHST is a flawed and even dangerous method to use. (I have not gone into the reasons why, but chapter 3 in Kline (2004) is a good place to start; you can download this chapter from www.apastyle.org/manual/related/kline-2004.pdf.) In addition, the *Publication Manual of the American Psychological Association* (APA), the style that most journals in the field use, gives the following recommendation about reporting CIs:

> The inclusion of confidence intervals (for estimates of parameters, for functions of parameters such as differences in means, and for effect sizes) can be an extremely effective way of reporting results. . . . Confidence intervals combine information on location and precision . . . they are, in general, the best reporting strategy. The use of confidence intervals is therefore strongly recommended. (APA, 2009, p. 34)

I recommend playing with Cumming's ESCI program, especially the "CIjumping tab", to watch the dance of the means, the dance of the CIs and the mean heap as ways to deduce how samples correspond to the actual parameters found in the population. I also wholeheartedly recommend reading Cumming (2012), if you can possibly find time to do so. I am summarizing some of his ideas here but the original is well worth reading.

For all these reasons, in this book I will largely refrain from using the NHST process and instead report and explain CIs when giving the results from studies. My hope is to help hasten along a change that I believe is in the best interests of our entire field.

4.1.3 Application Activities with Confidence Intervals

1. Larson-Hall (2008) examined scores on three tests by two groups of Japanese learners of English—those who studied English before age 12, and those who began their study of English at age 12 when it is compulsory in Japan. Please look at the CIs for the mean differences between the two groups on each of the three tests and answer the questions that follow. (Confidence intervals have been changed slightly for teaching purposes.)

    a. Aptitude test (37 points possible): (−1.57, 0.99)
    b. Grammaticality judgment test (200 points possible): (−5.62, 0.76)
    c. Phonemic discrimination task (96 points possible): (−10.8, −0.001)

    Is there an effect of group for any of the tests? How large is the effect? (Interpret this subjectively.) To what extent do you think having Japanese learners of English start their study before age 12 has a practical effect on any of the linguistic areas tested?
2. Ellis and Yuan (2004), which will be examined in more detail in Chapter 10, looked at the complexity and accuracy of written language produced by three groups who differed in the amount of time they had available to perform the task. Please look at Figure 4.6 for the mean differences between pairs of groups on the number of disfluencies (word crossed out and reformulated in the writing) in the groups' production and answer these questions: Is there an effect of group for any of the tests? How large is the effect? (Interpret this subjectively, bearing in mind that the mean number of disfluencies for the groups was around 0.05.) I am not explaining the exact procedure followed for each group here, but to what extent do you think having differing levels of time to perform the task had a practical effect on this particular linguistic measurement of disfluencies?
3. Chapter 6 features data from DeKeyser (2000) and Flege, Yeni-Komshian, and Liu (1999), where both studies used correlations. Consider the differences between these ways of reporting correlations, one using the old statistics (with *p*-values) and the other the new statistics. What do the CIs tell you that *p*-values cannot? In both cases, think of the *r*-value (which is the estimate that the 95% CI is giving) as a measure of the strength of the relationship, where $r = 0.50$ may be considered a strong relationship.

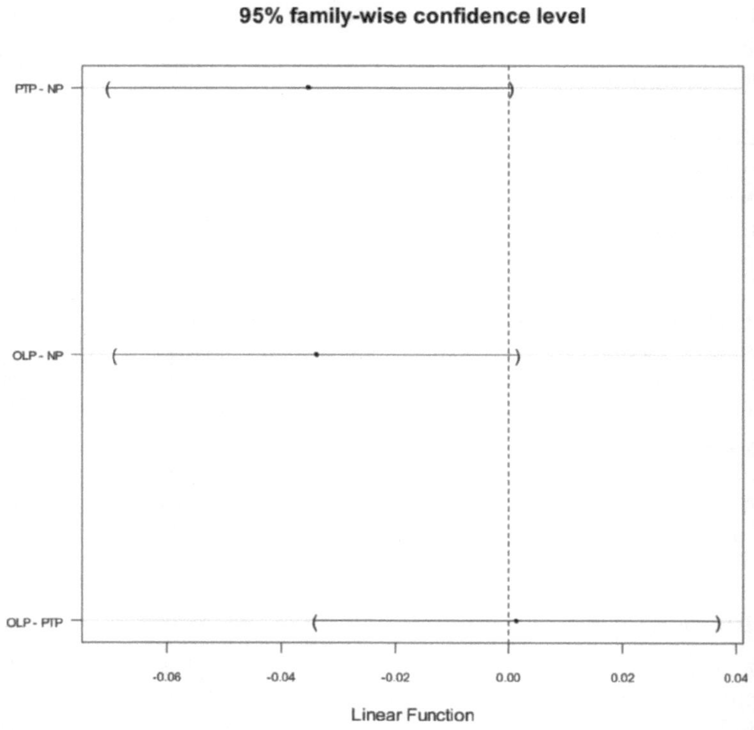

Figure 4.6 Ellis and Yuan's (2004) groups compared visually using 95% confidence intervals.

Variant 1a: DeKeyser (2000) found a statistical correlation between age of arrival and scores on the grammaticality judgment test ($r = -0.62$, $n = 57$, $p < 0.001$).

Variant 1b: Flege, Yeni-Komshian, and Liu (1999) found a statistical correlation between age of arrival and pronunciation scores ($r = -0.89$, $n = 264$, $p < 0.001$).

Variant 2a: DeKeyser (2000) found a statistical correlation between age of arrival and scores on the grammaticality judgment test (95% CI: −0.76, −0.42).

Variant 2b: Flege, Yeni-Komshian, and Liu (1999) found a statistical correlation between age of arrival and pronunciation scores (95% CI: −0.92, −0.87).

4 Poehner and Lantolf (2013) is a study that looked at how mediation, given as hints for understanding a listening comprehension passage on the computer, helped English-speaking learners of Chinese improve on the test. In this study, the author compared the results of the actual score on the test with the mediated score on the test to see whether the use of mediation was effective in helping Chinese learners improve their listening comprehension. Look at Figure 4.7. This figure is a bit complex at first, but when you understand it you will see it is elegant and beautiful, containing all of the data from the study plus the summarizing CIs. I created it using ESCI chapters 5–6, "Data Paired" tab. The data from 14 participants for the Actual scores on the test and their Mediated scores are represented by the dots and the lines connecting the two tests together for each individual. To the left of the dots there is a CI on the mean score of the Actual test, and to the right of the dots there is a CI about the mean of the Mediated test. Both tests had a maximum possible score of 76 points. Above the area labeled "Difference," the triangles represent the gain scores (the difference between the Actual and Mediated tests) for each individual and the CI to the farthest right is the 95% CI of

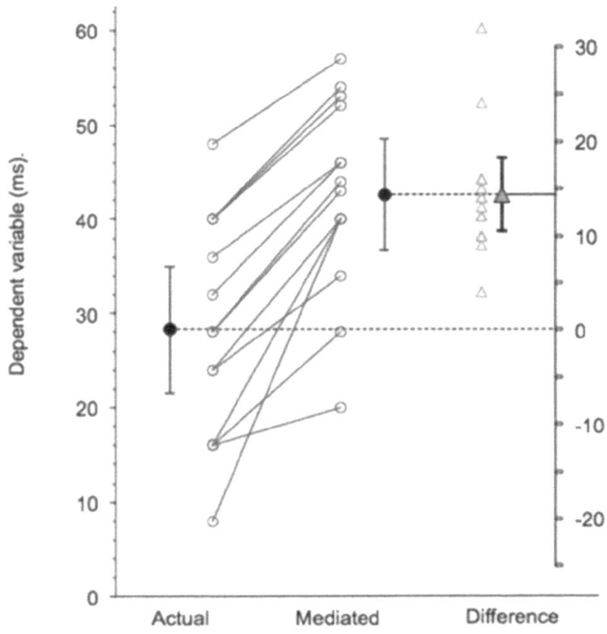

Figure 4.7 Data from Poehner and Lantolf (2013) showing improvements on a Chinese listening test when mediation was used.

the difference between the means, which is 95% CI [10.4, 18.3]. Considering the CI of the difference between the means, answer the question of whether there was an effect of mediation, how large the effect was and to what extent mediation was practically important for helping learners improve.

4.1.4 Confidence Intervals and the Imprecision of P-Values

When you first see CIs, you may feel that they are rather imprecise. Instead of giving you one nice number, like a mean score, a SD or a *p*-value, they give a range of plausible values for a parameter. Some readers may feel that *p*-values are better since you can make a black-and-white decision about the efficacy of a treatment instead of thinking that there is a range of possible answers.

In trying to implement a change to the new statistics, a change in thinking—from believing answers are black-and-white and there is no variation to understanding that there is variability inherent in any measurement—is desirable. I have noted that we could indeed use CIs to answer the same question as we use NHST thinking to answer, which is "Is there an effect?" for some treatment, or "Is there a relationship?" between some variables. But the new statistics claims that such thinking is not only inadequate (we want to go beyond simply asking if there is an effect to asking how large the effect is and how practically important it is), but that precise point values such as mean scores, *p*-values and even effect sizes have hidden from us the variability that has always been inherent in such measurements.

One of the most surprising facts Cumming (2012) brings out about *p*-values is that they are highly variable! We know there is sampling variability in mean scores and CIs. Remember Figure 4.2, where when we sampled from a distribution with a known mean and SD, we got different mean scores and different CIs for each sample. There is also sampling variability in *p*-values. In other words, if we took samples from a distribution with a known mean and SD, we could calculate a *p*-value for each sample, and this would give us a sampling distribution of *p*-values. The problem is that the sampling variability of *p*-values is quite large! We cannot calculate a CI for *p*-values (there is no population parameter that corresponds to *p*), but Cumming (2008) calculates *p* intervals. These are the prediction intervals for replication p. Cumming says that if we had a test where $p = 0.05$ in a two-tailed experiment, an 80% p-interval would range from 0 to 0.38, meaning "there's an 80% chance that a replication experiment gives two-tailed p somewhere between 0 and 0.38, and a fully 20% chance that p is greater than 0.38" (p. 132). If we increased the p-interval to 95%, the interval would be (0, 0.82). In other words, whatever p-value you get in an experiment, there is a high probability that it could have been completely different in another sampling of that same population.

Figure 4.8 shows what p-value is obtained in a simulated experiment with $N = 32$ in each of a control group and an experimental group. Power (this is the power to find a statistically significant result, meaning the p-value is less than 0.05) is set to 0.52, because this is similar to the average power in NHST disciplines like psychology (see Cohen, 1962, and Maxwell, 2004). In this case, the population mean and SD are known, and we draw random samples from this population to simulate an actual experiment. In each iteration of this experiment, a p-value is calculated for the difference between groups. The dots and lines in the middle of the figure show the dance of the CIs on the mean difference (the mean of the Control group is $\mu = 50$ while the mean of the Experimental group is $\mu = 60$, so the mean difference between groups is 10 points). The numbers to the left side of the figure show the p-value for each sampling from the population. They are marked in a very conventional way with one star for values less than $p = 0.05$, two stars for values less than $p = 0.01$ and three stars for values less than $p = 0.001$. A question mark is placed by values between 0.05 and 0.10, meaning a researcher might argue for the importance of such a result. The column labeled "Dance of the p-values" on the right shows little figures, which Cumming (2012) uses to indicate just how randomly the results are found. (He calls them "casino" figures, since as this simulation shows, "[o]btaining low p is a bit like winning a prize at a casino" (p. 137).) He speculates that a value of $p > 0.10$ might invoke deep sadness, as evinced by the crying figure under that column, while a p-value of less than 0.001 calls for celebration, as depicted by the joyful figure on the far right. If you are interested in trying the "dance of the p-values" yourself, I highly recommend trying the ESCI page, chapters 5–6, "Dance p" tab. There is also an entertaining video called "Dance p" at Cumming's website (under Videos), www.latrobe.edu.au/psy/research/cognitive-and-developmental-psychology/esci, which shows the program running and is accompanied by sounds for each result. (You can also access it directly in YouTube—just search for "statistics dance p.")

Figure 4.8 shows that the p-value is highly variable with each new sample, but the CI is not; the CI is in fact a much more accurate representation of the actual effect of each experiment. You can see that the mean scores and CIs fall within a much narrower range than the range of p-values that are found; the p-interval ranges from 0.001 to 0.974 while nearly all the CIs contain the 10-point mean difference in their range. We can conclude that the results of p-value testing are highly unreliable and that we cannot trust p! Cumming (2012) says he never worries about the difference between

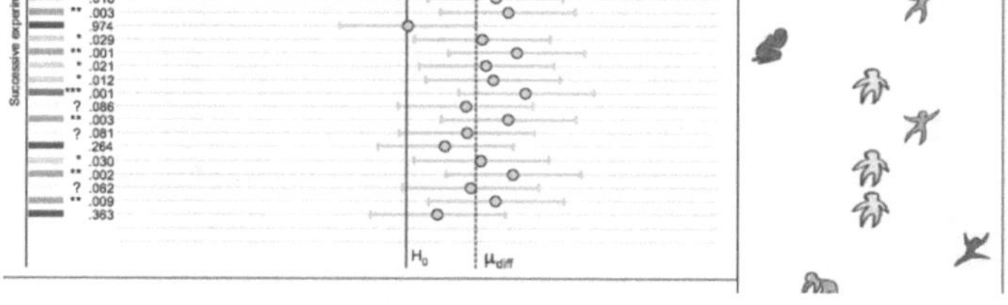

Figure 4.8 Dance of the p-values in an experiment comparing two independent groups, from Cumming's (2012) ESCI program.

$p = 0.03$ and $p = 0.08$, and that only very small *p*-values ($p < 0.001$) "give a reasonable basis for rejecting a null hypothesis" (pp. 134–135). However, he says that in such cases where the *p*-value is so small (< 0.001), the effect will be so large that it should be obvious without any actual statistical testing!

The point of this discussion then, is that although using CIs instead of NHST may feel at first like we are trading precision for imprecision, we are not. We actually get more precision with CIs than with *p*-values, along with more information about the current experiment as well as future ones.

Actually, the word *precision* can be defined in a more accurate way as well. The precision of a CI is one half of the width of the CI, which you may remember is called the MOE. By the way, you might feel you understand the MOE better if you think about hearing the results of a political poll reported. You will often hear something like "Candidate A leads Candidate B by 7 points, with a margin of error of plus or minus 3 points." That margin of error is the same MOE we are talking about! When you hear such a report you understand that although Candidate A is leading by 7 points, the lead might be as small as 4 points or as large as 10 points—there is wiggle room there, and Candidate B need not feel that all is lost quite yet.

The more precise a CI is, the smaller the MOE will be. In my political example, if you heard that the results from this poll had a margin of error of ± 0.01, you would feel more justified in thinking that Candidate B might not be able to make up this difference, as the true difference between the candidates seemed very settled around 7 points. It might at first sound counterintuitive that *increasing* the precision gives smaller MOEs, but you can see that the shorter the CI, the more precisely we are able to pinpoint the true effect of an experiment. Cumming (2012) states that precision contributes to the informativeness of an experiment. A CI that is less precise is less informative—we do not have as good an idea as we might like as to where the true parameter can be found.

How Can Precision be Increased?

- Increase sample size.
- Include repeated measures—either over time, over related types of tests or averaging the results of multiple tests.
- Use measures that have better reliability and validity.

4.1.5 Application Activities with Confidence Intervals and Precision

Look back at the application activities in Section 4.1.1 and answer the following questions about each item.

1 Larson-Hall (2008): What is the MOE of each CI for each of the three linguistic tests? Does this seem precise to you, given what you know about the total number of possible points? In other words, do you feel satisfied that you understand the real effect each test had?
2 Ellis and Yuan (2004). Looking at Figure 4.5, what is the approximate MOE of the CI for the comparison between the OLP and PTP groups? Just eyeballing, do the other group comparisons have a MOE similar to this? Does this MOE seem precise to you, given that this measurement is a count of disfluencies, and so has no fixed limit? In other words, do you feel satisfied you understand the real effect each test had?
3 What is the MOE for the DeKeyser (2000) CI? What is the MOE for the Flege, Yeni-Komshian, and Liu (1999) CI? Which is more precise? Why do you think that one is more precise?
4 What is the MOE of the CI in the Poehner & Lantolf (2013) study? Does this seem precise to you, knowing how many points are possible in the test? In other words, do you feel satisfied you understand the real effect of the test?

4.2 Introduction to Effect Sizes

Up to this point I have talked about effect sizes without defining them. I have stated that CIs provide a way to judge the size of the effect of a study using the original measurement, and in the application activity for CIs (Section 4.1.2) you made some judgments about the size of effects of studies. Now, it is time to define effect sizes more formally. The effect sizes we saw in CIs are done in original measurements, but there are also standardized effect sizes that are used to compare results across studies, and there are also some guidelines that could help you think about how big your effect is.

Effect sizes, whether the ones we see in CIs or in standardized form, are what Murphy and Myors (2004, p. 106) call "the most important parameter of all." In general an effect size is "the magnitude of the impact" (Kline, 2004, p. 97) of the independent variable on the dependent variable or of the relationship between variables. Effect size gives researchers the information that they may have thought they were getting from the NHST, which is whether the difference between groups or the association between variables is important or negligible. If the effect size is quite small, then it may make sense to simply discount the findings as practically unimportant (even if, in the old statistics terms, they were "statistically significant," meaning the *p*-value of the statistical test was less than 0.05). If the effect size is large, then the researcher has found something that it is important to understand.

Effect sizes do not change no matter how many participants there are (Maxwell & Delaney, 2004, p. 100). This makes effect sizes a valuable piece of information for answering the questions that research readers want to know, such as whether there was an effect, how big it was and how practically important it is (much more valuable than the old statistics question of whether a statistical test is simply "significant" or not). Effect sizes are also useful to those who are doing meta-analysis. Currently, several second language research journals require that authors report effect sizes, including *Language Learning*, *Language Learning & Technology*, *The Modern Language Journal* and *TESOL Quarterly*. This is a welcome advancement. As Larson-Hall and Plonsky (2015) have noted, "Every society which has produced recommendations with regard to statistics reporting practices has insisted that emphasis should be taken off of dichotomous *p*-value considerations of inferential statistical results, and that the focus instead should be on effect sizes and confidence intervals" (p. 132).

Indeed, any journal that uses APA format should expect authors to report effect sizes, as the *APA Publication Manual* (2009) clearly states the importance of doing so:

> For the reader to appreciate the magnitude or importance of a study's finding, it is almost always necessary to include some measure of effect size. . . . Effect sizes may be expressed in the original units (e.g., the mean number of questions answered correctly; kg/month for a regression slope) and are often most easily understood when reported in original units. It can often be valuable to report an effect size not only in original units but also in some standardized or units-free unit (e.g., as a Cohen's *d* value) or a standardized regression weight. (p. 34)

Although I am trying in this textbook to take the focus off the old statistics, with NHST and *p*-values, I also realize readers will be mostly surrounded by previous articles that do not yet use the new statistics. So I want to illustrate the difference between statistical significance and effect sizes with fictional data (idea taken from "Primer on statistical significance and *p*-values" available from http://ecp.acponline.org/julaug01/primer.pdf). Table 4.2 shows that a study with a resulting *p*-value of $p = 0.08$ might have much more practical significance than one whose *p*-value was $p = 0.003$. This is because the first study had only 10 participants but was still able to find a large effect size (here looking at effect size as simply the difference between means and not worrying about standardizing it yet). This means that teaching method A is very promising for increasing grammatical accuracy on a cloze test, but it lacked the power to find a lower *p*-value because of the small sample sizes. On the other hand, the study with 1000 participants did find a statistical difference between groups but the actual difference was quite small and probably not worth changing grammar teaching methods for.

In the same way, we can find articles that report results where the *p*-value is larger than 0.05, but the effect size shows that we have every reason to take notice of the result and not ignore it. For example, Poehner and Lantolf (2013) reported on a correlation between how much learners improved by receiving mediation (in the form of hints while they were taking a computer-administered test) and how well they performed on transfer items on a subsequent test of their ability. They reported that "significant low to moderate correlation coefficients . . . were obtained for the Chinese reading (r =.301, p < .01) . . . tests but not for the French reading test (r =.337, ns [not significant, meaning p-value over 0.05])" (p. 336). If we look at the size of the effect, found in the r-value, however, the effect was actually slightly higher for the French reading test than for the Chinese reading test. Why was the test statistically significant (p-value under 0.05) for the Chinese reading test but not the French one? Simply put, it was the size of the groups! There were 80 participants in the Chinese reading test but only 21 in the French group. Effect size does not take group size into account but p-values do, and here we see that the result for the French group is just as legitimate as the one for the Chinese group, despite the higher p-value for the French. I would advise authors to ignore the p-values and focus on the effect sizes as the more trustworthy and informative measure.

Table 4.2 An Illustration of the Importance of Effect Size

n, each group	*Change in accuracy on cloze test for grammar*		*Main effect*	*p-value*	*Appropriate conclusion*
	Teaching method A	*Teaching method B*			
10	25 points	5 points	20 points	.08	Not statistical at an α=.05 level, but promising
1,000	6 points	4 points	2 points	.003	Statistical but unimportant in practice

I do not want to imply that small effect sizes are never worth taking notice of, however. At times, something with a small effect size may be important for advancing our understanding. Rosenthal (1990, cited in Breaugh, 2003) noted that the correlation found between taking aspirin and having a reduced chance of heart attacks was based on a study that found a correlation of 0.03 (a small effect, by the standards I will present later).

What I want to emphasize is that *all* effect sizes should be reported, not just large ones. However, if CIs are given, standardized effect sizes do not strictly need to be reported—the choice will be up to the researcher. Again, the *APA Publication Manual* states that researchers should "mention all relevant results, including those that run counter to expectation; be sure to include small effect sizes (or statistically nonsignificant findings)" (2009, p. 32). Meta-analyses, which can only be conducted on studies for which effect sizes are reported or can be calculated, have found that a depressingly low percentage of journal articles report effect sizes (see Larson-Hall & Plonsky, 2015, figure 2). For example, Plonsky (2013), who surveyed 606 articles in the journals *Language Learning* and *Studies in Second Language Acquisition*, found that only 26% of the surveyed articles had effect sizes reported at all, and some of those articles only reported effect sizes for statistically significant results.

4.2.1 Understanding Effect Size Measures

Huberty (2002) divided effect sizes into two broad families—group difference indexes and relationship indexes—although it is important to note that in most cases there are algebraic calculations that can transform one kind into the other (Breaugh, 2003), and there are other kinds of effect sizes that do not fit into these categories, like **odds ratios** (Rosenthal & DiMatteo, 2001). Even mean scores can be considered a type of effect size measure according to Cumming (2012), since they answer the question of "how much?". Both group difference and relationship effect sizes are ways to provide a standardized measure of the strength of the effect that is found.

A **group difference index**, or mean difference measure, has been called the ***d*-family of effect sizes** by Rosenthal (1994). The prototypical effect size measure in this family is **Cohen's *d***. Cohen's d measures the difference between two independent sample means, and expresses how large the difference is in SDs. Therefore, if Cohen's $d = 1$, the two means differ by one SD. This means that the value of *d* can be higher than 1. Other group difference index measures include **Cohen's f^2** and Hedges' *g*. (This is similar to Cohen's *d* but adjusts for sample size.)

Relationship indexes, also called the ***r*-family of effect sizes** (Rosenthal, 1994), measure how much an independent and dependent variable vary together or, in other words, the amount of covariation in the two variables. The more closely the two variables are related, the higher the effect size. So, for example, the relationship between height and weight among adults is quite closely related, and would have a high *r*-value. Squared indices of *r* (R^2) and related quantities such as eta-squared (η^2), omega-squared (ω^2), partial eta-squared and partial omega-squared are also measures of association, but because they are squared they lack directionality (Rosenthal & DiMatteo, 2001). These squared measures indicate "the observed proportion of explained variance" (Kline, 2004, p. 100), and I will often call them percentage variance (PV) effect sizes in this book.

You may wonder which kind of effect size measure to use, the group difference or relationship effect size. In fact, either one can be used, and can even be easily converted into the other, but some effect sizes seem to be more associated with some statistical tests than others. For example, relationship indexes are almost always used with correlations or regression analysis. Olejnik and Algina (2000) note that relationship indexes may seem easier to understand because they vary between the fixed values of 0 and 1, unlike group difference indexes, which may go above 1. On the other hand, tests of group differences often use Cohen's *d* and you may be used to seeing this effect size by now so that if a PV effect size were used in a *t*-test it would seem quite strange. Thus, there is no overarching recommendation on which one type to use.

4.2.2 Interpreting Effect Sizes

The advice of statistical experts is that effect size is an important measurement and should be included in your research reports. I have stated that effect sizes answer the question of how large the effect was, and using them a researcher can make an estimation of how much of a practical significance any result has. So let us suppose you have now calculated your standardized effect sizes and included them in your research paper. You clearly need to also discuss the size of the effect. But this part is not straightforward or formulaic. Your conclusion of how large the effect size is can depend on a number of things. If other studies in your area have also included effect sizes, you can compare your effect with theirs. This comparison can help you see how large your effect is.

But in some cases you may not know much about effect sizes for other comparable research. In these cases, you could use guidelines first put forward by Jacob Cohen (1988), which are given in the tables in the following section. Cohen (1988) noted that effect sizes are likely to be small when one is undertaking research in an area that has been little studied, as researchers may not yet know what kinds of variables they need to control for. Cohen admitted that his proposed effect size magnitudes are subjective and based on his experience with the literature in the behavioral sciences. Still, he does have some general explanations for the guideline magnitudes. A small effect size is one that is not visible to the naked eye but exists nevertheless. Cohen (1988) stated this would be equal to the difference in IQ between siblings who were twins and non-twins. A medium effect is one that is visible to the naked eye or apparent to the observer, and would be equivalent to the difference in IQ between clerical and semiskilled workers. Lastly, a large effect is one that would be "grossly perceptible" (p. 27) and correspond to the difference in IQ between typical college freshmen and persons holding PhDs.

When one understands the reasoning behind Cohen's proposed magnitude sizes, one also understands that there is no imaginary line which would label a $d = 0.49$ a medium effect while $d = 0.51$ would be labeled a large effect. Cohen also noted that effect size magnitudes depend on the area, so that what may be a small effect size in one area may in fact be a rather large effect size in another area. The last thing advocates of effect sizes would like to see is effect sizes used as dichotomously as *p*-values!

Plonsky and Oswald (2014) found Cohen's guidelines somewhat too lenient for effect sizes in the SLA field. They analyzed a large number of SLA studies and then divided the effect sizes observed in published papers into the 25th, 50th and 75th percentile, labeling them as small, medium and large effects, respectively. I recommend these guidelines as a better starting point for SLA studies than Cohen's guidelines, but in the end, what Cohen as well as Plonsky and Oswald would like to see is researchers thinking for themselves about what their effect sizes mean. More comparison to effect sizes from other studies will help researchers come to their own conclusions about how big their observed effects are, and help the researcher make practical recommendations.

But one really important point to understand is that effect size need not be interpreted given these guidelines at all! For example, if some language learners are able to improve their use of the past tense by five points on a 60-point test, and the Cohen's d effect size for this is $d = 0.32$, this could be described as a small effect by Cohen's or Plonsky and Oswald's guidelines, but you may note that this increase in grammatical ability came after only 1 hour of use of your innovative computer program, and thus conclude that given the amount of time of the intervention and the low cost of using it (it is free on the Web) that the effect is rather impressive and could be called large.

Figure 4.9 shows one concrete example of how interpretation of results should differ if we move from a focus on dichotomous results to the new statistics. In Section 4.1.1, exercise #1 looked at my own 2008 study. Figure 4.9 compares how I reported the results in the published study to how I would report them now. (I *have* learned some stuff by writing a statistics textbook, after all!)

Note that in my "new statistics" report, I do not mention the t-test result nor p-values, but I answer all of the questions about the results that readers really want to know—whether there is an effect, how large the effect is and whether it has practical importance.

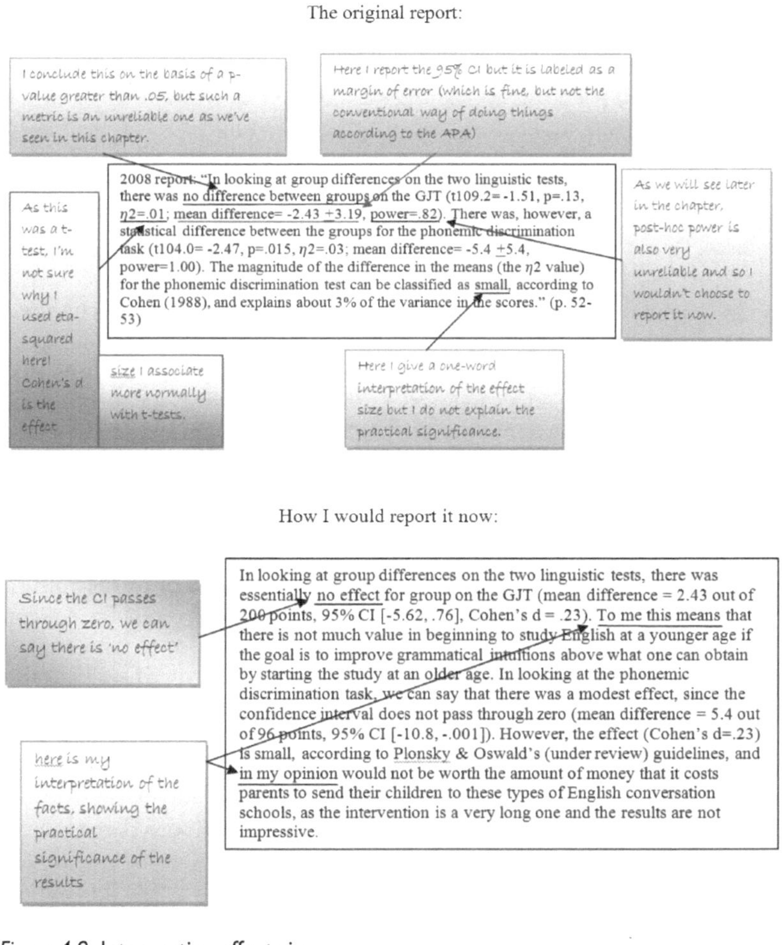

Figure 4.9 Interpreting effect sizes.

4.2.3 Calculating Effect Sizes Summary

In Part II of this book, I will provide information on how to calculate effect sizes for each statistical procedure as they are presented. In this chapter, however, I include a summary of effect sizes for each of the procedures outlined in this book. I imagine this section as more of a resource than something you will read through carefully all at one time.

In general, statistical tests that include a categorical variable that divides the sample into groups, such as the *t*-test or the analysis of variance (ANOVA), use the *d*-family of effect sizes to measure effect size. The basic idea of effect sizes in the *d*-family is to look at the difference between the means of two groups, as in $\mu A - \mu B$. However, if we just look at the mean difference, the scale of this effect will be different in every experiment. Therefore, we divide the mean difference by a standardizer, resulting in the basic formula $d = \frac{M_2 - M_1}{s}$, where M = the mean scores of the two groups and *s* = the standardizer. Olejnik and Algina (2000, p. 245) noted that there are at least three alternative methods for computing standardizers, which I have listed in Table 4.3. Cumming (2012) noted that Cohen's *d* values are not really interpretable unless you have stated *how* you calculated the *d*; in other words, you should clearly state in your report which of the standardizers you used in your calculation because the choice of standardizer affects the effect size, as we shall see.

Because choosing the standardizer (which is the SD) for the Cohen's *d* equation is not straightforward, I will explain here a little more about how to choose the best standardizer. However, note that the best standardizer can only be based on your own assessment of the situation, so that is why you should note in your report which standardizer you chose. Now, if you actually knew the true SD (σ) of the population, you would use that! But in reality you probably will not, so what is important is to understand the concept of the standardizer. If the variances of the groups being compared are equal (if you assume homogeneity of variances) then the pooled SD from the groups being compared (choice B from Table 4.3) or the pooled SD from all of the groups in the study (choice C, if you have more than two groups and you think they all have equal variances) would be the best one. However, in many cases in the field, we have a native speaker (NS) group versus a language learner group. In that case, most often variances will not be the same, and we will probably want to use the SD of just one group (choice A from Table 4.3) and have to think about which group we want to frame the effects in terms of.

Remember that Cohen's *d* expresses how large the difference between two groups is in SDs. Because you are dividing by the standardizer, the smaller the denominator (the standardizer), the larger the effect will be. So let us say you have two groups, a learner group and a NS group. The learners have an average mean of M = 120 and *s* = 40 on a grammaticality judgment test. The NS have an average M = 190, *s* = 10. The NS have performed much better and have much less variance in their performance. If we calculate Cohen's *d*, the effect size of the difference between groups, using the NS SD of *s* = 10, *d* = (190–120)/10 = 7, an extremely large effect size. However, if we calculate the effect size using the learners' *s* = 40, now *d* = (190–120)/40 = 1.75. This is still quite large, but obviously much smaller than the first calculation. So if we want to frame the effect in terms of how much better the NS are than the learners, and frame it in terms of the SD of the NS, we could say that *d* = 7.0. On the other hand, if we want to say how different the language learners are from NS and frame it in terms of the SD of the language learners (to me it seems this is the more likely thing a typical researcher would want to do), it is a smaller effect since the SD of the language learners is so much larger, and *d* = 1.75.

If we had a situation where we performed an experimental manipulation, such as teaching a certain type of mnemonic skill for learning vocabulary to one group, used a computer program for learning vocabulary to another group, and had a language learner control group, we might want to use the control group's SD as the standardizer. Then we would be using effect sizes that considered the control group's variance as the norm against which to compare change. Again, I emphasize that this is why when you report effect sizes you need to *tell the reader what standardizer you used* because the effect size could be different if the standardizer were different. Cumming (2012) suggested that "it's vital to think of *d* as a ratio whose value depends on both the numerator and denominator" (p. 288). Cumming further suggested that while the most common choice for the standardizer is the pooled SD (for the formula, see below), and combining SDs results in more precision since it includes a higher number of participants, the choice of the control group as the standardizer is a good choice if you think the homogeneity of variances assumption is not satisfied.

Note that effect size calculators available online may differ in which standardizer they use. Two that I recommended in Larson-Hall (2013) are www.uccs.edu/~lbecker/ and www.cognitiveflexibility.org/effectsize/. The first website uses the pooled SD while the second can use a control SD if only one SD is entered, but if two SDs are entered it uses the average of the two SDs (not the pooled SD as might be expected; justification for this choice is given on the website).

Table 4.3 Options for Computing Standardizers (the Denominator for *d*-Family Effect Sizes)

A	The standard deviation of one of the groups, perhaps most typically the control group
B	The pooled standard deviation of [only the groups] being compared
C	The pooled standard deviation [of all the groups] in the design

For option C, the formula to derive the pooled SD with any number of groups is:
$S_{pooled} = \sqrt{\frac{(n_1 - 1)S_1^2 + \ldots + (n_J - 1)S_J^2}{(n_1 - 1) + \ldots + (n_J - 1)}}$ where S_J = the SD of the *j*th group, and n_J = the number of participants or items in the *j*th group, and the formula for S_{pooled} with just two groups is:
$S_{pooled} = \frac{SS_{within}}{df_{within}} = \sqrt{\frac{(n_1 - 1)S_1^2 + (n_2 - 1)S_2^2}{n_1 + n_2 - 2}}$.

Table 4.4 contains a summary of the most useful formulas to use for the *d*-family of effect sizes. If *d*-family effect sizes are not normally used with certain statistical tests, I give a conversion from the *r*-family to the *d*-family. For example, Olejnik and Algina (2000) recommend *r*-family statistics for omnibus results of ANOVA tests, and these can be obtained as partial eta-squared statistics (*r*-family effect sizes) through computer output. If one wanted to, however, these could then be converted into *d*-family statistics and the conversion formula is given in Table 4.4 under the "One-way ANOVA" heading.

Note that the statistical tests in Table 4.4 do not go beyond one-way ANOVAs. Explanations for how to compute effect sizes for more complex kinds of ANOVA using *d*-family statistics are beyond the scope of this book. (Interested readers should consult Cohen, 1988; Grissom & Kim, 2005; and Olejnik & Algina, 2000.) In any case, it is probably better to stick with the most basic effect sizes that people understand the best, such as Cohen's *d* or *r*-values. In the first edition of this book, I did not make any recommendations for which effect sizes to use but at this point I think that the simplest effect sizes are the most effective at conveying information that readers will understand. So, for example, if you have a complex ANOVA design, I think the best effect sizes would be those at the very lowest level, between two groups, where you could use a Cohen's *d* effect size.

Table 4.5 summarizes effect size calculations for the *r*-family. In statistical tests that deal with continuous variables, such as correlation or regression, the *r*-family of effect sizes are generally used. If *d*-family effect sizes are more commonly used with a particular test, conversion formulas are given. Although *r* and R^2 are most commonly used with correlation and regression, indexes that are related to *r* are also used quite frequently for ANOVA designs. These are eta-squared (η^2), omega-squared (ω^2) and partial eta-squared. Maxwell and Delaney (2004) explained that eta-squared is a proportion that "indicates how much knowledge of group membership improves prediction of the dependent variable" (p. 104). Kline (2004, p. 100) explained that eta-squared is "the proportion of total population

Table 4.4 Calculation of *d*-Family of Effect Sizes

	d-family	*Cohen's guidelines*	*Plonsky and Oswald's guidelines*
t-test (one-sample)	$d = \frac{\overline{X}_{sample} - \mu}{S_{sample}}$, where μ = the known mean (Weinberg & Abramowitz, 2002)		
t-test (independent samples)	$d = \frac{\overline{X}_1 - \overline{X}_2}{\sigma}$ where $\overline{X}_k$ = the mean of group k, and σ = the appropriate standardizer from table 4.3 A shortcut: $d = \frac{2t}{\sqrt{df_{err}}}$, where t = the *t*-test statistic and df_{err} = degrees of freedom for the *t*-test (Murphy & Myors, 2004)	$d = 0.2$ (small) $d = 0.5$ (medium) $d = 0.8$ (large)	$d = 0.4$ (small) $d = 0.7$ (medium) $d = 1.0$ (large)
t-test (paired samples)	$d_{paired} = \frac{\overline{X}_1 - \overline{X}_2}{\sqrt{2}(S_1 - S_2)}$ (Volker, 2006) where S_k = the standard deviation of group k	$d = 0.2$ (small) $d = 0.5$ (medium) $d = 0.8$ (large)	$d = 0.6$ (small) $d = 1.0$ (medium) $d = 1.5$ (large)
one-way ANOVA	$f = \frac{\sqrt{\frac{\Sigma\left(\overline{X}_i - \overline{X}_{grand}\right)^2}{k-1}}}{\sqrt{MS_{within}}}$ where $\overline{X}_i$ = mean of each group, $\overline{X}_{grand}$ = grand mean or average of all of the individual group means, k = number of means or groups, and MS_{within} is the within-group sum of squares divided by the within-group degrees of freedom (the number found in an ANOVA table). This formula should only be used when group sizes are equal (Volker, 2006). Cohen's f^2 can be calculated in an easier way by using the ANOVA *F*-value and the degrees of freedom: $f^2 = \frac{(df_{hyp} \times F)}{df_{err}}$ or eta-squared: $f^2 = \frac{\eta^2}{1-\eta^2}$ (Murphy & Myors, 2004)	$f = 0.10$ (small) $f = 0.25$ (medium) $f = 0.40$ (large)	
contrasts instead of omnibus ANOVA	Insert the appropriate mean estimates into the numerator of the effect size *d* equation. For example, to compare the average of Groups A & B with Group C, the numerator will be: $\frac{1}{2}\left(\overline{X}_{GroupA} + \overline{X}_{GroupB}\right) - \overline{X}_{GroupC}$ For the denominator, we consider whether variances are equal (in which case, use the pooled SD across groups) or not (in which case, choose which one SD will be considered the control group's SD) (Volker, 2006).		
post-hoc contrasts (after ANOVA)	In a post-hoc contrast, there are only two groups, so matters proceed as outlined above for independent samples *t*-tests		
correlation	Normally, correlation effect size is reported in *r*, but to convert this to *d*: $d = \frac{2r}{\sqrt{1-r^2}}$ (Murphy & Myors, 2004)		

variance accounted for by an effect of interest when all factors are fixed." However, research by Pierce, Block, and Aguinis (2004) noted that eta-squared (η^2), an effect size that is often used by researchers in the field to report effect sizes, is biased compared to omega-squared (ω^2), especially when sample sizes are small. To make matters worse, partial eta-squared, which is the effect size that is produced automatically with SPSS reports of ANOVA results, overinflated the effect in published studies that these authors examined by at least 78% to as much as 143%. Partial eta-squared (found in SPSS computer output and, until SPSS version 11.0, mislabeled as "eta-squared") according to Pierce, Block, and Aguinis (2004) is used when there is more than one factor in the ANOVA design, and it gives a measure of the effect of the factor of interest when other factors in the design are controlled. Kline (2004) stated that partial eta-squared (and partial omega-squared) removes the variance of other factors that are not currently of interest from the calculation. Partial eta-squared, unlike the classical eta-squared statistic, can add up to more than 1, so it is important to clearly label results, especially so that those doing meta-analyses will not mistake partial eta-squared for the classic eta-squared value. Complications such as these may be further reason to prefer measures of effect size for individual contrasts (Cohen's d) or correlations (r-values) over omnibus results (η^2 or partial η^2) in published reports.

In considering which effect sizes to report for ANOVA designs, Kline (2004) has recommended that researchers report on either **omnibus test** effects (the first test you do when you have more than two groups, such as an ANOVA or a repeated measures ANOVA) or contrast effect sizes (where you get into the nuts and bolts of figuring out which groups, pairwise, differ from each other), but not both. For example, if you tested the hypothesis that three different kinds of treatments result in different test scores, an omnibus test would simply say whether the type of treatment was statistical, but would not indicate which groups were better than which others. Contrast effect sizes will be measured using **post-hoc tests** or **planned comparisons** and will specifically contrast only two groups at a time so they show which groups are better than which others.

One reason to report only the omnibus or contrast effect size is because omnibus effects will already include the effect sizes of the contrasts, so it is redundant to look at each. However, some authors, such as Volker (2006), have recommended reporting effect sizes for both omnibus effects and post-hoc contrasts. Confidence intervals can be computed for omnibus results as well as post-hoc contrasts, so both can be used just as well, but my own preference in reporting is to give the CIs or standardized effect sizes for just the post-hoc tests or planned comparisons as I think these are easier for readers to understand, and many times omnibus effects eventually get broken down into just comparisons between two groups anyway.

ANOVA effect size calculations also depend on whether factors are **fixed** or random, ideas explained in Chapter 2 (Olejnik & Algina, 2000). However, when eta-squared (not omega-squared) is calculated for a multifactor ANOVA, Olejnik and Algina (2000, p. 269) have suggested that the "distinction between random and fixed effects is not relevant" since eta-squared is a statistic that should not be used to make inferences to the population. (For more on random and fixed effects see the advanced topics Section 2.1.6.)

4.2.4 Effect Size Confidence Intervals

In this chapter I have emphasized that just because we give point estimates like a mean score or a p-value does not mean that these values are fixed. The mean score is a best estimate, but we can also find a CI around the mean where the true population mean is likely to be found. We can find a p-interval around a p-value that shows that many other p-values are just as likely as the one the computer printout returned to us. So it should not be surprising to know that effect sizes can also have CIs around them. An effect size is also not a fixed and precise value; it can vary.

Cumming (2012) stated that CIs can be calculated on Cohen's d effect size. However, there is no precise way to calculate them because the distribution is asymmetric. Instead, he noted that an iterative approximation is used that tries to narrow down the CI a little at a time. We will not worry about the mechanics or the details of how this CI can be calculated here. I simply want you to know that such CIs do exist, and Cumming's ESCI program can be used to calculate them.

Table 4.5 Calculation of *r*-Family of Effect Sizes

	r-family (also known as **percentage variance**, *or* **PV**)	*Cohen's guidelines*	*Plonsky and Oswald's guidelines*
correlation	The correlation coefficient *r* is an effect size in itself. The squared *r* (R^2) expresses the percentage of variance of the dependent variable that the independent variable explains	$r = 0.10$ (small) $r = 0.30$ (medium) $r = 0.50$ (large)	$r = 0.25$ (small) $r = 0.40$ (medium) $r = 0.60$ (large)
t-test (independent samples or paired samples)	the *t*-test effect size is most often calculated with Cohen's *d*. In the case of a *t*-test, *r* will be the point-biserial correlation. To convert *d* to *r* if sample sizes are equal: $r_{pb} = \frac{d}{\sqrt{d^2 + 4}}$ (Volker, 2006)	$d = 0.2$ (small) $d = 0.5$ (medium) $d = 0.8$ (large)	See Table 4.4 as it differs for independent or paired samples
one-way ANOVA (testing omnibus effects)	For eta-squared (η^2) and omega-squared (ω^2) with all factors **fixed** the general formulas are: $\eta^2 = \frac{SS_{between-groups}}{SS_{total}}$ where SS=sum of squares, found in ANOVA table $\omega^2 = \frac{SS_{between-groups} - (k-1)MS_{error}}{SS_{total} + MS_{error}}$ where k=# of groups or means, and MS=mean square, found in ANOVA table (Volker, 2006) *If ω^2 returns a negative value, it should be reported as zero (Olejnik & Algina, 2000).	$\eta^2/\omega^2 = 0.01$ (small) $\eta^2/\omega^2 = 0.06$ (medium) $\eta^2/\omega^2 = 0.14$ (large)	
factorial ANOVA	For a design where all factors have **fixed effects**, the calculations for η^2 and ω^2 are the same as in the one-way ANOVA. For partial η^2 and ω^2: $_{partial}\hat{\eta}^2 = \frac{SS_{effect}}{SS_{effect} + SS_{error}}$ $_{partial}\hat{\omega}^2 = \frac{df_{effect}(MS_{effect} - MS_{error})}{df_{effect}MS_{effect} + (N - df_{effect})MS_{error}}$ (Olejnik & Algina, 2000) Another way to calculate partial η^2 is $\frac{df_{hyp}F}{df_{hyp}F + df_{error}}$ (Murphy & Myors, p. 62)	Pierce, Block, and Aguinis (2004) note that partial eta-squared is often inflated relative to classical eta-squared; therefore, Cohen's guidelines for effect size should not be used for partial eta-squared. Cohen's *d* effect sizes for individual comparisons are preferable.	
chi-square	Cohen (1988) gives *w* as an effect size for chi-square. In cases of 2 × 2 tables, $w = \phi$(phi) (Howell, 2002). For larger designs, ϕ can be derived from Cramer's *V* by $w = V\sqrt{r-1}$ where V = Cramer's *V* and r = the number of row or columns (whichever is smaller of the two) (Volker, 2006). This type of effect size calculation is apparently only valid with naturalistic studies (no assigned groups trying to achieve random distribution); see Grissom and Kim (2005) for calculations when assignment is random	$w = 0.10$ (small) $w = 0.3$ (medium) $w = 0.5$ (large)	

To calculate these CIs, open up the ESCI chapters 5–6 Excel file. (See application activity 4.1.1 for detailed instructions on how to download these files.) The "Data two" tab allows you to cut and paste your own data about two groups that you are comparing into the program. I am going use the data found in the LarsonHall2008.sav file for a test of listening discrimination between R/L/W groups. (For more information about this data set, see Section 4.1.3, exercise #1.) Two groups who have different characteristics (having started studying English at an earlier age or not) performed the same test, and were found to have only slightly different mean scores (early age group mean = 54.7, SD = 14.7; not early age group mean = 49.3, SD = 13.2). The 95% CI for the difference between scores was [−9.5, −1.3], meaning that there was an effect for the difference between groups, with the difference ranging between 1.3 points and 9.5 points out of a 37-point test. The CI is fairly broad and the lower limit is a pretty small difference (just 1.3 points).

To get the effect sizes on the CI, enter the data in the yellow band, with the top row being a short name for the group that will be printed on the bottom of the figure. The measurement used can also be changed. (By default it is "cm" but it can be easily changed in the yellow band.) If you would like your figure to display the data points as well as the CIs, click on the box "Display Data Points" in the top blue band, near red 3. I think that having both the individual data and the group summary in the form of the CI is the best way to make figures, so I recommend this. You might also want to experiment with the "Display CI Overlap" button in the orange band, near red 4, which shows how much the CIs of the two groups overlap. The figure on the left shows the separate CIs for each group, while the figure on the right shows the separate CIs and then a CI for the difference between groups, which is really the number we are interested in. (If you do not see the figure on the right, click on "Reveal figure displaying differences" near red 9.)

To get Cohen's d as the effect size for the differences between groups, and a CI for that d, you will need to scroll a little to the right on this tab. There you will see, near red 11, an orange box that says "Display d and CI for δ" (note that δ is pronounced 'delta' and is the corresponding population effect size). After you click on this, go back to the original area and you will see a new orange band at the bottom, with a red 12. Now we can see a few pieces of data. The box labeled s_p is the pooled SD of the groups, so we know that the box with d uses the pooled SD. My $d = 0.396$, a fairly small effect. In this band I can also see $d_{unb} = 0.395$, which is the unbiased Cohen's d effect size. Cumming (2012) stated that "d overestimates δ, especially for small samples" (p. 294), so the d_{unb} corrects for this. Now, the ESCI page will also calculate the effect size on the d for me if I click on the "Calculate CI on d" button near red 12. For my data set the CI is [−0.70,−0.09], meaning the effect size could be as large as 0.70 or as small as 0.09. This result certainly shows me that my effect size point estimate is not very accurate at all. The interval is quite wide. So another way I could state my effect size is $d = 0.40 \pm 0.30$. I would conclude for my data that the expense of starting to study English early would probably not be worth the possibly very small gain in listening ability shown by this test.

4.3 Some Explanations of the "Old" Statistics

It is my intention in this textbook to move from thinking about statistics in terms of the "old" statistics, and most especially a reliance on NHST, to an analysis of statistics that relies on CIs and effect sizes. These two pieces of information will give all the information that NHST ever did, and much more. In this book, I will not feel the need after this chapter to even include p-values in my reports if CIs are available. However, I understand that readers will be looking at papers that use the NHST logic and reasoning, and beginning users of statistics may still be unclear on what exactly NHST involves and thus be unable to follow the logic of the "old" statistics if they do not receive further explanation of it. In the last sections of this chapter then, I present what I feel are the bare bones of explanation so that the reader of this book can be a confident consumer of research using the "old" statistics. However, I want the reader of this book to be a confident *user* of the "new" statistics, so this discussion will be slightly shorter than the one found in the first edition of the book.

4.3.1 Null Hypothesis Significance Tests

The first issue involved in understanding the NHST is to understand the logic of the hypotheses used for NHST. The research hypothesis is not the same as the hypothesis that is statistically tested.

To illustrate, let us say a researcher has a question in mind—will adults who practice meaningful grammar drills for 15 minutes every day learn and retain the grammar better than adults who tell a story that causes them to use the grammar for 15 minutes every day? We will call this the research hypothesis (R_H):

> R_H: *Will 15 minutes of practice of meaningful drills result in more accurate grammar scores than 15 minutes of telling a story where the grammar in question must be used?*

A researcher with this question in mind might then examine two groups: one group will do the explicit but meaningful grammar drills while in the other group students will use the grammar implicitly by telling stories to each other. The groups can then be tested and mean scores for their grammatical accuracy computed. Clearly, the two groups will not have exactly the same mean scores. There are two possibilities to explain the differences in mean scores between groups:

1 The difference in scores between groups is due to the fact that there were differential effects for the way grammar was practiced, and this effect was large enough that it cannot simply be attributed to chance variation.
2 The difference in scores between groups is small and can reasonably be attributed to the normal variation in scores we would expect to find between groups of people.

As discussed briefly in Chapter 2, the way to test which of these possibilities is correct is to transform our original question into a statement that there is no difference between groups, or no effect for treatment (the null hypothesis, H_0):

> H_0: *There is no [statistical] difference between a group that practices grammar using explicit meaningful drills for 15 minutes each day and a group that uses grammar implicitly by telling stories where the grammar is needed for 15 minutes each day.*

Now we also need to have an alternative hypothesis, something that we can use if we can reject the null hypothesis:

> H_a: *There is a [statistical] difference between the explicit and implicit group.*

Note that neither the H_0 nor the H_a are the same as the R_H. However, if we are able to reject the H_0 and accept the H_a, looking at the mean scores will tell us which group performed statistically better than the other, and we can thus address the R_H.

Now that the hypothesis has been formulated, a test statistic is used to assess the correctness of the hypothesis. Since only two groups are being compared, a *t*-test can be used. The *t*-test statistic is calculated based on three pieces of information: the mean scores of the groups, their variances and the size of each group (the sample sizes). The distribution of the *t*-statistic is known and has already been calculated by statisticians. However, the value of the *t*-test statistic depends on the degrees of freedom (df), because the distribution changes shape as the df change. As Baayen (2008, p. 68) noted, "What we want to know is whether the test statistic has a value that is extreme, so extreme that it is unlikely to be attributable to chance. . . . Whether a test statistic has an extreme value is evaluated by calculating how far out it is in one of the tails of the distribution."

In the NHST process, we should have already decided on a cutoff level that we can use to consider the results of the statistical test extreme. This is usually called the **alpha (α) level** or **significance level** and is commonly set at $\alpha = 0.05$ for our field. Before the advent of computers, after one calculated the *t*-statistic by hand, one then looked up the critical value for the statistic at a certain level of df in a table. For example, for a *t*-test with df = 18 (that would mean that there were 10 people in each group, minus 1 degree of freedom for each of the two groups), the critical values of *t* are 1.33 for $\alpha = 0.10$ and 1.73 for $\alpha = 0.05$. This means we would expect to find a value of *t* that was 1.33 or larger only 10% of the time, and a value of *t* that was 1.73 or larger 5% of the time, if H_0 were true. Figure 4.10 gives a graphic representation of the extreme ends of a curve where the test statistic must fall if the test is to be found statistically significant.

With computers then, the actual *p*-value that is returned when doing a statistical test is the probability that we would get a value of the *t*-statistic as extreme as we have found (one in the shaded areas under the curve in Figure 4.10), assuming that H_0 is true. In other words, there is no need to look up critical values anymore, since the computer will return them, but we still want to understand the process. This *p*-value is the proportion of the distribution that has a value as extreme as the *t*-statistic or larger. (It tells us how far out in the tails of the distribution we are.) If the *p*-value is lower than the alpha (α) level we set, we reject H_0 and accept H_a that there is a difference between the two groups. If the *p*-value is larger than the alpha (α) level, we "fail to reject" H_0. (This does not necessarily mean that H_a is correct, but most of the time that is what authors will assume.)

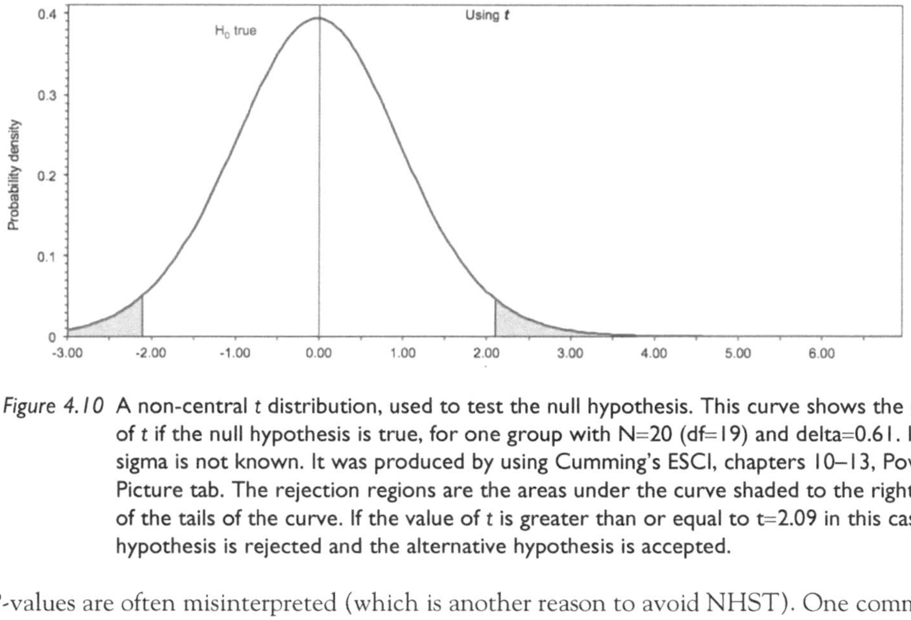

Figure 4.10 A non-central *t* distribution, used to test the null hypothesis. This curve shows the distribution of *t* if the null hypothesis is true, for one group with N=20 (df=19) and delta=0.61. It assumes sigma is not known. It was produced by using Cumming's ESCI, chapters 10–13, Power Picture tab. The rejection regions are the areas under the curve shaded to the right and left of the tails of the curve. If the value of *t* is greater than or equal to t=2.09 in this case, the null hypothesis is rejected and the alternative hypothesis is accepted.

P-values are often misinterpreted (which is another reason to avoid NHST). One common misinterpretation is that the *p*-value is the probability that H_0 is true. Not so. The *p*-value is the conditional probability of the data (the test statistic value that we found) given the hypothesis. In other words, if we were to repeat the experiment a large number of times, and if it were true that there was no difference between groups (or no relationship among variables), what is the probability that we would find this particular data outcome? For a *p*-value of 0.05, that probability is 5%. Notice that this is the probability of the data given the hypothesis or, written using logical notation, $p(\text{Data} \mid H_0)$, not the probability of the hypothesis given the data. Think it doesn't matter? Young (1993) said that a favorite example from statistical philosophers to illustrate this difference in perspectives is that the probability of being dead, if hung, *P*(Dead | Hung) is quite different from the probability of having been hung, if dead, *P*(Hung | Dead). You can see these are not the same thing at all! What you know from a *p*-value is the probability of the data given the hypothesis, so you cannot say anything at all about the probability that the hypothesis is true or not.

Meaning of the P-Value

The probability of finding a [insert statistic name here] this large or larger if the null hypothesis were true is [insert *p*-value].

Notice that the *p*-value is also *not* the probability that the results are due to chance. Since we have *assumed* that H_0 is true, we are looking at a conditional probability, not at the probability of chance.

4.3.2 One-Tailed versus Two-Tailed Tests of Hypotheses

In the type of hypothesis testing I have just described, the default method of testing the hypothesis is to use a **two-tailed test**. Thus, if we have an alpha level of $\alpha = 0.05$, this means that we would reject results that fell in the highest 2.5% of the distribution *or* the lowest 2.5% of the distribution, making up a total 5% probability that the data would be as extreme as or more extreme than what we found. A graphic depiction of the two-tailed test was seen in Figure 4.10, where the shaded areas were found on both the extreme high and extreme low sides of the distribution curve. In other words, in our H_0, we would be examining both the possibility that the explicit group was better than the implicit group and the possibility that the explicit group was worse than the implicit group. The hypothesis could go in either direction.

However, if the only thing we care about is just *one* of the possibilities, then we can use a **one-tailed test**. For example, let us say at the current moment we are already using the explicit way of practicing grammar in our classes. So we do not really care to know if the explicit way is better than the implicit way; we only want to know if the implicit way is better than the explicit one, because if it is we will then implement that into our curriculum. By the way, I have not often seen authors in our field using one-tailed tests, so this section may not be widely useful, but I also wanted to point out that CIs can also be one-sided, so this idea not only applies to NHST thinking, but also to "new statistics" thinking, so it may be worthwhile to try to understand the idea.

A one-tailed or **directional** test of a hypothesis looks only at one end of the distribution. A one-tailed test will have more power to find differences, because it can allocate the entire alpha level to one side of the distribution and not have to split it up between both ends. Figure 4.11 shows a distribution curve with the rejection region all concentrated at one end of the curve. If you compare this to Figure 4.10, where the rejection regions were distributed on both sides of the curve, you will see that having a one-tailed test gives you more area under the curve (AUC) in which to reject the

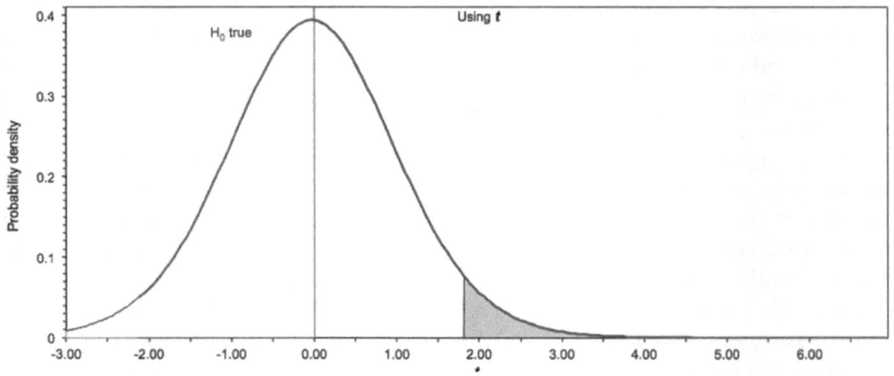

Figure 4.11 A one-tailed hypothesis rejection region, in which all of the rejection region is concentrated on just one side. This figure was created by digitally altering Figure 4.10, and the rejection area is approximate.

hypothesis, and thus gives you more power. Similarly, a one-sided CI will give you more room under the distribution curve on the side of the curve that you are investigating, thus resulting in a better chance of finding a statistically significant effect.

Figure 4.12 illustrates how power increases when using a one-tailed test. The crucial difference between the curves is in the location of the vertical line, representing the rejection AUC. The more darkly shaded curve shows a *t*-distribution and the more lightly shaded curve on the right is the amount of power. In the top diagram, a two-tailed test, both the left and right sides of the *t*-distribution are tested for difference, resulting in an area of alpha/2 on each side of the distribution. (The area to the right of the rightmost vertical line and to the left of the leftmost vertical line is the rejection AUC.) This means that the possibility of one group being better than the other and the possibility of that group being worse than the other are both tested. In the bottom diagram, a one-tailed test, all of the alpha is tested on the right side of the distribution (the area to the right of the vertical line), which could represent the possibility of one group being *better* than the other only. (The possibility that that group is worse than the other is not tested.) With all of the alpha concentrated on one tail, the critical value can be lower (in terms of its value on the x-axis), and it can be seen that there is more power to find differences because the AUC for alpha overlaps more with the power distribution than it did for the top diagram. (Look at the area to the right of the vertical line but under the critical *t* curve.)

If you do decide to conduct a one-tailed test, however, you will want to make sure that you can live with the result if no differences are found. It would be considered cheating to first examine which way

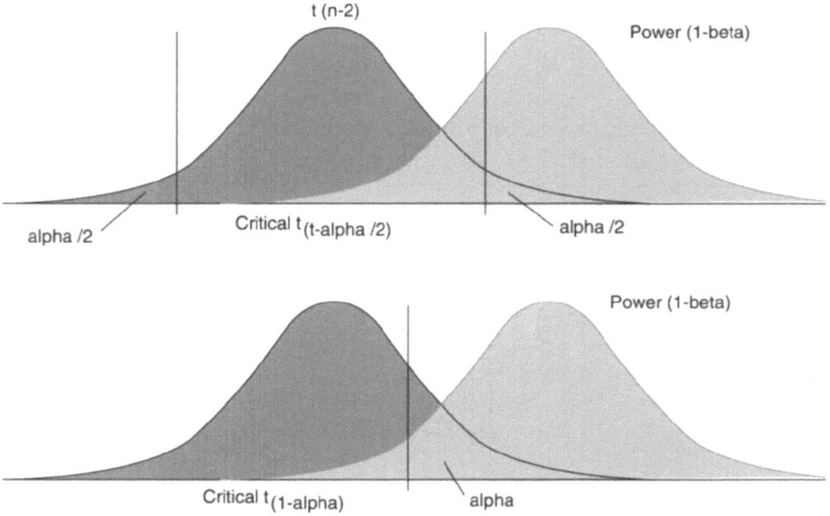

Figure 4.12 The top diagram shows the area under the curve used for testing a two-tailed hypothesis, while the bottom diagram shows a one-tailed hypothesis.

(*Source:* www.psycho.uni-duesseldorf.de/aap/projects/gpower/reference/reference_manual_02.html. With permission.)

the differences lay and then, after the fact, decide to change from a two-tailed to a one-tailed test. To calculate a one-tailed test in SPSS or R you can specify this choice in most statistical test menus. To calculate a one-sided confidence interval, Cumming (2012) has recommended calculating a 90% two-sided interval, then choosing the lower or upper limit of that CI as one end point of your one-sided 95% CI, while the other end will be infinity. For example, let us say that the 95% CI for the difference between our hypothesized explicit vs. implicit grammar teaching was [−0.05, 4.3] and the implicit mean score is slightly higher than the explicit mean score. We would not be able to conclude that the implicit

Table 4.6 Four Situations that a Researcher Might Encounter

		True situation in the population	
		No effect exists	Effects exist
Outcome observed in study	No effect exists	Correct situation (probability=$1-\alpha$)	Type II error (probability=β)
	Effects exist	Type I error (probability=α)	Correct situation (probability=$1-\beta$)
			↑ Power

teaching had an effect in that case, but if we had already decided beforehand that we only cared about one outcome, which was if the implicit teaching was better than the explicit, and we had decided to use a one-sided CI, then we would calculate the 90% CI for the difference between the teaching methods. Let us say this 90% CI was [3.2, 6.9]. Then we could say that the 95% one-way CI for the superiority of the implicit method is [3.2, infinity], and conclude that that teaching method did have an effect.

4.3.3 Outcomes of Null Hypothesis Significance Testing

Table 4.6 shows the four possible outcomes for testing NHST hypotheses when using inferential statistics. Two of the boxes in the table correspond to correct situations. In other words, this is when the actual situation that exists is correctly matched to the outcome of the statistical test. However, there are two boxes in the table that correspond to incorrect situations. These are outcomes that are mismatched to the real situation in the population.

The first is called a **type I error**, and this is when a researcher concludes that there was an effect for some treatment, but the truth is that there is actually no effect. Traditionally, researchers have been most concerned with avoiding type I errors. In this way, we avoid making mistakes and thinking there are statistical differences between groups when in fact there are none. A type I error has been called being gullible or overeager (Rosnow & Rosenthal, 1989).

A **type II error** is directly connected to the power of the study. This kind of error is made when a researcher concludes that there is no effect of a treatment when in fact there is an effect. A conclusion like this would result in researchers losing information because they were not able to detect the effect in their sample when it actually does exist in the population. Type II errors have been called errors of being overly cautious or blind (Rosnow & Rosenthal, 1989).

Avoiding type I errors is desirable, but it comes at the price of increasing the chance of type II errors. That is, the steps one takes to decrease the chance of a type I error (such as setting the alpha level lower) directly affect the amount of power in the study (power is defined in the next section), which will increase the chances of a type II error.

Readers may wonder how best to avoid both types of errors. The best answer is to stop using NHST! But to understand the reasoning of those who are still using it, I want to explain that the only way to change the probability of a type I error is to decrease the alpha level one sets as a cutoff. If a smaller cutoff is chosen (say, $\alpha = 0.01$), the probability of a type I error decreases but the probability of a type II error increases. There is thus a trade-off between the two types of errors.

To avoid a type II error, the alpha level can be *increased*. Increasing the chosen cutoff level (say, $\alpha = 0.10$) would increase the chance of a type I error but reduce the likelihood of a type II error (and result in more power). I advocated this in the first edition of this book, but this did not become a widespread standard. (I have to say, this is not surprising! The push to change NHST traditions has been going on for many years but has not been very effective!) The next and easiest way to avoid type II errors is to increase power through increasing sample sizes. Although some researchers may argue that it is difficult to increase sample sizes, fewer studies with more power to find results would be preferable to more studies which do not really have enough power to make any clear conclusions about treatment effects. These kinds of studies with low power lead to inconsistent results across similar studies and instability in the field (but if CIs are used, this is not an issue). If a study does not reject the H_0, the first place a researcher should look at is power. It is likely that power was not high enough in the study to make any conclusions. However, because researchers do not understand power, they most often try to explain their lack of results through some kind of alteration to their theory.

4.3.4 Power Analysis

Statistical power is an issue that is important to understand if one is using NHST. Power is an area where I feel people have become more knowledgeable and since the first edition of this book I have noticed more cases of people using power analyses, and that is a great thing. However, using the "new" statistics, power is not necessary, and we can instead talk about precision. Until the "new" statistics has taken hold, however, power will remain an important idea, so this section explores it in depth.

Power is the probability of detecting a statistical result when there are in fact differences between groups or relationships between variables. Sufficient power will ensure that real differences are found and discoveries are not lost.

If the power of a test is 0.50, this means that there is only a 50% chance that a true effect will be detected. In other words, even though there is in fact an effect for some treatment, the researcher has only a 50/50 chance of finding that effect. A survey of power in articles published in experimental psychology showed that the median power for medium effects at the $\alpha = 0.05$ level was only 0.37 (Sedlmeier & Gigerenzer, 1989), a dismally low level of power which means that, in many cases, when significant differences or correlations are not found, it is not because they do not exist but because there is not enough power in the study to discover them (Cohen, 1988). A lack of power leads to instability in results from similar studies, and researchers may look for theoretical explanations for the failure to distinguish between groups when their first question should be whether the study actually had enough power to adequately detect a difference in the first place.

Murphy and Myors (2004) stated that there is a consensus that the optimal level of power should be above 0.50 and would be judged adequate at 0.80. A power level of 0.80 would mean that four out of five times a real effect in the population would be found. A power level of 0.50 would mean that you as a researcher would "accept a .50 risk of failing to confirm a valid research hypothesis" (Tversky & Kahneman, 1971, p. 110).

Cumming (2012) points out that there is a difference, however, between a priori power analysis, and post-hoc power analysis. Calculating power *before* you conduct your study is really an exercise in thinking about how effect size and sample size will affect your statistical results. Previously when I read about calculating power, I was always put off by the fact that I had to estimate how large my effect size would be before I performed my experiment. I did not understand how I would do that. Now I understand that you do not know what your effect size will be, but you make an informed guess or use some guidelines for effect sizes (small, medium or large), and get an idea of how large your sample size will need to be to have enough power to find results if they are really there. Cumming (2012) has suggested that "power calculations often alarm researchers about how weak their contemplated experiment is, then guide them to some compromise between what size experiment is achievable and what target δ [delta; the population effect size] that experiment can seek with reasonable power" (p. 355). In this section I will show you how to do these calculations.

However, sometimes power is calculated *after* a study has already been run, resulting in a number for post-hoc power. This is the type of number that must have been used in a study like Sedlmeier and Gigerenzer, 1989 (cited above), which allows researchers to make conclusions about the power of tests that are already published. Perhaps using post-hoc power in this way to make a point about the importance of calculating a priori power is a permissible use of it, but Cumming (2012) calls post-hoc power "illegitimate" power and recommends never using it. One problem is that calculating power after a study has already been run is essentially circular. As Hoenig and Heisey (2001) have explained, "observed power is determined completely by the *p*-value and therefore adds nothing to the interpretation of results" (p. 20). The main problem, though, is that this post-hoc power is not a reliable and trustworthy number. Previously I followed Cumming's argument in demonstrating how variable the *p*-value can be, and since post-hoc power is dependent on the *p*-value, power is also similarly unstable and can range greatly with different replications of the same experiment. Cumming (2012) gives an example of a simulation replication where samples from a population where the true mean and SD are already known are repeatedly taken from two groups, and the *p*-value varies in 10 replications from a low of $p = 0.001$ to a high of $p = 0.90$. We saw this variation earlier in Section 4.1.4. But since post-hoc power is dependent on the effect size and the *p*-value, it too also ranges from a low of 0.05 to a high of 0.90.

It thus appears that power is just as fickle as *p*-values, and is part of the entire "old statistics" framework that we would be better off without. To understand better, think about this—power is the probability that H_0 will be rejected if an effect size of a specified amount is present. For example, if you think that your study will have a medium effect size of $d = 0.7$, then the a priori power you calculate will be the probability that the H_0 of no difference between groups will be rejected (if that effect size exists). For this reason, if we are using the new statistics and constructing CIs, it would not make sense to calculate power. Hoenig and Heisey (2001) stated that "[i]t is pointless to perform power calculations for hypotheses outside of the confidence interval because the data have already told us that these are unlikely values" (p. 22). The CI already gives you the range of values that are the most likely for (in this case) the difference between groups, so there is no need to test any hypothesis about there being no difference between groups, and thus no need to calculate the power to reject H_0. Power calculations are thus only useful within the NHST framework.

But understanding that, let us then continue with an exposition on how power can be calculated if that is what you would like to do. To calculate power, in the first edition of this book I used R, and that is still an option. I used the pwr package in R; interested users can check the help pages of that package for examples on how to use it. However, Cumming (2012) uses a free program called G*Power (Faul, Erdfelder, Lang, & Buchner, 2007), which can be set up more easily than R for those who are not using R, and also has some very nice graphics that accompany the numbers, so I would recommend it for users of both SPSS and R. I will demonstrate below how to calculate power using this program. To start, go to the website www.gpower.hhu.de and scroll down until you find a blue link to "Download G*Power" for Windows or Mac. The program downloads quickly and opens up smoothly when you click on the G*Power App.

4.3.5 Calculating Effect Sizes for Power Analysis

The biggest question in a researcher's mind for calculating power may be how to determine the effect size to expect. The best way to do this is to look at effect sizes from previous research in this area to see what the magnitude of effect sizes has been. If there is no previous research, or none that lists effect sizes, the researcher must make an educated guess of the size of the effect that they will find acceptable. Weinberg and Abramowitz (2002) suggested that one should "set the power of the test to detect a difference from the null hypothesis that is of practical importance" (p. 267).

In the case where there is no previous research to estimate effect sizes from, one may want to use the guidelines created by Cohen (1988) or Plonsky and Oswald (2014), as given in the tables in Section 4.2.3.

4.3.6 Examples of Power Analyses

In this section I will give examples of how one might approach performing a power analysis with some basic types of experimental design. In the first example, say we had a hypothesis that the students in our language institute who spoke most to native speakers while living abroad progressed the most in improving their Test of English as a Foreign Language (TOEFL) scores from the beginning to the end of the semester. We will first need to recognize that the experimental design is a correlation. (You will get more practice with recognizing designs in Chapter 5.) What we want to determine is how many participants we will need to carry out the study, but we will need to estimate the effect size that we think we will find, and also specify the *p*-value, power and whether the study will be one-tailed or two-tailed.

For G*Power, choose the appropriate statistical test first. Go to the TESTS menu and pull it down to see a large variety of choices. For this example we want a correlation, and when you hover your mouse over the correlation choice, you see many more choices for different types of correlation. But a correlation where both variables are continuous variables will be a "Correlations: Bivariate Normal Model" (the first choice on the list). Figure 4.13 shows the G*Power program open with this model chosen. In this case for "Tail(s)" I chose a two-tailed test because I do not know which way the variables will be affected and I want to get information about both positive and negative correlations. The next entry says "Correlation ρ H1" which is where you will enter your effect size, which in the case of the correlation is r (r is the correlation of the sample, ρ is the correlation of the population). Let us say we think there is an effect, but we suspect it is small. So we will use Plonsky and Oswald's (2014) number for a

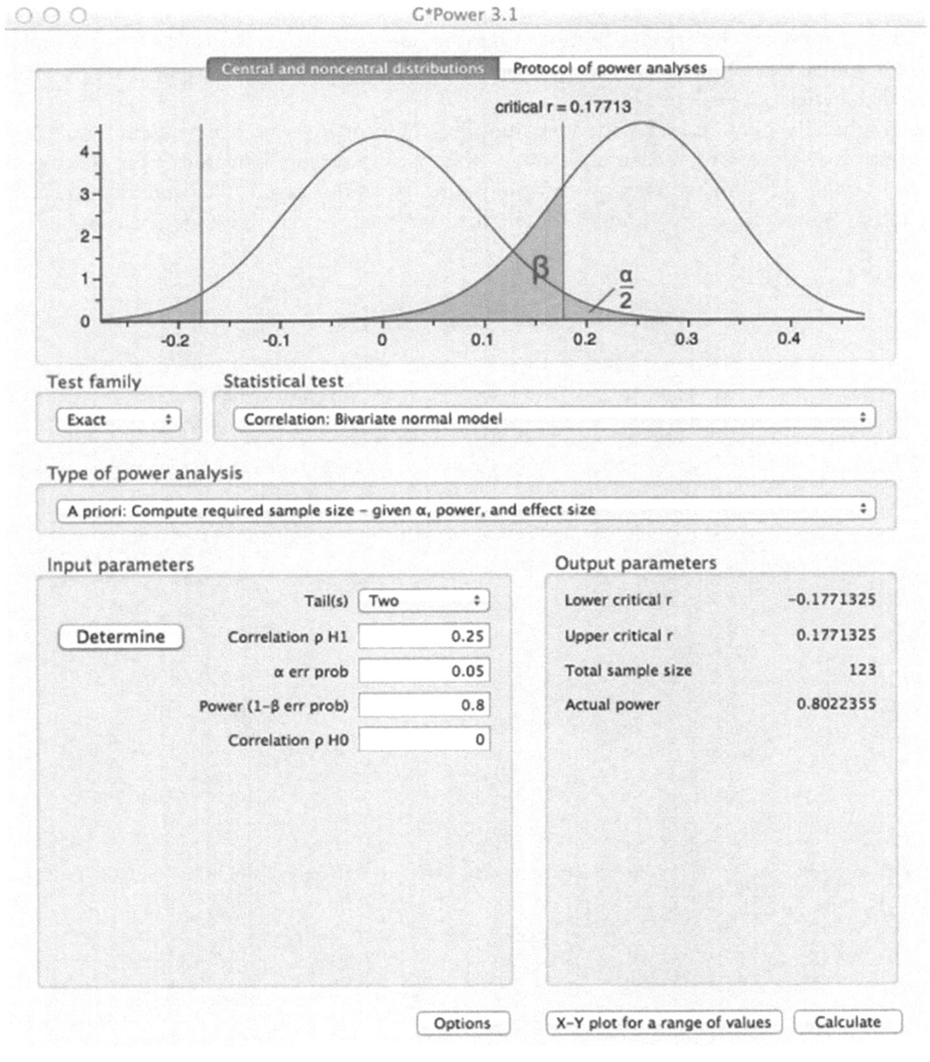

Figure 4.13 G*Power 3 program, open to show options for a correlation with two continuous variables.

small effect size for *r*, which is 0.25. The next entry is called "∝ err prob" and is your alpha level, which is normally found in our field at ∝ = 0.05. The "Power" entry asks you to set the level of power. Higher is better but results in a larger number of participants needed, so let us set it at 80% for a high but not overly demanding level. Last is the entry "Correlation ρ H0" which is the H0 we are testing against, which says that there is no correlation, so we will leave the zero in that box. Now press the "Calculate" button at the bottom of the box. Figure 4.13 shows the results after clicking on this button.

The results are shown in the right-hand panel labeled "Output parameters". We will need 123 participants with scores on the two measures (the TOEFL score change over time and the amount of hours the English learners spend speaking to native English speakers measured weekly, perhaps). If our institute is large this might be feasible but let us say we just cannot gather data from that many speakers. What can we do? Well, one of the major points of a power analysis is to experiment and see what will happen if we change some of the parameters of the analysis. For example, let us say we decide we could live with an alpha level of ∝ = 0.10. Changing that parameter means we only need 97 participants. That is still fairly high. What if we change the effect size? Let us say we hope we might have a medium effect size, so using Plonsky and Oswald's (2014) guidelines we put in 0.4 for the effect size. Now the sample size goes down to 37. It turns out that the most effective way to reduce to the sample size you need is to increase the effect size. If we change the effect size to 0.6 (large), our sample size reduces to 15. Change the alpha level back to ∝ = 0.05 but keep effect size at 0.6 and we only need 19 participants, if the effect size is large.

You can graphically play around with your numbers by plotting effect size against sample size. Choose the button to the left of "Calculate" called "X-Y plot for a range of values". For this example, I chose "Total sample size" for plotting on the y-axis, and plotted it against "Correlation ρ H1." But I want to explore how sample size changes for small to large effects, so I change the number in the

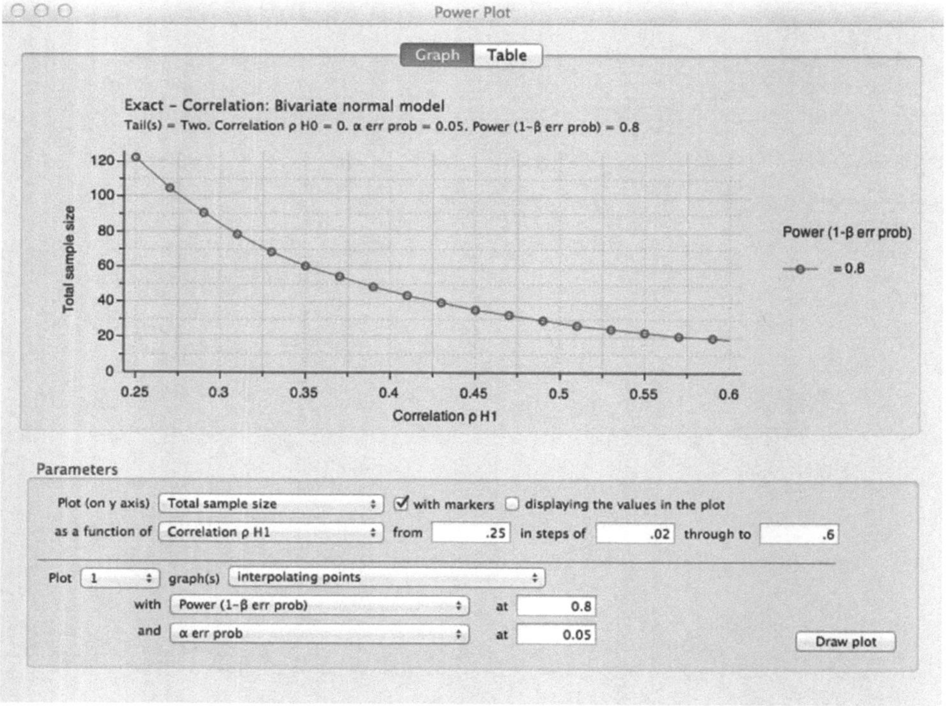

Figure 4.14 G*Power 3 Power Plot window, exploring the relationship between sample size and effect size for a correlation.

"from" box to the small effect size of 0.25, and enter 0.6 in the box after "through to." I also changed the steps from 0.01 to 0.02 to make the graph look cleaner. The result is shown in Figure 4.14. This figure shows that for total sample size to come down to below 20, the effect size has to be quite large, at least 0.55 or 0.60, so it does not look like we should have a sample size below 20 if we do not assume a large effect size. Even though gathering data from many participants might be hard, if we will not have enough power then it does not make a lot of sense to start an experiment that has a good chance of not having enough power to find real results. Murphy and Myors (2004) suggested that it is usually better to plan your power analysis by expecting small or small-to-medium effects, because if the effects are larger you will also find them. However, if you plan for a large effect but the effects are small, you will have little useful information.

Moving on to a second example, let us say we wanted to compare two groups of French language learners on their ability to remember French vocabulary. One group was being coached on different strategies for vocabulary learning, while the other group was left to their own devices, and we want to see whether one group will learn more vocabulary than the other. This experimental design will use a *t*-test, so in G*Power pull down the TEST FAMILY menu and then look at the choices for "means" tests. Here we want "two independent groups." Here the choices are exactly the same as they were for the correlation except that the effect size is labeled "Effect size d". Cohen's (1988) guidelines are that $d = 0.2$ is small, $d = 0.5$ is medium and $d = 0.8$ is large. Plonsky and Oswald's (2014) guidelines say that $d = 0.4$ is small, $d = 0.7$ is medium and $d = 1.0$ is large. Let us keep this a two-tailed test, assume a medium effect size of 0.5, keep $\alpha = 0.05$, set the power to 0.80, and keep the allocation ratio of participants as one-to-one. If you click on the calculate button, you will see that you need 64 participants in each group. If that is acceptable, plan to gather that number of participants. But in some situations, that might seem a number that would be difficult to reach. If we raise the alpha level of $\alpha = 0.10$ (and put power back down to 80%), the number of participants goes down a little bit to 51. If we assume the higher medium effect size of Plonsky and Oswald (0.7), the sample size goes down considerably to only 26 needed in each group. This seems a more reasonable number, but if the effect size is smaller than that, our study will not have enough power to find it, so it is worth considering whether you can realistically expect this large an effect size. Notice that even 26 in one group is a bit larger than many SLA experiments contain, so researchers in general need to realize that larger groups are necessary in many cases. Power calculations seem a good way to try to make a priori conclusions about how many participants will be needed in a study, and to make researchers aware that very small numbers of participants will result in less stability in results and less ability to find real differences between groups.

To graphically explore how effect size and sample size are related for tests with two independent groups, choose the button to the left of "Calculate" called "X-Y plot for a range of values". In the "Power Plot" window, choose "Total sample size" for plotting on the y-axis, and "Effect size d" for plotting on the x-axis. I then decided it would be most interesting to look at sample sizes needed for effect sizes between $d = 0.5$ and $d = 1.0$. I changed the steps to each 0.05 step and got the figure in Figure 4.15. It shows that sample size (this is total sample size, so each group would have half the number) decreases gradually as effect size increases, but is fairly high even at $d = 0.5$. Feel free to look at these factors with other ranges of effect sizes or other power levels.

Having the same groups do different tasks greatly increases the power of a study and lowers the number of participants needed. For example, say that we wanted to do the same type of vocabulary experiment as described above but have the *same* participants try learning one set of words with no training at all, and then learn another set of words with special vocabulary strategy training. Because we test the same participants on more than one measure, this is called a repeated measures test and it will be more powerful than an independent measures test. This time in the G*Power menu we choose STATISTICAL TEST > MEANS: DIFFERENCE BETWEEN TWO DEPENDENT MEANS (MATCHED PAIRS). Trying out the specifications we first used for the *t*-test with two independent groups (two-tailed, medium effect size of 0.5, $\alpha = 0.05$, power = 0.80) we see that we need only 34 participants, whereas with the independent groups we needed 64. We get a lot more statistical power from our participants if we use a repeated measures design, which is a good point to keep in mind when designing experiments.

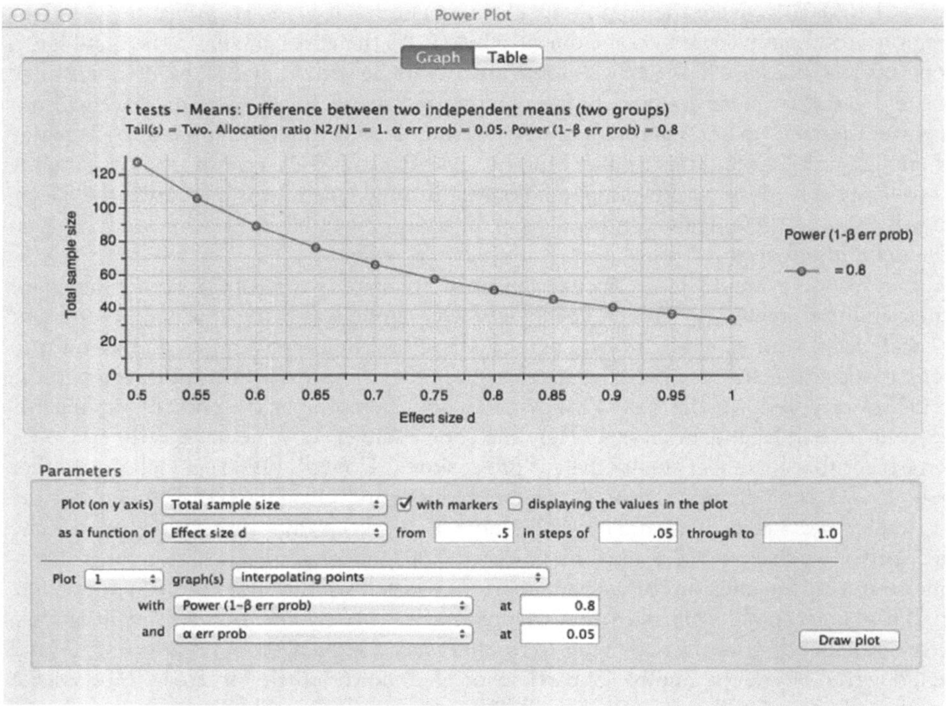

Figure 4.15 G*Power 3 Power Plot window, exploring the relationship between sample size and effect size for an independent *t*-test.

The three examples just given will probably be your basic ones when looking at power requirements (correlation between two variables; *t*-tests for two independent measures; and *t*-tests for two dependent measures). It is indeed possible to calculate sample size requirements on more complicated statistical designs such as ANOVAs and multivariate ANOVAs, but in the end you will probably be most interested in specific effects between just two groups or specific correlations between two variables, so these basic types of calculations for sample size may be all you need to know. However, it is up to you if you would like to calculate sample sizes for different kinds of designs. Once you know your design, it is not difficult to choose it in G*Power, and the effect sizes needed will be the same that are listed in Tables 4.4 and 4.5, so I will not give any further illustration of how to use the G*Power program here.

4.3.7 *Application Activities with Power Calculation*

1 Suppose you wanted to do a study to find out whether pronunciation training could help improve the comprehensibility of call center workers in Mexico. You have two treatment groups: one-on-one tutoring for individual pronunciation problems or a video course for pronunciation problems for L1 Spanish speakers. You want to see if there are any differences between the comprehensibility ratings for these two groups of speakers, but you do not know how many participants to include from each group. You assume that the effect size of the difference in training will be small ($d = 0.4$), and you have a large pool of participants you can use, so finding a large number of participants is not a problem. What does a power analysis say would be the number of participants to use to achieve a desired power level of 80% with α set at 0.05, using a two-tailed test (this is a *t*-test, independent groups design)? How many would you need for a power level of 95?

2 Pretend you have just read about a study that tried to look at the relationship between scores on the Words in Sentences aptitude test and scores for the personality trait of neuroticism. The study had 10 participants, and found that the Pearson's correlation coefficient was $r = 0.04$. The authors concluded that there was no relationship between these two variables. You suspect that the number of participants in the test was too small to have enough power to find any differences, and you decide you will do a replication of the study. Use power calculation to see how many participants you would need to find a correlation if you assume the effect size will be the same as what was found in the original study, and you want 80% power.

3 You are planning to do a study where you look at the effects on grammar acquisition of using L1 vs. L2 in the foreign language classroom. You will use the same group of students and teach one grammar rule where you will use the L1 and allow students to speak in the L1 while, for the second grammar rule, you will use the L2 and only allow students to speak the L2. Because you are using the same group of students, this is a repeated measures study and you will use a *t*-test, two dependent groups (matched pairs) design. Decide yourself what effect size you want to assume, what α and power level you will assume (choose a two-tailed test), and then report what your sample size will need to be.

4.4 Precision instead of Power

If power is an "old statistics" idea, then what should be put in its place? It turns out that the number of participants needed for studies may be calculated in the "new statistics" way by using a concept called **precision**. Precision refers to the length of the arms of the CI, which we also called the MOE. We can calculate how many participants we will need to test to obtain a target MOE that is some certain size. Precision is better than power because the target we are aiming at is measured in the exact same units as the result we get from conducting our experiment (the CI). The *APA Publication Manual* (2009) advises to "use calculations based on a chosen target precision (confidence interval width) to determine sample sizes" (p. 31), in other words, precision is a sanctioned alternative to power calculations.

Bearing in mind the problems we have seen previously in the amount of variability that one may get when calculating *p*-values, uncertainty is reduced by using a precision calculation rather than a power calculation (Cumming, 2012). In addition, Maxwell, Kelley, and Rausch (2008) stated that using precision is simpler to implement than power because the necessary sample size is not nearly so sensitive to the unknown effect size as a power analysis is. Cumming (2012) further advocates using precision calculated with **assurance**. Assurance is the probability that we will get a sample MOE that is larger than the target MOE (Cumming, 2012).

A normal precision calculation will only give on average an MOE that is no larger than the target MOE, so we have a 50% chance of getting a longer CI than the one that we judge to be useful. If we add assurance, however, we can be assured to some level of confidence (Cumming recommends 99%) that our MOE will not be longer than some certain length.

We can use Cumming's ESCI program to calculate precision for various scenarios. Cumming (2012) explains how to do so for one-sample tests, two-sample independent tests and two-sample paired tests. I do not think the one-sample test is very widely used, so I will explain only how to calculate precision for the two-sample test. Using the same example as found in Section 4.3.6, pretend that we want to compare two groups of French language learners on their ability to remember French vocabulary using two different methods. In this case we need to think about how large a difference in scores would be useful. We can think directly in the units we are using to measure the vocabulary. Let us say we have decided to have a 50-item vocabulary test. We might decide that the difference would need to be at least five points to establish any reason to prefer one method over another.

We need to open up ESCI chapters 10–13 and go to the "Precision two" tab. The light blue band, near red number 5, is an independent calculator that you can use to determine precision. Here we will enter our target MOE as five score units in the "Target MOE" box. ESCI also needs a SD to make the calculation.

This SD can be just an estimate. For example, we may assume that the SD will be around 10 points in a 50-point test. It probably could not be too much larger than this, given the 68–95–99.7 rule of thumb that 68% of the population will lie within ± 1 SD of the mean score, 95% will lie within 2 SDs and 99.7% will lie within 3 SDs. If we assumed the mean score was right in the middle of the 50 points at 25, then 1 SD would be [15, 35], 2 SDs would be [5, 45] and 3 SDs would include the entire range [0, 50]. If we had previous research or a meta-analysis to tell us what the SD was, that would be even better, but because we are working in the original scale of the test it should not be too hard to make some sort of estimate even if we have not run the test yet. Put this estimate in the "Population σ" box (shown in Figure 4.16). This will result in a number for *f* where the target MOE is calculated in SD units, something very akin to an effect size. Once the target MOE and SD are inserted, then *N* will be shown for a calculation using *z* (which you should use if you know σ), a calculation using *t* (which is used when you do not know σ and is a more realistic calculation) and a calculation using the assurance level specified on that same page in the band around red 2. A 99% level of assurance means that "there's a 99% chance that our sample MOE will not exceed the target MOE" (Cumming, 2012, p. 369). The resulting required *N* will of course be larger than the non-assurance *N* but will provide an excellent chance of finding a result within the target MOE.

So, continuing with the idea of the vocabulary experiment where the MOE is 5 and the SD is 10, the ESCI results show that we would need 44 participants in each group to assure a MOE as small as we wanted. (The assumption is that the *N* in one group equals the number of *N* in the other group.) Notice that this does not mean we would be assured of finding a difference between groups! All it assures us of is a more precise CI so we could be as sure as we wanted to be that the range of values in the CI centered on the most likely result, whether that be something close to zero (showing us that there is no difference between groups) or something farther away from zero (showing us a certain effect size). All of these calculations are done at a certain CI, usually 95%, which is set in the yellow band near red number 1 and could be changed if you wanted.

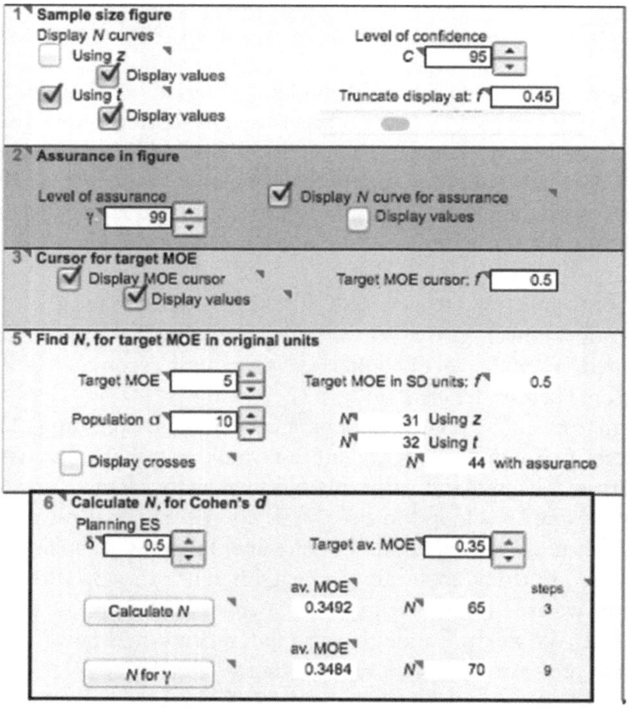

Figure 4.16 ESCI page, chapters 10–13, tab labeled "Precision two", for calculating sample size for confidence intervals.

This ESCI page also provides us with a way to calculate the number of participants needed to achieve a different end than that described in the previous paragraph, although it is still related to precision. The goal of the calculation in the green band near red number 6 on the same page is to calculate how many participants would be needed to achieve a certain CI around the effect size you assume you will find. This is different from how effect sizes were used in planning power (Section 4.3.6). Here, instead of just specifying the size of the CI you are interested in, you specify how wide the CI should be around the *d* itself. In this area, enter the Cohen's *d* that you expect to find in the box labeled "δ." In the box labeled "Target av. MOE," put in the average size of the MOE around the CI that would be acceptable. For example, if the effect size is $d = 0.5$, then how wide can the CI on this effect size be and still be of interest? If the CI is 0.3, that means the effect size may range from 0.2 to 0.8, thus varying in size from rather small to a larger medium effect size (see Figure 4.16). Obviously, the larger this number (the target average MOE), the less precise the estimation will be, and the less useful to the researcher in pinpointing the true effect size.

You could look back at the tab in ESCI labeled "CI for d" (found in the same chapter 10–13 file) to see how the target average MOE for the CI on *d* is calculated, and here you would see that you need a *d*-value as well as *N* sizes for groups. Because the calculation is done on a *t*-distribution, the arms are asymmetric and you must calculate lower and upper limits for the distribution. Once the CI is determined, the average MOE can be figured out and is given on this page. However, I suggest you simply think about how large the effect size could vary and still be worthwhile to you, and that is the number you enter into the "Target av. MOE" box in the "Precision two" tab.

So back to our example of the vocabulary experiment, if we decide to put in an effect size of Cohen's $d = 0.5$, and have an average MOE of 0.3, we would then click on "Calculate *N*" or "*N* for γ," which is the *N* needed for the assurance level specified near red 2 (set by default at 99%). Both of these calculations are done iteratively so they will take a number of steps and perhaps a minute or more to finish. (If ESCI cannot perform the calculation, a "No" will pop up instead of a number.) In this case, for *N* I get 89 and for *N* with a 99% assurance level I would need 94 participants. Is that number the total number of participants, or the number in each group? Check the red triangle near the calculation to see more notes on the topic, and in this case it says that *N* is the size of *each* group. Make the average MOE larger, say 0.35, and fewer participants are needed (65 for *N*, 70 for *N* with 99% assurance; see Figure 4.16), but the precision of the confidence interval around *d* will not be as good.

To calculate precision for a repeated-measures *t*-test, such as the example where we had the same group of French learners use two different methods for learning vocabulary and tested them on their recall ability after each method, we would move to the tab titled "Precision paired" in the Excel file for ESCI chapters 10–13. The entry for the paired situation is exactly similar to that for the independent groups, except that for the area where the CI around *d* is calculated, only *N*, and not *N* with assurance, is available. Cumming (2012) suggests this is because he has not been able to find any published work that provides the calculation for this factor. The area of precision is still in its infancy and in fact, the ESCI program does not provide any way to calculate sample size when performing a correlation because "considerable further statistical development is needed before we will have proven methods for all the ES measures researchers wish to use, and easily accessible software to do the work" (Cumming, 2012, p. 376). These gaps will surely be filled in as research advances in the area of new statistics.

4.4.1 Application Activities with Precision Calculation

1 Look at exercise #1 in Section 4.3.7. Your study will involve pronunciation ratings that will range from 1 to 30, that number being an aggregate of 10 judges' ratings on a 3-point comprehensibility measure. You decide that you would need to see an improvement of at least five points over the video course to decide to implement the more expensive one-on-one tutoring pronunciation training across your entire population of call center workers, and that you would only be willing to see a margin of error of at most two points either way. We will thus say that you want to have

a MOE of 2 in the original rating scale. You hypothesize that the SD in this 30-point rating scale might be somewhere around 5. How many participants will be needed to have a MOE of 2? How many are necessary if you want to have this MOE with 99% assurance?

2 Assume we are still thinking about the experiment from exercise #1 in Section 4.3.7. You want to have an effect size of Cohen's $d = 1$ (that is a numerator of 5, meaning the difference in mean scores for one group minus the other group, and a denominator of the SD of 5, resulting in 1) with at most a MOE on this confidence interval of 0.3 (so that is the target average MOE). How many participants will you need in each group to achieve this level of confidence around the effect size? How about with assurance = 99%?

3 Look at exercise #3 in Section 4.3.7. Assume that you will measure the acquisition of the grammar rule on a 10-point test. Decide for yourself what your target MOE will be and what a reasonable population σ value might be. Report what your sample size should be for 50% precision on the MOE. Report what it would be for 99% assurance for that MOE.

4.5 Summary

The field of second language research, like most other areas of scientific inquiry, would benefit from keeping current with changes in the field of statistics, and especially with changes in how statistical results are reported. In this chapter, I have noted some ways that researchers currently working in the area of applied statistics have proposed as ways to help researchers and journal readers better understand what they are doing when they use statistics to analyze their data.

A major shift in thinking about how to conduct statistical analyses, called the "new statistics" by Cumming (2012) has been the main thrust of this chapter. Although the types of statistical analyses promoted in this chapter are not actually new, their widespread use would be new, and would provide a much more intelligent, trustworthy and understandable way to conduct and report statistical results. This "new statistics" approach will be used in all reporting done throughout this book whenever feasible.

I also urge researchers to take the issue of the number of participants needed for a planned experiment seriously, as conducting experiments with too few participants results in a loss of real understanding of phenomena in the field. For a long time the way to determine the number of participants has been through a priori power calculations. Precision, the "new statistics" alternative to power calculation, is in its infancy and right now the only easily accessible method for computing precision involves only comparisons between two measures, but advances will surely be made in the near future so that we will not have to rely on power much longer. Post-hoc power is highly variable and since it depends on *p*-values, does not really give any new information that is not already found in a study, so its use is not recommended.

I would like to conclude my summary by discussing the idea of replication studies, which would surely enhance the reliability of findings in the field and strengthen theoretical claims, and their relationship to the idea of power.

4.5.1 Power through Replication and Belief in the "Law of Small Numbers"

Mackey and Gass (2005) and Polio and Gass (1997) have urged second language researchers to conduct more replication studies. Tversky and Kahneman (1971) have pointed out that replication studies will ideally have a larger number of participants than the original study. With a sample size that is larger than the original, the experimenter will have a better chance of finding a significant result. Why? As discussed earlier, sample sizes play a direct role in the amount of power that a study has.

Tversky and Kahneman noted that most social science researchers have a "belief in the law of small numbers" (the title of their article). The law of large numbers says that given a sufficient number of observations, or participant measurements, the sample statistic (such as the average) will approach the population statistic more and more closely. Tversky and Kahneman's proposed law of small numbers states that "the law of large numbers applies to small numbers as well" (p. 106). In other words, researchers believe that even a small sampling should represent the whole population well, which leads to an unfounded confidence in results found with small sample sizes. Hopefully, through the discussion of effect sizes and the importance of group sizes, the reader has seen that studies with small sample sizes will have significant drawbacks, including low power to find results, and most likely wide CIs, meaning that sampling error is large.

The "law of small numbers" led researchers in Tversky Kahneman's survey to believe that a statistical group difference found with groups of 40 participants each should still hold for groups of 20, when in fact the chances of finding a statistical group difference if this condition holds are only slightly above 50%! Researchers hold these erroneous assumptions because they do not understand power, and overestimate how much power a given study has. In fact, Tversky and Kahneman found that most of their colleagues in psychology would try to give a theoretical explanation for a non-statistical difference in such a replication study (where the original had 40 participants and the replication had 20) instead of noting differences in power as the most likely cause of the discrepancy or testing 20 more participants for the replication. The authors noted that reporting effect sizes, which are not affected by sample size, and CIs, which provide a range of sampling variability, and not just *p*-values, will help improve the statistical intuitions of researchers. I hope all of this just underscores the value of the ideas in this chapter, which we as researchers crucially need to understand well.

Part II

Statistical Tests

Chapter 5

Choosing a Statistical Test

> The hardest part of any statistical work is getting started. And one of the hardest things about getting started is choosing the right kind of statistical analysis. The choice depends on the nature of your data and on the particular question you are trying to answer.
>
> Michael Crawley (2007, p. 323)

Statistics is as much an art as it is a science. There is never just one way to analyze your data, which is why it is important to understand the reasoning behind the use of various tests. In my own research I often find myself revising my statistical analysis when I take a fresh look at it after setting it aside for some months. I may discover an alternative test, or a different idea for looking at the data. Part II of the book covers in depth a number of basic statistical tests including correlation, regression, the *t*-test and analysis of variance (ANOVA). These are by no means all of the statistical tools that are available for analyzing data, but they are the basic ones that are used most frequently in the second language research literature.

Of course, in getting started in analyzing your data, you do need to pick a statistical test. And getting started, as Michael Crawley suggests, may be the hardest part of statistical work. I have seen many approaches to trying to help students learn how to choose which test to use to analyze their data, but I am not sure any approach works very well! One common type of approach is to provide a step-by-step decision tree like that provided in Porte (2002) (reprinted from Hatch & Lazaraton, 1991) or Field (2005, 2012). I have found that such charts are quite helpful once you have a good deal of experience with statistics, but I remember as a beginning statistics user I found such charts frustrating. For example, I did not know if I wanted "to discover the effect of independent variables on dependent variables" or "discover a relationship between variables" (Porte, 2002, p. 248; this is the first question to divide the major types of statistical tests in Hatch and Lazaraton's flowchart).

So I have taken a different approach to the question of which test to choose in this chapter. Instead of providing a flowchart, this chapter is designed to give you a broad understanding of some basic types of statistical procedures illustrated by actual studies in the field that have used that test. The idea is to help you gain a feeling for the questions that various statistical procedures can answer. I hope an illustrative approach will *show* the difference between the types of tests instead of just tell it, but the fact of the matter is that understanding statistics does take some time and experience. This chapter is just a first step in helping you figure out where to start.

5.1 Statistical Tests that are Covered in this Book

A first step toward understanding what kind of statistical test you should choose is to understand the distinction between tests of relationships and tests of group differences, even though this dichotomy is somewhat of an oversimplification. Tests of relationships will look at questions of how strongly one variable influences another, or which variables can predict scores on another variable. Those covered in this book are correlation, partial correlation (online), and regression. Tests of group differences look at whether membership in a particular category or group influences the outcome of some test. Those covered in this book are the *t*-test, ANOVA, ANCOVA (online), and repeated-measures ANOVA (RM-ANOVA).

One way to tell if you want a test of relationships or a test of group differences is to look at the level of measurement of your variables. In general, you will want a test of relationships if all of your variables are continuous. In other words, they are measured on a scale where a difference of one point at the upper end of the scale is equal to the difference of one point on the lower end of the scale, and where a larger number has more of the quality than a smaller number. Examples include test scores, **Likert scale** scores (if the scale is wide enough) and age. If you have a mix of continuous and categorical variables you will probably want a test of group differences. Remember that categorical variables have labels that have no inherent numerical value, and these categories are often used to define the groups whose differences you want to explore. Examples of categorical variables are L1, experimental treatment group and a division into young/old age. (Remember from Chapter 2 that such a scale for age might also be called ordinal because there is some inherent ranking in younger vs. older, but in statistical tests we have to decide whether to treat such variables as either continuous or categorical, and this variable is clearly too small to be labeled continuous.) If you have *only* categorical variables, then you may want to use a chi-square test, which is a test of group differences (found online).

Another thing to keep in mind, as you decide which test to use, is whether your variables are dependent or independent. Remember from Chapter 2 that this dichotomy involves which variable we hypothesize may be influencing another (the independent variable (IV) influences the dependent (DV)). However, it is not always the case that we can clearly identify causation or influence. In some cases we are looking at mutual influence of the variables on each other, and usually in these cases we will use a test of relationships.

The following sections of this chapter lay out some information about the types of variables that are used in each type of test, whether they are dependent or IVs, and give several examples from the second language acquisition (SLA) literature that have used this particular technique. I have come up with some mnemonic devices that might be helpful for remembering which test to use, and although these are somewhat cheesy they might be helpful, so I will include them here. Also, I specify what alternatives exist for the test (both robust and classic non-parametric alternatives).

5.2 A Brief Overview of Correlation

5.2.1 Correlation: A Test of Relationships

Correlation looks at how two measurements vary together. The meaning of correlation in a statistical sense is very much related to the meaning you would think of in ordinary life; you might notice that people in your neighborhood seem to wear heavy coats more in the winter than in the summer. If there is a relationship between type of coat and weather there is a correlation between the two variables, and this means there is some kind of discernible linear pattern among the data. A test of correlation is thus looking for a pattern of relationships among data.

If we think of a graph that charts the relationship between two variables, then a relationship that shows a correlation has a linear trend (such as graph A in Figure 5.1 on the left) rather than being a collection of scattered points (as in graph B on the right).

A correlation has the following attributes:

- There are exactly two variables.
- These variables do not have any levels within them.

- If you took averages of the variables, you would have only two averages.
- Both variables are continuous.
- The variables cannot necessarily be defined as independent and dependent (having a cause-and-effect structure), although they might be.

Mnemonic device: A correlation has two variables, so stick out your two index fingers. A correlation involves a relationship, so bend your fingers toward each other as if they are having a conversation. Turn your fingers on the side and you have a "C" for correlation.

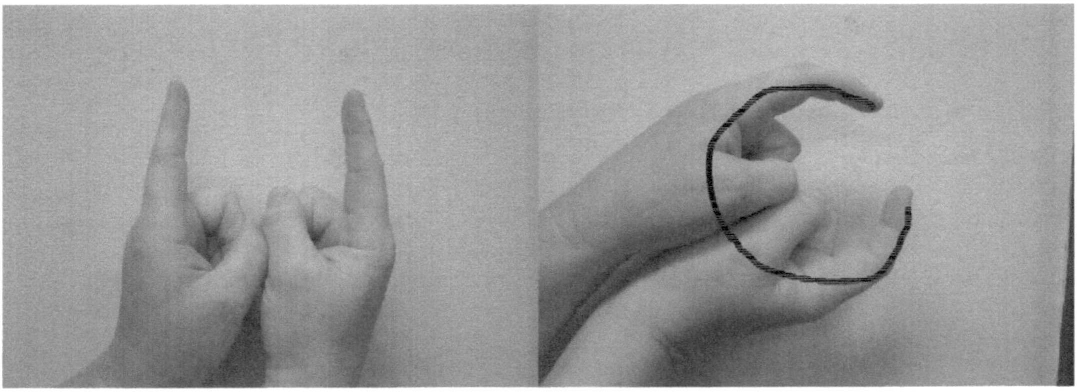

Research questions in SLA that have used correlation:

	Robinson (2005)
Research question	How does intelligence relate to the ability to abstract rules unintentionally and without awareness (implicitly) or intentionally and with awareness (explicitly)?
Answer examines	Whether intelligence and scores on implicit/explicit tests are related.

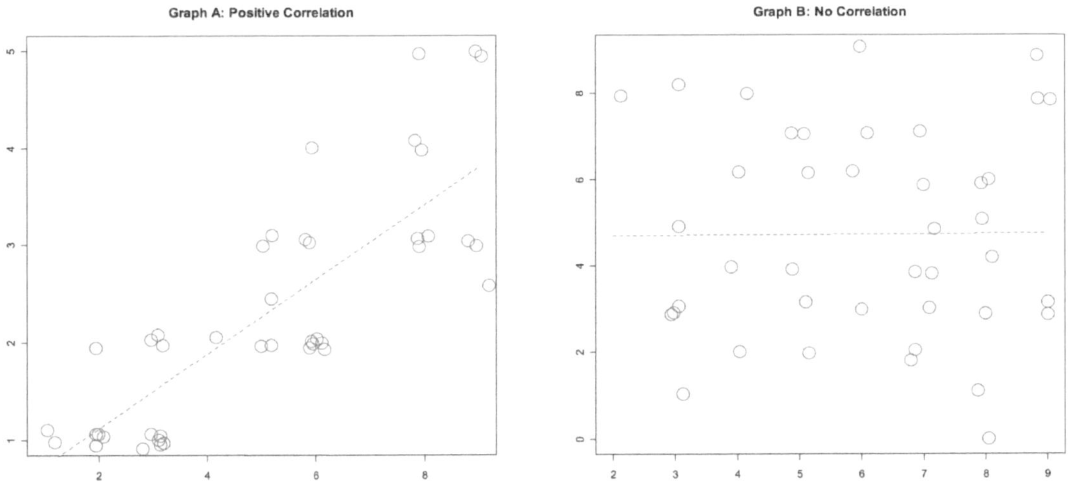

Figure 5.1 Scatterplots showing a correlation (A) or no correlation (B).

	Pearson, Fernandez, Lewedeg, and Oller (1997)
Research question	Does amount of input that a bilingual child receives matter to how much vocabulary they will learn in Spanish?
Answer examines	The relationship between input and amount of vocabulary in Spanish.

Robust alternative shown in this book: Robust correlations involving bootstrapping and robust estimation plots

Classical non-parametric alternative: Spearman's rank-order correlation test

5.3 A Brief Overview of Partial Correlation

5.3.1 Partial Correlation: A Test of Relationships

Partial correlation looks at the way two measurements vary together when a third variable has been factored out of their relationship. For example, you may have noticed while administering a timed vocabulary test that your older students struggled more with this than your younger students. You are actually interested in the relationship between the amount of vocabulary knowledge and scores on a reading test, but you decide you need to factor the effect of age out of the relationship to get an accurate view of it. For this you would use a partial correlation. For reasons of space the section on partial correlation has been moved online.

A partial correlation has the following attributes:

- There are three or more variables. (You may factor out the influence of more than one variable at a time.)
- These variables do not have any levels within them.
- If you took averages of the variables, you would have three or more averages.
- All variables are continuous.
- The variables cannot necessarily be defined as independent and dependent (having a cause-and-effect structure), although they might be.

Research questions in SLA that have used partial correlation:

	Larson-Hall (2006)
Research question	How does age at which a learner began studying English as a foreign language relate to scores on a grammaticality judgment test and a phoneme contrast test? Those who began studying earlier might have more total input, so this factor is statistically subtracted out of the equation by using partial correlation.
Answer examines	Whether there is a relationship between age and test scores when the amount of total input is factored out (in other words, input is partialled out).

Robust alternative shown in this book: Bootstrapped partial correlations

Classical non-parametric alternative: None

5.4 A Brief Overview of Multiple Regression

5.4.1 Multiple Regression: A Test of Relationships

Multiple regression looks at the relationship among multiple variables to try to make a prediction about how some variables (the independent or **explanatory variables**) may predict scores on another variable (the dependent or response variable). This is often done with an aim toward building an explanatory theory. Multiple regression tries to determine how much of the DV can be explained by variation in the scores on the IVs. What does it mean to explain the variance in scores? Basically, it means you are trying to explain why everyone did not get the same score. Why did some people get high scores and some get low scores? If you can explain the variance, you are explaining why people differ in their scores.

Figure 5.2 shows graphically how a nativeness rating in French might be explained to some extent by the age at which the participant began studying French, their level of motivation and their phonological training. Notice that these explanatory variables do not explain *everything*! When dealing with human beings, we will rarely find a combination of variables that can explain 100% of the DV.

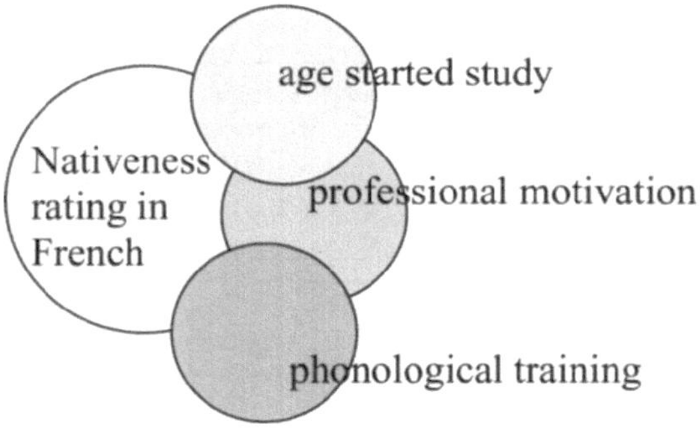

Figure 5.2 Visualizing how independent variables might help explain the dependent variable (areas of overlap show covariation).

A regression has the following attributes:

- It has two or more variables.
- These variables do not have any levels within them.
- If you took averages of the variables, you would have three or more averages.
- All variables are continuous.
- Unlike correlation, one variable must be dependent and the others are independent.

Mnemonic device: Regression usually has many variables, so hold out two fingers from each hand. Regression involves a relationship, so bend your fingers toward each other as if they are having a conversation. Join your forefingers and, if you were looking at yourself, you would see an "M" for multiple regression.

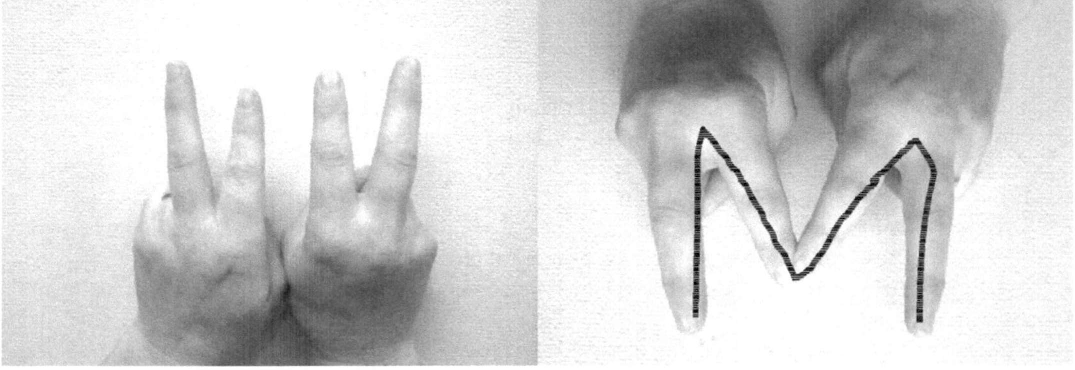

Research questions in SLA that have used multiple regression:

	Dethorne, Johnson, and Loeb (2005)
Research question	How much of the variance in children's mean length of utterance (the DV) can be accounted for by a syntactic measure of tense accuracy (TAC) and a vocabulary measure of the number of different words (NDW) (the IVs)?
Answer examines	Whether a morphosyntactic measure (TAC), a semantic measure (NDW), or both together can predict the length of children's utterances, and how much of that variance they predict.

	Zareva (2005)
Research question	To what extent could self-reported vocabulary knowledge, vocabulary size, vocabulary difficulty, native-like associational knowledge and number of associations made (the IVs) predict an actual measure of vocabulary knowledge (the DV)?
Answer examines	Which measures of vocabulary knowledge can be used to predict actual vocabulary knowledge and create a model with the fewest possible predictors.

	Paavola, Kunnari, and Moilanen (2005)
Research question	Does the amount of maternal responsiveness and number of child's intentional communications (the IVs) predict early linguistic abilities (the DVs)?
Answer examines	How well maternal responsiveness and infant intention can predict language development.

Robust alternative shown in this book: Bootstrapped regression
Classical non-parametric alternative: None

5.5 A Brief Overview of the Chi-Square Test of Independence

5.5.1 Chi-Square: A Test of Relationships

A **chi-square** test investigates whether there is a relationship between two categorical variables. The question is whether there is a relationship between the number of people in each category. (While it is important to understand when your data might fit into a chi-square test, it is not a highly used statistical test in SLA and this chapter has been moved online.) For example, we want to see if males and females differ in their choice of foreign language to study in high school, where the school offers Japanese, Spanish and French. The variable of gender (with two **levels** or two groups inside the variable) is categorical, as is choice of foreign language (with three levels). We might visualize this as a chart, as in Table 5.1.

Table 5.1 shows that the largest number of males chose Japanese and the largest number of females chose Spanish, but we also need to consider how many males and females took language classes overall, and how many of both genders chose each language to study.

A chi-square test for independence has the following attributes:

- It has exactly two variables.
- Each variable has two or more levels (categories) within them, so that the variable name is a word that generalizes (for example, gender, experimental group, L1 background).
- You cannot calculate averages of the variables; you can only count how many are in each category.
- All variables are categorical.
- The variables cannot necessarily be defined as independent and dependent (having a cause-and-effect structure), although they might be.

Table 5.1 Visualizing a Chi-Square Test of Relationships

	Language		
	Japanese	*Spanish*	*French*
Males	25	16	10
Females	14	27	18

Research questions in SLA that have used chi-square for independence:

	Geeslin and Guijarro-Fuentes (2006)
Research question	Will three groups (Spanish L1, Portuguese L1, and Portuguese L1, Spanish L2) differ in their choice of copula (*ser, estar* or both) in a contextual usage measure?
Answer examines	Whether first and second language knowledge plays a role in choice of *ser* versus *estar*.

	Wharton (2000)
Research question	Do high-proficiency learners use more of certain language learning strategies than low-proficiency learners, where use is measured as low, medium or high?
Answer examines	Whether proficiency and use of strategies are related.

Robust alternative shown in this book: None that I know of

Classical non-parametric alternative: The chi-square test of independence is already a non-parametric test and there is no parametric alternative when both variables are categorical

5.6 A Brief Overview of *T*-Tests

5.6.1 T-Test: A Test of Group Differences

The **t-test** is the simplest test of whether groups differ. Even if we tested two populations (or abstract groups of people under consideration, such as "ESL learners" and "native speakers") that we thought were exactly the same, there would be some variation in scores among the groups. Therefore, the *t*-test determines if the differences between groups are small enough to attribute them to the random variation in scores that would happen each time we take a new sample of the same population, or whether the differences are large enough that the two groups can be said to belong to two different populations.

In Figure 5.3 there are two distributions that have the same shape but have their peak at different places (meaning they have different mean scores). The *t*-test will tell us whether this amount of difference in mean scores (given the amount of variation that exists) is enough to say that the scores come from two different populations. There are two types of *t*-tests that we may be interested in. One is called the independent samples *t*-test, when the groups consist of different people, and the other is the paired samples *t*-test, which in our field is usually when the groups consist of the same people sampled at different time periods, although it could be something else, such as scores on related tests taken by the same people.

Mnemonic device: A *t*-test has two mean scores, so hold out two fingers. *T*-tests involve tests of group differences or how one variable intersects with the other, so cross one finger over the other to make a "T" for *t*-tests.

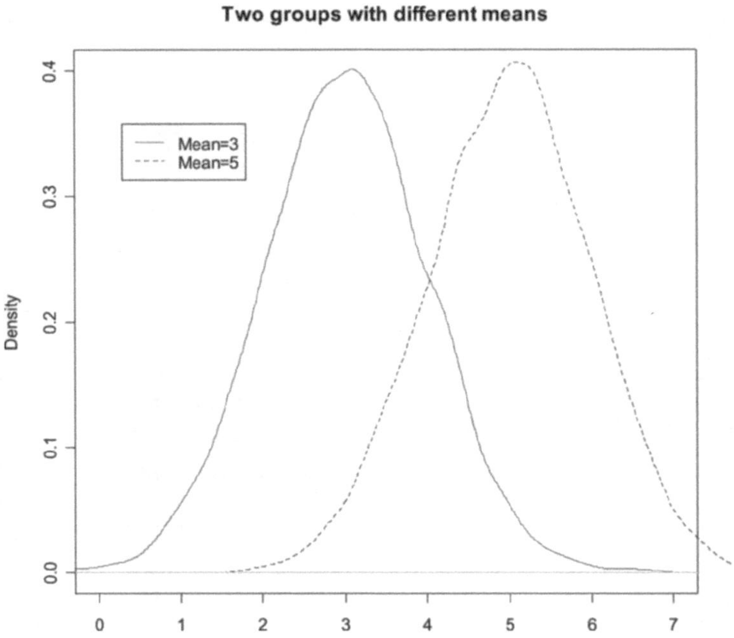

Figure 5.3 Two distributions with different means.

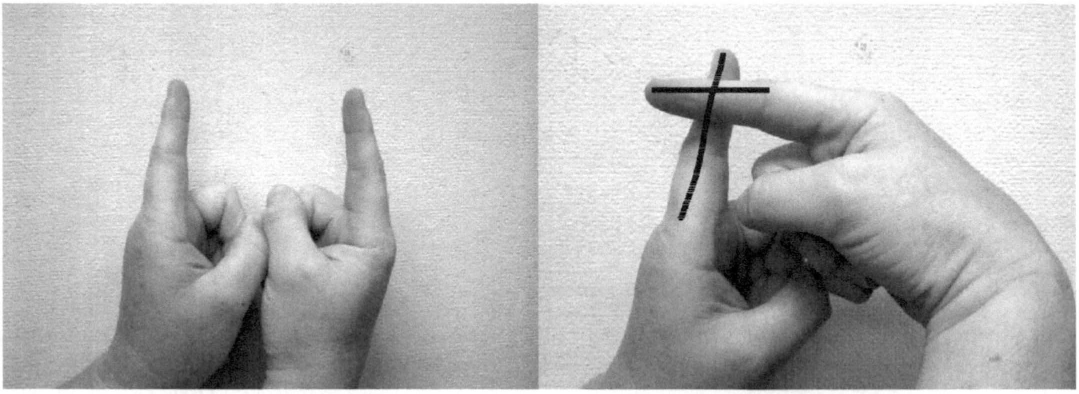

5.6.2 *A Brief Overview of the Independent Samples T-Test*

An **independent samples *t*-test** assumes that the two mean scores are independent of each other.

An independent samples *t*-test test has the following attributes:

- It has exactly two variables.
- One variable is categorical with only two levels and it is the IV.
  - People in each group must be different from each other. (If a person is in group X, for example, the experimental group, then they cannot have a score in a different group, for example, the control group.)
- The other variable is continuous and it is the DV.
- If you took averages of the variables, you would have two averages for two different groups on the same variable (for example, scores from the experimental group and scores from the control group on a test).

Research questions in SLA that have used independent samples *t*-tests:

	Hirata (2004)
Research question	Do English-speaking learners of Japanese who receive pronunciation training on a computer improve their performance on pitch and duration contrasts in Japanese more than controls?
Answer examines	Whether the difference between a group that received an experimental treatment and a group (the IV) that did not is large enough to conclude the groups are different from each other in pronunciation (the DV).

	Boers, Eyckmans, Kappel, Stengers, and Demecheleer (2006)
Research question	Will instruction that helps learners to "notice" formulaic sequences improve their perceived fluency in L2 English more than a group taught by the same teacher with the same materials but without a focus on formulaic sequences?
Answer examines	Whether the group that focused on formulaic sequences and the group that did not (the IV) have different enough mean scores to be considered as coming from two different populations on their fluency (the DV).

Robust alternative shown in this book: Bootstrapped *t*-test, means-trimmed *t*-test, bootstrapped and means-trimmed *t*-test

Classical non-parametric alternative: Mann–Whitney U test

5.6.3 A Brief Overview of the Paired Samples T-Test

A **paired samples *t*-test** is used when the people who are tested are the same, so the two mean scores cannot be independent of each other.

A paired samples *t*-test has the following attributes:

- It has exactly two measurements.
- There is one categorical distinction with only two levels and it is the IV (typically something like time, with a pretest vs. a posttest, but it could be grammatical score, as measured by the TOEFL and TOEIC, two related tests that all participants took, or phonemic ability as measured by scores on a perception task and a production task).
    - People in each group must be the same, so, for example, if a person is found in the pretest group, they must also have a score in the posttest group.
- There is one DV which is the score, a continuous measurement (but it is divided into the two different categories, so you feel that you have two measurements).
- If you took averages of the measurements, you would have two averages, but taken from two different times or from two different tests that you feel are measuring the same thing (such as grammatical ability or phonemic ability).

Research questions in SLA that have used paired samples *t*-tests are found below. Note that the Hirata study is the same as the one examined above using independent samples, but the question is now slightly different.

	Macaro and Masterman (2006)
Research question	Would English-speaking students studying French benefit from a short, intensive burst of explicit grammar training in their L2? The students were tested before the training and then after the training.
Answer examines	Whether the scores of the same group at different time periods can be said to differ, meaning that the group improved over time.

	Hirata (2004)
Research question	Do English-speaking learners of Japanese who receive pronunciation training on a computer statistically improve their performance on pitch and duration contrasts in Japanese from a pretest to a posttest?
Answer examines	Whether the group who received an experimental treatment performed differently enough on their second testing so we cannot say their scores reflect only random variation from test to test.

Robust alternatives shown in this book: Bootstrapped *t*-test, means-trimmed *t*-test, bootstrapped and means-trimmed *t*-test

Classical non-parametric alternative: Wilcoxon signed-rank test

5.7 A Brief Overview of One-Way Analysis of Variance

5.7.1 One-Way Analysis of Variance: A Test of Group Differences

A logical extension of a *t*-test is the case where you have more than two groups or levels of a variable. The one-way **analysis of variance (ANOVA)** is used when you want to test whether the scores of three or more groups or levels differ statistically. Figure 5.4 shows the distribution of three groups on a measure of pronunciation. All the groups have similar variances (roughly understood as the spread of points in the box), but their mean scores all differ. (Actually, the box plot shows the median but since these are perfectly symmetric distributions the mean and median will be the same.) The one-way ANOVA will test the probability that the groups are different from one another.

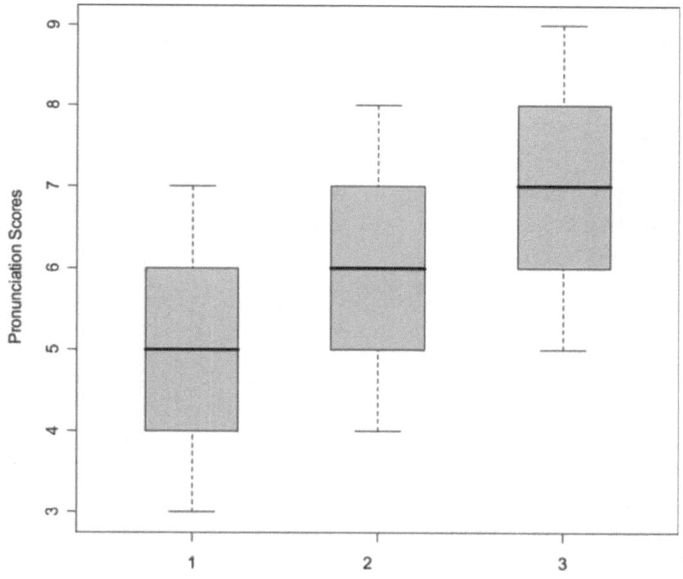

Figure 5.4 Distributions of data on a pronunciation measure for three groups.

A one-way ANOVA has the following attributes:

- It has exactly two variables.
- One variable is categorical with three or more levels and it is the IV. (This is typically something like experimental group or native language categorization.)
- The other variable is continuous and it is the DV.
- If you took averages of the variables, you would have measurements of three (or more) different groups.

Mnemonic device: A one-way ANOVA has at least three mean scores, so hold out three fingers. ANOVAs involve tests of group differences, so cross one finger over the other two, which will make an "A" for ANOVA.

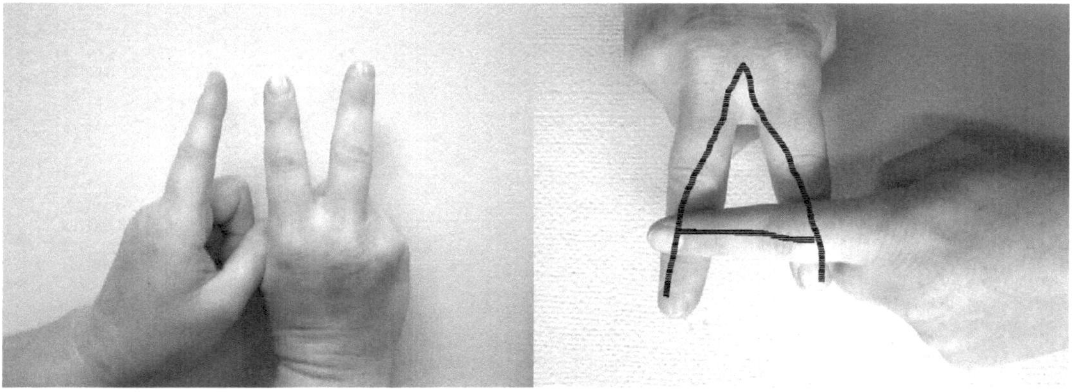

Research questions in SLA that have used one-way ANOVAs:

	Schauer (2006)
Research question	"Do learners in English as a foreign language (EFL) and English as a second language (ESL) contexts display differences in their recognition and rating of pragmatic and grammatical errors?" (p. 269). The third group tested were native speakers of English.
Answer examines	Whether the three groups (the IV) performed differently on correctly identifying pragmatic (one DV) and syntactic (a different DV) violations.

	Baker and Trofimovich (2006)
Research question	"Does the amount of L2 learners' experience influence their production of L2 suprasegmentals?" (p. 5). Three groups of Korean users of English were distinguished by their length of residence in the USA; native speakers of English were also tested.
Answer examines	Whether differences between four groups (the IV) are large enough to say that the groups differed in their production of suprasegmentals (the DV).

Robust alternative shown in this book: Bootstrapped one-way ANOVA, means-trimmed one-way ANOVA, bootstrapped and means-trimmed one-way ANOVA

Classical non-parametric alternative: Kruskall–Wallis test

5.8 A Brief Overview of Factorial Analysis of Variance

5.8.1 Factorial Analysis of Variance: A Test of Group Differences

A factorial ANOVA expands from *t*-tests and one-way ANOVAs by including more than one IV. If there are two IVs, we conduct a **two-way ANOVA**. If there are three IVs, it is a three-way ANOVA. As was seen in the one-way ANOVA section, each IV can have two or more levels. Therefore, these kinds of **factorial ANOVAs** are also sometimes labeled in a way that reports on the number of levels of the IVs. A study which had the IV of gender (levels: male or female) and experimental condition (A, B, or C) could be called a 2 (gender) × 3 (condition) ANOVA.

One advantage of a factorial ANOVA over a simple *t*-test or one-way ANOVA is that the interaction between factors can be explored. For example, it may be the case that males respond better to treatment A while females respond better to treatment B, as seen in Figure 5.5. With factorial ANOVAs we are beginning to use multivariate data sets, and although these are more complex they often reflect the more complicated nature of real people and real situations.

A factorial ANOVA has the following attributes:

- It has more than two variables.
- Two or more variables are categorical and they are IVs.
- Exactly one variable is continuous and it is the DV.

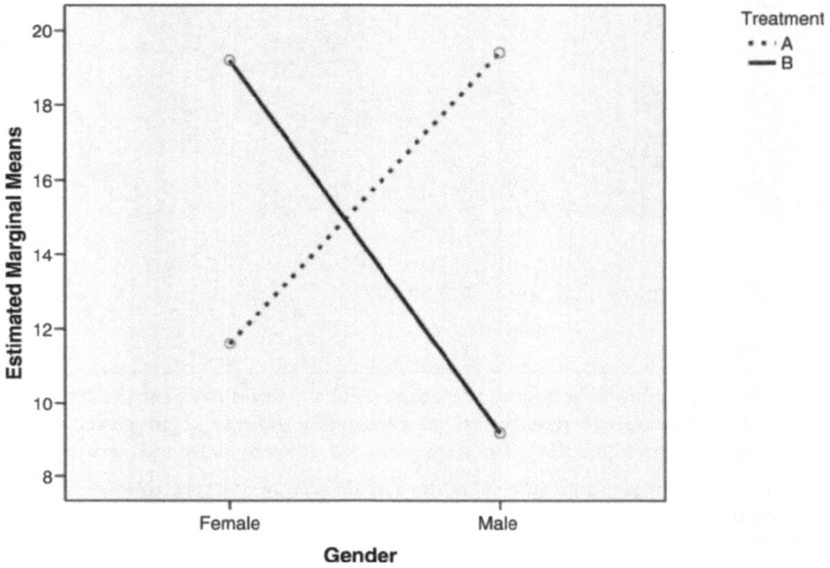

Figure 5.5 An interaction between gender and treatment type in a two-way ANOVA.

Mnemonic device: A factorial ANOVA, like multiple regression analysis, has many variables, so hold out two fingers from each hand. ANOVAs involve tests of group differences, so cross your fingers over the others. The result will look like a teepee, which you can think of as a "teepee factory" for *factorial* ANOVA. (I know, I am getting desperate here—so it is the last one!)

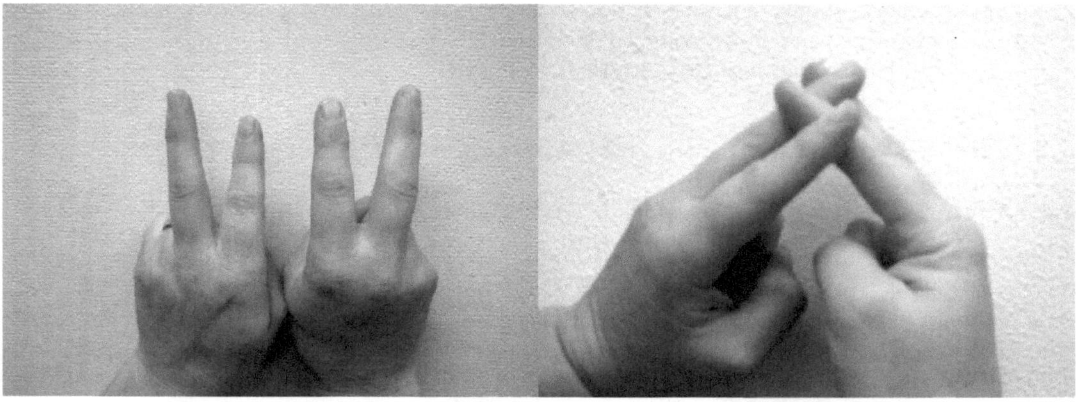

Two studies below reflect these more complicated research questions:

	Juffs (2005)
Research question	Does the L1 of learners from different language backgrounds affect how they process grammatical and ungrammatical wh-extraction in English sentences? Learners from four different L1 backgrounds were tested. Is there any effect for the specific kinds of structures that the wh-word is extracted out of? Three different kinds of structures were tested.
Answer examines	Whether the factors of first language and type of sentence structure (the IVs) affect the accuracy with which participants can judge sentences to be grammatical (or ungrammatical) (the DV), and whether these two factors interact. This would be a 4 (L1) × 3 (structure) ANOVA (in other words, a two-way ANOVA).

	Kondo-Brown (2006)
Research question	Do groups of readers who differ in their reading proficiency (more proficient versus less proficient) perform differently depending on whether they are guessing the meaning or pronunciation of unknown words, and also depending on whether they see the words in context or in isolation?
Answer examines	Whether groups performed differently on a test (DV) when the variables of task (guessing meaning or pronunciation) and context (words in isolation versus words in context) are taken into account, and whether task, context, and reading proficiency (the DV) interact. This would be a 2 (task) × 2 (context) × 2 (reading proficiency) ANOVA (in other words, a three-way ANOVA).

Robust alternative shown in this book (or online): Bootstrapped two-way ANOVA, means-trimmed two-way and three-way ANOVA, bootstrapped and means-trimmed two-way ANOVA, two-way percentile bootstrap using M-estimators

Classical non-parametric alternative: None

5.9 A Brief Overview of Analysis of Covariance

5.9.1 Analysis of Covariance: A Test of Group Differences

A slightly more complicated case of factorial ANOVA arises when the author wants to statistically control for some variable. This is called an **analysis of covariance**, or **ANCOVA**. The method of analysis is the same as for the factorial ANOVA, in that the **covariate** is also included in the analysis as the means of controlling for it. This chapter is available online.

An ANCOVA has the following attributes:

- It has more than two variables.
- One or more variables are categorical and they are IVs.
    - A catagorical IV may be a covariate.
- One or more variables are continuous.
    - Exactly one is the DV.
    - A continuous variable may be the covariate (this is more common than the categorical variable being the covariate).

This study has an ANCOVA design:

	Dromey, Silveira, and Sandor (2005)
Research question	Are there differences between groups with different language backgrounds (three groups) and different gender (two genders) in how accurately they recognize the affect in someone's voice when the participants' age is statistically controlled for?
Answer examines	Whether the factors of group membership and sex (the IVs) interact and have an effect on accuracy scores (the DV) in recognizing affective prosody. Age is a covariate, meaning its effect is subtracted. This would be a 3 (L1) × 2 (gender) ANCOVA controlling for age.

Robust alternative shown: Bootstrapped and means-trimmed ANCOVA with one covariate
Classical non-parametric alternative: None

5.10 A Brief Overview of Repeated-Measures Analysis of Variance

5.10.1 Repeated-Measures Analysis of Variance: A Test of Group Differences

Repeated-measures ANOVAs are ANOVAs for data in which the same participants were tested at more than one time (a longitudinal design), with more than one measure, or participated in more than one experimental condition (and were tested repeatedly). In other words, we cannot assume the independence of scores in the design because the same people were tested more than once. This type of design is also sometimes called a "mixed between/within ANOVA" if there are repeated measurements and the participants are also separated into groups for a different factor.

A repeated-measures ANOVA has the following attributes:

- It has more than two measurements, and can have any number of variables, although if there is only one independent variable it must have more than two levels.
    - There must be a within-group independent variable, meaning the same people are tested more than once and are in more than one of the groups. (This would usually be time, which is one variable, but it will have more than one level, such as pretest and posttest.)
    - There may be a between-group independent variable, meaning this variable splits people so each is found in only one group. (This could be experimental group, or gender, or native language, for example. This categorical distinction—experimental group, or native language—is one variable but will have at least two levels, such as control group vs. experimental group, or native speaker vs. non-native speaker.)
- Exactly one variable is continuous and it is the DV.

A design in which there is more than one DV is called a multivariate analysis of variance (MANOVA). However, in the field of second language research, few actual MANOVAs are used. In my search for linguistic studies in the Linguistics & Language Behavior Abstracts database, I found only a few articles that claimed to use the MANOVA. Of those, none actually tested more than one DV at a time. It may be that some authors are confused because one readout provided in SPSS when a repeated-measures ANOVA is performed is called "Multivariate." I personally can remember an article early in my career where I claimed to be using a MANOVA but I was actually doing repeated measures. Thankfully a reviewer corrected me! Because MANOVAs seem to be used so infrequently in the second language research field, I have not included them in this book.

Mnemonic device: There is no mnemonic device for repeated measures, but here is a hint—if you have a test conducted with the same people at different time intervals, it will be a repeated-measures test unless there is only one categorical variable with only two levels, such as testing time. (If the only variable is testing time with just pretest and posttest, it would be a paired samples *t*-test because there are only two mean scores.)

Here is a research question in SLA that has used a repeated-measures ANOVA:

	Toth (2006)
Research question	Will processing instruction provide any benefits over a communicative approach when participants must productively use Spanish *se* in a sentence production task? There were three groups, who all received different types of input. Will there be differences on a delayed posttest (24 days later) as well as an immediate posttest? There was also a pretest, resulting in three different times of testing. The use of three tests of the same participants results in the need for a repeated-measures statistical analysis.
Answer examines	Whether groups that were taught using different teaching methods (between-group IV) scored differently on a guided production test (the DV) using a pretest–immediate posttest–delayed posttest longitudinal design (within-group IV), and whether group and time of test had any interaction. This is a 3 (type of input) × 3 (time of test) repeated-measures ANOVA (repeated measures on time of test).

Robust alternative: Two-way bootstrapped and trimmed-means RM-ANOVA
Non-parametric alternative: None

A **repeated-measures ANCOVA** can also be conducted by simply including the covariate in the analysis. In this way, the researcher can examine the effects of the desired variables and their interaction knowing that the effects of the covariates have been mathematically factored out. The study below illustrates how an ANCOVA can be used with a repeated-measures design:

	Dewey (2004)
Research question	Do learners of Japanese progress more in their reading development in a situation of intensive immersion (where they do not leave the country where their L1 is spoken) or in a study abroad context living in Japan, over the course of a semester? Each of the two groups was tested at two time points, necessitating a repeated-measures ANOVA. In addition, because previous studies had shown that L1 and L2 reading ability affected reading development, measures of these constructs were also included in the analysis as covariates.
Answer examines	Whether two groups differ in their scores over time on a self-assessment task (the DV) when two variables shown to affect reading development are factored out (the covariates). This is a 2 (context, the between-group IV) × 2 (time of test, the within-group IV) repeated-measures ANCOVA (repeated measures on time of test), controlling for reading ability in L1 and L2 (in other words, L1 and L2 are partialled out).

5.11 Summary

I have now given you a quick overview of the types of statistical designs that can be used to answer certain kinds of research questions in the field of second language research. Although there was a lot of information contained in this chapter, I hope you realized that the major criteria for choosing which statistical test to use include:

- whether you are trying to test a relationship between variables or look for group differences;
- how many variables you have and how many levels or groups there are within the variable;
- whether the variables can be considered continuous or categorical; and
- whether the variables are seen as independent or dependent (or not really either, such as in a correlation).

In the coming chapters you will see these statistical tests illustrated by more actual studies in the field of second language research. The following application activity will give you some practice in putting the brief overview of this chapter into use in trying to figure out which test to use.

5.12 Application Activities for Choosing a Statistical Test

1 A researcher is interested in studying whether men and women differ in how politely they make requests in a second language.

  a What kind of statistical test could be used if the requests are categorized as either "polite" or "non-polite" so that we count how many men there are in the "polite" category and how many are in the "non-polite" category, and do the same for the women?
  b What kind of statistical test could be used if the requests are rated for politeness on an eight-point scale so there is one mean score for men and one mean score for women?

2 Robb, Ross, and Shortreed (1986) studied Japanese learners of English to see how four different kinds of written feedback for grammatical errors on weekly written work would affect the grammatical accuracy on a pre- and posttreatment cloze test.

  a What kind of statistical test could be used to compare the differences in the groups on the posttreatment cloze test, so there are four mean scores of the different groups on the test?

b What kind of test could be used to compare the differences in the groups on both the pre- and posttreatment cloze test, in order to test whether the groups were different and also whether there was any change from the pretest to the posttest?

3 Taguchi (2007) wanted to see whether having English-speaking learners of Japanese learn chunks would make them sound noticeably more fluent in a speaking test at the end of the semester when compared to one at the beginning. What kind of statistical test could be used to compare the mean scores of the Japanese learners at the beginning of the semester to their scores on fluency at the end of the semester?

4 Ellis, Heimbach, Tanaka, and Yamazaki (1999) conducted several tests to examine the effectiveness of learning vocabulary through different types of input and interaction.

a One study involved three groups, one group with unmodified input and no interaction, one group with modified input and no interaction and a third group with unmodified input and interaction. The authors measured how much vocabulary each group learned. What statistical test could be used to see whether the groups performed differently in the amount of vocabulary they learned?

b Another study looked at children in a group and counted the number of times each child negotiated for interaction. The children's comprehension scores were then examined to see if there was a relationship to the number of times they interacted. What statistical test should be used?

5 White, Spada, Lightbown, and Ranta (1991) wanted to see whether drawing learners' attention to grammar in question formation in English would change how accurately learners of English could create wh-questions.

a In Phase I, two groups, one which received form-focused instruction on question formation and another group which did not, were assessed on the accuracy of their question formation with a 15-item test. What kind of statistical test could examine whether there were differences in accuracy between the two groups?

b In Phase II more participants were studied and a third group of monolingual English speakers was added for comparison. What kind of statistical test could examine whether the non-native speakers were similar to the native speakers on the posttest?

c In Phase II the authors also wanted to see whether tests changed from pretest to posttest assessment. What kind of statistical test could examine whether the two non-native groups performed differently at the different time periods?

6 A researcher is interested in studying whether individual factors such as high language learning aptitude and strong motivation result in higher levels of tonal accuracy in second language learners of Thai.

a The researcher wants to know whether there was a relationship between aptitude and scores on a 20-point tone identification test. Which statistical test can be used to examine the relationship between these two variables?

b The researcher then examines how much of the difference in scores on the tone test can be explained by the factors of language learning aptitude and a motivation score. What kind of statistical test can be used to do this?

7 Bialystok, Craik, Klein, and Viswanathan (2004) performed a study to see whether being bilingual affected reaction time scores on a response task. The authors looked at a younger and an older bilingual group and also compared the bilinguals to monolinguals doing the same task. The task also involved congruent tasks (hitting a key on the keyboard that was on the same side as the stimulus on the computer) and incongruent tasks (hitting a key on the keyboard on the opposite side to the stimulus on the computer).

a In order to see whether age, language group, and type of task affected reaction times, what kind of statistical test could be used?

b The authors gave their participants an intelligence test. If they wanted to perform the same analysis as in (a) but factor out the possible effects of intelligence, what kind of statistical test could they use?

8 One of the questions Dixon (2012) examined was whether rates of identification for talented and gifted programs differed between Spanish L1 English L2 schoolchildren and monolingual English schoolchildren. What kind of statistical test could be used to examine this question?

9 Kim (2013) gave English language learners a pretest to see how well they could understand sarcasm. A subset of these learners participated in nine 1-hour sessions designed to teach them more about sarcasm. After these Schema for the Orienting Basis of Action interventions, teaching students about how to recognize facial expressions, gestures, body movements and language that indicate sarcasm, the learners completed an immediate posttest. A delayed posttest was given five weeks later. Native English speakers were also tested just once for comparison purposes.

a Which test could be used to compare the learners' pretest scores to their immediate posttest scores?

b Which test could be used to see how learners' pretest scores differed from their immediate posttest and delayed posttest scores?

c Which test could be used to compare the learners' posttest scores with those of native speakers?

10 Dewaele (2013) wanted to see what the relationship was between foreign language classroom anxiety and a personality trait of neuroticism. He measured both of these traits by means of a continuous variable. Which test did he use to investigate the relationship between these two measures?

Chapter 6

Finding Relationships Using Correlation

Age of Learning

> Probably the shortest true statement that can be made about causality and correlation is 'Empirically observed covariation is a necessary but not sufficient condition for causality.
>
> Edward Tufte (2003, p. 4)

In looking at individual statistical tests, I will start with **bivariate correlation**, which means the correlation between two variables. In my experience, correlation is the most intuitively understandable statistical test for those who are new to statistics because noticing that two properties are related is a common experience for all people. A correlation is thus looking for some relationship, some common variation, between two variables.

Correlation as a statistical test involves two variables that are both continuous. Some examples from daily life provide an intuitive feel for what correlation involves. For example, height and weight in individuals are usually highly correlated. The taller a person is, the more they will likely weigh. Although the area of intelligence quotient (IQ) is controversial, there has also been research showing that IQ scores of parents and children are highly correlated (Plomin, 1999). The number of alcoholic drinks you may choose to ingest on a given evening will directly affect (correlate with) your general sense of well-being the next morning.

Recent Examples of Correlation in the Second Language Acquisition Literature

Rodgers (2011)

This study looked at whether verbal morphology becomes more automatic with increasing practice by looking at correlations between reaction times and error rates in a picture identification task (receptive) and a picture description task (productive) among three different levels of L2 Italian learners. The design of the study seemed to have no hypothesis that one variable was causing the other, but rather was searching for whether there was indeed a relationship.

Foster, Bolibaugh, and Kotula (2014)

The authors investigated the relationship among Polish–English bilinguals between native language selection, as tested by two readings where participants were asked to underline odd expressions, and six variables: (1) engagement with L2 community; (2) motivation to acquire a high level of L2; (3) age of onset of learning the language; (4) length of exposure to the L2; (5) phonological short-term memory; and (6) context of acquisition (inside or outside target language country). The authors explicitly stated that native language selection was a dependent variable (DV) that could possibly be affected by the six independent variables (IVs) they examined.

Cherciov (2013)

The author wanted to explore how attitude affects first language attrition and second language proficiency in Romanian–English bilinguals. She measured attitude both using a questionnaire and through interviews, and found differences in a qualitative and quantitative approach to the same question. Her approach set up attitude as an IV to the DVs of attrition levels and L2 proficiency.

Dewaele (2013)

The author's main aim was to explore the correlation between foreign language classroom anxiety and the personality traits of psychoticism, extraversion and neuroticism, and the linguistic factor of knowledge of languages among adult language learners and users in England and Spain. In addition, levels of classroom anxiety among the different languages of the learners (L2, L3 and L4) were also differentiated. Dewaele's approach simply looked for relationships and did not assume that one factor was affecting another in any certain way.

Correlation can be either negative or positive. Figure 6.1 shows a positive correlation on the left side and a negative correlation on the right side. In the field of second language research, an example of a positive correlation would be the relationship between speaking and listening ability in a language. In other words, the larger the speaking ability, the larger the listening ability is. In a second language, listening and speaking are highly related, although not exactly the same thing. An example of a negative correlation would be the topic of this chapter, which is a decline in test scores as second language learners become older. In other words, as age gets larger (older), test scores get smaller. However, even though a correlation is negative the relationship between the two variables can be equally strong (the strength of the relationships shown in Figure 6.1 are about $r = \pm 0.80$).

Human beings also like to search for causes and effects. Thus, if in your experience you have seen that the attitude of students affects how proficient they become in a second language, you may have concluded that a positive attitude causes higher achievement in language learning. However, establishing cause and effect is a trickier proposition than simply establishing correlation. A statistical test can tell us whether two things we have measured have a relationship, but the test itself cannot tell us which one causes the other (or whether both mutually influence each other, as may be the case with language attitudes).

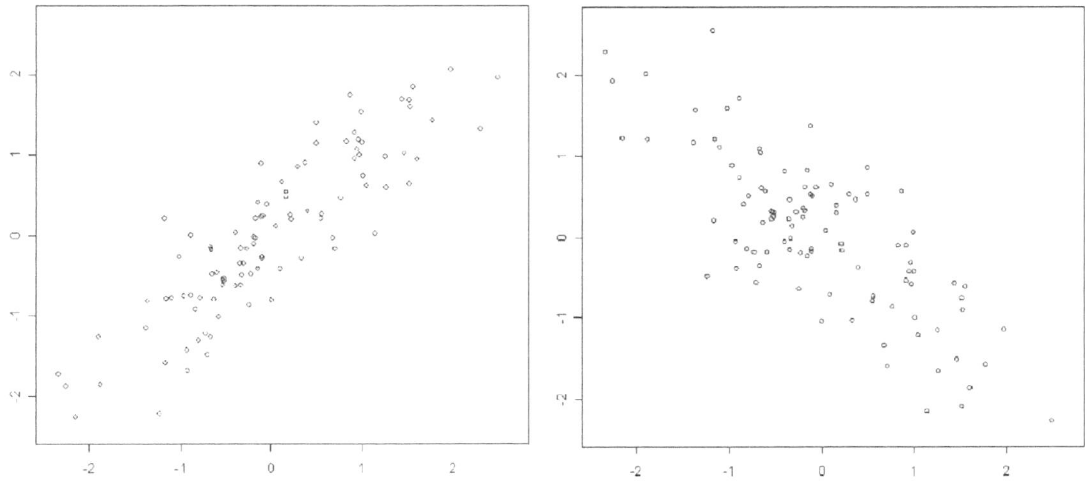

Figure 6.1 A scatterplot of a positive correlation (left side) and a negative correlation (right side).

There is a well-known and justifiable caution in statistics that "Correlation does not equal causation." In other words, we cannot conclude just because two measurements vary together that one has caused the other. However, in many cases, we are very interested in establishing causality when we do research, and there are ways to point toward a causal relationship even when using correlation. First, Maxwell and Delaney (2004) noted that an experiment where the researcher manipulates some variable that groups differ on, such as the type of input received, will more convincingly show evidence of causality than one where the groups are divided based on an already existing condition, such as age of learning. Second, one may use logic and reason. If you find a correlation between A and B, then logic dictates that A is the cause of B, B is the cause of A, or there is some external factor, C, which is the cause of both A and B. We can often make a good guess, depending on theory, previous research or just common sense, about which way causality might be running (Shadish, Cook, & Campbell, 2002). For example, Moyer (1999) found a correlation between satisfaction with pronunciation and accent scores for second language learners of German. If we exclude the possibility that a third variable (C) is involved, common sense tells us that it is more likely that good pronunciation causes the satisfaction rather than the satisfaction causing good pronunciation.

6.1 Visual Inspection: Scatterplots

Simple correlations tell us to what extent two variables are related or, in other words, vary together. If there is a correlation between two variables, we should be able to impose a line on the scatterplot data points, sloping either upward or downward through the data. The more tightly clustered around the line the data are, the stronger the correlation. Thus, the first assumption we must satisfy to test for correlation is that the relationship between the data is linear. It is possible but not desirable to find a statistical correlation for data that do not have a linear relationship, so the first step in performing correlation is to take a graphic look at your data.

6.1.1 The Topic of Chapter 6

One area of interest in the field of second language research is the relationship between age and ultimate outcomes in language ability. Many studies have shown that there is a relationship between the age at which a person begins learning a second language and how well that person can perform on tests of grammatical judgment (DeKeyser, 2000; Flege, Yeni-Komshian, & Liu, 1999; Johnson & Newport, 1989; McDonald, 2000) or be judged to sound like a native speaker of the language (Flege et al., 1999; Oyama, 1976; Patkowski, 1980).

Data from two of these experiments will be used in this chapter. DeKeyser (2000) gave 57 Hungarian immigrants to the USA a 200-point grammaticality judgment test of English. The participants varied in the age at which they first arrived in the USA and started learning English. DeKeyser found a negative correlation, meaning that, as age of arrival increased, scores on the grammaticality test decreased. Flege, Yeni-Komshian, and Liu (1999) examined 240 Korean immigrants to the USA on their ability to produce sentences as well as native speakers of English. The accent rating is the number from 1 to 9 that native English speakers gave to the learners' sentence-length productions. Again, the relationship here is negative in that the older the learners were when they arrived in the USA, the lower on average their accent scores tended to be. The line that Flege et al. (1999) fit to the data, however, is not linear, but a third-order (or cubic), non-linear fit to the data, which allows the line to change direction twice.

In performing a correlation, our first step should always be to examine the data to see whether the relationship between these two continuous variables is linear. Scatterplots allow us to judge whether the data are in fact linearly related, and are an excellent, information-rich graphic to publish in papers because they show all of your data to the reader.

6.2 Creating Scatterplots in SPSS

In this section I work with the DeKeyser2000.sav SPSS data file. Create a scatterplot by clicking on GRAPHS > LEGACY DIALOGS > SCATTER/DOT. (In SPSS version 12.0 the additional LEGACY

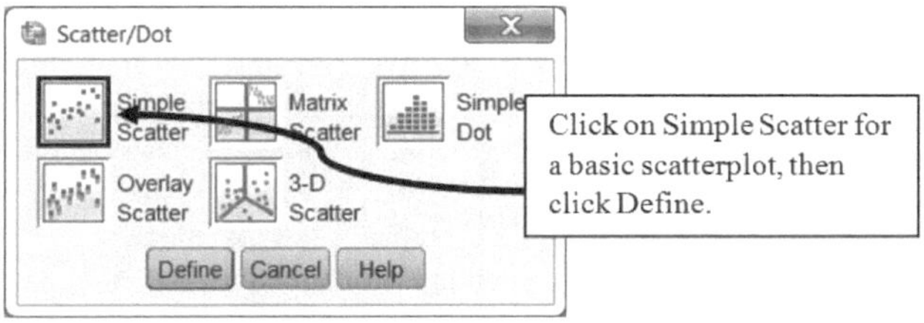

Figure 6.2 Choosing a scatterplot in SPSS.

Dialogs layer did not exist; in general, I still find the traditional way of doing graphs in SPSS more intuitive than the "Interactive" charts that SPSS currently provides; you may want to experiment with the Interactive option and see which you prefer.) A dialog box, shown in Figure 6.2, appears with several options for scatterplots. Pick the Simple Scatter scatterplot and then click on Define.

All of your variables will be listed on the left side of the scatterplot dialog box shown in Figure 6.3. Choose the two you want to plot and put them into the x-axis and y-axis boxes. Note that there is no good rule of thumb for which way to best plot your variables. If you decide to change the orientation afterward, you can easily do this with the Chart editor.

Tip: Note in Figure 6.3 that there is a ruler by all of the variables. The ruler means that the variables are numeric, or defined by numbers. Note that it does not mean that the variables are continuous. For example, the variable STATUS is a categorical variable with only two values, either the number "1" or the number "2." If your variable is not numerical, it is a string according to SPSS. You can use it in statistical calculations but only in places where you need a categorical variable, such as when you define groups. You would not be able to use a string variable in a correlation or scatterplot. You can change a variable's status by going to the Variable View tab and clicking on Type for the row (variable) you are interested in changing.

The scatterplot of the data in Figure 6.4 shows that, although the points do not lie in a perfect line, there is a general downward trend in the data. This means that, as participants started learning English at an older age, in general their performance on the morphosyntactic test grew worse. The inspection of the scatterplot shows that there is no other kind of non-linear relationship between the data, such as a U-shaped or curvilinear distribution. It is therefore appropriate to test for a linear relationship in the data by performing a correlation.

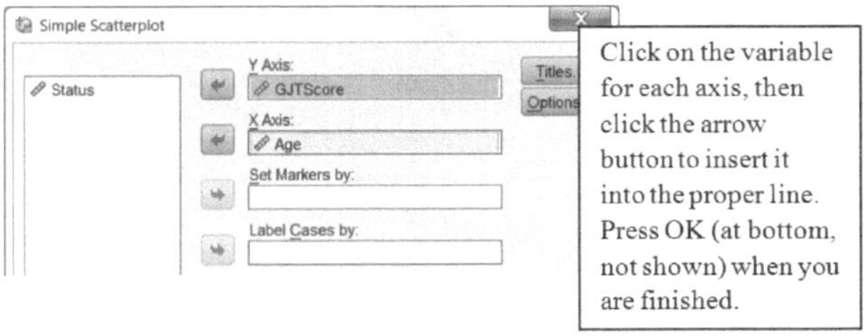

Figure 6.3 Scatterplot dialog box in SPSS.

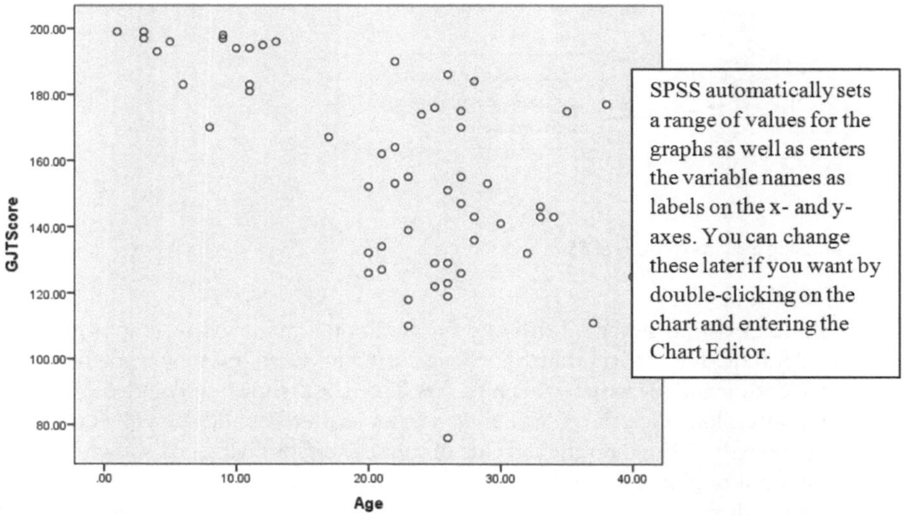

Figure 6.4 SPSS scatterplot of DeKeyser (2000) data.

> *Creating a Scatterplot in SPSS*
>
> 1 On the drop-down menu, choose GRAPHS > LEGACY DIALOGS > SCATTER/DOT. When a dialog box comes up, choose SIMPLE SCATTER for a two-variable scatterplot, and click on the Define button.
> 2 Put one variable in the x-axis box and another in the y-axis box. Click on OK.

6.2.1 Adding a Regression or Loess Line

Adding a **regression line** to a scatterplot can visually illustrate a linear relationship between variables. You may or may not want to include a regression line in published work, depending on your purposes for displaying the scatterplot. To add a regression line, first open the CHART EDITOR by double-clicking the graphic itself. The CHART EDITOR opens a reproduction of the graphic that you can change in a variety of ways (see Figure 6.5). All of the changes you make will be consolidated on your graph when you close the CHART EDITOR.

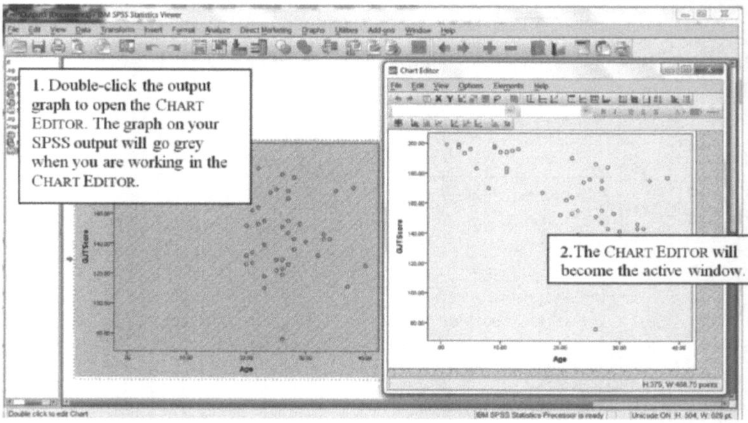

Figure 6.5 The Chart Editor in SPSS.

To fit a regression line, in the CHART EDITOR open the ELEMENTS > FIT LINE AT TOTAL menu choice or click on the "Fit Line at Total" button, shown circled in Figure 6.6. When you call on the CHART EDITOR to add a FIT LINE AT TOTAL, the PROPERTIES dialog box opens, as seen in Figure 6.6. A new feature of SPSS version 22.0 is that an equation for the regression line will be attached to the line. If you do not want this, tick off the button at the bottom of the properties box that says "Attach label to line."

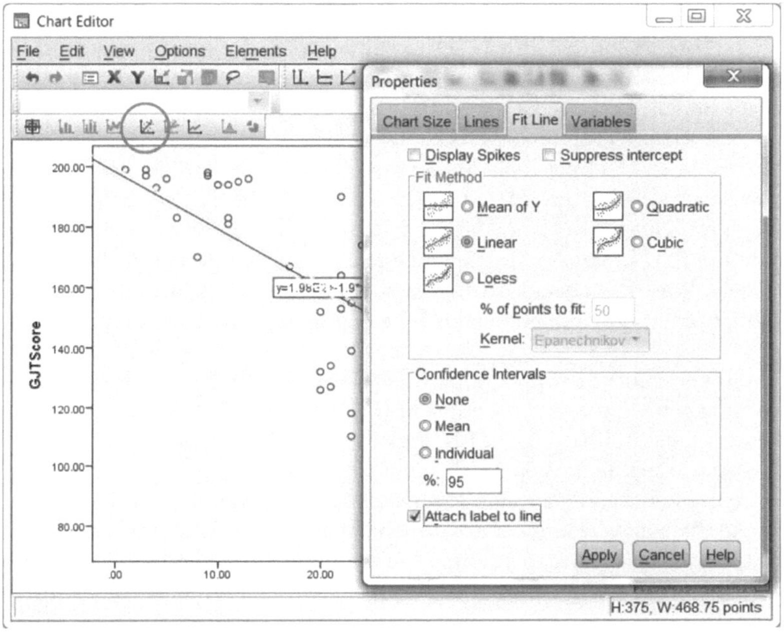

Figure 6.6 Using the Chart Editor to draw a regression line in SPSS.

> **Tip:** If you are working with older versions of SPSS like version 12.0, you add a regression line by first clicking on a data point while in the CHART EDITOR and then opening the menu sequence ADD CHART ELEMENT > FIT LINE AT TOTAL. If you want to add lines for separate groups, you need to click twice, slowly, on a point within the group, and then open the menu option. Repeat this process with a different group.

The option for LINEAR is already chosen in the PROPERTIES box, so if you want a regression line all you need to do at this point is click on CLOSE. (See Figure 6.7 for examples of regression lines drawn on the scatterplot.) Close the CHART EDITOR and you will see that the regression line has been drawn on your data, and that an "R Square Linear" value has been imposed on the chart to the right of the figure. This is the size of the shared variance between the two variables, and ranges from −1 to 1. The closer this value is to ±1, the more variance the factors share. If a variable were correlated with itself, the value would be a perfect ±1.

Another useful type of line listed in this PROPERTIES box is a Loess line. The **Loess** line is a locally weighted running-line smoother, and it considers only small chunks of the data at a time as it draws lines based on weighted least squares (Wilcox, 2001). In layman's terms, it fits the shape of the data by considering small intervals of the data at a time, instead of the overall pattern fit by a least-squares regression line. The Loess line is a way to examine the assumption of **linearity** in the data (Everitt & Dunn, 2001). This assumption says that the relationship between the two variables should approximate a straight line. I believe it is a good idea to provide both a regression line and a Loess line on published scatterplots (Larson-Hall & Herrington, 2009) so readers can evaluate the assumption of linearity (or other types of curves that you may want to claim fit the data better).

Let us take a look at the Flege et al. (1999) data now (FlegeYeniKomshianLiu.sav), since the authors found that a non-linear (third-order, or cubic) fit to the data was better than a straight regression line. First I create a scatterplot with the variables of age of arrival (the variable is called AOA) and scores on a pronunciation measure in English (PRONENG) using the command shown in the previous section (GRAPHS > LEGACY DIALOGS > SCATTER/DOT; then choose SIMPLE SCATTER). Next, I double-click on the graph that is shown in the SPSS output to open the CHART EDITOR. Now, from the CHART EDITOR's menus, I choose ELEMENTS > FIT LINE AT TOTAL. To get a Loess line, I choose Loess from the PROPERTIES dialog box. I also want to put a cubic fit line as well as a regression line on the data. To make the lines look different, after I have chosen the line, I change to the LINES tab of the PROPERTIES dialog box. Here I can change the weight, color and pattern of the line. I APPLY the changes, and CLOSE the dialog box. To additionally impose other fit lines on the scatterplot, I again open up the FIT LINE AT TOTAL command, pick a different fit line, and make sure to change the look of each line. If you decide to change some feature of the line later, simply click on the line until it is highlighted, then double-click and the dialog box that pertains to that part of the graphic will open.

Figure 6.7 shows an unbroken cubic fit line, a dotted regression line and a dot-dash line for the Loess fit on the Flege et al. data. The R^2 data for the cubic fit (0.749), printed on the graphic, is indeed larger than the value of the regression line (R^2=0.730). However, the Loess line seems to show that the data after age 20 scores do not so much go up (as the cubic fit shows) or down (as a regression line would predict) but rather taper off with only a slight downward trend. In any case, with all three lines on the data, you can evaluate the claims of a linear fit versus a cubic fit for yourself, which is definitely a point in favor of adding these kinds of lines to published scatterplots. I have argued (Larson-Hall & Herrington, 2009) that best practices for presenting scatterplots are to always draw both a regression line and Loess line over the data.

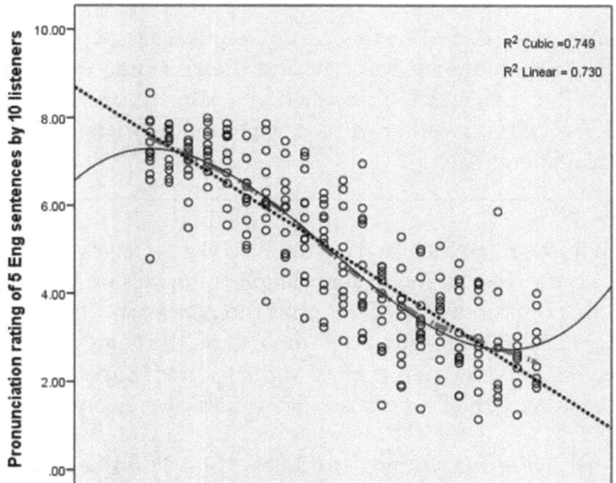

Figure 6.7 Scatterplot of Flege, Yeni-Komshian, and Liu (1999) pronunciation data, with a regression line (dotted), a cubic fit line (solid) and Loess line (dot-dash, in red) imposed on it.

Adding a Fit Line to a Scatterplot in SPSS

1 Double-click on your created scatterplot. This will open the CHART EDITOR, giving you a replica of your plot.
2 From the CHART EDITOR drop-down menu, choose ELEMENTS > FIT LINE AT TOTAL or click on the menu choice for the fit line. From the PROPERTIES dialog box, choose the LINEAR option for a straight regression line, the LOESS option for a line that fits the data more closely, or one of the other options.
3 When you are satisfied with the graph (and there are other options you may want to explore in the CHART EDITOR; just click on the area you would like to change and you usually can change it), close the CHART EDITOR and you will now have a graph that can be copied and pasted anywhere.

6.2.2 Viewing Simple Scatterplot Data by Categories

You can in effect add a third variable to your graph by using the SET MARKERS BY option in the SCATTERPLOT dialog box (see Figure 6.8). Use the menu sequence GRAPHS > LEGACY DIALOGS > SCATTER/DOT as before, but enter an additional categorical variable in the SET MARKERS BY box. DeKeyser (2000) had two categorical groups—participants who had begun to study English before age 15, and those who started after 15. To graphically see whether there appear to be differences between these two groups, we can use the SET MARKERS BY option to create a different look for each group. By entering a categorical variable into the SET MARKERS BY box, SPSS will then code the two groups with different colors and insert a legend.

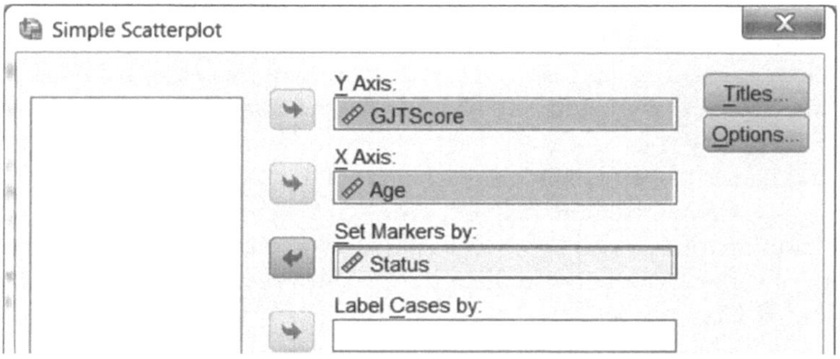

Figure 6.8 Dividing into groups in a scatterplot in SPSS.

You can make separate fit lines for each group by using the menu chain in the CHART EDITOR (after double-clicking on the graph to open the CHART EDITOR) ELEMENTS > ADD FIT LINE AT SUBGROUPS. There is also a menu button in the in CHART EDITOR that will do the job. It is to the right of the ADD FIT LINE AT TOTAL button and looks like this: . Figure 6.9 and especially the R^2 values show that the negative correlation is quite slight if each group is considered separately, although it slopes downward more for the earlier group (under 15) than for the later group (over 15).

Splitting Data into Groups on a Scatterplot in SPSS

In the SIMPLE SCATTERPLOT dialog box, add a categorical variable to the SET MARKERS BY box.

Customize the graph by adding fit lines or changing the properties of the plotting characters from the CHART EDITOR.

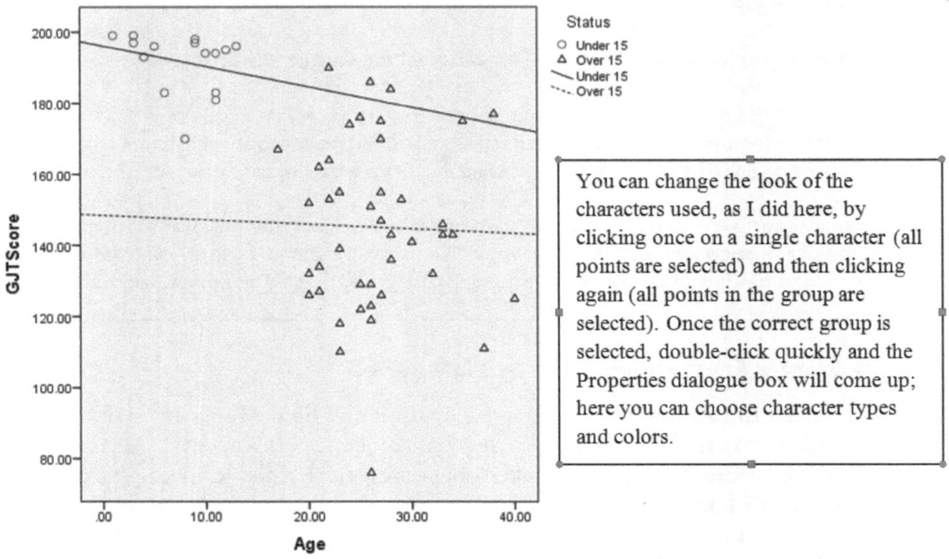

Figure 6.9 SPSS Scatterplot of DeKeyser (2000) data with division into groups.

6.3 Creating Scatterplots in R

In this section I work with the data from Flege et al. (1999) using the file FlegeYeniKomshianLiu.sav. (This file excludes the native speaker group.) In R, create a scatterplot by first opening up the R program, then the graphical interface R Commander with the command **library(Rcmdr)**. Use the menu sequence DATA > IMPORT DATA > FROM SPSS DATA SET to import the SPSS file called FlegeYeniKomshianLiu.sav and name it **flegeetal1999**. Your imported data set should have 240 rows and 9 columns. (See Section 1.3.2 if you need more help importing SPSS files into R.)

After calling for a scatterplot using the GRAPHS > SCATTERPLOT drop-down menu (Figure 6.10) you will subsequently see a list of variables for both the X and Y variable (Figure 6.11). The only variables that will appear are what R Commander calls "numeric" as opposed to "character" variables. This means that if you have any variables coded by letters instead of numbers, you will have to change them to numbers for them to be visible to the system. (See Section 1.4.5 for more information about types of data in R.)

The latest version of R Commander that I am using (2.0-0) provides several ways to change the look of your scatterplot in its OPTIONS tab (see Figure 6.11). The default will call for marginal box plots that illustrate just one dimension of the data spread on each axis, a least-squares line that is the straight regression line you can draw on correlational data (or at least, you assume you can), a smooth line that does Loess smoothing (in other words, it fits a line that follows the curve of the data) and an indication of spread showing the square root of the variance. Later you may decide you do not want your scatterplot to look so busy, and it is then easy to deselect some of these options.

The regression line (the straight line) on the Flege et al. (1999) data (Figure 6.12) shows a fairly steep negative correlation in the data set, while the Loess line (which smooth the data and is the heavier line on Figure 6.12) shows some curvature, with younger starters scoring higher than the regression line predicts until age 12 or so, and older starters scoring lower than the regression line predicts until about age 19 or 20, when the Loess line crosses the regression line. In layman's terms, it fits the shape of the data by considering small intervals of the data at a time, instead of the overall pattern fit by a least-squares regression line. The Loess line is a way to examine the assumption of linearity in the data (Everitt & Dunn, 2001), and if the regression and Loess line match, this provides confidence in the assumption of a linear trend to the data. In the case of the data from the Flege et al. (1999) study,

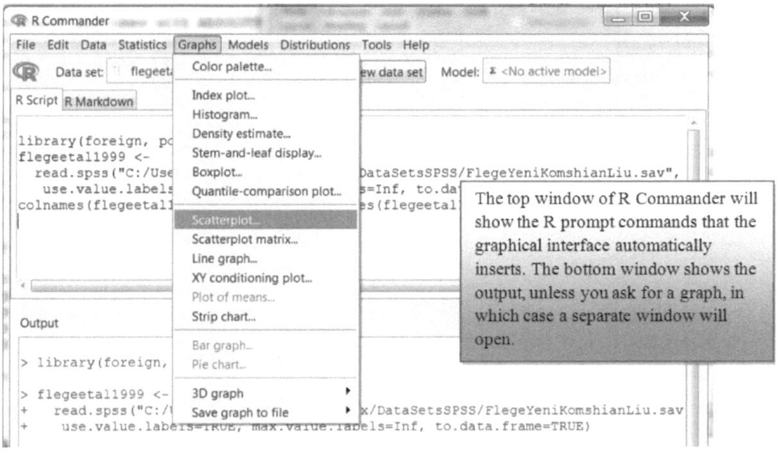

Figure 6.10 Calling for a scatterplot in R Commander.

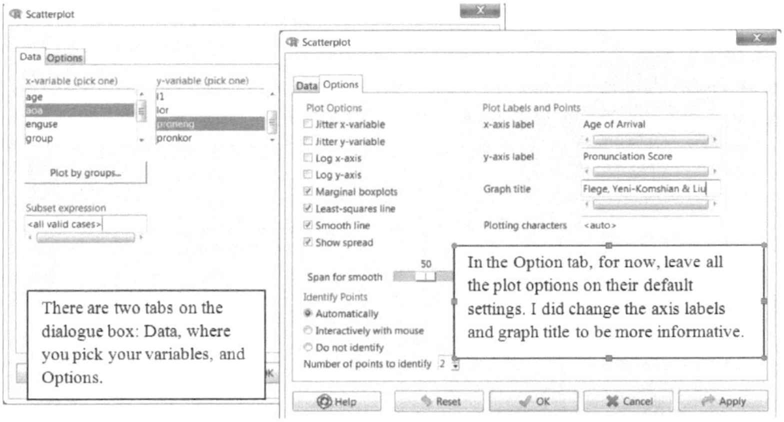

Figure 6.11 Choosing options when creating a scatterplot in R Commander.

the Loess line might be considered "close enough" to the regression line to treat the data as linear, but there would be justification for also considering a third-order (cubic) fit to the data, as Flege et al. (1999) did. I have argued (Larson-Hall & Herrington, 2009) that best practices for presenting scatterplots are to always draw both a regression line and a Loess line over the data. This way the readers can ascertain for themselves if your data satisfy the assumption of a linear relationship.

6.3.1 Modifying a Scatterplot in R Console

Although R Commander gives you the flexibility to modify variable names or the types of lines you put on your scatterplot, there may be other ways you will want to modify your graph as well. In general, the easiest way that I have found to do this is to copy the R Commander code and paste it to the R Console. This code can then be altered with various arguments to get the desired result. The syntax for making the scatterplot can be found in the upper Script Window of R Commander (see Figure 6.13).

I will now break down the code for the scatterplot in Figure 6.12. Use this template as a guide as you tweak various parts of the scatterplot, but you can always feel free to experiment by changing various parts one at a time to see what happens to your resulting graph. By the way, you can get a more complete list of all of the arguments of the scatterplot command by typing >help(scatterplot).

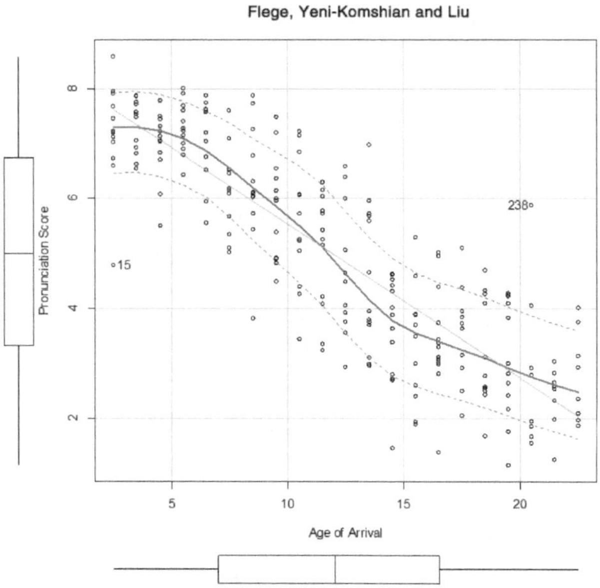

Figure 6.12 Scatterplot of Flege, Yeni-Komshian, and Liu (1999) pronunciation data, with a regression line (green, solid and straight), Loess smoother (red and solid) and a measure of variance around the Loess line (red and dotted lines) imposed on it. Extreme points are identified with their row numbers.

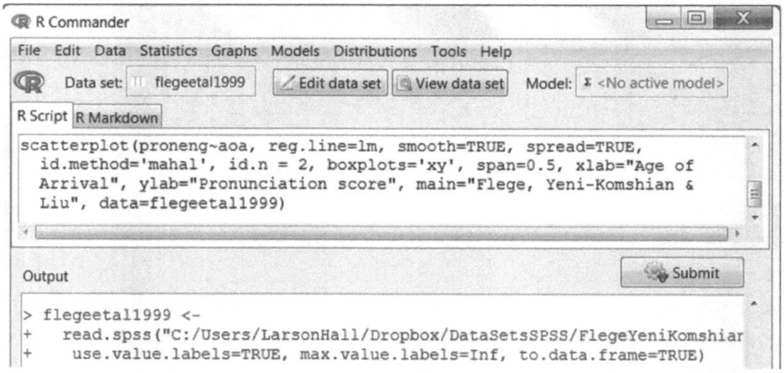

Figure 6.13 Obtaining R commands from the script window of R Commander.

> **Tip:** Use the up arrow on the keypad while in R Console to scroll through previously typed commands. This can be useful if you make a mistake in typing and need to correct an error in a previous command.

```
scatterplot(proneng~aoa, reg.line=lm, smooth=TRUE, spread=TRUE,
id.method='mahal', id.n = 2, boxplots='xy', span=0.5, xlab="Age of
Arrival", ylab="Pronunciation score", main="Flege, Yeni-Komshian &
Liu", data=flegeetal1999)
```

scatterplot (. . . ~ . . .)	Creates a scatterplot graphic, and needs two arguments.
proneng~age	Specifies the variables to use; the tilde (~) can be read as "is modeled as a function of," so here the GJT score is modeled as a function of age of arrival.
reg.line=lm	Tells R to draw a least-squares regression line.
smooth=TRUE	If TRUE, it calls for a Loess line.
spread=TRUE	If TRUE, it adds two lines outlining the variance to either side of the Loess line.
ld.method='mahal'	The method of identifying extreme points in the data is chosen here; this is the Mahalanobis distance from the mean of x and the mean of y; other choices are "x" (absolute value of x − mean of x) and "y" (absolute value of y − mean of y).
id.n = 2	Identifies the two most extreme points in the data.
boxplots='xy'	Produces box plots along the margin of the scatterplot.
span=0.5	Refers to how often the data are sampled to create the Loess line.
xlab="Age of arrival" ylab="Pronunciation score"	Put whatever you want to appear on the x- and y-axes in between the quotation marks.
main="Flege, Yeni-Komshian & Liu"	Put a title for the graph in between the quotation marks.
data=flegeetal1999	Specifies the data set that should be used. Without this command, the syntax will not know where to find the variables gjtscore and aoa, unless you have previously attached the data set, like this: attach(flegeetal1999).

Below is a list of some additional arguments you may want to add to make more changes to your scatterplot. A more complete list can be found by typing help(par), which gives a list of graphical parameters.

> **Tip:** Because the command can get long, you may want to paste it onto a different place, like a Word document, to add in different arguments easily and then paste the result into the R Console. One thing to be careful of here, however, is your quotation marks. R will not accept Word's "smart quotes" which are curly. Copy and use the quotes that you pasted over from R which are just straight up and down.

cex=1.6	Magnifies the size of the scatterplot dots relative to the graph; the default is 'cex=1'.
pch=2	The plotting character can be changed. Either an integer code for a symbol or an actual character can be used. Codes are 1 = circle, 2 = triangle, 3 = cross, 4 = 'x' and 5 = diamond (more are available; type help(points) to see more info). To use a single character, just be sure to put it in quotes. For example, if you type pch="Q" then all the points will be represented by the letter "Q".
font.lab=2	Changes the style of the fonts in the axis annotation, x and y labels and main titles. Integers are used and 1 = plain, 2 = bold, 3 = italic, and 4 = bold italic.
col=c("yellow", "orange", "pink")	Changes the color of the regression line, smooth line (and associated spread or variances lines if these are called for), and plotting characters, in that order; if using by.groups=T to look at different groups on the scatterplot (see Section 6.3.2 below) the first position specifies the color used for the plotting characters, regression line, smooth line and variance line of the first group. (Additional groups follow in order, so the second position of the argument will specify the color for the second group, etc.) Type colors() to see a full list of colors in R.
col.axis="orchid" col.lab="blue" col.main="red"	These parameters change the color of the annotation of the axis, the x and y labels and the main title (in that order, from the top).
legend=(x,y,legend=c("Name1", "Name2"), fill=c("grey", "red"))	Will plot a legend for groups in the area you specify with the x and y arguments. (Use the locator( ) command to let you find a place on the plot and get the coordinates returned to you.) Fill in the titles of the legend boxes using the fill argument.

The **plot()** command can also be used to create a scatterplot, but it takes more work to get it to look as nice as the graph called with the **scatterplot()** command.

Creating a Scatterplot in R

1. First import your data or, if the data are already imported, make sure your data set is the active one in R Commander by clicking on the "DATA SET" button in the upper left corner of R Commander's interface. From the drop-down menu, choose GRAPHS > SCATTERPLOT.
2. In the SCATTERPLOT dialog box, choose your x- and y-axes variables in the DATA tab. In the OPTIONS tab you can customize your graph by adding axes or labels or graph titles, removing or keeping the regression and Loess lines, spread (variance) lines and marginal box plots that are called with the standard command, or jittering the points (which spreads out your points if you have a limited range of numbers so there are many points at the same intersection). When finished, click on OK.
3. The basic scatterplot command in R is:

```
library (car) #this activates the car package, which has the scatterplot command
scatterplot (proneng~aoa, data=flegeetal1999)
```

6.3.2 Viewing Simple Scatterplot Data by Categories

To add a third variable to your scatterplot by graphically dividing your points up into different groups, open up the R Commander GRAPHS > SCATTERPLOT drop-down menu as before. I will illustrate this process using the SPSS file DeKeyser2000.sav that I have imported and named **dekeyser**. In the dialog box, I choose **age** for the x variable and **gjtsscore** for the y variable. Click on the "Plot by groups" button.

If you would like to divide your data by a categorical variable, only variables that are factors in R will be available. If you have imported a file from SPSS, if the variable was "Numeric" in SPSS but had defined groups in the Values area of the "Variable View" tab, it will automatically be imported as a factor into R. Also, if the variable was labeled as "String" in SPSS it will be imported as a factor. However, if the variable you want to use is *not* labeled as a character variable in R, you can change it into a character variable and a factor.

You can check the structure of your data set by using the **str( )** command, like this:

```
> str(dekeyser)
'data.frame': 57 obs. of 3 variables:
 $ age : num 8 11 9 11 13 4 1 12 3 10 ...
 $ gjtscore: num 170 181 198 194 196 193 199 195 197 194 ...
 $ status : Factor w/ 2 levels "Under 15","Over 15": 1 1 1 1 1 1 1 1 1 1 ...
```

This tells us that the **status** variable in the **dekeyser** data set is already a variable. However, if you have a variable whose status you want to change, use the following command:

```
dekeyser$status<-factor(dekeyser$status)
```

Then check the status of your data set and you should see that the variable that was supposed to change has indeed changed.

In the **dekeyser** data, however, this is already a factor, so you can just click on **status** when you click on the "Plot by groups" button (see Figure 6.14).

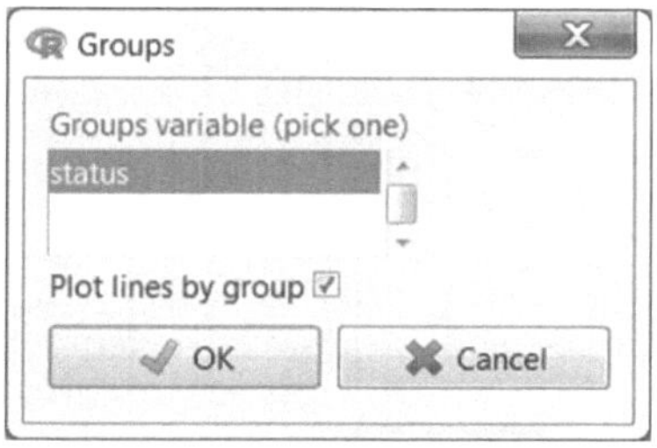

Figure 6.14 Plot by groups button in R Scatterplot command.

The resulting graph (Figure 6.15) shows the data split into two groups, one who arrived in the USA before age 15 and one who arrived after that age.

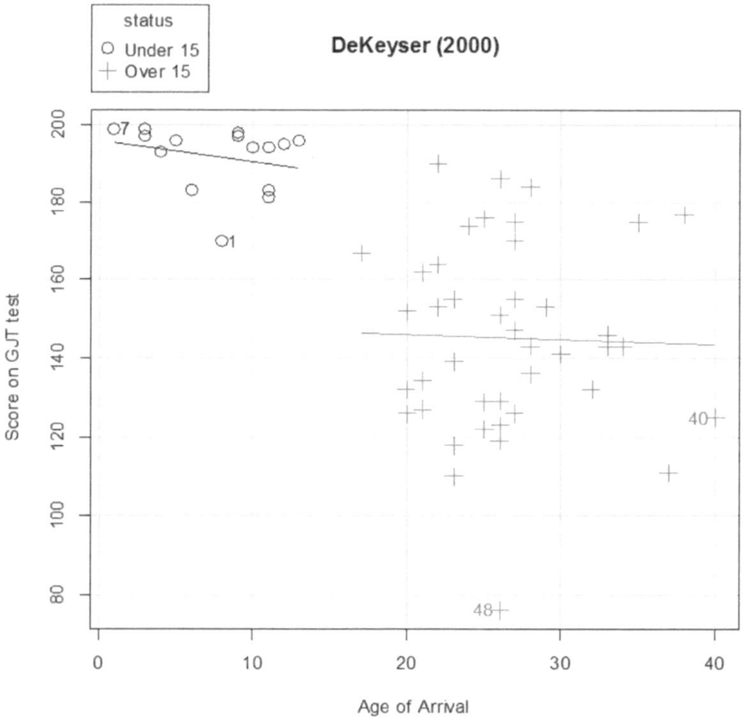

Figure 6.15 R Scatterplot of DeKeyser (2000) data with division into groups.

A legend is automatically added in the upper margin. The syntax of this command changes slightly from that found in the previous section. A simplified version is:

```
scatterplot(gjtscore~age | status, by.groups=TRUE, data=dekeyser)
```

The main difference is that status is added as a splitting variable, and the command by.groups=TRUE is added. If by.groups is set to FALSE, the regression and Loess lines will be drawn over the entire group.

Splitting Data into Groups on a Scatterplot in R

1. First make sure the variable you will use to split groups by is categorical and labeled a factor by R. If not, use the factor command in R Console:

```
dekeyser$status<-factor(dekeyser$status)
```

2. From R Commander's drop-down menu, choose GRAPHS > SCATTERPLOT and then use the "Plot by groups" button to choose the splitting variable. In the R Console, the basic command for a split-group scatterplot is:

```
library (car) #opening this package may not be necessary
scatterplot(gjtscore~age | status, by.groups=TRUE, data=dekeyser)
```

6.3.3 Application Activities with Scatterplots

1. Recreate the scatterplot for DeKeyser (2000). Use the file DeKeyser2000.sav. Create a simple scatterplot of the variables AGE and GJTSCORE. Draw a regression line and a Loess line over the scatterplot. Do the data appear to be linear?
2. DeKeyser noted that the results on the test for participants who had arrived in the USA before age 15 and after age 15 seemed to have different kinds of shapes. The data are already split along this dimension by the variable **Status**. Recreate the scatterplot in Figure 6.14 which adds a third dimension (group division) to the scatterplot. Draw regression and Loess lines on the data. What kind of relationship do age and test scores have for each of these groups?
3. Draw a new scatterplot for the Flege et al. (1999) data. Use the file FlegeYeniKomshianLiu.sav. Create a simple scatterplot of the variables LOR (length of residence) and PRONENG. Draw a Loess line over the scatterplot. What trends do you see?
4. Use the data from Larson-Hall (2008). Use the LarsonHall2008.sav file. This data set was gathered from 200 Japanese college learners of English. The students took the same 200-item grammaticality judgment test that the DeKeyser's (2000) participants took. Create a simple scatterplot of the variables GJTSCORE and TOTALHOURS of study to see whether students performed better on this test the more hours of study of English they had. Draw a regression line and a Loess line over the scatterplot. Is there a positive linear relationship among the variables of **totalhrs** (total hours studied) and **gjtscore**, so that we could say that with more hours of study of English, students perform better on the test? Do you note any outliers in the data? If so, identify them.
5. Using the same data set as in exercise #4 above, graphically divide the data into two groups—early and later learners—using the variable ERLYEXP. I wanted to know whether students who had taken private English lessons before age 12 (early learners) would ultimately perform better on morphosyntactic tests than Japanese learners who started study of English only in junior high school at age 12 (later learners). Separate your graph into these two groups and draw regression and Loess lines over both groups. What trends can you see? Comparing the regression and the Loess lines, would you say the data are linear?
6. Dewaele and Pavlenko Bilingual Emotions Questionnaire (2001–2003). Use the BEQ.Swear.sav file. Dewaele and Pavlenko gathered these data online from a large number of bilinguals. Explore whether there is a correlation between the age that bilinguals started learning their L2 and their own self-ratings of proficiency in speaking their L2. Create a scatterplot between the variables of AGESEC and L2SPEAK. Put a regression line and a Loess line on the data. What trend can you see? Are the data linear?
7. Abrahamsson and Hyltenstam (2009) examined data from 195 Spanish L1 participants who started learning Swedish L2 at various ages of onset for learning Swedish, but had lived in Sweden for at least 10 years. Ten native speakers of Swedish listened to speech samples and

rated each participant as a native speaker or not, and those scores were totaled up for a maximum of 10 points if every judge thought the speaker was a native speaker of Swedish. Open the Abrahamsson&Hyltenstam.NoNS.sav file and see how strong the relationship between score as a native speaker of Swedish and age of onset for learning Swedish L2 is. Plot both a regression line and a Loess line on the scatterplot. Are the data linear?

6.3.4 Multiple Scatterplots

In some cases you may have a large number of variables to correlate with each other, and in these cases it would be very tedious to graphically examine all of these correlations separately to see whether each pairing were linear. Statistics programs let us examine multiple scatterplots at the same time. I will use data from my own research, Larson-Hall (2008), to illustrate this point. (In R, import the LarsonHall2008.sav file "as lh2008".) I will examine a subset of Japanese learners of English who began studying formally outside of school when they were younger than age 12. To make the graphics manageable, I will only show scatterplots from a 3 × 3 matrix of the variables of language aptitude test scores, age, and a score for use of English.

6.3.5 Creating Multiple Scatterplots with SPSS

As you did for simple scatterplots, choose GRAPHS > LEGACY DIALOGS > SCATTER/DOT. Now, however, choose the MATRIX SCATTER option and insert any number of variables that you want. For Figure 6.16, I put in the variables AGE, USEENG and APTSCORE. You can also use SPSS to put a regression or Loess line on this data, just open up the CHART EDITOR and use the menu sequence ELEMENTS > FIT LINE AT TOTAL.

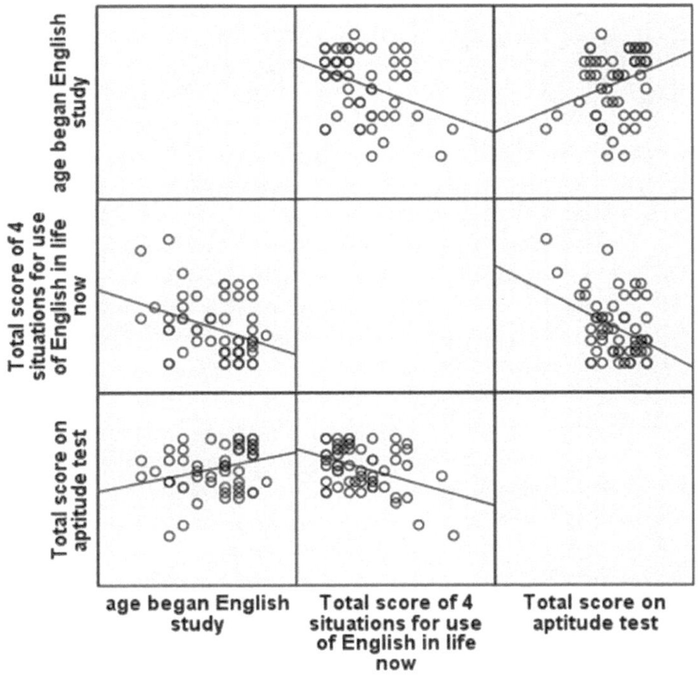

Figure 6.16 SPSS multiple scatterplot of three variables in Larson-Hall (2008) data.

Creating a Multiple Scatterplot

1. On the drop-down menu, choose GRAPHS > LEGACY DIALOGS > SCATTER/DOT. When a dialog box comes up, choose MATRIX SCATTER and press the DEFINE button.
2. Insert as many variables as you are examining into the MATRIX VARIABLES box. If you wanted to split variables by groups, you can put a categorical variable in the SET MARKERS BY box. Click on OK. Fit lines can be added by using the CHART EDITOR as explained in Section 6.2.1.

6.3.6 Creating Multiple Scatterplots with R

In R Commander, choose GRAPHS > SCATTERPLOT MATRIX. In the SCATTERPLOT MATRIX dialog box DATA tab, choose three or more variables in the normal way that you would select multiple items in Windows. (Hold down the "Ctrl" key while left-clicking separate variables, or use "Shift" and scroll down with the left mouse key to highlight adjacent variables.) I chose the variables **age, aptscore** and **useeng**. In the OPTIONS tab, you will find your choice of graphics to insert in the diagonal: density plots, histograms, box plots, one-dimensional scatterplots, normal Quantile-Quantile (Q-Q) plots or nothing. You can experiment with which of these extra plots may be the most informative and understandable. The one shown in the Figure 6.17 is the default, which is the density plot. This plot gives you a good sense of the distribution of the data, if the variable is not a categorical one. (If it is, the distribution will be very discrete, as in the density plot for age.) You can also decide whether to put regression lines, Loess lines and the variance around the Loess line (in the option "Show spread") on each graph, just as in the single scatterplot. Additionally, you can decide to label extreme points by changing the spinner after "Number of points to identify in each panel and group." R Commander's multiple scatterplot is shown in Figure 6.17.

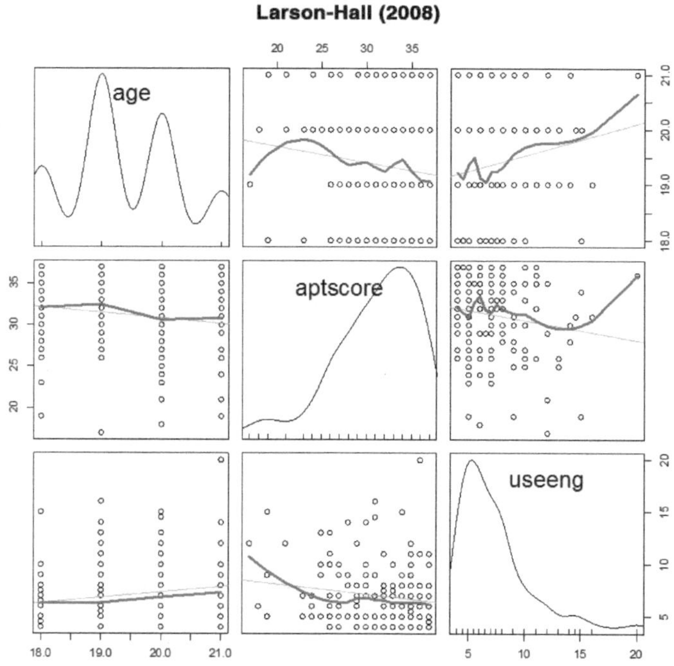

Figure 6.17 R multiple scatterplot of the Larson-Hall (2008) data with density plots of separate variables on the diagonal.

This graphic is implemented with the following syntax:

```
scatterplotMatrix(~age+aptscore+useeng,reg.line=lm,smooth=TRUE,spread=FALSE,span=0.5,id.
n=0, diagonal = 'density', data=lh2008)
```

The command scatterplotMatrix creates the matrix, and the variables are listed after the tilde. They are combined using a plus sign. The only other command that is different from the simple scatterplot command is diagonal = 'density', which plots a density plot along the diagonal. (Other choices are 'histogram', 'boxplot', 'oned' (one-dimensional scatterplots), 'qqplot', and 'none'.)

If you have a data frame that contains only the variables you want to examine, you can call a multiple scatterplot with the simple command plot( ).

Creating a Multiple Scatterplot in R

1 From the R Commander drop-down menu, choose GRAPHS > SCATTERPLOT MATRIX. When a dialog box pops up, select multiple variables by holding down the Ctrl button and clicking on the variables. All of the variables must be numeric, not character. (In other words, they cannot be categorical variables.) Use the "Plot by groups" button if you would like to split groups. Choose an additional graph to put on the diagonal, such as a density plot or histogram. When finished, click on OK.
2 The basic command in R Console for a 3 × 3 scatterplot matrix is:

```
library (car) #opening this package may not be necessary
scatterplotMatrix(~age+aptscore+useeng, reg.line=lm, smooth=TRUE, span=0.5,
diagonal = 'density', data=lh2008)
```

6.3.7 Interpreting Multiple Scatterplots

The matrix scatterplot is necessarily information-rich, so take some time to really study it. You are basically looking to see whether you are justified in assuming the linearity of your variables. In the previous examples, there were nine boxes in the 3 × 3 matrix, but the three main graphs you should be looking at were either above or below the diagonal line that runs from the top left to the bottom right. These three boxes (the three in the upper right-hand diagonal or the lower left-hand diagonal) are mirror images of the other side. For the three boxes that lie along the diagonal, SPSS leaves them blank while R fills them with other types of graphs. If you compare the two kinds of scatterplot matrices, you can see the R matrix is easier to read and more informative.

R adds more information by giving graphs along the diagonal. In Figure 6.17, the graphs along the diagonal are the density plots of each separate variable, showing how many points are contained at each discrete point along the x-axis. For example, for the box labeled "age," there are only four ages at which the participants were tested, so the data here are quite discrete. (You can see the ages labeled to the right of the top row as 18, 19, 20 and 21.) The graphs above (or below) the diagonal show the intersection of two variables. So the middle graph in the top row is the intersection of the two variables "age" and "aptscore."

Interpreting these scatterplots may be more difficult than looking at individual scatterplots because the plots are smaller. However, at this point you should just be checking to make sure the data only have linear or randomly scattered patterns, not curvilinear or U-shaped patterns, so that you can ascertain whether the linearity assumption of the correlation test has been met. Therefore, a quick glance at the scatterplot matrix can be quite helpful when many variables are involved. In looking at Figures 6.16 and 6.17, we can see that the relationships among the three intersections we are considering appear to be linear or perhaps random, and do not follow any specific non-linear pattern, so we may proceed with further correlational analysis.

6.4 Assumptions of Parametric Statistics for Correlation

If you wanted to conduct what is considered a "normal" type of correlation that you will see reported in research in the field, you want to use a Pearson product-moment correlation. In this section I discuss which assumptions you should fulfill to perform a parametric correlation (i.e. Pearson's). However, a word of caution here. Statistics is about finding the best fit for the data, and it may turn out that a linear model of correlation may not be the best fit for your data. The previous sections have shown how to graphically examine your data to test the assumption of linear relationships between variables by using scatterplots. There are a variety of different models that may be used to characterize non-linear data, such as non-linear regression, non-parametric rank correlation (Spearman's rank-order correlation), tree models and Loess models (a comprehensive look at all of these alternatives is beyond the scope of this book, but see Crawley, 2012, for a very clear exposition of these models). What I am trying to say is that you may be looking for relationships between variables, but if you use a correlation you are making an assumption that the best way to describe the relationship is with a straight line. A correlation is a linear model of the data. Chapter 7 on multiple regression will explore in more detail what a statistical model of the data entails.

The first assumption of correlation is that the data are related linearly. As seen above, this assumption must be tested by examining the data visually. Besides linearity, further assumptions for a parametric correlation are that the data should be independently gathered, normally distributed and homoscedastic (i.e. having equal statistical variances) (Hatch & Lazaraton, 1991; Miles & Shevlin, 2001). Table 6.1 summarizes these assumptions.

Hatch and Lazaraton (1991) suggested that the assumption of **independence** means that the scores of one person must not influence the scores of another person in the data set. In other words, good old participant AB should not be influenced by the way that participant YZ took the test. (In other words, we sure hope YZ did not tell AB the answers to the test before AB took it!) For this kind of independence assumption, maintaining independence needs to be addressed in the research design. However, another thing to keep in mind is that independence means that each line of data in your data set needs to be independent from the others. This may mean that each row consists of data from one person and one person only. Therefore, having each row represent one entire group of data is unacceptable in any kind of statistical calculation. (See the **Watch Out!** box for an illustration of this.) Another problem would be if the same person was repeated in more than one row of data. If this occurs, then you have repeated measures data and you cannot use a correlation.

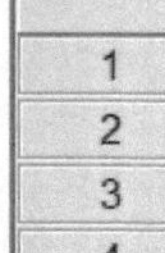

Watch Out!

Data for a correlation should look like this:

	id	age	LOR	aptitude
1	EG227	46	20.0	45
2	FS228	50	13.0	22
3	HD230	38	12.5	56
4	JF233	55	35.0	18

where each row contains data from a separate person. (Usually in SLA it is a person, although it could be something else like a particular textbook I suppose!) You cannot do correlations across *groups* of people. For example, let us say you tested 10 participants at 4 different sessions on their ability to correctly produce irregular past tense verbs, and you wanted to see how their scores, which were produced in a spoken and a written situation, were related. That sounds like a correlation! You calculated their group performance score at each session like this:

	Group	Spoken	Written
1	Session 1	.83	.62
2	Session 2	.88	.52
3	Session 3	.74	.89
4	Session 4	.85	.73

You might think you can then run a correlation on the two variables of Spoken vs. Written but this would violate the independence of observations assumption. Because your participants all participated in multiple sessions, these data would need to be analyzed with a repeated-measures test to look at whether their performance had changed over time and with the condition of a written or spoken environment. You would need to go back to a data set where each person was found in one row only, like this:

ID	S1.Spoken	S1.Written	S2.Spoken	S2.Written
EG227	.56	.89	.73	.25
FS228	.50	.52	.55	.48
HD230	.70	.70	.56	.63
JF233	.92	.57	.91	.60

Table 6.1 Assumptions of Parametric Correlation (Pearson's *r*)

Meeting correlation assumptions		*Correlation*
(1) Linear relationship between each pair of variables	Required?	Yes
	How to test assumption?	Examine scatterplots to rule out non-linear relationships; use multiple scatterplots to look at many variables at one time.
	What if assumption not met?	(1) Transform the variables to make the relationship linear; (2) try other kinds of models to better describe the data (cubic, quadratic, Loess models, etc.).
(2) Independence of observations	Required?	Yes, but should ideally be addressed in research design before experiment is conducted.
	How to test assumption?	Plot residuals against case number (see p. 262).
	What if assumption not met?	Gather new data.
(3) Variables are normally distributed	Required?	Yes, both for individual variables and for the relationship between variables
	How to test assumption?	Examine plots for normality (histograms, Q-Q plots)
	What if assumption not met?	(1) Use a robust correlation instead of a parametric one to avoid assumption of normality or remove outliers while preserving independence of observations; (2) transform variables to make distribution more normal; (3) use a non-parametric Spearman's rank test.
(4) Homogeneity of variances (constant variance)	Required?	Yes
	How to test assumption?	Plot studentized residuals against fitted values and look for equal spread across entire graph (see Chapter 7).
	What if assumption not met?	(1) Use robust methods in order to avoid assumption of homoscedasticity; (2) transform variables to make variances more equal; (3) use a non-parametric Spearman's rank test

The best way to satisfy the assumption of independence is to introduce randomness in how data are gathered, judged or graded. Usually participants are not selected truly randomly in the second language research field, but one can strive to at least randomize assignment to groups, so that each volunteer for a study is randomly assigned to a specific group, but often intact classes are used in second language research and this is definitely not random assignment to groups.

The assumption of a normal distribution is not a trivial one and it has been addressed earlier in this book in Chapter 3. As mentioned in that chapter, robust statistical tests are a good alternative to or even as companions to parametric methods. Robust methods mean that data do not have to satisfy the assumption of an exactly normal distribution. Since it is often impossible to tell whether the data from your small sample are indeed normally distributed, it is a nice idea to use robust methods as a companion to or a replacement for the parametric statistics.

The assumption of **homoscedasticity** (sometimes also spelled homoskedasticity) means that the variance of the **residuals** (residuals are what is not accounted for in the model) for every pair of points on the IV is equal (Miles & Shevlin, 2001). This assumption is equivalent to the assumption of homogeneity of variances required for *t*-tests or analysis of variance (Miles & Shevlin, 2001). The way to check this assumption is by examining the residuals plot, but do not worry about how this can be done until you have read Chapter 7 on multiple regression. If the variances are not equal then the data are **heteroscedastic**. Note that robust methods can also alleviate the need for data to be homoscedastic as well as normally distributed (Wilcox, 2012a, 2012b).

Note that for the most part the statistical procedure is not going to tell you if you have violated any of these assumptions! It is up to you to check them and to report this in your results. I do recommend using robust statistics, which deal better with the data if they do not satisfy the assumptions of normality and homoscedasticity, and will deal just as well with the data if they do satisfy those assumptions (Wilcox, 2012a, 2012b). Non-parametric versions of correlation can also be useful if the data do not satisfy these assumptions either, and they include Spearman's rank correlation coefficient or Spearman's rho (ρ), or the Kendall rank correlation coefficient or **Kendall's tau-b** (τ). These non-parametric correlations are generally preferred when the data is ordinal, meaning that the measurements are ranked (Howell, 2002). For example, if you had 20 students perform an oral interview and did not give them a numerical score but instead ranked them relative to one another in proficiency level, you would have a rank ordering.

One more question might be whether there is any minimum sample size needed to perform a correlation. There is not, although in general a larger sample provides more reliable results because it results in less sampling variability and narrower confidence intervals (CIs). However, the correlation coefficient (which, we shall see, is called r) is an effect size and will reflect the strength of the correlation regardless of the sample size. We will see the effect of a small sample size in the CIs though, which will necessarily be quite wide, meaning we cannot have a lot of faith in the point estimate of the correlation coefficient (which is also the effect size).

6.4.1 Effect Size for Correlation

The effect size that is calculated for correlations is R^2, which is usually described as a measure of how much of the variance in one variable is accounted for by the other variable. This definition can be confusing for those not yet familiar with statistics, however, and so I will borrow a very nice example from Crawley (2002, p. 235), which I think portrays what effect size means in a much clearer way.

Look at the two scatterplots in Figure 6.18, produced using the TeachingDemos package in R (Snow, 2013). Remember that you can obtain a package in the R Console by typing `install.packages("TeachingDemos")`. The command to get a window with sliders to adjust for r is: `run.cor.examp(n=50) #set n to whatever you want`. You'll need the tkrplot package to run this demo. The two graphs have the same y intercept and slope of the line, but they differ in the amount of distance that the points are scattered from the regression line.

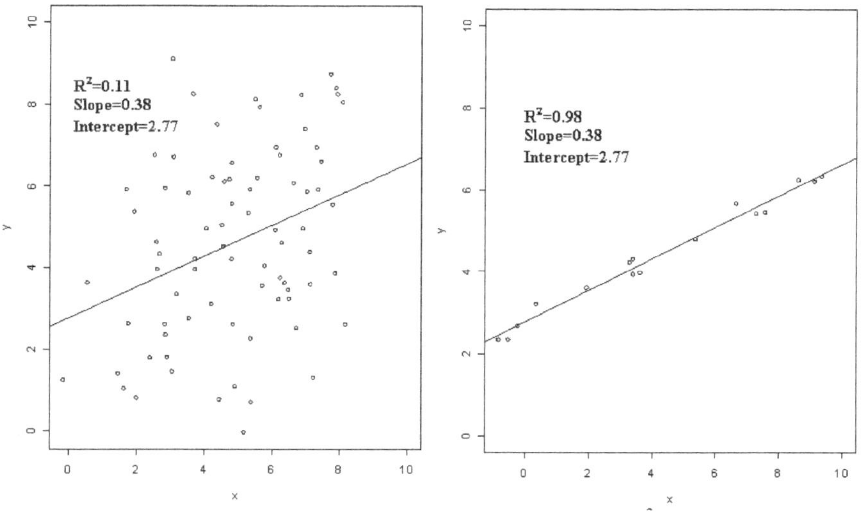

Figure 6.18 The effect of scatter on the correlation effect size (R^2).

R^2 is a measurement of how tightly these points fit the regression line. If the fit is perfect and all the points are lined up exactly on the regression line, R^2 will equal 1. In Figure 6.18, the scatterplot on the right has almost a perfect fit, meaning that almost all of the variance away from the line is accounted for. If there is a very poor fit and the points are widely scattered away from the regression line, R^2 will be low and close to 0. The scatterplot on the left in Figure 6.18 shows that the regression line does not account for a large amount of the variance between the variables, although it does account for some, because R^2 is greater than 0. This illustrates graphically how the variance in scores, or scatter away from the regression line, is accounted for by the R^2 statistic.

R^2 is a percentage of variance effect size, from the *r*-family of effect sizes. Cohen (1992) defined effect sizes for R^2 as $R^2 = 0.01$ is a small effect, $R^2 = 0.09$ is a medium effect and $R^2 = 0.25$ is a large effect, but he also encouraged researchers to define effect sizes for their own fields. Plonsky and Oswald (2014) have provided some guidelines for the second language acquisition (SLA) field that are more stringent than Cohen's. Extrapolating from their guidelines for the correlation coefficient for *r*, we would then say that: $R^2 = 0.06$ is small, $R^2 = 0.16$ is medium and $R^2 = 0.36$ is large. Once again, however, these numbers are not set in stone and interpretation can be given within subfields as well. For example, thinking about some of the effect sizes that have been found with regard to age and language learning, DeKeyser and Larson-Hall's (2005) survey of critical period studies found that age of arrival accounted for at least 50% of the variance in scores ($R^2 = 0.50$) in all studies, with other factors such as length of residence and motivation having much smaller effect sizes, such as $R^2 = 0.05$ or less. In this subfield I might argue that R^2 needs to be at least 0.40 to be considered large, while anything below 0.10 might be considered small.

Just in case you think such pronouncements make everything easy and clear, Cumming's (2012) ESCI program has a nice demonstration page where you can look at scatterplots for different values of *r* and see what amount of scatter you will find for that value of *r*. In many cases it is hard to tell the difference in the amount of correlation just by looking at the scatterplot, but it is definitely a good idea to try to visualize what different *r*-values look like on a scatterplot. To do so, go to ESCI chapters 14–15 and click the "See *r*" tab. For example, Figure 6.19 shows scatterplots for the values of *r* that would make up some of Cohen's and Plonsky and Oswald's values. (I just took the square root of the R^2 value listed; $R^2 = 0.25$ would be equal to $r = 0.5$, for example.)

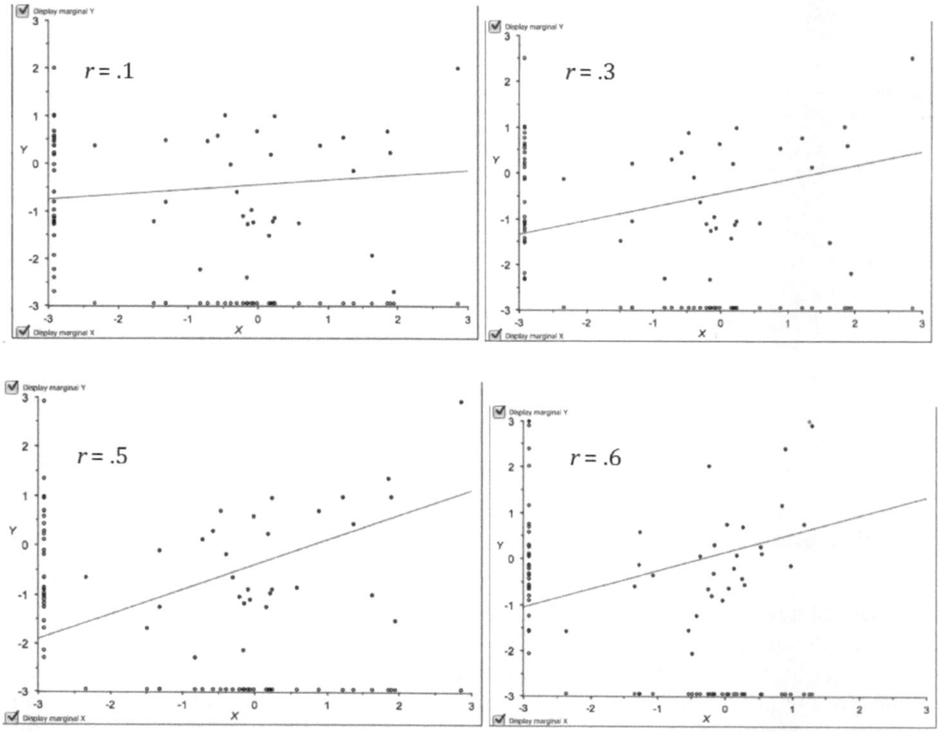

Figure 6.19 Four scatterplots, each with $N=30$, with differing levels of r, drawn with Cumming's ESCI program. Regression lines of x against y are drawn over the scatter, and each plot also shows the marginal points for both the x and y axes (where the dots would be found on the axis if they were dropped down to the axis)

6.4.2 Confidence Intervals for Correlation

Chapter 4 discussed CIs and how important they are for understanding statistics better. Confidence intervals can be calculated for correlations, but there is an additional wrinkle. Correlation coefficients are bounded, and can only be calculated from −1 to 1. So a CI cannot be $r = 0.8 + 0.24$, because then the r-value would be larger than 1! Cumming (2012) suggested that an approximate but very good way to calculate CIs for correlations is to transform the r-value into a z-score on a normal curve. Confidence intervals can then be calculated for the z-score value, and these are transformed back into r-values for the appropriate CI. Because you are using software, you will not need to actually perform this transformation yourself, but I just wanted to make you aware of what is happening when CIs are calculated.

6.5 Calculating Correlation Coefficients and Confidence Intervals

We have now arrived at the point in this chapter when you will actually calculate the correlation coefficient! It has taken a while to get here. To me, it is kind of like painting a wall of your house—you have to do a lot of preparation work before you can actually slap the paint on the walls, such as make sure the walls are clean, sand off any parts that are flaking off, tape up the edges and put down something so the paint does not splatter on your furniture and floor. That is all hard work to get you to the point where you can put the paint on, which is pretty fun. If you just start painting without any preparation though, you will have a big mess on your hands and your paint job will not look good. In the same way, if you start doing your correlation without actually looking at your data with scatterplots, and thinking about whether the assumptions of correlations are fulfilled, you will end up with garbage. As they say in the computer world, "Garbage in, garbage out"! So do not skip the previous steps outlined in this chapter before you undertake the relatively easy and fun step of computing the correlation coefficient and its accompanying CI.

In the output for a correlation, you will want three pieces of information:

1 The correlation coefficient and which test it came from (Pearson's *r*, Spearman's rho, etc.).
2 The 95% CI of the correlation coefficient, if it is possible to calculate it. (It is for Pearson's *r*.)
3 The number of items or participants (*N*) involved in the correlation.

In contrast to the first edition of this book, I am throwing away the requirement to list a *p*-value. As discussed in Chapter 4, in this book I will use statistics that emphasize what researchers are actually interested in, which is asking whether there is an effect, how large the effect is and to what extent it is practically important. Because the actual test statistic of a correlation is itself an effect size (*r*, which can be squared to make another effect size, R^2), it is easy to see how large the effect is right away. The *p*-value is not necessary to understand anything about a correlation; if the sample size is large enough, any correlation will be "statistically significant" and if the sample size is quite small, almost any correlation will be "statistically insignificant." One problem with authors listing *p*-values is that they often dismiss an interesting finding as unimportant because the *p*-value is larger than 0.05. Readers should get used to understanding the importance of the size of the *r* or R^2 value, and understand the size of a correlation without worrying about whether the *p*-value is lower than 0.05 or not. Researchers should take care to calculate CIs that give an idea of how precise the *r*-value is, but need not worry about the exact *p*-value associated with that effect size.

In both SPSS and R you have a choice of three different types of correlation coefficients: Pearson's, Kendall's tau-b and Spearman's. Pearson's is the parametric test and is also used for reporting the results of a bootstrapped test, while the other two are the older type of non-parametric tests, and use rank-order to calculate correlation coefficients. Given the discussion in Chapter 2 (Section 2.3), I will not advise using these older types of non-parametric tests, but will provide information about how to generate robust correlation coefficients with the newer type of non-parametric tests instead. (If you really want to know about the Spearman or Kendall tests, see the online document "Classic non-parametric statistics".)

6.5.1 Calculating Correlation Coefficients and Confidence Intervals in SPSS

Start a correlation in SPSS by choosing ANALYZE > CORRELATE > BIVARIATE. Enter any of the continuous variables that you want from the list on the left into the box on the right titled VARIABLES, as shown in Figure 6.20.

> **Tip:** In SPSS the order in which you transfer variables is the order in which you see them in your output. Therefore, I advise you to transfer the variables you are *most* interested in to the VARIABLES box first.

Using the Flege et al. (1999) data, I entered AOA and pronunciation ratings of English sentences. (The same data that were examined graphically in Figure 6.7.) Here we are interested in the relationship between AOA of the Korean immigrants to the USA, and their pronunciation rating for English.

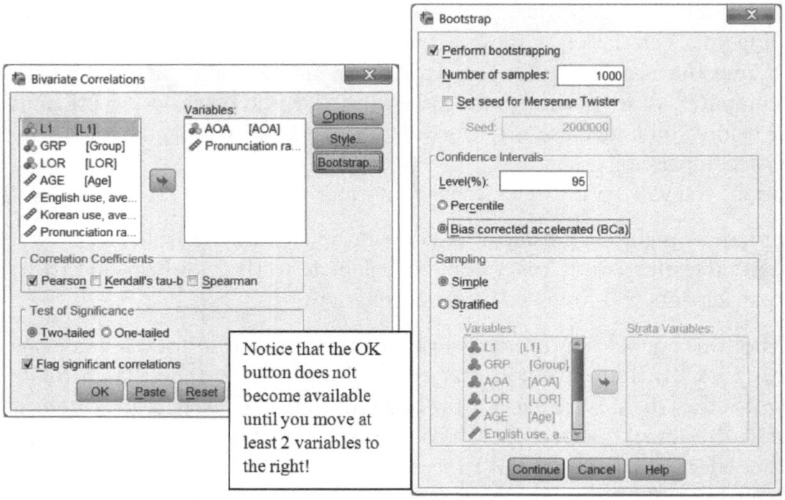

Figure 6.20 Calling for a correlation in SPSS.

We saw previously in the scatterplots that the relationship is negative, with pronunciation ratings becoming lower as the age of arrival was higher.

Figure 6.20 also shows the dialog box that opens when you click on the "Bootstrap" button. Here you can perform one type of robust correlation by using bootstrapping, and you will receive CIs for that bootstrap. These are non-parametric bootstraps, which mean we do not have to have normally distributed data nor equal variances for the procedure to work well, according to Efron and Tibshirani (1993), although they say that "coverage accuracy can still be erratic for small sample sizes" (p. 178). You can call for either a percentile or bias-corrected and accelerated (BCa) CI. The BCa is the percentile method adjusted for bias and skewness, so it should be preferred as it will tend to be closer to the true CI than the simple percentile method (ibid). The percentile method is the default for SPSS, but I recommend choosing the BCa, as shown in Figure 6.20. Keep the sampling at "Simple" unless you wanted to stratify it by some type of group or level in your data. (See LaFlair, Egbert and Plonsky (2015) for an example of stratification.)

The output from a **Pearson's correlation** with bootstrapping is shown in Table 6.2. The output shows that for the correlation between age of arrival and pronunciation rating, the effect size is $r = -0.855$ and $N = 240$. This is a large effect size and shows there is a strong negative relationship between AOA and pronunciation rating. (It explains $R^2 = 0.65$, or about 65% of the variance in scores.) The negative sign means that as one variable goes up (age), the other variable goes down (scores for nativeness on the pronunciation). We would like to have a CI for this parametric correlation test but SPSS does not provide it. However, we do see from the output that a bootstrapped BCa 95% CI is [−0.83, −0.88]. Because the number of participants is rather large, the CI is fairly narrow and lets us know that we can be fairly confident (95% confident) that the actual correlation coefficient is contained within these bounds from $r = -0.83$ to $r = -0.88$. Note that I have ignored the fact that the *p*-value is less than 0.001—the printout says it is 0.000 but it is never just zero; however, we can assume it is less than .001— as it does not really provide me with any important information beyond what I already know from the CI: there is an effect for age on pronunciation scores, and the effect explains about 65% of the variation between persons in the scores, meaning that practically speaking there is a very large effect for age!

The bootstrapped CI is a robust estimator and is the only robust test that SPSS has available at the time for correlations. The R statistical software provides more choices for different types of robust tests with correlations.

Table 6.2 Output from a Correlation in SPSS

Correlations

				AOA	Pronunciation rating of 5 Eng sentences by 10 listeners
AOA	Pearson Correlation			1	-.855
	Sig. (2-tailed)				.000
	N			240	240
	Bootstrap[a]	Bias		0	.000
		Std. Error		0	.016
		BCa 95% Confidence Interval	Lower	.	-.882
			Upper	.	-.825
Pronunciation rating of 5 Eng sentences by 10 listeners	Pearson Correlation			-.855	1
	Sig. (2-tailed)			.000	
	N			240	240
	Bootstrap[a]	Bias		.000	0
		Std. Error		.016	0
		BCa 95% Confidence Interval	Lower	-.882	.
			Upper	-.825	.

a. Unless otherwise noted, bootstrap results are based on 1000 bootstrap samples

Calculating Correlations in SPSS

1 In the drop-down menu choose ANALYZE > CORRELATE > BIVARIATE. Move any number of variables from the list on the left to the "Variables" box.
2 For a parametric test, choose Pearson's in the "Correlation Coefficients" area. To obtain a CI, click on the "Bootstrap" button and tick the "Perform bootstrapping" box. Choose the BCa method of computing the 95% CI. Click on "Continue" and then on OK.
3 The method described in #2 is a robust test for the CI. This is the only type of robust test that SPSS currently provides for correlations.

6.5.2 Calculating Correlation Coefficients and Confidence Intervals in R

In this section I will use the Flege et al. (1999) data set (file named "FlegeYeniKomshianLiu.sav"). You can import this into R by going to the menu choice DATA > IMPORT DATA > FROM SPSS data set. I named the data set flege etall 999.

To perform a correlation using R Commander, choose STATISTICS > SUMMARIES > CORRELATION TEST or STATISTICS > SUMMARIES > CORRELATION MATRIX. With the first choice, you can only test the relationship between two variables at a time, but the test will return a 95% CI as well as the correlation coefficient. With the second choice you can choose any number of variables but will only get the p-value, not a CI.

Choose at least two variables by using the Ctrl button and the mouse to click on the variables you want to use. To parallel the illustration for the SPSS data, I chose the variables "aoa" and "proneng". This means we are concerned with the relationship between the participants' AOA in the USA and an objective rating of their pronunciation in English by native speakers of English. From previous research we will expect this to be a negative correlation, meaning that as the AOA goes up, the pronunciation score gets lower and less native-like, and indeed we saw this relationship in the scatterplot earlier in the chapter. Now we will get the exact effect size by calculating the correlation coefficient.

Leave the "Type of Correlations" in its default at "Pearson product-moment," which is the parametric test (see Figure 6.21). In this dialog box you can choose to use only variables for which all of the values are completely filled out (the "complete observations" choice) or obtain all the possible results you can by using variables that are missing data for some variables but not others (the "pairwise-complete observations" choice). Chapter 1 talked about how to use imputation to fill out data sets that may be incomplete, and this would be a better solution than the pairwise deletion choice, so I recommend keeping the default choice of "Complete observations" and if you have missing data take care of this beforehand.

You can also choose to get *p*-values for the correlations. I have argued that *p*-values are not necessary and I stick by that assertion, but in this case the results are more complete when you choose to see the "Pairwise *p*-values" so I recommend calling for them. Specifically, you will see how many cases (your *N*) were tested if you choose to also get the *p*-values.

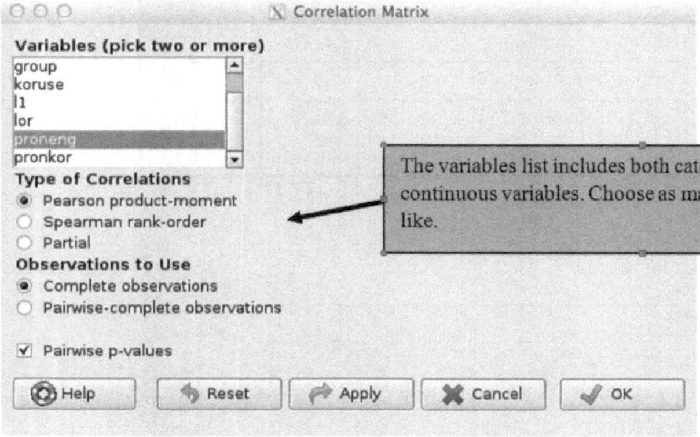

Figure 6.21 Calling for correlation coefficients in R Commander.

Tip: R will enter variables in alphabetical order no matter in what order you choose to enter them.

The results print out in the output window of R Commander. Below is the information you would get from either R Commander or running the code in R from the command line:

```
 Pearson correlations:
             aoa proneng
aoa       1.0000 -0.8545
proneng  -0.8545  1.0000

 Number of observations: 240

 Pairwise two-sided p-values:
        aoa proneng
aoa          0
proneng 0

 Adjusted p-values (Holm's method)
        aoa proneng
aoa          0
proneng 0
```

The first table of numbers ("Pearson correlations") is the correlation coefficient. Thus, we can see that the correlation between AOA and pronunciation score in English is $r = -0.85$, a very large and very strong effect size. This is based on $N = 240$ cases, as noted underneath the correlation coefficients. The last two tables are tables of *p*-values, and they are mirror images of each other along the diagonal line, so you only need to look at one of them if you were going to report a *p*-value. (I am not advocating this, just explaining these numbers.) The second table gives *p*-values adjusted for having multiple comparisons, and uses the Holm adjustment. (In this case there was just one comparison so nothing was adjusted.) The Holm adjustment is more liberal than the more commonly known Bonferroni correction.

> **Tip:** In the R Console, to bring up your previous command line and modify it instead of typing the entire command all over again, click on the up arrow.

Here is the R code for obtaining this correlation:

```
library(Hmisc, pos=4) #open Hmisc package (Harrell & Dupont, 2014) at lower position (#4) on R's search
rcorr.adjust(fyl[,c("aoa","proneng")], type="pearson", use="complete")
```

rcorr.adjust	Runs a correlation matrix that also shows raw and adjusted *p*-values for pairwise correlations between each two variables. Observations are filtered for missing data and only complete observations are used if the use="complete" argument is included (as it is here).
FYL[,c("aoa","proneng")]	Specifies the variables to use from this data set. (I am using the Flege, Yeni-Komshian and Liu data, which I named fyl); the blank before the comma means to use all of the rows, and variables listed after the comma specify the columns to use.
c("aoa","proneng")	Tells R to use these two columns from the data set.
type="pearson"	Calls for Pearson correlation coefficients; Pearson is default but you can also choose "spearman".

> **Tip:** To get a list of the variable names in R, type names(fyl), inserting your own data set name instead of "fyl." This will produce a list of the variable names in the data set.

Now we would like to get a CI for this correlation coefficient. We will calculate bootstrapped CIs, just as was found in the previous SPSS section. We will have to move to R to do this, as there are no menu commands in R Commander for calculating bootstrapped CIs. (I am using the syntax given in LaFlair, Egbert, and Plonsky, 2015, for this command.)

```
library(boot) #open up the boot package
f <- function (data, indices) {
obs <- data[indices,]
return(cor(obs$aoa, obs$proneng))}
```

f <- function (data, indices) {	To run the bootstrap, we need a function that indicates what type of statistical test we are doing, and which accesses the data using random indexes. Here we write the function, arbitrarily name it "f" and begin defining it with the two arguments it needs, which are the data and the indexes. (In making your own function, it does not really matter what you call these, but I have tried to use informative names here.)
obs <- data[indices,]	This line makes a data frame (with rows from the bootstrap sample) that has the same structure as the original data set. It is arbitrarily named "obs" meaning observations. This line refers to the names of the arguments we set up in the first line, so in making your own function, keep this the same.
return(cor(obsaoa, obsproneng))	This line returns the results from a correlation between the two variables, but repeated over and over (we will specify how many times to repeat it in the later boot command) with different observations. In making your own function, replace the names of the variables with your own variables.
{. . . .}	Curly brackets are normally used to group statements in R, and conventionally the first one goes at the end of its own line (no statement after it on the same line), while the last one is at the end of the statement.

With this command we create a function that makes a correlation between random pairings in your two data vectors (here, AOA and pronunciation rating in English). The only thing to change in this command to use for your own correlation data would be the underlined names of the variables.

```
bootcorr <-boot(fyl, f, R=500) #bootstrap the data
```

Use the name of your own data set; the name of my data set is underlined in the first argument. The second argument is f, the function we wrote above, and the argument "R" specifies how many bootstrap replicates to use; 500 is probably sufficient but 1000 is often the norm for bootstrapped samples.

```
bootcorr #get the results
```

```
ORDINARY NONPARAMETRIC BOOTSTRAP


Call:
boot(data = FYL, statistic = f, R = 500)


Bootstrap Statistics :
      original          bias    std. error
t1* -0.8545445 -0.0007350577  0.01646056
```

In the results, the result labeled "original" is the function applied to the original data set, so we can see that it is exactly the same as the parametric correlation coefficient obtained above in the Pearson correlation.

The "bias" result is the average difference of the bootstrapped estimates from the original value (LaFlair, Egbert, & Plonsky, 2015). Here we can see that there is very little bias in the Pearson correlation coefficient and the bootstrapped coefficient. We would ideally like this to be 0, but if it is not we know that there is a difference between the parametric test and the bootstrapped test. The result labeled "standard error" is the standard error (SE) of the replicated statistic, and the lower it is, the more precise the results are. (Remember from Section 3.1.2 that the SE is the standard deviation of the sampling distribution of the sample mean.)

Notice that the bootstrapped results give us a normal, "garden-variety" Pearson correlation as well as a bootstrapped estimate. The bootstrapped CI is one type of robust correlation that you might want to use.

If you are following along with me, you may get a slightly different result, as bootstrapping randomly samples with replacement from the data set so that the statistics will vary slightly each time you run the analysis.

Note that this non-parametric bootstrap is not the same thing as the non-parametric Spearman correlation coefficient. A Spearman non-parametric correlation would calculate the correlation coefficient only once, but without assuming a normal distribution. For this calculation the data has been bootstrapped, meaning it has been resampled randomly and 500 times, and a correlation coefficient for that randomly sampled data has been computed.

This calculation might be more visible if we look at a histogram of the *r*-value. In our case the histogram will display the accumulation of 500 *r*-values of the randomly sampled data. In fact, you should definitely check a plot of your data every time you use bootstrapping. You need to check that your results make sense and that no unanticipated complications have arisen. Davison and Kuonen (2003, p. 11) stated that "the aim of computing is insight, not numbers; garbage in, garbage out." In other words, do not just rely on the numbers you get from the calculations—look at graphs too to get a holistic sense of your data. Canty (2002) suggested that if the results are too discrete you may need to increase the number of replicates, or the issue may be a fundamental problem with using a certain type of statistic, in which case you will see that the bootstrap cannot be used in that case.

The command for plots will produce a histogram and a Q-Q plot of the simulated *r*-values:

```
plot(bootcorr)
```

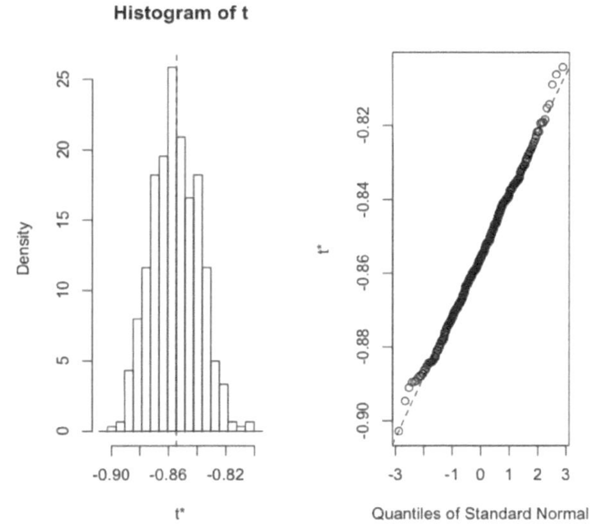

Figure 6.22 Histogram and Q-Q plot of bootstrapped correlation coefficient.

Notice that, in the histogram, there is a dashed line around $r = -0.85$ representing the correlation coefficient of the original data set (the non-bootstrapped one). As you can see, with so many replications of the data, the distribution looks fairly normal in both the histogram and the Q-Q plot.

Lastly, we can use the command to obtain the numbers for the CI, but here again things are not so simple; the **boot.ci( )** command brings up four different types of CIs! Here I called for two different confidence levels (90% and 95%) to illustrate how to call for different confidence levels, should you want to do that. If you only want a 95% CI, you do not need to specify it as that is the default argument (as is the last argument that calls for all the different types of CIs).

```
boot.ci(bootcorr, conf=c(.90,.95), type="all")
```

```
BOOTSTRAP CONFIDENCE INTERVAL CALCULATIONS
Based on 500 bootstrap replicates

CALL :
boot.ci(boot.out = bootcorr, conf = c(0.9, 0.95), type = "all")

Intervals :
Level      Normal                Basic
90%   (-0.8809, -0.8267 )   (-0.8811, -0.8258 )
95%   (-0.8861, -0.8215 )   (-0.8869, -0.8228 )

Level     Percentile             BCa
90%   (-0.8832, -0.8280 )   (-0.8792, -0.8239 )
95%   (-0.8863, -0.8222 )   (-0.8840, -0.8187 )
```

Which type of CI should you report? The "Normal" CI assumes that the statistic is normally distributed and calculates a CI in the normal way. The "Basic" CI is used when the distribution of the statistic is not normal. If you believe the resampled data are normally distributed, then any of the methods should provide quite similar coverage, but for distributions that are not normal the BCa method is the most accurate one available from these choices (see Carpenter & Bithell, 2000, for explanations of why) and I would recommend using that one.

Thus, with the Flege, Yeni-Komshian and Liu data we could report that the correlation between AOA and pronunciation rating is 95% BCa CI [−0.88, −0.82], which would explain anywhere between 67% (r=.82 $R^2 = 0.67$) and 77% (r=.88 $R^2 = 0.77$) of the data. The CI is quite small and precise, and even the lower end of the CI leads us to believe that it is very likely that the AOA explains a very substantial portion of the pronunciation rating.

Obtaining Correlation Coefficients with R

1. In R Commander, choose STATISTICS > SUMMARIES > CORRELATION MATRIX. Choose variables by holding down the Ctrl key and mouse clicking, and tick the box for "Pairwise *p*-values" to see the *N* value. This will return a correlation coefficient and an *N* value.
2. A Pearson correlation between just two variables can be obtained using the R code:

```
library(Hmisc)
rcorr.adjust(fyl[,c("aoa","proneang")])
```

3. To calculate a CI around the true correlation coefficient, use the R code, substituting in your own data in the underlined portions:

```
library(boot)
f <- function (data, indices) {obs <- data[indices,]
return(cor(obs$aoa, obs$proneng))} #this needs to be on a separate line to work!
bootcorr <-boot(FYL, f, R=500) #you can also change R to a higher number if desired
bootcorr
plot(bootcorr)
boot.ci(bootcorr) #use the BCa confidence intervals as a default
```

6.5.3 Robust Correlations

As has been mentioned previously, "classical" correlation is not robust to violations of assumptions, especially the assumption that the data are normally distributed and that there are no outliers. The sections in 6.5 for both SPSS and R showed how to calculate a bootstrapped CI, which is definitely one type of correlation that can help lessen problems due to outliers (Sheskin, 2004). This section outlines other methods that can be used to generate robust results.

One command that can be informative for thinking about your data is cor.plot in the mvoutlier package (Filzmoser & Gschwandtner, 2015). It does not provide CIs, so the main output I recommend looking at here is a graph that plots an ellipse around the data points that would be included in the "classical" correlation and those that would be included in the robust correlation. The mvoutlier documentation on this command says that "Robust estimation can be thought of as estimating the mean and covariance of the 'good' part of the data." The calculation is based on the Fast Minimum Covariance Determinant described by Pison, Van Aelst, and Willems (2002) and more information about robust detection of outliers can be found in Rousseeuw and Leroy (1987).

Note that this command will not work on a data set that has any missing data. Missing data can be fixed through imputation (see Section 1.5) or removing rows that contain missing data. (This is "listwise deletion" and in Chapter 1 I argued that it is the worst way to deal with missing data.)

To demonstrate the use of the cor.plot( ) command, I will look at the correlation between age and scores on the GJT in the DeKeyser (2000) study. We have previously worked with this data set and seen that DeKeyser would like to divide the group up into participants who arrived in the USA before and after the age of 15. However, if we try to do an overall correlation on the entire data set, the "classical" correlation command of cor will assume a linear relationship and calculate a correlation coefficient for *r*. Let us see what kind of correlation we obtain with the robust correlation commands.

```
library(mvoutlier) #use install.packages("mvoutlier") first if you don't have this package
attach(dekeyser)
corr.plot(age,gjtscore)
```

```
$cor.cla
[1] -0.6191344

$cor.rob
[1] 0.02849056
```

The output reminds us that the classical correlation was strong and negative ($r = -0.62$). This robust correlation says that the correlation is positive but very small, with $r = 0.03$ (rounding up from 0.028). The graph that is plotted, shown in Figure 6.23, is what I would use to examine my data. It shows a dotted line ellipse around the data that would be considered in a classical correlation (which actually has outliers, so it is slightly different from previous calculations that did not remove any outliers), and a solid line around the data that is considered to be a "good" representative of the center of the bivariate relationship between the data. In fact, the correlation has basically done what we already knew we should do with the data, which is to consider it as coming from two separate groups and calculate correlations individually. The robust correlation includes just the data from the participants who arrived in the USA later, around age 10 or 11. This type of analysis would provide a mathematically principled way for making a decision on where to split the data for consideration as separate groups.

Another way to call for a number of robust correlation measures is to use Rand Wilcox's R libraries (Wilcox & Schönbrodt, 2014). Install Wilcox's libraries by using the following commands:

```
install.packages(c("MASS", "akima", "robustbase")) #install dependent packages
install.packages(c("cobs", "robust", "mgcv", "scatterplot3d", "quantreg", "rrcov", "lars", "pwr",
"trimcluster", "multicore", "mc2d", "psych", "Rfit"))
#install suggested packages
install.packages("WRS", repos="http://R-Forge.R-project.org, type="source") #install WRS
```

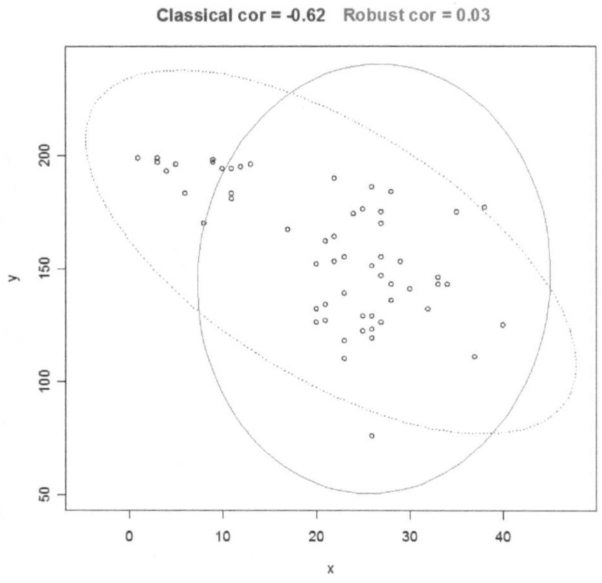

Figure 6.23 Comparison of data included in classical and robust correlations.

If this does not work for some reason, you can download the functions in the most current version of the Rallfun file, which as of the writing of this second edition was Rallfun-v26, from http://dornsife.usc.edu/labs/rwilcox/software/ where you should look for the small link in red. Download the file by right-clicking on it and choose "Save link as". Save it to your working directory for R. To find out your working directory, type getwd() first, or you can find the downloaded file by typing: source(file.choose()). Then use this command to get the file into R:

```
source(file.choose( ))
```

Once you have Wilcox's libraries loaded, you should open the WRS package (library(WRS)), although this is not necessary if the files are sourced in. Wilcox (2012b) explained that there are two basic types of approaches to correlation. One is the M-type, which guards against outliers but does not take overall structure into account. This includes the classical non-parametric tests like Kendall's tau-b. The other type is called the O-type and it downweighs or eliminates outliers taking the overall structure into account. Wilcox (2012a, 2012b) also explained how to use the scor( ) function, which uses an OP correlation. In this approach, outliers are detected and removed through mathematical methods, and then a Pearson correlation is calculated with the remaining data, which seems to be an effective method if there are outliers. Let us try this command with the DeKeyser data:

```
scor(dekeyser$age, dekeyser$gjtscore, plotit=T, xlab="Age", ylab="GJT Score", STAND=T)
```

You can see that you just put one variable in the first position and the other variable in the second position. The argument plotit=T returns a scatterplot with a polygon enclosing the central half of the data. The next two arguments are used to label this graph, and the final argument is suggested if the measures are on different scales, which they are here. The output tests the hypothesis that the OP correlation is equal to 0, testing at the α = 0.05 level, so the hypothesis is rejected if the test statistic (labeled $test.stat in the output) exceeds the critical value (labeled $crit.05 in the output). The output here shows that the test statistic is larger than the critical value, so we can conclude there is a correlation between the variables.

```
$cor.values
[1] -0.6431184

$test.stat
[1] 6.22839

$crit.05
[1] 2.441577
```

Wilcox (2012a, 2012b) noted that if you want to use a correlation with data that violates the homoscedasticity requirement, a basic percentile bootstrap is a good method. Section 6.4.2 explained how to do this with your own function, but Wilcox (2012 a, b) has also provided a function for bootstrapping data that might be easier if you are having any problems with writing your own code. The following function uses the percentage bend correlation by default, which is an M-type correlation, but can also be set to use the OP correlation (substitute in corfun = scor):

```
corb(dekeyser$age, dekeyser$gjtscore, corfun = pbcor, nboot = 599)
```

This command returns a 95% CI and a correlation estimate (r) as well as a p-value. You can set the number of bootstrap samples higher if you like.

```
$cor.ci
[1] -0.7959392 -0.4100159

$p.value
[1] 0

$cor.est
[1] -0.6374295
```

Here we can get a better idea of the effect size of the correlation since we can see the CI.

6.5.4 Application Activities for Correlation

1 Use the file DeKeyser2000.sav. Find the correlation coefficient and 95% CI between AOA (AGE) and scores on the GJT (GJTSCORE) over the entire data set. DeKeyser (2000) divided participants into two groups based on their AOA (STATUS). Find the correlation coefficients and 95% CIs between AOA (AGE) and scores on the GJT (GJTSCORE) for each group separately. Before performing any of the correlations, check the assumptions about linearity and normal distribution (check histograms and skewness and kurtosis numbers). Say something about effect size.
2 Use the FlegeYeniKomshianLiu.sav file. What is the correlation coefficient and 95% CI between AOA and scores on a Korean pronunciation test (PRONKOR)? Before performing any of the correlations, check assumptions about linearity and normal distribution (check histograms and skewness and kurtosis numbers). The scatterplot in Figure 6.7 leads us to believe that up until age 20, a line appears to describe the model well, so look at correlation over the entire data set, and also up to age 20 only. Say something about effect size.
3 Use the LarsonHall2008 file. There are a variety of variables in this file; let us look for relationships between use of English (USEENG), how much participants said they liked learning English (LIKEENG) and score on the GJT test (GJTSCORE). In other words, we are looking at three different correlations. First, check for assumptions for parametric correlations. Do you note any outliers? Note which combinations do not seem to satisfy parametric assumptions. Then go ahead and check the correlations between these variables. Say something about effect size.

4 Dewaele and Pavlenko Bilingual Emotions Questionnaire (2001–2003). Use the BEQ.Swear.sav file. What correlation was found between the age that bilinguals started learning their L2 (AgeSec) and their own self-ratings of proficiency in speaking (L2Speak) and comprehending their L2 (L2_Comp)? In other words, look at three different correlations. First, check for assumptions for parametric correlations. Do you note any outliers? Note which combinations do not seem to satisfy parametric assumptions. Then go ahead and check the correlations between these variables. Say something about effect size.
5 Abrahamsson and Hyltenstam (2009). In Section 6.3.3, you looked at a scatterplot of these data from Spanish L1 participants who started learning Swedish L2 at various ages of onset. Use the Abrahamsson&Hyltenstam.NoNS.sav file and first use a robust correlation to examine what the "good part" of the data is. Then find the correlation coefficient and 95% CI for the strength of the correlation between score as a native speaker of Swedish and age of onset for learning Swedish L2.

6.5.5 Reporting a Correlation

Report a correlation by including the name of the test used (a Pearson correlation, Spearman's rho or a Pearson correlation on a bootstrapped data set), the r or R^2 value and CIs. Here is an example for the Larson-Hall (2008) data on Japanese learners of English:

A Pearson correlation (r) between reported hours of study of English and scores on the GJT found the effect size of the correlation was small, and the CI fairly wide (95% CI [0.05, 0.32], r = 0.18, N = 200, R^2 = 0.03), meaning the correlation coefficient is not highly reliable. No correlation between aptitude score and scores on the GJT was found, with a negligible effect size and a CI spanning 0 (95% CI [−0.06, 0.22], r = 0.08, R^2 = 0.006).

Table 6.3 Correlation Table Example

Variable	*GJT (r)*	*N*	*CI*	*Effect size (R^2)*	*RLW phonemic discrimination (r)*	*N*	*CI*	*Effect size (R^2)*
Age began English study	−.37	61	−.58, −.13	.14	.07	61	−.19, .32	.00
English speaking ability (1–10, 10=native-like)	.29	196	.16, .42	.08	.13	196	−.01, .27	.02
English reading ability (1–10, 10=native-like)	.18	196	.04, .31	.03	.08	196	−.06, .22	.01
English usage	.31	187	.18, .44	.10	.09	187	−.05, .23	.01
How much like studying languages	.32	199	.19, .44	.10	.18	199	.04, .31	.03
Aptitude test score	.08	200	−.06, .22	.01	.12	200	−.02, .26	.01

You can see that it takes a lot of words to report on correlations. For this reason, many writers report correlations in a tabular form when there are quite a number of variables involved. Here is an example using a number of variables from the Larson-Hall (2008) data, where correlations of the explanatory or predictor variables (the rows) with the GJT and phonemic discrimination tasks (the columns) are of most interest.

Table 6.3 shows that, while most of the effect sizes associated with the GJT are small (0.01–0.14), those associated with phonemic discrimination are tiny (0.00–0.03). Thus, whether the CI (which does not change sign from positive to negative) is statistical, is not nearly so important to understanding what is happening with regard to the effect size.

6.6 Summary

The main use of correlation in second language research studies is to examine whether two continuous variables show a relationship. In looking at variables, the most useful first step is to examine a scatterplot. The scatterplot can show visually how or whether the variables are related. A correlation assumes that the relationship is linear, in other words that it is best described by a straight line through the data. A Loess line, which follows the trend of the data closely, is a useful tool for visually ascertaining whether a straight line is a good approximation to the data.

To use the parametric correlation statistic (Pearson's *r*), various assumptions, such as normal distribution of the variable and a linear relationship between variables, should be examined. In the exercises you have seen that, in many cases, assumptions are not fulfilled but parametric statistics are still used. An alternative is to use non-parametric statistics such as bootstrapping.

I have suggested that the most important points to report in looking at a statistical association are the effect size and CIs. R^2 is a percentage of variance effect size and indicates to what degree a straight line through the data effectively accounts for the variation between the two variables. The larger this number is, the more strongly the variables are related. The CI can tell you whether the association is statistically significant (if the CI does not pass through 0) as well as show how precise the correlation coefficient (the *r*) is by giving an upper and lower limit for the coefficient.

There are three more advanced topics concerning correlation and they can be found online. One topic is partial correlation. This technique can factor out the effects of one variable that, you may decide after the fact, is interfering with revealing the true extent of the correlation between your variables. The example I use is of a study where the older age of the test takers affects some of them negatively, so age is factored out of the correlation between the variables of interest. See the online version "Partial Correlation" for this section. Another use of correlation, fast becoming outdated, is the use of the **point-biserial correlation** to determine which items are useful in test construction when answers are dichotomous (with only two choices, such as yes/no or correct/incorrect). The online section "Point-Biserial Correlation" covers this area. Another advanced topic in correlation is the question of reporting **inter-rater reliability** when judges are used in your experimental design and can be found in the online version on "Inter-Rater Reliability." This same statistic can be used to report on the reliability of a test you have used if you have raw scores for each item in the test.

Chapter 7

Looking for Groups of Explanatory Variables through Multiple Regression

Predicting Important Factors in First Grade Reading

> Assuming that the regression [you fit] adequately summarizes the data does not make it so.
>
> John Fox (2002b, p. 28)

One of the goals of scientific research is to try to explain and predict phenomena. For example, if you are a teacher you know that some students in your classes excel, while others just cannot seem to grasp the concepts you are teaching. To explain these differences, you might look for explanatory variables such as intelligence quotient, motivation, amount of time spent on homework, reading speed, socioeconomic status or any other number of variables. Regression is a technique that allows you to look at a number of explanatory variables and decide which ones have independent power to explain what is going on with the variable you have measured, for example, scores on a Test of English as a Foreign Language (TOEFL) test. We will call this property you measure the response variable, and the variables you think might explain what is going on the explanatory variables. The explanatory variables are also sometimes called independent variables (IVs), but we will avoid that since these variables are often correlated with the response variable, and thus not very "independent."

As a statistical test, multiple regression involves two or more continuous variables. One of the variables will be the response variable, and one or more variables will be the explanatory variables. As an example of how multiple regression might apply to the real world, say that you run a small business in Korea helping students to score highly on the TOEFL test. You know that how hard students work to learn grammar and vocabulary has an impact on how well they can do. But you also sense that some students are just more gifted than others at learning languages, and this also affects how highly they can score. You measure how much time your students spend per week in classes and studying English, and you also give them a language aptitude test. You can use multiple regression to determine whether these two factors do indeed independently affect scores on the TOEFL test, and how much they affect scores.

Recent Examples of Multiple Regression in the Second Language Acquisition Literature

Huang (2014)

The author wanted to know how a variety of factors including age of learning, length of residence, years of education and aptitude, among others, would affect proficiency in L2 English grammar and pronunciation. A multiple regression was used to look at which of the factors produced the strongest effects and contributed the most toward explaining the performance of Mandarin L1 English L2 speakers on the grammatical test, and found that age of arrival and language aptitude were the strongest explanatory factors. A different regression analysis looked at which of the factors was most influential in explaining ratings on a speaking test. This analysis found age of arrival to be the strongest factor followed by current oral English input, although the study used standardized coefficients instead of R^2 change to compare the impact of the factors, which is not recommended (see Section 7.4.2).

Mu (2014)

This combined qualitative and quantitative study used a multiple regression to quantitatively examine the contribution of two factors on the language proficiency of Chinese heritage speakers living in Australia. The factors were "habitus of Chineseness" (heritage learners' disposition toward the language) and investment of capital (how they used their resources). The author reported that these two factors helped explain 62% of the variance in language proficiency.

Plakans and Gebril (2013)

This study investigated how integrating writing from other sources can help shape language learners' writing scores. The authors analyzed data from the Internet-based TOEFL writing portion where test takers were asked to integrate data from other tasks (listening and reading) that addressed the same information. The multiple regression looked at how importance (i.e. how important the ideas that the TOEFL writers integrated into their writing were in the source document), reading source use, listening source use and total verbatim words affected the assessment score of the writing. The authors reported that a regression with these four factors accounted for 55% of the variance in writing scores, and noted that the factor that predicted the largest amount of score variation was using ideas from the listening source texts.

Kang (2012)

The author wanted to understand how Korean students' individual differences (measured by the Neuroticism-Extraversion-Openness personality inventory) predicted the use of language learning strategies (measured by the Oxford strategy inventory for language learning). A simultaneous regression found that the five personality factors that were measured explained 22% of the variance in language strategy scores.

7.1 Understanding Regression Design

Mathematically, the default for a regression equation will be:

$$Y_i = \alpha + \beta_1 x_{i1} + \cdots + \beta_k x_{ik} + \text{error}_i$$

To put this in terms of our example that has two explanatory variables:

> TOEFL score = some constant number (the intercept) + time spent on English per week + aptitude score + a number that fluctuates for each individual (the error)

This mathematical equation is one that defines a line for a data set. (Although multiple regression does not always have to define a line, for this chapter it will.) If it has been a while since you thought about how to draw a line, let me remind you that mathematically a line needs to be defined by a number representing its intercept (**alpha** or α) and a number representing its slope (**beta** or β). In Figure 7.1, you can see how the line is formed by knowing just these two values—the intercept and the slope. In the regression formula, the α is the intercept and the β is the slope. The slope is divided up into different parts if there is more than one explanatory variable. These betas are thus called **partial coefficients** if there is more than one explanatory variable. The error part at the end of the equation is necessary to explain all of the other parts of the real data that do not actually land straight on this regression line. This error is also called the residual.

In multiple regression, then, we can try to see whether the explanatory variables we have posited explain very much of what is going on. For example, we might find that time spent on English per week plus aptitude scores explains about 60% of the variation in TOEFL scores (in other words, $R^2 = 0.60$). The rest, the part we cannot explain, gets dumped into the error, and we might want to add other variables to try to explain more later.

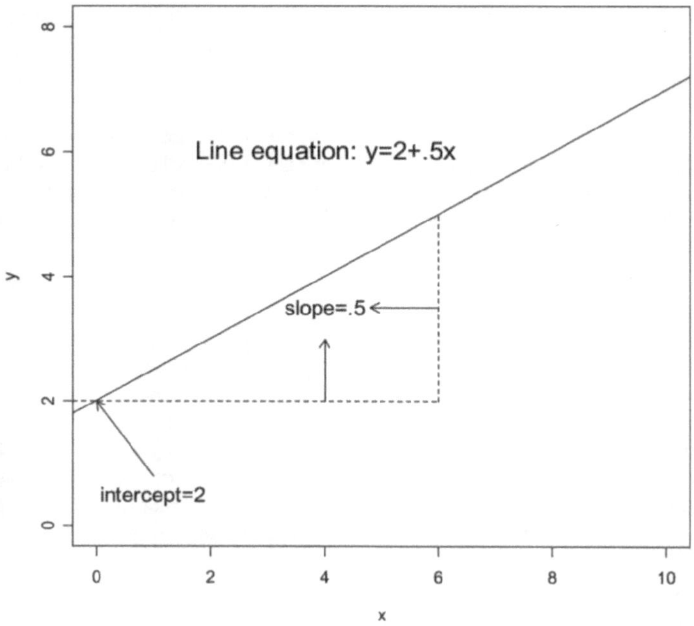

Figure 7.1 The mathematical formula of a line.

Besides seeing whether the explanatory variables we picked do a good job of explaining what is happening, we can also use multiple regression to predict how people in the future will score on the response variable. Since we can have an equation for the response variable, we can just plug in the x values for each individual (the scores on each of the explanatory variables) and calculate the y value mathematically (the response variable). In the TOEFL example, if it turns out that with my current students the combination of language aptitude and hours spent in study explains a lot of the variation in TOEFL scores, then with future students, if I know how many hours a week they are studying and I measure their language aptitude, the regression equation will spit out a predicted TOEFL score *for each individual* that should be fairly close to what they will actually score.

To put this into concrete terms, let us suppose one of our students, Jun, scored 486 on the TOEFL. He reported to us that he studies English five hours a week and he got a score of 25 on the short form of the Modern Language Aptitude Test (MLAT). We have analyzed the data of our 20 students through multiple regression and found out that alpha = 29.2. The beta coefficient for hours of study is 10.1, and the beta coefficient for the MLAT is 12.6. If we were going to predict what score Jun would get, we could calculate it like this, putting the numbers we obtained into the TOEFL score equation found at the beginning of this section:

$$\text{TOEFL score} = 29.2 + 10.1*(\text{Jun's hours of study} = 5) + 12.6*(\text{Jun's MLAT} = 25)$$

$$\text{TOEFL score} = 29.2 + 51 + 315 = 395.2$$

In other words, if we were predicting Jun's score, we would predict he would score 395 on the TOEFL. But in fact he scored 486, so we have some error in the equation. The error for Jun is 486−395 = 91. You can see that, even though this regression equation explains a good deal of variation in TOEFL scores (60%), it is not perfect.

Although the regression equation is a linear equation, and the regression line we will draw is a straight line, another way to visualize what is happening in multiple regression is to look at a Venn

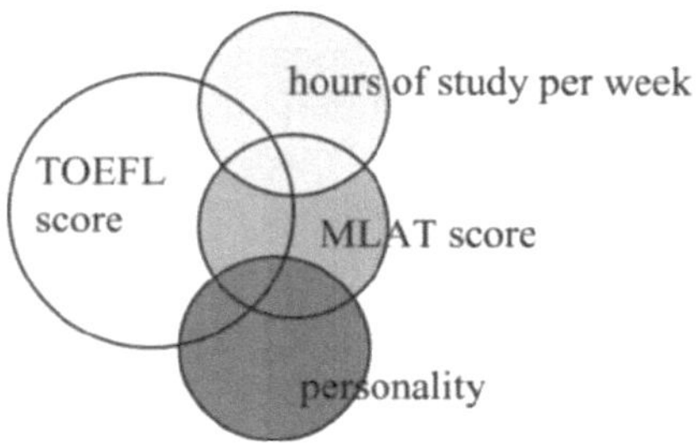

Figure 7.2 Venn diagram of regression variables.

diagram. We can think of the response variable being what we want to explain, and we can think of the explanatory variables as overlapping with the response variable. The overlapping portions of the circles in Figure 7.2 are areas of shared variance (Tabachnick & Fidell, 2001). Using our previous example of trying to explain TOEFL scores, we can add another variable to hours of study per week and MLAT score, that of personality, to try to improve the predictive ability of the model.

What we see is that there are overlapping areas of variance *among* the explanatory variables as well as with the response variable (the TOEFL score). For example, the score on the MLAT may correlate in part with how many hours an individual studies per week as well as with some part of the personality measure. The way these overlapping parts are measured is the basis for a division into two types of regression—**standard** and **sequential** (also called **hierarchical**). As I explain these types you should understand how the choice of **regression model** (the type of regression you do and what variables are included) can make a difference to the final conclusions that a researcher may draw, and will answer different questions.

7.1.1 Standard Multiple Regression

If standard multiple regression is used, the importance of the explanatory variable depends on how much it *uniquely* overlaps with the response variable. In Figure 7.3 then, the MLAT score has the largest unique contribution to the variance of the TOEFL score (the area in c), because it overlaps more with the TOEFL score than with any of the other explanatory variables and more than those variables uniquely overlap with TOEFL score.

Thus, in standard multiple regression only the areas of each explanatory variable that overlap with the response variable, but not with any other variables, contribute to the overall estimation of how much the variables predict the response. In other words, each variable is evaluated "as if it had entered the regression after all other IVs [independent variables] had entered" (Tabachnick & Fidell, 2001, p. 131). Tabachnick and Fidell (2001) explain that standard multiple regression answers two questions:

1 What are the nature and size of the relationship between the response variable and the set of explanatory variables?

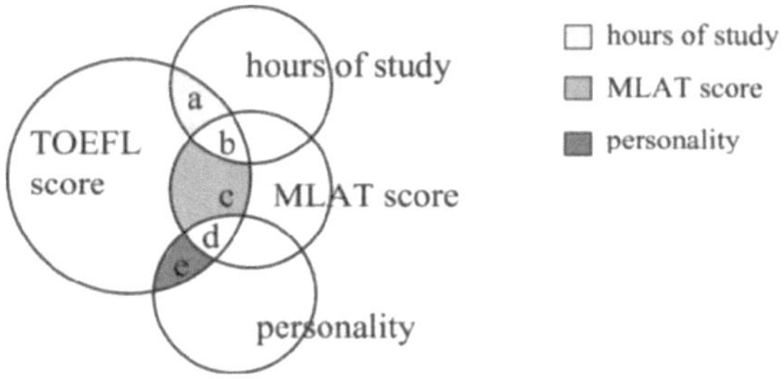

Figure 7.3 Venn diagram of standard regression design.

2 How much of the relationship is contributed uniquely by each explanatory variable?

If one of the explanatory variables is very highly correlated with another explanatory variable, it may appear to contribute very little to the overall regression equation in spite of being highly correlated with the response variable. For this reason, you should consider both the canonical correlation of the variables and the information about the unique contribution made by the explanatory variable from the regression analysis.

7.1.2 Sequential (Hierarchical) Regression

For sequential (hierarchical) regression, all of the areas of the explanatory variables that overlap with the response variable will be counted (unlike in standard multiple regression), but the way that they will be included depends on the *order* in which the researcher enters the variables into the equation. Therefore, the importance of hours of study in our example will increase with sequential multiple regression if it is entered first, because it will account for both areas a and b (see Figure 7.4). If the MLAT score is added second, it will account for even more of the variance than it did in standard multiple regression because it will be able to "claim" areas c and d.

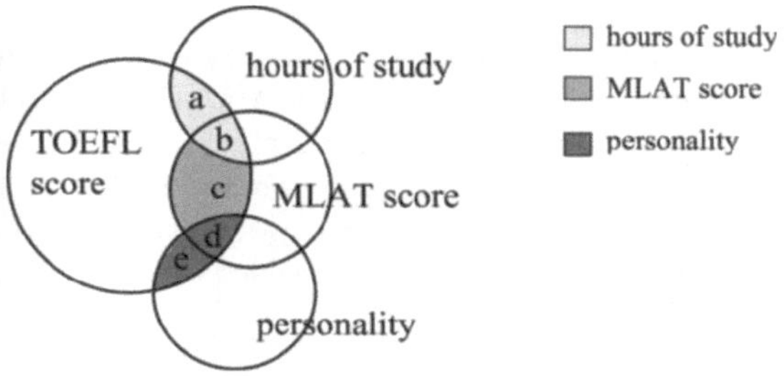

Figure 7.4 Venn diagram of sequential regression design.

The importance of any variable, therefore, can be emphasized in sequential multiple regression, depending on the order in which it is entered. If two variables overlap to a large degree, then entering one of them first may leave little room for explanation for the second variable. Tabachnick and Fidell (2001) therefore advise researchers to assign the order of variables depending on a theoretical or logical reason.

They state that the main research question that a sequential regression can answer is:

> Do the subsequent variables that are entered in each step add to the prediction of the response variable after differences in the variables from the previous step have been eliminated? (Tabachnick & Fidell, 2001, p. 139)

The data set illustrated in this chapter from Lafrance and Gottardo (2005) basically asked this question by examining whether differences in phonological awareness add to the prediction of First Grade L1 word reading performance after differences in non-verbal reasoning, L2 word reading ability in kindergarten, L2 naming speed and L2 working memory measures have been eliminated.

In fact, if the authors had done a standard multiple regression, the only explanatory variable included in the model would have been phonological awareness. This is because apparently it is the only explanatory variable that overlaps with First Grade L1 reading scores in a unique way that does not overlap with any of the other explanatory variables. Thus to see the contributions of the other variables, the authors used a sequential multiple regression with phonological awareness entered last.

7.1.3 Data Used in this Chapter

In this chapter, I have used data from a study by Lafrance and Gottardo (2005), who tried to predict reading performance by French–English bilinguals, and took an uncommon look at whether

L2 abilities affected L1 reading skills. The study was longitudinal and looked at the same children, being schooled in French, from kindergarten to Grade 1.

The response variable is:

- scores on L1 (French) word reading skills in Grade 1 (Woodcock Reading Mastery Test-Revised).

The five explanatory variables are:

- L2 (English) phonological awareness measured in kindergarten;
- L2 working memory measured in kindergarten;
- L2 naming speed measured in kindergarten;
- non-verbal reasoning ability (Matrix Analogies Test);
- L2 word reading skills in kindergarten.

7.2 Visualizing Multiple Relationships

Before you begin a multiple regression it is imperative that you examine your data graphically and get to know what is going on. Actually conducting a multiple regression is extremely easy using computer software, but multiple regression also has a large number of assumptions that must be met to be satisfied that the statistical techniques that are employed are going to give accurate results. These assumptions are traditionally examined *after* you have run the regression, however, since many of the assumptions involve looking at plots of the residuals, which cannot be determined until after the regression model has been determined. (In other words, you have to decide which variables you will include in the model before you can test assumptions.)

One assumption that can be examined before running a multiple regression is that of linearity. The assumption is that each explanatory variable has a linear relationship with the response variable. To examine this assumption let us take a look at a multiple scatterplot for the Lafrance and Gottardo (2005) data set. (I have included only four of the five variables we will examine in the regression in this scatterplot for reasons of space.) The scatterplot has the Loess line (not the regression line) on each graph, and a histogram of the distribution of the variable on the diagonal. Since Chapter 6 explained how to create scatterplots and scatterplot matrices, I will not explain how to perform scatterplots in this section; I will merely comment on the Lafrance and Gottardo (2005) data. The R statistical program provides a way to examine several other kinds of graphics that SPSS cannot, and so I will use R to examine the Lafrance and Gottardo's data in this section.

Here are some of my thoughts on looking at the matrix scatterplot in Figure 7.5, where Grade 1 French (L1) word reading skills (L1G1WR) is the response variable and the others are the explanatory variables. (I am looking specifically down the far right column where L1G1WR is matched with the other variables.)

- The relationship between L1 word reading and L2 phonological awareness seems reasonably linear.
- The relationship between L1 word reading and the other variables does not seem as clearly linear but also does not seem to show any curvature or other defined patterns.
- There may be some outliers in the relationship between L1 word reading and non-verbal reasoning.

The one scatterplot not shown here, that between Grade 1 French (L1) word reading skills and kindergarten English (L2) word reading skills, is shown in Figure 7.6 with a Loess line drawn over the data.

The scatterplot in Figure 7.6 shows some clear curvature. In this chapter, I will recreate the regression as Lafrance and Gottardo (2005) conducted it, but it is worth keeping in mind that, because the relationship between these two variables is not linear, a better approach might be to try a polynomial fit for this variable.

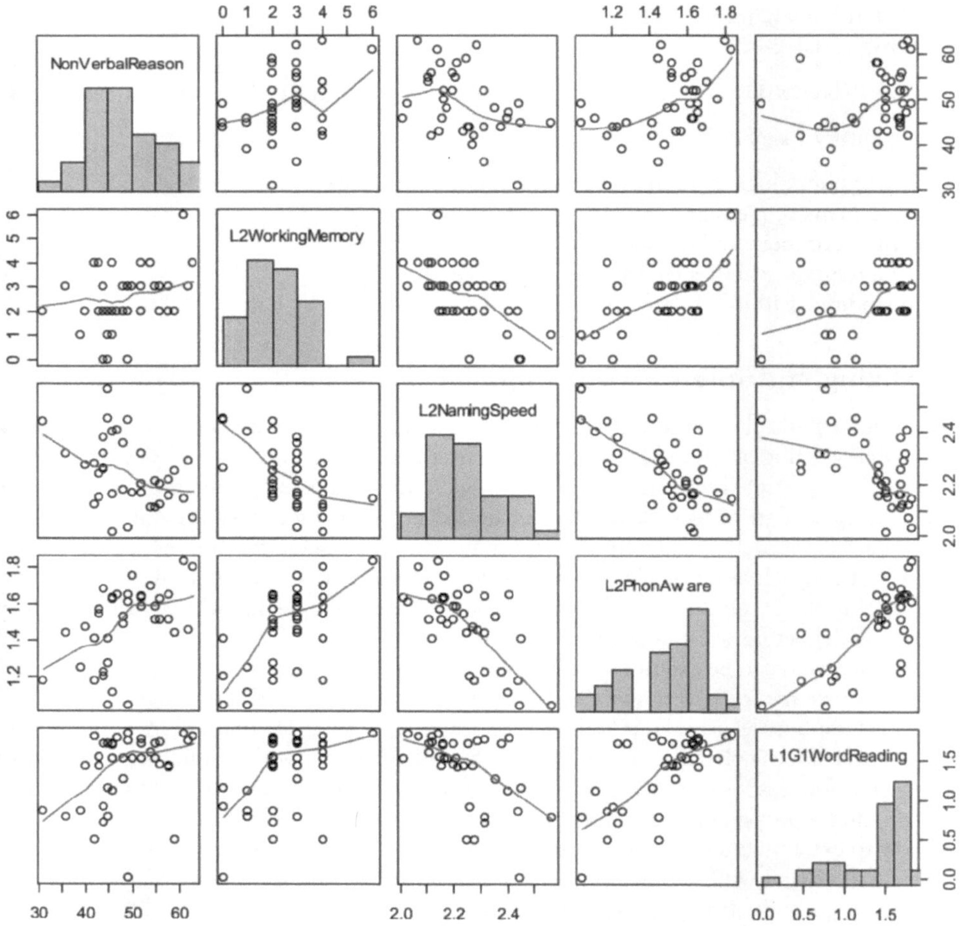

Figure 7.5 Scatterplot matrix of the Lafrance and Gottardo (2005) variables.

7.2.1 Graphs in R for Understanding Complex Relationships: Conditioning Plots

A conditioning plot or "**coplot**" shows the effects of a third variable in a step-by-step fashion on scatterplots of two variables together. This plot can perhaps best be understood by looking at an example from geography in Figure 7.7. (This coplot and several others can be recreated by typing example(coplot) in R; make sure to click on the Graphics Device to advance to the next graphic.)

The conditioning variable in the figure is depth of the ocean and the scatterplots show the location of 1000 earthquakes near Fiji at various latitude and longitude points. Each bar of the six conditioning variables (depth) corresponds to one scatterplot. This correlation begins on the left-hand side for depth and this first bar (around 100 km) corresponds to the scatterplot on the bottom row, left-hand corner. The scatterplots are then read from left to right and from bottom to top. Thus the fourth depth bar (spanning from 200 to 500 km) matches up with the leftmost scatterplot on the upper row (#4). Physically what is seen as the eye travels along the scatterplots from 1–6 is a concentration of the earthquakes into a smaller area as the depth of the ocean increases. Note that the conditioning bars overlap so that there is a sense of physically moving deeper and deeper as one's eyes skim over the scatterplots.

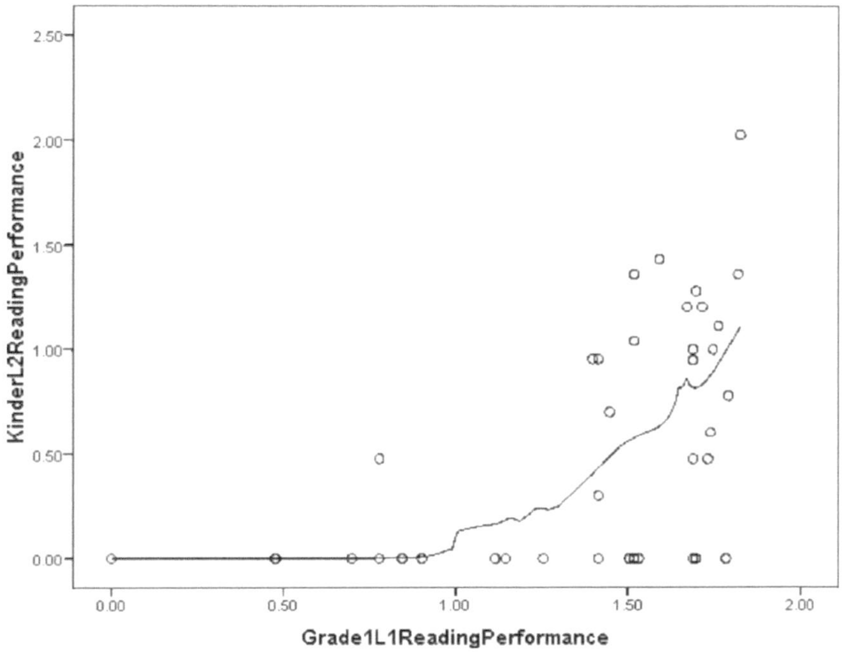

Figure 7.6 Scatterplot between Grade 1 L1 reading and kindergarten L2 reading skills.

The previous coplot was made with three variables: depth, latitude and longitude of earthquakes. Coplots can also be constructed with four variables. Figure 7.8 shows a coplot (again, taken from R's example coplots) of how state region and levels of illiteracy (percentage of population) affect the

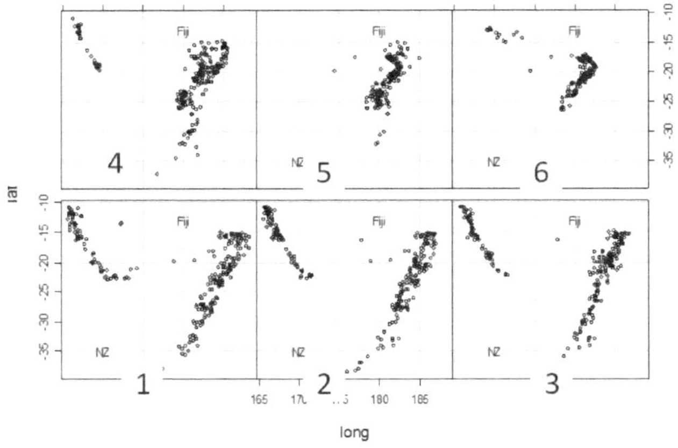

Figure 7.7 Coplot for the quakes data in the base R system.

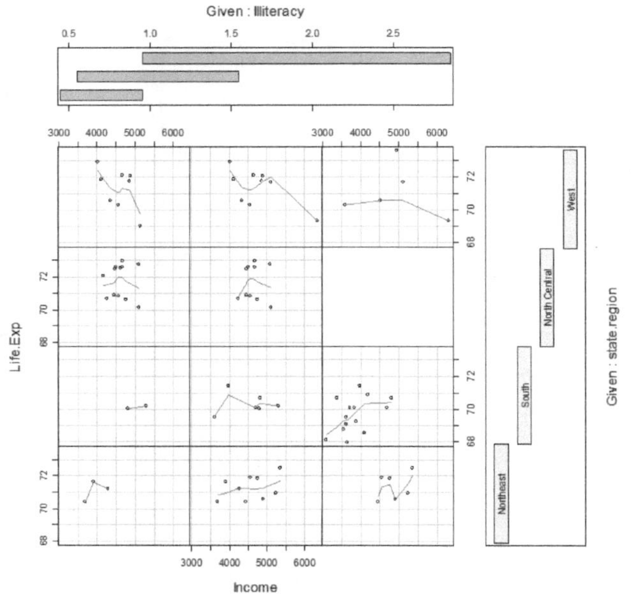

Figure 7.8 **Coplot for the data.frame(state.x77) data in the base R system.**

interaction of income and life expectancy. This coplot also shows how a smooth line (Loess line) can be drawn over the data to give an indication of the trend of the data.

There are few data points in each scatterplot so we would need to be careful about drawing strong conclusions from the data, but in the Northeastern and Southern USA we see somewhat of a trend toward higher life expectancies with higher income, whereas in the West there seems to be a trend of lower life expectancy with higher income. None of these seem to show any clear pattern with increases in illiteracy rates.

Now, using the Lafrance and Gottardo data (if you are working along with me, import the SPSS file "LafranceGottardo.sav" and name it **lafrance**), we will look at how non-verbal memory affects the relationship between L2 phonological awareness and L1 word reading scores in First Grade.

The coplot in Figure 7.9 roughly shows that reading ability (Grade 1 L1 reading) and phonological awareness (L2 phonemic awareness) are positively correlated, in that as phonological awareness increases, word reading becomes better. In other words, the Loess lines generally show an upward trend in each scatterplot. The conditioning variable of non-verbal reasoning just seems to show that there is more variability in the levels of phonological awareness and word reading ability when non-verbal reasoning is lower. That is, the bottom row of scatterplots shows more spread over both reading ability and phonological awareness, while the top row, indicating higher levels of non-verbal reasoning, is more tightly clustered among higher word reading and higher phonological awareness levels (except for one apparent outlier in panels 4 and 5).

Coplots are not available in R Commander, so you must use the R Console to obtain them. I used the following command to obtain the coplot in Figure 7.9.

```
coplot(l2phonemicawareness~grade1l1reading|nonverbalreasoning,
panel= function(x,y,...)
panel.smooth(x,y,span=.8,...),data=lafrance)
```

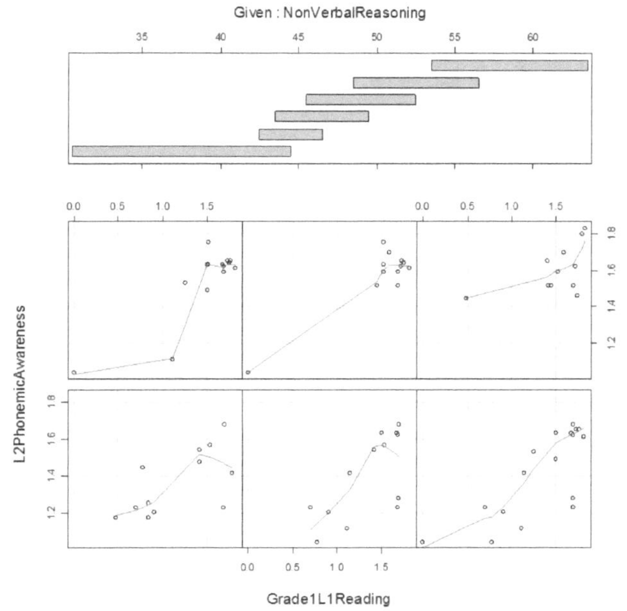

Figure 7.9 Coplot for three variables in the Lafrance and Gottardo (2005) data set.

coplot(A~B|C)	The coplot( ) command needs to have at least three arguments. The argument after the upright bar is the conditioning variable, the one that will be seen in the bars at the top of the graph.
panel=function(x,y,…)	Because coplot is a high-level function that draws more than one plot (really, a matrix of scatterplots), using the "panel" functions is one way to perform an action that will affect each plot (Murrell, 2006). Here, the panel function is specified as the smoother that follows. (Notice that there is no comma in between the function and the panel.smooth command.)
panel.smooth(x,y,span=.8,…)	According to Murrell (2006), panel.smooth is a predefined panel function that will add a smooth (Loess) line through points. The span affects how detailed the line is, with larger numbers spreading over a wider number of points and thus being smoother, while smaller numbers take more details into account and result in a choppier line.
data=lafrance	This specifies which data set the variables come from.

Creating a Coplot

The basic R code for this command with *three* variables is:

coplot(L2PhonemicAwareness~Grade1L1Reading|NonVerbalReasoning, panel= function(x,y,...) panel.smooth(x,y,span=.8,...),data=lafrance)

The basic R code for this command with *four* variables is:

coplot(L2PhonemicAwareness~Grade1L1Reading|NonVerbalReasoning*NamingSpeed, panel= function (x,y,...) panel.smooth(x,y,span=.8,...),data=lafrance)

Put the conditioning variable(s) after the upright line ("|")

7.2.2 Graphs in R for Understanding Complex Relationships: 3-D Graphs

Another way of looking at three variables at a time is to use a **three-dimensional (3-D) graph**. There are several libraries that can draw 3-D graphics but the coolest and easiest to use is definitely the one available through R Commander. In R Commander, choose GRAPHS > 3D GRAPH > 3D SCATTERPLOT. This command will not be available unless you have a data set active that has at least three variables! The dialog box is shown below (Figure 7.10). If you are working with me, I am still using the lafrance data set.

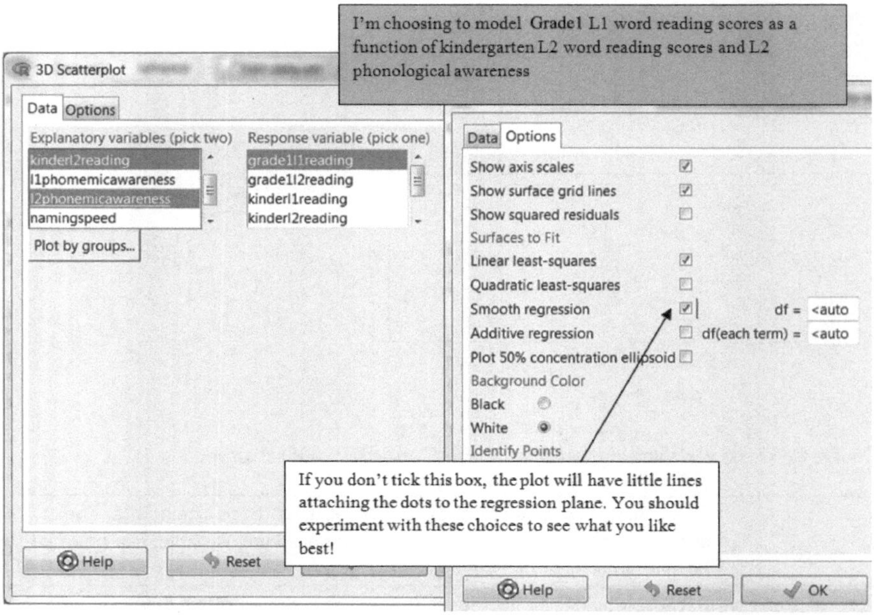

Figure 7.10 Three-dimensional scatterplot dialog box in R Commander.

After you click on OK, an RGL device will launch, and you can move the 3-D object with your mouse to rotate it to various positions. The graphs in Figure 7.11 are screenshots of two positions I found informative, but they cannot do justice to the ability to rotate the graph around that you get in the actual program.

You can save the graph as the RGL file by going back to the GRAPHS drop-down menu, choosing 3D graph again and then choosing SAVE GRAPH TO FILE. (You must do this while your RGL file is still open.) You can also identify particular points by going back to the GRAPHS menu with the 3D graph still open (GRAPHS > 3D GRAPH > IDENTIFY OBSERVATIONS WITH MOUSE).

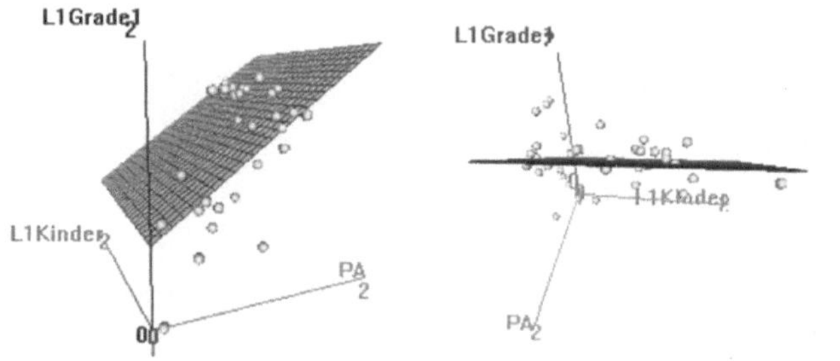

Figure 7.11 3-D scatterplots of the Lafrance and Gottardo (2005) data.

Tip: If you have a mouse with a wheel, rolling the wheel forward will make the graph smaller (recede it into the background) and rolling it backward will enlarge your view of the graph.

What can be deduced from the 3-D scatterplot is that scores on the Grade 1 reading test are better when phonological awareness is increased. The regression plane is fairly flat when looking from the kindergarten word reading scores axis, however, seeming to show there is not a lot of effect of this score on the other two.

Creating a 3-D Plot

In R Commander, go to GRAPHS > 3D GRAPH > 3D SCATTERPLOT. Choose one response variable and two explanatory variables (use the Ctrl button to choose more than one variable). Your 3-D graph will open up and you can move it around with your mouse. The basic command in R is:

```
scatter3d(lafrance$kinderl2reading, lafrance$grade1l1reading,
lafrance$l2phonemicawareness, fit=c("linear","smooth"), bg="white",
axis.scales=TRUE, grid=TRUE, ellipsoid=FALSE, xlab="kinderl2reading",
ylab="grade1l1reading", zlab="l2phonemicawareness")
```

7.2.3 Graphs in R for Understanding Complex Relationships: Tree Models

Tree models give a more intuitive sense of what is going on with the data than the regression coefficient numbers of a multiple regression. Crawley (2002) suggested that tree models are useful for cases where there are many explanatory variables and you do not know which ones to select. It takes a little bit of effort to understand how tree models work, but once you have figured them out they can be quite useful for deciding which variables to include in a regression and for deciding which types of interactions are taking place. For the code below to work properly you will need to import a data frame that contains the response variable that you want to model in the first column. I have imported the SPSS file "Lafrance5.sav" which contains the response variable in the first column, and only the five explanatory variables that Lafrance and Gottardo (2005) investigated with Grade 1 L1 reading performance as the response variables in columns 2–6. In R, I named it lafrance5.

This graph is only available using the R Console. The code for the tree model is from the tree package (Ripley, 2015):

```
install.packages("tree") #install the package if you do not already have it
library(tree) #there is a warning that it was built under an earlier version of R
model=tree(lafrance5)
plot(model)
text(model)
```

In this case I used the file lafrance5 which contained only the five explanatory variables that Lafrance and Gottardo (2005) investigated with Grade 1 L1 reading performance as the response variable. The model will assume that the first column contains the response variable that you want to model, but if it does not, you can specify which variable is the response variable using the regression model notation, where the "tilde dot" following the response variable means to include all other variables in the data frame as explanatory ones:

```
model=tree(grade1l1readingperformance~., lafrance.tree)
```

The data before the first comma is the formula for the tree model, while the second item is the name of the data. I have changed the variable names for the lafrance5 file for Figure 7.12 to make them more informative, which is why the code gives the name of the file as lafrance.tree. If you run this command with the lafrance5 file, it will have the same structure but the labels will be different.

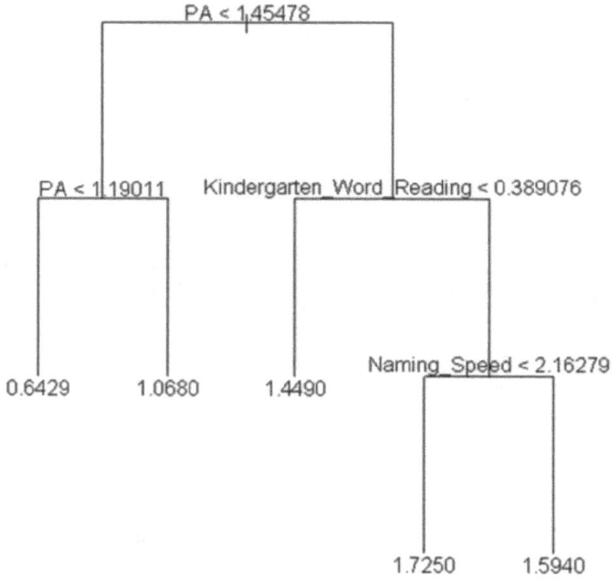

Figure 7.12 **Tree model for some variables in the Lafrance and Gottardo (2005) set.**

To understand the tree figure in Figure 7.12, you should know that all of the numbers at the terminal nodes refer to the response variable, Grade 1 L1 reading performance. Looking at the tree you should follow a path from the top (called the root) to the nodes (called the leaves). The first important split in the data is between those whose phonological awareness (PA) is below 1.45 and those who are above it. For those who have lower levels of phonological awareness (on the left branch of the first node), no other variable is important, as the next split also occurs with the same variable of PA. The group can be split into those who have PA lower than 1.19 and higher than 1.19. The mean score on the Grade 1 L1 word reading test is 0.64 for those whose PA is lower than 1.19, and it is 1.07 for those who PA is higher than 1.19.

For those who have higher levels of PA (above 1.45, on the right branch of the first node), scores on the reading test in kindergarten are the next most important variable. For those who scored below 0.39 on the kindergarten measure, their mean score on the Grade 1 word reading test is 1.45. For those children who scored higher than .39 on the kindergarten reading test, naming speed is the next most important variable. Those children who were faster at naming pictures (less than 2.16) got higher scores on the Grade 1 word reading test (mean = 1.73). Those who scored higher on naming speed had an average score of 1.59 on the Grade 1 L1 reading measure.

The data can also be seen in a different way by using the print command:

```
print(model)
```

```
node), split, n, deviance, yval
      * denotes terminal node

 1) root 37 7.36000 1.3670
   2) phonologicalawarenessinl2 < 1.45478 12 2.75400 0.8911
     4) phonologicalawarenessinl2 < 1.19011 5 0.72190 0.6429 *
     5) phonologicalawarenessinl2 > 1.19011 7 1.50400 1.0680 *
   3) phonologicalawarenessinl2 > 1.45478 25 0.58540 1.5950
     6) kinderl2readingperformance < 0.389076 7 0.05779 1.4490 *
     7) kinderl2readingperformance > 0.389076 18 0.32070 1.6520
      14) namingspeed < 2.16279 8 0.04694 1.7250 *
      15) namingspeed > 2.16279 10 0.19760 1.5940 *
```

A star marks the terminal nodes for this data. The numbers are the node numbers and they are labeled by the variable which made the split. So node #2 was split by Phonological Awareness, and this was split for the criteria of being below 1.45478. The number of cases going into the split for node #2 was 12. The next number (2.754) is the deviance at the node, and the last number is the mean score of the response variable (here, First Grade L1 word reading scores) at that node. The lowest score for First Grade word reading was at node 4, and the highest was at node 14.

This model can help us understand better how PA is involved in scores on the response variable. Crawley (2002, p. 585) says, "This kind of complex and contingent explanation is much easier to see, and to understand, in tree models than in the output of a multiple regression." The results of the tree model might lead us to choose to include PA, kindergarten reading scores, and naming speed in our model, and leave out working memory and non-verbal reasoning.

Creating a Tree Model

Use the R Console with the basic commands:

```
library(tree)
model=tree(grade1l2reading~., data=lafrance)
plot(model)
text(model)
```

The first argument is the variable you are trying to explain (the response variable). The "~." (tilde and dot) mean that all other variables contained in the data file should be used as explanatory variables. To specify exactly which variables in the file should be used, use the "+" or "-" sign to add or subtract variables after the first argument but before the comma.

7.2.4 Application Activities in R with Graphs for Understanding Complex Relationships

Since the graphs I explored in this section can only be performed using the R statistical software, only R exercises will be given here.

Coplots

1 Use the Lafrance and Gottardo (2005) data (import the SPSS file "LafranceGottardo.sav" and name it lafrance; it has 40 rows and 9 columns). Do a 3-variable coplot with Grade 1 reading measures in L1 (grade1l2reading) and working memory measures (workingmemory) conditioned by L2 PA (l2phonemicawareness) (put the conditioning, or given, variable after the vertical line in the equation). Be sure to include the smooth line. What happens to the relationship between working memory values and Grade 1 L1 reading scores as phonemic awareness in L2 increases?

2 Use the same data set as in #1. Do a 3-variable coplot with L2 reading measures from kindergarten (kinderl2reading) and First Grade (grade1l2reading) conditioned by L2 PA (l2phonemicawareness) (put it after the vertical line in the equation). What effect does increasing L2 PA seem to have on the relationship between word reading measures in kindergarten and First Grade?

3 Use the Larson-Hall (2008) data set (use SPSS file LarsonHall2008.sav, import as lh2008). Explore the relationship between the age that early learners began studying English (earlyage) and their performance on a pronunciation measure (rlwscore) and grammar measure (gjtscore) as adults. Use age as the conditioning variable (put it after the vertical line in the equation). What effect does increasingly later starting age have on outcomes?

3-D plots

1 Use the Lafrance and Gottardo (2005) data set. Create a 3-D plot with L2 reading measures from First Grade (grade1l2reading) as the response variable, conditioned by L1 PA (l1phonemicawareness) and L2 reading measures from kindergarten (kinderl2reading). What trends in the data can you describe?

Tree models

1 Lafrance and Gottardo (2005). Use the LafranceGottardo.sav file (not the Lafrance5.sav) which has nine variables. Set up the Grade 1 L2 reading performance to be the response variable (grade1l2reading) and note which variables the tree model says are explanatory out of the eight that are entered. Run a tree model again, excluding all other measures of reading performance besides those that turned out to be explanatory in the first run. To exclude a variable, simply subtract it from the item in the parenthesis, before the tilde and dot, like this: tree(grade1l2reading-kinderl2reading~., data=lafrance). Which variables are explanatory now?

2 Use the Dewaele and Pavlenko (2001–2003) data set. Use the file concerning the use of swear and taboo words, which I have put into the BEQ.Swear.sav SPSS file. (Import it as beq.swear.) Dewaele (2004) examined the frequency of use of swear words in the languages of multilinguals and the emotional weight they carry in each language (weight1, weight2) with a linear regression involving age, age of onset of acquisition for each language, self-rated proficiency in four areas and frequency of language use. Dewaele (2004) looked at attriters only and we will not recreate his regression. I have put the relevant variables into this file, plus a couple more that looked interesting, such as level of educational degree (degree) and number of languages, frequency of swearing in L1 and the weight it carries in L1. Use this data set to examine one tree model for the frequency of swearing in L2 (swear2) and another for the weight it carries in L2 (weight2), and report on what variables seem to be pertinent to explaining how often multilinguals swear in their second language and what weight they give to swear words.

7.3 Assumptions of Multiple Regression

Regression presents a large number of assumptions that must be satisfied, and indeed this area is quite a complex one that cannot be totally covered in this book. I will focus only on the most basic assumptions and tests of the assumptions. Assumptions such as a normal distribution and linearity may be familiar from previous chapters, but the methods used to check them differ. Regression fitting is done *after* a regression model has been selected. Assumptions cannot be tested until the model has been decided on, because in many cases the variables you are testing are results from the model, such as the residuals (what is left over after the explanatory variables have done their part). Table 7.1 may thus not make sense until after you have gone through later sections of the chapter that show how to check assumptions of multiple regression.

7.3.1 Assumptions about Sample Size

There are a variety of "rules of thumb" for the number of samples that should be collected for a multiple regression. Porte (2002) recommends 30 participants per explanatory variable. Tabachnick and Fidell (2001, p. 117) give the formula: $N \geq 50 + 8m$ where m = number of explanatory variables. Stevens (2002) recommends about 15 per variable based on his own experience and some statistical studies. Howell (2002, p. 548) cites (but does not necessarily support) a widespread rule of thumb of 10 observations for each variable. Thus, for Lafrance and Gottardo's regression with five explanatory variables, Porte would say they should have 150 participants, Tabachnick and Fidell would recommend 90, Stevens would say 75 and Howell's rule of thumb would ask for 50 (quite a difference!). Tabachnick and Fidell quote Green (1991), who gives a rule that includes effect size: $N \geq (8/f^2) + (m - 1)$ where

Table 7.1 Assumptions for Multiple Regression

Assumptions		*How to test assumption?*	*What if assumption is not met?*
Normal distribution	Errors normally distributed (note that this is *not* the distribution of the variables, but rather the distribution of the error that should be examined)	Examine Q-Q plots	(1) Use robust methods of regression such as the bootstrap found in this chapter; (2) transform variables
	No outliers	Look at graphs of studentized residuals, Cook's and Mahalanobis distances; look for values beyond usual ones	(1) Use robust methods of regression such as the bootstrap found in this chapter to minimize the influence of outliers while preserving independent of observations; (2) remove outliers and rerun analysis; report on both results to your readers
Homogeneity of variances (constant variance)	"The variance of Y for each value of X is constant (in the population)" (Howell, 2002, p. 267)	Plot studentized residuals against fitted values and look for equal spread across entire graph	(1) Use robust methods of regression such as the bootstrap found in this chapter; (2) transform to equalize spread (try square root or log)
Linearity	The relationship between X and Y is linear	(1) Examine scatterplot matrices; (2) plot residuals against individual variables and look for curvature	Use a polynomial model instead (put in x^2 or x^3 terms to model the curvature)
Multicollinearity	Explanatory variables involved in the regression should not be highly intercorrelated	(1) Look at numerical matrix of correlations; (2) check VIF	Delete a variable from the regression if it is highly correlated with another explanatory variable

$f^2 = 0.01$, 0.15 and 0.35 for small, medium and large effects, respectively. Given this rule and estimating a medium effect size from previous research with reading and PA, Lafrance and Gottardo would need $N \geq (8/0.15) + (5 - 1) = 58$ participants (rounding up). Note that such a number would enable the authors to find a medium or large effect size, but not a small effect size. Cohen et al. (2003) combined both power and effect size to determine that, with five explanatory variables, for an $R^2 = 0.20$ and power of 0.80, 53 subjects would be required. This wide divergence of sample size recommendations is daunting, giving support for any number of observations, ranging in the case of five predictors from 50 to 150. It is clear though, as Gelman and Hill (2007) stated, that "Sample size is never large enough" (p. 438). They suggested that just as you can never have enough money, you can never have too large a sample size either.

I include here Table 7.2, calculated from Cohen et al. (2003), for various levels of R^2 and various numbers of predictors, but all at the same $\alpha = 0.05$ and power = 0.80 level. The formula is: $\frac{L}{f^2}$ + number of predictors; to calculate this you must use Cohen et al. (2003)'s table to look up the values of L, and can then calculate $f^2 = R^2/1 - R^2$.

It can be seen that the higher or more obvious you expect the effect size to be (the R^2), the fewer participants are needed. Because the effect size in Lafrance and Gottardo's study is so high ($R^2 = 0.58$ for the regression I am examining), their sample size of 40 turns out to be more than adequate.

Table 7.2 Sample Size Needed for Various Effect Sizes at 80% Power in Regression

Number of predictors	R^2=.10	R^2=.15	R^2=.20	R^2=.25	R^2=.30	R^2=.50
2	74	47	34	21	21	10
3	91	58	42	26	26	13
4	104	66	48	30	30	15
5	114	73	53	33	33	17
6	123	79	58	36	36	19
7	131	85	62	39	39	21
8	139	90	66	42	42	23
9	146	95	70	44	44	25
10	153	99	73	47	47	26

However, one important idea to take away from this discussion is that you should not try to "throw in the kitchen sink" and include every variable you can think of. The more variables you have, the more observations or participants you will need to have a strong statistical case. The number of variables and your choice of them should include the costs of obtaining the data in sufficient numbers so as to be statistically valid. The best-case scenario would be if researchers chose a power level and estimated an effect size to have a principled reason for the number of participants in a study.

7.4 Performing a Multiple Regression

Before doing a multiple regression, I need to explain one more type of regression that Tabachnick and Fidell (2001) have discussed. In Section 7.1 I discussed standard and sequential types of regression. In the former case, only the unique contribution of the explanatory variable to the response variable was counted, while in the latter the entire amount of overlap of the explanatory variable with the response variable was counted, so that order of entry mattered.

Another type of regression mentioned by Tabachnick and Fidell (2001) is **statistical regression**. Like sequential regression, this type of regression counts all of the area where the explanatory variables overlap with the response variable and add variables one at a time to determine the best fit. However, statistical regression (called **stepwise regression** in SPSS) is not recommended. This is because using stepwise regression leaves the model determination up to the computer and the variables are entered based "solely on statistical criteria," which makes this a "controversial procedure" (Tabachnick & Fidell, 2001, p. 133). The choice of which variable is entered first is based on the strength of the correlation.

Let us say for the TOEFL example we were looking at in Section 7.1 that all three variables had nearly the same strength of correlation with the TOEFL score, but the MLAT score had a slightly higher correlation with the TOEFL score than the other two explanatory variables (see Figure 7.13). In that case, the MLAT score would be entered first, and thus b, c and d would count for the variance

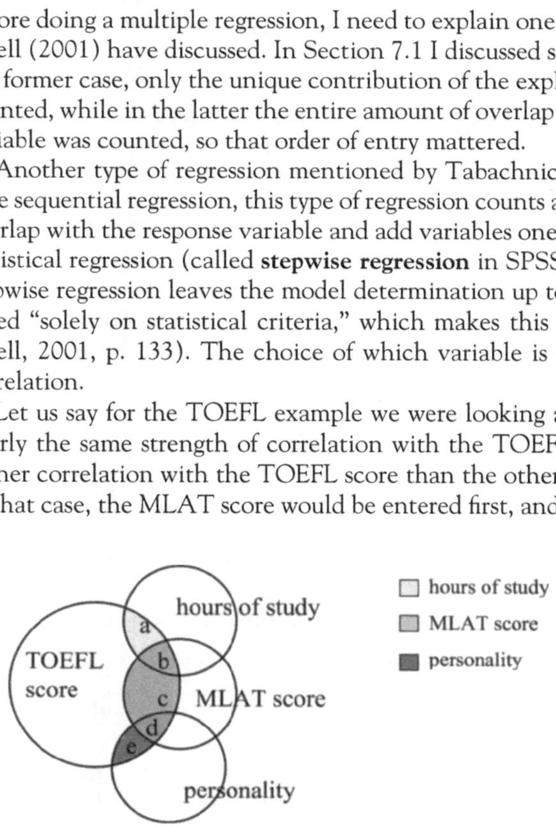

Figure 7.13 Venn diagram of stepwise regression design.

of MLAT. Next, the algorithm for a statistical regression would evaluate whether the remaining variables contributed significantly to the R^2 (the part of the variance in the response variable that the explanatory variables account for). If they did not, because much of their variance has been claimed by the MLAT, they would not be entered in the equation, in spite of the fact that initially their correlation levels were about the same strength.

For the Lafrance and Gottardo (2005) data, we find fairly high correlations between naming speed and the response variable ($r = -0.57$), kindergarten measures of reading and the response variable ($r = 0.55$) and working memory and the response variable ($r = 0.51$). If only these three variables were included in a regression model, a statistical regression would pick naming speed first, even though the difference between $r = -0.57$, $r = 0.55$ and $r = 0.51$ may not be practically important.

In a statistical regression, you as the researcher are letting the computer pick the regression configuration based on purely statistical information, with no logical or theoretical assumptions involved. For this reason, most writers recommend against it. Tabachnick and Fidell (2001, p. 135) have cautioned that it should be used only if samples are "large and representative," and even then researchers should be cautious about generalizing results to a wider population. Howell (2002, p. 565) suggested that it can "capitaliz[e] on chance" and thus the computer may choose a model that is only slightly better than a more "logically appropriate model." It should not be used unless you truly "have no particular theoretical axe to grind" (p. 564).

Before running the regression you should have examined your data set for linearity by using scatterplots. If the data look reasonably linear, you may begin your regression. (Note that Lafrance and Gottardo transformed some of their variables with the log transformation to correct for skewness.) We will examine assumptions of multivariate normality and homogeneity of variances through residual plots called for in the regression analysis itself.

7.4.1 Starting the Multiple Regression in SPSS

To perform a regression, choose ANALYZE > REGRESSION > LINEAR. (To follow along with my analysis here, use the Lafrance5.sav file.) Put your response variable in the box labeled "Dependent" (see Figure 7.14). A crucial step, and one that will determine how you enter the explanatory variables in the box labeled "Independent(s)," is determining which method you want to use to analyze the regression. Pull down the menu next to METHOD and use the explanations in Figure 7.14 to decide which method to choose. Also, open three of the buttons on the right-hand side of the dialog box: STATISTICS, PLOTS and SAVE. (Open the OPTIONS button when you are using stepwise regression.)

To follow along with my analysis here, use sequential regression. For the Lafrance and Gottardo data, first put Grade1L1Reading Performance into the "Dependent" variable box. Then put Nonverbal Reasoning in the Independent(s) box first and click on the "Next" button, then kindergarten L2 reading scores in kindergarten (and click on "Next"), then Naming Speed ("Next"), then Working Memory ("Next") then PA in L2. (Do not push Next after this last one!)

Figure 7.15 shows subdialog boxes you should open from the main LINEAR REGRESSION dialog box. From the STATISTICS button you will choose to view graphs that will be used to assess the assumptions of the regression model (normality, homogeneity, etc.). From the PLOTS button, you will choose to view graphs that will be used to assess the assumptions of the regression model (normality, homogeneity, etc.). From the SAVE button you will be able to call for some diagnostic tests. From the OPTIONS button you have the chance to choose how to deal with missing data and also to specify the stepwise criteria if you should choose this method of regression. For missing data, the default option is listwise exclusion, which is preferable to pairwise exclusion even though it may reduce sample size. Howell (2002) says that excluding pairwise in a regression can result in strange correlations. Replacing missing values with the mean can be appropriate if you have only a small amount of missing data that does not display any patterns for being missing. Remember from Section 1.5 Wilkinson (1999) labeled both listwise and pairwise deletion the worst ways of dealing with missing data, and I suggested in that section that one good way to deal with missing data would be imputation. In fact, the LafranceGottardo.sav file that is used later in this chapter is one where I imputed a few missing values for the Naming Speed variable.

Once you have configured your regression as noted in Figures 7.14 and 7.15, click on OK and run your regression. The output that is shown in the next section results from following the steps that I have shown in Figure 7.15, so to get the same analysis as I show here, perform a sequential regression as explained in this section on the Lafrance5.sav data set.

7.4.2 Regression Output in SPSS

The first box in the regression output is the descriptive statistics (Table 7.3). Here we see that the mean scores are quite different for the different predictors. For example, the mean score for non-verbal

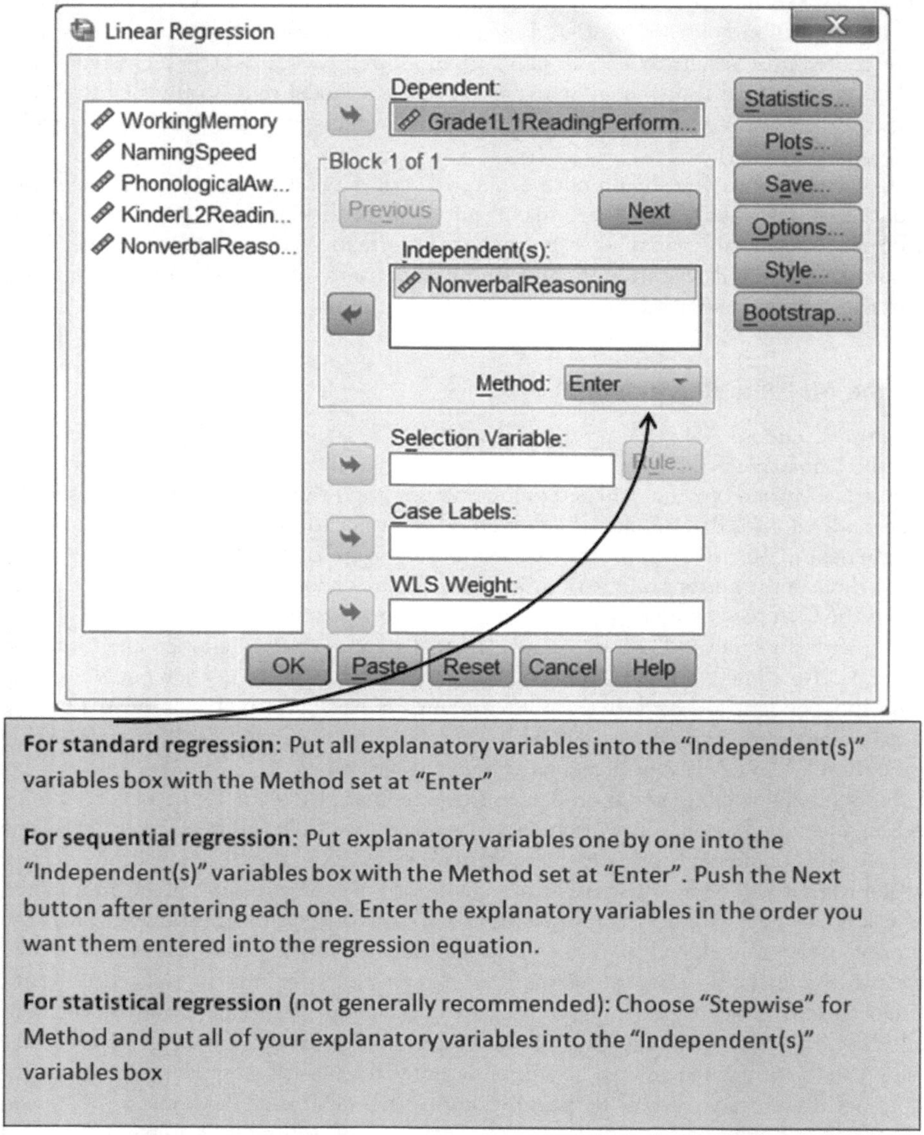

Figure 7.14 Main dialog box for linear regression in SPSS.

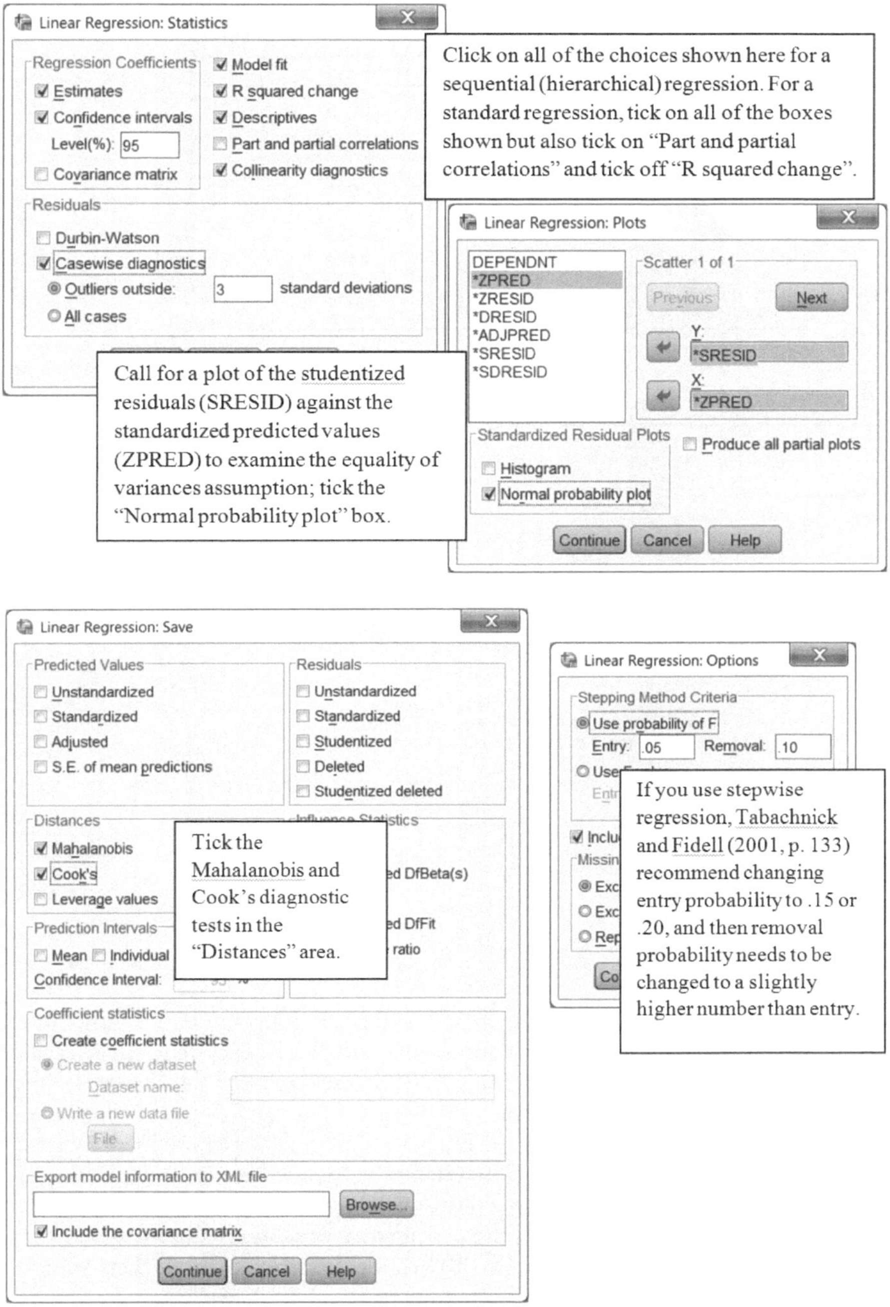

Figure 7.15 Sub-dialog boxes for linear regression in SPSS.

reasoning is 48.9, but for naming speed it is 2.2. All this means is that the variables were measured on different types of scales. We also see that using listwise deletion means that we have only 37 cases for the regression, even though 40 participants were included in the experiment. (To follow along with the analysis in this section, use the Lafrance5.sav file, which is not imputed; it will recreate Lafrance

Table 7.3 Regression Output: Descriptive Statistics

Descriptive Statistics

	Mean	Std. Deviation	N
Grade1L1Reading Performance	1.3669	.45215	37
NonVerbal Reasoning	48.9459	7.28753	37
Kinder L2 Reading Performance	.5464	.58691	37
Naming Speed	2.2414	.12846	37
Working Memory	2.6486	1.27402	37
Phonological Awareness in L2	1.4926	.20815	37

Table 7.4 Correlations between Variables in Lafrance and Gottardo (2005)

		Nonverbal reasoning	Kindergarten L2 reading	L2 naming speed	L2 working memory	L2 phon. awareness
Grade 1 L1 reading	*r*	.34	.57	-.57	.52	.75
	95% CI*	[.00, .63]	[.40, .73]	[-.75, -.36]	[.16, .75]	[.56, .87]
	N	37	37	37	37	37
Kindergarten L2 reading	*r*	.42				
	95% CI*	[.14, .64]				
	N	37				
L2 naming speed	*r*	-.41	-.40			
	95% CI*	[-.62, -.17]	[-.65, -,14]			
	N	37	37			
L2 working memory	*r*	.26	.5	-.61		
	95% CI*	[-.03, .49]	[.21, .74]	[-.75, -.41]		
	N	37	37	37		
L2 phon. awareness	*r*	.49	.71	-.70	.59	
	95% CI*	[.28, .68]	[.55, .84]	[-.84, -.48]	[.25, .78]	
	N	37	37	37	37	

*BCa bootstrapped confidence interval (see Section 7.4.4)

and Gottardo's (2005) results, table 3, under L2 phonological processing variables, Grade 1 word reading L1.)

The second box of the output is a correlation matrix. The format of this in SPSS is rather messy, so Table 7.4 shows the same data in a more readable form, giving the *r*-value, confidence interval (CI), which can only be calculated if you use bootstrapping in SPSS (see Section 7.4.4 for more information), and *N* for each cell of the correlation matrix.

Although we will examine **multicollinearity** measures later (e.g. variance inflation factor (VIF); multicollinearity measures how much a number of variables vary together), it is important to note here whether there are any high correlations between the explanatory variables and the response variable (these are shown in the first row), or among the explanatory variables themselves (shown in the second through fifth row). Tabachnick and Fidell (2001) cautioned against correlations as high as or higher than $r = 0.70$, and a couple of correlations with kindergarten L2 PA reach that level. However, Lafrance and Gottardo (2005) knew from previous studies that PA is highly correlated with reading measures, and they wanted to see whether any other factors could be predictive before PA was added, so they probably did not want to throw out PA.

The next part of the output shown in Table 7.5 is the Variables Entered/Removed table. Because Lafrance and Gottardo performed a sequential (hierarchical) regression, this table importantly shows the order in which the variables were entered. If this were a standard regression, this table would just list the variables entered, as shown in the smaller table on the right.

Table 7.5 Regression Output: Variables Entered/Removed

Variables Entered/Removed[b]

Model	Variables Entered	Variables Removed	Method
1	NonVerbal Reasoning[a]	.	Enter
2	Kinder L2 Reading Performance[a]	.	Enter
3	Naming Speed[a]	.	Enter
4	Working Memory[a]	.	Enter
5	Phonological Awareness in L2[a]	.	Enter

a. All requested variables entered.

b. Dependent Variable: Grade1L1Reading Performance

Variables Entered/Removed[b]

Model	Variables Entered	Variables Removed	Method
1	Phonological Awareness in L2, NonVerbal Reasoning, Working Memory, Kinder L2 Reading Performance, Naming Speed[a]	.	Enter

a. All requested variables entered.

b. Dependent Variable: Grade1L1Reading Performance

The next part of the output, the Model Summary table, provides a summary of how much of the variance in the response variable is accounted for by the predictors (Table 7.6). In the sequential regression there are five models because SPSS tests each of the models listed as (a) through (e). Thus, in the first model (a), SPSS tests how much of the variance in word reading can be accounted for by just non-verbal reasoning. In other words, this equation is tested:

Grade 1 L1 word reading = intercept (Constant) + non-verbal reasoning + error

Model 2 tests how much of the variance can be accounted for by two factors:

Grade 1 L1 word reading = intercept (Constant) + non-verbal reasoning + kindergarten L2 reading + error

Table 7.6 Regression Output: Model Summary (Sequential Regression)

Model Summary[f]

					Change Statistics				
Model	R	R Square	Adjusted R Square	Std. Error of the Estimate	R Square Change	F Change	df1	df2	Sig. F Change
1	.335[a]	.112	.087	.43209	.112	4.422	1	35	.043
2	.582[b]	.339	.300	.37819	.227	11.686	1	34	.002
3	.683[c]	.467	.418	.34489	.127	7.884	1	33	.008
4	.688[d]	.473	.407	.34814	.006	.385	1	32	.539
5	.761[e]	.580	.512	.31585	.107	7.879	1	31	.009

a. Predictors: (Constant), NonVerbal Reasoning

b. Predictors: (Constant), NonVerbal Reasoning, Kinder L2 Reading Performance

c. Predictors: (Constant), NonVerbal Reasoning, Kinder L2 Reading Performance, Naming Speed

d. Predictors: (Constant), NonVerbal Reasoning, Kinder L2 Reading Performance, Naming Speed, Working Memory

e. Predictors: (Constant), NonVerbal Reasoning, Kinder L2 Reading Performance, Naming Speed, Working Memory, Phonological Awareness in L2

f. Dependent Variable: Grade1L1Reading Performance

By the end, Model 5 tests how much variance is explained by all five predictors added into the regression equation. You can see how the regression equation used in each model can easily be derived from the predictors listed underneath the model summary box in the lettered footnotes. (The equation is just missing the error term and plus signs between the variables.)

The number that we are most interested in from Table 7.6 is in the R Square column or R Square Change column. The results tell us that Model 1 with just non-verbal reasoning accounts for $R^2 = 11\%$ of the variance, as seen in the R Square column in the Model Summary (the R^2 number can range from 0 to 1). This model has 35 degrees of freedom (df) (see the column called df2), because there are 37 rows of data, and we have to subtract 1 df for the response variable and 1 df for the one explanatory variable. The Adjusted R Square corrects for positive bias in the R^2 estimate, but few people report this number because it is usually lower than the R^2!

The second model tested adds the predictor of kindergarten L2 Woodcock reading test results. Now the R^2 is 0.339, but what we really want to know is how much R^2 kindergarten L2 reading independently added to the total model. To know this we just subtract 0.112 from 0.339 (= 0.227) or simply look in the R Square Change column to see 0.227. In other words, kindergarten L2 reading independently adds 23% of explanation for the variation in scores on the Grade 1 L1 reading test.

The model with five explanatory variables can explain 58% of the variance in scores on the Grade 1 L1 reading test. This is a very high percentage! However, we should realize that there is a trade-off between the amount of explanatory value and the number of predictors. Adding more predictors always results in a higher R^2, so if we fit the model with 37 predictors we might have a R^2 coefficient of 1 but we would have little explanatory value.

What Lafrance and Gottardo (2005) were interested in examining with this sequential regression was if other predictors besides PA have an independent ability to account for variance. The output in Table 7.6 shows that they did, except for working memory, which added only about 0.01% in explanation of the variation in scores on the Grade 1 L1 reading measure.

Going on to explain a couple more of the columns of output in Table 7.6, the F Change column of the sequential regression Model Summary gives the result of an analysis of variance (ANOVA) comparing the current model with the previous model to see whether the two models are statistically different. Model 2, for example, is statistically different from Model 1 ($F = 11.69$, $p = 0.002$). Model 1 is compared to the null model, which is just the average mean score of all of the variables. Model 4 is not statistically different from Model 3, as shown by the fact that the significance of the F change is $p = 0.539$ (not less than $p = 0.05$). If you are interested in a good fit for predictors, you would probably want to leave out the predictor added in Model 4, which was working memory (WM).

Note that the Model Summary output, shown in Table 7.7, will not contain any part of the "Change Statistics" if the regression is a standard regression with all variables added at once. If you performed a standard regression, your Model Summary table will look much simpler, and you will basically be interested in the R^2 statistic.

Moving on to the next part of the output, Table 7.8 shows a table which gives the results of an ANOVA performed on each model. The ANOVA tests the null hypothesis that the predictive power of the model is equal to zero. This is probably never a very realistic hypothesis, so a statistically

Table 7.7 Regression Output: Model Summary (Standard Regression)

Model Summary

Model	R	R Square	Adjusted R Square	Std. Error of the Estimate
1	.761[a]	.580	.512	.31585

a. Predictors: (Constant), NonVerbalReason, WorkingMemory, KinderL2Reading, NamingSpeed, L2PhonAware

Table 7.8 Regression Output: ANOVA Table

ANOVA[a]

Model		Sum of Squares	df	Mean Square	F	Sig.
1	Regression	.826	1	.826	4.422	.043[b]
	Residual	6.534	35	.187		
	Total	7.360	36			
2	Regression	2.497	2	1.248	8.729	.001[c]
	Residual	4.863	34	143		

significant result is not too much to get excited about, and there is probably nothing from this table you will want to report.

The next part of the output is the Coefficients table (Table 7.9). This is an important piece of the output. This table gives information about each explanatory variable in the equation. Here you find the unstandardized (**B**) and standardized **regression coefficients** (named beta or β) for each of the five explanatory variables (plus 95% CIs for the B). The unstandardized coefficients are the coefficients you would use to write the regression equation. For example, Model 2 would predict that scores in Grade 1 L1 reading performance could be modeled by:

Y = 0.795 + (0.007)*non-verbal reasoning + (0.404)*kindergarten L2 reading performance + error

The 0.795 is the intercept (alpha), taken from the row named "Constant" under Model 2. The B coefficients are then multiplied by each factor in the equation. However, unstandardized coefficients cannot be compared to each other well. Standardized coefficients give the coefficients that would result if they were fitted to standardized data. Tabachnick and Fidell (2001) reported these in their results, but I am not sure that that is necessary, since coefficients are not really the thing to look at to report on the effect size or importance of the variables. For that, look at the R^2 and the squared semipartial correlation (sr^2). (More on these coming up.)

The *t*-test associated with each line in the Coefficients table tests whether each explanatory variable contributes uniquely to the equation (Tabachnick & Fidell, 2001). In their paper, Lafrance and Gottardo reported, for each model, the total R^2 (from the Model Summary output), the change in R^2 (from the Model Summary output), the standardized coefficients for each model (from the Coefficients output) and whether each coefficient was statistical (from the Sig. column next to the *t*-test in the Coefficients output) by putting stars next to the statistical coefficients. In following the "new statistics" model of reporting CIs, instead of reporting the *p*-value from the "Sig." column of the Coefficients table (Table 7.9), we would report the CI for the unstandardized coefficient.

Table 7.9 Regression Output: Coefficients (Sequential Regression)

Coefficients[a]

Model		Unstandardized Coefficients		Standardized Coefficients			95.0% Confidence Interval for B		Collinearity Statistics	
		B	Std. Error	Beta	t	Sig.	Lower Bound	Upper Bound	Tolerance	VIF
1	(Constant)	.350	.489		.716	.479	-.643	1.342		
	NonverbalReasoning	.021	.010	.335	2.103	.043	.001	.041	1.000	1.000
2	(Constant)	.795	.447		1.777	.085	-.114	1.704		
	NonverbalReasoning	.007	.010	.116	.754	.456	-.012	.027	.825	1.212
	KinderL2ReadingPerformance	.404	.118	.525	3.418	.002	.164	.644	.825	1.212
3	(Constant)	4.415	1.352		3.265	.003	1.664	7.166		
	NonverbalReasoning	.000	.009	-.002	-.014	.989	-.019	.018	.757	1.320
	KinderL2ReadingPerformance	[illegible]	[illegible]	[illegible]	[illegible]	[illegible]	[illegible]	[illegible]	[illegible]	[illegible]

In their paper, Lafrance and Gottardo (2005) noted that, when L2 PA was entered (Model 5), it became the only statistical predictor of Grade 1 L1 reading performance. They concluded that L1 and L2 PA were highly related and that cross-language transfer of PA was taking place.

Both Tabachnick and Fidell (2001) and Howell (2002) have argued that the change in R^2 (which can be seen in Table 7.6, under the "R Square Change" column) is a better measure of the "importance" of each variable than the regression coefficients, which do not really measure the effect of each variable independently of each other, vary greatly from sample to sample and are affected by the size of their standard deviations (SDs).

The last column of the Coefficients table provides information about multicollinearity. The VIF column shows the variance inflation factor. (Tolerance, the column before it, is just 1/VIF.) Heiberger and Holland (2004, p. 243) suggested that VIF values of over 5 are evidence of collinearity, which would be evidence that the variables are too highly intercorrelated and may harm the model. Most of the VIF for this data set are around 1 or 2, and the highest value is for PA in L2 in Model 5 at 3.47 (not shown). These are all under 5, so we do not find anything problematic.

If you do a standard regression, you will see additional columns in the Coefficients output, notably the columns under the "Correlations" section (see Table 7.10). These columns contain the correlations labeled "partial" and "part." In a partial correlation the effect of the variable is taken out of both the IV and DV, while in semipartial correlation (the one labeled "part" in SPSS), the effect of the variable is taken out of only the IV (Tabachnick & Fidell, 2001). The column labeled "Part" gives the sr^2 for each term (Tabachnik & Fidell suggested that what SPSS returns as "Part" needs to be squared to obtain the sr^2; see p. 162), and it "expresses the unique contribution of the IV to the total variance of the DV" (Tabachnick & Fidell, 2001, p. 140). The sr^2 should be reported as a way of comparing the importance of each term in the model, but because of shared variances between the explanatory variables, the sum of all of the semipartial correlations often does not actually sum up to the total R^2 for the entire model. Tabachnick and Fidell (2001) suggested that it is often common to see a large R^2 but an sr^2 for each IV that is quite small, which means that much of the R^2 comes from effects between IVs. As you can see, if Lafrance and Gottardo's regression were done as a standard regression, L2 phonemic awareness would be the most important factor by far (with "part" of 0.37).

For a sequential (hierarchical) regression like the one we called for here, beyond the Coefficients table there will be three more tables included in the output (Excluded Variables, Collinearity Diagnostics and Residuals Statistics). For a sequential regression, the sr^2 can be seen "as the amount of variance added to R^2 by each IV at the point that it enters the equation" (ibid, p. 142), so the size of the sr^2 will depend on what point it was entered into the equation; sr^2 is labeled as "R Square Change" for each IV in the SPSS output (ibid).

We will not worry about excluded variables, but we will see in the next section that the Collinearity Diagnostics and Residuals Statistics are important for examining assumptions for the model. For a standard regression, there is no Excluded Variables table because all variables were entered at the same time and there are no excluded variables. In an analysis like the one performed here, after the tables there will be two graphics we will use to examine regression assumptions.

Table 7.10 Regression Output: Coefficients (Standard Regression)

Coefficients[a]

Model		Unstandardized Coefficients		Standardized Coefficients			Correlations			Collinearity Statistics	
		B	Std. Error	Beta	t	Sig.	Zero-order	Partial	Part	Tolerance	VIF
1	(Constant)	-1.015	1.832		-.554	.583					
	NonVerbalReasoning	-.002	.009	-.037	-.270	.789	.346	-.046	-.031	.714	1.400
	WorkingMemory	.042	.057	.116	.735	.468	.505	.125	.085	.537	1.863
	NamingSpeed	.097	.599	.028	.162	.872	-.491	.028	.019	.465	2.151
	L2PhonemicAwareness	1.453	.452	.672	3.218	.003	.730	.483	.373	.308	3.247
	KinderL2Reading	.029	.136	.037	.211	.834	.550	.036	.024	.442	2.260

a. Dependent Variable: Grade1L1Reading

7.4.3 Examining Regression Assumptions Using SPSS

We have already examined the assumption of multicollinearity, but in this section we will look at the assumptions of normal distribution of data, including outliers, and the equality of variances (homogeneity of variances). The last table of the output before the charts is labeled Residuals Statistics. There are several tests here that look for outliers or influential points, and the output is shown in Table 7.11.

Table 7.11 Regression Output: Residuals Statistics

Residuals Statistics(a)

	Minimum	Maximum	Mean	Std. Deviation	N
Predicted Value	.5996	1.9967	1.3669	.34430	37
Std. Predicted Value	-2.228	1.829	.000	1.000	37
Standard Error of Predicted Value	.076	.185	.124	.027	37
Adjusted Predicted Value	.5437	2.0857	1.3710	.34588	37
Residual	-.73580	.72589	.00000	.29309	37
Std. Residual	-2.330	2.298	.000	.928	37
Stud. Residual	-2.540	2.473	-.006	1.022	37
Deleted Residual	-.87468	.84074	-.00411	.35654	37
Stud. Deleted Residual	-2.808	2.716	-.012	1.078	37
Mahal. Distance	1.120	11.372	4.865	2.475	37
Cook's Distance	.000	.267	.037	.066	37
Centered Leverage Value	.031	.316	.135	.069	37

a Dependent Variable: Grade1L1ReadingPerformance

In examining the assumption of normality, there are two ideas we need to look at. The first is the distribution of data, but for a regression we do not look at the distribution of individual variables; instead we look at the distribution of the residuals. The first chart that will appear in the regression output (if you have followed my instructions to request one, as in Figure 7.15) is a Probability-Probability (P-P) plot of the standardized residuals. The P-P plot is similar to the Q-Q plot in that the points should follow a linear distribution if they are normally distributed. Figure 7.16 shows this plot, and we can detect some areas where the distribution strays away from the straight line that it would follow if it were normally distributed. This may be evidence of non-normality in data distribution, although, as was seen in Figure 3.20, there can be departures from the line even with data generated from a known normal distribution, and the data here do not veer too far away from the line. Another point to consider, however, is that with data generated from a normal distribution, as in Figure 3.22, the data usually leave the line at the tails of the distribution, and not in the middle, as is seen here. As discussed in Chapter 3, Section 3.5, it is almost impossible to know if data are exactly normally distributed or not, but the requirement for normality is exact. This is just another argument for implementing robust methods of data analysis instead of the more common parametric analyses, and I will illustrate how to do that in subsequent sections.

The second idea we want to look at for normality is to check whether there are any outliers. One way to do this is to look at the row in the Residuals Statistics output (Table 7.11) that is labeled Std. Residual. No points should be above 3.0 or below −3.0. (Because the numbers are standardized, they reflect the number of SDs they are away from the mean.) The table tells us that there is nothing below −2.33, and nothing above 2.298, so in this test no signs of outliers are found.

Outliers that are influential data points can be checked for by looking in the Residuals Statistics output (Table 7.11) at the row for **Cook's distance**. A value over 1.0 would be cause for concern, but the largest value in this data set is 0.267. If you found a value over 1.0 you could then look at your data set and search for the value or values that are over 1.0. The **Mahalanobis distance** value is another diagnostic for influential outliers. Tabachnick and Fidell (2001) noted that the Mahalanobis distance is "distributed as a chi-square variable, with degrees of freedom equal to the number of IVs" (p. 157). Thus, one would need to look up the critical chi-square value at the appropriate df, but a rule of thumb

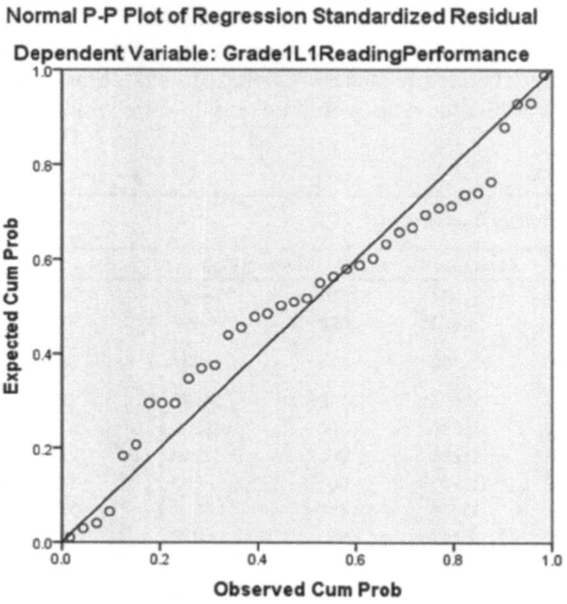

Figure 7.16 P-P plot for diagnosing normal distribution of data.

is that if your sample size is small (less than 30 and with only two explanatory variables), values greater than 11 would be problematic, but with larger data sets and more IVs, cases above 15 would be cause for worry. Again, Table 7.11 does not indicate any problems with influential points in the data using the Mahalanobis distance diagnostic.

The next assumption we want to check is for homogeneity of variances. The way to check this is to examine the scatterplot between the studentized residuals (what SPSS calls *SRESID) and the predicted value of the standardized residuals (*ZPRED). In the SPSS output, look at the section labeled "Charts" for this graph.

Figure 7.17 shows this graph. The shape of this scatterplot should show a cloud of data scattered randomly. Instead, the data here show a more restricted range on the right side of the graph, indicating that the assumption of homogeneity of variances has been violated. Often variables are transformed to correct this problem, but Lafrance and Gottardo (2005) already performed a log transformation on their variables, so it may be unlikely that further transformation would help.

The conclusion we can draw after examining the various regression assumptions is that the data may be non-normally distributed and violate the homogeneity of variances assumption. There does not seem to be excessive multicollinearity, nor do there seem to be any obvious outliers or influence points. The assumption of linearity (seen in the scatterplot matrix at the beginning of the chapter) may not always be a good assumption either. There are many assumptions inherent in a regression analysis, and it seems that few researchers in the field report on whether these assumptions are satisfied. Performing a robust regression as is detailed in the following section is one way to address the violation of assumptions. Another option would be to take out some of the variables that might be causing problems (such as the PA here) and try running the regression again.

7.4.4 Robust Regression with SPSS

Using bootstrapping with a regression can change several things about the analysis that was previously shown in Section 7.4.2, but the main one is that you can get bootstrapped estimates of the

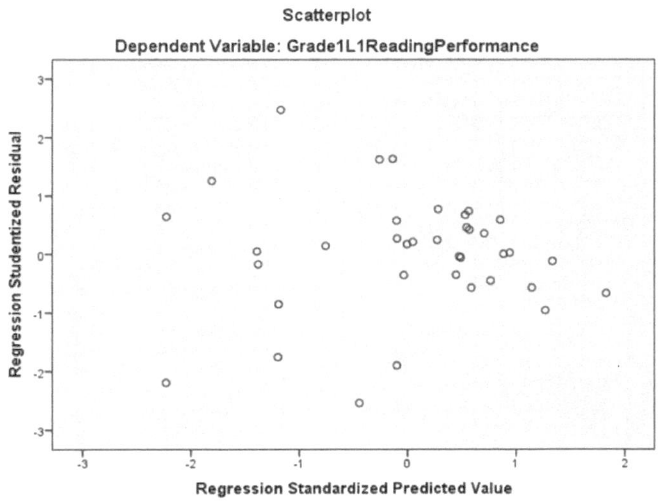

Figure 7.17 Plot of studentized residuals cross with fitted values.

unstandardized coefficient B and bootstrapped correlation coefficients. You can also get bootstrap estimates for the mean and SD of each variable in the "Descriptives" box (Table 7.3) but since we do not really use or report those numbers in a regression analysis this does not seem useful.

In calling for a bootstrap in SPSS, from the main LINEAR REGRESSION dialog box choose the BOOTSTRAP button. Set the number of samples to 2000 and the CIs to BCa, as shown in Figure 7.18. If you then run the analysis with the options shown in Figure 7.15, you will get an error message that the command stops. This is apparently because the bootstrap option does not like to run when you are also saving information about residuals. It also does not seem to run residual plots when bootstrapping is activated. Therefore, when running a bootstrapped analysis, open only the STATISTICS button from the LINEAR REGRESSION dialog box and follow the same directions as were given in Section 7.4.2. Do not run PLOTS and do not use any of the choices from the SAVE button. You also do not need the OPTIONS button, unless you run a stepwise regression, which I recommended against.

Since you are running the bootstrap, which is doing some computer-intensive work, the output may take a few minutes to appear in SPSS. Be patient—it will eventually appear!

You will then see that your output got a little more complicated, but not by too much. You will now have bootstrapped CIs to add to the correlation matrix (Table 7.4; just a warning—these correlation results look really messy in SPSS, so do not be surprised that they look so different from what I report in the book!) and bootstrapped B (unstandardized) coefficients for your regression model. These are found in the "Bootstrap for coefficients" output, shown here in Table 7.12. The B in the first column is the standard coefficient (unbootstrapped) and you should be able to recreate this number if you use the same file, but remember that your results for the BCa CI will not be exactly the same as mine because of the way bootstrapping works (randomly creating an empirical distribution from the data).

The bootstrapped CIs for the correlation coefficients (Table 7.4) show that the correlation coefficients are not very precise as the confidence intervals are quite wide. *P*-values are not included in Table 7.4, because a determination as to whether the correlation is statistical or not can be found in examining whether the CI passes through zero (see Chapter 4).

The bootstrapped CIs for the B coefficients can be reported along with the (unbootstrapped) unstandardized coefficient point estimates, just as in Table 7.4 with correlations, or instead of them. The bias statistic shows the difference between the B of the original point estimate and the bootstrapped point estimate (not shown).

Table 7.12 Bootstrapped Unstandardized Beta Coefficients in SPSS

Bootstrap for Coefficients

Model		B	Bootstrap[a]					
			Bias	Std. Error	Sig. (2-tailed)	BCa 95% Confidence Interval	
						Lower	Upper
1	(Constant)	.350	.021	.448	.435	-.386	1.340
	NonverbalReasoning	.021	.000	.009	.029	.000	.036
2	(Constant)	.795	.014	.441	.093	.100	1.764
	NonverbalReasoning	.007	.000	.010	.457	-.015	.024
	KinderL2ReadingPerformance	.404	.000	.119	.008	.175	.656
3	(Constant)	4.415	-.056	1.524	.010	1.518	7.383
	NonverbalReasoning	[illegible]	[illegible]	[illegible]	[illegible]	[illegible]	[illegible]

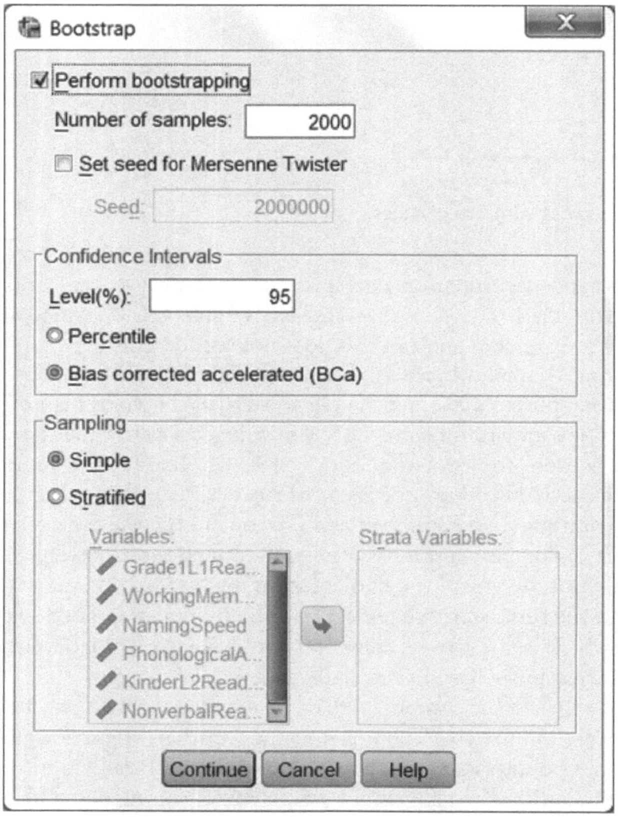

Figure 7.18 Calling for the bootstrap in SPSS regression.

7.4.5 Linear Regression in R: Doing the Same Type of Regression as in SPSS

This section of the book explains how to fit a model of the type that many software programs, such as SPSS, for example, by default apply to a regression. I am not saying that this is the best approach to your data; in fact, I do not think it is. However, I understand you may want to know how to recreate the type of analysis found in those software programs, and in any case, it is a fine place to start thinking about how regression is conducted. We will want, in the end though, to go beyond this simplistic thinking and begin thinking about the *best* fit for the data.

Before running the regression you should have examined your data set for linearity by using scatterplots. Most of the regression assumptions that we examine in a multiple regression involve the residuals of the regression model, so we will look at those in the next section, after we have created our model. However, another assumption besides linearity that we should actually examine before we create our model is that of multicollinearity by examining correlations between the explanatory variables and the response variable, and also among the explanatory variables themselves. You can do this through R Commander by using the menu choice STATISTICS > SUMMARY > CORRELATION MATRIX. Choose all of the variables in the file (there should be six for the Lafrance5.sav file that you will have already imported as "lafrance5"), keep the type of correlation as Pearson, and click on OK. You will first want to check the results for Grade1 L1 reading (the response variable) with all the five explanatory variables, and make sure the correlation is not higher than $r = 0.70$ (Tabachnick & Fidell, 2001). For this data set the correlation with PA *is* higher than $r = 0.70$, but Lafrance and Gottardo (2005) already knew this from previous studies and what they were doing was modeling what happens if they put in other variables before PA, so we do not want to get rid of this explanatory variable. We can then skim through the rest of the correlations (see Table 7.4 for my summarized version) and see that only correlations having to do with PA are high, so we will not worry about those.

Having satisfied these beginning assumptions, we can move on to making a regression model. Fitting a regression model in R is extremely easy in the sense that writing the regression equation is quite intuitive once you understand how regression works. For example, to fit the five-factor model that SPSS would create for a standard regression using the Lafrance and Gottardo data, one would simply tell R to create a linear model (use the lm( ) command) with the five explanatory factors:

```
model=lm(grade1l1readingperformance~nonverbalreasoning+kinderl2readingperformance + nami
ngspeed+workingmemory+phonologicalawarenessinl2, data=lafrance5)
```

In other words, you put the response variable in the first position after the parentheses, then model a fit that involves all of the other five variables just being added together. To obtain the information about R^2 and regression coefficients that you will need to report for a multiple regression, you can simply ask for a summary of the model:

```
summary(model)
some results deleted . . .

Coefficients:
                            Estimate Std. Error t value Pr(>|t|)
(Intercept)                 0.156062   1.979867   0.079  0.93768
NonverbalReasoning         -0.003540   0.008471  -0.418  0.67888
KinderL2ReadingPerformance  0.073145   0.134886   0.542  0.59151
NamingSpeed                -0.310744   0.638273  -0.487  0.62979
WorkingMemory               0.025168   0.056629   0.444  0.65982
PhonologicalAwarenessInL2   1.322462   0.471151   2.807  0.00857 **
---
Signif. codes:  0 '***' 0.001 '**' 0.01 '*' 0.05 '.' 0.1 ' ' 1

Residual standard error: 0.3158 on 31 degrees of freedom
  (3 observations deleted due to missingness)
Multiple R-squared: 0.5798,     Adjusted R-squared: 0.512
F-statistic: 8.555 on 5 and 31 DF,  p-value: 3.538e-05
```

Note that R uses scientific notation in reporting the *p*-value: 3.538e^5; "e" raised to some number means you should move the decimal place to the left that number of spaces, so 3.538e^5 is equal to 0.00003538.

The unstandardized regression coefficients (under "Estimate" in the readout) are the population regression parameters (the α and β of our regression equation), and estimating these numbers is "the central object of simple-regression analysis" (Fox, 1997, p. 112). The regression coefficients provide information about the strength of the association between the explanatory variable and the response variable. For example, the estimate of 1.32 for Phonological Awareness in L2 means that a 1% increase in PA is associated with a 1.32% increase in Grade 1 L1 word reading scores when all the other explanatory variables are held constant (Fox, 2002b, p. 27). The standard error (SE) of this estimate, which is something like the SE of a mean, but calculated slightly differently (see Crawley, 2007, p. 398 for the mathematical formula for calculating SEs of slopes and intercepts), measures the amount of unreliability surrounding the coefficient. A smaller SE is therefore always preferable.

The *t*-value in the third column for the coefficients area tests the hypothesis that the slope is equal to zero (H_0: $\beta_k = 0$), and the *p*-value in the fourth column tests the probability that we would find a *t*-value this large or larger if this hypothesis were true.

The next-to-last line at the bottom of the output ("Multiple R-Squared") shows how much of the variance in scores this model explains (58%). Because R^2 varies from 0 to 1 and can never be negative, it is always positively biased. For this reason, an adjusted R^2 is also provided that corrects for the positive bias, and this number says that the model accounts for 51% of the variance in scores. Whichever number you use, both are quite large as effect sizes go and mean the model explains a large amount of variance.

The last line at the bottom of the output ("*F* statistic") shows the results of an ANOVA test of the hypothesis that the regression slopes are all equal to zero. In other words, it tests the hypothesis that the unstandardized regression coefficients (except for the intercept coefficient) are all equal to each other and are all zero (Fox, 1997, p. 122). Logically, there is little chance that this null hypothesis will be true, so it will almost always be statistical, as it is here, and should not be given too much attention.

This type of standard regression answers the question of how much power all five variables have together to predict scores on the response variable, Grade 1 reading performance. The R^2 effect size tells us that all five variables together explain 58% ("Multiple R-squared: 0.5798) of the variance in scores in Grade 1 reading. However, remember that the more variables we put in, the higher the R^2 effect size is, and our sample size is really not very big. (This file had 40 observations, but the summary printout tells us that 3 were deleted due to some missing values in some of the columns, so we have 37 cases.) The *t*-test values tell us that in this model, only L2 PA is a statistically significant predictor of scores.

The unstandardized coefficients would help us write a mathematical model that we could plug more students' values into, and get a predicted score on L1 reading:

Grade 1 L1 reading = 0.16 (the intercept) – 0.004*Nonverbal Reasoning + 0.07*kindergarten L2 Reading – 0.31*Naming Speed + 0.03*Working Memory + 1.32*Phonological Awareness

You may think that these coefficients tell us something about the relative importance of the variables in the equation, but since all of the variables were measured on different scales, they do not. Accordingly, many people want to also see the standardized regression coefficients. If you wanted to pull out the standardized regression coefficients, you can do this by adding the scale command before each part of the equation, which standardizes all variables to mean 0 and SD 1, around every variable. I gave the model a new name, "model.standard," like this:

```
model.standard=lm(scale(grade1l1readingperformance)~scale(nonverbalreasoning) + scale(kinderl2readingperformance) + scale(namingspeed) + scale(workingmemory) + scale(phonologicalawarenessinl2), data=lafrance5)
```

Now, in the summary (summary(model.standard)), the estimates are standardized regression coefficients.

```
Coefficients:
                                       Estimate
(Intercept)                            -0.03730
scale(NonverbalReasoning)              -0.05672
scale(KinderL2ReadingPerformance)       0.09386
scale(NamingSpeed)                     -0.08883
scale(WorkingMemory)                    0.07049
scale(PhonologicalAwarenessInL2)        0.61181
```

However, I do not think this step is really necessary. The reason most people want standardized coefficients is because they have read that if coefficients are standardized, their effect sizes can be compared. Both Tabachnick and Fidell (2001) and Howell (2002) have argued that R^2 and sr^2 (more on these coming up) are better measures of the "importance" of each variable than the regression coefficients, which do not really measure the effect of each variable independently of each other, vary greatly from sample to sample and are affected by the size of their SDs. Most statisticians stay away from standardized coefficients.

A much better way to compare the relative importance of terms in a regression is to use the **calc.relimp( )** command in the **relaimpo** package (Grömping, 2006). This command returns five different estimates for assessing relative importance of terms in linear regression (Grömping, 2006). The estimates assess each individual term's contribution to the multiple regression model, and the lmg metric is the recommended one. (The pmvd metric is also recommended but is not available to users in the USA.) The lmg metric is appropriate for assessing relative importance no matter what order the term comes in the model, and, after being squared, is akin to the sr^2. This measure "expresses the unique contribution of the IV to the total variance of the DV" (Tabachnik & Fidell, 2001, p. 140). The sr^2 should be reported as a way of comparing the importance of each term in the standard regression model, but because of shared variances between the explanatory variables, the sum of all of the semipartial correlations often does not actually sum up to the total R^2 for the entire model. Tabachnick and Fidell (2001) stated that it is often common to see a large R^2 but that the sr^2 for each IV is quite small, which means that much of the R^2 comes from effects between IVs. So the relative importance metrics are effect sizes for each term in the regression model, and are appropriate for making comparisons as to how much of a contribution each term adds to the overall R^2 value. Even better, they are simple to calculate using the **relaimpo** package:

```
install.packages("relaimpo")
library(relaimpo)
calc.relimp(model) #just put in the name of the model you created here

data deleted . . .
```

```
Relative importance metrics:

                                  lmg
NonverbalReasoning         0.02743436
KinderL2ReadingPerformance 0.10740872
NamingSpeed                0.10360432
WorkingMemory              0.07554998
PhonologicalAwarenessInL2  0.26581778
```

The relative importance metrics show that Phonological Awareness was the most important factor by far out of the five, contributing about 7% (0.26^2) of the variance. However, kindergarten L2 reading and naming speed each contributed about 1% to the model with five factors.

You can obtain the 95% CI of the unstandardized coefficients with the **confint** command:

```
confint(model)
```

```
                  2.5 %      97.5 %
(Intercept) -3.88190436 4.19402818
NR          -0.02081698 0.01373652
KL2WR       -0.20195750 0.34824771
NS          -1.61251062 0.99102199
WM          -0.09032847 0.14066421
PAL2         0.36154270 2.28338092
```

Remember that this data set has missing data, however, so I will show how you could work with these data if you wanted to impute it (see Section 1.5.3), and had five different imputed models to work with:

```
imp<-mice(lafrance5, 5) #open the mice package if not open
model=with(imp, lm(grade1l1readingperformance~nonverbalreasoning+kinderl2readingperformance+
namingspeed+workingmemory+phonologicalawarenessinl2, data=lafrance5))
model.pooled<-pool(model)
```

The output (not shown) actually gives estimates for the coefficients, *p*-values and CIs for the coefficients, but it does not provide the R^2 information. Additionally, the calc.relimp( ) command does not work for the pooled data. So, here I would complete the data matrix and reduce it down to just one:

```
complete(imp)
implafrance<-complete(imp)
```

Now a model and summary with this new file (implafrance) will give the same results as everything previously shown in this section.

The model shown up to this point provides the standard regression that Tabachnick and Fidell (2001) described, whereas the sequential (hierarchical) regression that was the focus of the SPSS analysis of Lafrance and Gottardo's data in Section 7.4.2 could easily be done in R by just creating five different models, each with increasing numbers of variables, like this:

```
model1 = lm(grade1l1readingperformance~nonverbalreasoning, data=lafrance5)
model2 = lm(grade1l1readingperformance~nonverbalreasoning+kinderl2readingperformance, data=lafrance5)
model3 = lm(grade1l1readingperformance~nonverbalreasoning+kinderl2readingperformance+ namingspeed,
         data=lafrance5)
model4 = lm(grade1l1readingperformance~nonverbalreasoning+kinderl2readingperformance+
         namingspeed+workingmemory, data=lafrance5)
model5 = lm(grade1l1readingperformance~nonverbalreasoning+kinderl2readingperformance+ namingspeed+
         workingmemory+phonologicalawarenessinl2, data=lafrance5)
```

If you then run a summary() for each model, you will be able to list the R^2 for each model and change of R^2 for each successive model, just as was seen in Table 7.6 with the SPSS output. For a sequential regression, the sr^2 can be seen "as the amount of variance added to R^2 by each IV at the point that it enters the equation" (Tabachnick & Fidell, 2001, p. 142), so the size of the sr^2 will depend on what point it was entered into the equation; sr^2 is the *R* square change for each IV. For example, a summary of model 3 shows that the multiple $R^2 = 0.4667$. A summary of model 4 shows that the multiple $R^2 = 0.473$. Therefore, the change in explanatory value from model 3 to model 4 is only 0.006, meaning the sr^2 for naming speed is $sr^2 = 0.006$. The point of this section is to show that linear multiple regression can easily be done as well in R as in SPSS. However, subsequent sections are going to show how regression can be done better by finding a better fit to the data rather than just assuming a linear regression.

Doing this modeling in the R Console seems to me easier and more transparent than doing it in R Commander, but there are some advantages to doing it in R Commander, which are that once you have your model created, menu choices will lead you to many things you can do with your model, including diagnostics and graphs.

So if you want to do regression modeling in R Commander, the first step is to create your model. In R Commander, you do this by first making sure the data set you want is active. (I am using lafrance5, which I imported from Lafrance5.sav.) Next, choose STATISTICS > FIT MODELS > LINEAR REGRESSION. As you can see from the dialog box in Figure 7.19, you can now pick your response variable and explanatory variables. In keeping with the information given in this section, this regression model will be simple addition of main effects, as in the original model written with R code. Use the CTRL key to choose more than one explanatory variable on the right side of the dialog box.

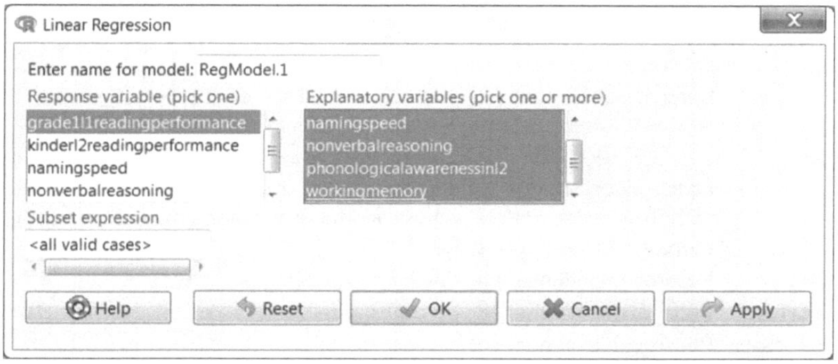

Figure 7.19 Dialog box for simple regression in R Commander.

Once you click on OK, you will now have a model called "RegModel1" (of course you could have changed this name if you wanted to). Now you can go to the MODELS drop-down menu. If this is your first model you do not need to do anything special, but if you have other models and need to select which one is active, you can pick MODELS > SELECT ACTIVE MODEL (see Figure 7.20).

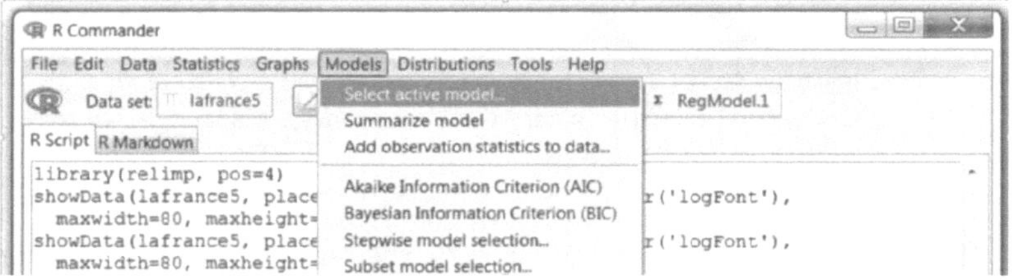

Figure 7.20 Creating regression models in R Commander.

Once you have selected your model (and this one was named RegModel1 if you did not change the name), you can now use any drop-down menu under the MODELS menu. Table 7.13 gives you an idea of all of the things you can do.

One thing you should do for sure with your model as created in this section is call for statistics that help examine data assumptions. In R Commander, follow the MODELS > ADD OBSERVATION STATISTICS TO DATA Choice. If using only R, copy these commands. (You might begin to see why you would want a more descriptive name than "model" but we are going to stick with it for now!)

```
lafrance5$fitted.model <- fitted(model)
lafrance5$residuals.model <- residuals(model)
lafrance5$rstudent.model <- rstudent(model)
lafrance5$hatvalues.model <- hatvalues(model)
lafrance5$cooks.distance.model <- cooks.distance(model)
lafrance5$obsNumber <- 1:nrow(lafrance5)
```

By doing this you are adding columns of diagnostic data to the end of the "model" you created previously.

If, after reading further along in the following sections you would like to make a more complicated model and still have all of these choices in R Commander available to you, use the STATISTICS >

Table 7.13 R Commander "Models Menu" Explanations

Models menu	
Summarize model	Returns coefficients with *t*-tests, residual standard error, R^2 value, ANOVA *F*-test (as seen above in R)
Add observation statistics to data	Lets you add columns of data to the end of the active data set, including fitted values, residuals, studentized residuals, hat-values, Cook's distances and observation indices. (These will be used when you are examining regression assumptions later.)
Confidence Intervals (CIs)	Returns confidence intervals for coefficient parameters
Akaike Information Criterion	Returns this number for current model
Bayesian Information Criterion	Returns this number for current model
Stepwise model selection	Lets you select between stepwise models that go backward, forward, and a combination of backward/forward or forward/backward. You can also choose whether you want the BIC or AIC to be the criterion for stepping
Subset model selection	Model selection by exhaustive search, forward or backward stepwise, or sequential replacement (read help for more details)
Hypothesis tests	
ANOVA table	Returns ANOVA output for model
Compare two models	Lets you perform an ANOVA for two models (used to see if simplified model is better; see subsequent section to see how this is used to find a better fit to the data)
Linear hypothesis	Conducts a comparison between your model and a linearly restricted model that you can specify
Numerical diagnostics	
Variance inflation factors (VIFs)	The VIF tests for multicollinearity, something you want to avoid to satisfy data assumptions (see following section)
Breusch–Pagan test for heteroscedasticity	Tests for heteroscedasticity
Durbin–Watson test for autocorrelation	(Seems to be used mainly in econometrics.)
RESET test for nonlinearity	(Diagnostic for correctness of functional form)
Bonferroni outlier test	Tries to identify outliers
Graphs	
Basic diagnostic plots	Returns the four graphs shown in Figure 7.21 in the following section on examining regression assumptions
Residual quantile-comparison plots	Returns Q-Q plot with 95% CIs drawn
Component + residual plots	These plot partial residuals against predictors; they are used to detect nonlinearity if data do not follow regression line
Added variable plots	Show leverage and influence of observations on subsets of the data; look for influential points far from regression line
Influence plot	Plots the studentized residuals against the hat values using a bubble plot; area of circle represents observations proportional to Cook's distances
Effect plots	Returns a plot that is useful to help in interpreting interactions; see Fox (2003)

FIT MODELS > LINEAR MODEL dialog box (not the LINEAR REGRESSION choice I advocated in this section), which will give you the option of including interaction terms, nested terms, quadratic terms, etc.

Creating a Basic Regression Model in R

1 First, write a simple linear regression model by using the lm() command and modeling your response variable as the function of (~) the explanatory variables joined by the plus sign. Do this in the R Console:

```
model=lm(grade1l1readingperformance~nonverbalreasoning+kinderl2readingperformance + namingsp
eed+workingmemory+phonologicalawarenessinl2, data=lafrance5)
```

To see basic information about this model, use the summary() command:

```
summary(model)
```

2 For further work you might want to use R Commander. Choose your model from MODELS > SELECT ACTIVE MODEL and then you can use the other commands in the MODELS menu. One command you should definitely use is MODELS > ADD OBSERVATION STATISTICS TO DATA to get information for checking regression assumptions. You can also do this manually in R. (See the text for the commands.)

7.4.6 Examining Regression Assumptions in R

In creating your regression model in Section 7.4.5 you created additional columns at the end that you will now use as diagnostic data to examine regression assumptions for your model. The assumptions of multiple regression are that the distribution of the data is normal, that the variances of variables are equal (homoscedasticity), that the variables are not too highly intercorrelated (multicollinearity) and that the data are independent. Crawley (2007) suggested that the most important assumptions are those of constancy of variance and normal distribution, and these are the most common problems that occur in real data sets.

In R, the one simple command plot(model) will call up a series of residual plots:

```
plot(model,cex=1.5) #the cex argument makes the circles bigger
```

The results of the plot( ) command are found in Figure 7.21. The Residuals vs. Fitted plot (top left) is used to diagnose heteroscedasticity in the data. If the data are normally distributed, this plot will show a random scattering of points both above and below the line at zero, and to the left and right of the graph. However, the distribution on the right side is more restricted than that on the left, indicating that the variance is not the same at every point in the distribution and that the homogeneity of variances assumption has been violated. Sometimes a transformation of some of the variables can help correct this problem, but Lafrance and Gottardo (2005) already transformed several of their variables to begin with.

The Normal Q-Q plot (top right of Figure 7.21) examines the normality distribution assumption. The standardized residuals are plotted against a normal distribution. This Q-Q plot shows a deviation away from a straight line, especially at the ends of the distribution. Fox (2002b, p. 29) stated that such a pattern of pulling away from the comparison line at the ends indicates that the residual distribution is heavy-tailed. Again, this would indicate that the response variable needs transformation to fit the normality assumptions, or that we would do better to use a method of robust or resistant regression rather than the least-squares fit used here.

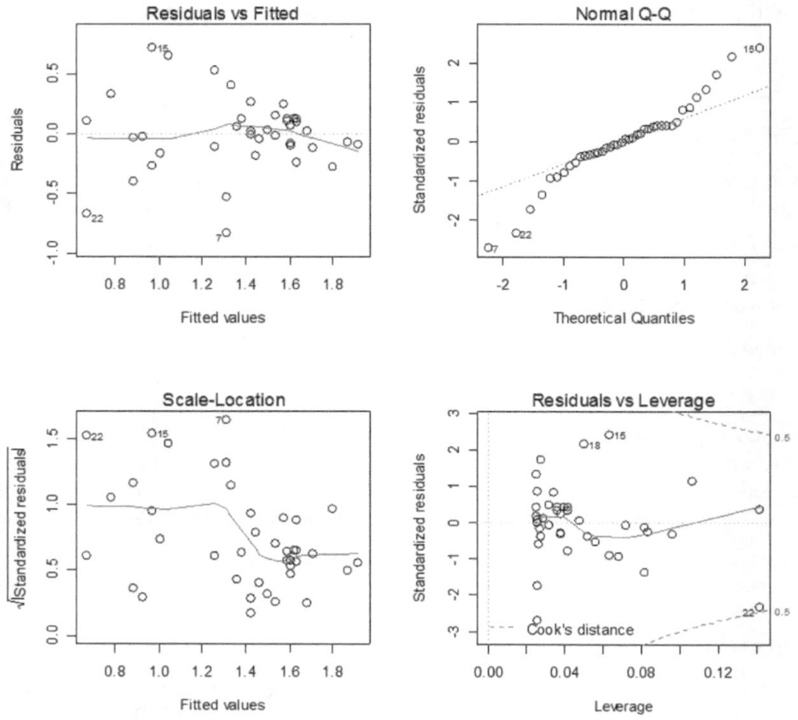

Figure 7.21 **R regression diagnostic plots.**

The Scale-Location plot (bottom left) is very much like the Residuals plot except that the square roots of the standardized residuals are plotted. According to Crawley (2002), this plot is useful for detecting a non-constant variance. Again, we see the cramping of values toward the right end of the graph, indicating a non-constant variance.

The Residuals vs. Leverage plot (bottom right) is intended to help you identify possibly outliers that may have an undue amount of influence over the analysis. The dotted lines identify Cook's distance, a measurement designed to highlight particularly influential data points. Point 22 is the highest in leverage (looking along the x-axis) and it is also quite close to Cook's distance, which means it is having a large effect on the analysis. According to Crawley (2007), we could try removing this data point and check what influence it has on the regression analysis and assumptions, and report the results both with and without the data point to the reader. However, it seems to me more objective to use robust regression analysis.

Here is how we could model the fit of the data without point 22 (where the exclamation point ('!') indicates "is not"):

```
model2<-update(model, subset=(lafrance !=22))
```

If we run the plots again (plot(model2)), this update does not substantially change the problems we find with non-normality and inequality of variance, and knowing that manually removing outliers results in non-independence would lead me to leave it in.

Another plot that can investigate the influence of outliers can be also found in the plot(model) command, but must be called for by the which argument. This diagnostic measures how much the analysis would change if each point were removed. Therefore smaller values are better while a value larger than 1.0 would be unusual (Howell, 2002, p. 561). The result for our original model is found in Figure 7.22.

```
plot(model,which=4)
```

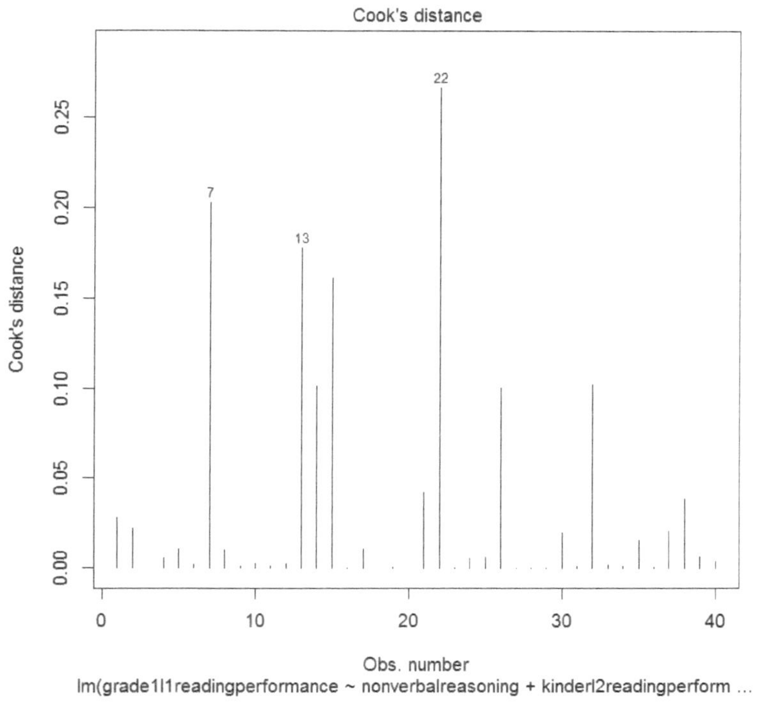

Figure 7.22 Cook's d influential point graph.

In Figure 7.22, point 22 seems quite different from the rest of the points, but if you cut out 22, you might then also consider 7 and 13 as outliers. In fact, point 22 is not above 1.0 so it is probably not a real problem. The problem with just looking for outliers (instead of using robust methods) is that it is a subjective method. If you do find outliers in your data set, you need to understand that this can radically alter the accuracy of your model. You should first check to make sure the outliers have been accurately entered and are not a data entry mistake. If they are fine, you should consider using a robust regression that can deal with outliers. (Robust regression is detailed further on in this chapter.)

Another assumption of multiple regression is that the variables will not be highly intercorrelated (multicollinearity is undesirable). One way of checking for multicollinearity is the VIF diagnostic. (Remember, VIF stands for variance inflation factor.) Heiberger and Holland (2004, p. 243) have suggested that VIF values of over 5 are evidence of collinearity. According to Fox (2002b), the square root of the VIF indicates "how much the confidence interval for β_j (the standardized regression coefficient) is expanded relative to similar, uncorrelated data" (p. 217) and thus provides a very direct measure of the harm that collinearity may be doing to the model.

To call for the VIF in R, use the command vif(model). Note that this command does not work if there is only one explanatory variable, as there cannot be multicollinearity with only one explanatory variable!

```
     nonverbalreasoning kinderl2readingperformance
               1.375244                   2.261691
            namingspeed              workingmemory
               2.425874                   1.878376
phonologicalawarenessinl2
               3.470786
```

The VIF values are all under 5 so we do not see any strong evidence of multicollinearity.

For the assumption of independence of observations, if the data are ordered in some way, for example, if we inadvertently tested the most eager students first while the least eager students came in last, there would be some sort of ordering dependency that would be visible in a scatterplot of the residuals against their case number. If your data points are numbered by some kind of ID number, you can plot by using the name of that column. For the Lafrance and Gottardo (2005) data, the participants are not numbered, so we just use their row number to identify them. We will use the function **stdres** in the **MASS package** (Venables & Ripley, 2002) to examine independence:

```
library(MASS)
plot(row.names(lafrance),stdres(model),cex=1.5)
```

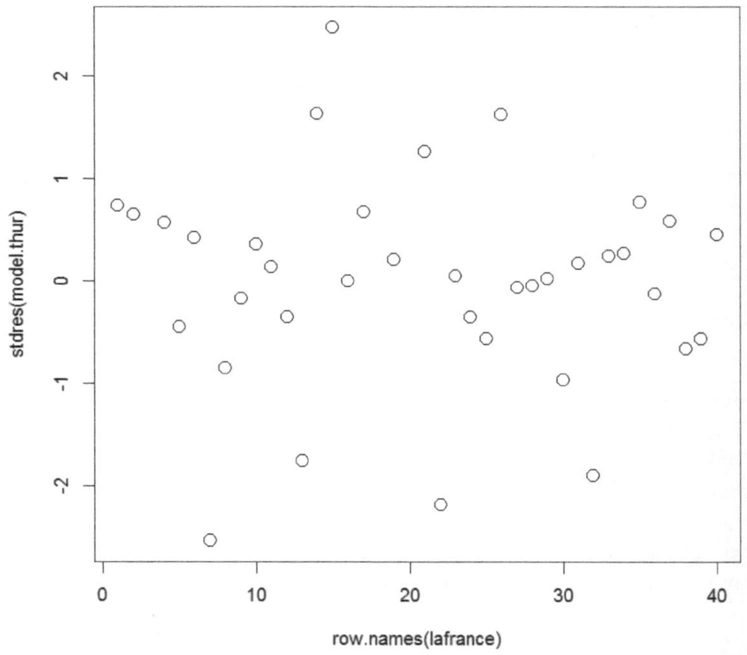

Figure 7.23 **Plot of standardized residuals against ID to check for independence.**

In looking at the output of this plot in Figure 7.23, you should see whether you perceive any order or pattern to the residuals. If there is no pattern you can conclude there is independence of observations. I do not see any particular pattern here so I conclude that the residuals are independent.

From this inspection of all four assumptions for regression we can conclude that there are problems in the data set with non-constant variance and non-normality. As has been noted previously, sometimes transformation of variables can help to correct some of these problems, but Lafrance and Gottardo (2005) already transformed these variables and the problems remained. Because of this, I suggest that robust regression/ bootstrapping may help to gain a more accurate picture of what is happening. Of course, one could always simply report the results of the regression and let readers know that certain assumptions are not satisfied. The practical importance of not satisfying assumptions is that power is lost, so if you find results in the direction you wanted, not having satisfied assumptions does not invalidate your results.

Examining Regression Assumptions in R

1 **Plotting your model will return four diagnostic graphics:**

plot(model)

Residuals vs. fitted values—tests for homoscedasticity, you want random points
Normal Q-Q plot—tests for normal distribution, data should be linear
Scale-Location—tests for homoscedasticity, you want random points
Residuals vs. Leverage—identifies influential outliers

2 **You can also call one other plot to check for outliers:**

plot(model, which=4)
returns a plot of Cook's d—identifies influential outliers. Values over 1 problematic.

3 **Check for multicollinearity using VIF. Problematic scores are over 5.**

vif(model)

4 **Call for a plot of standardized residuals against ID—tests for independence of observations. You want random distribution of points.**

library(MASS)
plot(row.names(lafrance),stdres(model))

7.4.7 Robust Linear Regression in R

Using bootstrapping with a regression can change several things about the analysis that was previously shown in Section 7.4.5, but the main one is that you can get bootstrapped estimates of the unstandardized coefficient B and the CI of B. You can achieve this same thing with a function from Wilcox's WRS library (Wilcox & Schönbrodt, 2014). First, you will need to get Wilcox's WRS library, as detailed in Section 6.5.3 or 8.4.4. Open the package (library(WRS)) and use the already sourced functions. For all of Wilcox's functions shown in this section, the first argument for the function (x) needs to be a matrix containing the predictors, while the next argument (y) should contain the response variable. The lafrance5 data contains both of those together, so we will need to massage the data a little bit first before using the function:

```
lafrance4<-subset(lafrance5, select=c(2:6)) #choose only columns 2 through 6
lafrance1<-subset(lafrance5, select=c(1))
```

Wilcox's function lsfitci( ) can return 95% CIs for regression parameters, based on the ordinary least-squares estimator, using a percentile bootstrap method:

```
lsfitci(lafrance4, lafrance1, alpha=.05, nboot=599)
```

```
[1] "Taking bootstrap samples; please wait"
$intercept.ci
[1] -3.209349  2.980318

$slope.ci
            [,1]       [,2]
[1,] -0.07825026 0.15741646
[2,] -1.35244460 0.75877152
[3,]  0.38249907 2.16327707
[4,] -0.16964594 0.28143174
[5,] -0.02284200 0.01462635

$crit.level
[1] 0.01

$p.values
     Slope    p-value
[1,]     1 0.72787980
[2,]     2 0.54757930
[3,]     3 0.01669449
[4,]     4 0.44741235
[5,]     5 0.83806344
```

The output gives bootstrapped CIs for (first) the intercept, and then the slopes of the five predictor variables. *P*-values are also returned, but would only be statistical if under the critical level, which in this case is 0.01, so that only the third variable in our set (which is Phonological Awareness) is even close to having a slope that is statistically different from zero. (Perhaps it is statistical since we can see that the CI does not pass through zero? The documentation on this function is minimal and I am not sure about the answer.)

Besides giving bootstrapped estimates of coefficients there are several things we would like a robust regression to help us with. One is when we have heteroscedasticity in our variables. Another is when there are outliers or influential points, because we would like to lessen their influence. Wilcox (2012a, 2012b) provided information about how to use a number of robust regression estimators but also noted that there is no one approach that is always optimal.

A good approach to robust regression might be something similar to that used by Adler (2010), which is to try the fit of a regular regression (with lm( )) and compare it to a couple of other types of regression. Adler (2010) then examined the fit of the different regressions on a graphic plot and decided which type of regression made the most sense, but this was possible as he used only one predictor.

This section will thus give a number of possible types of regression that may be used, with the understanding that no one approach is likely to be optimal all the time, and that you will have to decide which approach is best able to handle your particular data.

The **MASS** package has a function lqs( ) that fits a resistant regression using the least trimmed squares estimator. The help files for this function says that it fits "a regression to the good points in the data set" (lqs help, undated), so it is useful if you think you have outliers. You model this in exactly the same way that you do with the regular lm( ) function for regression, but just specify the method you want after the formula and data:

```
library(MASS)
lqs(grade1l1readingperformance~nonverbalreasoning+kinderl2readingperformance+
namingspeed+workingmemory+phonologicalawarenessinl2, data=lafrance5, method=c("lts"))
```

```
Coefficients:
                (Intercept)           nonverbalreasoning
                   0.880579                     0.003592
kinderl2readingperformance                  namingspeed
                   0.186991                    -0.551729
              workingmemory    phonologicalawarenessinl2
                  -0.106723                     1.204486
```

The relevant information relates to the coefficients of the regression.

Another function in the **MASS** package helps with outliers and also if you think you have violated the homoscedasticity requirement. This approach uses MM estimation:

```
rlm(grade1l1readingperformance~nonverbalreasoning+kinderl2readingperformance+namingsp
eed + workingmemory + phonologicalawarenessinl2, data = lafrance5, method = c("MM"))
```

7.4.8 Reporting the Results of a Regression Analysis

What to report for your regression analysis depends on your question. Throwing in too much data can confuse readers, but there is a lot of information returned in a multiple regression. Pick carefully what is most important to you and your reader—you do not have to report all of the numbers you have obtained while doing your analysis.

You will want to tell your readers what kind of regression you performed, whether standard, sequential or stepwise (not recommended). For all regression models you should report regression coefficients. Most statistics books recommend reporting the unstandardized coefficient (labeled B), which are necessary to write a predictive equation, including the coefficient for the intercept (labeled as "Constant" in the SPSS output). Include 95% CIs for the unstandardized coefficients. If you performed a sequential regression I do not think it is necessary to report on the *t*-tests for the contribution of each variable to the model (this is apparent from the significance of the R^2 change for each model), but you should probably include this information when performing a standard regression.

I think the information most readers are interested in is how much variance each term adds to the regression equation. In other words, how important is any particular variable when it is part of the regression model? This question can be answered by reporting the sr^2 for each term of the model along with the total R^2 for the model. Remember that the sr^2 provides a way of assessing the unique contribution of each variable to the overall R^2. Then the R^2 value expresses how much variance can be explained by the explanatory variables as a whole. For a standard regression, report the R^2 value and the sr^2 for each IV. For a sequential (hierarchical) regression, report the R^2 value and then the R^2 change for each step of the model, which is the sr^2 for each IV that is added to the model. These numbers are already an effect size, so there is no need to require any additional reports of effect sizes, although of course you should discuss the practical importance of your effect sizes.

Another thing to report to your readers about a regression analysis is the correlations between the explanatory variables and the response variable as well as the correlations among the explanatory variables. Tabachnick and Fidell (2001) explained that these correlations are important to report because, depending on the type of regression and how much intercollinearity there is (how much the IVs correlate among themselves), some variables may seem to be less important than they really are because most of their variability is shared with another IV. This can be seen if individual correlations are provided. If at all possible, a correlation matrix with *r*-values, CIs and *N* should be provided to readers (such as that found in Table 7.4). Of course, information about whether your data satisfy the requirements for a parametric analysis should also be reported.

The following gives an example of how the results of a standard regression with the Lafrance and Gottardo (2005) data could be reported, based on the analysis in the previous text. Notice that this is not the same as what they actually reported, which was a sequential regression.

> Lafrance and Gottardo (2005) examined the question of how predictive PA (measured in L2) was for Grade 1 L1 reading performance when the variables of kindergarten L2 reading performance, non-verbal reasoning, L2 measures of naming speed and working memory were also included in the regression equation. The total R^2 value for this model was 58%, meaning the inclusion of all of the variables explained 58% of the variance in scores.
>
> A standard regression resulted in the unstandardized regression coefficients shown in the following table (coefficients and CIs from R regression analysis). The table also includes a measurement of the relative importance of each variable to the regression equation, where it can be seen that PA added the most unique variance to the model. The low value of the unique variances of the variables (all of the sr^2 added together equals only about 9%) means that most of the variance in the model comes from shared variances between the IVs (58 – 9 = 49%).

	Total R^2	*Intercept*	*Nonverbal reasoning*	*Kinder reading*	*Naming speed*	*Working memory*	*Phono awareness*
B	0.58	0.16	–0.003	0.07	–0.31	0.03	1.32
95% CI		[–3.88, 4.19]	[–0.02, 0.01]	[–0.20, 0.35]	[–1.6, 0.99]	[–0.09, 0.14]	[0.36, 2.28]
relative import. (sr^2)			0%	1%	1%	.01%	7%

> In this model the only statistical predictor was PA. Certainly, PA is the most important variable for predicting reading performance.

If you perform a sequential (hierarchical) regression, you will need to report some different types of data. For the Lafrance and Gottardo data set we have been considering, the authors' question was *not* how much explanatory power all five variables had to predict Grade 1 reading ability, but how much predictive power PA has on Grade 1 reading ability after other variables are taken out. The reader would thus be interested in seeing the predictive power of the model with variables besides PA.

One way to compare the explanatory power of the variables is to report the change in R^2 for each model before PA is added. This information can be gleaned from the "Model Summary" information. (Table 7.6 shows these numbers for SPSS and I will not repeat them for R, although the details are a little different using R.) These numbers are already a **percentage variance effect size** (of the *r*-family), so there is no need to give any additional reports of effect sizes. Because it contains a lot of information a table is often the most compact way to report results.

Here is an example of what I would report with the Lafrance and Gottardo data (and this is the way that Lafrance and Gottardo reported their data):

> Lafrance and Gottardo (2005) examined the question of whether phonological awareness (PA) (measured in L2) would add in predictive power for Grade 1 L1 reading performance after the variables of kindergarten L2 reading performance, non-verbal reasoning, L2 measures of naming speed and working memory were already added to the regression equation.
>
> It was assumed from previous research that PA would be the most significant factor in a standard regression, so a sequential regression was run to examine the effects of the other variables before PA was added. The variable of kindergarten L2 reading measures added the most explanatory power to the model ($R^2 = 0.20$) when it was added before PA, as can be seen in the ΔR^2 column of the table below. After all other variables were added, PA accounted for 11% of the variance, but it was the only statistical variable in the regression model with all five explanatory variables. (You can tell that because it is the only CI that does not go through zero.) Total R^2 for the model, change in R^2 and CIs for the unstandardized regression coefficients (B) are shown in the following table. (These numbers are taken from the R analysis using five different models; note that they are a little bit different from the SPSS numbers.)

Model	*Total R^2*	*ΔR^2*	*Intercept*	*Non-verbal reasoning B*	*Kindergarten reading B*	*Naming speed B*	*Working memory B*	*Phono awareness B*
1	0.12	0.12	[−0.62, 0.27]	[0.002, 0.04]				
2	0.32	0.20	[−0.11, 1.68]	[−0.01, 0.03]	[0.14, 0.62]			
3	0.47	0.15	[1.66,7.17]	[−0.02, .02]	[0.09, 0.54]	[−2.47, −0.39]		
4	0.473	0.003	[0.56, 7.18]	[−0.02, 0.02]	[0.03, 0.53]	[−2.47, −0.12]	[−0.09, 0.17]	
5	0.58	0.11	[−3.9, 4.2]	[−0.02, 0.01]	[−0.20, 0.35]	[−1.61, 0.99]	[−0.09, 0.14]	[0.36, 2.28]

> The answer to the question of whether PA added to the prediction of Grade 1 L1 word reading performance after differences in other predictors were eliminated was yes. Phonological awareness added 11% to explaining the total variance of Grade 1 L1 reading scores.

7.4.9 Application Activities: Multiple Regression

1 Lafrance and Gottardo (2005) data. Using the Lafrance5.sav file, replicate the results I got in the text for the sequential regression using Grade 1 L1 reading scores as the response variable and the five explanatory variables shown in the text. (If using R, import this file and name it lafrance5; it has 40 rows and 9 columns). If using R, use the summary( ) function for your five models to get the *R*, R^2 and unstandardized regression coefficient information (also 95% CIs for the unstandardized regression coefficients).

2 Lafrance and Gottardo (2005) data. Lafrance and Gottardo (2005) also looked at a multiple regression using Grade 1 L2 reading scores as the response variable and the same five explanatory variables (L2 measures) used in the text. Using the LafranceGottardo.sav file (if using R, import this file and name it lafrance), perform a standard regression to determine which variables were statistical predictors of Grade 1 L2 reading scores, what their standardized regression coefficients were and what the R^2 of the model is. Also report relative importance metrics (sr^2). Mention whether this model satisfies the assumptions of regression.
3 French and O'Brien (2008). Use the French & O'Brien Grammar.sav file. (If using R, import it and call it French.) The authors examined French L1 children in an intensive English program and tested their phonological memory abilities. In order to see whether phonological memory predicted later abilities in learning vocabulary and grammar in English, the authors performed several hierarchical multiple regressions. We will look only at one where the response variable was Time 2 grammar (GRAM_2). The explanatory variables were, in the order they were entered, Time 1 grammar (GRAM_1), scores on an intelligence test (INTELLIG), language contact (L2CONTA), then an Arabic non-word phonological memory test at Time 1 (ANWR_1) and lastly an English non-word phonological memory test at Time 2 (ENWR_1). (French and O'Brien actually used Time 2 but we will use Time 1.) First take a look at a scatterplot matrix to make sure the relationships are linear and look at a correlation matrix to check for high multicollinearity. Then perform this sequential (hierarchical) regression and report the overall R^2, the change in R^2 for each of the explanatory variables and the unstandardized regression coefficients (with which you would write a regression equation; in R, use the summary() command to get this information), and the 95% CIs for the unstandardized regression coefficients. Also report relative importance metrics (sr^2) and mention whether this model satisfies the assumptions of regression.
4 Howell (2002). Use the HowellChp15Data.sav file. (If using R, import it and name it howell.) Chapter 15 included a data set where students rated their courses overall and also aspects of the courses on a 5-point scale (where 1 = very bad and 5 = exceptional). Use the OVERALL variable as the response variable and the other variables—teaching skills of instructor, quality of exams, instructor's knowledge of subject matter, the grade the student expected in the course where F = 1 and A = 5, and the enrollment of the course—as explanatory variables. First take a look at a scatterplot matrix to make sure the relationships are linear and look at a correlation matrix to check for high multicollinearity. Perform a standard multiple regression and look at which factors statistically predict the response variable. Report the overall R^2 for the model. Run a new regression using just the statistical factors and report the regression equation, the R^2, and comment on regression assumptions.
5 Dewaele and Pavlenko Bilingual Emotions Questionnaire (2001–2003). Use the BEQ.Swear.sav file; import it into R as beqswear. Results from exercise #6 in Section 7.2.4, the application activity where a tree plot was used, showed that the variables that might help explain how frequently a person swears in their L2 (SWEAR2) are the frequency that the person uses their L2 (L2FREQ), the weight they give to swearing in their L2 (WEIGHT2) and their evaluation of their speaking and comprehension skills in L2 (L2SPEAK, L2_COMP). First take a look at a scatterplot matrix to make sure the relationships are linear and look at a correlation matrix to check for high multicollinearity. Conduct a multiple regression analysis to determine which of these variables effectively predicts frequency in swearing in an L2, and perform another regression with only statistical predictors. Report the unstandardized coefficients, 95% CI for the coefficients and the R^2 for the model with only statistical predictors, and comment on regression assumptions.
6 Larson-Hall (2008). Are number of hours of input in a foreign language (TOTALHRS), aptitude (APTSCORE) and scores on a phonemic task (RLWSCORE) useful predictors of scores on a grammaticality judgment test (GJT)? Use the file LarsonHall2008.sav; import into R as lh2008. First take a look at a scatterplot matrix to make sure the relationships are linear and look at a correlation matrix to check for high multicollinearity. Perform a hierarchical

regression using the GJT (GJTSCORE) as the response variable and the three other variables as explanatory variables. There are six possible combinations, but try three by entering each variable as the first variable once. See which order gives the highest overall R^2, and which results in the highest change in R^2 for each of the three explanatory variables. Comment on regression assumptions.

7.5 Summary

There are two main uses of regression in second language research studies. One is to decide to what extent the explanatory variables the researcher has measured can account for some response variable of interest. To answer this question the researcher will use standard regression and report on the R^2 statistic, letting readers know how much of the variance in the response variable can be accounted for by the combination of the explanatory variables. In a standard regression the researcher can also provide information about how much each explanatory variable uniquely contributes to the equation. Rather than use the standardized coefficients for this, I have suggested that researchers provide information about the sr^2 of each term of the equation. The sr^2 provides information about the relative importance of each term of the regression equation.

The other main use of regression analysis in second language research studies is to try to find a predictive model that will best account for the variance in the response variable. Using a sequential (hierarchical) regression can help answer this question by examining whether the addition of a term adds to the predictive power of the equation. It is up to the researcher to specify in what order terms are added, and we have seen in this chapter that order does matter when using a sequential regression.

I have suggested that stepwise regression is probably not a type of regression that most researchers will be looking for, as it lets the computer decide which terms to eliminate, often based on non-statistical differences between terms of similar importance. It is better for researchers to have a theoretical reason to examine the addition or elimination of terms in a regression.

Consumers of research on regression ought to realize that the order that variables are entered into a sequential regression matters, and that those variables that are entered first will account for the most variance. It is also important to note the correlations among variables. If the author has included several variables that are highly intercorrelated, it is highly likely that one of those variables will be seen as inconsequential. This is not because it really is necessarily inconsequential, but because the regression gets rid of terms that substantially overlap with each other.

One more section on regression that was not included in this chapter is an advanced look at regression which suggests that the lock-step format, whereby a linear regression includes only the main variables added together (as a linear regression in SPSS forces users to do), is not the best approach to linear regression. Assuming only one way to fit data does not make it the best way! A regression formula can include interaction terms between the main variables as well as variables squared or raised to higher levels that can model curvature in the data. The best use of standard regression is for researchers to find the minimal adequate regression model and report on that. SPSS software, because of its "black box" approach to statistics where researchers do not really control how the regression equation is created, makes it more difficult to try out and test different models, but it can be done by manually adding interaction and possibly quadratic (squared or cubic) terms to the regression equation. R software makes the process quite visible, and the online section "Finding the Best Regression Fit" shows how to create a model with the best balance between explanatory value and simplicity.

Chapter 8

Looking for Differences between Two Means with *T*-Tests

Think-Aloud Methodology and Teaching Sarcasm

> Far better an approximate answer to the *right* question, which is often vague, than an *exact* answer to the wrong question, which can always be made precise.
>
> Quote attributed to Tukey (1962)

A *t*-test answers a very simple question—are two scores the same or different? In spite of the apparent simplicity of this test, it is very useful in a variety of settings. All of the statistical tests investigated in this chapter involve looking at two mean scores on the same testing instrument. Owing to random chance, scores from two groups on the same test are unlikely to be exactly the same, even if the two scores come from the same set of people. A *t*-test can tell us if the differences between the two scores are big enough that we can assume they come from two different groups, or that scores at Time 1 differ from scores at Time 2. If the differences are not big enough we will assume that the scores come from the same group or that there are no differences between Time 1 and Time 2 scores. This chapter looks at two main types of *t*-tests that are very frequently used in second language research studies: (1) the independent samples *t*-test; and (2) the paired samples (or matched samples) *t*-test.

8.1 Types of *T*-Tests

This section will help you understand how to choose which *t*-test to use. The independent samples *t*-test is used when you perform an experiment and you have obtained mean scores from two independent groups. You have measured both scores yourself and you only have two of them. (If you had three groups, you could not use a *t*-test.) For example, you might assign students randomly to one of two treatments, and then at the end of the experiment you would test them and have two mean scores. You want to know whether one group performed better or worse than the other group.

An example of the independent samples *t*-test that will be used in this chapter comes from Leow and Morgan-Short (2004), who addressed the methodological question of whether doing a think-aloud while completing a task affected learners' comprehension ability and subsequent production ability. Leow and Morgan-Short had a think-aloud group and a non-think-aloud group who were compared on their scores, which is why the independent samples *t*-test was needed. For example, on the comprehension task, there was one mean score from the think-aloud group and one mean score from the non-think-aloud group. There were thus two mean scores to be compared, and the question was whether there was any difference between the two groups.

The paired samples *t*-test, or matched samples *t*-test, is used when you have performed an experiment and you have two mean scores but the groups are not independent of each other. This may be because you measured the same group at two different time periods, and you want to see if they perform better or worse at the second time period. Or maybe you measured the same group on two related measures, such as a morphosyntactic and phonological measure, and you want to see if they performed better on one type of test than the other. In these cases, because you are measuring the same people more than once, you cannot assume the groups are independent, and a paired samples *t*-test takes this lack of independence into account.

Data from Kim (2013) illustrate the paired samples *t*-test in this chapter. We looked at descriptive statistics for these data earlier in Chapter 3. In this study, students took a pretest to check on their ability to understand sarcasm in their L2, English. After nine weekly sessions designed to help the students understand sarcasm, they took a posttest in the week after their sessions ended, then a posttest five weeks later. The same nine participants took all three tests, so these data should be analyzed with paired samples *t*-tests, since the same participants took the test, just at different time periods.

There is actually another type of *t*-test, called the one sample *t*-test, but it is much less common in second language research data than the other two types of *t*-tests. The one sample *t*-test is used when you have measured only one mean score, but you would like to compare this mean to some idealized mean or otherwise already known mean score. For example, let us say that you know from literature put out by your college that incoming graduate students have an average of 600 on the graduate record examinations (GRE) test. You want to compare the GRE scores of the group of graduate students coming into your program to this known mean to see whether your students are better or worse than the average students entering the university. A second example would be that you measured students' reactions to a new curriculum change on a scale of 1–7. You want to know whether there is a statistical difference in the result from a purely neutral attitude (which would be 4 on this scale). You can use a one-way *t*-test to see whether the results are statistically different from neutral. This type of *t*-test will not be discussed in detail in this chapter but can be found online ("One Sample *T*-Tests").

Recent Examples of *T*-Tests in the Second Language Acquisition (SLA) Literature

Schmid, Gilbers, and Nota (2014)

One question in this study was whether advanced and highly motivated second language learners of English (Dutch–English bilinguals, $N = 20$) would be able to score as highly on a foreign accent rating task as native speakers of English living in a Dutch environment (English–Dutch bilinguals, $N = 9$; thus comparing bilinguals to bilinguals, instead of monolinguals, as is often done in such studies). The participants retold the story of a silent movie video, and a 15- to 20-second excerpt was played twice for 16 judges, who rated it on a 1–6-point scale. An independent samples *t*-test tested the hypothesis that there was no difference between the groups (L1 vs. L2 English speakers). The test found that there was indeed a difference between groups in their global pronunciation ability ($t(19.8) = 5.5$, $p < 0.01$), with the Dutch–English bilinguals scoring a mean of 2.5 (SD = 1.2) on the task while the English–Dutch bilinguals scored 1.1 (SD = 0.1).

Wang, Shang, and Briody (2013)

Fifty-seven Taiwanese college freshmen participated in a semester-long study where approximately half the students ($N = 31$) used an automated writing evaluation instrument that provided feedback on their essays for 14 weeks. The control group ($N = 26$) wrote essays every week, just as the experimental group did, but received feedback from their teachers on the essays. The authors reported that an independent samples *t*-test found a statistical difference between the experimental group's mean number of errors (M = 4.8, SD = 3.0) and the control group's larger number of errors (M = 15.6, SD = 9.9), $p = 0.000$ (no *t*-value is given). They also reported that a paired samples *t*-test comparing writing accuracy (number of errors) in a pretest vs. posttest writing assignment found an important difference for the experimental group (Time 1: M = 14.8, SD = 7.6; Time 2: M = 4.8, SD = 3.0), with a 95% confidence interval (CI) on the mean difference of [7.5, 12.5], suggesting a quite substantial and reliable reduction in errors. (No mention is made of whether a parallel paired samples *t*-test was made for the control group.)

Poehner and Lantolf (2013)

This study conducted from the sociocultural theory viewpoint aimed to test Vygotsky's idea that mediation, here implemented in the form of hints while doing an online L2 listening and reading task, would help learners improve their language abilities, even in just a single session. Poehner and Lantolf had learners doing the listening comprehension task listen to spoken passages in Chinese or French, and then respond with multiple choice answers concerning vocabulary, grammar, discourse or culture. The innovative part of the study was that when learners missed an answer, mediation in the form of a repetition of the relevant chunk of text would focus the learner's attention on the relevant part, with successive prompts narrowing the focus of the help if learners did not narrow in on the correct answer in the first try. The research question was whether this form of mediation would result in improved scores on the test, and on transfer items which were embedded in the test. For the Chinese listening test, a paired samples *t*-test (because the same participants' scores on two tests were compared) between the actual score ($N = 62$, mean = 29.9, SD = 15.6) and the mediated score ($N = 62$, mean = 41.7, SD = 10.6) found a statistical difference between the two tests ($t(61) = 3.1$, $p < 0.01$, $d = 1.4$).

Jiang, Novokshanova, Masuda, and Wang (2011)

This study aimed to test the hypothesis that if learners have a particular morphological structure in their L1, they will be sensitive to this morpheme in their L2, while if they do not, they will not be sensitive to that morpheme. This was tested with the plural morpheme in Japanese L1 ($N = 26$) and Russian L1 ($N = 24$) learners of English L2. Russian contains a plural morpheme so the Russian–English readers were expected to be sensitive to the incongruous use of the plural while the Japanese–English readers were not. The task was a self-paced reading task where only one word at a time appeared on a screen, and it was assumed that any delay in reading the target word (such as the underlined words in the sentence *They met several of the board <u>member</u> during <u>their</u> visit*) would indicate an automatic sensitivity to the structure and align with a hypothesis that the speaker had acquired the morpheme. Paired samples *t*-tests were conducted between grammatical and ungrammatical sentences for the plural morpheme among each group. So, for example, the Russian L1 group took statistically longer to read sentences with plural errors than sentences with all plural morphemes correctly inserted ($t(23) = 2.1$, $p = 0.05$) while the Japanese L1 group had no difference in the time it took them to read ungrammatical vs. grammatical sentences with the plural morpheme ($t(25) = 0.5$, $p = 0.64$).

8.1.1 Application Activity: Choosing a T-Test

Read the following descriptions of possible linguistic experiments. Decide whether you would use an independent samples or paired samples *t*-test:

1 Reading attitudes. English as a second language (ESL) students randomly received either a scripted or a non-scripted version of a reading program. Twenty students from the scripted version were interviewed about their attitudes about reading before the semester started, and then near the end of the semester. You want to know whether the students' attitudes toward reading changed over the course of the year.
Choose one: independent paired

2 Reading ability. In the study above, you also want to know whether students using the scripted version of the reading program performed better on a reading test at the end of the year than the ESL learners who used the non-scripted version.
Choose one: independent paired

3 Listening comprehension. One group of advanced French as a second language (FSL) users and another group of beginning FSL users performed a listening comprehension task that had two components. One component was linguistic processing ability and the other was pragmatic processing ability. You want to know whether the beginning and advanced learners differed from each other in their ability to process pragmatic information on the test.
Choose one: independent paired

4 Pitch. A group of English–Spanish bilinguals were recorded speaking to monolingual English and monolingual Spanish speakers. Their average fundamental frequency (pitch) was recorded in each language. You want to know whether these bilinguals use a different pitch when speaking in each of their languages.
Choose one: independent paired

5 Learning strategy instruction. A group of ESL learners in Taiwan received a class detailing how to ask higher-order questions and give more elaborated responses. The learners were measured as to the accuracy of their questions before this training, and again at the end of the course. You want to know whether the students improved in their accuracy over the course of time.
Choose one: independent paired

6 Vocabulary learning I. Students in an English Language Institute were randomly assigned to watch one episode of either *Friends* or *Seinfeld* each day for eight weeks. A recorded interview with an unknown but same-sex and same-age native English speaker was recorded for every participant before and after the term. You want to know whether students used more slang terms at the end of the semester.
Choose one: independent paired

7 Vocabulary learning II. You also want to know whether there were any differences between the *Friends* and *Seinfeld* groups in the number of slang terms used in the final interview.
Choose one: independent paired

8 Morphology. You hypothesize that Japanese learners of Russian will not be sensitive to mistakes with a marker of verbal aspect but that Spanish learners of Russian will be, since Japanese does not mark aspect with different verbal pairs while Spanish does. You want to compare the reading times of Japanese learners with the reading times of Spanish learners on ungrammatical sentences.
Choose one: independent opaired

8.2 Data Summaries and Numerical Inspection

The first data set featured in this chapter is that of Leow and Morgan-Short (2004), who wanted to know whether performing a think-aloud task while also performing a language task would affect scores on the language tasks. Leow and Morgan-Short thus had two independent groups of students, and they compared scores from the two groups using an independent samples *t*-test. The SPSS file used here from Leow and Morgan-Short contains scores from two language measures—one a recognition task measure and the other a controlled written production measure.

Table 8.1 contains the mean scores and standard deviations (SDs) of the two language measures from Leow and Morgan-Short (2004). Leow and Morgan-Short noted that neither of these variables was normally distributed and in fact analyzed both of them with the non-parametric Mann–Whitney U test. Leow and Morgan-Short did in fact use both pretest and posttest measures, but not to confuse you at this point I will include just the comparison at the posttest. This author conducted their analysis of the groups by comparing them at the posttest point, so this analysis is in keeping with the spirit of their paper. Consider the mean scores of the think-aloud and non-think-aloud groups on the receptive posttest. The total number of points on the test was 17, and one group scored 5.89 while the other scored 3.92. This is not a very big difference in the

Table 8.1 Summary Data for the Leow and Morgan-Short (2004) Data

	Receptive posttest			*Production posttest*		
	Mean	*SD*	*N*	*Mean*	*SD*	*N*
Think-aloud	5.89	6.04	39	1.34	3.45	38
Non-think-aloud	3.92	4.31	39	1.15	3.11	39

context of 17 points. Notice that the SDs are also quite large, even bigger than the mean score, indicating skewness in the data. (If the data were normally distributed, we would expect to be able to find two to three SDs in either direction from the mean; we will look at the distribution visually in the next section.) Notice that mean scores for the production test are quite low overall.

Summary scores when there is more than one group can be obtained in several ways. For SPSS you can use ANALYZE > DESCRIPTIVE STATISTICS > EXPLORE and put the group variable into the "Factor List" box and the test variables into the "Dependent List" box. It would also be possible to use the ANALYZE > DESCRIPTIVE STATISTICS > DESCRIPTIVES choice, but since there are two groups you would want to split the data first by going to DATA > SPLIT FILE and putting GROUP into the "Groups based on" box. In R Commander, the command STATISTICS > SUMMARIES > NUMERICAL SUMMARIES is a good way to summarize group data.

The second data set featured in this section comes from Kim (2013). Kim analyzed language acquisition from the sociocultural theory viewpoint, and the study actually contains both qualitative and quantitative data. Qualitative data is analyzed differently from quantitative data but is of course equally valid. Kim's main aim was to understand how to help L2 learners of English to better understand a very difficult concept in a second language, that of sarcasm. A very important part of Kim's study was pre-instruction and post-instruction interviews, where she asked the participants about how they understood sarcasm in English and talked about how the series of Schema for the Orienting Basis of Action (SCOBAs) they used helped them better understand how to recognize sarcasm in English. The quantitative part of Kim's study was when she asked the participants, after their instruction was finished, to watch 10 different videoclips and underline, in a written transcript of the dialogue, sarcastic utterances. They also needed to check off from a list 3 cues they noted for each instance of sarcasm, resulting in a maximum score of 30 in this test. Table 8.2 shows the summary statistics for this data set, showing a strong improvement in mean score from pretest to posttest, along with a desirable decrease in SD (meaning more of the students scored closer to the mean score). The delayed posttest showed an even further increase in mean score.

8.2.1 Visual Inspection: Box Plots

In this chapter I will talk about visual ways to explore data used in *t*-tests. Two good visuals are the histogram and the **box plot**. Histograms have been explained in Chapter 3, so this chapter will show how to call up box plots. I have found that box plots are fairly rare in second language research reports. Larson-Hall (2013) examined the graphs that were provided in the history of three second language acquisition (SLA) journals (*Language Learning*, *Studies in Second Language Acquisition* and *The Modern*

Table 8.2 Summary Data for the Kim (2013) Data

	Mean	*Standard Deviation*	*N*
Pretest	7.4	5.2	9
Posttest	16.6	3.0	9
Delayed posttest	19.7	3.0	9

Language Journal) and found that out of the articles that contained graphics, about 75% of the time the graphics were line or bar graphs. In the combined 196 years of these journals being published up to 2011, by my count, a total of only 18 articles contained some form of a box plot.

Box plots are far superior to bar graphs because they provide much more data. While a bar graph usually provides only a mean score, box plots provide information about group centers, spread and shape of a distribution. Box plots are also a useful device for spotting outliers in your data points that distort group means, especially in groups with small sizes.

However, because many readers may not be familiar with box plots, I would like to discuss them in a little more detail here. (For more information, see Larson-Hall & Herrington, 2009.) Figure 8.1 shows a box plot with a skewed distribution (on the left) and a normal distribution (on the right). The line drawn in the box marks the median, which is the point at which 50% of scores are above and 50% of scores are below. For the skewed distribution, you can see that this median is not in the middle of its box—it is somewhat off-center—while for the normal distribution the line is directly in the center of the box.

The shaded box is called the interquartile range (IQR) and contains the scores that fall within the 25th to 75th percentile. If two distributions have equal variance, the length of their boxes (or IQR) will be very similar. For these two distributions we see that the skewed distribution has a much longer box than the normal distribution, so we could not say these two distributions had equal variance.

Lines called whiskers extend out from the box. These whiskers extend to the minimum and maximum points of the data set, unless those lie beyond a point calculated by 1.58x the IQR divided by the square root of N. Points that lie outside one and a half times the length of the box are identified as outliers with a circle in Figure 8.1. These whiskers show the range of the data, excluding outliers. The range is certainly much wider for the skewed distribution than for the normal distribution.

In summary, the box plot, at a glance, gives us the following information:

- the midpoint of scores (at the median);
- the area that contains the central scores (the box) and gives a visual sense of the variance;
- the minimum and maximum points, which show the range of data;
- outliers (if present);
- if the distribution is symmetrical.

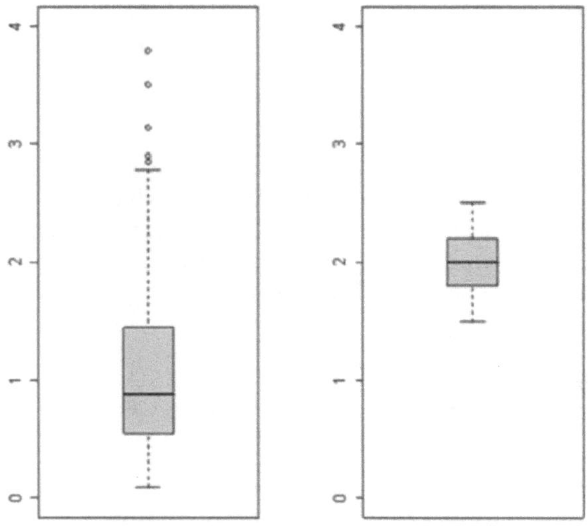

Figure 8.1 Box plot of a skewed and a normal distribution.

8.2.2 Box Plots for One Variable Separated by Groups in SPSS

To look at the data from the Leow and Morgan-Short (2004) experiment, we will want to look at a box plot that shows distributions on one variable for the two different groups. Let us look then at scores on the recognition posttest from the LeowMorganShort.sav file. To make a box plot, open GRAPHS > LEGACY DIALOGS > BOXPLOT. Choose the box labeled "Simple" and the button under "Data in the chart are" as "Summaries for groups of cases." Click on the DEFINE button. When you define the box plot, put the dependent variable (DV) (RECPOSTSCORE) into the line labeled "Variable." Put the group variable (GROUP in this case) into the line labeled "Category Axis." Additionally, if you put your ID variable in the "Label Cases by" box, any outliers will be labeled with their ID number. These steps are shown in Figure 8.2.

Figure 8.3 shows the box plot for the posttest scores on the recognition test. Since box plots are not very common in our field, let me walk you through the graph. (Section 8.2.3 walks the reader through a different box plot, so you might want to look at that too.) Box plots contain all the data

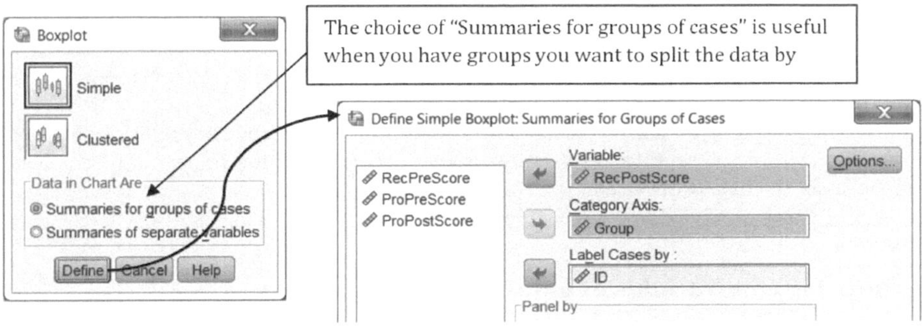

Figure 8.2 How to make a box plot of one variable separated into groups.

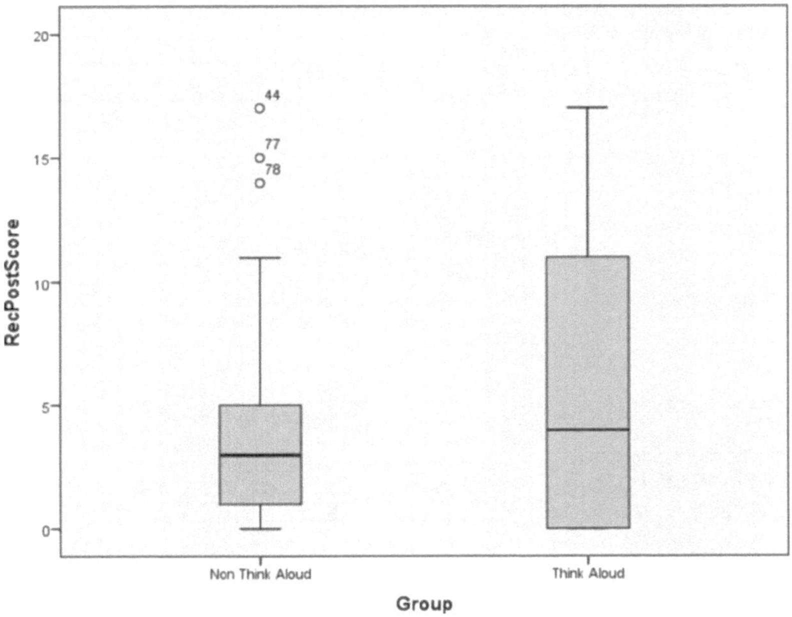

Figure 8.3 A box plot of Leow and Morgan-Short's (2004) posttest receptive measure.

from the first to the third quartile in their box. The median line marks the spot where 50% of the participants are above that line and 50% are below it. The lines that extend out from the box mark the minimum and maximum points of the distribution, and any points beyond that are labeled as outliers.

Notice that, although the median scores do not seem to be that different between the think-aloud and non-think-aloud groups, the distributions are clearly not normal because the boxes and whiskers of the box plot are not symmetrical around the median lines. Both are positively skewed (meaning the tail extends farther to the right than the left if we were looking at a histogram, or if we turned the box plot on its side). In the think-aloud group, the median line is clearly non-symmetric in relation to the box. The whiskers are also non-symmetric. For the non-think-aloud group, although the median seems symmetric to the box, the distribution of the whiskers is not symmetric. There are also three outliers in the non-think-aloud group, identified by their subject numbers (44, 77 and 78).

Creating a Box Plot for an Independent Samples T-Test in SPSS (One Variable Split into Groups)

1 Choose GRAPHS > LEGACY DIALOGS > BOXPLOT. When a dialog box comes up, choose SIMPLE for a one-variable box plot, and choose the "Summaries for groups of cases" radio button. Press the DEFINE button.
2 Put the group or splitting variable in the "Category Axis" box. Put the variable you have measured in the "Variable" box. If you want to identify outliers with row names, put a column of ID numbers in the "Label cases by" box. Press OK.

8.2.3 Box Plots for One Variable Separated by Groups in R

To look at the data from the Leow and Morgan-Short (2004) experiment, we will want to look at a box plot that shows distributions on one variable for the two different groups. If you are following along with me, import the LeowMorganShort.sav file (**library(Rcmdr)**) and save it as **leow**. To make a box plot of one DV split into two groups with R Commander, click on GRAPHS > BOXPLOT to open up your dialog box, as shown in Figure 8.4.

Figure 8.5 shows the box plot for the pretest scores on the recognition test. Since box plots are not very common in our field, let me walk you through the graph. (Section 8.2.2 walks the reader

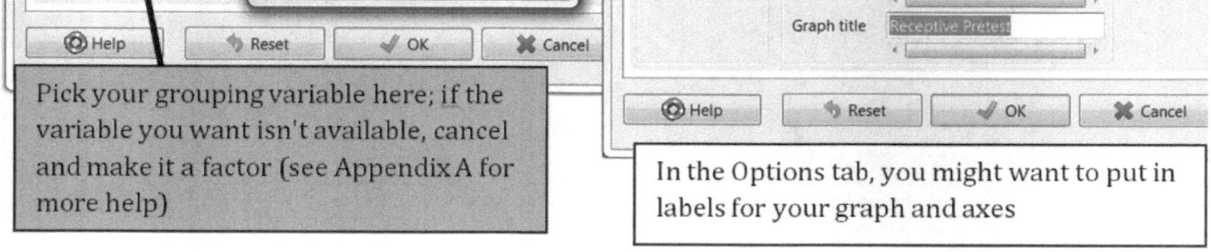

Figure 8.4 How to make a box plot in R of one variable separated into groups.

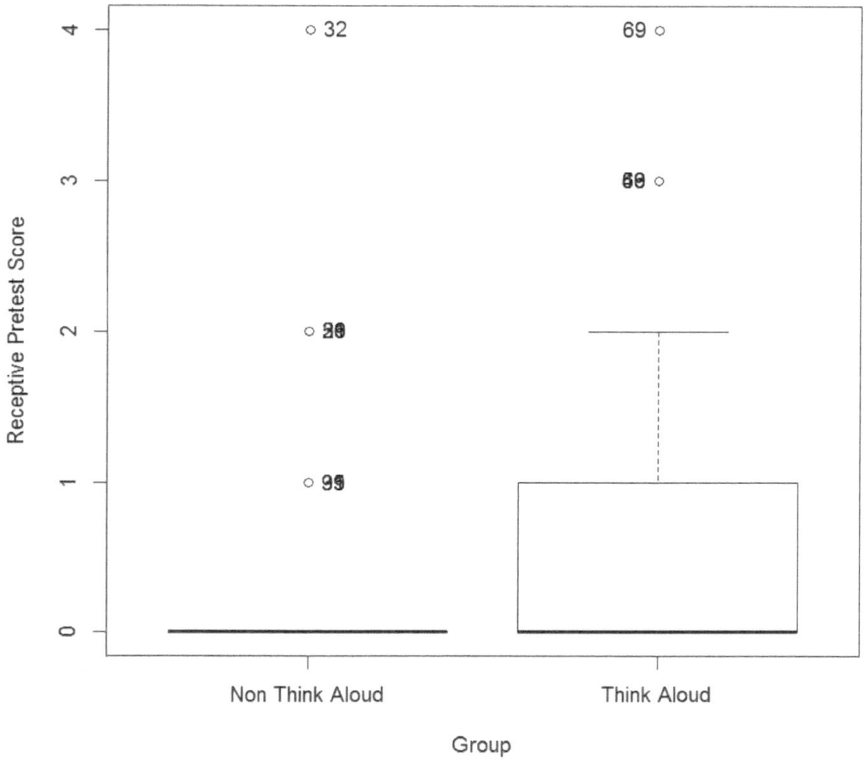

Figure 8.5 An R Commander box plot of Leow and Morgan-Short's (2004) pretest receptive measure.

through a different box plot, so you might want to look at that too.) Box plots contain all the data from the first to the third quartile in their box. The median line marks the spot where 50% of the participants are above that line and 50% are below it. The lines that extend out from the box mark the minimum and maximum points of the distribution, and any points beyond that are labeled outliers.

From Figure 8.5, we can immediately see that the distribution of scores on this task is non-normal for both the think-aloud and non-think-aloud groups because we do not see symmetrically distributed boxes and whiskers around the median line. In fact, for the non-think-aloud group, there is nothing but a median line and no box at all! In addition, there is a problem with this box plot; there are a number of outliers, and these were automatically numbered with their row number, but some of them overlap so that you cannot see the row number well. This is a problem with R Commander's built-in box plot, and so at this point I will move to showing you a command for a box plot that can deal more easily with outliers, plus automatically plot each point of the distribution, which I think is a much more informative graph. Once we have seen this second graph, I will walk you through how to understand the information in the box plot. (This one seems especially weird since the median for both groups is at zero.)

Get the ggplot2 package (Wickham, 2009) (install.packages("ggplot2")) and open it (library(ggplot2)). The following command will produce Figure 8.6:

```
ggplot(data=leow,aes(x=group,y=recprescore))+geom_boxplot(outlier.shape=NA)+geom_
jitter(position=position_jitter(width=.3, height=0))+labs(x="Group", y="Receptive Pretest Score")
```

Here is the analysis of the ggplot2 box plot syntax.

ggplot(data=leow	The ggplot2 package, written by Hadley Wickham (2009), is a very useful graphics tool. The first argument of this command is the name of the data set.
aes(x=group,y=recprescore))	aes is a function in ggplot2 that generates aesthetic mappings and can use traditional R style names, such as cex for size. Here we put the grouping variable in the x-axis and the interval-level variable in the y-axis.
geom_boxplot(outlier.shape=NA)	A geom "specifies the objects that define the graph type" (Kabacoff, 2011, p. 390). Here, we tell the geom not to plot outliers because they will already be plotted with the jitter command and we do not want to overplot.
geom_jitter(position= position_jitter(width=.3, height=0))	This geom jitters the points, which is important because there are only four discrete-point values, so if more than one person gets that point we cannot tell how many dots there are. The jitter spreads the dots out, here with a width of 0.3, but no height because the scores are discrete.
labs(x="Group", y="Receptive Pretest Score")	Gives custom names to the x- and y-axis labels.

For the non-think-aloud group in Figure 8.6, almost all of the scores are concentrated on zero, which indicates that this group knew very few of the four imperative forms they were shown. This was good, because the authors wanted to include people who had only a limited knowledge of imperative

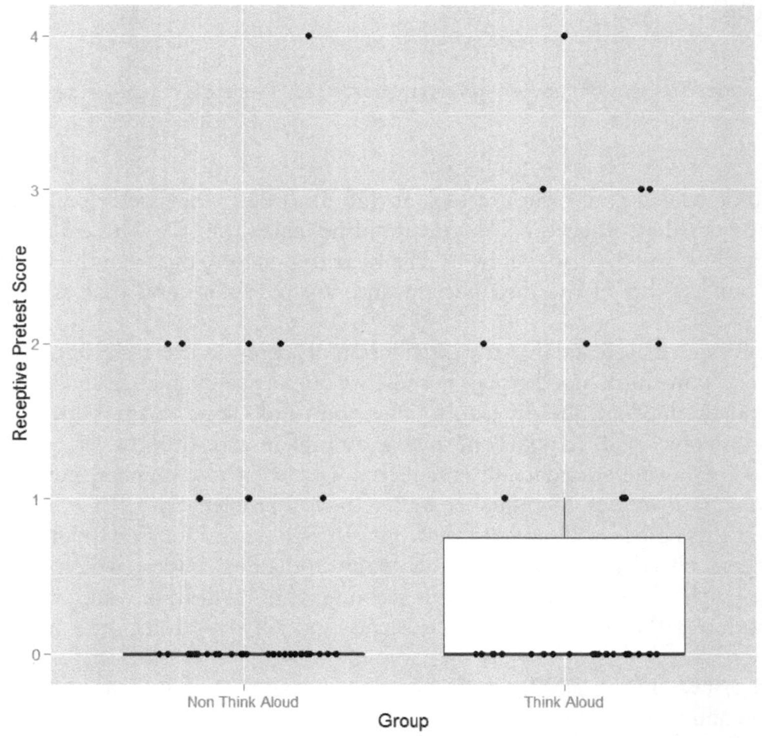

Figure 8.6 A better box plot with jittered data points of Leow and Morgan-Short's (2004) pretest receptive measure.

forms before the treatment. There were 39 participants in the non-think-aloud group, and we can see that the majority of them received a zero on this task. The others are labeled as outliers because they got one, two or four points on the pretest. We know that they are outliers from the box plot because they are plotted beyond the length of the whiskers of the box. Actually, for the non-think-aloud group, the box is only one line along zero and so it does not have any whiskers (but you can see that the think-aloud group does have a box with a line going above it, which is the more normal situation).

For the think-aloud group in Figure 8.6, we can tell that a majority of the 38 participants received a zero, because the black median line lies on zero, and the median marks where half of the participants are below and half are above. (In such a discrete-point test as this one, we will only get a line on the points themselves.) The box of the box plot contains 50% of the participants, from the first to the third quartile, although in this case there is no bottom whisker to the box that extends down to the minimum score, since there is nothing less than zero. The whisker of the box plot for the think-aloud group extends upward to 1, which is categorized as the maximum score of the distribution. (Note that in Figure 8.6 the whisker is just a vertical line, while in Figure 8.5 the end of the whisker is marked with a horizontal line; this is just a cosmetic difference.) Seven participants, one who scored 4, three who scored 3 and three who scored 2, are classified as outliers to the distribution.

Notice that, although the median scores do not seem to be that different between the think-aloud and non-think-aloud groups, the distributions are clearly not normal because the boxes and whiskers of the box plot are not symmetrical around the median lines. Both are positively skewed, meaning the tail extends to the right if we were looking at a histogram, or if we turned the box plot on its side, with the majority of scores concentrated toward the lower end of the scale. In the think-aloud group, the median line is clearly non-symmetric in relation to the box. (The non-think-aloud group does not have a box!) The whiskers are also non-symmetric, meaning the data are not normally distributed. The presence of outliers also means that data distribution is not normal.

If you want to use the built-in command for box plots that R Commander uses, I have broken down this command too.

```
Boxplot(recprescore~group, data=leow, id.method="identify",
xlab="Group", ylab="Receptive Pretest Score", main="", col="grey")
```

Boxplot(x~y)	Makes a box plot modeling x as a function of y.
recprescore~group	Scores on the pretest recognition task are modeled as a function of group.
data= leow	Gives the name of the data set.
id.method="identify"	This command will allow the identification of points on the plot with the mouse; the default is "y," which will automatically label all points; another choice is "none."
xlab="Group", ylab="Receptive Pretest Score"	Gives custom names to the x- and y-axis labels.
main=""	Indicates that there is no main title, but one could be put in between the quotation marks.
col="grey"	This command fills in the box with a gray color; this was not original to the R Commander command, I just added it to make it look nicer.

Creating a Box Plot for an Independent Samples T-Test in R (One Variable Split into Groups)

1 On the R Commander drop-down menu, choose GRAPHS > BOXPLOT. Pick your dependent variable. To split the variable into groups, use the "Plot by Groups" button. (If your grouping variable is not a factor, you will need to change it to one; see Appendix A.) On the OPTIONS tab, decide how to identify outliers, if at all, and put in informative titles.
2 The basic R code for this command in the built-in system is:

```
Boxplot(recprescore~group, data=leow)
```

3 A nicer box plot that inserts dots for all of your data points comes from the ggplot2 library. Install and open the library, and then the R code for this command is:

```
ggplot(data=leow,aes(x=group,y=recprescore))+geom_boxplot(outlier.shape=NA)+geom_jitter
(position=position_jitter(width=.3, height=0))+labs(x="Group", y="Receptive Pretest Score")
```

8.2.4 Box Plots for More than One Variable Plotted on the Same Graph in SPSS

To look at the data from the Kim (2013) study, we will want to look at three variables—scores on the sarcasm test in a pretest, posttest and delayed posttest. To see these variables side by side in a box plot, choose GRAPHS > LEGACY DIALOGS > BOXPLOTS, and when the BOXPLOT box comes up choose SIMPLE plus "Summaries of separate variables." This choice will let you look at the summaries of several DVs not divided into groups; thus there is no place to enter a group variable in the dialog box seen in Figure 8.7. The "Label Cases by" box will simply label outliers in the box plot if you put an identifier label in it (Participant for the Kim data). By the way, if you have a sharp eye you might have noticed in Figure 8.7 that SPSS has marked the pretest with a different symbol from the posttest and delayed posttest. This is usually the symbol used for grouping variables, but the pretest is a numeric variable just like the other tests in this data set, and when imported into R also has the structure of an interval-level variable, so I cannot figure out why the symbol is different! It does not seem to make a difference.

The resulting box plot in Figure 8.8 shows the distribution of all three variables that measure performance on the sarcasm test. There are no outliers identified for any test, but notice that the only distribution that looks fairly normally distributed is the posttest. The pretest and posttest distributions are not normal because the boxes and whiskers of the box plot are not symmetrical around the median

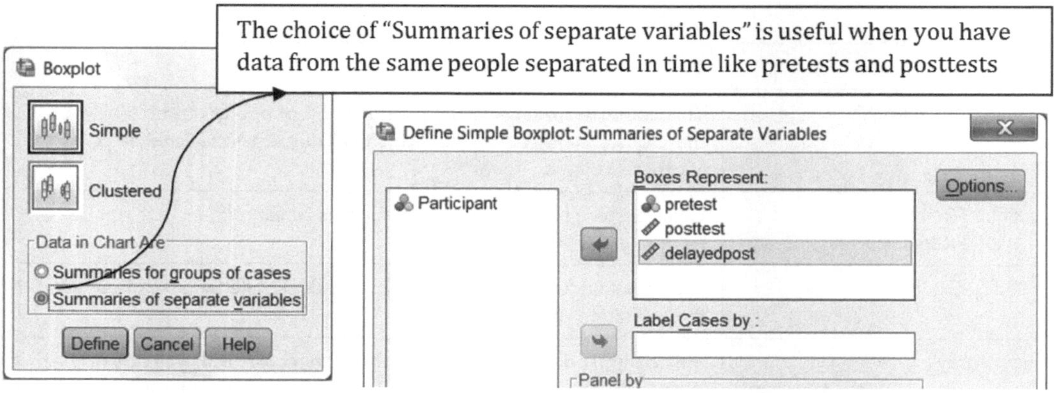

Figure 8.7 How to make a box plot of several variables (perhaps separated in time) side by side.

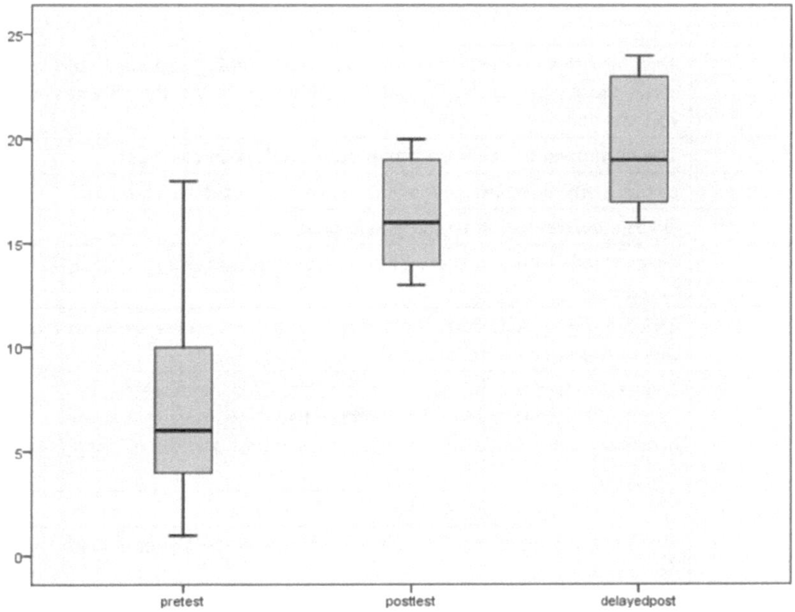

Figure 8.8 A box plot of Kim's (2013) data from SPSS.

lines. Both are positively skewed, meaning the tail extends farther to the right than the left if we were looking at a histogram, or if we turned the box plot on its side.

Creating a Box Plot for a Paired Samples T-Test (Several Variables Side by Side)

1 Choose GRAPHS > LEGACY DIALOGS > BOXPLOT. When a dialog box comes up, choose SIMPLE and choose the "Summaries of separate variables" button. Click on the DEFINE button.
2 Put the dependent variables in the "Boxes represent" box. If you want to identify outliers with row names, put a column of ID numbers in the "Label cases by" box. Click on OK.

8.2.5 Box Plots for More than One Variable Plotted on the Same Graph in R

To look at the data from the Kim (2013) study, we will want to look at three variables—scores on the sarcasm test in the pretest, posttest and delayed posttest. If you are following along with me, import the SPSS file Kim2013.sav and call it kim2013. In R Commander you cannot choose more than one variable at a time, so our only choice to get a figure similar to Figure 8.8 that SPSS provides is to use the R Console. Here the box plot command (a little different from the Boxplot( ) command seen in Section 8.2.3) provides us the easiest way to view the data and also add a few more bells and whistles (see Figure 8.9).

```
attach(kim2013)
boxplot(pretest, posttest, delayedpost, ylab="Score on sarcasm test out of 30",
names=c("Pretest", "Posttest", "Delayed Posttest"),
```

```
las=1,notch=FALSE,col="grey", boxwex=.5, ylim=range(c(1,40)),medcol="white")
detach(kim2013)
```

attach(kim2013)	Attaching this means I do not have to type "kim2013$pretest" but can instead just type "pretest". (Just remember to detach the data set when you are done!)
boxplot( )	The command to call for a box plot in the R base package.
pretest, posttest, delayedpost	List as many variables as you want here, separated by commas.
ylab="Score on test out of 30"	Gives a custom name to the y-axis label.
names=c("Pretest", etc.)	Gives x-axis labels to the variables; otherwise they appear only as numbers.
las=1	Orients the variable labels horizontal to the axis (las=2 would orient them perpendicular to the axis).
notch=FALSE	Makes notched box plots, where the 95% CI is indicated by the notches; I like notches but in this case I got a warning that some notches went outsides the hinges on the boxes so I did not apply the notches.
col="grey"	Fills the box plots with a color.
boxwex=.5	Boxwex is a scale factor for all boxes. It makes the boxes thinner than normal.
ylim=range(c(1,40))	Specifies that y-axis limits should range from 1 to 40.
medcol="white"	Makes the median line the indicated color.

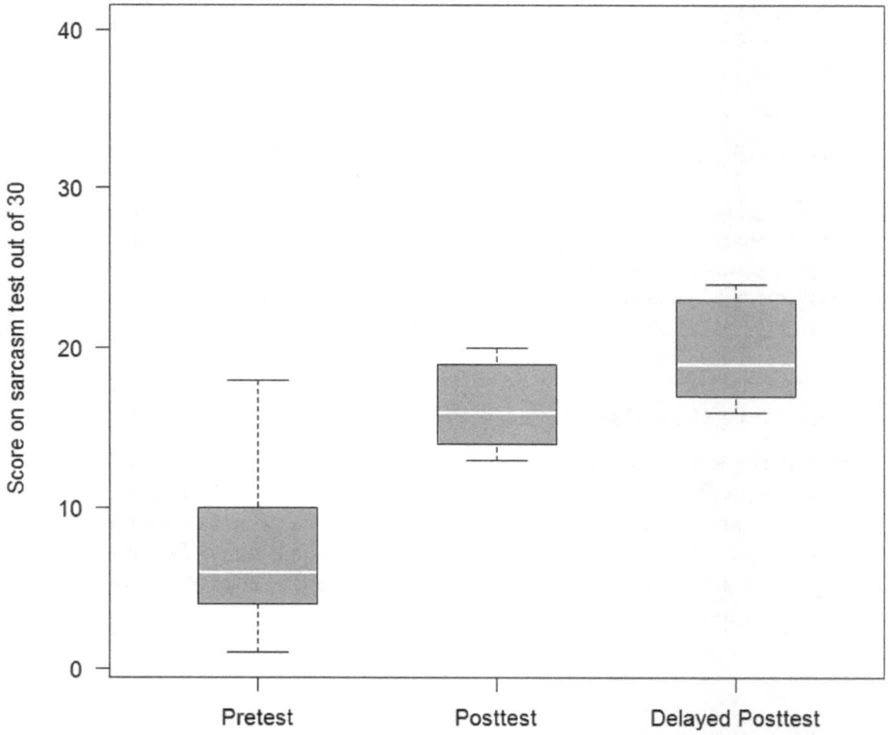

Figure 8.9 A box plot of Kim's (2013) data from R.

Tip: If you cannot remember the names of your variables, you can go back to R Commander and pull up the Data Editor with the Edit data set button. Alternatively, type the command names(kim2013) in R Console.

The following table gives additional commands that could be useful for customizing any box plot that you make. For even more, type help(box plot) or see Paul Murrell's 2006 *R Graphics* book.

varwidth=TRUE	Draws box plots with width proportional to the number of observations in a group.
outline=FALSE	Will not draw in outliers if set to FALSE.
names=FALSE	Will not print labels under each box plot if set to F.
horizontal=TRUE	Draws box plots horizontally if set to T.
par(mfrow=c(1,2))	Sets the parameter so that two graphs can be displayed side by side in the Graphics Device; the first number in c( ) gives the number of rows, the second number gives the number of columns.

Creating a Box Plot for Several Variables Side by Side

The basic R code for this type of box plot is:

```
attach(kim2013)
boxplot(pretest, posttest, delayedpost)
detach(kim2013)
```

I have also included commands in this section for many ways to customize box plots.

8.2.6 Box Plots for More than One Variable Separated by Groups in SPSS and R

There is one more box plot that might be useful to look at. This is the case where we have more than one DV, but the scores are split into groups. The Leow and Morgan-Short (2004) data had two different groups, and perhaps we might like to see the data from different but related tests (the productive pretest and posttest measures) side by side. This type of box plot can do that. Use the LeowMorganShort.sav file for SPSS or leow for R. The data will be split by the think-aloud and non-think-aloud groups. Figure 8.10 shows an example of these side-by-side box plots.

Figure 8.10 shows that in the pretest, where participants had to produce the imperative form, basically everyone in both groups scored zero. The box plot labels all those who scored above zero as outliers. In the posttest, both groups have the same distribution, although there are more outliers in the think-aloud group than the non-think-aloud one. (At least in this portion of the data; it actually goes to 15 but I have limited it since the distribution is so close to zero in both cases.) Still, in the productive posttest, at least half of the participants scored zero, as evidenced by the median line on zero.

For SPSS, call for this type of side-by-side box plot by choosing GRAPHS > LEGACY DIALOGS > BOXPLOT, then CLUSTERED and "Summaries of separate variables." Put the grouping variable in the "Category axis" box.

The best way to get such a box plot in R is to set the par(mfrow) command to include the number of plots you want, set side by side. Here I set it to include two sets of variables.

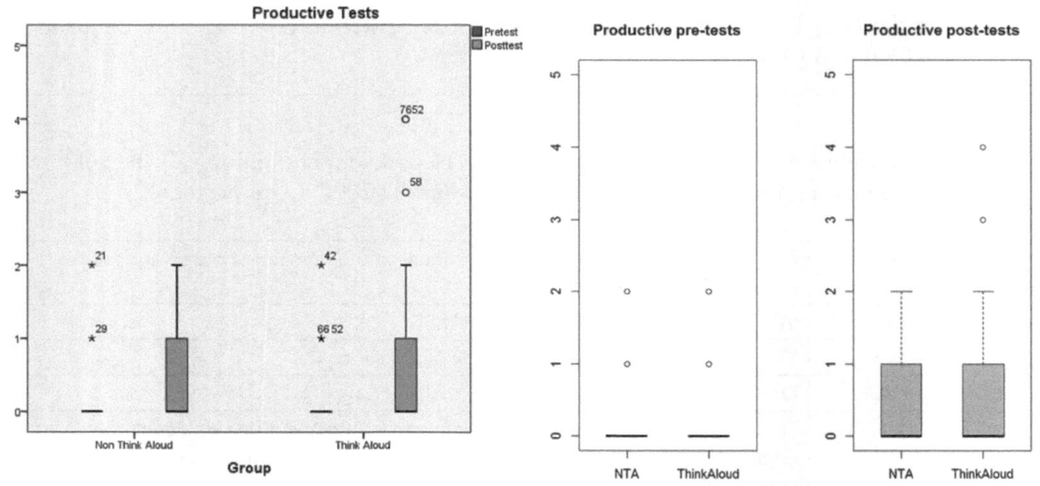

Figure 8.10 Leow and Morgan-Short's (2004) variables split by groups using multiple box plots, shown in SPSS and R versions.

```
par(mfrow=c(1,2)) #1 row, 2 columns of data
levels(leow$group)=c("NTA", "ThinkAloud") #make labels shorter so they'll print
boxplot(proprescore~group,data=leow,ylim=range(c(0,5)),col="gray", main="Productive
pretests",boxwex=.5)
boxplot(propostscore~group,data=leow,ylim=range(c(0,5)),col="gray", main="Productive
posttests",boxwex=.5)
```

I will not analyze this command because it is not substantially different from the **boxplot( )** command I analyzed in Section 8.2.5. However, I will point out that to split by groups, you model the DV (**proprescore**) by the IV (**group**) by using the tilde syntax (**proprescore~group**). Also notice that it is especially important to use the **ylim()** argument here, which limits the range of the y-axis, so graphs that are being compared are using the same scale.

The problem with this graph from R is that the points are not jittered so I cannot really see how many outliers there are, and I cannot use the **ggplot** command (which does show jittering) with the **par(mfrow)** syntax so I can put it side by side. Of course, one workaround is always to just make the box plots the way you want them and then use a program like Paint to place them side by side.

Creating a Box Plot for Multiple Variables Split into Groups

1 In SPSS, follow the command syntax:
GRAPHS > LEGACY DIALOGS > BOXPLOT, then CLUSTERED and "Summaries of separate variables"

2 The way to do this in R is to concatenate a series of box plots split by groups. In R, use the R Console with this basic code:

par(mfrow=c(1,2)) #the first entry tells # of rows, second tells # of columns

Now put in as many split-group box plots as you planned for:

boxplot(<u>proprescore</u> ~ <u>group</u>,data=<u>leow</u>,ylim=range(c(<u>0,5</u>)))
boxplot(<u>propostscore</u> ~ <u>group</u>,data=<u>leow</u>,ylim=range(c(<u>0,5</u>)))

8.2.7 Application Activities with Box Plots

1 Use the data from the study by Leow and Morgan-Short (2004) (LeowMorganShort.sav). Create two new variables (gainscores) by subtracting the pretest score from the posttest score in both the receptive and productive conditions. (The receptive conditions are preceded by the prefix "rec-" and the productive ones by the prefix "pro-".) Plot these two new variables. (I called them "recfinal" and "profinal." Do NOT divide the box plots by experimental group right now.) Did the participants seem to perform differently in the receptive versus productive condition? Would you say these distributions have the same size of box (the IQR)? Are there any outliers? Do these groups have normal distributions?

2 Using the same data as in activity #1, make box plots of the variables you calculated in activity #1 (the gain scores), but this time divide the box plots into the think-aloud and non-think-aloud groups. Are there any outliers? Which group improved the most on the receptive measure? Which improved the most on the productive measure? Which group has more spread? What do you think it means if one box plot is larger (has more spread) than another?

3 Use the Yates2003.sav data set. This is data from an MA thesis by Yates (2003) which examined whether pronunciation practice that emphasized suprasegmentals (by having participants mimic the actors in *Seinfeld*) was more effective than laboratory segmental practice in improving the accent of English learners. Did the lab group seem to improve over the semester? What about the mimicry group? Are there any outliers? Which group has more spread?

4 Use the DeKeyser (2000) data (DeKeyser2000.sav). Look at the distribution of the grammaticality judgment test (GJT) score variable split by DeKeyser's age groups (under 15 and over 15). Did the groups seem to perform differently? Would you say these distributions have the same size of box (the IQR)? Would you say the groups are normally distributed? Are there any outliers?

5 Use the Inagaki and Long (1999) *t*-test data (InagakiLong1999.Ttest.sav). The authors tested the hypothesis that learners of Japanese who heard recasts of target L2 structures would have a greater ability to produce those structures than learners who heard models of the structures. These data were for adjectives and the authors compared the differences between the recast and model groups. Examine the distributions. Did the groups seem to perform differently? Would you say these distributions have the same size of box (the IQR)? Are there any outliers? Do these groups have normal distributions?

6 Use the Larson-Hall and Connell (2005) data (LarsonHall.Forgotten.sav). These are data from an experiment with Japanese speakers who lived in the USA when they were children (early), as adults (late) or never (non). I had them produce words beginning in /r/ and /l/ and then judges decided whether they thought they heard an /r/ or /l/. Let us look at their judged accent on words beginning with /r/ (ACCENTR) and /l/ (ACCENTL), splitting the data into the three groups according to the STATUS variable. (Here you want to look at multiple variables, but split by groups.) In this case a higher accent score is more native-like. Did the learners in general produce words beginning with /r/ or /l/ better? Would you say the variances are equal across the groups? Which box plots represent approximately normal distributions?

7 Use the French and O'Brien (2008) data. The authors examined 104 French Canadian students in Grades 4 and 5 who were taking a five-month intensive English course. These students were measured at the one-month mark and again at the end of the five months. French and O'Brien wanted to find out whether scores on two measures of phonological memory would improve at the end of the five months of study. Since children's phonological memory has been shown to develop as children get older and cognitively more mature, French and O'Brien wondered whether they could find a measure of phonological memory that would not be influenced by changes in language proficiency (in other words, a measure that was language independent). Two phonological memory measures were used, one using English non-words (ENWR) and the other using Arabic non-words (ANWR). Arabic was a language unknown to the children. Make a box plot that compares the four variables of Arabic at time 1 (anwr_1) and time 2 (anwr_2) and English at time 1 (enwr_1) and time 2 (enwr_2). Did the learners improve from time 1 to time 2 in either

measure? Would you say the variances are equal from time 1 to time 2? Which box plots represent approximately normal distributions?

8.3 Assumptions of *T*-Tests

There are four main assumptions for *t*-tests:

1 The DV should be measured in interval-level measurements.
2 The data should be independent.
3 The data should be normally distributed.
4 Groups should have equal variances.

The first two assumptions are covered well in most books about general research design and must be addressed when you are planning your research study (Mackey & Gass, 2005; Porte, 2002, 2010). Because there is no way statistically to examine or help fix a research study that has violated these assumptions, they will not be discussed further in this chapter. The last two assumptions are the ones that can be examined through the use of statistical software.

The assumption of equal variances is very often violated in second language research studies if a group of native speakers versus non-native speakers is included, since the native speakers usually have a far smaller variance than the group of non-native speakers. Fortunately, for *t*-tests there are estimators that can take unequal variances into account.

Although there are statistical tests to check for both the normality of your data and equal variances, according to Wilcox (2003) a basic problem with such tests is that these tests "do not always have enough power to detect situations where the assumption should be discarded" (p. 241). He does not recommend using them. Table 8.3 shows the assumptions for each test and alternatives that can be used if the assumptions do not hold.

Table 8.3 Assumptions for *T*-Tests

Meeting t-test assumptions		*Independent samples t-test*	*Paired samples t-test*
(1) Normal distribution of data	Required?	Yes	Yes
	How to test assumption?	Examine box plots, plot normal curve over histogram; use Q-Q plots (see Chapter 3)	Examine box plots, plot normal curve over histogram; use Q-Q plots (see Chapter 3)
	What if assumption not met?	(1) use a robust method with means trimming or bootstrapping; (2) use non-parametric Mann–Whitney U test	(1) use a robust method with means trimming or bootstrapping; (2) use non-parametric Wilcoxon signed-ranks test
(2) Equal variances	Required?	Yes; homogeneity especially important if group size unequal (Maxwell & Delaney, 2004)	Yes but traditionally just assumed to be true for paired samples to simplify mathematical calculations
	How to test assumption?*	Examine box plots; look at summary statistics for variance (see Chapter 3)	
	What if assumption not met?	(1) Choose Welch procedure readout (equal variances not assumed); (2) use robust methods	

*Note that SPSS provides a test called Levene's test for the independent samples *t*-test which is supposed to check whether the variance of two groups is similar enough to satisfy this requirement. The problem is that, if sample sizes are small, large differences in variances may not be seen as problematic, while, if sample sizes are large, even small differences in variances may be counted as a problem (Clark-Carter, 2005).

8.3.1 Adjustments for Multiple T-Tests (Bonferroni Adjustment, False Discovery Rate)

If you are following my recommendation and showing your readers CIs, there is no need to worry about the following problem. However, if you are still using the "old statistics," you will need to think about this issue.

Another type of assumption associated with doing statistical testing the old way is the alpha level (α), the level of tolerance for type I errors. Remember that a type I error is a false positive—when you mistakenly conclude there was an effect for a treatment when, in fact, there was not one. In our field alpha is generally set to $\alpha = 0.05$. In many cases, however, researchers do not perform only *one* statistical test; in fact, they perform many! This is often the case when *t*-tests are used. For example, Leow and Morgan-Short (2004) looked at *t*-tests comparing their think-aloud and non-think-aloud groups on three different language measures, and then, because they did pretests and posttests, they also did comparisons across time.

The problem with conducting multiple statistical tests is that the possibility of a false positive increases. In other words, each time you conduct a statistical test such as a *t*-test, you have a 5% chance of getting a false positive error. If you have 10 *t*-tests, then this 5% chance gets added together 10 times to give a 50% chance overall that you will get a false positive somewhere in your batch of tests. (The truth of what exactly this chance may be is a little more complicated, but it is close enough for us.)

One way to address this conceptual problem is with a **Bonferroni adjustment**. A Bonferroni adjustment corrects the problem by decreasing the acceptable alpha rate depending on how many tests are done. Bonferroni found that the type I error rate (the false positive) is less than or equal to the number of comparisons done, multiplied by the chosen alpha level. Again, for 10 *t*-tests at an $\alpha = 0.05$, this would be $10 \times 0.05 = 0.50$. To correct for this increase in false positive error, Bonferroni advised the researcher to divide the desired alpha level by the number of comparisons. In other words, you are distributing the chance of finding a false positive equally across all of your *t*-tests. Thus, if you had four *t*-tests, you should not consider the *t*-test to be statistical unless the alpha level was less than $\alpha = 0.05/4 = 0.0125$.

Herrington (2002) pointed out that this approach is much too conservative when many comparisons are being made. He advocated using Benjamini and Hochberg's (1995) **False Discovery Rate (FDR)** method. The FDR has more power than the Bonferroni adjustment, as it seeks only to control the proportion of errors that are found in tests where the null hypothesis (H_0) was rejected, but keeps the overall number of decision errors at the 5% alpha level. You can use R to calculate the FDR. (SPSS will not calculate it presently.) Simply enter your *p*-values into a file, then use the p.adjust() command to return adjusted *p*-values. Here is an example where you enter the 10 different *p*-values you got from your tests, then run the p.adjust( ) command:

```
p <-c(.045, .003, .0001, .000, .10, .94, .67, .003, .01, .053)
p.adjust(p, method="fdr", n=length(p))
 [1] 0.07500000 0.00750000 0.00050000 0.00000000 0.12500000 0.94000000 0.74444444
 [8] 0.00750000 0.02000000 0.07571429
```

The result shows that what was previously $p = 0.045$ should now be considered = 0.075, and would thus be non-statistical, and so on. This is a much more reasonable approach than the Bonferroni adjustment, which would say that the cutoff point was 0.05/10 = 0.005, so that anything larger than 0.005 would not be considered statistically significant.

8.3.2 Data Formatting for Tests of Group Differences (the "Wide Form" and "Long Form")

Up to this point in the book we have not worried about how your data were set up because there really was not anything to worry about—variables were all entered with the variables in columns and the rows representing individual cases (see Section 1.1.2). However, with the advent of tests that examine group differences (where you need to divide the data into groups, such as the independent samples *t*-test discussed in this chapter) you will need to be aware that you may have to reformat to have your data in the correct format.

There are two basic ways that you might have your data set up in a spreadsheet:

1 Data is split so that the results for each group for each variable are found in different columns. We will call this the "wide" format because the columns are shorter than they would be in the "long" format, thus making the whole file wider (see Table 8.4).
2 All the data for one variable are in one column, and there is another column that codes the data as to which group they belong to. Everitt and Dunn (2001) call this the "long" form because the columns will be longer in this case (see Table 8.5).

Table 8.4 is an example of data in the wide format. Let us say we are looking at the correlation between test scores of children and adults on regular and irregular verbs. We would have one column that represented the scores of the children on regular verbs, another column containing the scores of adults on the regular verbs, another one with scores of children on irregular verbs and finally a column with scores of adults on irregular verbs. In the wide format, we do not need any indexing (or categorical) variables, because the groups are already split by those variables (adult vs. child and regular vs. irregular verbs in this case) into separate columns.

These data can be put into the long format (see Table 8.5). We put all of the irregular verb scores together, in the same order (let us say children first and then adults). Then the group membership column indexes the scores on both verb columns so we know which group the data came from, children (= 1) or adults (= 2). If it were necessary for our analysis, we could even reduce this further, so that all of the interval data were in one column, and the group column would then have to index both adult vs. child and regular vs. irregular (say, with a scheme such as 1 = child, regular; 2 = adult, regular; 3 = child, irregular; 4 = adult, irregular).

Table 8.4 Data in the "Wide" Format

ChildRegVerb	*AdultRegVerb*	*Child/IrregVerb*	*Adult/IrregVer*
14.00	13.00	14.00	15.00
13.00	15.00	15.00	15.00
15.00	15.00	11.00	15.00
15.00	13.00	15.00	14.00
13.00	8.00	14.00	15.00
8.00	13.00	14.00	15.00
13.00	13.00	14.00	13.00

Table 8.5 Data in the "Long" Format

RegularVerbs	*IrregularVerbs*	*Group*
15.00	11.00	1.00
14.00	13.00	1.00
12.00	8.00	1.00
15.00	13.00	2.00
14.00	9.00	2.00
15.00	15.00	2.00
11.00	6.00	2.00

For independent samples *t*-tests (and for analysis of variance (ANOVA) in the chapters to follow), the data should be arranged in the "long form." This means that, if you have entered your data in the "wide" form, you will need to combine columns and also make up a separate variable that indexes groups. If you do not have a categorical group variable, you will not be able to run a *t*-test or an ANOVA using the menu commands.

8.4 The Independent Samples *T*-Test

Leow and Morgan-Short (2004) tested 77 learners of Spanish on their knowledge of the Spanish impersonal imperative using two receptive tasks (a reading passage comprehension and a recognition of correct imperative forms) and one productive task (produce the correct imperative forms). The learners were divided into a think-aloud group (n = 38) and a non-think-aloud group (n = 39). The authors essentially performed three independent samples *t*-tests to see whether there were any differences in scores on each of the three tasks depending on which group the learners belonged to. In this analysis, we will consider only the receptive recognition task and the productive task (not the reading comprehension task).

We have seen repeatedly that real data sets only rarely fulfill the requirement of having a normal distribution. Figure 8.11 shows box plots of both the recognition and the productive task side by side. Both tasks had 17 points. Figure 8.11 shows that scores on the productive task were quite low overall, and heavily skewed. Scores on the receptive task were more varied, but the distributions were still somewhat skewed (since the whiskers were not symmetric around the boxes). There were some outliers in each task, especially for the very positively skewed production task. In summary, neither one of these tasks had perfectly normally distributed data, but to illustrate how *t*-tests work I will analyze the receptive task with an independent samples *t*-test.

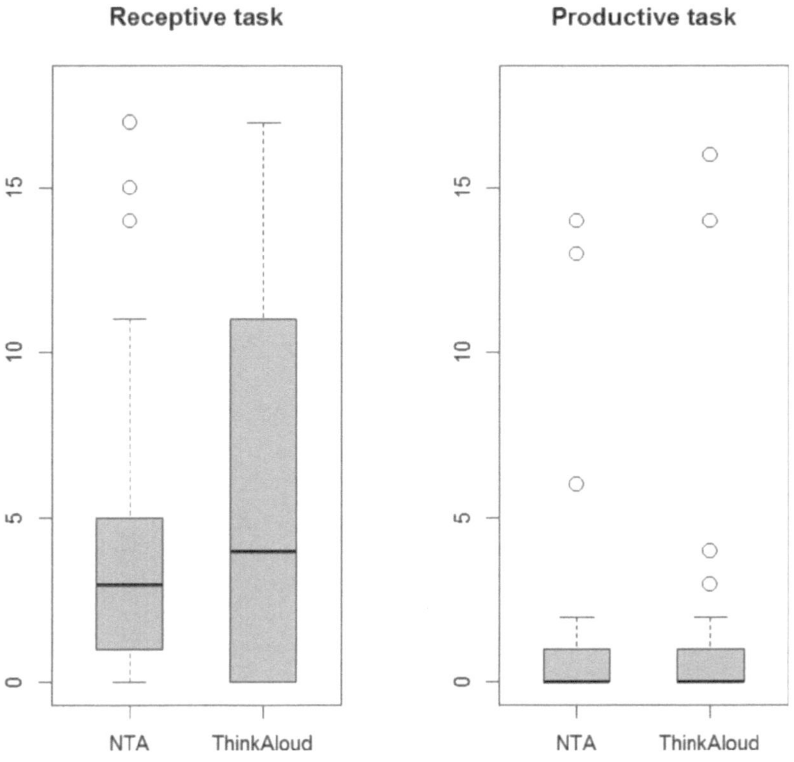

Figure 8.11 Box plots of Leow and Morgan-Short's posttest receptive and productive tasks.

In this section I will also show how to perform robust types of *t*-tests on our data and not have to worry that the data are not normally distributed or that there may be outliers in the data. In both SPSS and R we can use bootstrapping, and with R we can also add means trimming to increase the robustness of the data to non-normality or outliers.

> **Tip:** In this book I use real data sets that authors have published. This means that data are often messy and do not turn out perfectly. We see with the Leow and Morgan-Short data set that the data are not normally distributed, which turns out to be true of almost every data set in this book, and probably true of your data set as well. The Kim data set has very small numbers of participants (only nine). But one of the best ways for dealing with these issues is to use robust methods, such as bootstrapping to generate an empirical distribution that confidence intervals can be drawn from, or means trimming as a principled way of getting rid of outliers. This approach is better than using traditional non-parametric statistics (Wilcox, 2003).

In case you are interested, here is the R syntax I used for Figure 8.11:

```
par(mfrow=c(1,2))
levels(leow$group)=c("NTA", "ThinkAloud")
boxplot(recpostscore~group,data=leow,ylim=range(c(0,18)),col="gray", cex=1.5,main="Receptive
task",boxwex=.5)
boxplot(propostscore~group,data=leow,ylim=range(c(0,18)),col="gray", cex=1.5, main="Productive
task",boxwex=.5)
```

As regards the assumption of homogeneity of variances, the box plots indicate that the variances are different in the receptive task because the width of the boxes is highly different. (In the productive task the variances are quite similar.) Also, numerically the variances are quite different. The variance is just the SD squared, and the SD (found in Table 8.1) in the receptive task for the think-aloud group was about 6, making its variance around 36, while the SD for the non-think-aloud group was about 4, making its variance around 16. Thus, numerically and visually we can see that the two groups in the receptive task do not have homogeneous variances. However, we do have a procedure in the *t*-test to take unequal variances into account, so we will proceed with the analysis.

8.4.1 Performing an Independent Samples T-Test in SPSS

To perform an independent samples *t*-test, go to ANALYZE > COMPARE MEANS > INDEPENDENT SAMPLES T-TEST (see Figure 8.12). Remember that the data for the independent samples *t*-test need to be in the "long" format. That is, you must have one interval-level variable that contains data for both groups, and then a categorical grouping variable.

> **Tip:** In order to "Define groups" correctly you will need to use a variable with categories specified by numbers, not names (SPSS "strings"). If you have only strings you will need to recode your variable (see online document "Manipulating Variables"). It is, however, perfectly valid to have *values* for your numbered categorical variables. These can be entered in the "Variable View" tab, in the Values column. These will describe the variable while still keeping it classified as numerical in SPSS.

In the dialog box, move the DV (RECPOSTSCORE in this case) into the "Test Variable(s)" box. Move the categorical grouping variable (GROUP in these data) into the "Grouping Variable" box. You should then be able to click on the "Define groups" button. If you cannot, click again on the

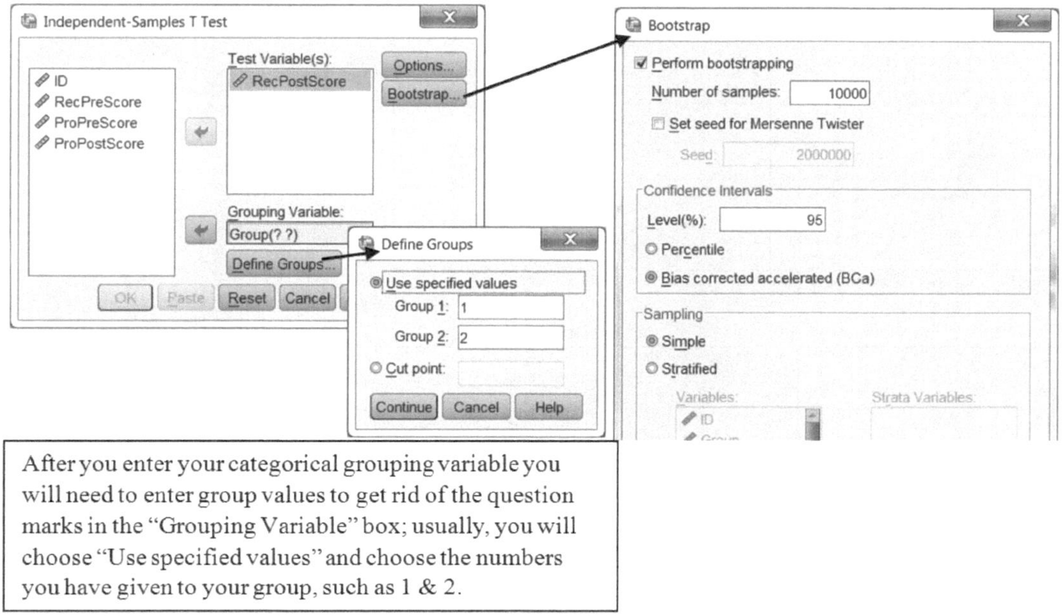

Figure 8.12 Opening an independent samples *t*-test dialog box in SPSS.

variable that is now in the "Grouping Variable" box but says "Group(? ?)" and highlight it, and then the "Define groups" button should work.

The reason you have to define groups in the "Independent Samples T-Test" dialog box is that you may want to perform *t*-tests among different pairs of groupings. For example, if you had three different groups but decided to use *t*-tests to test them, you could do this by specifying that Group 1 = 1 and Group 2 = 2 the first time you run it (so you test Group 1 against Group 2), then Group 1 = 1 and Group 2 = 3 the second time you run it (now testing Group 1 against Group 3) and finally Group 1 = 2 and Group 2 = 3 the last time you run it (last of all testing Group 2 against Group 3).

We also would like to bootstrap the data, so click on the Bootstrap button and check the "Perform bootstrapping" box. Change the number of samples to 10,000 instead of 1000 (Chernick, 2007). Change the CIs to "BCa." (According to Crawley (2007, p. 322), statisticians prefer this interval.)

There are three tables produced as the output to this test, and these are shown in Table 8.6. The first table, titled "Group Statistics," shows descriptive statistics. You should always check descriptive statistics first to get a sense of your data and make sure the *N* is correct. This table further contains bootstrapped BCa CIs for the mean scores of the groups. The "Bias" shows how different the bootstrapped score is from the originally calculated score, but in the case of the mean it is zero so the bootstrapped mean score is not any different from the original parametric mean score. (The bootstrapped SD does have some bias away from the original parametric SD though.) The "Std. Error" is the SD of the simulated bootstrap values for that statistic, so you can see that the SD of the bootstrapped samples (0.69 for the non-think-aloud group) is smaller than the original parametric SD (4.31 for the non-think-aloud group). The CI gives us the range with which we can be 95% confident that our true statistic lies in. So we believe the true mean of the non-think-aloud group lies between 2.72 and 5.31. We are not that interested in bootstrapped statistics for the mean and SD of each group, however. We are more interested in the bootstrapped CI for the difference between means, which is in the third box.

The second table in the output is labeled "Independent Samples Test," and this table has the results of *two* different tests, and *two* columns labeled "Sig." Be sure not to interpret the first significance

Table 8.6 Output from the Independent Samples *T*-Test

Group Statistics

Group			Statistic	Bootstrap[a] Bias	Bootstrap[a] Std. Error	BCa 95% Confidence Interval Lower	BCa 95% Confidence Interval Upper
RecPostScore	Non Think Aloud	N	39				
		Mean	3.92	.00	.69	2.72	5.31
		Std. Deviation	4.313	-.121	.699	2.969	5.280
		Std. Error Mean	.691				
	Think Aloud	N	38				
		Mean	5.89	.00	.96	4.09	7.77
		Std. Deviation	6.044	-.100	.483	5.114	6.669
		Std. Error Mean	.980				

a. Unless otherwise noted, bootstrap results are based on 10000 bootstrap samples

Independent Samples Test

		Levene's Test for Equality of Variances F	Levene's Test for Equality of Variances Sig.	t-test for Equality of Means t	df	Sig. (2-tailed)	Mean Difference	Std. Error Difference	95% Confidence Interval of the Difference Lower	95% Confidence Interval of the Difference Upper
RecPostScore	Equal variances assumed	10.565	.002	-1.651	75	.103	-1.972	1.194	-4.350	.407
	Equal variances not assumed			-1.644	66.808	.105	-1.972	1.199	-4.365	.422

Bootstrap for Independent Samples Test

		Mean Difference	Bootstrap[a] Bias	Bootstrap[a] Std. Error	BCa 95% Confidence Interval Lower	BCa 95% Confidence Interval Upper
RecPostScore	Equal variances assumed	-1.972	.003	1.190	-4.318	.319
	Equal variances not assumed	-1.972	.003	1.190	-4.318	.319

a. Unless otherwise noted, bootstrap results are based on 10000 bootstrap samples

Note: The p-value of Levene's test is *lower* than $\alpha = 0.05$, so we cannot assume equal variances.

level as the *t*-test! The first test is Levene's test for the equality of variances. You can see that the Independent Samples Test table has two rows—one if you assume that variances are equal, and another if you assume they are not. The Levene's test for the equality of variances will indicate whether you can use the first line, labeled "Equal variances assumed." If the p-value is *greater* than 0.05, you can use the first line; if not, use the second line.

The output in Table 8.6 shows that the p-value for the Levene's test is $p = 0.002$, which means that the variances of the two groups are not equal. In this case, Levene's result lined up with our intuitions gained from looking at the box plots and the numerical summaries, namely that in the receptive task the group variances were not equal. You should be aware that there can be problems of power in testing assumptions of parametric tests as the Levene's test does (Wilcox, 2003), so it may be safer to always use the second line with equal variances *not* assumed, which is also called Welch's *t*-test.

> **Tip:** Because it might seem counterintuitive to look for a significance value *greater than* 0.05 for the Levene's test, here's an explanation. For the Levene's test, the null hypothesis is that the variances are equal. If the p-value is less than $p = 0.05$, you reject this hypothesis. Therefore you will assume that the variances are not equal.

The results of the *t*-test for independent samples is found under the part of the table labeled "*t*-test for Equality of Means." However, we can get all of the important information out of the 95% CI for the difference between groups. For equal variances not assumed, the CI ranges from −4.37 to 0.42. This means that the actual difference in scores between the groups will lie, with 95% confidence, in this interval. Since zero is found in this CI, we know that we should not reject H_0. We also see that the interval is wide, almost 5 points in the test where the maximum score is 17, and so we do not have a precise estimate of the mean difference between groups.

We could report this normal parametric CI or we could report the bootstrapped BCa CI, which is found in the third box of the output. In this case, there is not much difference in the numbers. Still using the unequal variances row, we could report that the bootstrapped BCa 95% CI was [−4.32, 0.32]. This interval still goes through zero and is still quite wide.

Leow and Morgan-Short concluded that doing a think-aloud concurrent with a language task made no difference to participants' scores. However, remember that failing to reject H_0 does not prove there was no difference between groups. We can only report our findings and explain that we were not able to find any differences in our current population, and that the CIs show that there could be a true difference as large as 4.32 points in the population, but it is more likely to center closer to the mean difference of about 2 (remember the cat's eye in Figure 4.4), and that statistically we cannot conclude that there is any real difference.

Performing an Independent Samples T-Test in SPSS

1. On the drop-down menu, choose ANALYZE > COMPARE MEANS > INDEPENDENT-SAMPLES T-TEST. When a dialog box pops up, put your independent variables into the box labeled "Test Variables." Put your categorical grouping variable in the "Grouping Variable" box.
2. Define which two groups you will compare in the DEFINE GROUPS button. If you have only two groups, you will just enter "1" and "2" in these boxes (if those are the labels you have used in the "Data View").
3. Open the BOOTSTRAP button and check the "Perform bootstrapping" box. Change the number of samples to 10,000 and the CIs to "BCa." Click on CONTINUE. Run the test.

8.4.2 Performing an Independent Samples T-Test in R

Perform an independent samples *t*-test in R Commander by clicking on STATISTICS > MEANS > INDEPENDENT SAMPLES T-TEST (see Figure 8.13).

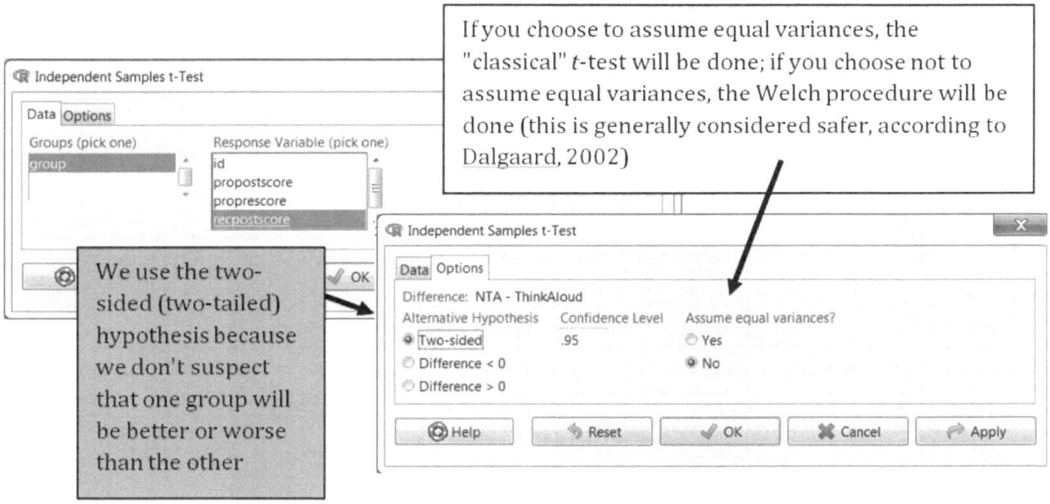

Figure 8.13 Opening an independent samples *t*-test dialog box in R Commander.

The R code for the independent samples *t*-test is:

```
t.test(recpostscore~group, alternative='two.sided', conf.level=.95, var.equal=FALSE, data=leow)
```

Here is the output:

```
        Welch Two Sample t-test

data:  recpostscore by group
t = -1.6441, df = 66.808, p-value = 0.1049
alternative hypothesis: true difference in means is not equal to 0
95 percent confidence interval:
 -4.3654956  0.4221757
sample estimates:
       mean in group NTA mean in group ThinkAloud
                3.923077                 5.894737
```

We see from the last line that the means for the posttest production task in the two groups are different numbers (NTA (non-think-aloud) group = 3.92, ThinkAloud (think-aloud) group = 5.89), but our question is whether they are different enough to say they come from two different populations. (The actual difference in mean scores between our groups is thus 1.97.) To answer this question, look at the 95% CI. The interval in which we expect, with 95% confidence, to find the true difference between the means is quite wide, from −4.37 to 0.42. This means that the actual difference in scores between the groups will lie, with 95% confidence, in this interval. Since zero is found in this CI, we know that we should not reject H_0. We also see that the interval is wide (almost 5 points in the test where the maximum score is 17) and so we do not have a precise estimate of the mean difference between groups.

Leow and Morgan-Short (2004) concluded that doing a think-aloud concurrent with a language task made no difference to participants' scores. However, remember that failing to reject H_0 does not prove there was no difference between groups. We can only report our findings and explain that we were not able to find any differences in our current population, and that the CIs show that there could be a true difference as large as 4.37 points in the population, but it is more likely to center closer to the mean difference of about 2, and that statistically we cannot conclude that there is any real difference.

The R code for this test is:

```
t.test(recpostscore~group, alternative='two.sided', conf.level=.95,
var.equal=FALSE, data=leow)
```

t.test (x, . . .)	Calls a *t*-test.
recpostscore~group	Syntax for modeling the DV by the IV (group).
alternative="two.sided"	This default calls for a two-sided hypothesis test; other alternatives: "less", "greater."
conf.level=.95	Sets the confidence level for the mean difference.
var.equal=FALSE	Calls for Welch's *t*-test, which does not assume equal variances; note that this is the default and that this is generally regarded as the safer option.
data=leow	Specifies the data set.

Tip: The only variables that will appear in the Groups list for the Independent Samples *t*-test in R Commander are those that *only* have two dimensions, as the Leow and Morgan-Short (2004) data set has. Thus, if you have three groups that you would like to compare using three different *t*-tests, you should subset your original data set to contain just two groups at a time. For example, with my data set (SPSS file called LarsonHall.Forgotten.sav, imported as forget) that had three groups, here is a command to subset that will exclude the group "Non":

```
forgetNoNon <- subset(forget, subset=status!="Non")
#note that the "!=" symbol means "does not equal"
```

The R Commander *t*-test does not give us the option of bootstrapping the results. The following two sections give two options for robust approaches to independent samples *t*-tests.

Performing an Independent Samples T-Test in R

1 On the R Commander drop-down menu, choose STATISTICS > MEANS > INDEPENDENT SAMPLES T-TEST. In the DATA tab, pick your group variable (the IV) and the "Response Variable" (the dependent variable). On the OPTIONS tab, unless otherwise strongly compelled, leave the "Assume equal variances" button at its default of "No."
2 The basic R code for this command is:

```
t.test(recpostscore~group, var.equal=FALSE, data=leow)
```

8.4.3 Performing a Bootstrapped Independent Samples T-Test in R

In this section, I use code created by LaFlair, Egbert, and Plonsky (2015) to bootstrap the mean difference between two groups, applied to the Leow and Morgan-Short data that I have been working with in Section 8.4.

To run a bootstrap, first we write up a function for running an ANOVA and then a Tukey's honest significant difference (HSD) post-hoc test. If you want to bootstrap this statistic, you should type the following lines into the R Console *exactly* as they are here, except for the three places that are underlined, where you should put in your own data names (recpostscore is the name of the DV in the Leow and Morgan-Short data set, and group is the name of the IV that splits the groups). You also do not have to worry about the spaces being exactly the same, and you can trade the "<-" symbol for "=."

```
MeanDifference <- function(data, i) {
temp <-data[i, ]
aov.temp <-aov(recpostscore ~ group, data = temp)
Tuk <- TukeyHSD(aov.temp)
return(Tuk$group[ , 1])
}
```

Then, we run the bootstrap using the boot( ) command from the boot package, so if you do not have this package, first download it (install.packages("boot")) and then open it (library(boot)).

```
MeanDifferenceBoot <- boot(leow, MeanDifference, 10000) #this will take a minute to run
MeanDifferenceBoot.ci <-boot.ci(MeanDifferenceBoot, conf=0.95, type="bca")
print(MeanDifferenceBoot.ci)
```

```
BOOTSTRAP CONFIDENCE INTERVAL CALCULATIONS
Based on 10000 bootstrap replicates

CALL :
boot.ci(boot.out = MeanDifferenceBoot, conf = 0.95, type = "bca")

Intervals :
Level       BCa
95%   (-0.372,  4.296 )
Calculations and Intervals on Original Scale
```

The output shows that the 95% BCa CI is [−0.37, 4.30], slightly smaller than we found for the normal CI. In any case, the CI still runs through zero and we would say that we were not able to find a statistical difference between the groups.

> **Tip:** If this R code does not work for you, the first thing to check and double check is that you have typed it in exactly as written here. I struggled to get it to work for a while, and my first problem was that I replaced the temp in the data=temp line with my own data's name. After I fixed that, I got an error code when I ran the boot.ci line. It turned out I was typing ="bcA" instead of "bca"! But it took me a while to figure that out.

8.4.4 Performing a Bootstrapped, 20% Trimmed Means, Independent Samples T-Test in R

Another way to do a bootstrapped independent samples *t*-test is to use Rand Wilcox's R libraries (Wilcox & Schönbrodt, 2014). Wilcox (2003) has suggested that using 20% trimmed means and the non-parametric (percentile) bootstrap procedure is the best overall approach for a robust test of data. You could adjust the amount of means trimming to be larger or smaller if you had reason to, but for general purposes stick to 20%.

Install Wilcox's libraries by using the following commands:

```
install.packages(c("MASS", "akima", "robustbase")) #install dependent packages
install.packages(c("cobs", "robust", "mgcv", "scatterplot3d", "quantreg", "rrcov",
"lars", "pwr", "trimcluster", "multicore", "mc2d", "psych", "Rfit"))
#install suggested packages
install.packages("WRS", repos="http://R-Forge.R-project.org") #install WRS
```

If this does not work for some reason, you can download the functions in the most current version of the Rallfun file, which as of the writing was Rallfun-v27, from the www-rcf.usc.edu/~rwilcox/ website. You should then click on the Software tab and then look for the small link in red that says Rallfun-v27. Download it (right-click to "Save link as"), put it in your working directory then use this command to get the file into R (find out your working directory by typing getwd() first):

```
source("Rallfun-v27")
```

Once you have Wilcox's libraries loaded, you should open the WRS package (library(WRS)) unless you have sourced it in ; in that case, all the commands will just be available. According to Wilcox, when you are comparing means, a percentile bootstrap is not very good unless you are using means trimming, in which case it is "one of the most effective methods for obtaining accurate probability coverage and achieving relatively high power" (2012, p. 336). To run this type of test, use this function, which is given here with its default arguments:

```
trimpb2(x, y, tr=0.2, alpha=.05, nboot=2000)
```

The type of bootstrap used here is the percentile bootstrap. The argument x contains the data from one group, while y contains the data from the other group being compared. The argument tr=0.2 refers to means trimming, which is the procedure of trimming off the most extreme ends of the data set. The nboot() function specifies how many bootstrap replicates to use.

So here is how I would perform a percentile bootstrapped and 20% trimmed means independent samples *t*-test on the Leow and Morgan-Short data (follow the steps in the left-hand column):

names(leow)	Remind myself of the names of the variables.
leow$group	See which rows contain which group data; I see that the NTA group is from row 1 through row 39.
NTA<-leow$recpostscore[1:39] NTA	This makes a new variable with the data for the receptive post-task score for just the NTA group; typing the name lets me check that the data I think is in the vector is really there.
TA<-leow$recpostscore[40:77]	Repeat for the other group, ThinkAloud (TA).
trimpb2(NTA, TA)	Run the test, with the default arguments (20% means trimming, 2000 bootstrap replicates).

Here is the output:

```
$p.value
[1] 0.177

$ci
[1] -5.140  0.735

$est.dif
[1] -1.95
```

The output shows that the 95% CI is [−5.14, 0.74]. This is a little bit different from any of the other CIs we have seen up to now for these same data but that is OK. First, because the means have been trimmed so that is one difference already, and second because bootstrapping is a random procedure and there will be small differences even when running the exact same procedure. The value labeled $p.value is the *p*-value, which does not give us any more information than the CI because we already see that the CI runs through zero and so the test is not statistically significant. The value $est.dif is the difference in means between the two groups.

We can also find out what the trimmed means value is, because it will be different from the untrimmed means value:

```
mean(NTA, tr=.2)
[1] 2.8
```

When choosing not to trim means, Wilcox (2012b) has suggested that bootstrap-t methods are preferable to the percentile bootstrap. To perform a bootstrapped test on the difference between the means of two groups without any means trimming or with very low means trimming, use the following function:

```
yuenbt(x, y, tr=0.2, alpha=0.05, nboot=599, side=F)
```

The only argument here that is different is side=F, which means that a symmetric or equal-tailed CI will be used. If this is set to side=T a different, symmetric CI will be used, and a *p*-value can be calculated.

Running this test on the Leow and Morgan-Short data, the output shows that the 95% CI is [−4.67, 0.94]. The value labeled $test.stat is the *t*-value, although there is no valid *p*-value unless side=T is included. The value $est.1 is the mean of our first group, which is NTA, and $n1 is the number of participants in this group, and the values with "2" are for the other group. I leave it to the reader to conduct this test to see the output.

I want to note that the way you order your two variables does matter slightly. It does not matter in the sense that the outcome will change, but it does matter in the sense that your CI will change depending on which variable is being subtracted from the other. So, in a case where you have a CI that uses negative numbers given one ordering of the variables (say, for example, it is [−10.75, −1.28] in one case), it will use positive numbers given the opposite ordering of the variables. (Now the CI is [1.28, 10.75] in the opposite order.) This of course is of no consequence as the difference between the groups is the same.

Wilcox's procedure involves a few more steps than just the built-in function t.test, but it is more foolproof than writing your own code for a bootstrap, and has the added bonus of being able to include means trimming as a possibility. Actually, Wilcox's system has many more functions that provide other ways of testing the differences between groups, such as testing medians, M-estimators or even only the top 0.75 quantile. For more information, see Wilcox (2012b), chapter 8.

Performing a Robust Independent Samples T-Test in R

1 First, the Wilcox R libraries must be loaded or sourced into R. (See p. 296 for how to do this.)
2 If you have your data in the long format, which is what you need to use SPSS or most R functions, you will have to subset your data to use Wilcox's commands. For example, the NTA file holds only the information for the receptive posttest variable and only for the non-think-aloud group.
3 The basic R code for a percentile bootstrap with means trimming is:

```
trimpb2(NTA, TA, tr=0.2, alpha=.05, nboot=2000)
```

The basic code for a bootstrap-t, which works best without means trimming, is:

```
yuenbt(NTA, TA, tr=0.2, alpha=0.05, nboot=599, side=F)
```

8.4.5 Effect Sizes for Independent Samples T-Tests

Unfortunately, neither SPSS nor R include an effect size for independent samples *t*-tests in their output. In some cases you can find a quick calculation using the Internet, but first I need to explain the idea of a standardizer so you know what your best choice for an effect size is.

Cohen's index of effect size for independent samples called *d* can be calculated as: $d = \frac{\hat{X}_1 - \hat{X}_2}{\sigma}$ where σ = the appropriate standardizer, selected from the following choices (Olejnik & Algina, 2000, p. 245):

A The SD of one of the groups, perhaps most typically the control group (Glass, 1976);
B The pooled SD of [only the groups] being compared (Cohen, 1988);
C The pooled SD [of all the groups] in the design (Hedges, 1981).

If the groups do not have equal variances, then A is considered the best choice for a standardizer (Olejnik & Algina, 2000). This variant is sometimes called Glass's δ (delta) because Glass (1976) proposed this method. Leow and Morgan-Short's (2004) receptive task did not have equal variances, so we will use the SD of the non-think-aloud group as the standardizer. When you have to pick one group's SD as the standardizer, Olejnik and Algina noted that the control group, or the group least affected by the experiment, should be the one used as the standardizer. This makes calculation of the effect size for the receptive task rather easy using the data from Table 8.1:

$$\frac{3.92-5.89}{4.31}$$

$d = -0.46$ (We can ignore the negative sign as it is an arbitrary result of which mean is put first.) This effect size is medium, according to Cohen (1992) but small, according to Plonsky and Oswald (2014). (See Table 4.4 for a list of Cohen's guidelines for effect size.)

If the groups do have equal variances, then with only two mean scores there is no difference between choices B and C, and a way to save time is to use an online calculator. I found one at www.uccs.edu/~lbecker/. This calculator lets you compute Cohen's d if you know the means and SDs of two groups, or the t-test value and degrees of freedom. Another shortcut is to use the equation found in Table 4.4, which requires only the t-value and the degrees of freedom:

$$\frac{2t}{\sqrt{df_{err}}}$$

where df_{err} for a t-test is simply the degrees of freedom.

Here are the summary statistics for the Leow and Morgan-Short's productive task:

	Mean	*SD*	*0%*	*25%*	*50%*	*75%*	*100%*	*n*
NTA	1.153846	3.108041	0	0	0	1	14	39
Think Aloud	1.342105	3.450627	0	0	0	1	16	38

An effect size calculator online returns $d = -0.06$, which is a negligible effect size. The calculation for the pooled SD for any number of groups, for anyone without online access, is

$$S_{pooled} = \sqrt{\frac{(n_1-1)S_1^2+\ldots+(n_J-1)S_J^2}{(n_1-1)+\ldots+(n_J-1)}}$$

For Leow and Morgan-Short's productive task, the calculation for the standardizer (the denominator for d) is:

$$S_{pooled} = \sqrt{\frac{(39-1)3.11^2+(38-1)3.45^2}{(39-1)+(38-1)}} = \sqrt{\frac{367.54+440.39}{75}} = 3.28.$$

With the correct standardizer we can now calculate the effect size for the production task:

$$d = \frac{1.15-1.34}{3.28} = -.06.$$

8.4.6 Reporting the Results of an Independent Samples T-Test

For a parametric t-test, you will want to make sure to report on the appropriateness of assuming normality and homogeneity of variances to do a parametric test. You will want to report a CI for the mean difference as well as the N, the mean and SDs of the groups, and effect sizes (with a mention of what standardizer you used) along with an interpretation of their magnitude. If you feel you must, you may also report a t-value and associated p-value, although these are unnecessary if the CI is present.

Here is how I would report the results of an independent samples *t*-test on the receptive posttest for the Leow and Morgan-Short data if I used a parametric *t*-test:

> Data from Leow and Morgan-Short (2004) showed departures from non-normality in that there were outliers, distributions were not symmetric and variances were not equal. An independent samples *t*-test found no evidence of a difference between scores on the receptive posttest task for the think-aloud group (mean = 5.89, SD = 6.04, *N* = 38) and the non-think-aloud group (mean = 3.92, SD = 4.31, *N* = 39), 95% CI [−4.37, 0.42]. Since the 95% CI contains zero, we conclude that there is no statistical difference between groups. The wide CI, almost 5 points on a test where the maximum score was 17 points, shows that the estimate of how different the groups are is uncertain, but not likely to be far from zero. The effect size for this comparison, calculated with the SD of the non-think-aloud group, was Cohen's *d* = −0.46, which by Plonsky and Oswald's (2014) guidelines for effect sizes for SLA can be considered a small effect.

In reporting the results of a robust test, you will want to mention which robust method was used, the *N*, the mean for each group and a CI for the mean difference between the groups. It is not clear to me that you can calculate an effect size with trimmed means, so I have not. Here is an example of what you could say:

> Using 20% trimmed means and a percentile bootstrapping method, an independent samples *t*-test found no evidence of a difference between scores on the receptive posttest task for the think-aloud (20% trimmed means = 4.75, *N* = 38) and the non-think-aloud group (20% trimmed means = 2.8, *N* = 39). The 95% CI for the difference in means was [−5.14, 0.74]. Since the 95% CI contains zero, we conclude that there is no statistical difference between groups. The wide CI, almost 6 points on a test where the maximum score was 17 points, shows that the estimate of how different the groups are is uncertain.

8.4.7 Application Activities for the Independent Samples T-Test

1. Larson-Hall (2008) examined 200 Japanese college learners of English. They were divided into two groups, one called early learners (people who started studying English before junior high school) and the other later learners (people who only started studying English in junior high). Open the Larsonhall2008.sav file and see whether the groups (divided by the variable ErlyExp) were different in their language learning aptitude (AptScore), use of English in everyday life (UseEng), scores on a GJT and scores on a phonemic listening test (RLWScore). Be sure to explore whether the data are normally distributed and have equal variances. Run bootstrapped *t*-tests as well as normal parametric tests. Report results for all variables regardless of meeting assumptions: 95% CIs, means, SDs, *N*s and effect sizes. Discuss what the numbers mean.
2. Use the Inagaki and Long (1999) *t*-test data (InagakiLong1999.Ttest.sav). Test the hypothesis that learners of Japanese who heard recasts of adjectives would have a greater ability to produce this structure than learners who heard models of the structure. Remind yourself of whether these data are normally distributed and have equal variances by looking back to your answer on activity 4 in Section 8.2.7. Report results regardless of meeting assumptions: 95% CIs, bootstrapped 95% CIs, means, SDs, *N*s and effect sizes. Discuss what the numbers mean.
3. Practice doing a *t*-test with a data set that contains more than two groups at a time. Use the LarsonHall.Forgotten.sav file and import it as "forget" There are three groups in these data, called "Non," "Early" and "Late." (I examined Japanese users of English who had either never lived abroad (Non), lived abroad as children (Early) or lived abroad as adults (Late). Perform three independent samples *t*-tests on the variable of SentenceAccent to see if the groups are different in how well they pronounced entire sentences. Use the Status variable to divide the groups. Report effect sizes for the tests as well.

4 In activity #1 you examined several comparisons. The phonemic test **gjtscore** did not show a statistical difference between groups. Run robust tests on this variable (as many kinds as you can; with R you have a number of options including bootstrapping and means trimming, while with SPSS you only have bootstrapping) with the two groups (**erlyexp**) and compare the results of the CIs of the mean difference in the robust tests to the CI of the mean difference in the parametric *t*-test.
5 Cole (1927). Cole did an experiment testing whether different types of teaching methods would help high school students perform better on a number of different types of French tests (vocabulary, grammar, reading). Cole's results are found in the file Cole1927.sav. One teaching method was the traditional grammar translation method, while the other involved less grammar and more writing of original compositions. Calculate a gain score for each of the three types of tests (subtract Time 1 from Time 2, and use the Time_XXX_Percent variables instead of the original data labeled "Feb" and "June") and then do three independent samples *t*-tests to test whether teaching method had any effect on test scores. Try out different robust tests to see whether you are able to get any statistical results!

8.5 The Paired Samples *T*-Test

Kim (2013) investigated the question of whether an intervention using concept-based instruction that taught English language learners to recognize sarcasm would result in a conceptual and functional understanding of this idea. Kim's study took an approach that used both qualitative and quantitative measures to see whether and how students understood sarcasm better. Kim's qualitative data was very interesting, and involved many different facets of testing the participants' understanding, such as observing in-class interaction, having students produce their own SCOBAs and write interpretive essays. This wealth of data cannot be summarized in the numbers of quantitative research, and adds a rich dimension to her study, which did find development in the English learners' understanding of sarcasm.

On the quantitative side, Kim tested whether the learners performed better on a test where they had to uncover instances of sarcasm in the videos they were watching. The learners took this test before they received a series of eight weekly lessons that sometimes involved SCOBAs and always involved watching videoclips and examining homework. The SCOBAs refer to pedagogical tools (e.g. diagrams, flowcharts, figures, images) that Kim developed for the concept-based instruction. The learners also took the same test one week after they finished the lessons. A delayed posttest was given five weeks after the immediate posttest. Thus, the learners in this study were given the same test at three different time periods. Because the same people were tested at multiple time periods, an independent samples *t*-test cannot be used. We expect that there will be quite a bit of correlation between the three samples since the same people took the test, and a paired samples *t*-test explicitly takes this into account.

Figure 8.8 showed a box plot of the distribution of scores on all three tests, which contained 10 items worth 3 points each. Participants got one point for correctly identifying an instance of sarcasm and correctly identifying one cue that indicated sarcasm, such as gestures like arms on hips, or body movements like rolling the eyes. They could also get 2 more points for each item if they correctly identified two more cues, for a total of 30 possible points on the test. The box plots show that there were no outliers in the data but the distributions were not normal—all were positively skewed. The sizes of the boxes were fairly similar, and numeric reports of the SDs in Table 8.2 showed that variances were equal for the posttests, but the variance of the pretest was larger than that of the posttests.

8.5.1 Performing a Paired Samples T-Test in SPSS

To perform a paired samples *t*-test, go to ANALYZE > COMPARE MEANS > PAIRED SAMPLES T-TEST. You will see the dialog box that is shown in Figure 8.14. (This box looked slightly different before SPSS version 16.0; specifically, it did not have two columns to show the pairing in the "Paired

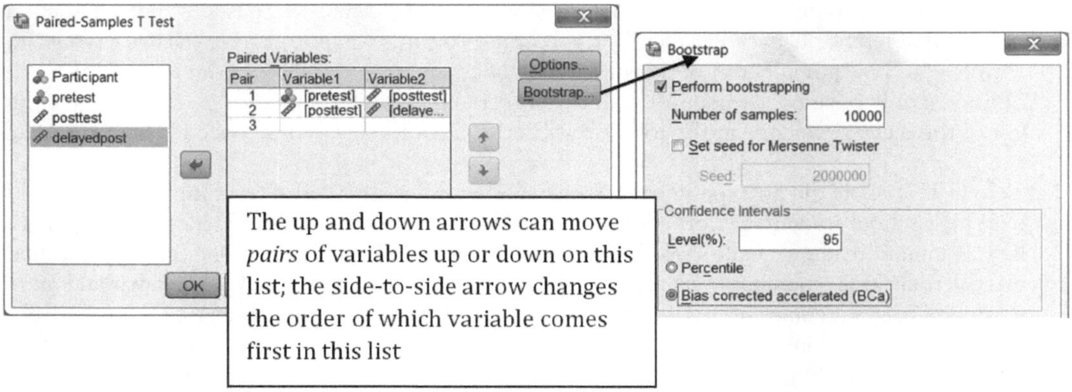

Figure 8.14 Opening a paired samples *t*-test dialog box in SPSS.

Variables" box.) Because the paired samples *t*-test must have a pairing of variables, the first variable you click from the list of variables on the left will go into the area labeled "Variable1" and the second will go into the area labeled "Variable2." (In previous versions of SPSS you needed to hold down the Ctrl key to select two variables at once to move to the right. You do not need to do that now.) Also, I recommend opening the Bootstrap button and checking the "Perform bootstrapping" box. Change the number of samples to 10,000 instead of 1000 (Chernick, 2007). Change the CIs to "BCa" because, according to Crawley (2007, p. 322), statisticians prefer this interval.

The output from this test is shown in Table 8.7. The first box of the output gives the summary statistics (mean, sample size, SD) which we saw previously in Table 8.2, so that table is not reproduced here. The second table of the output is labeled "Paired Samples Correlations" and shows the strength of the correlation between the two measures. Remember that the paired *t*-test assumes that the variables will be correlated, and that it could be problematic if they are not. You will want to examine the correlation assumption in this table, but do not be confused— this is not the statistical test itself! Here we see that there are correlations between both sets of variables. Notice that, if you have given the variable a label (usually longer and more descriptive than your variable name), it will be shown in the output here. My names are simple so I did not add any descriptive labels, and so there is no difference in names here.

The third table of the output (the lower table shown in Table 8.7) contains the results of the paired samples *t*-test. The first column is the mean difference between the two scores. If it is quite small in terms of the scale used, you would not expect to see a statistical difference for the *t*-test. Given that there were 30 points on the test, the first comparison between the pretest and posttest with a mean

Table 8.7 Output from the Paired Samples *T*-Test

Paired Samples Correlations

		N	Correlation	Sig.
Pair 1	pretest & posttest	9	-.340	.371
Pair 2	posttest & delayedpost	9	.586	.097

Paired Samples Test

		Paired Differences					t	df	Sig. (2-tailed)
					95% Confidence Interval of the Difference				
		Mean	Std. Deviation	Std. Error Mean	Lower	Upper			
Pair 1	pretest - posttest	-9.111	6.846	2.282	-14.373	-3.849	-3.993	8	.004
Pair 2	posttest - delayedpost	-3.111	2.713	.904	-5.197	-1.026	-3.440	8	.009

difference of about 9 points might be big enough to find a statistical difference, but the second comparison with a mean difference of only 3 points might not be.

Looking at the CIs for the parametric test, we see that the 95% CI for the mean difference between Kim's pretest and posttest is [−14.37, −3.85]. This is good news, as it tells us that there was a statistical difference between the pretest and posttest, but because the interval is so wide it tells us that the actual mean difference could be as small as about 4 points, or as large as about 14 points. We cannot pinpoint very precisely how much of an effect the sarcasm teaching had, but we can definitely say it made a difference. This CI could probably be made narrower if the number of participants were larger.

For the comparison between the immediate and delayed posttest, the CI was [−5.20, −1.03]. So it turns out that there was a statistical difference in scores here as well! The difference was not as large, but still there was improvement in the five weeks from the immediate posttest to the delayed posttest, which seems to point to the English learners really understanding the concept of sarcasm well and improving as time went on, and they were able to more and more reliably identify it in everyday life. Kim (2013) concluded from both her qualitative and quantitative analysis that "[s]tudents gained mature knowledge of the concept and improved their ability to comprehend different intentions and attitudes conveyed by sarcasm users" (abstract).

What about the bootstrapping we called for? I did not print it, but when I ran the test with two comparisons, the output gave a warning about the bootstrapping and said that because the variable **posttest** was specified more than once, the bootstrap execution stopped. So I went back and ran the test again with just one pair at a time. This time, the first box of the *t*-test output (the descriptive statistics) included bootstrapped information about the variables (you can see an example of what it looks like in Table 8.6 for the independent samples *t*-test), but that is not really the information we are interested in. We want to know about the bootstrapped CIs for the difference between the pairs, and Table 8.8 shows that output for both pairs.

Table 8.8 Output from the Bootstrapped Paired Samples *T*-Test

Bootstrap for Paired Samples Test

			Bootstrap[a]				
						BCa 95% Confidence Interval	
		Mean	Bias	Std. Error	Sig. (2-tailed)	Lower	Upper
Pair 1	pretest - posttest	-9.111	-.009	2.139	.051	-12.333	-5.444

Bootstrap for Paired Samples Test

			Bootstrap[a]				
						BCa 95% Confidence Interval	
		Mean	Bias	Std. Error	Sig. (2-tailed)	Lower	Upper
Pair 1	posttest - delayedpost	-3.111	-.006	.856	.026	-4.667	-1.444

a. Unless otherwise noted, bootstrap results are based on 10000 bootstrap samples

The BCa bootstrapped 95% CI for the pretest vs. posttest comparison is [−12.33, −5.44], which indicates a statistical difference between the testing times, and is also a narrower CI than the non-bootstrapped CI. This is good, as it gives us more of an idea of where the true mean difference between the groups lies, although the CI is still pretty wide. The BCa bootstrapped 95% CI for the immediate vs. delayed posttest is [−4.67, −1.44], which again still shows a statistical difference between these two testing periods, and is also a slightly narrower CI than the non-bootstrapped CI. Because we know that the data were not normally distributed I would definitely be inclined to report the bootstrapped results as closer to the true population values.

Performing a Paired Samples T-Test in SPSS

1 On the drop-down menu, choose ANALYZE > COMPARE MEANS > PAIRED-SAMPLES T-TEST. When a dialog box pops up, move your variables to the box labeled "Paired Variables."
2 Make sure the pairs of variables are put together in the way you want to test. Any number of paired groups can be selected, although if you insert more than one pair that contains the same name, you will not be able to run the bootstrapping.
3 Click on the BOOTSTRAP button and check the "Perform bootstrapping" box. Change the number of samples to 10,000 and the CIs to "BCa." Click on CONTINUE. Run the test.

8.5.2 One-Sided versus Two-Sided Confidence Intervals

Notice that for both the paired and the independent samples *t*-test, SPSS gives CIs and significance levels for the two-tailed case; there is no way to specify the one-way hypothesis using the drop-down menus. If you want to test a one-tailed hypothesis (meaning you want to see if there are differences in one direction only), you could report a *p*-value that has been divided by two. However, this is not true for the 95% CI; the calculated two-tailed CI cannot be halved to get the appropriate one-tailed CI. If you wanted to calculate a 95% CI for a one-tailed hypothesis, Cumming (2012) suggested you could calculate the 90% CI, then choose the upper or lower limit of that CI as your single limit of the one-sided 95% CI. For example, Kim's data might be an example of a situation where you could genuinely commit to using a one-sided hypothesis before you run your statistics, because you could say that you are only interested in knowing if the participants improved after the teaching. (Because you are confident they could not get worse, since you deliberately picked participants whose knowledge of sarcasm was quite low to begin with.)

If I ran the paired samples *t*-test again, I would click on the OPTIONS button in SPSS and change the "Confidence Interval Percentage" to 90. I can also do that for the bootstrapping case. The non-bootstrapped 90% CI for the comparison between the pretest and posttest is now [−13.35, −4.87], but we are not interested in the upper limit (13.35), just in the lower limit (4.87), since we are interested in how much the group will gain *at least*. You can see that this lower limit in the 90% CI is bigger than the lower limit in the 95% CI (which was 3.85). The terminology here might be a bit confusing since in Table 8.7 the value −3.85 is labeled as the upper limit, but it is negative and we are interested in the smallest difference between the groups, so we can just reverse signs and with a positive on both numbers, 3.85 will be the lower limit. With a two-sided hypothesis at 95% confidence level we consider the most extreme 2.5% of the curve on both the left and right to be outside of our confidence level. However, with the 95% one-sided hypothesis, we put all of the 5% of the curve that is outside the confidence level on one side or the other. Thus we will need to choose which side to put the 5% on, and since we are interested in maximizing the difference between groups, we will put the 5% on the left-hand or lower side, thus increasing the minimum difference between the groups. The other side of the curve will then extend to infinity. In other words, here we are interested in knowing how much better the difference will be in the posttest, so we are looking at the lower end point or the lower limit. Therefore, we could say that the one-sided 95% CI for this test was [−4.87, −infinity]. Actually, Cumming (2012) suggested that the name "lower end point CI" is the least ambiguous term for this type of interval.

Tip: If you use a directional one-tailed hypothesis for a *t*-test, you will have more power to find differences. If you use a one-tailed test however, the CI will not specify an upper range. This makes sense if you think it through because if you are testing the hypothesis that one group will be better than another, then you are not testing for how much *greater* the difference could be; you simply want to know the *least* the difference will be. Note that the *p*-value that will be given is already adjusted for a **one-tailed** (or **directional**) **hypothesis**.

8.5.3 Performing a Paired Samples T-Test in R

To perform the paired samples *t*-test in R, use R Commander and choose STATISTICS > MEANS > PAIRED T-TEST (see Figure 8.15). In the DATA tab, click on one variable from the "First variable (pick one)" box and one variable from the "Second variable (pick one)" box. In the OPTIONS tab you can choose a one-sided hypothesis instead of a two-sided, and also set your confidence level.

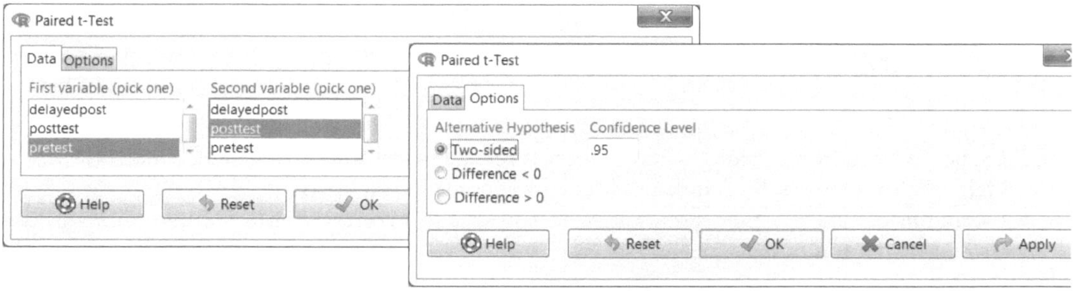

Figure 8.15 Opening a paired samples *t*-test dialog box in R Commander.

The output below shows that the CI for the mean difference between the tests goes from −14.37 to −3.85. This is good news, as it tells us that there was a statistical difference between the pretest and posttest, but because the interval is so wide it tells us that the actual mean difference could be as small as about 4 points, or as large as about 14 points. We cannot pinpoint very precisely how much of an effect the sarcasm teaching had, but we can definitely say it made a difference. This CI could probably be made narrower if the number of participants were larger.

```
        Paired t-test

data:  kim2013$pretest and kim2013$posttest
t = -3.9929, df = 8, p-value = 0.003989
alternative hypothesis: true difference in means is not equal to 0
95 percent confidence interval:
 -14.37304  -3.84918
sample estimates:
mean of the differences
              -9.111111
```

The R code for the paired samples *t*-test is:

with(Kim2013, (t.test(pretest, posttest, alternative='two.sided', conf.level=.95, paired=TRUE)))
conf.level=.95, paired=TRUE)

with(kim2013,	Evaluates an R function, and lets us specify the data/set of the variables
t.test (pretest, posttest, . . .)	Calls a *t*-test: gives two variables for the test from Kim2013
kim2013$pretest, kim2013$posttest	Put in two variables that are pairs; here I have to put kim2013$ before the variables because I have no other way to specify which data set the variable comes from.
alternative="two.sided"	This default calls for a two-sided hypothesis test; other alternatives: "less," "greater."
conf.level=.95	Sets the confidence level for the mean difference.
paired=TRUE	This argument specifies that a paired samples test should be done.

To test another pairing, such as the difference between the immediate and delayed posttest, you will need to run the test again. Here is the output from a test of the two posttests.

```
        Paired t-test

data:  kim2013$posttest and kim2013$delayedpost
t = -3.4401, df = 8, p-value = 0.008823
alternative hypothesis: true difference in means is not equal to 0
95 percent confidence interval:
 -5.196613 -1.025610
sample estimates:
mean of the differences
              -3.111111
```

Another choice for running a paired samples *t*-test is the **pairwise.t.test( )** command, which is set up a little differently from the **t.test( )** command. It is a little more powerful in that it lets you test more than just two columns of data at a time, and it also lets you specify a correction for multiple comparisons. However, it does not return CIs.

Performing a Paired Samples T-Test in R

1 On the R Commander drop-down menu, choose STATISTICS > MEANS > PAIRED T-TEST. Pick your two paired variables. The order will not be important unless you have a one-tailed hypothesis.
2 The basic R code for this command is:

```
t.test(with(kim2013, pretest, posttest, alternative='two.sided',
conf.level=.95, paired=TRUE)
```

8.5.4 Performing a Robust Paired Samples T-Test in R

I would like to give you an analog to Section 8.4.3 where I used the **boot()** function to bootstrap data, but I do not have the expertise to write up a function on my own. Really smart people who know R well seem to think it is not hard to figure this out and so they have not institutionalized the syntax for these tests in any package, as far as I can tell. However, I am not that smart, and I would not trust myself to write the correct syntax to make it work. So this section will use Wilcox's **WRS** package to perform robust paired sample *t*-tests. I am assuming that you have read through Section 8.4.4 and have installed all of the packages that are necessary and have loaded the **WRS** package.

There are several different types of tests we could use. Wilcox (2003) noted that when using paired groups, there are two hypotheses that could be tested—that the difference between the groups is zero, or that the group means are equivalent. For the first choice, the hypothesis is:

$$H_0: \mu_D = 0$$

In this case, bootstrapping will be done by resampling the difference values for each pair. Resampling takes place with replacement, meaning the picked value is put back into the pool of values and could be resampled again. For the second choice, the hypothesis is:

$$H_0: \mu_1 = \mu_2$$

When we want to test this hypothesis that the group means are equivalent, pairs of observations will be resampled. The difference in these two hypotheses is not merely academic. At times, it may affect the outcome of the statistical test. It should be noted that the paired *t*-test used in SPSS tests the hypothesis that the difference score is zero (Wilcox, 2003, p. 363), and this is also true for R. (Note that the paired *t*-test output in R explicitly states the alternative hypothesis: "true difference in means is not equal to 0".) I shall follow along with what SPSS and R do and test the first hypothesis, that the difference in means is zero. Wilcox (2012b) noted that if the goal is to maximize power, in the general case it is best to use the difference scores approach, but of course there could be situations where, depending on how the groups differ, the optimal choice is to use the equal means approach. Wilcox (2012b, chapter 9) provided three different tests that use the difference scores approach ($\mu_D = 0$). They are:

Function name	*Function syntax*	*Description*
trimci	trimci(x, tr=.2, alpha=.05), where x = difference data.	Non-bootstrap method for trimmed mean
trimcibt	trimcibt(x, tr=.2, alpha=.05, nboot=599, side=T), where x = difference data. (Side = T results in a symmetric CI; side = F results in an equal-tailed CI.)	Bootstrap-t for trimmed mean
trimpb	trimpb(x, tr=.2, alpha=.05, nboot=2000), where x=difference data	Percentile bootstrap for trimmed mean

In Section 8.4.4 we learned that the percentile bootstrap works quite well with means trimming, while the bootstrap-t works better when you are not performing any means trimming. Since the data from Kim (2013) we are working with here are skewed, it would be better to perform means trimming, so let us use the trimpb( ) function to test the hypothesis that the difference between the pretest and posttest is equal to zero.

So here is how I would perform a percentile bootstrapped, 20% trimmed means, paired samples *t*-test on the Kim pretest–posttest data (follow the step in the left-hand column):

names(kim2013)	Remind myself of the names of the variables.
attach(kim2013)	Now I do not have to specify which data set the variables come from.
kimdif<-posttest-pretest kimdif	This makes a new variable with the difference data. I put the posttest first since I assume (and know from previous investigation of the data) that the posttest scores are greater than the pretest scores. Once created, I look at the data to make sure it makes sense. I see one person lost five points (participant #4).
trimpb(kimdif)	Run the test with the default arguments (20% trimmed means, 2000 bootstrap replicates).

Here is the output:

```
$ci
[1]  4.857143 13.285714

$p.value
[1] 0.003
```

We can see that the 95% CI is [4.86, 13.29]. Again, this is good news as it tells us that the instruction on sarcasm had a result, and that result was at least about five points increase from pretest to posttest. Also, this bootstrapped CI is slightly smaller than the non-bootstrapped CI from the previous section, which was [−14.37, −3.85]. Bootstrapping and means trimming has helped us narrow down the interval where we can expect to find the true mean of the difference in the population, but it is still wide given that the test only contains 30 points.

Performing a Robust Paired Samples T-Test

1 First, the Wilcox library must be loaded into R and opened:

```
library(WRS)
```

2 If you want to test the hypothesis that the difference in means is zero (H_o: $\mu_D = 0$), the basic code for a trimmed means, percentile bootstrap test is:

```
trimpb(kimdif, tr=.2, alpha=.05, nboot=2000)
```

8.5.5 Effect Sizes for Paired Samples T-Tests

The method for calculating effect size for paired sample *t*-tests is different than that of independent samples tests, although researchers do not agree on exactly the same methods for calculating the effect size. Volker (2006) stated that for descriptive purposes in published research it is acceptable to use the same calculations as were used for the independent samples *t*-test. However, other researchers have suggested that the correlation between scores in the paired samples *t*-test should be taken into account (Morris & DeShon, 2002). The website www.cognitiveflexibility.org/effectsize/ lets you correct for correlation, and returns a Cohen's *d* of $d = -1.93$ for the pretest–posttest pairing of Kim's (2013) data, and $d = 1.15$ for the immediate posttest–delayed posttest pairing. What these numbers mean is that the difference between the pretest and posttest was equal to about twice the SD of the difference between the groups. This is quite a large effect size. The effect size is smaller for the immediate posttest–delayed posttest comparison, but is still over 1 SD in size, so it is rather large.

These calculations were based on this summary data:

	Mean	*SD*	*Correlation*
Pretest–posttest	7.44 – 16.56	5.25 – 2.96	−0.34
Posttest–delayed posttest	16.56 – 19.67	2.96 – 3.00	0.59

Because it is a choice, report what kind of standardizer you used to calculate the effect size. In the online calculator, it is the average of the two SDs, according to what the author says on the website.

8.5.6 Application Activities with Paired Samples T-Tests

1 French and O'Brien (2008) tested French Canadian students in Grades 4 and 5 to see whether scores on two measures of phonological memory would improve at the end of the five months of language study. Two phonological memory measures were used, one using English non-words (ENWR), the other using Arabic non-words (ANWR). Arabic was a language unknown to the children. Did the learners improve from time 1 to time 2 in either measure? Use the French and O'Brien grammar.sav file. First comment on the distribution of the data by using box plots; then report on the *t*-tests no matter whether distributions are normal or not. Report descriptive statistics, CIs and calculate effect sizes for the comparisons.

2 French and O'Brien (2008) also performed paired samples *t*-tests to see whether the participants in their study improved on receptive vocabulary (RVOCAB), productive vocabulary (PVOCAB) and grammar measures (GRAM). Maximum points were 60 on both vocabulary measures and 45 on the grammar measure. Perform three *t*-tests to investigate whether the schoolchildren made progress on these measures over the course of their English immersion. First comment on the distribution of the data by using box plots; then report on the *t*-tests no matter whether the distributions are normal or not. Report CIs and calculate effect sizes for the comparisons.

3 Yates (2003). You examined box plots from this data in Section 8.2.7. Compare the accent scores of the lab group before and after training, and also the mimicry group before and after training and calculate CIs for the comparisons. Be sure to look at effect sizes. How might you explain the results?
4 The Larson-Hall and Connell (2005) data (LarsonHall.Forgotten.sav) that you examined in Section 8.4.7 can be analyzed with a paired samples *t*-test. A paired samples *t*-test will answer the question of whether the participants performed the same way with their accent on words beginning with /r/ (AccentR) and /l/ (AccentL). Be sure to look at effect sizes. What are the results?
5 The Cole (1927) data that you examined in Section 8.4.7 can be analyzed with a paired samples *t*-test. Answer the question of whether students in each group performed better on the three types of French tests (vocabulary, grammar, reading) from Time 1 (February) to Time 2 (June). You should split the file into separate groups and answer this question for the different groups. For example, calculate whether scores increased from Time 1 to Time 2 just for the grammar translation group first, then calculate it for the composition group second. Try out different robust tests and see whether results change depending on the test used.

8.5.7 Reporting the Results of a Paired Samples T-Test

For a parametric *t*-test, you will want to make sure to report on the appropriateness of assuming normality and homogeneity of variances to do a parametric test. You will want to report a CI for the mean difference as well as the *N*, the mean and SDs of the groups, and effect sizes (with a mention of what standardizer you used) along with an interpretation of their magnitude. If you feel you must, you may also report a *t*-value and associated *p*-value, although these are unnecessary if the CI is present.

Here is how I would report the results of a paired samples *t*-test for the Kim (2013) pretest–posttest data, analyzed with a parametric paired samples *t*-test:

> Data for the pretest, posttest and delayed posttest showed some departures from normality in having a skewed distribution. Standard deviations showed that the scores at testing times did not have homogeneous variance, with the variance being less on the immediate and delayed posttests (pretest mean = 7.44, SD = 6.24, $N = 9$; posttest mean = 16.56, SD = 2.96, $N = 9$; delayed posttest mean = 19.67, SD = 3.0, $N = 9$). A parametric paired samples *t*-test found that a 95% CI for the difference between the pretest and posttest showed a statistical and important difference [−14.37, −3.85]. Because this CI does not go through zero, it means the difference between groups is statistical, and the size of the interval tells us that the actual mean difference could be as small as about 4 points, or as large as about 14 points. Because the interval is wide I cannot say precisely how much of an effect the sarcasm teaching had, but I can definitely say it made a difference, and possibly a very large difference. A Cohen's *d* effect size for this comparison was $d = 1.93$ (using the average of the two SDs as a standardizer), which meant that the difference between the pretest and posttest was equal to about twice the SD of the difference between the groups. This is a very large effect size and shows that the sarcasm SCOBAs were quite effective.

In reporting the results of a robust test, you will want to mention which robust method was used, the *N*, the mean for each group and a CI for the mean difference between the groups. It is not clear to me that you can calculate an effect size with trimmed means, so I have not. Here is an example of what you could say:

> I conducted a 20% trimmed means, percentile bootstrapped, paired samples *t*-test on the pretest–posttest data (pretest 20% trimmed mean = 6.86, posttest 20% trimmed mean = 16.57). There were nine participants in each group. The 95% CI was [4.86, 13.29], showing that there was at least a nearly 5-point improvement from pretest to posttest, and possibly an increase as large as 13 points. The 95% CI shows that the mean gain from pretest to posttest can be assumed, with 95% confidence, to lie within this interval, and so it is a real and large gain. However, the variability in the interval shows that we cannot be very confident of exactly where the real mean gain lies. With further testing this interval could be narrowed.

8.8 Summary of *T*-Tests

In this chapter we started out by noting that *t*-tests are used when you have exactly two mean scores to compare and your research question is whether the two groups those mean scores come from are different from each other (or whether the same group performed differently at different times or on different tests). One good way for visually examining the distribution of scores from two groups is to use a box plot. Box plots provide more information than bar graphs and can be a quick visual check on the assumptions of normality and homogeneity of variances that are necessary for using a parametric *t*-test.

In the independent samples *t*-test, scores from two different groups on the same measure are compared. We mainly relied on 95% CIs to give us the statistical information we were looking for: whether there was a statistical result, how large the effect was and to what extent it was practically important. Beyond CIs, I also showed how to calculate effect sizes, although these should be taken with a grain of salt because, as with all discrete-point values, they have CIs too and are not fixed numbers (see Section 9.4.9 for more information).

In the paired samples *t*-test, scores from the same group at two different times or on two related measures are compared. Paired *t*-tests take into account the violation of the assumption of independence to report on whether the two mean scores are considered to be different from one another.

One more topic is found online for one sample *t*-tests, which are used when you have measured only one group but want to compare that group's scores to another, externally devised standard. See the online version "One Sample *t*-tests".

Chapter 9

Looking for Group Differences with a One-Way Analysis of Variance

Effects of Planning Time

> Most of the time, when you get an amazing, counterintuitive result, it means you screwed up the experiment.
>
> Michael Wigler, quoted by Angier (2007, p. 206)

In the previous chapter we examined *t*-tests, which look for group differences when there are only two groups. Although it was not framed this way when talking about *t*-tests, essentially we had one variable that was independent and measured categorically (the group splitting factor) while we had another that was dependent and measured on an interval or continuous scale (the measurement we took from the groups). When we want to ask the same question of whether the groups come from the same or different populations but we have more than two groups, we will use a one-way analysis of variance (ANOVA). For example, in this chapter we will look at the question of whether groups who differed in the kind of time they got to plan and write an essay performed differently on an evaluation of that essay. In this case there is one dependent variable (DV), which is the evaluation of the essay, and one independent variable (IV), which is group membership. In Ellis and Yuan's study (2004) there were three different levels of planning/writing time, so we cannot use a *t*-test; we must use a one-way ANOVA.

Recent Examples of One-Way Analysis Of Variance in the Second Language Acquisition Literature

Ayoun (2014)

Ayoun gave two measures of proficiency to 34 L2 French learners: a scalar grammaticality judgment task and a preference/grammatically judgment task. On the basis of scores on these tests, the French learners were divided into three levels of proficiency—Intermediate-Mid, Intermediate-High and Advanced. Later, these participants completed a cloze test. Native speakers of English also completed this test. A one-way ANOVA asked whether these four groups (the three French learner groups and native speakers (NS) of English) performed differently on the cloze test. There was a main effect for the ANOVA and post-hoc tests found that the NS were different from the Intermediate-Mid and Intermediate-High learners, but not the Advanced learners of French. The Advanced learners were also statistically different from the Intermediate-Mid learners.

Dahlen and Caldwell-Harris (2013)

Dahlen and Caldwell-Harris examined the question of whether how language learners rehearse new vocabulary can affect how well they retain new vocabulary. Participants learned Turkish nouns in one of four different conditions: (1) vocal rehearsal where they could hear themselves speak (Vocal group); (2) vocal

(continued)

(continued)

rehearsal where their own auditory feedback was masked by white noise (White Noise Group); (3) subvocal rehearsal where they were not allowed to speak (Subvocal group); (4) and no rehearsal allowed (Articulatory Suppression). One facet of the analysis was looking at response times for a recognition task. The question was whether any of the four groups performed differently in reaction times from any of the other groups. A one-way ANOVA found a main effect for group, meaning that not all of the groups performed in the same way, and subsequent pairwise comparisons found that statistically, the Subvocal group and the Vocal group were different from each other. It turned out that the groups that rehearsed aloud (the Vocal group and the White Noise Group) had the longest reaction times, and the Subvocal group had the shortest reaction time, with the Articulatory Suppression group (no rehearsal allowed) in the middle as far as reaction time.

Reali (2014)

Reali provided evidence that usage-based models, where learners construct representations of abstract linguistic constituents on the basis of experience, are plausible accounts of the processing difficulty of nested grammatical structure. Reali assumed that frequency of occurrence predicts complexity judgments and reading time patterns. This study specifically looked at head noun phrases that are the object of the verb in the relative clause, called object relative clauses, such as "The reporter that the senator attacked admitted the error." When the head noun phrase is the subject of the embedded verb, these sentences are called subject relative clauses. An example sentence is "The reporter that attacked the senator admitted the error." Subject relative clauses have been shown to be easier to process than object relative clauses, but the question is why. Here Reali looked at the phenomenon in Spanish. A look at a Spanish corpus led Reali to predict, given a usage-based theory, that "pronominal object relative clauses should be easier to process when the embedded subject is a null pronoun and, if the pronoun is present, O(SV) clauses should be judged easier than O(VS) ones" (pp. 695–696). Thus, three types of sentences with object relative clauses were tested: (1) null embedded pronouns; (2) pronoun present in object–subject–verb (OSV) clauses; and (3) pronoun present in object–verb–subject (OVS) clauses. Thirty NS of Spanish completed a questionnaire in which they judged the complexity of the sentences and rated them on a 1–7 scale, where 1 = easy to understand and 7 = hard to understand. There were 12 sentences of interest and 34 filler sentences. The difficulty of the three different types of sentences was analyzed with a one-way ANOVA. This ANOVA found a main effect, and pairwise comparisons among the three conditions showed that the third condition (pronoun present in the OVS clause) was statistically rated more complex than the other two conditions. The best explanation for this result, Reali suggested, is the fact that null pronoun clauses are quite rare in object relative clauses, and when they are present, they occur more often with the OSV word order than with the OVS order.

Cuza and Frank (2015)

Cuza and Frank designed a study that compared the results of adult Spanish L2 speakers, Spanish heritage learners (those born in the USA who had heard Spanish spoken in their home since birth) and monolingual Spanish speakers from Cuba. The authors looked at double complementizer questions in Spanish, a grammatical form that does not exist in English. An example is "Ramón le dijo a Celina que dónde cenó anoche," translated as "Ramon asked Celina where she ate dinner last night." The Spanish structure for embedding wh-questions is much more complex than that for English, so the authors wondered how learners with different ages of exposure would perform on a number of tests designed to measure sensitivity to the semantic and syntactic constraints involved with this grammatical structure. One test was an aural sentence completion task where the participants heard the researcher read a sentence with the pertinent information, and then were given a prompt that they should complete. A one-way ANOVA with group as the independent variable found a main effect for group on scores on the sentence completion task. Post-hoc tests showed a statistical difference between L2 learners and Spanish NS but no statistical difference between the heritage speakers and Spanish NS.

9.1 Understanding the Analysis Of Variance Design

You might wonder why ANOVA is called an analysis of *variance*. Are we not looking to see whether the mean scores of the groups are different from one another? The fact is, the mathematics of ANOVA indeed compares the variances of groups; an ANOVA compares the variance *within* the group to the variance *between* the groups to see whether the differences between groups are "big enough" to say that the groups come from different populations. A graphical example may help illustrate this idea and make the process of ANOVA seem less mystical. (This example and the code to generate the figures are borrowed with permission from Crawley, 2002, p. 244.)

First, let us say we have two groups, A and B. Figure 9.1 plots the data from both group A and group B, and the horizontal line is the mean score for both groups taken together. The vertical lines from the mean to the points represent the variance, or error, between the mean and the actual points. We subtract this error from the mean, and square it, to get a sense of the magnitude of how much the actual points differ from our estimate of their middle point. This is called the **total sum of squares (SST)**, and is written mathematically as $SST = \Sigma\,(yi - \mu)^2$, where yi = each point and μ = the overall mean score. This measures the total variance, and this number is what is found in the "Total" row of an ANOVA table in SPSS. In R, the total is not given but if you add the output of the column labeled "SumSq" for the two lines "Group" and "Resid" together, you will get the SST.

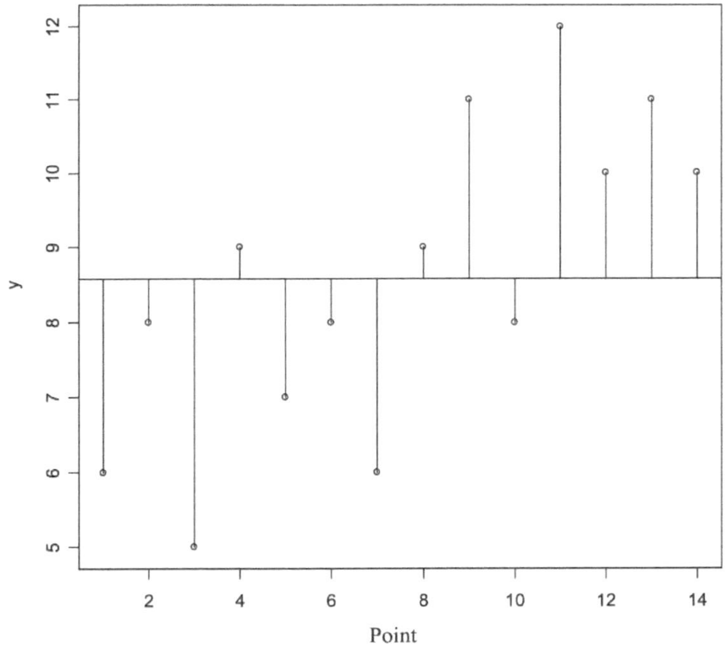

Figure 9.1 Total variance illustrated graphically (one total line for Groups A and B).

Next, we can divide the groups up and calculate a mean score for each group. Figure 9.2 shows that the mean for group B is larger than the mean for group A. Again, we calculate the difference between the mean inside each group (the horizontal line) and the actual fitted points and square the result, which becomes what is called the **error sum of squares (SSE)**: $SSE = \Sigma\,(yA - \mu A)^2 + \Sigma\,(yB - \mu B)^2$, where yA = each point in the A group and μA = the mean of group A, and yB = each point in the B group and μB = the mean of group B. This number represents the variance *within* the groups and shows the variability in scores due to the treatments. This number is found in the "Within" row of an

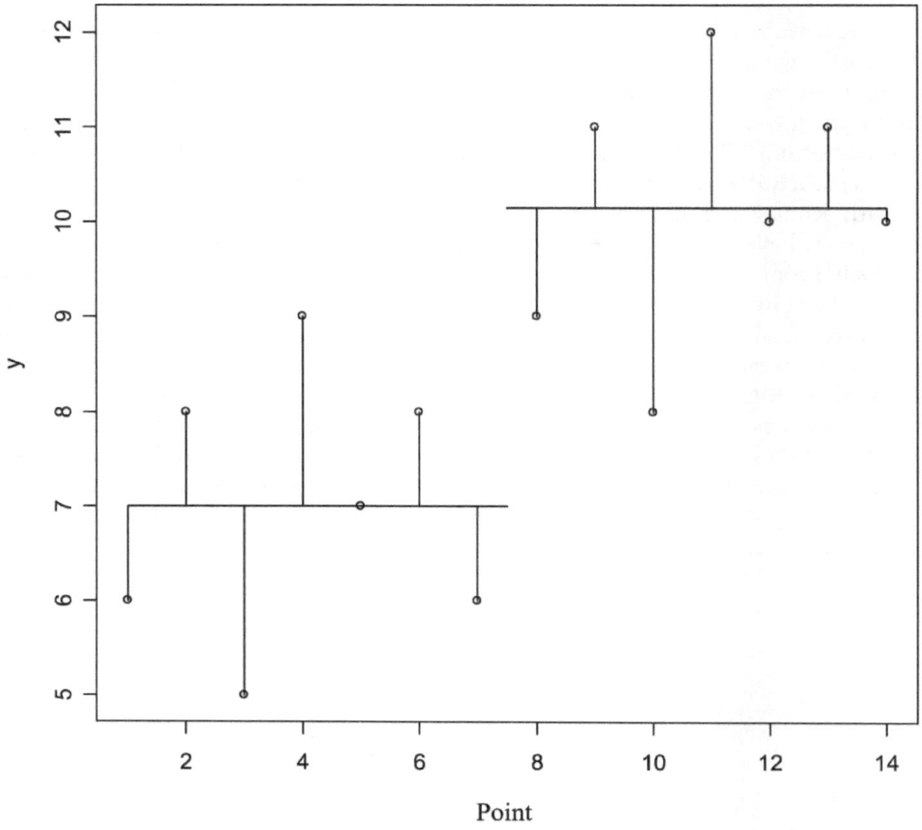

Figure 9.2 Variance *within* groups illustrated graphically (one line each for Group A and Group B).

ANOVA table in SPSS or the figure in the column "SumSq" with the line labeled "Resid" in the R output.

The value of the variation between groups, the part that is explained by your independent variable (something like "group"), is actually the SST minus the SSE. In other words, take the overall variance (SST), subtract from it the variance due to the differences within groups (SSE), and you have the treatment sum of squares, or the variance that is explained. This number is found on the "Between" row of an ANOVA table in SPSS or the figure in the column "SumSq" with the line labeled "Group" (or whatever your IV is called) in the R output.

If the means of the groups A and B were the same (which they are not in Figures 9.1 and 9.2), then the SST (the calculations illustrated in Figure 9.1) would be the same as the SSE (Figure 9.2). However, if the mean values are quite different, the SSE will be less than the SST because the separate group fits will be more accurate (and thus the difference between the mean and the points less), and the *F*-value will end up being large, which means we can reject the null hypothesis (H_0). Note that the actual ratio that gives the *F*-value is between the explained variance (the "Between-groups" line in the SPSS printout) and the unexplained variance within groups (SSE, the "Within-groups" line in the SPSS printout), illustrated in Figure 9.2. The total variance is used to make calculations about the explained variance, but is not used in calculating the *F*-ratio. Hopefully this explanation will help make sense of why we are most concerned about *variances* in ANOVA. Crawley claims that we can "make inferences about differences between means by looking at variances" (2002, p. 245).

A visual table you can play with, changing the variances and means to see the effects on *F*, can be found at www.psych.utah.edu/stat/introstats/anovaflash.html. Figure 9.3 shows two examples where I have manipulated the mean scores and the variances. In the picture on the left of Figure 9.3, the variance within groups is larger than the variance between groups, and the *F*-value is low, under 1. In the picture on the right, the mean scores are quite different from each other, and the variances are not too different, so that the variance between groups is much greater than the variance within groups, so the *F*-value is quite large, somewhere close to 3, so that the ANOVA results will be statistical.

9.2 The Topic of Chapter 9

The data set used in this chapter comes from Ellis and Yuan (2004), who examined the effect of planning on writing—would planning time help writers produce more fluent, accurate, or complex language on a writing instrument? The population investigated was Chinese foreign language learners of English. The dependent measure was a story, written according to visual story prompts, and the groups differed in how much planning time they received for their writing, how much time they had to write and whether they had a length requirement. The different levels in this independent variable were:

- no planning group: had 17 minutes to write and were asked to write at least 200 words;
- pre-task planning group: had 10 minutes to plan what they would write and 17 minutes to write, and were asked to produce at least 200 words;
- online planning group: had as long as they wanted to write and had no minimum word requirement

For the dependent measure, fluency, complexity and accuracy on the writing task were measured by means of seven different measures. This means that there were seven DVs in the study. A one-way ANOVA has only one DV and one IV, so Ellis and Yuan (2004) conducted a series of seven separate one-way ANOVAs. The box in Figure 9.4 represents one of the seven one-way ANOVAs.

The design box in Figure 9.4 shows that a one-way ANOVA has one DV, which will be continuous (interval-level), and one IV, which will be categorical. The IV will have at least three levels. If it

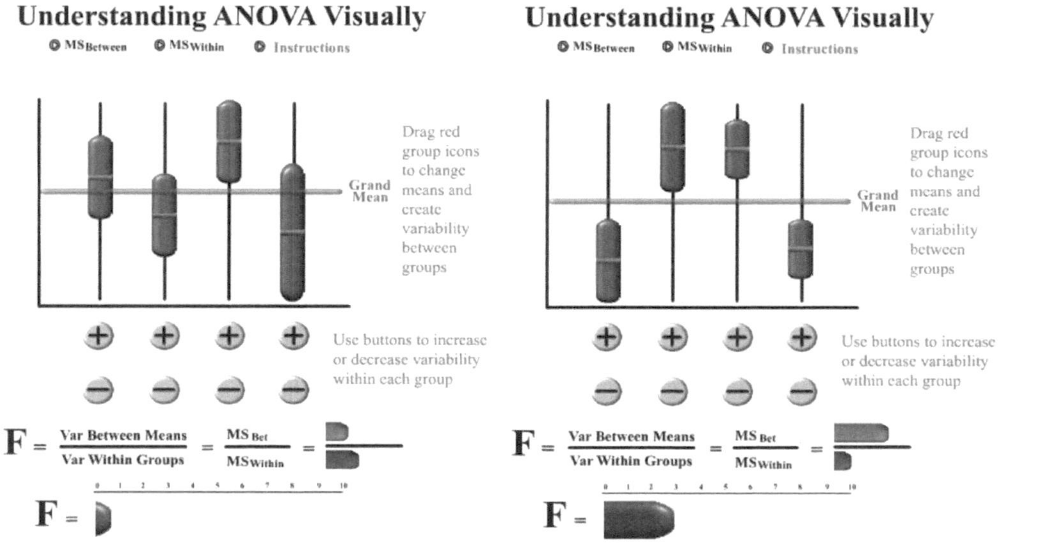

Figure 9.3 ANOVA variance between and within groups illustrated graphically from website (www.psych.utah.edu/stat/introstats/anovaflash.html).

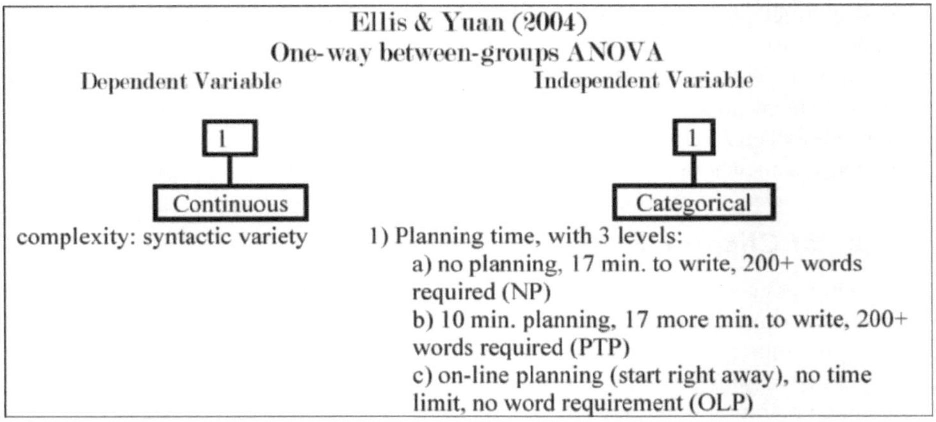

Figure 9.4 Design box for Ellis and Yuan one-way ANOVA.

only had two levels, we could analyze it using a *t*-test. If there is more than one IV, the test that will be needed is a factorial ANOVA, treated in the next chapter.

9.2.1 Numerical and Visual Inspection of the Data in this Chapter

To get a sense first of what is happening with the Ellis and Yuan (2004) data, let us take a look at a numerical summary of the DV of syntactic variety. Use the EllisYuan.sav file, and if you are using R, import it into R Commander as EllisYuan, open R Commander with library(Rcmdr)).

In SPSS, to get means and standard deviations (SDs) in a more compact form I split the data by Group (DATA > SPLIT FILE, then click on the radio button "Compare groups" and move the GROUP variable to the "Groups Based on" box) and then called for descriptive statistics using ANALYZE > DESCRIPTIVE STATISTICS > DESCRIPTIVES. I put SYNTAXVARIETY in the "Variable(s)" box and ran the analysis.

In R Commander, I went to STATISTICS > SUMMARIES > NUMERICAL SUMMARIES. I chose the variable of syntaxvariety, then opened the "Summarize by groups" button and chose group. The code for the summary is:

```
numSummary(EllisYuan["syntaxvariety"], groups=EllisYuan$group,statistics=c("mean","sd"))
```

Table 9.1 shows the means and SDs for each of Ellis and Yuan's three groups.
The group that received the planning time scored the highest on the amount of syntactic variety they included in their writing (the pre-task planning (PTP) group). The group that scored the lowest was the group with no planning (no-planning or NP group). Another thing we can note from the numerical summary is that there were the same number of participants in each group, and their variances are roughly equal.

Turning now to visual examination of the data, box plots would be good for examining whether the distribution of the data was normal and whether the variances looked similar. Section 8.2 had more

Table 9.1 Numerical Summary for Ellis and Yuan's (2004) SYNTAXVARIETY

	Mean	*Standard deviation*	*N*
No planning (NP)	16.2	4.1	14
Pre-task planning (PTP)	22.1	3.6	14
Online planning (OLP)	18.9	3.2	14

detail about how to understand box plots and create different kinds, so I will only briefly describe how I got box plots for these data.

To make the box plot in SPSS choose GRAPHS > LEGACY DIALOGS > BOXPLOT and then SIMPLE and "Summaries for groups of cases." I put SYNTAXVARIETY into the "Variable" box and GROUP into the "Category Axis" box. I found when I did this that I still had the data split and I got three different box plots, so I went back and told SPSS to analyze all groups together (DATA > SPLIT FILE, "Analyze all cases").

To make the box plot in R Commander, an easy way is to choose GRAPHS > BOXPLOT and then pick the variable of syntaxvariety. Click on the "Plot by groups" button and choose group, then run the graph. However, with a little more work I can make a box plot with the data points plotted on it using the ggplot2 package, and I use this code in the R Console to do so:

```
ggplot(data=EllisYuan,aes(x=group,y=syntaxvariety))+geom_boxplot(outlier.shape=NA)+
geom_jitter(position=position_jitter(width=.3, height=0))+labs(x="Group",y="Amount of syntax variety")
```

A box plot of the data in Figure 9.5 shows visually that none of the distributions is exactly normal; the NP group has an outlier (it is not labeled as such in the ggplot box plot, but it is the point at 25), and none of the groups has a perfectly symmetrical median or whiskers. However, the size of the box is approximately the same for all three groups, which is one indication that variances are approximately equal.

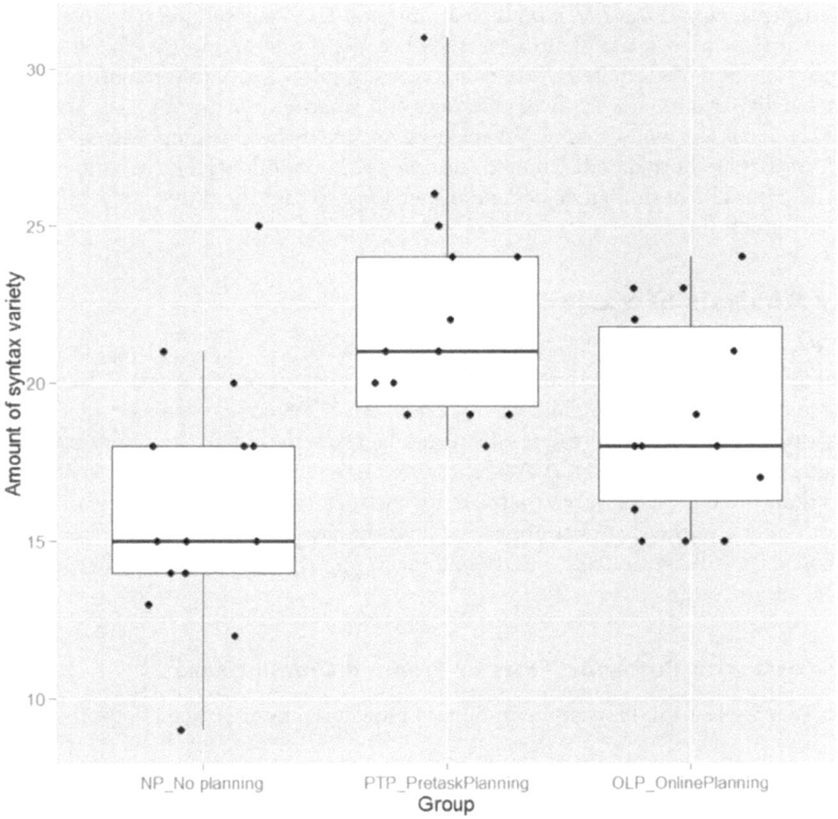

Figure 9.5 Box plot of SyntaxVariety from Ellis and Yuan (2004).

Table 9.2 Assumptions for a Parametric One-Way ANOVA

Meeting assumptions		*One-way ANOVA*
1. Normal distribution of data (looking at the data according to groups)	Required?	Yes
	How to test assumption?	Examine box plots, plot normal curve over histogram (see Chapter 3); use Q-Q plots to check for outliers
	What if assumption not met?	Use 20% trimmed means and/or bootstrap
2. Equal variances (looking at the data according to groups)	Required?	Yes
	How to test assumption?	Examine side-by-side box plots, look at summary statistics for variance (see Chapter 3); Howell (2002) notes that if sample sizes are unequal *and* variances are unequal it leads to an appreciable loss of robustness (pp. 340–341); use Levene's test for homogeneity.*
	What if assumption not met?	Use 20% trimmed means and/or bootstrap.

*Be careful in trusting the results of this test (see note under Table 8.3 for more information).

9.3 Assumptions for an Analysis of Variance

The four main assumptions for ANOVA are the same as those found for the *t*-test. Again, the first two (data should be independent and the DV should be an interval-level measurement) are requirements that need to be met at the time you are planning a study because there is no way to statistically examine or fix a research study that has violated these assumptions. Table 9.2 gives a summary of how to test assumptions for normality and homogeneity of variances and what to do if assumptions are not met.

As Howell (2002) notes, the logic of ANOVA makes sense given these assumptions. If we have two or more distributions that are normally distributed (not skewed) and if they all have similar variances, this means all of the groups have similar shapes and dispersions, so that the only question left to ask is whether their mean values differ.

9.4 One-Way Analysis of Variance

A one-way ANOVA asks whether the differences between mean scores of three groups or more are so great that we could not just ascribe the differences to chance fluctuations in scores. This question is exactly analogous to that of the *t*-test, and in fact a one-way ANOVA could be used in place of a *t*-test if there were only two mean scores, and the results would be the same. (The *t*-test statistic squared is equal to the *F*-value of the one-way ANOVA.) The difference between a one-way ANOVA and a *t*-test, of course, is that, since there are more than two mean scores, a statistical outcome on a one-way ANOVA does not really end the question of exactly how the groups differ. Because there are more than two mean scores, we still are not sure whether all mean scores are different or whether some are different but others are the same.

9.4.1 Omnibus Tests with Post-Hoc Tests or Planned Comparisons

In a one-way ANOVA we test the H_0 that any number of mean scores are equal:

$$H_0 = \mu 1 = \mu 2 = \mu 3 = \ldots = \mu k$$

If we reject this H_0, we still want to know which mean scores are different from others. Wilcox (2003) noted that there are two ways to test the means of more than two groups. One way is the traditional and popular way of conducting an overall (or *omnibus*) test to see whether the means of all the groups are equal (the H_0 shown above). If this test is statistical, then researchers generally go on to perform so-called post-hoc tests, which test all of the possible pairings of groups for statistical differences. This may seem equal to performing a series of *t*-tests, but post-hoc tests are different in that they control the **familywise error rate (FWER)**, the overall level of type I error in all tests of a related research question. If, instead of an ANOVA, a large number of *t*-tests were performed, the type I error rate of $\alpha = 0.05$ for each test would be compounded, and the overall FWER would be larger than $\alpha = 0.05$. Post-hoc tests employ different methods to reduce this FWER. The other way to test the mean is to use planned comparisons. In planned comparisons you do not conduct all of the possible tests of groups but instead focus on only a subset of groups.

Although an omnibus (overall) test followed by post-hoc tests is the traditional way of testing more than two groups, there is usually nothing to be gained by performing the omnibus test itself (Howell, 2002), as the researcher is most likely interested in the actual comparison between groups. In this case, it is claimed that performing an omnibus test (the initial test of the ANOVA) actually reduces the power to find differences between groups because an additional test is performed and has to be controlled for in order not to increase the FWER. Actually, when conducting one-way tests and post-hoc tests, SPSS does not adjust the post-hoc alpha value to take the omnibus test effect into account; that would have to be done by the author, something I have never actually seen done in the literature, so in practice this point may be moot.

The main reason to use planned comparisons is to increase the power you have to find statistical differences between groups. You will gain power if you have a large number of groups but you do not care about testing all possible comparisons. For example, if you had several groups who differed on their first language, and what you were interested in was how various groups differed from NS (but not among themselves), you could use planned comparisons to effectively increase your power. Do note, however, that the planning for such comparisons needs to be done before you conduct your statistical analysis. It should not be used to fish for a way to make your comparisons statistical! Both omnibus tests with post-hoc tests and comparisons without an overall test will be illustrated in this chapter.

9.4.2 Testing for Group Equivalence before an Experimental Procedure

Many researchers would like to show *before* experimental treatment is begun that the groups used in their studies are not different when they are compared on some proficiency measure, such as a Test of English as a Foreign Language (TOEFL). The goal is to show that any differences found after the experimental treatment can be attributed to the actual effects of the treatment and not to inherent differences between groups.

Although this kind of pretesting for group homogeneity or heterogeneity is a common practice in our literature, Rietveld and van Hout (2005) asserted that it does not make statistical sense and is pointless because it does not generalize to an entire population (p. 48, exercise #5 and answer on p. 235). Blackwelder (1982) noted that an observed *p*-value can only be used as "a measure of evidence against the null, not for it" (p. 346). However, the real problem with testing for group equivalence before an experimental procedure is that just because a statistical test does not find evidence to reject the null hypothesis does not mean that the groups are indeed equal. It could be that the groups are different but the test does not have enough power to find this difference (Clark-Carter, 2005). Indeed, in general the absence of evidence does not mean that there is evidence of absence (Kline, 2004). Possibly the best that can be said after using the conventional **null hypothesis significance testing (NHST)** method is that a lack of statistical difference between groups before experimental testing is "comforting" (Howell, 2002, p. 500). If we did see a statistical difference between groups before an experimental procedure, we would want to then use the pretest as a covariate to subtract its effect out of the equation.

There is in fact a way to test for equivalence of groups by using confidence intervals (CIs) that was outlined by Tryon (2001), and it is not very complicated. I suggest that anyone who wants to claim that their experimental groups are equivalent before an experimental treatment takes place use this method instead of fallaciously claiming that comparing the groups and getting a *p*-value higher than 0.05 means that the groups are equivalent. My thanks to Mike Clark (2014a, 2014b) for pointing me to this possibility.

Tryon suggested that we must calculate an "inferential CI" by taking the descriptive CI and reducing it by some factor E. For example, say that two groups took a 100-point test and the descriptive statistics for group A are mean = 75, SD = 3.2, *N* = 20, and that the calculated inferential 95% CI is [73.95, 76.06]. (I will show below how to calculate this, but for now do not worry about it.) Now for group B, mean = 76, SD = 2.4, *N* = 20, and the calculated inferential 95% CI is [75.21, 76.79]. If the inferential CIs do not overlap, we may say there is a statistical difference between groups. But in this case, clearly the CIs *do* overlap. Now, to determine that the groups are statistically equivalent, we need to first pick an amount of difference that we are willing to accept as inconsequential. For example, we may decide that 3 points of difference is an inconsequential amount in the 100-point test our students took. Next, we need to look at the range of the CIs, going from the lowest point to the highest point, meaning we now have a range of [73.95, 76.79], or 2.84 points. This amount is less than three points, so we may conclude that the groups are statistically equivalent. On the other hand, say that we had previously decided that only two points of difference was all we could accept to say that the groups were equivalent. (This choice must be determined by the researcher and is not statistically determined.) In that case, the result would be indeterminate. We could neither say that the two groups were statistically equivalent nor could we say they were statistically different. Tryon (2001) suggested that this is "not evidence for or against anything; it is not evidence of any kind" (p. 381) and that further evidence may either shed more light on the issue or the indeterminacy may persist. However, he thinks that accepting a verdict of "indeterminate" is less harsh than accepting the H_0.

An important step in applying Tryon's (2001) method is calculating the inferential 95% CI. The formula Tryon gives for calculating the conventional CI for independent groups using descriptive data is mean score ± $t.\text{value}_{\text{reduced by E}}$(standard error). Next, a factor by which the *t*-value should be reduced is put forward (he calls it E), which is equation 3 in Tryon (2001), and uses the standard errors (SEs) of the groups like this:

$$t_{95}E = \frac{\sqrt{S_{Y_1}^2 + S_{Y_2}^2}}{S_{Y_1}^2 + S_{Y_2}^2}$$

Here S_{Y1} is the SE of the first group and S_{Y2} is the SE of the second group. (Remember from Section 3.1.2 that the SE is the SD of the sampling distribution of the sample mean.) Tryon says that the least the E factor could be in an independent groups design where the SEs are equal, is E = 0.7071, so if you do not want to bother with any calculations you could just use that number, but the number you will get by doing your own calculations will probably be higher.

To show you how this works with independent groups, compare two new groups, group C (M = 68.0, SD = 12.0, *N* = 20, df = 19, *t*(df) = 2.09, SE = 2.6920) and group D (M = 75.0, SD = 3.2, *N* = 20, df = 19, *t*(df) = 2.09, SE = 0.7054). (These data are taken from table 1 in Tryon, 2001.) The *t*-value is 2.09, which we will reduce by factor E. In this case we decide not to worry about calculating E and just choose the minimum number since we expect these groups to be different to start with, so the appropriate *t*-value is 2.09(0.7071) = 1.4778. Next, we calculate the inferential CI for group C using the following formula: mean score ± $t.\text{value}_{\text{reduced by E}}$(standard error). This results in: 68 ± 1.4778(2.6920) = 68 ± 3.9782 = [64.02, 71.98]. Now, we calculate the inferential CI for group D: 75 ± 1.4778(0.7054) = 75 ± 1.0424 = [73.96, 76.04]. For these two groups the inferential CIs do not overlap, so we may say that the groups are statistically different.

For two dependent means (i.e. two means produced by the same participants, such as the pretest and posttest scores on a test, or scores on related tests taken by the same participants), the calculation of the inferential CIs is the same: mean score ± $t.\text{value}_{\text{reduced by E}}$(standard error). However, the calculation of E is different and takes the relationship between the variables into account. The formula for E for two dependent means, given in equation 5 in Tryon (2001), is:

$$t_{95}E = \frac{\sqrt{S_{Y_1}^2 + S_{Y_2}^2 - 2r_{12}S_{Y_1}S_{Y_2}}}{S_{Y_1}^2 + S_{Y_2}^2}$$

Here again S_{Y1} is the SE of the first group and S_{Y2} is the SE of the second group, and then r_{12} is the correlation between the two groups. Take now data from two new groups, group E (M = 50.0, SD = 5.3, N = 20, df = 19, t(df) = 2.0930, SE = 1.1916) and group F (M = 54.0, SD = 5.6, N = 20, df = 19, t(df) = 2.0930, SE = 1.2552) (this data taken from table 2 in Tryon, 2001), and stipulate that the correlation between the two data sets is 0.521. First we will calculate E:

$$t_{95}E = \frac{\sqrt{(1.1916)^2 + (1.2552)^2 - 2(.521)(1.1916)(1.2552)}}{(1.1916)^2 + (1.2552)^2}$$

which is 0.4002. Now the t-value, reduced by E, equals (0.4002)(2.0930) = 0.8376. Now we can calculate the inferential CI for group E: 50 ± 0.8376(1.1916) = [49.00, 51.00]. For group F, the inferential CI is 54 ± 1.0254(1.2552) = [52.95, 55.05]. Again, we see that the CIs do not overlap so we must say these groups are statistically different.

For more detailed information about how to correctly calculate an E factor when making multiple comparisons, consult Tryon (2001).

9.4.3 Performing an Omnibus One-Way Analysis of Variance Test in SPSS with Subsequent Post-Hoc Tests

There are two ways to perform a one-way ANOVA in SPSS. Both use the ANALYZE drop-down menu, but one uses the COMPARE MEANS > ONE-WAY ANOVA and the other uses the GENERAL LINEAR MODEL (GLM) > UNIVARIATE choice. One difference is that the GLM procedure offers the chance to specify IVs as **random** or **fixed**. (Just briefly, this distinction has to do with whether the levels cover all possible divisions; more will be said on this topic in Chapter 10.) Since the GLM approach will be needed for two-way and higher ANOVAs and will be shown in Chapter 10, in this chapter I illustrate the use of the COMPARE MEANS > ONE-WAY ANOVA menu. Be aware, though, that you could equally well use the univariate method for a one-way ANOVA.

I will illustrate how to perform a one-way ANOVA using Ellis and Yuan's (2004) variable of syntax variety, which was explored graphically at the beginning of this chapter. The research question we are interested in is whether the groups with differing amounts of planning time are statistically different in the amount of syntactic variety they produce. The IV is the experimental group. To conduct a one-way ANOVA in SPSS, open ANALYZE > COMPARE MEANS > ONE-WAY ANOVA. Put your DV in the "Dependent List" box and your IV in the "Factor" box as shown in Figure 9.6.

You should also click on some of the other buttons on the one-way ANOVA dialog box. In the POST-HOC area you can choose which post-hoc tests to use. You would want to use a post-hoc test because you have more than two groups, so if you have a main effect of the ANOVA, the post-hoc tests will help you pinpoint which groups are different from the others. However, if we are using the "new statistics" approach, the CIs are what we are interested in, not the p-values, in which case the choices in the POST-HOC button are really moot. Thus, it is up to you to decide if you want to choose any post-hoc tests at all or not.

If you are still using the "old statistics" approach, here are my recommendations for which post-hoc tests to choose (shown in Figure 9.7). If you want more detail on other post-hoc tests that are available to you, I recommend Maxwell and Delaney (2004), who discuss the choice of post-hoc tests in quite some detail.

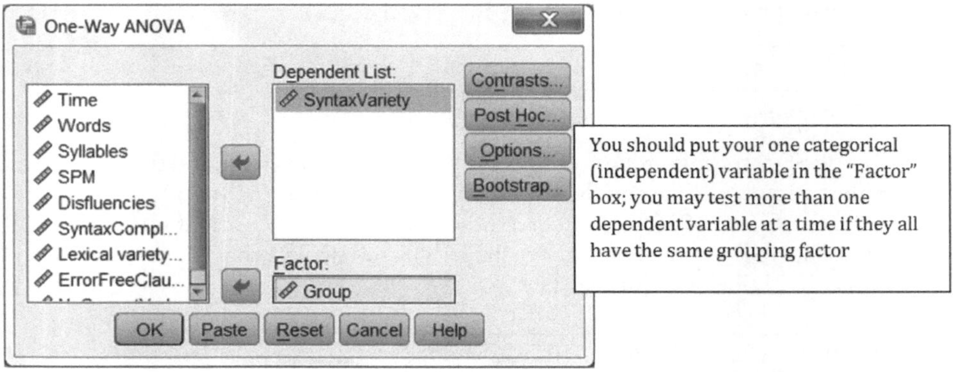

Figure 9.6 Opening a one-way ANOVA dialog box in SPSS.

- If you are making three or fewer comparisons, choose the least significant difference (LSD) post-hoc and do not adjust the means (Howell, 2002).
- If you are making more than three comparisons and cannot be bothered to go to R to use the false discovery rate (FDR) adjustment, choose Tukey's post-hoc test (Howell, 2002; Maxwell & Delaney, 2004).
- If you are making more than three comparisons and want the most power to find differences between your groups, choose the LSD post-hoc test to get unadjusted *p*-values, then go to R to use Benjamini and Hochberg's FDR adjustment (Maxwell & Delaney, 2004). This is discussed in more detail in Section 9.4.6.
- If variances are not equal, use the Games–Howell post-hoc test (Howell, 2002; Maxwell & Delaney, 2004).

For the Options button, click on the boxes I have shown in Figure 9.8, which include "Descriptives" to get descriptive statistics, and "Homogeneity of variance test" to get Levene's test for homogeneity of variances. In the Bootstrap section, check the "Perform bootstrapping" box, change the number of samples to 10,000 (Chernick, 2007) and choose the "Bias corrected accelerated (BCa)" CIs.

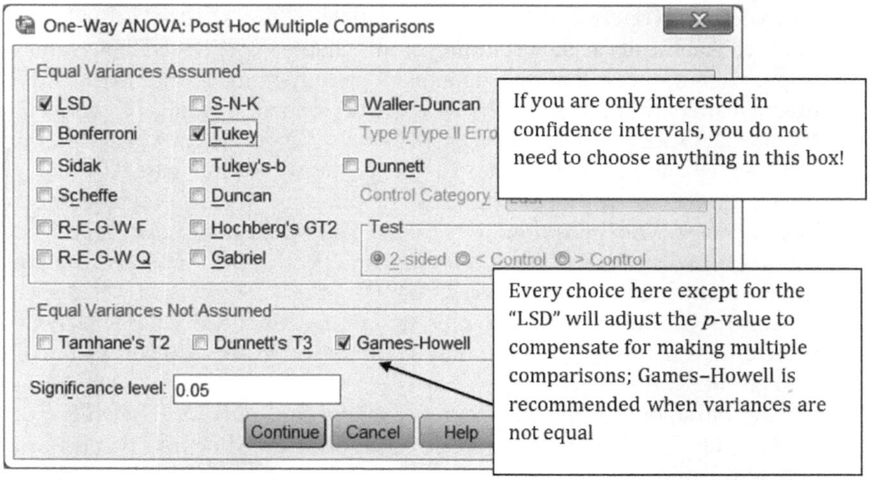

Figure 9.7 Post-hoc comparisons for a one-way ANOVA in SPSS.

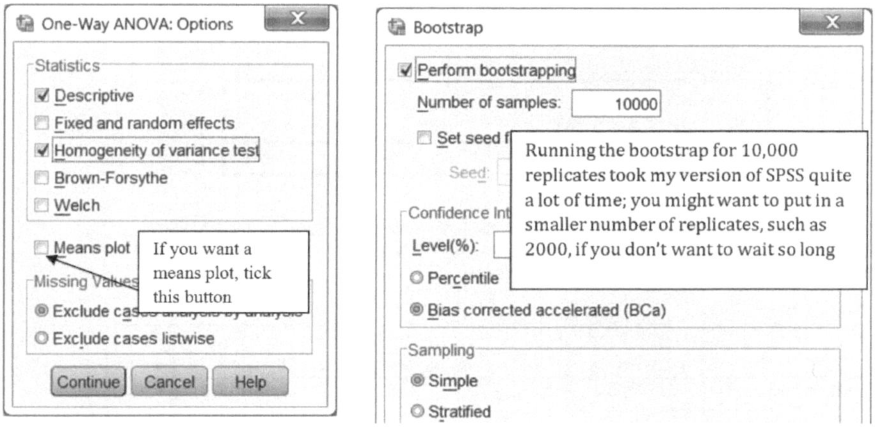

Figure 9.8 Options and Bootstrap for a one-way ANOVA in SPSS.

After you have selected all of these choices, you can run the ANOVA. The first part of the output you will see, after a box about bootstrap specifications, will be the descriptive statistics for your group, shown in Table 9.3. (I have shown this table without the bootstrapped CIs because we will not use the bootstrap for the descriptive statistics and also to make a more compact box visually.) Check this box, especially the sample size in the first column, to make sure all the participants you expected were included. Notice that the Ellis and Yuan (2004) data has equal numbers of participants in each group, which is nice to have and to be preferred if you can achieve it.

The next piece of output, shown in Table 9.4, is the test for homogeneity of variances. I have included this as one more way of checking on the assumption that we have equal variances, but there is controversy in the literature about whether such formal tests have enough power to test their own assumptions (Wilcox, 2003). More informal ways of testing equal variances are equally helpful, such as looking at box plots and numerical summaries. While it is good to understand the shape of your data and know whether your data are normally distributed and have equal variances, robust measures such as the bootstrap can act as a measure of protection against violations of these assumptions. For the Ellis and Yuan data, the Levene's test does not contradict the assumption of equal variances that we already gained from looking at the box plots in Figure 9.5, since, for the Levene's test, a significance level above 0.05 means that you do not reject the hypothesis that the groups have equal variances.

The next part of the output is the omnibus ANOVA test, shown in Table 9.5. For the variable of SyntaxVariety, the omnibus ANOVA shows a statistical difference between groups. To report this you will note the value of the *F*-test (9.05), the degrees of freedom (df) between groups (2) and within groups (39), and the *p*-value ($p = 0.001$). Remember, the *p*-value does *not* mean that there is, for this case, a 0.1% chance that the result happened by chance; rather, it means that there is less than a

Table 9.3 Output from the One-Way ANOVA: Descriptives

Descriptives

SyntaxVariety

	N	Mean	Std. Deviation	Std. Error	95% Confidence Interval for Mean: Lower Bound	95% Confidence Interval for Mean: Upper Bound	Minimum	Maximum
NP_No planning	14	16.21	4.098	1.095	13.85	18.58	9	25
PTP_PretaskPlanning	14	22.07	3.583	.958	20.00	24.14	18	31
OLP_OnlinePlanning	14	18.86	3.207	.857	17.01	20.71	15	24
Total	42	19.05	4.305	.664	17.71	20.39	9	31

Table 9.4 Output from the One-Way ANOVA: Levene's Test for Homogeneity of Variances

SyntaxVariety

Levene Statistic	df1	df2	Sig.
.290	2	39	.750

Table 9.5 Output from the One-Way ANOVA: Omnibus One-Way ANOVA

ANOVA

SyntaxVariety

	Sum of Squares	df	Mean Square	F	Sig.
Between Groups	240.905	2	120.452	9.051	.001
Within Groups	519.000	39	13.308		
Total	759.905	41			

1 in 1000 chance you would find a value more extreme than the observed one if H_0 were true. Notice that we do not get a CI for this result. Instead, the CIs are found in the post-hoc comparisons between groups that we have called for.

Tip: When reporting the results of main effects from an ANOVA, you need to report two numbers for degrees of freedom. The first is the degrees of freedom for your independent variable (such as "Group" or "Gender"), which is shown as the "Between groups" row for a one-way ANOVA. The second is the degrees of freedom of the error, which is listed as the "Within groups" row for a one-way ANOVA. Do not get confused and report the "Total" degrees of freedom for this second number. For example, for the output in Table 9.5 you could say: "The main effect of group was statistical, $F_{2,39} = 9.05$, $p = .001$."

Technically, if your omnibus ANOVA is not statistical then you should stop your analysis and not continue with post-hoc tests. Since you have called for post-hoc tests before seeing the omnibus test, however, SPSS will provide them. Also, since we are using the "new statistics" and looking at CIs, we will still be interested to see what the CIs are for the comparisons between groups, even if the omnibus ANOVA is not statistical, especially as we were not able to look at a CI for the omnibus result.

If you called for post-hoc tests, the next piece of the output ("Post-Hoc Tests: Multiple Comparisons") contains the results of the requested post-hoc comparisons, but not the bootstrapped versions of these comparisons. Go to the next piece of output, shown in Table 9.6, to see the bootstrapped CIs of the

Table 9.6 Output from the One-Way ANOVA: Bootstrap for Multiple Comparisons

Bootstrap for Multiple Comparisons

Dependent Variable: SyntaxVariety

			Mean Difference (I-J)	Bootstrap[a]			
						BCa 95% Confidence Interval	
	(I) Group	(J) Group		Bias	Std. Error	Lower	Upper
Tukey HSD	NP_No planning	PTP_PretaskPlanning	-5.857	-.001	1.456	-8.643	-3.122
		OLP_OnlinePlanning	-2.643	.008	1.374	-5.308	.058
	PTP_PretaskPlanning	NP_No planning	5.857	.001	1.456	2.941	8.872
		OLP_OnlinePlanning	3.214	.010	1.272	.907	5.729
	OLP_OnlinePlanning	NP_No planning	2.643	-.008	1.374	-.150	5.387
		PTP_PretaskPlanning	-3.214	-.010	1.272	-5.917	-.748

comparisons between groups. If you called for post-hoc tests as shown in Figure 9.7 there will be three different tests shown in the output (the Tukey's (HSD) post-hoc, the LSD post-hoc and the Games–Howell post-hoc) but they all have exactly the same results. This is not true for the CIs in the previous piece of output, the parametric results in "Post-Hoc Tests: Multiple comparisons," but apparently for the bootstrap no adjustment takes place so here I am only showing the top part of the output.

Since there were three groups, three unique comparisons are made (NP vs. PTP, NP vs. unpressured online planning (OLP) and PTP vs. OLP). We see that the difference in mean scores between the NP and PTP group could be as low as three points or as high as almost nine points (95% BCa bootstrapped CI [−3.12, −8.64]). On a test with no maximum score but mean scores between 16 and 22 points, even 3 points of difference seems like a substantial amount, and 9 points would be quite remarkable! In other words, the effect of the difference between these two methods seems important (and descriptive statistics tell us that the PTP group had higher scores than the NP group), although the CI is wider than we might like it to be. However, the difference between NP and OLP is not statistical (95% BCa bootstrapped CI [−5.31, 0.06]). Lastly, the comparison between PTP and OLP groups shows that there is a real difference, but it may be small (95% BCa bootstrapped CI [0.91, 5.7]), as low as about one point of difference. The effect of this difference is not so large as the difference between the NP and PTP groups.

If you want to stick with the "old statistics" and look at the results in the "Post-Hoc Tests: Multiple comparisons" output, you can see that choice of post-hoc test can matter. Table 9.7 shows comparisons for the Tukey's HSD post-hoc and the LSD post-hoc (which has no adjustment for multiple comparisons). Table 9.7 shows that, whether looking at *p*-values or CIs, for the Tukey's HSD post-hoc test, there is a statistical difference between the NP and PTP groups (the significance level is shown as 0.000, but because the difference is never really zero we would say that $p < 0.0005$), but not for the NP vs. OLP group ($p = 0.15$) or the PTP vs. NP group ($p = 0.06$). The results are different for the LSD test, reflecting more power to find differences. The LSD post-hoc test finds statistical differences for the PTP vs. OLP group ($p = 0.025$) and the CI does not go through zero. This example shows us how silly it is to look only at *p*-values, however, because in the Tukey's HSD post-hoc test, for the PTP vs. NP group the CI is [−0.14, 6.57], while in the LSD post-hoc test, the same CI is [0.43, 6.00]. These 95% CIs are nearly the same range, but the Tukey's HSD test just barely goes through zero. Instead of looking at a black-and-white "accept-or-reject" decision of NHST, it is better to report CIs and note that the true effect could be very small and close to zero.

Table 9.7 Output from the One-Way ANOVA: Post-Hoc Tests

Multiple Comparisons

Dependent Variable: SyntaxVariety

	(I) Group	(J) Group	Mean Difference (I-J)	Std. Error	Sig.	95% Confidence Interval Lower Bound	Upper Bound
Tukey HSD	NP_No planning	PTP_PretaskPlanning	-5.857*	1.379	.000	-9.22	-2.50
		OLP_OnlinePlanning	-2.643	1.379	.147	-6.00	.72
	PTP_PretaskPlanning	NP_No planning	5.857*	1.379	.000	2.50	9.22
		OLP_OnlinePlanning	3.214	1.379	.063	-.14	6.57
	OLP_OnlinePlanning	NP_No planning	2.643	1.379	.147	-.72	6.00
		PTP_PretaskPlanning	-3.214	1.379	.063	-6.57	.14
LSD	NP_No planning	PTP_PretaskPlanning	-5.857*	1.379	.000	-8.65	-3.07
		OLP_OnlinePlanning	-2.643	1.379	.063	-5.43	.15
	PTP_PretaskPlanning	NP_No planning	5.857*	1.379	.000	3.07	8.65
		OLP_OnlinePlanning	3.214*	1.379	.025	.43	6.00
	OLP_OnlinePlanning	NP_No planning	2.643	1.379	.063	-.15	5.43
		PTP_PretaskPlanning	-3.214*	1.379	.025	-6.00	-.43

Performing a One-Way Analysis of Variance

1 ANALYZE > COMPARE MEANS > ONE-WAY ANOVA (or use ANALYZE > GENERAL LINEAR MODEL (GLM) > UNIVARIATE; this method is explained in more detail in Section 10.5.1).
2 Put your DV(s) into the "Dependent List." (Move more than one variable if you are doing multiple one-way ANOVAs at the same time.) Put your independent (group or splitting variable) into the "Factor" box.
3 Click on the OPTIONS button and tick "Descriptive" and "Homogeneity of variances test." Open the Bootstrap button and check the "Perform bootstrapping" box, change the number of samples to 10,000 (or possibly less if you do not have much time to wait), and change the "Confidence Intervals" to BCa. Click on Continue then on OK and run the test.
4 If you are using the "old statistics" and *p*-values, open the Post Hoc button and choose an appropriate post-hoc test.

9.4.4 Performing an Omnibus One-Way Analysis of Variance in R with Subsequent Post-Hoc Tests

I will illustrate how to perform a one-way ANOVA using Ellis and Yuan's (2004) variable of syntax variety, which was explored graphically at the beginning of this chapter. The research question we are interested in is whether the groups with differing amounts of planning time are statistically different in the amount of syntactic variety they produce. The IV is the experimental group. To answer the research question using R Commander, pull down the menu sequence STATISTICS > MEANS > ONE-WAY ANOVA, as shown in Figure 9.9. Pick **group** for the "Groups" box and **syntaxvariety** for the "Response Variable." Tick the "Pairwise comparisons of means" box. Click on OK.

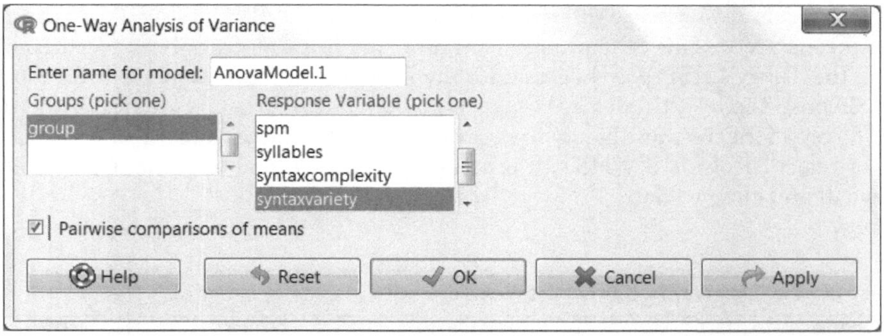

Figure 9.9 Opening a one-way ANOVA dialog box in R Commander.

Although the dialog box is simple, the output produced by this command is quite extensive! The first piece of information returned is the omnibus *F*-test.

```
            Df Sum Sq Mean Sq F value    Pr(>F)
Group        2  240.9 120.452  9.0513 0.0005901 ***
Residuals   39  519.0  13.308
```

This output shows that there is a statistical omnibus effect, so there is some difference between the groups, with $F_{2,39} = 9.05$ and $p = 0.0006$. When reporting the results of main effects from an ANOVA, you need to report two numbers for the df. The first is the df for your IV or hypothesis (such as "Group" or "Gender"), which is called in SPSS the "Between groups" row, and which is $df_{hyp} = 2$ here. The second is the df of the error, which is listed as the "Within groups" row in SPSS, and is called "Residuals" here. It is $df_{err} = 39$.

Note that we get a *p*-value for the omnibus result of the one-way ANOVA, not a CI. To report the result of the omnibus ANOVA, you will apparently need to report a *p*-value. Even though the *p*-value is small ($p = 0.0006$), remember that this does not mean that there is a 6 in 10,000 chance that the result happened by chance. What it really means is that *if* H_0 were true (that all the groups have equal means), the probability that you would get this particular result is very small. So we reject H_0 that the groups are all the same.

Technically, if your omnibus ANOVA is not statistical then you should stop your analysis and not continue with post-hoc tests. Since you have called for post-hoc tests before seeing the omnibus test, however, R Commander will provide them. Also, since we are using the "new statistics" and looking at CIs, we will still be interested to see what the CIs are for the comparisons between groups, even if the omnibus ANOVA is not statistical, especially as we were not able to look at a CI for the omnibus result.

The next pieces of output give vital descriptive statistics for the groups—means, SDs and the counts (*N*). Notice that the Ellis and Yuan (2004) data has equal numbers of participants in each group, which is nice to have and to be preferred if you can achieve it.

```
                         mean       sd  n
NP_No planning       16.21429 4.098378 14
PTP_PretaskPlanning 22.07143 3.583387 14
OLP_OnlinePlanning   18.85714 3.207135 14
```

We see from the means that the group who got the most pre-task planning (PTP) time produced the most syntactic variety, on average (22.07).

The next piece of output performs the post-hoc tests to find out exactly which of the groups are different from the others. By default, Tukey's post-hoc tests are used. When analyzing the syntax of this command, below, we will see ways to call for other post-hoc tests, but if we are focused on the "new statistics," we are not particularly interested in this part of the output since it does not contain CIs. If you are interested in the "old statistics" results, I will discuss what choices I recommend for post-hoc tests later in this section in the syntax notes.

Moving on to the next part of the output, we have reached the output that contains the CIs for the post-hoc tests.

```
> confint(.Pairs) # confidence intervals

         Simultaneous Confidence Intervals

Multiple Comparisons of Means: Tukey Contrasts


Fit: aov(formula = syntaxvariety ~ group, data = EllisYuan)

Quantile = 2.4366
95% family-wise confidence level


Linear Hypotheses:
                                             Estimate lwr     upr
PTP_PretaskPlanning - NP_No planning == 0     5.8571   2.4976  9.2167
OLP_OnlinePlanning - NP_No planning == 0      2.6429  -0.7167  6.0024
OLP_OnlinePlanning - PTP_PretaskPlanning == 0 -3.2143  -6.5738  0.1453
```

Since there were three groups, three unique comparisons are made (NP vs. PTP, NP vs. OLP and PTP vs. OLP). We see that the difference in mean scores between the NP and PTP group could be as low as two and a half points or as high as more than nine points (95% BCa bootstrapped CI [2.50, 9.22]). On a test with no maximum score but mean scores between 16 and 22 points, even 2.5 points of difference seems like a substantial amount, and 9 points would be quite remarkable! In other words, the effect of the difference between these two methods seems important (and descriptive statistics tell us that the PTP group had higher scores than the no planning group), although the CI is wider than we might like it to be. However, the difference between NP and OLP is not statistical (95% BCa bootstrapped CI [−0.72, 6.00]).

Lastly, the comparison between PTP and OLP is not statistical (95% BCa bootstrapped CI [−6.57, 0.14]. We will see later that we can massage this number to make it "statistical," that is, not pass through zero, by not applying any correction for multiple comparisons. (The Tukey's post-hoc test used here corrects the numbers to adjust for the fact that multiple comparisons were made.) However, even if the CI does not pass through zero, we see that the effect of this comparison produces a CI range that has a smaller effect than the difference between NP and PTP, and could be very close to nothing.

The last part of the output from R Commander produces a graphic that plots these three CIs for the mean difference between groups, which shows graphically what we find from the numerical output above. (I have not shown this because I will show you a better graphic later in the chapter.)

The R code for performing a one-way ANOVA is actually the same type of syntax that is used for performing regression analysis, except that we used the lm( ) command for regression analysis in the Chapter 7 while we use the aov( ) command in this chapter. ANOVA is simply a special form of the linear regression model and this is reflected in the syntax that R uses to perform the one-way ANOVA. (Miles & Shevlin, 2001, is a fairly accessible book that explains how regression analysis and ANOVA are related.) This is made explicit in the code that R Commander uses for the omnibus ANOVA:

```
AnovaModel.1 <- aov(syntaxvariety ~ group, data=EllisYuan)
```

aov( )	The aov( ) command creates an analysis of variance model. It actually uses the lm( ) command seen in Chapter 7, but differs in that the output from the summary( ) and print( ) commands is more suitable for an ANOVA.
AnovaModel.1 <- aov( )	Put the aov model into an object which R Commander labeled AnovaModel.1 automatically. (We can change this name, of course.)
aov(syntaxvariety ~ group)	The model says that the scores on the syntactic variety variable (syntaxvariety) are modeled as a function of group.
data=EllisYuan	Specifies which data set should be used.

So the first command is to create a regression model (an ANOVA model) and put it into an object. But to see the ANOVA table and find the omnibus *F*-test, then, one will need to call for a summary of the regression model. Thus, this is the next step of the syntax that R Commander uses:

```
summary(AnovaModel.1)
```

This command gave the results of the omnibus one-way ANOVA, the first piece of output that we saw from R Commander. The last part of the R Commander call is this:

```
with(EllisYuan, numSummary(syntaxvariety, groups=group, statistics=c("mean", "sd")))
local({
 .Pairs <- glht(AnovaModel.5, linfct = mcp(group = "Tukey"))
 print(summary(.Pairs)) #pairwise tests
 print(confint(.Pairs)) #confidence intervals
 print(cld(.Pairs)) #compact letter display
 old.oma <- par(oma=c(0,5,0,0))
 plot(confint(.Pairs))
 par(old.oma)
})
```

The following table explains the output of each of the following lines that R Commander uses:

with(EllisYuan, . . .)	The with( ) command is a generic command that is used to simplify calls to functions and in this case acts like attach( ) so the data set name does not have to be specified in the following functions
numSummary(syntaxvariety , groups= group, statistics=c("mean", "sd"))	Gives descriptive statistics for the data, split by group; other possible descriptive statistics that could be called for are "IQR" (interquartile range), "quantiles," "cv" (coefficient of variation, equal to sd/mean), "skewness" or "kurtosis."
local({	This call is similar to with( ) in that it is generic, and it evaluates arguments in the environment specified by the envir argument. In this case, it makes it possible to not worry about opening up the multcomp package which the glht( ) command comes from.
.Pairs <- glht(AnovaModel.1, linfct = mcp(group = "Tukey"))	To call post-hoc tests, R Commander uses the glht( ) command from the multcomp package. This command sets up multiple comparisons, but it provides more detail if the result is placed into an object (.Pairs) and then a summary and CIs can be called for. For more detailed analysis of this command, see below
print(summary(.Pairs)) # pairwise tests	The summary( ) command will return *t*-values and *p*-values for the pairwise comparisons (since I am using the "new statistics" I did not show this output), and the print( ) commands prints it out.
print(confint(.Pairs)) # confidence intervals	The confint() command will return CIs, as shown in the R Commander output previously for the pairwise comparisons
print(cld(.Pairs))	This gives a compact letter display
old.oma <- par(oma=c(0,5,0,0)) plot(confint(.Pairs)) par(old.oma)	These commands call for a graphic, but I will provide a better one later on, so they are not very important.

I want to explain the **glht( )** command from the **multcomp** package listed above in more detail:

```
.Pairs <- glht(AnovaModel.1, linfct = mcp(group = "Tukey"))
```

glht(AnovaModel.1)	The general linear hypothesis test (glht) needs a model, and we specified this previously.
linfct=	Specifies which linear hypothesis should be tested.
mcp	Multiple comparisons are returned by using this argument.
(group="Tukey")	Tells mcp to use Tukey's post-hoc comparisons using the group variable divisions; see below for an explanation of how to change the type of post-hoc.
alternative=c("two.sided")	This argument is a default one and not included but you could change it to a one-sided hypothesis by using "less" or "greater."

Should you use a Tukey's post-hoc test? If you are still using the "old statistics" approach, here are my recommendations for which post-hoc tests to choose:

- If you are making three or fewer comparisons, do not adjust the means (Howell, 2002).
- If you are making more than three comparisons, choose the Tukey's HSD test or Benjamini and Hochberg's FDR adjustment (Maxwell & Delaney, 2004).

What if you do not want to use the Tukey's adjustment, and instead would like to use a different type of adjustment for multiple *p*-values? You can add an additional argument to the **summary( )** command to get the FDR adjustment:

```
summary(.Pairs,adjusted(type=c(p.adjust.methods=c("fdr"))))
```

For a summary without any adjustment, use "none". The summary() command will return *p*-values but not CIs. For CIs with this package, only CIs adjusted with a Tukey's HSD adjustment can be returned.

For parallelism with SPSS, you might want to call for Levene's test for homogeneity of variances. With the usual caveat that this test may not have enough power to be useful and should be used in conjunction with visual and numerical reports of variances of different groups, use the following command to use this formal test of homogeneity of variances:

```
levene.test(EllisYuan$syntaxvariety, EllisYuan$group)
```

```
Levene's Test for Homogeneity of Variance
      Df F value Pr(>F)
group  2  0.1639 0.8494
      39
```

For the Ellis and Yuan (2004) data, Levene's test shows that there is no reason to reject the assumption that the variances of the groups are homogeneous. (Reject this assumption only if $p < 0.05$.) Previous inspection of graphs and numerical summaries has also shown us that there does not seem to be a great difference in variances between the groups.

The last piece of data that R Commander calls for is a plot of the CIs for the pairwise comparisons. R Commander uses this code: plot(confint(.Pairs)). However, a mean–mean multiple comparisons (MMC) plot that I like even better can be found in the HH package (Heiberger, 2015). Create a new object using the mmc( ) command, then plot it, like this:

```
library(HH) #open the package first (get it by using install.packages("HH") first)
ellisyuan.mmc<-mmc(AnovaModel.1,linfct=mcp(group="Tukey"))
plot(ellisyuan.mmc)
```

The plot contains not only the CIs of the comparisons which correspond to the actual width of the interval if one consults the contrast value along the x-axis, but also shows means of each group along the left-hand y-axis.

The line type and color of statistical comparisons differ from non-statistical comparisons as well on this plot. The solid line in the middle is red and indicates a statistical comparison, while the dotted black lines go through zero and indicate non-statistical comparisons. The height of the comparison is also plotted along the average mean of the two groups. You can see the mean scores on the left-hand y-axis, so, for example, the average mean of the NP vs. OLP group is between 16.21 and 18.86. The gray triangles that are constructed in the background also reflect the relative distances of the means, although because they are fairly equidistant in this case it is not readily apparent (Heiberger & Holland, 2004).

Conducting a One-Way Analysis of Variance Using R

1 In R Commander, choose STATISTICS > MEANS > ONE-WAY ANOVA. Choose a Group (= IV) and Response variable (= DV). Tick the box for pairwise comparison of means. Change the name of the regression model if you like.
2 I have suggested the following R code to obtain the same results as R Commander, but sometimes with an improvement:

```
AnovaModel.1= aov(syntaxvariety ~ group, data=EllisYuan) #create model
Anova(AnovaModel.1) #omnibus test
levene.test(EllisYuan$SyntaxVariety, EllisYuan$Group) #test homogeneity of variances
numSummary(EllisYuan [,"syntaxvariety "], groups = EllisYuan$group) #descriptives
library(multcomp)
.Pairs=glht(AnovaModel.1,linfct=mcp(group="Tukey")) #model for multiple comparisons
confint(.Pairs) #returns confidence intervals for comparisons
summary(.Pairs, adjusted(type=c(p.adjust.methods=c("fdr")))) #returns p-values for comparisons, gives
#choice of p-value adjustment methods
library(HH)
ellisyuan.mmc=mmc(AnovaModel.1,linfct=mcp(group="Tukey")) #model for MMC
plot(ellisyuan.mmc) #MMC plot
```

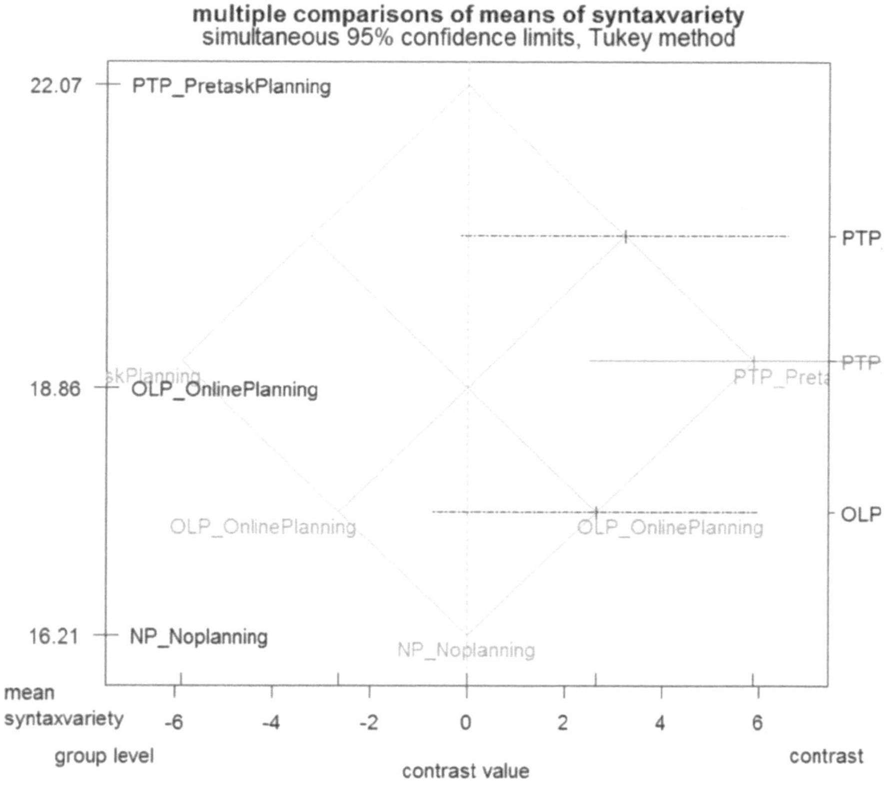

Figure 9.10 MMC (multiple comparison of means) plot with Ellis & Yuan (2004) data.

9.4.5 Performing a Bootstrapped One-Way Analysis of Variance in R

As in Chapter 8, I can show you two ways to perform bootstraps on your data. This section uses the code used by LaFlair, Egbert, and Plonsky (2015) to bootstrap a one-way ANOVA. (See their chapter for more examples.) The other way is to use Rand Wilcox's **WRS** library, and instructions to do this can be found online chapter "Bootstrapped and Means-Trimmed One-Way ANOVA in R". The advantage of the bootstrap in this section over Wilcox's commands, as I see it, is that your data do not need to be changed around into a different form.

Actually, the code used for the bootstrap function of the one-way ANOVA is exactly the same as the code used in Section 8.4.3, but this time the group variable contains more than two different groups, and LaFlair, Egbert, and Plonsky will provide further code to put the CI results into a nice format. I will keep working with the Ellis and Yuan (2004) data, the syntax variety variable. The underlined parts of the code are the only parts where you will put in your own data and change the code as given here. In fact, in trying to make this code work for me, I found that the easiest way to do it was to run the code exactly as given in LaFlair, Egbert, and Plonsky with their data, then when I could run their data set and was sure the code was typed in right, I ran my own data set. So you might want to try to run this code exactly as it is, with the Ellis and Yuan data, and then use it with your own data if you have problems getting it to work.

```
MeanDifference <- function (data,i){
temp<-data[i,]
aov.temp<-aov(syntaxvariety ~ group, data=temp)
Tuk <-TukeyHSD(aov.temp)
return(Tuk$group[,1])
}
```

Next run the bootstrap using the **boot()** command from the **boot** package, so if you do not have this package, first download it (**install.packages("boot")**) and then open the package (**library(boot)**).

```
MeanDifferenceBoot <- boot(EllisYuan, MeanDifference, 10000) #this will take a little time to run
print(MeanDifferenceBoot)
```

```
ORDINARY NONPARAMETRIC BOOTSTRAP


Call:
boot(data = EllisYuan, statistic = MeanDifference, R = 10000)


Bootstrap Statistics :
     original        bias    std. error
t1*  5.857143 -0.0005911158    1.428281
t2*  2.642857  0.0061298104    1.373872
t3* -3.214286  0.0067209262    1.260620
```

I do not find this output particularly helpful. The output shows the original mean difference between the groups, the bias. (If the bootstrapped comparison is different from the original mean, the "bias" column will contain the numerical amount the two means differ and the SE.) In other words, if the original difference between group A and group B was 6.32 points, and the bootstrap comparison found that the difference was 6.30 points, the bias will be 0.02. Another problem with this output is that we only get titles like "t1*" and "t2*" and we do not know exactly which comparisons these are. With further commands we will get more useful information and also see which comparisons are which, so we need to be patient for now.

In the next step, LaFlair, Egbert, and Plonsky created a structure (a data frame) that would return CIs for the bootstrapped data, which is what we are really interested in seeing. There is nothing in this code that needs to be changed for your own data, so just type it all as is (although you could change the type of CI if you liked; for the **boot.ci()** command, you can choose from the following types of CIs: **"norm"** (uses the normal approximation), **"basic"** (uses the basic bootstrap method), **"stud"** (uses the studentized bootstrap method), **"perc"** (uses the bootstrap percentile method), **"bca"** (adjusted bootstrap percentile method) or you could write **"all"** and get all five types of CIs.

```
PAIRci.s <- NULL
PAIRt0 <- as.data.frame(MeanDifferenceBoot[1])
for(i in 1:length(MeanDifferenceBoot[[1]])){
CI <- boot.ci(MeanDifferenceBoot, conf = .95,
  type = "bca", t0 = MeanDifferenceBoot$t0[i] ,
  t = MeanDifferenceBoot$t[,i])
PAIRci.s[[paste("lwr",i,sep=".")]]<- CI$bca[c(4)]
PAIRci.s[[paste("upr",i,sep=".")]]<- CI$bca[c(5)]
}
Pci <- matrix(PAIRci.s, ncol = 2, nrow = length(PAIRt0[[1]]),
byrow=TRUE)
 PAIRboot.ci <- data.frame(PAIRt0[1], lwr = Pci[, 1], upr = Pci[, 2])
 print(PAIRboot.ci)
```

```
                                             t0        lwr        upr
PTP_PretaskPlanning-NP_No planning      5.857143  3.1692053  8.7847772
OLP_OnlinePlanning-NP_No planning       2.642857 -0.1023239  5.3369514
OLP_OnlinePlanning-PTP_PretaskPlanning -3.214286 -5.8547641 -0.9277621
```

This output shows us the original mean difference between the groups again (t0), but also the 95% BCa CI for the three comparisons that were made (PTP vs. NP, OLP vs. NP and OLP vs. PTP). We see that the difference in mean scores between the PTP and NP group could be as low as three points or as high as almost nine points (95% BCa bootstrapped CI [−3.17, −8.78]). On a test with no maximum score but mean scores between 16 and 22 points, even 3 points of difference seems like a substantial amount, and 9 points would be quite remarkable! In other words, the effect of the difference between these two methods seems important (and descriptive statistics tell us that the PTP group had higher scores than the NP group so we know it was the PTP group that comes out ahead), although the CI is wider than we might like it to be. However, the difference between OLP and NP is not statistical (95% BCa bootstrapped CI[−0.10, 5.34]). Lastly, the comparison between OLP and PTP shows that there is a difference, but it may be small (95% BCa bootstrapped CI [−5.85, −0.93]), as low as about one point of difference. The effect of this difference is not so large as the difference between PTP and NP. In fact, the difference between the OLP and NP test and the OLP and PTP test is very similar: the 95% CIs are nearly the same range, but the CI just barely goes through zero for the OLP vs. NP comparison. Instead of looking at a black-and-white, "accept-or-reject" decision of NHST, it is better to report CIs and note that the true effect could be very small and close to zero for both the second and third comparisons, although the third comparison does not go through zero so we can say it does have an effect while the second comparison may have an effect of zero.

9.4.6 Conducting a One-Way Analysis of Variance Using Planned Comparisons

You have seen in the sections up to now that when you do a one-way ANOVA, you usually do not stop at the omnibus test. Instead, you go on to conduct post-hoc tests, which are also called multiple comparisons. These tests will compare every group in your ANOVA to every other group. If you only have three groups, there will only be three comparisons. But once you start getting a larger number of groups, the number of comparisons can really multiply. For example, for 4 groups, comparing each group to the other will result in 6 tests, while for 5 groups there will be 10 tests!

Using planned comparisons is a sensible way to give yourself more statistical power and to simplify your statistics so that your readers may more easily understand your main hypotheses. Wilcox (2003) recommends performing post-hoc tests without the omnibus *F*-test of the one-way ANOVA. Wilcox recommends this as a way of increasing the statistical power of the test although in SPSS, and in R as far as I can tell, the omnibus test is not taken into account when adjustments are made for running multiple statistical tests.

Using planned comparisons means that you test only *some* of the possible comparisons among your groups. For example, if you have four different groups where one is a native speaker group and the rest are different kinds of language learners, perhaps you are really only interested in testing whether the NS differ from the language learner groups, and not whether each language learner group differs from the other. In this case, you could perform only three comparisons (NS vs. each of the three learner groups) rather than the six that would result from testing every group against every other group. In the "old statistics," reducing the number of comparisons would mean that you could divide up your $\alpha = 0.05$ among fewer comparisons. In the "new statistics," where we focus on CIs, this could also matter (we have seen that CIs can be adjusted for multiple procedures as well) and it is also just nicer to your readers if you only make them look at the statistics that you really care about.

The easiest way to set this up is through the one-way ANOVA procedure. You could also, of course, just use a series of *t*-tests. However, if you did this you might be concerned about inflating the error rate by having multiple tests. Howell (2002) suggested that if you have only one or two comparisons to make then the *t*-test approach is not unreasonable, but if you have a really large number of comparisons then using planned comparisons is better.

To illustrate this procedure, we will look again at the comparison among the three groups of the Ellis and Yuan (2004) data for the syntactic variety variable without doing the omnibus *F*-test. Suppose that we wanted to test all of the possible comparisons among the groups. In this case, there are three groups, so there will be three possible comparisons. In each comparison, we want to ignore one of the groups and compare the other two. Study Table 9.8 to examine the pattern of coefficients that need to be used to do an ordinary comparison of the three groups.

Table 9.8 Planned Comparison Coefficients for Two-Way Comparisons

Groups	*Compare Group 1 to Group 2*	*Compare Group 1 to Group 3*	*Compare Group 2 to Group 3*
NP = Group 1*	1	1	0
PTP = Group 2*	−1	0	1
OLP = Group 3*	0	−1	−1

*These numbers are just arbitrarily assigned to the groups and have nothing to do with the coefficients.

From Table 9.8 you can see that you put a number in the row of the groups you want to compare. The number could be 1, 2 or 1000, but there needs to be an equally large number to be subtracted so that, when the columns are added up, they add up to zero. Any row of the column that contains a non-zero number will be included in the comparison. For the planned comparison shown in Table 9.8, only two groups at a time are being compared. All possible pairings are made (i.e. NP vs. PTP, NP vs. OLP and PTP vs. OLP). The results from such a comparison will be exactly what we have found up to this point, because this is exactly the kind of comparison we have done (the $con in the output for the linconb( ) command in the online section "Bootstrapping and Means-Trimmed One-Way ANOVA in R," shows the same exact numbers as are seen in Table 9.8).

However, let us say what we really wanted to know was whether having planning time made a difference or not, and whether having unlimited time made a difference or not. For the question of planning time, we could compare the group with planning time (PTP) to the two others without planning time (NP and OLP). For the question of unlimited writing time, we could compare the group with unlimited time (OLP) to the groups who only had 17 minutes of writing time (NP and PTP). Study the coefficients in Table 9.9 to see how we would enter coefficients to test these two different hypotheses.

Table 9.9 Planned Comparison Coefficients for Multiple Comparisons with Ellis and Yuan (2004)

Groups	*Compare PTP to NP and OLP*	*Compare OLP to NP and PTP*
NP=Group 1	−1	−1
PTP=Group 2	2	−1
OLP=Group 3	−1	2

In each case, the numbers in the column add up to zero. However, by distributing the "−1" over both the NP and OLP group in the first column of Table 9.9, we balance those two groups *together* against the PTP group, with its "2." The same is true for the second hypothesis, where we balance the NP and PTP groups together against the OLP group.

Lastly, consider the case I made earlier of a situation where you have four groups but only want to make three comparisons—that of the NS group against each of the language learner groups. In Table 9.10, you can again see that the numbers in each column add up to zero, but this time every time the NS group gets a 1, and the "−1" is put in the row of just one of the three learner groups. The other two groups get zeros so that they are not involved in the comparison.

9.4.7 Conducting Planned Comparisons in SPSS

To translate this idea to SPSS, we will bring up the dialog box for the one-way ANOVA (ANALYZE > COMPARE MEANS > ONE-WAY ANOVA). The same variables are moved into the same boxes as shown previously in Figure 9.6. The difference is that now we click on the CONTRASTS button, and we enter coefficients to test the two hypotheses outlined in Table 9.9.

Table 9.10 Planned Comparison Coefficients with L1 Groups

Groups	*Compare NS to Spanish L1*	*Compare NS to Portuguese L1*	*Compare NS to Japanese L1*
Native speakers (NS)	1	1	1
Spanish L1	−1	0	0
Portuguese L1	0	−1	0
Japanese L1	0	0	−1

In the CONTRASTS dialog box we enter the coefficients for each of our planned comparisons. Figure 9.11 shows the coefficients added for the first contrast in the box that says "Contrast 1 of 1." The presence of a negative number "−1" for the NP group and an additional "−1" for the OLP group means their data will be combined and will be used in contrast to the balancing positive "2" of the PTP group. The reason I used the number "2" for the PTP group is that it is the smallest whole number that equals the two other groups if I assign them whole numbers; I could have given both the NP and OLP groups a "−0.5" and then the PTP group a positive "1." The numbers themselves do not matter as long as they sum to 0. I then clicked on the NEXT button to move to "Contrast 2 of 2," where I entered the coefficients −1, −1 and 2, which result in comparing the NP and PTP group *together* to the OLP group. As those are the only two hypotheses that I have determined I want to compare, I click on the CONTINUE button and then on OK in the main dialog box.

The output we are interested in from this planned comparison is shown in Table 9.11. The first table shows the contrast coefficients you have entered. (Confusingly, the contrast is shown in the *row*, not the column!) The main output of interest is labeled "Contrast Tests" and shows the results of the two planned comparisons. From the *p*-value, we see that the first hypothesis, that planning time affected the amount of syntax variety, was upheld because the *p*-value for Contrast 1, whether assumed to have equal variances or not, was less than 0.05. (I do not like doing this the "old statistics" way, but SPSS gave me no options for returning a CI, even when I tried to do bootstrapping.) The second hypothesis, that unlimited writing time affected the amount of syntax variety, cannot be upheld, however, because $p = 0.81$.

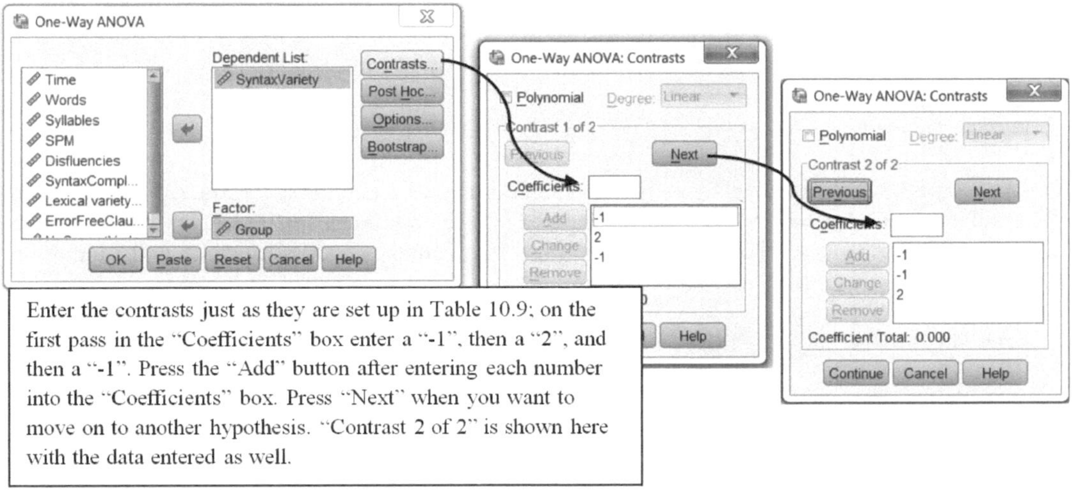

Figure 9.11 Calling for planned comparisons in SPSS.

Performing Multiple Comparisons

1 ANALYZE > COMPARE MEANS > ONE-WAY ANOVA.
2 Move the DV and IV into appropriate boxes. Open the CONTRASTS button. Enter comparison coefficients in Coefficients box; click on Add after every number, and "Next" after each comparison is finished. Make sure that the "Coefficient Total" at the bottom of the dialog box equals zero for every contrast. Click on "Continue" and then OK.

Table 9.11 Output from a Planned Comparison in SPSS

Contrast Coefficients

	Group		
Contrast	NP_No planning	PTP_Pretask Planning	OLP_OnlineP lanning
1	-1	2	-1
2	-1	-1	2

Contrast Tests

		Contrast	Value of Contrast	Std. Error	t	df	Sig. (2-tailed)
SyntaxVariety	Assume equal variances	1	9.07	2.388	3.799	39	.000
		2	-.57	2.388	-.239	39	.812
	Does not assume equal variances	1	9.07	2.367	3.832	26.436	.001
		2	-.57	2.248	-.254	30.437	.801

9.4.8 Conducting Planned Comparisons in R

To translate the idea explained in Section 9.4.6 to R, we will need to use the syntax of the one-way ANOVA.

Creating your own planned comparisons in R is straightforward using the **glht( )** command seen in Section 9.4.4 and used to conduct post-hoc multiple comparisons. To set up planned comparisons like those in Table 9.8, simply specify your contrasts by naming your contrast anything you like, then putting in a column of numbers that correspond to the comparison coefficients, using the order that the levels in your IV come in. For example, for the **groups** variable in Ellis and Yuan (2004), the names of the levels can be obtained with the levels command:

```
levels(EllisYuan$group)
[1] "NP_No planning" "PTP_PretaskPlanning" "OLP_OnlinePlanning"
```

I can see that NP is the first level of the variable, PTP is the second and OLP is the third. Now I can specify the coefficients for the comparisons I want to make in an object I will call **contr.** (Look to the columns of Table 9.8 to understand the numbers I use.) The numeric coefficients refer to the inclusion of the levels in the order they are found in R in the **levels( )** command you just looked at:

```
contr=rbind("NP-PTP"=c(1,-1,0),
"NP-OLP"=c(1,0,-1),
"PTP-OLP"=c(0,1,-1))
```

Next, I run the **glht( )** command again, specifying that the testing for Group will be the object I just created. I can then run **summary( )** and **confint( )** on this object. To be more clear, I would first create an ANOVA model, then I have to open the **multcomp** package and then I can run the **glht( )** command. In the **glht( )** command I specify that the group will be formed from the matrix of contrasts that I put together and called **contr**:

```
AnovaModel.1 <- aov(syntaxvariety ~ group, data=EllisYuan)
library(multcomp)
Ellisyuan.Pairs=glht(AnovaModel.1,linfct=mcp(group=contr))
summary(Ellisyuan.Pairs)
confint(Ellisyuan.Pairs)
```

The results will be exactly the same as those reported in Section 9.4.4 since I am specifying the same contrasts. (They are reversed in sign, but this does not make any difference ultimately.) To make planned comparisons with more than three groups, or only among certain groups the idea is the same, but the number used in the comparison needs to be adjusted so that each column adds up to zero.

However, let us say what we really wanted to know was whether having planning time made a difference or not, and whether having unlimited time made a difference or not. For the question of planning time, we could compare the PTP group to the NP and OLP groups. For the question of unlimited writing time, we could compare the OLP group to the NP and PTP groups. Study the coefficients in Table 9.9 to see how we would enter coefficients to test these two different hypotheses.

Here is what I would write for the matrix I need to create for the **glht( )** command:

```
contr=rbind("Planning Time vs. No Planning Time"=c(-1,2,-1),
"Unlimited writing time vs. Limited"=c(-1, -1, 2))
```

Run the third line of code above again (the **glht** command), then the **confint( )** command:

```
Fit: aov(formula = syntaxvariety ~ group, data = EllisYuan)

Quantile = 2.2949
95% family-wise confidence level


Linear Hypotheses:
                                        Estimate lwr     upr
Planning Time vs. No Planning Time == 0  9.0714   3.5909 14.5519
Unlimited writing time vs. Limited == 0 -0.5714  -6.0519  4.9091
```

Notice that there is no adjustment for multiple comparisons here. The results for the first hypothesis, that planning time affected the amount of syntax variety, was upheld because the 95% CI for the first hypothesis runs from 3.60 to 14.55. This is a rather wide CI and it means the influence on planning time for syntax variety could have been as small as 3.6 points, or as large as 15 points! We do not have a very precise idea of how much influence planning time really had, but we do have an idea that it did have an effect. On the other hand, the second hypothesis, that unlimited writing time affected the amount of syntax variety, cannot be upheld, because the CI is [−6.05, 4.91].

Last of all, to conduct a comparison like the one in Table 9.10, create a matrix of coefficients like this:

```
contr=rbind("NS vs. Spanish L1"=c(1,-1,0,0),
 "NS vs. Portuguese L1"=c(1,0,-1,0),
 "NS vs. Japanese L1"=c(1,0,0,-1))
```

We do not have a data file to try this out on but hopefully this helps you see how you would write up the matrix for whatever coefficients you wanted. If you do not need any labels and just want to make the matrix (as might be the case for Wilcox's linconb( ) command in the online section "Bootstrapped and Means-Trimmed One-Way ANOVA in R"), you can simply type in the numbers you want after the "c", then specify the number of rows and columns in the matrix. Remember that the contrasts should add up to zero in each column, so for the matrix written just above this paragraph, you would need four rows and three columns, and for Wilcox's linconb( ) command you could type this, so that the argument in the linconb( ) command would be con=MAT:

```
MAT<-matrix(c(1,-1,0,0,1,0,-1,0,1,0,0,-1), 4, 3)
MAT
     [,1] [,2] [,3]
[1,]    1    1    1
[2,]   -1    0    0
[3,]    0   -1    0
[4,]    0    0   -1
```

Conducting Planned Comparisons in R

1 Specify the coefficients for the comparisons you want to make and rbind( ) the coefficients together into a matrix. It would probably help to first write the coefficients down in a table like the ones I have shown in the text (Tables 9.8, 9.9 and 9.10). List the coefficients in the order that the levels of your group variable are found in (check this with the levels( ) command). Make sure the column adds up to zero. Create a new object with the rbind( ) command. Here is an example for comparing all of the comparisons in an independent variable (IV) with three levels:

```
contr=rbind("NP-PTP"=c(1,-1,0),
"NP-OLP"=c(1,0,-1),
"PTP-OLP"=c(0,1,-1))
```

2 Run the glht( ) command again, using the new object (contr) as the type of contrast for the IV:

```
Ellisyuan.Pairs=glht(AnovaModel.1,linfct=mcp(group=contr))
```

3 You may now obtain the statistics from this model with summary( ) and confint( ).

9.4.9 Effect Sizes in One-Way Analysis of Variance

When you do a one-way ANOVA you have a choice as to what effect size you will report—that of the omnibus ANOVA *F*-test, or that of the post-hoc or planned comparisons tests. Kline (2004) recommended reporting on only one or the other. For the omnibus test you will use a percentage variance (PV) effect size, while for the post-hoc tests or planned comparisons you will use Cohen's *d*. When researchers in second language research do report effect sizes, I have mostly seen the effect sizes for the individual comparisons, not for the omnibus test, and my feeling is that this is the most appropriate place to look at effect sizes.

However, if you wanted to report the omnibus PV effect size, you can use the ANOVA output. The basic formula for eta-squared from Volker (2006) is to divide the number for the sum of squares (SS) of the IV (found in the "Between Groups" row of the SPSS output or in the line titled by your own variable, such as "Group" for the Ellis and Yuan data) by the total SS (found in the "Total" row in the SPSS output, or calculated by adding together the sum of squares in the "Group" line and the "Residuals" line of the R output). Thus, for the Ellis and Yuan (2004) omnibus test, looking at the output in Table 9.5, PV = 240.9/759.9 = 0.32, meaning the between-groups differences account for 32% of the variance in scores. However, eta-squared is slightly biased positively so omega-squared, which adjusts for the bias, can be calculated with the same information as for the eta-squared and also the information about the number of groups and the mean square of the error (the line labeled "Within groups" in the SPSS output, or the line labeled "Residuals" in the R output). In this case, the equation is:

$$\omega^2 = \frac{SS_{hyp} - (k-1)(MS_{error})}{SS_{total} + MS_{error}} = \frac{240.9-(3-1)(13.31)}{759.91+13.31} = 0.28$$

where k = the number of groups, SS_{hyp}= the sum of squares of the hypothesis, labeled as "Between Groups" in SPSS or "**Group**" (my name) in R, and MS_{error} = mean square of the within-subjects line (in SPSS) or the "**Residuals**" line (in R). We see the omega-squared is slightly smaller than the eta-squared value, but still represents a large effect.

However, remember that effect sizes, which are point estimates, also have CIs. LaFlair, Egbert and Plonsky (2015) created code that allows us to look at the R^2 (eta-squared) effect size CIs calculated by bootstrapping to see the values that we can be confident our real effect size will fall into. Here is the code I used to calculate the effect size for Ellis and Yuan's **syntaxvariety** variable. As with the other bootstrapping codes written for R, I urge you to make this work with the original syntax first, then substitute your own data into the areas with the underlines second:

```
m<-lm(syntaxvariety~group, data=EllisYuan)
resid<-m$residuals
EllisYuan$resid<-resid
EllisYuan$g.hat<-predict(m)
Rsqstat<-function(data,i) {
  temp<-data
  temp$r<-temp$g.hat + temp$resid[i]
  aov.temp<-summary(lm(r~group,data=temp))
  return(aov.temp$r.squared)
}
Rsqboot<-boot(EllisYuan, Rsqstat, 10000)
print(Rsqboot)
```

For this ordinary non-parametric bootstrap, here is the output (cut down to the essentials for brevity):

```
Bootstrap Statistics :
     original      bias     std. error
t1* 0.3170197 0.03191241    0.108793
```

This tells us that our original R^2 (or η^2) was 0.32; however, the bootstrap finds that this estimate is biased by 0.03, meaning that the average value of the resampled distribution was different by about 0.03 points. Moving on, the CI is quite wide, we find:

```
Rsqboot.ci<-boot.ci(Rsqboot, conf=.95, type="bca")
print(Rsqboot.ci)
```

```
Intervals :
Level        BCa
95%    ( 0.0688,   0.4879 )
```

Again, cutting down the output to the bare minimum, we see the CI for this effect size is [0.07, 0.49], meaning that the real effect size could be almost negligible at 7%, or quite large at 49%. What this tells us is that our point estimate effect size of 0.32 is not very accurate. We cannot really depend on the effect size being 32% because the actual interval where we are confident of finding it in is so wide. In other words, our point estimate effect size is almost worthless, and what we really need to do is just list the CI of the effect size and tell our reader that we are not very confident of the exact effect size.

To calculate Cohen's *d* effect sizes for post-hoc tests or planned comparisons, use the same approach as was used for independent group *t*-tests in Chapter 8. (You can also use an online calculator, such as the one found at www.uccs.edu/~lbecker/.) In other words, you will divide the mean difference between groups by a standardizer, which can be either the pooled SD, if variances are equal, or the SD of the control group, if variances are unequal.

Since the Ellis and Yuan (2004) data had equal variances, I calculated the following using the data in Table 9.1 and the formula for d on p. 148 with the standardizer formula from p. 147:

$$d(NP-PTP)=\frac{16.2-22.07}{\sqrt{\frac{13(4.1)^2+13(3.6)^2}{13+13}}}=-1.53.$$

The effect size for the comparison between NP and PTP is the largest at 1.53, meaning the difference between the groups is 11/2 times the SD of the group. The effect sizes for the other comparisons are not negligible: between NP and OLP $d = -0.72$, and the effect size for the comparison between PTP and OLP is $d = 0.95$.

We can use the R package **bootES** (Kirby & Gerlanc, 2013) to calculate CIs for Cohen's *d* effect sizes. The following code specifies that we want to test the contrast between the NP and PTP group using Cohen's *d* results, with BCa bootstrapping.

```
install.packages("bootES")
library(bootES)
bootES(EllisYuan, R=2000, data.col="syntaxvariety", group.col="group",
contrast=c("NP_NoPlanning"=1, "PTP_PretaskPlanning"=-1), effect.type=c("cohens.d"), ci.type=c("bca"))
```

The output shows the original statistic is nearly identical to the one we already calculated (original $d = 1.53$, bootES $d = 1.52$), but shows that the CI ranges from 0.61 to 2.29. There does seem to be a real effect for the contrast between these groups.

In the documentation for the **bootES** package, Gerlanc and Kirby (2013) noted that with BCa CIs, it is best to use an unbiased estimator of the effect size, which is called Hedges' *g* and will be somewhat smaller than Cohen's *d*. We can easily implement this by changing the argument to **effect.type = c("hedges.g")**. With this change, the CI for the NP–PTP contrast is [0.61, 2.24] (not much of a change). The **bootES** package also offers the choice of a robust version of Cohen's *d* proposed by Algina, Keselman, and Penfield (2005), called with the command **effect.type=c("akp.robust.d")**. It uses trimmed means and Winsorized SDs. This approach provides good coverage for groups with as few as 20 subjects per group, even with strongly non-normal distributions, but its interpretation will be different from that of Cohen's *d* or Hedges' *g*, since it is measuring the middle 60% of the population (since 20% gets cut off of each end of the distribution).

I therefore recommend using Hedges' *g* instead of Cohen's *d* if you are bootstrapping the CIs of the effect size.

Here is a little more detail about the **bootES( )** command:

```
bootES(EllisYuan, R=2000, data.col="syntaxvariety", group.col="group",
contrast=c("NP_NoPlanning" =1, "PTP_PretaskPlanning"=-1), effect.type=c("cohens.d"), ci.type=c("bca"))
```

bootES()	Performs a bootstrap (you can choose which kind) on any number of effect sizes and returns a CI for the effect size.
EllisYuan	The first argument represents the data, which need to be a numeric vector or data frame that needs to contain at least one DV and optionally, one or more columns of categorical data.
R=2000	This is the default number of bootstrap samples.
data.col="syntaxvariety"	The data.col argument should contain the DV (the outcome data). Notice that the name of the variable should have quotation marks around it.

group.col="group"	The group.col argument should contain the IV (the categorical data). Notice that the name of the variable should have quotation marks around it.
contrast=c("NP_NoPlanning"=1, "PTP_PretaskPlanning"=–1)	When doing a Cohen's *d* type of effect size with more than two groups in the IV, this argument lets you specify which groups should be compared against each other; notice that the numbers refer to how we should balance the comparison weights; these are the same types of numbers as we saw in Section 9.4.6 when we talked about planned comparisons. Note that you use the names of the variable exactly as given in your file.
effect.type=c("cohens.d")	Here is where we specify the type of effect size we want to look at; we can choose from "unstandardized", "cohens.d", "hedges.g", "cohens.d.sigma", "r", and "akp.robust.d". See Gerlanc and Kirby (2013), which is quite readable and not too technical, for more information about these choices.
ci.type=c("bca")	By default bootES uses the BCa method for computing bootstrap CIs, as this calculation has been shown to have the best coverage for many different types of data. Gerlanc and Kirby (2013) recommend using the default (in which case you do not actually have to type this argument) unless you have a strong reason for changing the method. Other possible methods include: "norm", "basic", "perc", "stud", and "none".
plot=T	If you add this command to your effect size call, you will get a histogram and a normal Quantile-Quantile plot of the bootstrapped samples. You should examine these plots to see if the data appear to be normally distributed.

Bootstrapping the other comparisons using bootES, I find that the 95% BCa CI for the NP vs. OLP comparison (remember the original Cohen's $d = -0.72$) is [0.10, 1.54] and Hedges' g is [0.11, 1.47]; for the PTP vs. OLP comparison (original Cohen's $d = .95$), the CI is [0.23, 1.65] and Hedges' g is [0.20, 1.61].

The entire chapter has shown that there is not too much difference between the NP vs. OLP and PTP vs. OLP comparisons, even though under various types of analyses the NP vs. OLP comparison is not statistical (using "old statistics" thinking) while sometimes the PTP vs. OLP comparison is. We might conclude that each of the planning conditions provided the participants with an opportunity to increase their statistical variety, with a clear effect for PTP being much better for syntax variety than no planning. In any case, using the "new statistics" we can lay out the CIs for the mean difference and the effect sizes for our readers, and let them see what the possible range of values may be instead of making black-and-white decisions about which effects are important and which are not.

9.4.10 Application Activities with One-Way Analysis of Variance

1 Using the Ellis and Yuan data (EllisYuan.sav), look at the variables of error-free clauses, MSTTR (a measure of lexical variety) and speed per minute (SPM). First examine the data visually. What do you find with regard to normality, homogeneity of variances and outliers? Next, perform a one-way ANOVA on each of the three variables along with post-hoc tests. Report omnibus F-results; find 95% CIs for the difference in means and calculate effect sizes along with their effect sizes for the contrasts. What would you remark upon here?

2 Pandey (2000) conducted research on how well NS of different English dialects performed on the TOEFL and reported the raw data scores in her article. Pandey's research design is shown in the following diagram:

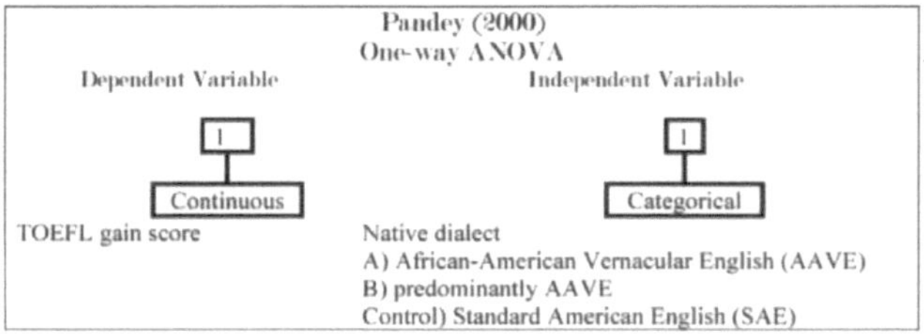

Pandey did not perform statistics on her data, but merely observed the trend that both focus groups had quite low TOEFL scores the first time they were tested (mean for Focus Group A—443; mean for Focus Group B—429), but, with comparative instruction, both focus groups improved their scores over time. In comparison, the control group's scores hardly changed at all the second time they took the test. Using the Pandey2000.sav file, investigate statistically the research question of whether Groups A and B are different from each other in their first gain scores (GAIN1), and also whether Group A and B *together* are different from the control group in the first gain scores. You will need to use planned comparisons to answer this question. Be sure to first visually examine the data. (Even if it does not fit assumptions, go ahead and analyze it here.)

3 Thought question. Imagine a research design that investigates the pragmatic development of Chinese learners of Russian. The researcher asked participants to complete discourse completion tasks at three separate times during the semester. The participants were in three different classes, and each class received each of the three treatments (Control—no pragmatic discussion; explicit pragmatic discussion; implicit pragmatic discussion), with five weeks between each treatment. Immediately following the treatment, participants took the discourse completion task. The researcher wants to know whether the groups differed depending on their treatment, and plans to conduct a one-way ANOVA with GROUP as the IV and score on the discourse completion task at every time period as the DV, as is shown in the table below. What is wrong with this research design?

	Participant	Group	Time	DCTScore
1	ChiWei	1	1	68
2	ChiWei	1	2	49
3	ChiWei	1	3	87
4	TsiWen	1	1	53
5	TsiWen	1	2	56

4 Inagaki and Long (1999) conducted an experiment with Japanese learners to see whether asking participants to repeat a correct model after they heard it would be as effective as recasting after an incorrect utterance (and whether these would differ from a control condition where participants simply studied *kanji* characters). Two structures, that of correct adjective formation when there are multiple adjectives (GainAdj), and subject placement after a locative phrase (GainLoc), were examined with 24 participants. If possible, conduct two separate one-way ANOVAs to determine whether there was any difference between the three experimental groups on each of the two structures. Be sure to first visually examine the data. Examine comparisons of the three different groups, and report omnibus *F*-results; find CIs for the difference in means, and also perform robust tests to find robust CIs. Find effect sizes and, if possible, CIs for the effect sizes. Use the InagakiLong.sav file.

5 Dewaele and Pavlenko's Bilingual Emotions Questionnaire (2001–2003). Use the BEQ.Context.sav file. Multilinguals who answered the questionnaire rated their proficiency in L2 speaking, comprehension, reading and writing on a 1–5 scale (where 5 = fully fluent). Multilinguals also differed in the context in which they had acquired their L2, if it was naturalistic, instructed or both. Examine the question of whether there are differences in proficiency on L2 speaking and L2 reading depending on the context of instruction. Be sure to first visually examine the data, report omnibus *F*-results; find CIs for the difference in means, and also perform robust tests to find robust CIs. Find effect sizes and, if possible, CIs for the effect sizes.

6 Jensen and Vinther (2003). The authors experimented with the presentation of input at either a fast or slow speed and one of the variables they tested for was phonological decoding based on the experimental condition (Fast-Slow-Fast, Fast-Slow-Slow or control, who did not hear dialogs at any speed). Participants took a pretest and a posttest, and their gain scores are recorded in the file JensenVinther2003.sav. (These scores were estimated from their graph in figure 2 of their paper.) Calculate whether there are differences between the three groups in their gains at phonological decoding. Be sure to first visually examine the data, report omnibus *F*-results; find CIs for the difference in means, and also perform robust tests to find robust CIs. Find effect sizes and, if possible, CIs for the effect sizes.

9.4.11 Reporting the Results of a One-Way Analysis of Variance

The pieces of information that you will want to report from a one-way ANOVA depend on whether you decide to include the omnibus *F*-test. In most cases, it makes little sense to include an omnibus test, as what most researchers are interested in is not whether there is an overall effect or not, but specifically how each group differs from the others. However, it may be traditional to report this omnibus test, and it does not seem to subtract from the power of subsequent comparisons, so you can choose to report it or not.

In reporting the results from an omnibus test, include at least the df between groups (also called the hypothesis df), the df within groups (also called the error df or residuals), the *F*-value and the *p*-value. Some people like to report the entire ANOVA table, with SS and mean squares, but I prefer just to report the raw data so that people can recreate my analysis or, if the sample size is too large, tell people I would be happy to send them the raw data. If you do not want to do that, I still do not see any compelling reason to give SS or mean squares information, but you can report them if you wish.

The information that should be reported from the post-hoc tests or multiple comparisons of the groups should start with means, SDs and counts for each group. The type of comparison used (post-hoc or planned comparison) and method used for controlling the FWER (for example, Tukey, FDR, etc.) should also be specified. Include the 95% CI for the mean difference between the tests. Depending on which way the comparison was made (for example, NP–PTP or PTP–NP), the mean difference will be negative or positive, but is not practically important.

Effect sizes should also be reported, but statisticians specify that you should give the effect size for either the omnibus test *or* the comparisons, not for both. Most readers will probably be more interested in the effect size of the comparisons, not of the omnibus test. Here is an example of reporting the results of the test for syntactic variety from the Ellis and Yuan (2004) data, ignoring the omnibus test and focusing instead only on the post-hoc comparisons and using bootstrapping (results come from Sections 9.4.4, 9.4.5 and 9.4.9):

> In looking at the amount of syntactic variety produced by the participants in the groups with differing levels of planning time, planned comparisons were made among all three groups. The descriptive statistics for the groups were: no planning (NP), X = 16.2, SD = 4.1, *N* = 14; online planning (OLP), X = 18.9, SD = 3.2, *N* = 14; and pre-task planning (PTP), X = 22.1, SD = 3.6, *N* = 14. Comparisons using bootstrapping and calculating 95% BCa CIs (unadjusted for multiple comparisons) found the following CIs for the mean differences between groups and Cohen's *d* effect sizes:
>
> - NP and PTP (mean difference = 5.86, 95% BCa CI [3.17, 8.78], Cohen's *d* = 1.53, 95% BCa CI for Hedges' *g* is [0.61, 2.24]
> - NP and OLP (mean difference = 2.64, 95% BCa CI [−0.10, 5.34], Cohen's *d* = 0.72, 95% BCa CI for Hedges' *g* is [0.11, 1.47]
> - PTP and OLP (mean difference = 3.2, 95% BCa CI [−5.85, −0.93], Cohen's *d* = 0.95, 95% BCa CI for Hedges' *g* is [0.20, 1.61]
>
> All of the CIs for the mean differences between groups are large, but it can be seen that the comparison between NP and PTP produced the CI farthest away from zero, indicating the strongest effect. On a test where the maximum score was 17, we are confident that there was a real difference of *at least* 3 points between the NP and PTP group, with the PTP getting higher scores, indicating that amount of planning time had a noticeable effect on the amount of syntactic variety produced in writing, with pre-task planning producing the largest amount of syntactic variety. The other comparisons show that there was also an effect for PTP time being slightly better than online planning time, although the effect might be as low as just one point of difference. Effect sizes show the largest effect for pre-task planning, with a *d* = 1.52 indicating a difference of 1.5 times the SD between the two groups, but CIs for the effect sizes are large and differences could be as small as only 0.5 a SD. Confidence intervals for the effect sizes for the two other comparisons

show both effect sizes could be quite small, and we cannot place too much confidence in them. In summary, I conclude that amount of planning time had a noticeable effect on the amount of syntactic variety produced in writing, with PTP producing the largest amount of syntactic variety.

9.5 Summary of One-Way Analysis of Variance

A one-way ANOVA is just one conceptual step away from a *t*-test. *T*-tests are used when you want to examine whether two groups differ; one-way ANOVAs are used when you want to examine the effect of groups and you have three or more groups to examine. There is only one DV and only one IV.

We saw at the beginning of the chapter that ANOVAs mathematically compare the difference in the fit of a line between all the data points (the within-subjects effects) to the fit of lines for each of the groups (the between-subject effects). If the groups are not very different this ratio will be close to 1, but if they are different from each other the ratio will be larger than 1 and the *p*-value of the *F* statistic will be less than 0.05. This indicates an overall omnibus effect for the one-way ANOVA.

The assumptions of the parametric one-way ANOVA are the same as those of the *t*-test, and include a normal distribution and homogeneous variances. In going through the examples and doing the exercises you will have probably noticed that there are very few if any instances when data are exactly normally distributed. I have suggested here that using robust methods of analysis, such as bootstrapping empirical distributions (resulting in non-parametric statistics) and also possibly trimming means if distributions are highly skewed (possible only in R at the moment and shown in the additional online document "Bootstrapping and Means-Trimmed One-Way ANOVA in R") can deal better with non-normal distributions or non-equal variances than simply ignoring the matter and using parametric statistics (see Larson-Hall & Herrington, 2009).

A concept we discussed with regard to ANOVAs that goes beyond *t*-tests was the difference between an omnibus test and post-hoc tests or planned comparisons. Because ANOVAs look at three or more groups, a statistical ANOVA result (reporting an *F*-value) will not really tell us all that we need to know. If this *F*-test, or omnibus test, is statistical, we may proceed to look at post-hoc tests that compare only two groups at a time. Indeed, I asserted that we may want to ignore the omnibus test altogether and go straight to the comparisons we are interested in as the *F*-test does not tell us what we really want to know. This is possible by using planned comparisons. If you are not interested in all the possible pairings of groups, it is always a good idea to use planned comparisons.

Effect sizes and CIs for effect sizes should also be reported. For one-way ANOVAs we saw that there are effect sizes for both the omnibus test and the comparisons. I suggested that most readers would be more interested in the effect sizes for comparisons than for the omnibus effect, and this effect size is calculated in much the same way as we saw for *t*-tests.

Chapter 10

Looking for Group Differences with Factorial Analysis of Variance When there is More than One Independent Variable

Learning with Music

> Although statistical analysis can objectify, to some extent, the process of looking for patterns in data, statistical methods . . . do not assure that the most appropriate ways of organizing the data will be found.
>
> Maxwell and Delaney (2004, p. 5)

A one-way ANOVA examines group differences when there is one independent variable (IV) and one dependent variable (DV). However, sometimes, we may be interested in a more complex situation where the DV can be explained by several different IVs. When we conduct an ANOVA with two IVs it is called a two-way ANOVA. (See that? The one-way ANOVA had one IV and the two-way ANOVA has two IVs— it makes sense!) In general, once we get past the one-way ANOVA, these types of models are called factorial ANOVAs. Table 10.1 lists the terminology of ANOVAs that we use and then tells how many DVs and IVs each type of ANOVA has.

Table 10.1 Types of Factorial ANOVAs

One-way between-groups ANOVA
IV: 1 categorical variable
DV: 1 continuous variable
Two-way between-groups ANOVA
IV: 2 categorical variables
DV: 1 continuous variable
. . .
K-way between-groups ANOVA
IV: K categorical variables
DV: 1 continuous variable

In this chapter, we look at a study by Obarow (2004) that asked whether music affected how much vocabulary English as a second language (ESL) children learned, and also whether picture book illustrations affected vocabulary learning. These ANOVAs can be called "factorial," because we have more than one factor or IV. In fact, because there are two IVs that split the participants into separate groups we can also call this a two-way **between-groups design**.

Recent Examples of Factorial Analysis of Variance in the Second Language Acquisition Literature

Muñoz and Llanes (2014)

The goal of this study was to examine how foreign accent would change over a three-month time period for language learners living in their own native country vs. those who studied abroad. The researchers also brought the issue of age into the picture by testing adults and children learning a second language in both situations. Therefore, there were four groups: (1) children who studied abroad ($N = 13$); (2) children who studied at home ($N = 15$); (3) adults who studied abroad ($N = 15$); and (4) adults who studied at home ($N = 12$). There was a pretest and a posttest. The participants told a narrative based on pictures they saw, and also spoke in a semistructured interview task; 20-second excerpts from the story narration were played for judges who rated them on a 1–7 point scale, where 1 = no foreign accent and 7 = very strong foreign accent. Child and adult native speakers' (NS) data were included in the rating task. A 2 (age) × 2 (context) factorial ANOVA on the gain score from pretest to posttest was conducted to answer the research question of whether degree of accent changes as a result of age and learning context. There was no interaction between the independent variables (IVs) of age and context (partial eta-squared = 0.00) nor a statistical effect for age (partial eta-squared = 0.02), but there was a main effect for learning context ($F_{1,51} = 6.9$, $p = 0.01$, partial eta-squared = 0.12), with those studying abroad having greater gains than those who studied at home.

Dahl and Ludvigsen (2014)

Research on gestures has been increasing, and this study aimed to extend previous work on the benefit of gestures in connection with listening comprehension among second language learners. The authors chose a foreign language population to test their hypothesis on, and also tested NS to see whether gestures helped improve their comprehension or not. The tests were conducted on middle school students in the USA ($n = 28$) and Norway ($n = 46$). Study participants listened while a speaker described four funny cartoons, and either saw a video with the speaker's entire body and her natural gestures (the Gesture condition) or saw an edited video with only the speaker's head (the Non-Gesture condition). The listeners' task was to draw the cartoon after they had listened to the entire description. The research question was whether gestures would help improve comprehension, and whether native listeners and foreign language listeners would differ in how they responded to the gestures, thus creating a research design with two independent variables—Condition (gestures or no gestures) and Language (NS of English or foreign language learner of English). A 2 (Condition) × 2 (Language) factorial ANOVA conducted on comprehension of the material showed a statistical interaction between Language and Condition, $F_{1,70} = 6.31$, $p = 0.01$, partial eta-squared = 0.08 (this is a medium-sized effect). The native language learners performed better than the foreign language students, and performed better regardless of whether they saw gestures or not, while the foreign language learners performed better in the Gesture condition.

Albirini and Benmamoun (2014)

The overriding question held by the researchers was how heritage language learners differ from second language learners. To this end, they examined three groups of Arabic speakers: Arabic L1, Arabic L2 and Heritage language learners ($n = 30$ in each group). The focus of the study was plural morphology in Arabic, with a basic distinction between so-called sound plurals, which are formed through agglutinative suffixation only, and broken plurals, which use stem changes along with affixes. The participants completed three oral tasks that involved formation of this morphology. One of these tasks was a plural formation task, where participants were shown pictures of words and asked to form the plural of the words. A factorial ANOVA that only examined the heritage learners and the L2 speakers (2 groups) and the effect of the plural form (sound vs. broken) found a statistical interaction, $F_{1,53} = 5.5$, $p < 0.05$, partial eta-squared = 0.09. Albirini and Benmamoun stated that "the performance gap between sound and broken plurals was more pronounced in the case of the L2 learners than the heritage speakers" (p. 862).

Letts, Edwards, Sinka, Schaefer, and Gibbons (2013)

Several studies have found a relationship between low socioeconomic status (SES) and delayed language development. The authors noted that there are difficulties in defining both SES and language development, and while some studies have found a relationship, others have not. They intended this study to add clarifying information to the debate as they tested a very large sample and tried to look at a number of characteristics of the children and the types of tests that are being used to establish the link between low SES and language delay. A newly created standardized language test, the New Reynell Developmental Language Scales, was developed by the first three authors of the study and includes items for comprehension and production which "cover early vocabulary (nouns and verbs), relating two objects, simple sentences, grammatical inflections and complex sentences" (p. 134). A sample of 1266 British children between ages 2 and 7 were tested. Socioeconomic status was measured by two measures—maternal education level and a governmental index regarding indicators of the geographical area of the child's school. A 2 (maternal education level) × 11 (child's age in a six-month band) factorial ANOVA was done to examine the effects of these IVs on the comprehension portion of the test. The authors reported that there was "a trend that approached significance" for the interaction of maternal education level and age ($F_{10,1070} = 1.82$, $p = 0.054$; no effect size reported). For production, the *p*-value was below 0.05 ($F_{10,1064} = 2.22$, $p < 0.02$, partial eta-squared = 0.2). A line graph showed that for the most part in production, children whose mothers had gone on to more than the minimum 16 years of education performed at a higher level than children whose mothers had a higher education, but there is a period from ages 4 to 5 when that trend is reversed (thus creating the interaction). The authors concluded that their test did find evidence of a relationship between SES (as measured by maternal education) and language development, but that it was modest and showed the most effects at the extremes of the age scales.

10.1 Analysis of Variance Design

There are several factors to consider when thinking about the design of factorial ANOVAs and how to interpret the output. One factor we will explore in this section is interaction. Another is distinguishing between the number of variables and the number of levels in a variable. If these two areas are not clear, it will be difficult to understand the ANOVA design.

10.1.1 Analysis of Variance Design: Interaction

Although one-way ANOVAs and higher-order ANOVAs are very similar in many ways, one reason to treat them in different chapters is that, once we have more than one independent variable, there is a chance of **interaction** between the variables. An interaction is when one level of a variable affects the levels of a second variable differently. To give a concrete example, look at Figure 10.1, which uses made-up data about the effects of two types of homestay programs and which country the student stayed in as explanatory factors for a Test of English for International Communication (TOEIC) bridge score. (The TOEIC bridge is a low-level version of the TOEIC test.) This figure, created in R using the HH package and the interaction2wt( ) command, shows an interaction between the homestay program and country. (See Section 10.2.1 for code to create a plot like this.) If there were no interaction, all of the lines would be parallel, but they are not. The top left panel shows that students in program A all performed about the same on the TOEIC bridge no matter what country they spent their homestay in, but students in program B seemed to do much better if they stayed in Australia or Korea, and worst if they stayed in Thailand. The same information is seen reversed in the bottom right panel of Figure 10.1. Here we might see more easily that program B produced higher results overall, but not when the homestay was in the country of Thailand.

Once we can look at the effect of two or more variables, we may see that the effects of a variable are not constant in all situations. If two IVs show an interaction, then participants do not score the same way on both variables. If there had been no interaction, then students in any country would have performed the same way regardless of the program, and students in either program would have performed the same way regardless of the country. In an interaction we cannot really talk about the effect of just one variable, because its effect depends on the other variable. So we cannot say that overall, program B was better than program A, because it depended on the country the participant stayed in. Likewise, we cannot say that all participants were better off doing a homestay in Australia, because that also depended on which program they were in. If they were in program A, it really did not matter which country they stayed in.

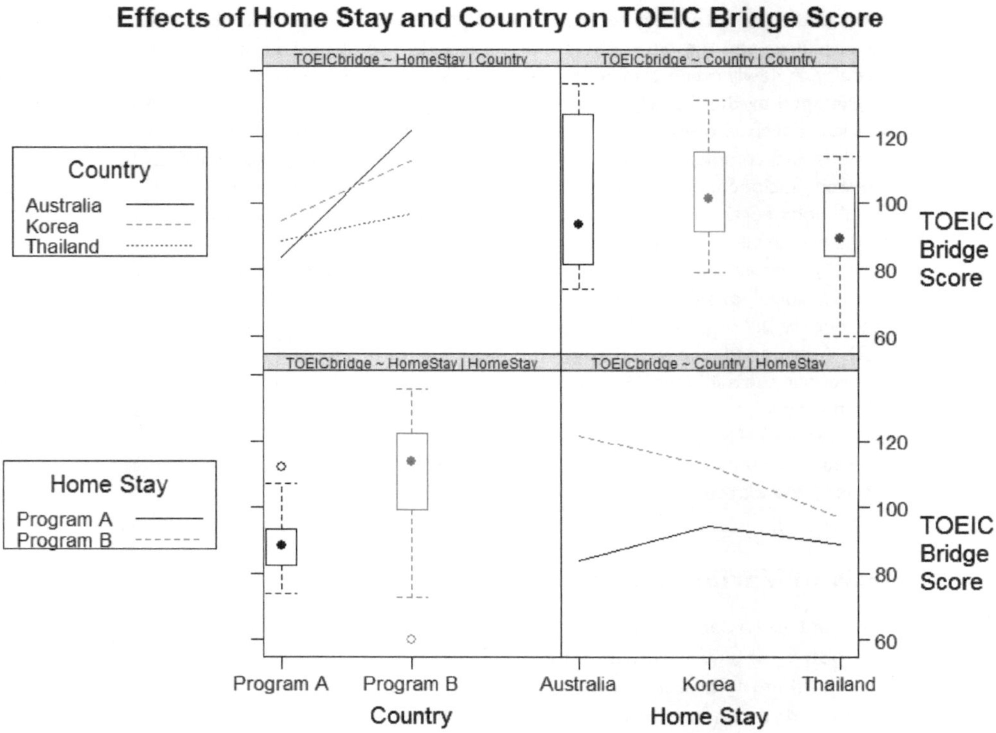

Figure 10.1 Interaction plot example with made-up data about effects of country and study abroad program on TOEIC bridge scores (this plot used the interaction2wt( ) command in R).

By the way, I like the graphic in Figure 10.1 because it shows box plots for the TOEIC score as it is affected by each variable (the top right panel shows scores in a box plot depending only on the country, and the bottom left panel shows scores depending only on the program) as well as the interaction plot in reversed formats. It thus shows both main effects (Program, Country) as well as the interaction effects (Program*Country). It is quite an informative and helpful graphic for understanding your data. See Section 10.2.1 for more information about how to make these types of plots.

> **Tip:** As the number of independent variables becomes larger, the number of possible interactions becomes larger too. Many statistical experts recommend not including more independent variables in an ANOVA than you are able to understand if the highest possible number of interactions occurs. This often means you should stick to three independent variables at the most.

10.1.2 Application Activity in Understanding Interaction

Look at the graphs in the following exercises, which show an interaction between variables. Try to state the interaction in your own words. All of these data are invented. First, here is an example of what I want you to do. I describe the interaction in Figure 10.2:

Interaction: When there were pictures present, it did not matter if music was present or not—participants scored about the same. However, when there were no pictures, participants did much better if they had music.

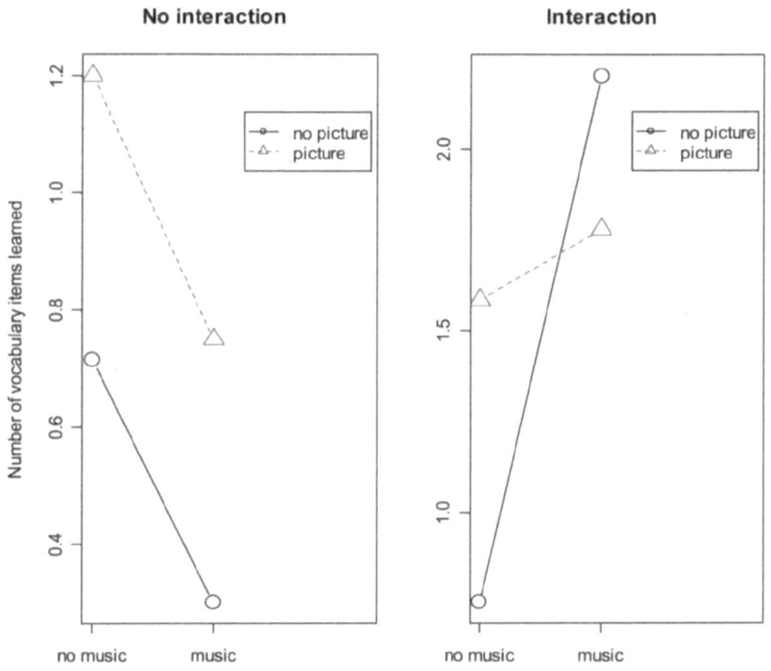

Figure 10.2 Interaction plot example with made-up data about effects of music and pictures on vocabulary learning (modeled after Obarow's data but not her actual data).

1 The use of feedback and explicit vs. implicit instruction and its effect on test scores.

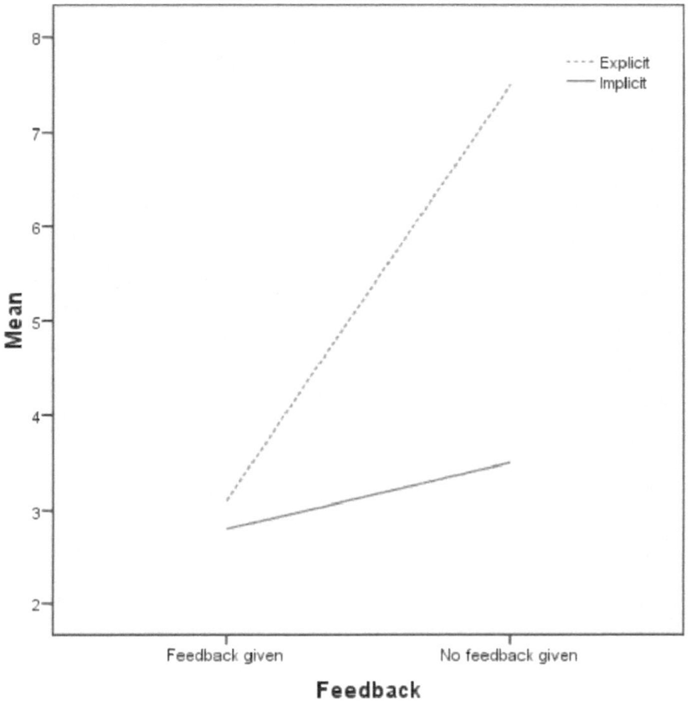

2 Type of pronunciation input and type of production data examined (segmental or intonation) and their effect on pronunciation accuracy.

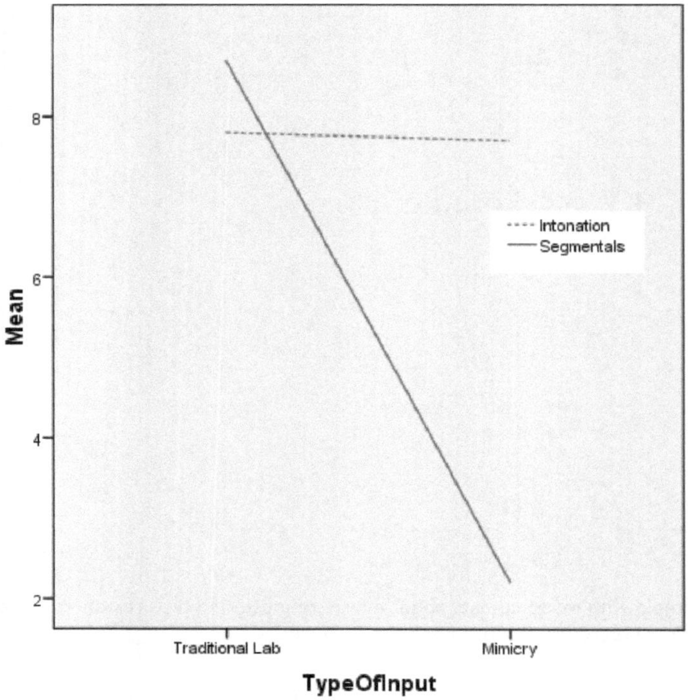

3 The effects of length of immersion, language aptitude and motivation on the proficiency levels of study abroad learners.

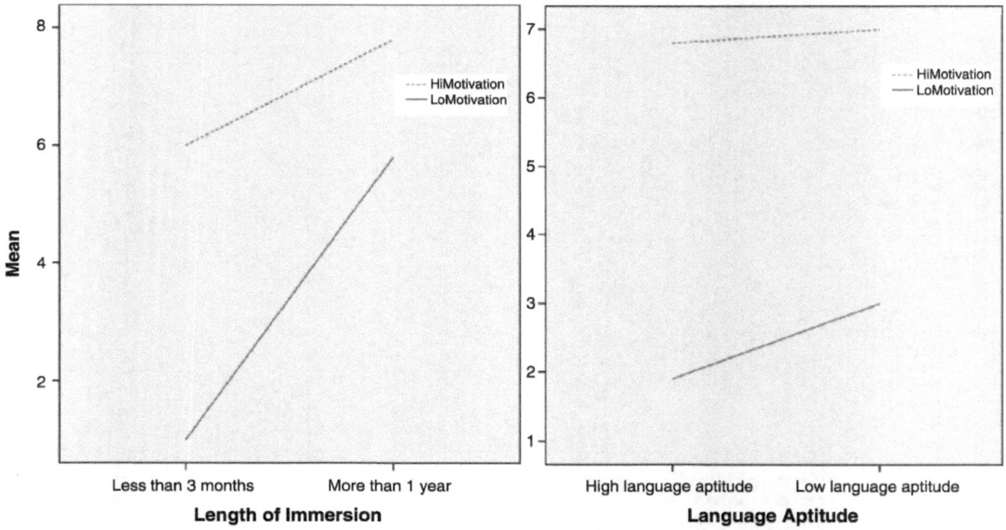

4 The effects of age (child or adult) and context (studying abroad or studying at home) on gain scores on a language proficiency test. (This is modeled on the study by Muñoz and Llanes (2014) but does not use their actual data.)

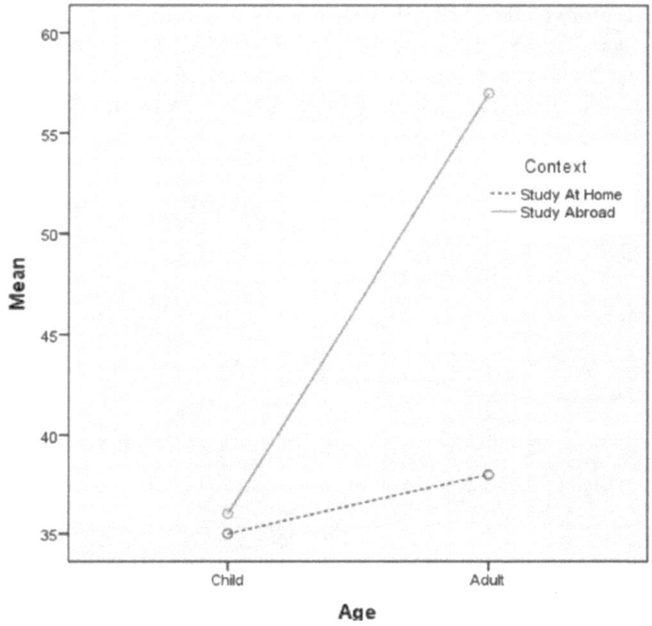

5 The effects of language background (NS, L2 learner or heritage speaker) on scores for correctly forming two different types of plural formation in Arabic. (This is modeled on the study by Albirini and Benmamoun (2014) but does not use their actual data.)

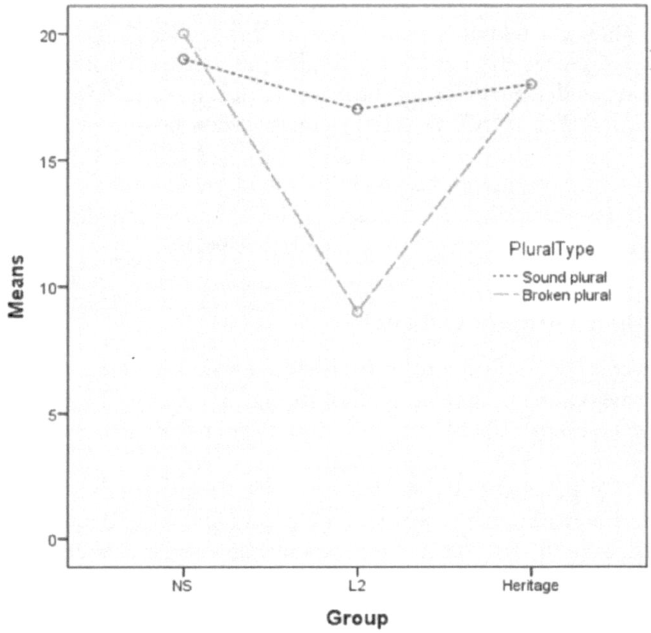

10.1.3 Analysis of Variance Design of the Obarow Study

The study featured in this chapter is the one done by Obarow (2004). Obarow investigated whether the method of presenting storybooks to young children would influence how much vocabulary they would incidentally learn. Obarow had two IVs: music (singing the story) and illustrations. Thus, there were four different conditions that the story could be heard in—with or without music, crossed by the variable of with or without illustrations. This is a two-way factorial ANOVA because there is more than one IV. This ANOVA can also be called a 2 (music) × 2 (illustration) ANOVA (two-by-two ANOVA), to represent the number of levels in each factor. The design box in Figure 10.3 lays out this design.

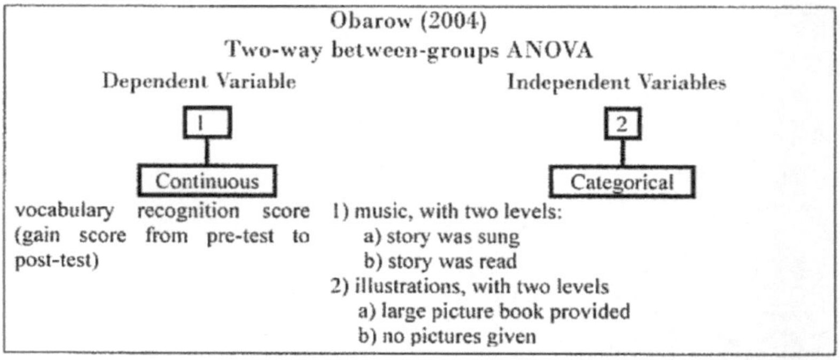

Figure 10.3 Obarow (2004) design box.

Both variables in the Obarow study are **between-groups variables**. This means that each person participated in only one level of the variable. For example, the children tested either had music or did not have music with their story, and either had pictures or not. (In fact, this statement is not accurate, since actually Obarow tested the children on four different stories and each time they did it she varied the experimental group they were in, but for purposes of this chapter and this part of the data I will maintain this assertion.)

If you have any **within-groups variables** you will need to use a repeated-measures design. A within-groups variable, where the same people repeat the experiment under different conditions, such as everyone hearing the book with music and later everyone hearing it without music, would result in more than one DV. Therefore, for factorial ANOVA, the IVs must always be a between-groups variable.

In this chapter, to illustrate a more complex design, I will add the IV of Gender to the ANOVA. This is also a between-groups variable, as each student is classified as either male or female. This now makes the factorial ANOVA a 2 (music) × 2 (illustrations) × 2 (gender) ANOVA.

10.1.4 Analysis of Variance Design: Variable or Level?

Once we have more than one IV, it can get confusing to distinguish between separate IVs and the levels of the IVs. I suggest that if the measurement applies to all of the participants in the study then it is a separate variable, while if the measurement applies to only a section of the participants it is a level of a variable.

Let us say you want to do a study that looks at reaction times for participants reading sentences online and you want to figure out whether reading sentences with long-distance dependencies results in longer reaction times than sentences with short-distance dependencies. Some participants will read sentences with short-distance dependencies and some will read sentences with long-distance dependencies. You also include speakers from three different L1s in your experiment—Spanish, Chinese and Russian. You know you have more than one IV, but you are a little confused about what to label your variables, and whether they are separate variables or just levels. For example, are sentences with long-distance dependencies IVs or just a level of a variable? So ask yourself whether all participants are reading sentences with long-distance dependencies. They are not, so this is just a level of a variable. That means your variable is something you could label "Sentence Type," with two levels—long-distance and short-distance dependencies. It might be more natural in an experiment like this to have all participants read sentences with both short-distance and long-distance dependencies to compare the two. However, in that case this would be a repeated-measures design, since all participants would have a score on short-distance dependencies (which would be one DV) and all the same participants would have a score on long-distance dependencies (which would be an additional DV). Then you wonder if L1 is a separate variable or just a level. Does L1 apply to all participants? Yes, they all fall into one category of L1, so L1 is a variable. Of course, they are not all Russian, so Russian is a level within the variable of L1. The following application activity will give you practice in identifying the number of IVs in an ANOVA design, and the number of levels in each variable.

10.1.5 Application Activity: Identifying Independent Variables and Levels

Look at the following descriptions of actual research studies. First, label the study. Then list the IVs (there may be one, two or three) and how many levels each IV has.

1 Pandey (2000) wanted to see whether first language dialect would affect scores on the Test of English as a Foreign Language (TOEFL) test. She hypothesized that monodialectal African American Vernacular English (AAVE) speakers would score similarly to ESL speakers. Simplifying Pandey's design, it consisted of testing each of four classes by giving them the TOEFL test at the end of the semester.

This is a __________-way	IV(s):	No. of levels:
ANOVA	1	1
	2	2
	3	3

2 Takimoto (2006) was interested in whether explicit instruction would be useful in helping Japanese learners of English learn to perform requests with more pragmatic accuracy. Simplifying the research design, it consisted of three different experimental groups—a structured input group with no feedback, a structured input group with feedback and a control group who did not receive any input or feedback on pragmatic appropriateness of requests. The groups were tested before and after the experimental treatment.

This is a __________-way	IV(s):	No. of levels:
ANOVA	1	1
	2	2
	3	3

3 Smith, McGregor, and Demille (2006) looked at the phonological development of two-year-olds, and compared those who had advanced vocabulary levels with those who were just average in

their vocabulary. The children were further divided by their age into two groups—those who were 24 or 30 months old.

This is a ___________-way ANOVA	IV(s):	No. of levels:
	1	1
	2	2
	3	3

4 Sanz and Morgan-Short (2004) examined how explanation and explicit feedback could affect whether English learners of Spanish would choose the correct interpretation for preverbal direct object pronouns in Spanish. There were four groups of learners, who differed as to whether they received an explanation or not, and whether they received implicit or explicit feedback on their answers.

This is a ___________-way ANOVA	IV(s):	No. of levels:
	1	1
	2	2
	3	3

5 Muñoz and Llanes (2014) compared children and adults who either studied abroad or studied at home on their level of foreign accent. They computed a gain score from pretest to posttest. (Try to do this question and the next three without looking back at the information at the beginning of the chapter!)

This is a ___________-way ANOVA	IV(s):	No. of levels:
	1	1
	2	2
	3	3

6 In the study by Dahl and Ludvigsen (2014), middle school students watched a video of someone describing a cartoon and could either see the person's whole body or just their head. Listeners had to draw the cartoon and were rated on how closely it resembled the description. The research question was whether seeing gestures would help the listeners or not. The listeners were either NS of English or foreign language learners of English.

This is a ___________-way ANOVA	IV(s):	No. of levels:
	1	1
	2	2
	3	3

7 Albirini and Benmamoun (2014) examined NS of Arabic, heritage learners of Arabic and L2 learners of Arabic to see how well they would be able to form the plural form of two kinds of plural nouns—so-called "sound plurals" and "broken plurals."

This is a ___________-way ANOVA	IV(s):	No. of levels:
	1	1
	2	2
	3	3

8 In the study by Letts, Edwards, Sinka, Schaefer, and Gibbons (2013), 11 groups of children at different age bands (six-month bands) took a newly developed language development test. One question the study examined was whether maternal levels of education (finished only the mandatory 16 years or finished more than the mandatory) affected scores on the production portion of the test.

This is a ___________-way ANOVA	IV(s):	No. of levels:
	1	1
	2	2
	3	3

10.2 Numerical and Visual Inspection

To inspect Obarow's data, let us first look at the mean scores and standard deviations (SDs) of the gain scores for the first story from the Obarow (2004) data (using the Obarow.Story1.sav file), which are shown in Table 10.2. The data are found in the Obarow.Story1.sav file. We will be looking at immediate gain scores of how much vocabulary children learned. There were 20 possible vocabulary words to learn, but the pretest score was an average of 15.6 for all 64 participants in the study, with a minimum score of 11 and a maximum score of 17. This is why you will note that gain scores are fairly low.

Table 10.2 Numerical Summary from Obarow (2004) Story 1

Immediate posttest gain score (gnsc1.1)			N	*Mean*	*SD*
Male	No pictures	No music	8	0.75	2.12
	No pictures	Music	5	2.20	1.79
	Pictures	No music	12	1.58	1.16
	Pictures	Music	9	1.78	2.11
Female	No pictures	No music	7	0.71	0.95
	No pictures	Music	10	0.30	1.49
	Pictures	No music	5	1.20	0.45
	Pictures	Music	8	0.75	1.04

In SPSS, you can get the information in Table 10.2 by first splitting the file by all of the IVs (DATA > SPLIT FILE, then click on the "Compare groups" radio button and move the variables GENDER, PICTUREST1 and MUSICT1 to the "Groups based on" box). To call for descriptive statistics looking at the immediate gain scores, choose ANALYZE > DESCRIPTIVE STATISTICS > DESCRIPTIVES and put GNSC1.1 into the box called "Variable(s)." Click on OK and do not forget to unsplit the data after you are finished.

In R you can get all the information you need to fill in Table 10.2 by actually running your ANOVA. We will do it now, but ignore the ANOVA output. Use the menu sequence in R Commander, STATISTICS > MEANS > MULTI-WAY ANOVA. For "Factors" choose gender, musict1 and picturest1. (Use the Ctrl button plus click the mouse to choose more than one variable at a time.) For "Response variable" pick the immediate gain score (gnsc1.1). Press OK.

Toward the end of the output, you get output to a command called with( ). You will then see the mean scores, SDs and counts that you need:

```
with(obarowStory1, (tapply(gnsc1.1, list(gender, musict1, picturest1), function(x)
sum(!is.na(x)))))
```

with(obarowStory1, . . .)	The with( ) command is a generic command that is used to simplify calls to function and in this case acts like attach( ) so the data set name does not have to be specified in the following functions.
tapply()	This command is an object-oriented wrapper, which means it takes data and applies some function on them. The general syntax of the tapply( ) command is tapply(data, index, function).
gnsc1.1	These are the data that we want to get a numerical summary for. The tapply( ) command says its first argument is "an atomic object, typically a vector." You need to specify the variable name (gnsc1.1).
list(gender, musict1, picturest1)	Because the second argument of the tapply( ) command is some kind of index which we want to be the three different groups, we can combine them using the list() command. The list() command takes whatever data are put into it and makes a list of them. Tip: For the tapply( ) command we can specify which name it prints out though, so actually we could write PresenceOfMusic=musict1 instead of just musict1, which would alter that specification so that instead of printing out music in the results, it would label the data as PresenceOfMusic if we ran this command in the R Console.
function(x) sum(!is.na(x))	This argument is the function that the tapply( ) command uses. This function returns a count of the number in each of the divided groups we made. We can put in mean and sd directly, but this command for counts is a little tricky. It asks R to count up the number of items that are *not* missing. (The "!" means "do the opposite" of the next thing, which asks R to sum up the number of missing values, so the command sums up the number of not missing values.)

The way that the command sets up the output, the descriptive statistics show the number of vocabulary items learned when, first of all, pictures are present vs. absent, and splits those data up into variables of gender and music. If this is not the organization of the data that you want, you could just change the order that the factors are listed in the tapply( ) command and run it again in the R Console.

Considering that there were 20 vocabulary words tested from the story, as we look at the means for each of the 4 groups in the immediate gain scores (the day after treatment ended), there does not seem to be a big difference between conditions. Overall, scores were higher for all groups in the delayed gain scores (one week after treatment), but they are still not large gains (somewhat fewer than two words). The numerical summary also shows that the SDs are quite large, in most cases larger than the mean.

For the visual summary, since we are looking at group differences, box plots would be an appropriate way of checking the distribution of data. But since we are also looking for interactions, means plots are a helpful tool for visualizing the trends of the data. R can produce a very nice visual, as was seen earlier in the chapter and again in Figure 10.4, which contains both box and means plots.

Figure 10.4 shows box plots of the immediate gain score for each of the three main effects: gender, the presence of music and the presence of pictures. All of the box plots show a number of outliers or a skewed distribution of data, so we already know that these data are not normally distributed. Also included in Figure 10.4 is a means plot of the interaction between the three IVs, gender, music and pictures. In most of the cases the lines are pretty much parallel to each other. Visually, no interaction would be shown by parallel lines, meaning that the effects of pictures were the same whether music (or pictures) were present or not and regardless of the person's gender. In a couple of cases there are crossed lines or lines that are not parallel, but the differences do not look very large, so here, visual methods lead us to not expect to see an interaction between variables in these data (maybe with the exception of the interaction plot for Music and Gender). However, visual methods can be misleading depending on the scale of the plot.

Figure 10.5 shows a means plot where it appears that there is an interaction in the immediate gain score, although not in the delayed gain score, between Music and Pictures. Why did we not think we saw an interaction between these two in Figure 10.4? The very detailed scale of the graph

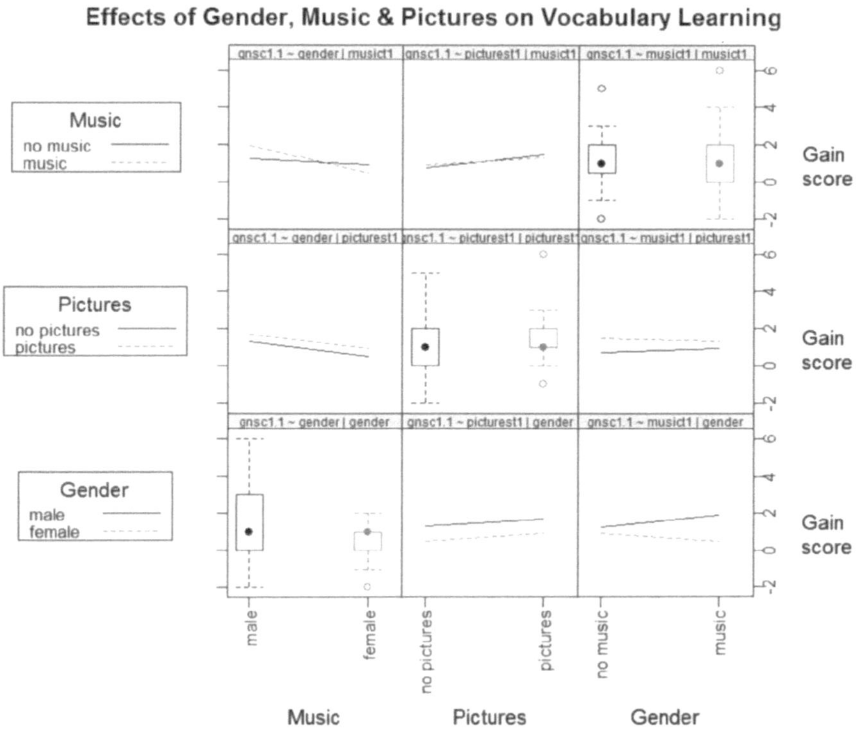

Figure 10.4 Box plots and means plots for immediate gain scores for vocabulary in Story 1 in Obarow's data.

in Figure 10.5 makes the lines look non-parallel. Notice the scale for Figure 10.5 is of only one point, from 0.60 to 1.60, whereas the scale for Figure 10.4 is from eight points, from −2 to 6. Actually, the panel of Figure 10.4 that matches Figure 10.5 (there are two panels where you see Music crossed with Pictures) does show a slight non-parallelism at the larger scale of Figure 10.4, but we can ignore it as unimportant. If the scale of your graph is small enough, the lines may not look parallel, but when you pull back to a larger scale that difference can fade away.

Although means plots are often given for ANOVA data and are useful for discerning trends in the data, I urge caution in including them in published reports. Means plots often provide only one piece of information per group—the mean, which means they are an impoverished type of graphic and are not data accountable (Larson-Hall, in preparation). I like the R graphic that provides the more data-accountable box plot alongside the means plot, and I would urge researchers to use R to create this graphic instead of just inserting a means plot. (See the following section for information about how to make it.) Since I think that means plots alone are useful for personal analysis but not publication, and since they can be called for in the statistical output when running a factorial ANOVA (in SPSS), I will explain commands for how to call up means plots in SPSS and R only in the later sections of the chapter on running ANOVAs.

Note that means plots will only be appropriate with two-way and higher ANOVAs since a means plot with a one-way ANOVA would have only one line. A different type of graphic, the parallel coordinate plot, is shown in Chapter 11 on repeated-measures ANOVAs, and could be used with factorial ANOVAs as well.

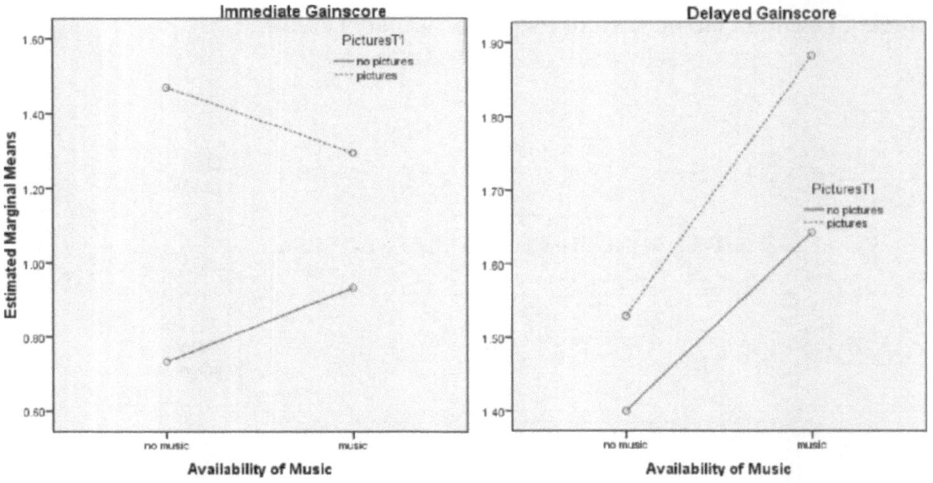

Figure 10.5 Means plots of gain scores from Obarow (2004) Story 1.

10.2.1 Creating a Combination Box Plot and Means Plot in R

The following explains the code used to create Figure 10.4, a combination box plot and means plot. This command comes from the HH package, so please install this package and open the package with the following commands first:

```
install.packages("HH")
library(HH)
attach(obarowStory1)
interaction2wt(gnsc1.1~gender*picturest1*musict1, par.strip.text=list(cex=.6), main.in="Effects of Gender, Music & Pictures on Vocabulary Learning", box.ratio=.3, rot=c(90,90),
factor.expressions=
c(musict1=expression("Music"),
picturest1=expression("Pictures"),
gender=expression("Gender")),
responselab.expression="Gain\nscore")
```

attach(obarowStory1)	Attaching this means that I do not have to type this long file name every time with my variable name; use search( ) to check which objects you already have attached on your desktop; frequently clean up and remove objects you do not want anymore: use detach(package:HH), for example, to detach or rm(obarow) to remove data sets you do not need anymore.
interaction2wt( )	This command from the HH package (make sure you install and open the HH package before using) creates a combination main effects/box plots and interaction effects/means plot graphic.
gnsc1.1~gender*picturest1*musict1	The command says to model the DV (immediate gain score) interval-level scores by the three independent variables gender, picturest1 and musict1. It is no problem to have more than two variables, they just need to be set up in the form of a linear model, with either a plus sign (+) adding main effects together, a colon (:) showing interactions or an asterisk (*) showing an expansion in the main effects and all of the interactions. (See further on in this chapter for more about linear models.)
par.strip.text=list(cex=.6)	This argument sets the size of the fonts in the top strip of each of the panels; I set mine smaller than I so the whole name could fit and could be seen.

main.in="Effects of Gender, Music & Pictures on Vocabulary Learning"	Gives custom name to the title of the graphic.
main.cex=1.2	Sets the size of the main title font (not used here).
box.ratio=.3	Sets the scale of the box plot, with smaller numbers thinner and larger numbers fatter; at a larger size the box plots go off the side of the graphic so I set them smaller.
rot=c(90,0)	Rotates the labels along the x-axis 90 degrees in the first argument; if you set 90 in the second argument, the ticks along the rightsided y-axis will also rotate; the help info says that only the settings of 0 and 90 will look good.
factor.expressions= c(musict1=expression("Music"), picturest1=expression("Pictures"), gender=expression("Gender"))	Use this syntax to specify the title of the legend on the left of the plot. (Do not forget the extra parentheses at the end.) Note: Even if you do not attach your data file, do not put the name of the file in front of the name of the variable, like this: obarowStory1$musict1. The command will not work if you do that.
Colors of lines	See Tip 1 for this section.
ylim=range(c(-2, 6))	I did not use this argument, but you could use it if you wanted to specify limits of the data on the y-axis.
responselab.expression= "Gain\nscore"	Allows the user to determine the string given on the right of each panel, explaining the measurement of the DV. The "\n" tells R where to make a new line.
detach(obarowStory1)	Be sure to detach your data when you are finished so you do not get confused later; use the argument data=obarowStory1 inside of your interaction2wt() command if you have not attached your data set.

Tip 1: It is a little complicated to change the color and types of lines but it may well be something you would want to do for publication of your graphic. We will use a method where you will change the global settings of the graphic parameters of the lattice functions. Since interaction2wt( ) uses lattice function parameters, you will need to use this system to change things. Here is how I changed the colors and line types for my graphic (this worked for a PC but not a Mac):

show.settings()	
mysettings<-trellis.par.get()	Create an object that you will put your changed parameters into.
mysettings$superpose.line $alpha [1] 1 $col [1] "#0080ff" "#ff00ff" "darkgreen" "#ff0000" "orange" [6] "#00ff00" "brown" $lty [1] 1 1 1 1 1 1 1 $lwd [1] 1 1 1 1 1 1 1	This will show the current parameters for your superimposed lines. You can see that $col, the color, has seven default colors, which will recycle if there are more than seven lines. We will reset all seven colors. Colors can be specified by number or name, as shown here in the default. To choose colors by looking at a color wheel, use the epitools package (Aragon, 2012) and type colors.plot(TRUE). For $lty, the line type, all of the lines use the same type. If you type help(par) you can see definitions for many of the graphics. Here you will see that a line type of 1 = solid, 2 = dashed, 3 = dotted, 4 = dot-dash, 5 = long-dash, 6 = two-dash, or you could use these names as is.
mysettings$superpose.line$col<-c("black", "red", "blue", "hotpink", "darkgreen", "orange", "gray94")	Set your new colors as you like.
mysettings$superpose.line$lty<-c(1:6)	Here I just set the line types to vary from one to six.
trellis.par.set(mysettings)	This last command now sets the trellis settings to your own settings. Run the command and you should see your own defaults being used now.

If the interaction2wt( ) command does not work for you, or does work but lines do not show up that should be there, consider whether you have any missing data in your data set. I tried to make this same graph with the delayed gain score data, but some of the graphs showed up with only one line instead of two. I figured out that the delayed gain score data had a missing value.

If you have missing data, the command will still produce a graphic but it will not print out a line of a group with missing data. Probably the fastest way to find missing data is just to click on the VIEW DATA SET button in R Commander and look through your data set. Figure 10.6 shows an "NA" in the gnsc1.2 column of the obarowStory1 data set that I have imported from the .sav file.

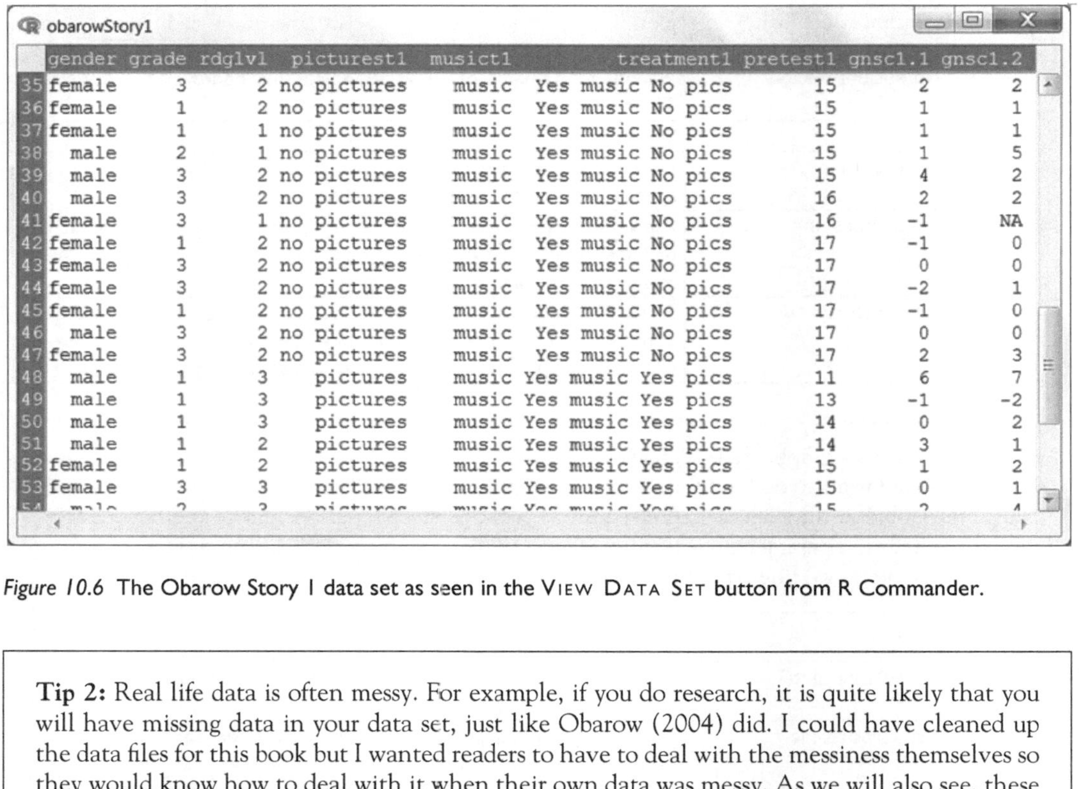
obarowStory1

	gender	grade	rdglvl	picturest1	musict1	treatment1	pretest1	gnsc1.1	gnsc1.2
35	female	3	2	no pictures	music	Yes music No pics	15	2	2
36	female	1	2	no pictures	music	Yes music No pics	15	1	1
37	female	1	1	no pictures	music	Yes music No pics	15	1	1
38	male	2	1	no pictures	music	Yes music No pics	15	1	5
39	male	3	2	no pictures	music	Yes music No pics	15	4	2
40	male	3	2	no pictures	music	Yes music No pics	16	2	2
41	female	3	1	no pictures	music	Yes music No pics	16	-1	NA
42	female	1	2	no pictures	music	Yes music No pics	17	-1	0
43	female	3	2	no pictures	music	Yes music No pics	17	0	0
44	female	3	2	no pictures	music	Yes music No pics	17	-2	1
45	female	1	2	no pictures	music	Yes music No pics	17	-1	0
46	male	3	2	no pictures	music	Yes music No pics	17	0	0
47	female	3	2	no pictures	music	Yes music No pics	17	2	3
48	male	1	3	pictures	music	Yes music Yes pics	11	6	7
49	male	1	3	pictures	music	Yes music Yes pics	13	-1	-2
50	male	1	3	pictures	music	Yes music Yes pics	14	0	2
51	male	1	2	pictures	music	Yes music Yes pics	14	3	1
52	female	1	2	pictures	music	Yes music Yes pics	15	1	2
53	female	3	3	pictures	music	Yes music Yes pics	15	0	1

Figure 10.6 The Obarow Story 1 data set as seen in the VIEW DATA SET button from R Commander.

> **Tip 2:** Real life data is often messy. For example, if you do research, it is quite likely that you will have missing data in your data set, just like Obarow (2004) did. I could have cleaned up the data files for this book but I wanted readers to have to deal with the messiness themselves so they would know how to deal with it when their own data was messy. As we will also see, these data are messy in the sense that we cannot find evidence that the treatment Obarow applied in her experiment had any effect on vocabulary learning. Usually when you go to the trouble of creating a treatment and testing its effect you are hoping the treatment is better than nothing (a control group). This chapter shows how to deal with both missing data and also with the fact that no effect can be found for the main experimental factors. Pilot testing your experiment might be one way to avoid getting disappointing results in your experiment as well (although this would need to be taken care of at the planning level, not the statistical level).

Chapter 1 had a section on missing data (Section 1.5). Since we believe the missing piece of data was missing at random, probably just because a child was absent on the testing day, and because we already have a rather small data set, and also because deleting a case (a row) is one of the worst ways to deal with missing data, we will go ahead and do multiple imputation to help fill in the missing data. I leave it to you to go back to Section 1.5.3 to read the details, but the Obarow data can be imputed rather easily by using the mice package, creating an object that contains the imputed data sets, and then completing the imputation and renaming it with our original data set name. Here is the R code for doing that:

```
library(mice)
imp <-mice(obarowStory1)
obarowStory1 <-complete(imp)
```

If you now take a look at your data set, you will find the missing value filled with the number "2," which seems a reasonable value. (By the way, if you are using R Commander to look at your data, you may need to open a different package, then come back to the obarowStory1 to see the updated version of your data set.)

10.3 Assumptions of a Factorial Analysis of Variance

The four main assumptions for ANOVA are the same ones we have seen for the *t*-test and the one-way ANOVA, but, with factorial ANOVAs, meeting the assumptions is more complicated because the model is more complicated. For factorial ANOVAs, the residuals are often examined as to how well they meet these requirements, as was done in the case of multiple regression. The four assumptions are:

1 The DV should be measured in interval-level measurements.
2 The data should be independent.
3 The data should be normally distributed.
4 Groups should have equal variances.

The first two assumptions need to be addressed in the design of the study, and so are an issue for your research design. The last two assumptions are the ones that can be tested *before* parametric ANOVA statistics are run and should also be examined by residual plots *after* the ANOVA is run. Just as for multiple regression, creating an ANOVA involves making a model, and that model needs to be examined for normal distribution and equal variances as well. Table 10.3 gives a summary of assumptions that can be tested for the ANOVA. Assumptions 1 and 2 can be tested before the model is run, and assumptions 3 and 4 can be tested only after the model is run.

Table 10.3 Assumptions for Factorial ANOVA

Meeting assumptions		*Factorial ANOVA*
1 Normal distribution of data (looking at the data according to groups)	Required?	Yes
	How to test assumption?	Examine box plots; plot normal curve over histogram (see Chapter 3); use Q-Q plots, robust diagnostics to check for outliers.
	What if assumption not met?	Use 20% trimmed means and/or bootstrap.
2 Equal variances (looking at the data according to groups)	Required?	Yes
	How to test assumption?	Examine side-by-side box plots; look at summary statistics for variance (see Chapter 3); examine spread versus level plot (called for in analysis of variance).
	What if assumption not met?	Use a bootstrap.
3 Normal distribution of residuals	Required?	Yes
	How to test assumption?	Call for residuals and then examine a histogram of their distribution.
	What if assumption not met?	Use 20% trimmed means and/or bootstrap.
4 Equal variances of residuals	Required?	Yes
	How to test assumption?	Examine scatterplot of predicted values versus studentized residuals. You should see random horizontal scatter and no patterns of data.
	What if assumption not met?	Use a bootstrap.

10.4 Getting Ready to Perform a Factorial Analysis of Variance

When we move to two-way and higher ANOVAs, we are finally moving into the world of multivariate analyses for groups. Factorial ANOVAs allow us to test for the effects of more than one IV at a time. For example, in the data set that will be used in this section, that of Obarow (2004), the factor of both music and pictures was used to investigate how well these two factors would facilitate vocabulary acquisition among kindergarten and Grade 1 children who were being read stories containing some unfamiliar words. Although Obarow only included these two factors in the analysis, for purposes of illustrating a higher-level ANOVA (and because the inclusion of this factor leads to interesting interactions), I will also include the factor of gender.

One important reason for doing a factorial ANOVA, in this case, a 2 (levels of music) × 2 (levels of pictures) × 2 (levels of gender) ANOVA, is to uncover possible interactions among the variables. In other words, if we performed a *t*-test separately on the data by investigating the performance of males vs. females, or by those who heard the stories sung (with music) vs. those who heard them read (without music), we would not know whether these factors worked together. As we will see, in the Obarow data there is a difference in how males and females react to the presence of music in how well they learn vocabulary. This result could not be uncovered in separate *t*-tests or separate one-way ANOVAs.

Obarow was extending a previous study by Medina (1991), which found that Grade 2 second language learners had higher vocabulary gain scores in conditions where they heard a story either sung or read with illustrations, and had the highest scores of all when both conditions were in effect. Medina's results did not find differences between groups; however, there were only seven students in each group. Obarow thus hoped to find statistical differences between groups by using a higher number of participants in each group (originally about 20 in each experimental condition, although through attrition her final numbers were slightly lower). She also had each child participate in each of the four conditions, once for each of four stories. Obarow thus in essence had a repeated-measures ANOVA because each child participated in each condition. However, Obarow's original analysis was to run separate factorial ANOVAs for each of the stories, and that is what we will look at here. (You can look at Obarow's results again in the exercises for Chapter 11 on repeated-measures ANOVA.)

This chapter introduced the idea of **main effects** and interaction in an ANOVA. The variance of a factorial ANOVA is partitioned into different parts, including main (or simple) effects and interaction. In the Obarow example, we have three IVs—music, pictures and gender. The ANOVA will partition variance into seven separate parts:

1 effects due to music alone;
2 effects due to pictures alone;
3 effects due to gender alone;
4 effects due to the interaction between music and pictures;
5 effects due to the interaction between music and gender;
6 effects due to the interaction between pictures and gender;
7 effects due to the interaction between music, pictures and gender.

Effects 1 through 3 in this list are called main effects or **simple effects**. Effects 4 through 7 are interaction effects. If we find an interaction effect, then very rarely will the main effect still be of interest. This is because the main effects can only be interpreted in light of the interaction. For example, we would not care that musical delivery of vocabulary was more effective than non-musical delivery if we knew that, when there were pictures, music was effective but, when there were no pictures, music was not effective.

10.4.1 Making Sure Your Data is in the Correct Format for a Factorial Analysis of Variance

The Obarow data set provides a good example of the kind of manipulations one might need to perform to put their data into the correct format for an ANOVA. A sample of Obarow's original data set is shown in Figure 10.7.

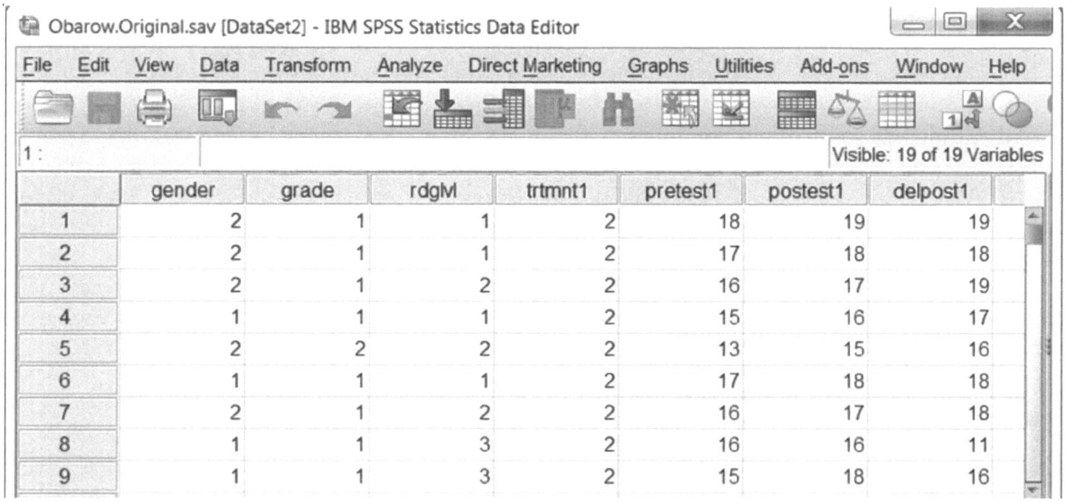

	gender	grade	rdgM	trtmnt1	pretest1	postest1	delpost1
1	2	1	1	2	18	19	19
2	2	1	1	2	17	18	18
3	2	1	2	2	16	17	19
4	1	1	1	2	15	16	17
5	2	2	2	2	13	15	16
6	1	1	1	2	17	18	18
7	2	1	2	2	16	17	18
8	1	1	3	2	16	16	11
9	1	1	3	2	15	18	16

Figure 10.7 The Obarow.Original.sav file, showing the original configuration of the Obarow (2004) data, which needs to be changed.

It can be seen in Figure 10.7 that Obarow had coded students for gender, grade level, reading level (this was a number from 1 to 3 given to them by their teachers) and then treatment group for the particular story. Obarow then recorded their score on the pretest, as it was important to see how many of the 20 targeted words in the story the children already knew. As can be seen in the pretest columns, most of the children already knew a large number of the words. Their scores on the same vocabulary test were recorded after they heard the story three times (immediate posttest) and then again one week later (delayed posttest). The vocabulary test used in the pretest and posttest was a four-item, multiple choice format test.

The format found here makes perfect sense for entering the data, but it is not the form we need to conduct the ANOVA. First, to do a factorial ANOVA, and not a repeated-measures ANOVA, we need to look at gain scores. This is because pretest, posttest and delayed posttest are all DVs collected from the same participants. If we have more than one DV, collected from the same participant, we would be forced to use a repeated-measures analysis. To calculate a gain score for the immediate posttest, we will simply subtract the pretest score from the posttest score (and a delayed gain score will be done by subtracting the pretest score from the delayed posttest score).

But there is an issue we should think about before we start to rearrange the data. Although the vocabulary words were chosen to be unfamiliar to this age of children, there were some children who achieved a perfect score on the pretest. Children with such high scores will clearly not be able to achieve any gains on a posttest. Therefore, it is worth considering whether there should be a cutoff point for children with certain scores on the pretest. Obarow did not do this, but it seems to me that, unless the children scored 17 or below, there is really not much room for them to improve their vocabulary in any case. I do not think it violates the independence assumption to throw these cases out because it is equal to excluding children from the experiment if their pretest scores are too high. With such a cutoff level, for the first story there are still 64 cases out of an original 81, which is still quite a respectable size. In the subsequent sections, I will demonstrate how I cut out these cases.

The next thing to rearrange in the original data file is the coding of the IVs. Previously I have discussed the issue of the wide vs. long format of data. For a factorial ANOVA, the data need to be in the long format, meaning that DV data from all of the groups is contained in just one column of data. For example, the DV for the Obarow data is now the calculated gain score, and the data for all four of the groups are contained in this one column called gnsc1.1 (the immediate gain score). This is probably not a surprise, but what I want to point out here is that because you have two or more IVs, the DV will be in one column but the IVs that index the DV will be in separate columns.

Because music and pictures are going to be two separate IVs, we need two columns, one coded for the inclusion of music and one coded for the inclusion of pictures in the treatment (Gender is already coded). The way Obarow originally coded the data, Trtmnt1 was coded as 1, 2, 3 or 4, which referred to different configurations of music and pictures. Using this column as it is, we would be able to conduct a one-way ANOVA (with Trtmnt1 as the IV), but we would not then be able to use a factorial ANOVA and test for the presence of interaction between music and pictures. However, for other purposes, like graphics, you may want one column that combines both of the factors and thus separates the data into smaller groups, as the Trtmnt1 variable does.

So to put these data into the correct format for the factorial ANOVA, we need to make two new columns, one for music and one for pictures, indicating the presence or absence of these for each category. The following sections explain how to complete all of these actions in either SPSS or R.

10.4.2 Rearranging Data for a Factorial Analysis of Variance Using SPSS

First, I will calculate the gain scores. I use the menu choice Transform > Compute Variable to create a new variable called gnsc1.1, which involves subtracting the Pretest1 variable from the Posttest1 variable. Follow this menu choice and you will see the dialog box in Figure 10.8. Use the calculator-type box (called "Numeric Expression" in the Compute Variable dialog box) to tell SPSS what to calculate, moving the correct variables over to the middle box and adding in the correct arithmetic functors. Add a name for your new variable in the "Target Variable" box. Thus, in Figure 10.8 you can see that in the "Numeric Expression" box I have "posttest1-pretest1," and in the "Target Variable" box I have put the name "gnsc1.1".

Notice that in this dialog box, you can select a box at the bottom that says "If . . ." This opens the dialog box shown on the right of Figure 10.8, which lets you select cases just for this variable. In this case, we want to select the cases where the pretest score is 17 or below, so enter that information in the Numeric Expression box. (It is not labeled as "Numeric Expression" in the "Compute Variable: If Cases" dialog box, but the whole calculator-type setup is the same as in the "Compute Variable" box). Click on Continue, then on OK on the main dialog box, and you will see a new column appear at

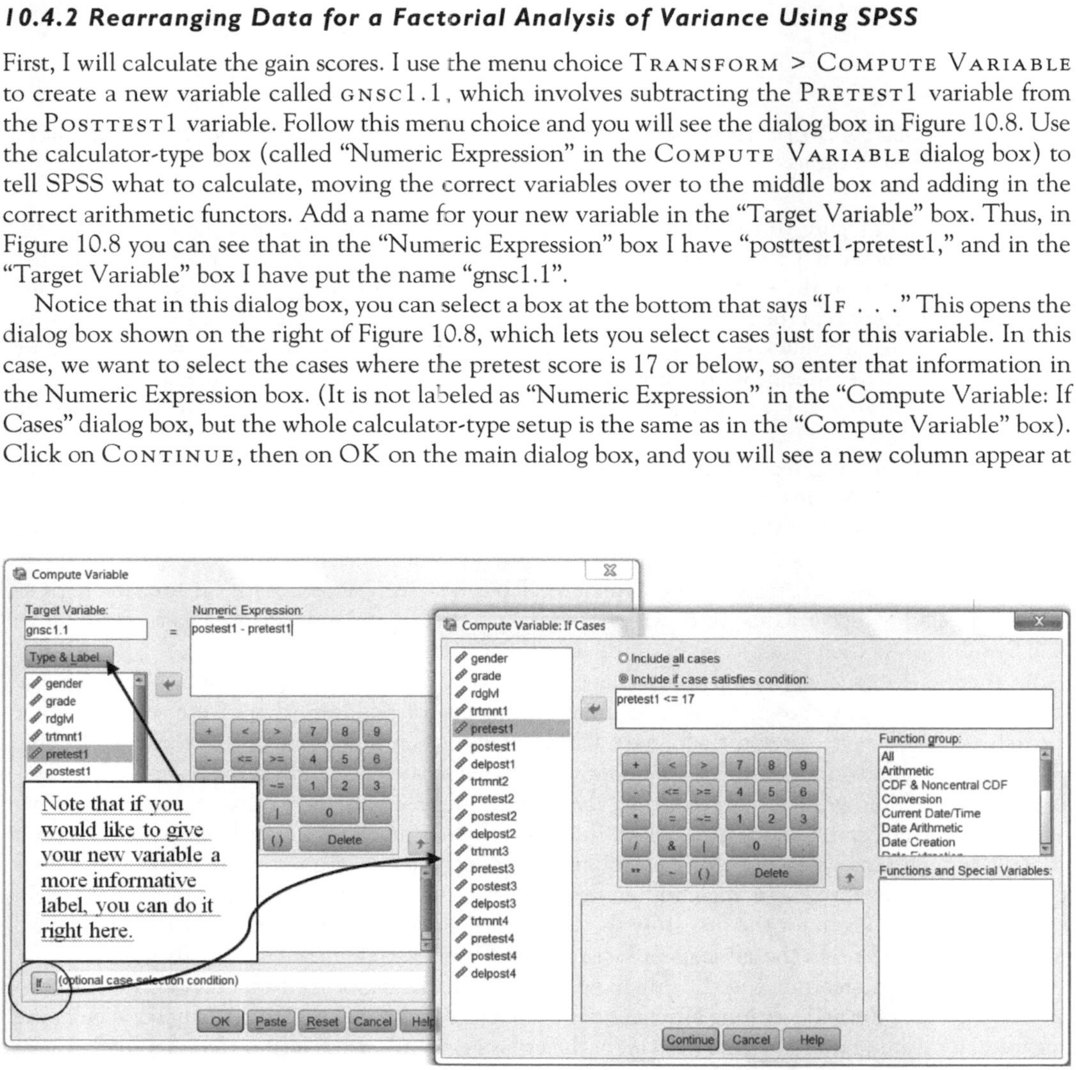

Figure 10.8 Calculating a new variable in SPSS with the Obarow (2004) original data set.

the end of your data file. In the case of the pretest in Story 1, no participant scored higher than a 17, so no cases have been cut out. If they had been, the cell for that row would not show any number, it would just be blank.

So, using the IF . . . button in the COMPUTE VARIABLE box is one way to select certain participants for inclusion in the analysis. This way might be the most appropriate for a data set like Obarow's, where you have different pretests for different stories, so a more global method would not be sufficient. If you had a data set where you wanted to cut out data for all participants in the data set, for example, say we wanted to look only at students who had a lower reading level of 1 or 2 in the Obarow data set, we could use the DATA > SELECT CASES menu choice. This dialog box looks similar to the one in Figure 10.8, but there are a couple of differences, so I have shown this menu choice in Figure 10.9. For selecting cases there are more choices than just the conditional argument that I used here, such as random sampling or using a range of values. I would click on the "If condition is satisfied" radio button. Remember, we are going to select the cases we want to *keep*. (I often get confused and work the opposite way, selecting the cases I want to get rid of!) Figure 10.9 shows the SELECT CASES dialog box and the dialog box that opens when you press the IF. . . button. If you choose to filter cases, you will see a slash line through those row numbers. If you delete your unselected cases, the rows will simply be gone.

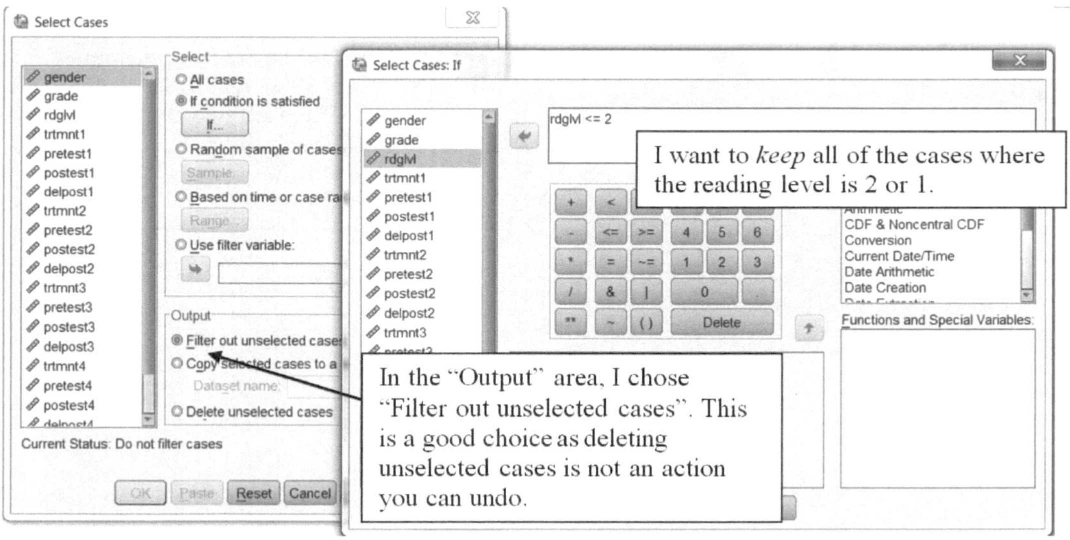

Figure 10.9 Selecting cases for the Obarow (2004) original data set.

The last chore is to change the TRTMNT1 variable into two separate variables. To add the two extra columns, I used the TRANSFORM > RECODE INTO DIFFERENT VARIABLES command. Figure 10.10 shows this dialog box. I set the recoding up for the Music variable knowing that 1 and 2 indicate the absence of music, and 3 and 4 the presence of music. After I created these variables I went to my data file and clicked on the VARIABLE VIEW tab, where I added values so I would know later whether 1 meant music was present or not. (This part is not shown but is important to do!) I then did the recoding for pictures, with the directives for transforming pictures being: 1 = 1, 2 = 2, 3 = 1, 4 = 2, where 1 = no pictures and 2 = pictures.

After all of this manipulation, I saved this new file as Obarow.Story.1.sav and I am ready to get to work on my ANOVA analysis! Notice from Figure 10.11 that I now have a gain score (GNSC1.1) and two columns coding for the presence of pictures (PICTUREST1) and music (MUSICT1). There are only 64 rows of data. I have called this file Obarow.Story1.sav.

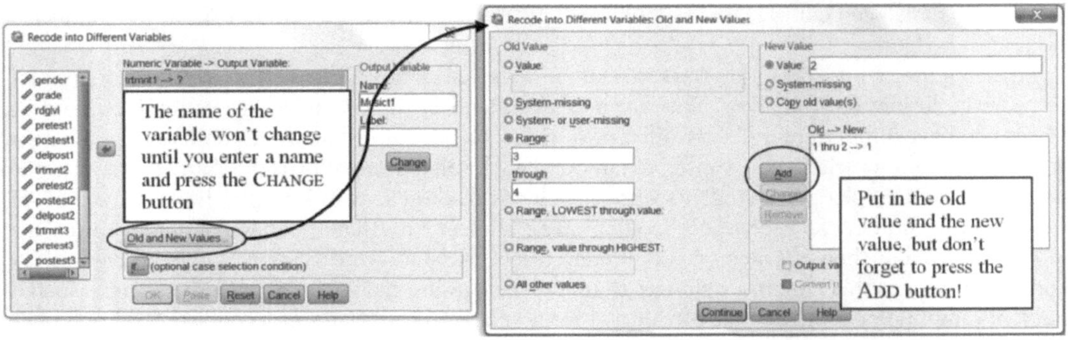

Figure 10.10 Recoding into new variables for the Obarow (2004) original data set.

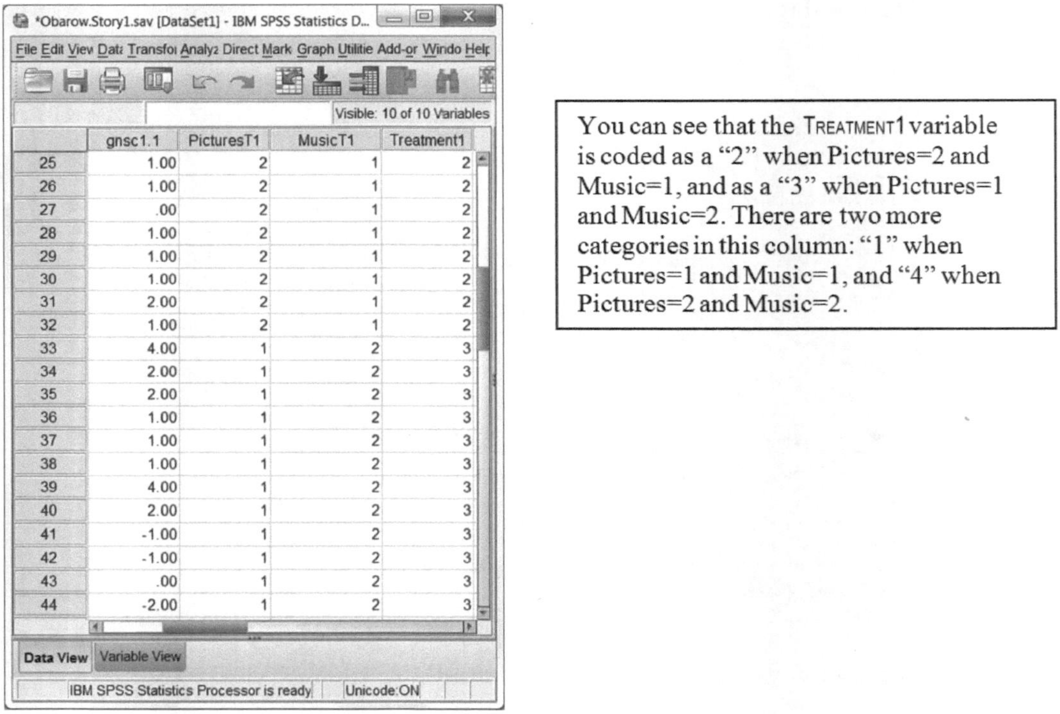

Figure 10.11 The Obarow Story 1 data set showing the presence of two separate columns of data for two independent variables, plus a column that combines the two variables called Treatment1.

10.4.3 Rearranging Data for a Factorial Analysis of Variance Using R

Import the Obarow.Original.sav file as obarow. To cut out some rows in R, the simplest way is to use the R Console:

```
new.obarow<-subset(obarow, subset=pretest1<18)
length(obarow$pretest1)
[1] 81
```

```
length(new.obarow$pretest1)
[1] 64 #I've made sure the file has been cut down from its original length
```

Note that there are data for four different stories in the original Obarow file. We cut the data out where the pretest was too high, but this only applies to the first story. If we wanted to get rid of all of the variables except those that pertain to the first story, do this in R Commander by making sure new.obarow is in the "Data set" box, then go to DATA > MANAGE VARIABLES IN ACTIVE DATA SET > DELETE VARIABLES FROM ACTIVE DATA SET. Here you can just pick all of the variables with a number greater than 1 appended to them. (So keep delpost1, but get rid of delpost2, delpost3, etc.) This is easier than the R code, because there you have to write a line of code for every one of the variables you want to get rid of, and you will probably have to look at a list of names as you write it, whereas using the menu option you can easily pick and choose which ones you want to delete. Here is an example of how to get rid of one column:

```
new.obarow$delpost2 <- NULL
```

Calculating gain scores is also very simple using the R Console. The only thing we need to worry about is that the new variable we create gets added to the new.obarow file. For example, the following code would easily create the immediate gain score and should be straightforward to understand:

```
gnsc1.1<-new.obarow$postest1-new.obarow$pretest1
```

However, this variable will not be added to the new.obarow data set; you can verify this by asking for the names of the data set (names(new.obarow)), where you will not see gnsc1.1. So what needs to be done is to specify that the new variable is part of the new.obarow data set with the code on the left side of the arrow:

```
new.obarow$gnsc1.1 <- new.obarow$postest1-new.obarow$pretest1
```

You could also use this code, which saves you time in writing the new.obarow data set name twice:

```
new.obarow$gnsc1.1 <- with(new.obarow, postest1- pretest1)
```

I will leave it to you to compute the delayed gain score.

The last thing is to change the trtmnt1 variable into two separate variables. Because music and pictures are going to be two separate IVs, we will need two variables, one coded for the inclusion of music and one coded for the inclusion of pictures in the treatment. I can see the way the trtmnt1 variable is coded by using the levels() command. This is important because I will have to use the exact same label to recode:

```
levels(new.obarow$trtmnt1)
[1] "No music No pics" "No music Yes pics" "Yes music No pics" [4] "Yes music Yes pics"
```

The plyr package (Wickham, 2011) has a nice command that lets us recode intuitively and automatically sets the new variable up as a factor, if it originally started out as a factor.

```
library(plyr) #if needed, install.packages("plyr")
new.obarow$musict1<-revalue(new.obarow$trtmnt1, c("No music No pics"="no music",
"No music Yes pics"="no music", "Yes music No pics"="music", "Yes music Yes pics"="music"))
```

Repeat this coding for the Pictures variable.

After this manipulation, we are ready to get to work on the ANOVA analysis! If you are following along with me, you will see that in the coming section I import the data from the SPSS file Obarow.Story1 and call it obarowStory1. We could just use the new.obarow file that we just manipulated, but to be safe, import the file that I have already put into order. Notice in Figure 10.11 that I now have a gain score (gnsc1.1), and two columns coding for the presence of music (musict1) and pictures (picturest1). There are only 64 rows of data since I excluded any participants whose pretest score was 18 or above.

10.4.4 Excursus on Type II vs. Type III Sums of Squares (Advanced Topic)

It is mainly when we are examining ANOVA tables that the issue of which type of sum of squares (SS) is used will arise. Within ANOVA, four methods of partitioning error into SS have been distinguished. However, it is only when experimental designs are unbalanced, meaning that the group sizes are not all equal, that differences according to the type of SS used will arise. Langsrud (2003) noted that most major statistical programs use Type III SS as the default in calculation, and this includes SPSS. Many researchers, including Maxwell and Delaney (2004), have concluded that Type III SS are best. However, several other researchers have argued strongly that, as a general rule, Type II SS are best, provide the most power and generally test more interesting hypotheses than Type III sums of squares (Fox, 2002a, 2002b; Langsrud, 2003; Nelder, 1994; Nelder & Lane, 1995).

With all types of SS, differences in analysis will arise only in conjunction with the analysis of the main effects, not of the interaction effects. Therefore, say we have factor A and factor B. The differences in what SS are reported for the effect of A and the effect of B will differ according to the type of SS used (if the design is unbalanced), but the effect of AB will be the same whatever the type of SS used.

Type II SS consider the main effects of variables A and B by assuming that any interaction involving them is not statistical. This results in each effect being adjusted for all other terms in the model except for terms that contain the effect. Langsrud (2003, p. 163) gave the following example: "in a three-way table (A, B and C) the main effect for factor A is not adjusted for the interaction AB, AC, and ABC. And the two-factor interactions are not adjusted for ABC." In contrast, using the Type III SS adjusts for all other factors in the model, which means that, when looking at the main effect of A, adjustments are made for the interactions of AB, AC and ABC as well as for all other factors. In practice this means that Type III SS evaluate the main effect of A regardless of whether the interaction is statistical or not.

Although it may at first seem logical to use Type III sums of squares because you do not want to assume that interactions are not statistical, Langsrud gave a convincing argument for the superiority of Type II SS: "[i]f a main effect is found to be significant, this result is correct if there is no interaction. If the interaction is present, both main effects will also be present. In any case, the statement about a significant main effect will be correct" (2003, p. 165). The logical argument, then, actually favors Type II SS because it is not logical to assume that the interaction AB could be statistical without the main effects A and B also being statistical (Langsrud, 2003). For this reason, several authors have argued the hypotheses that Type III SS test are unrealistic or uninteresting hypotheses.

Langsrud (2003) also noted that one would like to choose the most powerful test. He says that, when there is no interaction, Type II SS will be the most powerful. When there is an interaction, some limited simulation studies have concluded that on average Type II is still more powerful than Type III. Therefore, when one is choosing between a Type II and Type III test, my advice is to prefer the Type II test, which means changing the default in SPSS. The default in R programs is Type II, which means that if you want to change to Type III, you will have to do that manually. How you actually do it depends on the particular command.

Summary of a Comparison between Type II and Type III Sums of Squares

A Type II SS approach looks at a main effect A without adjusting for the interactions that A is involved in, such as AB, AC and ABC. The hypothesis that is tested is whether the main effect of A is statistical given the other interactions that A is involved in.

A Type III SS approach looks at a main effect A by adjusting for all interactions that A is involved in, such as AB, AC, and ABC. The hypothesis that is tested is whether the main effect of A is statistical whether or not the interactions that A is involved in are statistical.

It was pointed out that logically it does not make sense to ignore an interaction if it is statistical. Fox (2002) claims that, thus, Type III SS test uninteresting hypotheses.

10.5 Factorial Analysis of Variance: Extending Analyses to More than One Independent Variable

As you will see in the coming sections, factorial ANOVA gets more complicated than one-way ANOVA. In some ways, complications arise the more variables you have in your analysis. So, for example, a three-way ANOVA is going to be harder to work with in some ways than a two-way ANOVA. However, in other ways, having a lot of levels in your variables also makes for complications. So even if you have a two-way ANOVA, if each variable has four or five levels, there are other things that are going to get complicated! In this chapter I show a three-way ANOVA on a data set that has only two levels per variable. For more practice with analyzing variables with more levels, see the online section "Two-Way Factorial ANOVA." This document will provide an analysis of a two-way ANOVA that has many levels. In the two-way ANOVA I will also show how to do planned comparisons if you do not want to compare every level to every other in your analysis. Finally, in the online section "Finding a Minimal Model Using R" I will show (only in R) how to do model simplification to cut out parts of your ANOVA model that are not adding any explanatory value.

10.5.1 Performing a Three-Way Factorial Analysis of Variance with SPSS

To perform an ANOVA when you have more than one IV, use the ANALYZE > GENERAL LINEAR MODEL > UNIVARIATE menu. The dialog box that appears is shown in Figure 10.12. I have put all three IVs into the "Fixed Factors" box. Figure 10.12 also show the dialog box that opens up when you click on the MODEL button. Here, I suggest you change the type of SS from III to II and click on CONTINUE. (For a justification for this, see Section 10.4.4.) SPSS uses Type III SS as a default, but from my readings I think it is better to use Type II.

To use the "new statistics" approach to our ANOVA, we need to do something a little bit tricky with SPSS. This involves using SPSS syntax instead of just the drop-down menus, but it is not anything you should not be able to do. Later we will come back and use most of the buttons on this menu, but for now, in the box under "Factor(s) and Factor Interactions" that you see when you open the OPTIONS button, move all of your ANOVA parts that involve interactions over to the right to the DISPLAY MEANS FOR box. Figure 10.13 shows all of the parts moved over to the right without any other boxes ticked. Click on CONTINUE then on OK to run the entire ANOVA.

If we look at the output so far, it is rather simple. Under the line "Univariate Analysis of Variance," the first box will list what your IVs are, how many levels each variable has and how many participants are in each level (in the table labeled "Between-Subjects Factors"). Next, you will see a box labeled "Tests of Between-Subjects Effects" (Table 10.4). This is the box that we would mainly use to report on our ANOVA if we were using an "old statistics" type of approach. If you quickly glance through

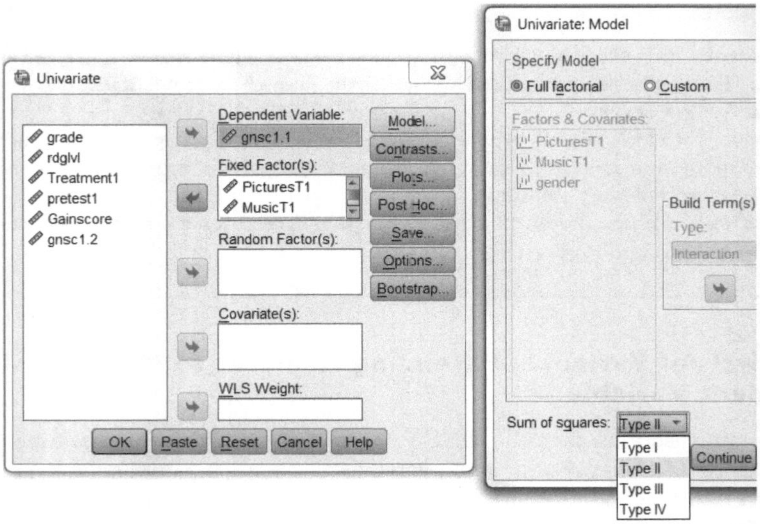

Figure 10.12 The Univariate dialog box for conducting a factorial ANOVA in SPSS and the Model dialog box.

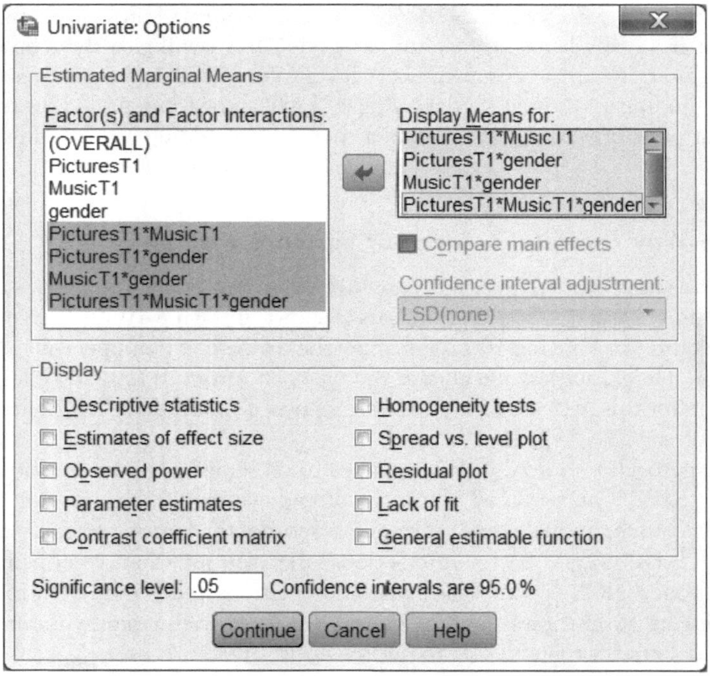

Figure 10.13 The Univariate: Options dialog box for a factorial ANOVA in SPSS.

it, you can see that by just using the criterion of looking for $p < 0.05$, the only comparison that is statistical is "Gender," which has a p-value of 0.042. But we know that using p-values is just the luck of the draw, and that p-values have a very wide sampling variability (see Chapter 4). We might even remember that Cumming (2012) stated that only p-values under 0.001 give any basis for reasonably rejecting the null hypothesis (H_0), and $p = 0.042$ is certainly not close to that! So although we might be tempted to look at this box and shout "hooray" for our *p*-value of less than 0.05, remembering the "dance of the *p*-values" (Figure 4.8) reminds us that it is really the confidence levels that we should be examining. And we will be getting to that soon!

For your further information, I will point out that the first two and last two lines of this table are generally of no interest to us. The "Corrected Model" specified in the first line is a test of "the null hypothesis that performance is a function of the full set of effects (the main effects and the interactions)" (Howell, 2002, p. 464); if group sizes are exactly equal this line will be exactly equal to the SS of all the main effects and interactions (SS model). The second line, "Intercept," tests the hypothesis that the grand mean is equal to zero (Howell, 2002), and we are generally not interested in this question. The information of interest is the between-groups factors (the three main effects of gender, music and pictures, and the four interaction effects with these factors) and the within-groups factor, which is also called the "Error" (since the variation within and not across the groups represents variation we cannot account for, and thus this is all put into the error term). A large SS in the Error line relative to the main and interaction effects tells us our model has not accounted for very much of the variation in the model (which is true in this case).

Finally, in this initial SPSS output of our first run, you will see "Estimated marginal means." This will give mean scores for the intersection of the IVs. We have a lot of different intersections (corresponding to the seven parts of the ANOVA), so there are a number of different tables here, starting with the "Grand Mean," going through the main effects of pictures, music and gender, and then moving on to the two-way and three-way interactions of the data. We get a 95% CI for these data, but as the CI is not the CI for the *difference* between groups, we cannot make any inferences about which groups are different from the others with this information.

The real reason we called for these marginal means is that calling for them produces the syntax we need to make comparisons between the differences between groups (Weinberg & Abramowitz, 2002). There is no way to perform post-hoc tests for the interaction using the drop-down menus (Landau & Everitt, 2004). I am not sure that the syntax method is really the best way to go about looking at the pairwise comparisons in the interactions, but it is the only way I have found to get CIs on these comparisons.

Table 10.4 Univariate ANOVA Output: Test of Between-Subjects Effects

Tests of Between-Subjects Effects

Dependent Variable: gnsc1.1

Source	Type II Sum of Squares	df	Mean Square	F	Sig.	Partial Eta Squared
Corrected Model	22.399[a]	7	3.200	1.393	.226	.148
Intercept	81.000	1	81.000	35.272	.000	.386
PicturesT1	2.388	1	2.388	1.040	.312	.018
MusicT1	.365	1	.365	.159	.692	.003
gender	9.990	1	9.990	4.350	.042	.072
PicturesT1 * MusicT1	1.669	1	1.669	.727	.398	.013
PicturesT1 * gender	.270	1	.270	.117	.733	.002
MusicT1 * gender	5.551	1	5.551	2.417	.126	.041
PicturesT1 * MusicT1 * gender	1.369	1	1.369	.596	.443	.011
Error	128.601	56	2.296			
Total	232.000	64				
Corrected Total	151.000	63				

a. R Squared = .148 (Adjusted R Squared = .042)

So, to continue with our "new statistics" analysis, open the UNIVARIATE ANOVA box again (menu sequence: ANALYZE > GENERAL LINEAR MODEL > UNIVARIATE). Click on the PASTE button on the UNIVARIATE dialog box. This will bring up the **Syntax Editor**. The first line will read "UNIANOVA," and you are looking for the lines that use the **EMMEANS** (estimated marginal means) syntax, like this:

```
/EMMEANS = TABLES(PicturesT1*MusicT1)
```

This line tells SPSS to create a table of means for the interaction. To create post-hoc tests for the interaction, copy the line and add the command **COMPARE(PicturesT1)** to it. Copy it again and also add **COMPARE(MusicT1)** to it to get both types of comparisons. You should only do this with the lines where two or more IVs are crossed. So here is the syntax I would paste in after the line shown above:

```
/EMMEANS = TABLES(PicturesT1*MusicT1)COMPARE(PicturesT1)
/EMMEANS = TABLES(PicturesT1*MusicT1)COMPARE(MusicT1)
```

The first line (with **PicturesT1**) will divide the data up into Pictures vs. No Pictures and within each condition compare the Music vs. No Music conditions. The second (with **MusicT1**) will divide the data up into the Music vs. No Music condition, and then compare the Pictures vs. No Pictures condition. In this case, because there are only two levels for each of these variables, the effect will be exactly the same and you do not really need both lines. In other cases, where there are different numbers of levels within the groups, you would get different results from the two lines. In order not to cause confusion, I will just go ahead and run two lines of comparison, one with the first variable, and the other with the second variable. You can see how I copied and added to these lines in Figure 10.14.

Next, I pasted the lines underneath each "Tables" command just to keep track of what I was doing. You can actually paste the lines anywhere, but if you put them at the end, put a period to show that it is the end of the commands and erase the previous period at the end of the syntax. Now choose the RUN menu, and either RUN ALL or highlight the part you want and choose RUN SELECTION (see Figure 10.14).

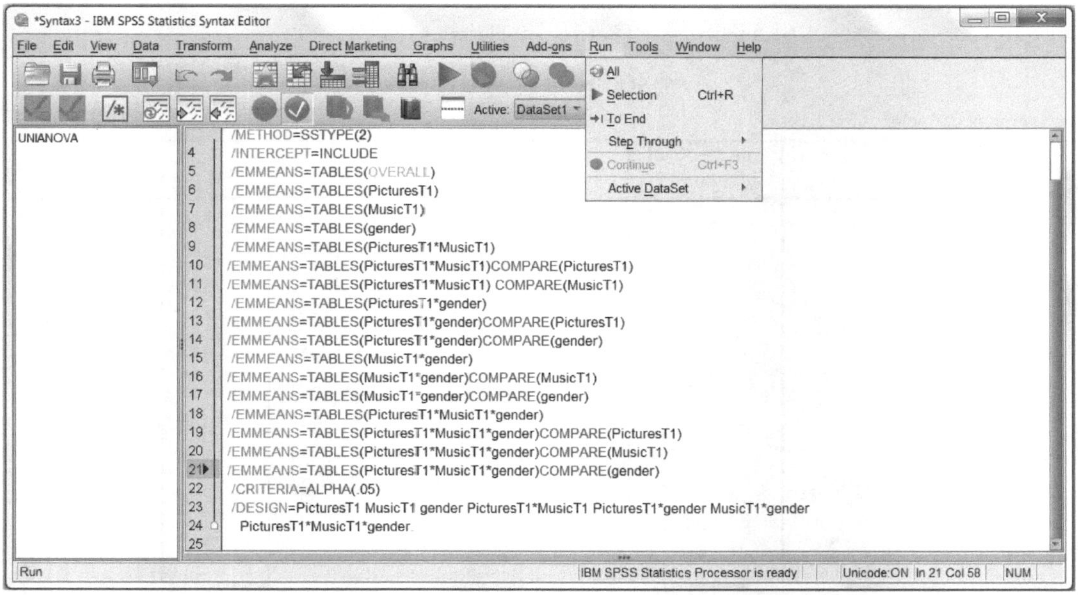

Figure 10.14 Syntax to obtain post-hocs for interaction effects.

You will then be looking for a title in the output that says "Pairwise Comparisons" somewhere below the "Estimated Marginal Means." Actually, you will see the two-way interactions first, but let us start with the most complicated interaction first, because if any of the three-way interactions are statistical, then we do not care as much about the two-way interactions or the main effects. So look down your output until you see PicturesT1*MusicT1*gender. (Actually, if you ran three lines of comparison, you will have three of these titles.) First, it will have mean scores and CIs in the "Estimates" table, but below that you will see the table labeled "Pairwise Comparisons" (see Table 10.5). Each of the three entries will examine the data in a different way. Table 10.6 shows the data divided into Music/No Music first, then Gender, then Pictures/No Pictures.

Looking at the pairwise comparisons in Table 10.5, we can see that all of the CIs go through zero, and they are all about three points wide, approximately centered around zero. So there is a mean difference of 0.83 among males who heard no music but comparing whether they saw pictures or not, with a 95% CI of [−2.22, 0.55]. And there is a mean difference among females who heard no music but comparing whether they saw pictures or not of 0.49, with a CI of [−2.26, 1.29]. In both cases, we do not have much reason to doubt that among males who heard no music there was no effect of pictures, and that among females who heard no music there was no effect of pictures. The situation is similar for males and female who did hear music: again, CIs show that there was no effect for pictures.

Table 10.5 Interaction Post-Hoc Tests (pictures*music*gender)

15. PicturesT1 * MusicT1 * gender

Estimates

Dependent Variable: gnsc1.1

PicturesT1	MusicT1	gender	Mean	Std. Error	95% Confidence Interval Lower Bound	95% Confidence Interval Upper Bound
no pictures	no music	male	.750	.536	-.323	1.823
		female	.714	.573	-.433	1.862
	music	male	2.200	.678	.842	3.558
		female	.300	.479	-.660	1.260
pictures	no music	male	1.583	.437	.707	2.460
		female	1.200	.678	-.158	2.558
	music	male	1.778	.505	.766	2.790
		female	.750	.536	-.323	1.823

Pairwise Comparisons

Dependent Variable: gnsc1.1

MusicT1	gender	(I) PicturesT1	(J) PicturesT1	Mean Difference (I-J)	Std. Error	Sig.[a]	95% Confidence Interval for Difference[a] Lower Bound	95% Confidence Interval for Difference[a] Upper Bound
no music	male	no pictures	pictures	-.833	.692	.233	-2.219	.552
		pictures	no pictures	.833	.692	.233	-.552	2.219
	female	no pictures	pictures	-.486	.887	.586	-2.263	1.292
		pictures	no pictures	.486	.887	.586	-1.292	2.263
music	male	no pictures	pictures	.422	.845	.619	-1.271	2.115
		pictures	no pictures	-.422	.845	.619	-2.115	1.271
	female	no pictures	pictures	-.450	.719	.534	-1.890	.990
		pictures	no pictures	.450	.719	.534	-.990	1.890

Based on estimated marginal means

a. Adjustment for multiple comparisons: Least Significant Difference (equivalent to no adjustments).

Table 10.6 Interaction Post-Hoc Tests (pictures*gender*music)

16. PicturesT1 * MusicT1 * gender

Pairwise Comparisons

Dependent Variable: gnsc1.1

PicturesT1	gender	(I) MusicT1	(J) MusicT1	Mean Difference (I-J)	Std. Error	Sig.[a]	95% Confidence Interval for Difference[a]	
							Lower Bound	Upper Bound
no pictures	male	no music	music	-1.450	.864	.099	-3.181	.281
		music	no music	1.450	.864	.099	-.281	3.181
	female	no music	music	.414	.747	.581	-1.082	1.910
		music	no music	-.414	.747	.581	-1.910	1.082
pictures	male	no music	music	-.194	.668	.772	-1.533	1.144
		music	no music	.194	.668	.772	-1.144	1.533
	female	no music	music	.450	.864	.604	-1.281	2.181
		music	no music	-.450	.864	.604	-2.181	1.281

Based on estimated marginal means

a. Adjustment for multiple comparisons: Least Significant Difference (equivalent to no adjustments).

The "Univariate Tests" box below the "Pairwise Comparisons" gives us F-values, p-values and degrees of freedom (df) for these contrasts, but since we are interested in CIs, we will not worry about these numbers.

If you go on to look at the next part that also says PicturesT1*MusicT1*gender (the pairwise comparisons are shown in Table 10.6), you will see that now the comparison is switched around to have Pictures/No Pictures first, then Gender, then Music/No Music. So we are seeing that there is a mean difference of 1.45 among males who saw no pictures but comparing whether they heard music or not, with a 95% CI of [−3.18, 0.28]. Here the CI is a little less balanced around zero and it looks like there might be some reason to suspect that for males who saw no pictures music might be close to being a helpful factor (looking back at the "Estimates" box I see that the mean for males who saw no pictures and heard no music is 0.75 while the mean for males who saw no pictures but heard music is 2.20), but this is not true for the females who saw no pictures. For them the mean difference between having music or not is 0.41, CI [−1.08, 1.91], a CI centered pretty much around zero. For participants who did see pictures, I will not give you the exact numbers, but they do not look much different from most of the others and do not show much evidence that there was any effect for having music or not.

Finally, there will be a third box of "Pairwise Comparisons" that says PicturesT1*MusicT1*gender and organizes the data by Pictures/No Pictures first, then Music/No Music next, then Gender (Table 10.7). Here again the comparison gets turned around so that we can say that among those who saw no pictures and heard no music, the mean difference between males and females is 0.04, CI [−1.54, 1.61]. Among those who saw no pictures but did hear music, the mean difference between males and females is 1.90, with a CI of [0.24, 3.56]. So, in this one case, we can find a difference that is real, although the CI range lets us know that it could be a very small difference (only 0.24 of a point). The estimates show that the mean for males who heard music but saw no pictures was 2.20, but for females it was only 0.30, so it is the males who did better with music when they saw no pictures. Among participants who saw pictures but heard no music, the difference between males and females was small (0.38, CI [−1.23, 2.00]), while for those who saw pictures and did hear music, the mean difference between males and females was larger (1.03), but the CI still ran through zero [−0.45, 2.5], although not as centeredly as some of the other CIs.

The pairwise comparisons all break the data up into comparisons of three variables, but the ways of looking at the data are different and in fact we find different ideas in all of them. Since we found a case

Table 10.7 Interaction Post-Hoc Tests (pictures*music*gender)

17. PicturesT1 * MusicT1 * gender

Pairwise Comparisons

Dependent Variable: gnsc1.1

PicturesT1	MusicT1	(I) gender	(J) gender	Mean Difference (I-J)	Std. Error	Sig.[b]	95% Confidence Interval for Difference[b]	
							Lower Bound	Upper Bound
no pictures	no music	male	female	.036	.784	.964	-1.535	1.607
		female	male	-.036	.784	.964	-1.607	1.535
	music	male	female	1.900*	.830	.026	.237	3.563
		female	male	-1.900*	.830	.026	-3.563	-.237
pictures	no music	male	female	.383	.807	.636	-1.233	1.999
		female	male	-.383	.807	.636	-1.999	1.233
	music	male	female	1.028	.736	.168	-.447	2.503
		female	male	-1.028	.736	.168	-2.503	.447

Based on estimated marginal means

*. The mean difference is significant at the .05 level.

b. Adjustment for multiple comparisons: Least Significant Difference (equivalent to no adjustments).

where there was a real effect for a three-way interaction, we may not be all that interested in looking at the two-way interactions, or the main effects. We saw from the CIs that there seems to be a real effect with males who hear music but do not see pictures, that they did better than the females, but the effect size for this is fairly small, so we should be careful of claiming any strong effect.

You might have noticed that the three tables given here do not represent *all* of the possible comparisons that could have been made with this three-way interaction! For example, there are no comparisons like: Male/Music/ Pictures: No Pictures or Music/Pictures/ Male: Female. In fact, there are 24 possible permutations of the data. We can calculate how many possible permutations there are by figuring out how many possibilities there are in our first choice (6, which is 2 levels of gender × 2 levels of music × 2 levels of pictures), then, having chosen our first variable, how many choices are left for the second slot (which equals 4: say we choose gender; then for the second slot we have 2 levels of music × 2 levels of pictures), and then in the last slot there is just one variable left, and since it only has 2 levels, which will be compared to each other, there is only 1 possibility there, making for 6 × 4 × 1 = 24 possibilities. However, a comparison like Male/Music/Pictures: No Pictures is the same as Music/Male/Pictures: No Pictures, which was tested here. So, although there are 24 possible permutations, we cut the possibilities in half because there will be no difference to the results in how we order the first two constituents. (In other words, Music/Male or Male/Music, it does not matter!) So SPSS tested 12 possibilities, and that does constitute all of the possible unique combinations of the data.

If you want to look at the two-way interactions, of course, you could just repeat the process I went through in the earlier entries of the output, looking at the two entries for, say, Music*Gender. (These are #12 and #11 in my output.) In this case there are only four possibilities for testing (4 choices for the first slot, which is 2 levels of music × 2 levels of gender, and 1 choice for the second slot because it only has two levels which will be compared to each other, meaning 4 ×1 = 4 possibilities). Note that these possibilities for numbers of permutations would get exponentially larger as the number of levels in a variable increased. For a two-way interaction, if both your variables had 3 levels, you would have 9 × 3 = 27 choices (9 choices for the first slot, which is 3 levels of A × 3 levels of B, and 3 choices of comparisons for the second slot, because comparing every level to every other level when you have 3 levels takes 3 comparisons). In the online section "Two-Way Factional ANOVA" there is an example that has more than two levels of variables, so take a look at that section too if you have a number of levels in your variables.

I find the only CI that does not run through zero is the difference between males and females when they have music (mean difference = 1.46, 95% CI [0.35, 2.58]), with mean scores telling us that males gained more than females in this condition (males = 1.99, females = 0.53). This comparison collapses the difference between having pictures and not having pictures though, and the three-way interaction already told us that males do better than females with music when they do not see pictures. My point is thus that the two-way interaction does not add any more to our understanding than the three-way interaction, and in fact, obscures some things, such as that the comparisons show a real difference only when pictures are not present.

Thus, in reporting on the results of this factorial ANOVA, because there is a real difference for one part of the three-way interactions, I would likely report on all 12 of the pairwise comparisons in the three-way interaction, reporting the mean scores in each case, the mean difference between the groups and the 95% CIs of the mean difference between the groups. My conclusion for this data set would be that the interaction of music, pictures and gender produced a possible (but weak) difference only in the case where there was music, but not pictures, and that males gained more than females in this case.

What about the fact that we have carried out many comparisons? In the "old statistics" we used corrections like the Tukey's honest significant difference (HSD) test or Bonferroni correction to correct for the fact that having many comparisons might capitalize on the fact that just by chance some of our comparisons will be statistically significant. Cumming (2012) suggested that the multiple comparison problem does not go away just because we are using estimation, but he noted that there is no well-established CI adjustment comparable to the Bonferroni correction. According to Cumming, that is not so much of a problem, because it would still be preferable to rely on CIs than "calculating a 'corrected' criterion for evaluating a *p*-value when on replication *p* could easily be markedly different" (2012, p. 422). However, if you have carried out several comparisons, and noted any statistical results as "interesting possibility[ies] needing further investigation, rather than [being] established finding[s]" (Cumming, 2012, p. 421), it is fine to explore your data and not worry too much about adjusting for multiple comparisons. Crawley (2007) suggested that if you have factors with many levels, meaning you will have many more comparisons to make than I made here, mixed-effect models that treat "the factors as random effects rather than fixed effects" (p. 483) might be a good idea. You can find mixed-effect models described in the online section for Chapter 11 called "RM-ANOVA the Mixed Effects Way" and in Cunnings and Finlayson (2015).

In SPSS, it is possible to make adjustments to the pairwise comparisons, and thus to the CIs you call up. You would just add an "**ADJ(BONFERRONI)**" or "**ADJ(SIDAK)**" to the end of the line you paste in, like this:

```
/EMMEANS = TABLES(PicturesT1*MusicT1)COMPARE(PicturesT1) ADJ(BONFERRONI)
```

However, Bonferroni is a very conservative adjustment and may be too penalizing if you are doing as many comparisons as we have done here. Šidák correction is also quite conservative and only slightly less punishing than Bonferroni.

Now, let us go back and run the analysis again, this time asking for more information to test the validity of the assumptions we made, such as a normal distribution of data and homogeneity of variances, and add bootstrapping into the analysis. Go to Analyze > General Linear Model > Univariate. Keep everything the same as before, but this time click on the Plots button. From this button you can call for a means plot. Remember that I did not discuss in Section 10.2 how to make means plots since I said we could call for them while conducting the ANOVA, and here they are!

In the Plots box (see Figure 10.15), we already know which configuration produced a difference between groups, so we want something that will show that well, but it is not immediately obvious which configuration to choose. I found that putting Gender into the "Separate Plots" box, Music into the "Separate Lines" box and Pictures into the "Horizontal Axis" box resulted in the panels on the left of Figure 10.16. However, changing the scale of the picture to about eight points instead of three (see the panels on the right of Figure 10.16) makes the interaction between music and pictures for males look far less impressive. In any case, I warned in Section 10.2 that I do not think actually printing

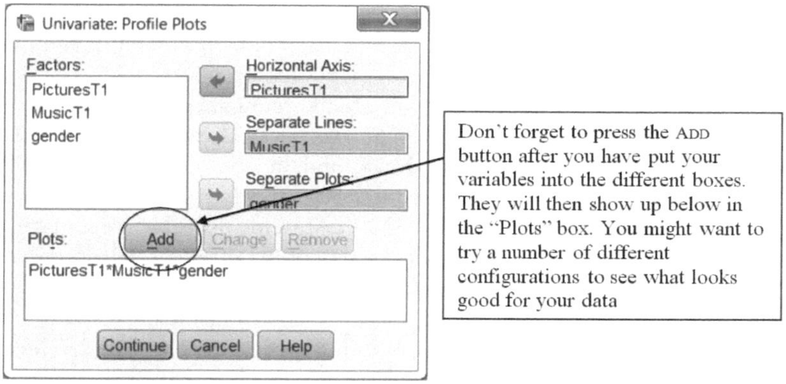

Figure 10.15 The UNIVARIATE: PROFILE PLOTS dialog box for a factorial ANOVA in SPSS.

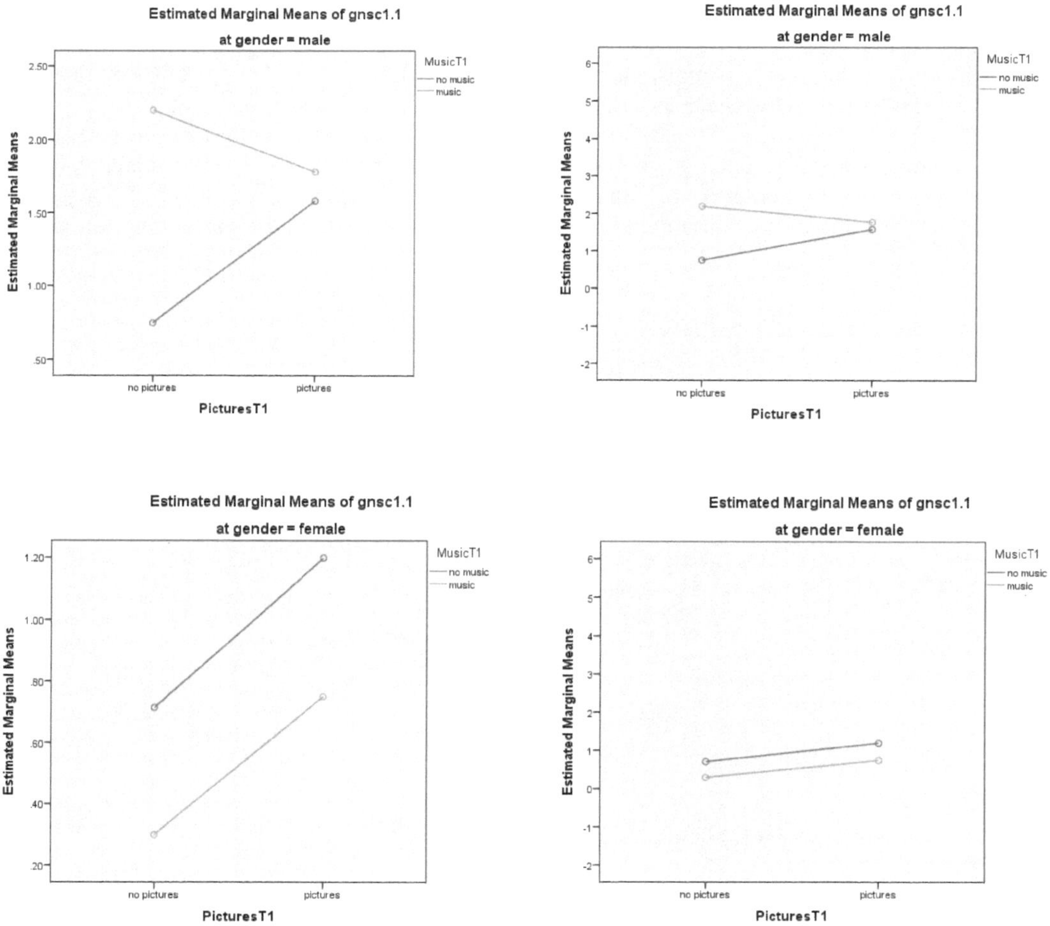

Figure 10.16 Means plots for the Obarow (2004) data at two different scales for the same data.

only means plots in your published research is a good idea, as there is very little data. I think you can get the same sense of the difference between the interaction of music and pictures from the numbers.

Figure 10.17 shows the Post Hoc dialog box. This box is actually not very useful to you in running your factorial ANOVA. It will only give you post-hoc information on main effects, not on any of the interaction effects. In other words, it will only tell you which groups are different for the main effects of Pictures, Music and Gender, but it will not give you any information about how to interpret the data if you have a statistical interaction, such as Music and Gender, or Pictures and Music. Referring back to the list of parts of the ANOVA from Section 10.4, this post hoc will only tell you about parts 1–3 and not about any of the other parts of the ANOVA. Remember that we said you may not be very interested in the main effects of just one variable if any of the interactions are statistical. You would want to use the Post Hoc dialog box only in the case where: (1) none of your interaction effects were statistical; (2) the "Tests of Between-Subject Effects" showed a statistical result for the main effect (Table 10.4 shows this box for the Obarow data); and (3) you had more than two levels in any of your variables. The last caveat is because if you only have two levels to any of your IVs in the data set, if you found a main effect you would know from the descriptive statistics which group performed better than the other. Since we have already found a statistical interaction effect, even though one of the main effects is statistical (that of gender) we have no need for a post-hoc test for these data.

Next, click on the Save and Options buttons and click on the boxes that I have selected (see Figure 10.18) to call for plots and diagnostic numbers that will help us understand if our statistical model satisfied the assumptions of normality and homogeneity of variances. Run your analysis again.

The first two tables in the output will be descriptive, telling you what your IVs are, how many levels each variable has and how many participants are in each level (in the table labeled "Between-Subjects Factors"), and giving the mean, SD and *N* for each intersection of your variables. (This table is labeled "Descriptive Statistics".) Here we might notice that there are actually very few participants in the comparisons we were making, when they get divided up into these parts. For example, for the one intersection we found an effect for, no pictures*music*male vs. female, we only had 5 males and 10 females in the comparison. This might lead us to think the effect was quite robust if we found it for

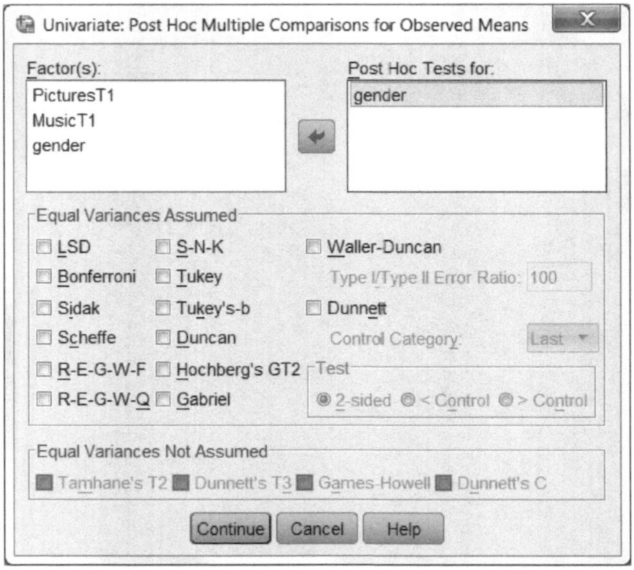

Figure 10.17 The Univariate: Post Hoc Multiple Comparisons for Observed Means dialog box for a factorial ANOVA in SPSS. Do **not** use this box unless you only have statistical main effects.

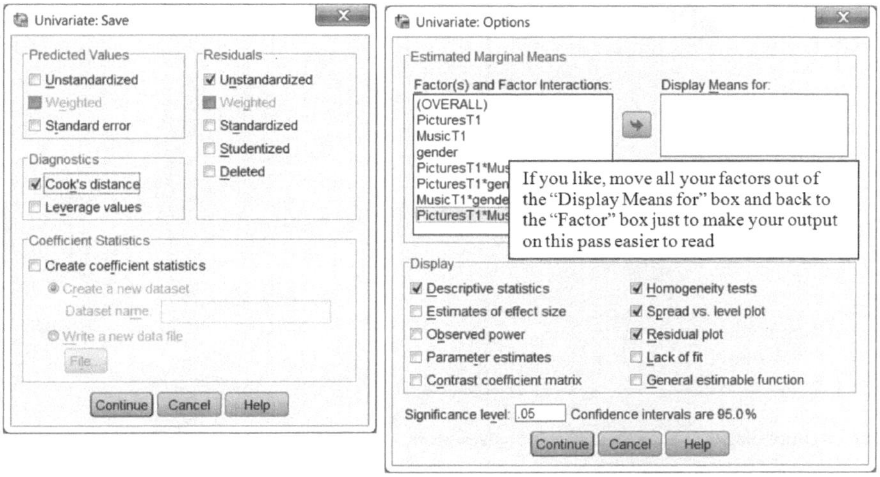

Figure 10.18 The UNIVARIATE: SAVE and UNIVARIATE: OPTIONS dialog boxes.

such a small number of participants. (Obarow (2004) did not conduct an investigation of gender, so her groups would not have been divided up so small.)

The next piece of output is Levene's test for homogeneity of variances, shown in Table 10.8. It is not statistical ($p > 0.05$), meaning that the assumption of homoscedasticity is not violated (or, at least, that is what Levene's test says). The other thing to notice about Levene's test is that in the footnote (a) the regression equation is given explicitly. In just the same way that multiple regression used an equation, ANOVA also uses an equation. The difference is that, for multiple regression, SPSS included only main effects, while, for an ANOVA, SPSS automatically includes main effects and all interactions. You can see that the equation for the ANOVA has all seven parts of the variance I said we would test in the ANOVA in Section 10.4.

Table 10.8 Univariate ANOVA Output in SPSS: Levene's Test

Levene's Test of Equality of Error Variances [a]

Dependent Variable: gnsc1.1

F	df1	df2	Sig.
1.882	7	56	.090

Tests the null hypothesis that the error variance of the dependent variable is equal across groups.

a. Design: Intercept + PicturesT1 + MusicT1 + gender + PicturesT1 * MusicT1 + PicturesT1 * gender + MusicT1 * gender + PicturesT1 * MusicT1 * gender

The next piece of output is the "Test of Between-Subjects Effects"; somewhere after this box you will find a few plots that have been called for to check the assumptions of the ANOVA model. Figure 10.19 shows the spread vs. level plot. There are two spread vs. level plots, one comparing SDs and the other comparing variances. Both plots test the assumption of equal variance for the data and should show no pattern of data, just random scattering. This seems true of the spread vs. level plots seen here. For the residual plot, shown in Figure 10.20, the Predicted vs. Std. Residual box (center column, bottom

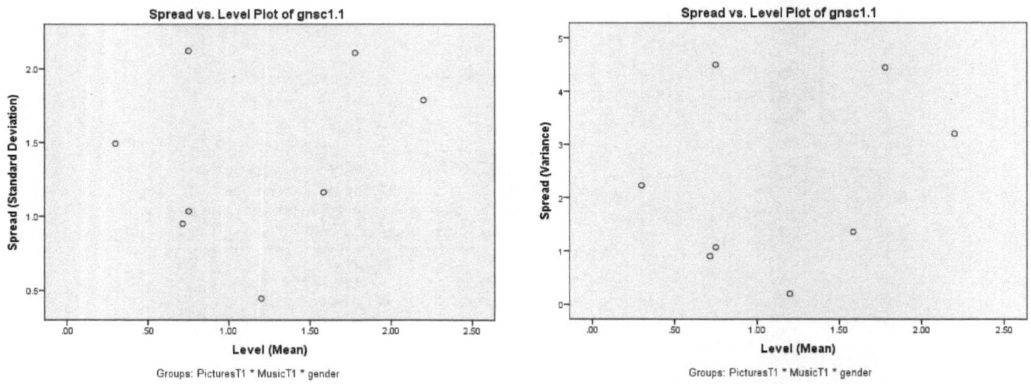

Figure 10.19 Equal variance diagnostic: SPSS spread vs. level plots.

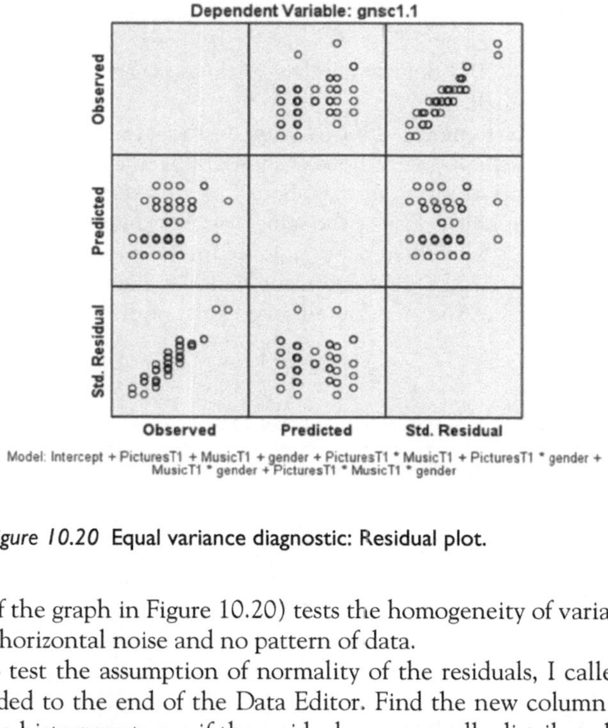

Figure 10.20 Equal variance diagnostic: Residual plot.

row of the graph in Figure 10.20) tests the homogeneity of variances of the residuals. This should also show horizontal noise and no pattern of data.

To test the assumption of normality of the residuals, I called for the unstandardized residuals to be added to the end of the Data Editor. Find the new column in the data that says Res_1. We can make a histogram to see if the residuals are normally distributed (GRAPHS > LEGACY DIALOGS > HISTOGRAM). The histogram to the left in Figure 10.21 seems to have some deviation away from normal. Cook's distance is a measure of influential outliers, and values over 1 would be cause for concern. There are many ways you could check this; I just went ahead and did another histogram (see the right side of Figure 10.21) and saw that the largest value of Cook's was only 0.15, so it seems the assumptions for the residuals are satisfied.

It appears then, that our original data were not normally distributed and in some cases variances were not equal; there is also some question as to whether the residuals are normally distributed. We might want to see what a bootstrap analysis would do with our data. But what would we want to

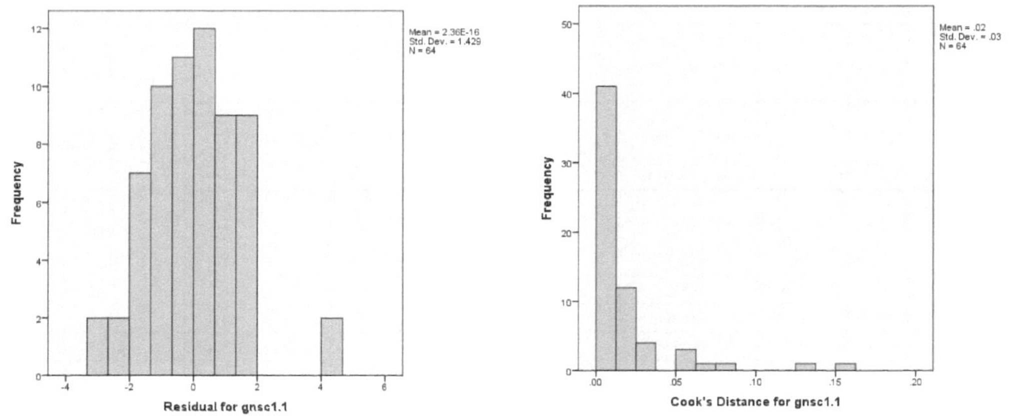

Figure 10.21 Normality of residuals diagnostic: Histograms of unstandardized residuals and Cook's distance.

bootstrap? When we call for a bootstrap in SPSS, we get bootstrapped CIs on the mean scores of the data and on the estimated marginal means, but what we really want are bootstrapped CIs on the differences between groups. That means we will need to return to the OPTIONS button and move over the means we want to test. I am just going to put the three-way interaction into the box and see if there are any differences from my previous analysis. While I am there, I am going to tick off all of the boxes I ticked previously (shown in Figure 10.18) because I want to keep my output as simple as I can. I might also click on the SAVE button and tick off the boxes I had ticked previously.

Now, click on the BOOTSTRAP button. I have shown this button a number of times previously so I will not show it again (see Figure 10.17); open it and check the "Perform bootstrapping" box, leave the number of samples at 1000 and change the "Confidence Intervals" to bias-corrected and accelerated (BCa) bootstrap. (The analysis is getting more complicated and bootstrapping can take quite a while now. I am finding that it stops computing around 1000 samples anyway, for this data set.) Click on CONTINUE. Run the factorial ANOVA but do not worry about the output yet. When the bootstrapping is done, open the ANALYZE > GENERAL LINEAR MODEL > UNIVARIATE again and click on the PASTE button. As before, add three Compare lines after the three-way interaction syntax (/EMMEANS=TABLES(PicturesT1*MusicT1*gender). Run the analysis from the RUN menu, and this time, under the "Pairwise Comparisons" that we analyzed earlier (Tables 10.5–10.7), you will find a box labeled "Bootstrap for Pairwise Comparisons." I will look at the box where we found the statistical comparison before, shown in Table 10.9.

Here we see that the bootstrap found some bias away from the original mean difference score, but still only found one situation where there was a difference between groups, which was when there were no pictures but there was music, with males doing better than females, 95% BCa bootstrapped CI [0.13, 3.70]. This CI is even closer to zero than the non-bootstrapped one was, making us feel very cautious about being too exultant about finding a difference between males and females. We may say there is an interesting possibility that males and females are different in how much vocabulary they will learn with music only, but we would not consider it an established finding.

One point to take away from the Obarow data is that when the expected results fail to materialize, it can pay to explore your data a bit to look for other explanatory variables. Obarow (2004) looked at her data using only the music and pictures variables and found no interesting results. We added in the variable of gender, which she had measured, and found an interesting possibility.

Table 10.9 Bootstrapped Interaction Post-Hoc Tests (pictures*music*gender)

Bootstrap for Pairwise Comparisons

Dependent Variable: gnsc1.1

PicturesT1	MusicT1	(I) gender	(J) gender	Mean Difference (I-J)	Bootstrap[a] Bias	Std. Error	Sig. (2-tailed)	BCa 95% Confidence Interval Lower	Upper
no pictures	no music	male	female	.036	-.017[b]	.810[b]	.974[b]	-1.400[b]	1.600[b]
		female	male	-.036	.017[b]	.810[b]	.974[b]	-1.714[b]	1.483[b]
	music	male	female	1.900	.007[c]	.940[c]	.037[c]	.133[c]	3.699[c]
		female	male	-1.900	-.007[c]	.940[c]	.037[c]	-3.734[c]	-.070[c]
pictures	no music	male	female	.383	-.002[c]	.366[c]	.302[c]	-.440[c]	1.072[c]
		female	male	-.383	.002[c]	.366[c]	.302[c]	-1.000[c]	.368[c]
	music	male	female	1.028	-.024	.783	.204	-.291	2.382
		female	male	-1.028	.024	.783	.204	-2.738	.708

a. Unless otherwise noted, bootstrap results are based on 1000 bootstrap samples

b. Based on 999 samples

c. Based on 993 samples

Performing a Factorial (Three-Way and Higher) Analysis of Variance

1 ANALYZE > GENERAL LINEAR MODEL > UNIVARIATE.
2 Put DV into "Dependent Variable" box. Put IVs into the "Fixed Factor(s)" box.
3 Click on the MODELS button; change Sum of Squares from Type III to Type II.
4 Click on the OPTIONS button and move all the parts under "Factor(s) and Factor Interactions" to the box called "Display Means for." Click on CONTINUE, then OK and run the entire ANOVA.
5 Manually add syntax to examine pairwise comparisons of interactions. Open ANALYZE > GENERAL LINEAR MODEL > UNIVARIATE again and click on the PASTE button. Look for the syntax with /EMMEANS = TABLES(PicturesT1*MusicT1). Copy the line and underneath paste it in twice, adding COMPARE(PicturesT1) the first time, then COMPARE(MusicT1) the second time. Here is what the first line of added syntax looks like:

   EMMEANS = TABLES(PicturesT1*MusicT1) COMPARE(PicturesT1)

   Choose RUN > ALL and look for the output that says "Pairwise Comparisons."
6 Check the ANOVA model for normality and equal variances. Open ANALYZE > GENERAL LINEAR MODEL > UNIVARIATE again and click on the PLOTS button. Put variables in in different orders. Click on CONTINUE.
7 Click on the Save button and tick "Cook's distance" under "Diagnostics," and "Unstandardized" under "Residuals." Click on CONTINUE.
8 Click on the OPTIONS button and move all of the factors out of the "Display Means for" box to simplify your output. Under "Display," tick "Descriptive Statistics," "Homogeneity tests," "Spread vs. level plot" and "Residual plot." Click on CONTINUE and then on OK.
9 If you think it necessary, run the analysis again with bootstrapping. Open ANALYZE > GENERAL LINEAR MODEL > UNIVARIATE again and click on the BOOTSTRAP button. Tick the "Perform bootstrapping" box and change the CIs to BCa. Try to increase the replicates to 2000 but leave at 1000 if your analysis has problems running.

10.5.2 Performing a Three-Way Factorial Analysis of Variance Using R

To replicate the type of full factorial ANOVA available in most commercial statistics programs, you can use a factorial ANOVA command in R Commander. Choose STATISTICS > MEANS > MULTI-WAY ANOVA.

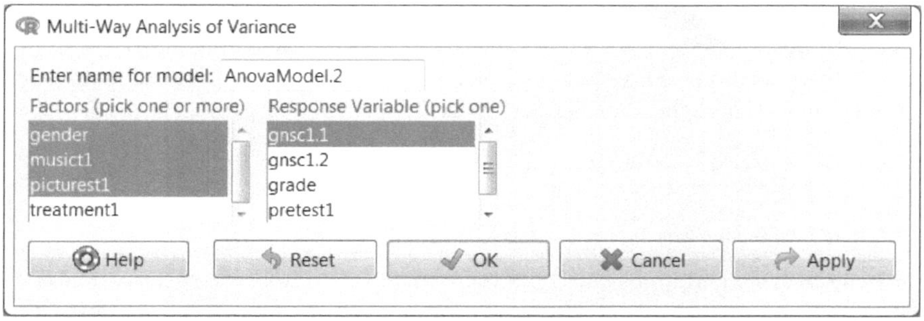

Figure 10.22 Calling for a factorial ANOVA in R Commander.

Using the Obarow (2004) data set, I am testing the effect of three IVs (gender, presence of music, presence of pictures), which I choose from the FACTORS box. The response variable I will use is the gain score for the immediate pretest (gnsc1.1). Click OK to run the analysis.

The R Commander output will give an ANOVA table for the full factorial model, which includes all main effects and all interaction effects:

y=Gender + Music + Pictures + Gender:Music + Gender:Pictures + Music:Pictures + Gender:Music:Pictures

where ":" means an interaction. (These seven parts would actually all be called for in a model that was written as Gender*Music*Pictures in R syntax; the asterisk syntax means expand into all of the main effects and all of the interactions.) Notice that these parts of the model correspond to the seven parts we said we would have in the factorial ANOVA at the beginning of Section 10.4. They are also the same parts listed in the ANOVA table in the output.

```
Anova Table (Type II tests)

Response: gnsc1.1
                            Sum Sq Df F value  Pr(>F)
gender                       9.990  1  4.3504 0.04157 *
musict1                      0.365  1  0.1588 0.69176
picturest1                   2.388  1  1.0399 0.31223
gender:musict1               5.551  1  2.4174 0.12563
gender:picturest1            0.270  1  0.1175 0.73308
musict1:picturest1           1.669  1  0.7266 0.39763
gender:musict1:picturest1    1.369  1  0.5959 0.44338
Residuals                  128.601 56
---
Signif. codes:  0 '***' 0.001 '**' 0.01 '*' 0.05 '.' 0.1 ' ' 1
```

This ANOVA table only gives us the "old statistics" approach to the data. In the "old statistics" approach we would just look for the parts of the ANOVA that had a *p*-value less than 0.05, and rejoice because we found a "statistically significant" effect. We would say that the output of the ANOVA analysis shows that only the main effect of gender is statistical ($F_{1,56} = 4.35$, $p = 0.04$) and noted that since males have a higher mean score, males are statistically better than females. In other words, separating the numbers strictly by gender and not looking at any other factor, there is a difference between how males and females performed on the task. But we know that using *p*-values is just the luck of the draw, and that *p*-values have a very wide sampling variability (see Chapter 4). We might even remember that Cumming (2012) suggested that only *p*-values under 0.001 give any basis for reasonably rejecting H_0; $p = 0.042$ is certainly not close to that! So although we might be tempted to look at this box and shout "hooray" for our *p*-value less than 0.05, remembering the "dance of the *p*-values" (Figure 4.8) reminds us that it is really the confidence levels that we should be examining. We will be getting to that soon, but for now, bear with me as I finish out an explanation of the "old statistics" approach, because some parts will be applicable to the "new statistics" approach also.

Because we only have two levels in the gender variable, we can look at mean scores and see who gained more vocabulary words. The automatic ANOVA output only gives mean scores for divisions with all three variables, but we can call for the mean scores by using the menu choice STATISTICS > SUMMARIES > NUMERICAL SUMMARIES, picking the gnsc1.1 variable, clicking on the "Summarize by groups" button and choosing gender. Press OK.

```
            mean        sd IQR 0% 25% 50% 75% 100% data:n
male   1.5294118 1.762149   3 -2   0   1   3    6     34
female 0.6666667 1.124441   1 -2   0   1   1    2     30
```

The output shows that the males performed better than the females. The ANOVA analysis here does not show any statistical effects for interactions, and here only the main effect of gender shows any difference.

The last line of the ANOVA output, called Residuals, is the error line. This part is called error because it contains all of the variation we cannot account for by the other terms of our equation. Thus, if the SS for the error line is large relative to the SS for the other terms (which it is here), this shows that the model does not account for very much of the variation.

Notice that the numbers you can obtain here may be different from the identical analysis run in a different statistical program such as SPSS. This is because R is using Type II SS (and this is identified clearly in the output), while SPSS or other statistical programs may use Type III SS, although I actually urged readers in the SPSS section to use the Type II SS. (See the previous Section 10.4.4 for more information.)

The last part of the output from R Commander gives descriptive statistics (mean, SD and count) for the permutation of the IVs in the order they are placed in the regression. Since these numbers were already discussed in Section 10.2 on numerical summaries, I will not go over them again here.

We would also like to check whether our statistical model fulfills the assumptions of normality and homogeneity of variances. R makes this easy by providing a series of plots that will be created when you use the plot() command on a linear model, like the one R Commander created when you called for an ANOVA. If you look at the syntax from that command, the first line is:

```
AnovaModel.1 <- (lm(gnsc1.1 ~ gender*musict1*picturest1, data=obarowStory1))
```

Now, run this command in the R Console:

```
par(mfrow = c(2, 2), oma = c(0, 0, 2, 0)) #this asks for all 4 plots to be on one page
#oma gives parameters for the outer margins
plot(AnovaModel.1)
```

This provides a series of four diagnostic plots. If you do not change the parameters with the par() command line, you will see the plots one at a time but will need to pull down the NEXT menu and choose the only option available (NEXT PLOT). You might need to turn on the recording to go back and see all of the figures. (Go to HISTORY > RECORDING.) Figure 10.23 shows all four plots together.

The first plot, shown in the upper left-hand corner of Figure 10.23, is a residual plot; if the data have equal variances, it should show only a random scattering of data. Since the data values are so discrete we do not really see a scattering, but extreme values at the top of the plot may indicate a problem with heteroscedasticity. The second plot, shown in the upper right-hand corner, is a Quantile-Quantile (Q-Q) plot. It tests the data against the assumption of a normal distribution. The data should be reasonably linear, and, although the discreteness means that the middle points form little parallel lines instead of following the diagonal, there also does not seem to be any clear pattern of non-normality (such as an S-shaped or J-shaped pattern in the Q-Q plot). The third plot, shown in the lower left-hand corner, is, like the first plot, meant to detect heteroscedasticity, and if there were problems the data would show a pattern and not be randomly scattered. This plot looks OK. The last plot, in the lower right-hand corner, is meant to test for influential points. Cook's distance, shown by the dashed line, is a measure of influential outliers, and values over 1 would be cause for concern. It looks close to zero here so that seems to be fine. Crawley (2002, p. 240) suggested that the two biggest problems

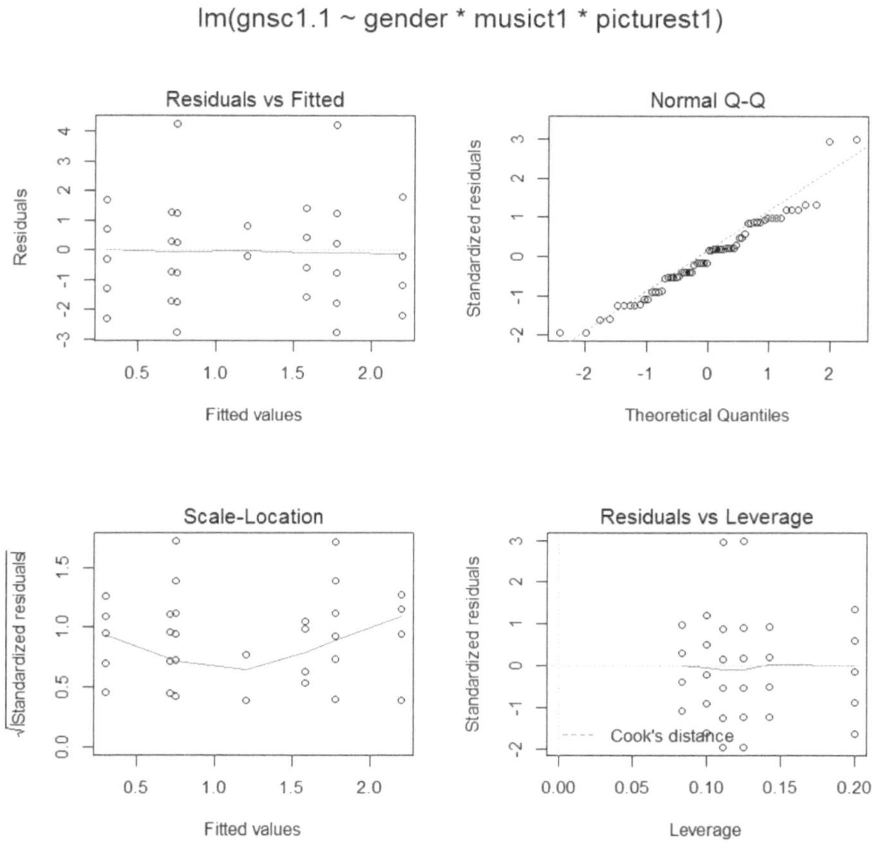

Figure 10.23 Diagnostic plots for the Obarow (2004) data file, a 2 x 2 x 2 factorial ANOVA.

for regression/ANOVA are heterogeneity of variance (non-constant variance across the x-axis) and non-normal errors. There do not seem to be large problems in this model with anything.

If you did find problems though, my suggestion would be to use a robust ANOVA order to address the issues of both non-normality and possible heterogeneity of variance (for SPSS use bootstrapping; for R, see the online section "Two-Way Factorial ANOVA-R").

10.5.3 A Confidence Interval Approach to Factorial ANOVA (Advanced Topic)

Now we want to move on to try to see a "new statistics" approach to these data, one where we can look at CIs and estimates of differences between mean scores instead of *F*- and *p*-values. What we need to do is perform multiple comparisons of the data, starting with the most complicated interaction. This is because simple effects (like gender) may not be of much interest if any of the interaction effects are statistical; if we knew that, for example, the three-way interaction were statistical, this would tell us that males and females performed differently depending on whether music was played *and* depending on whether pictures were present. In that case, our interest would be in how all three factors together affected scores, and we would not really care about just the plain difference between males and females. The omnibus results of the ANOVA given above do not show any interaction effects, but it is possible that CIs of differences between mean scores will.

In a sense, we are ignoring the omnibus ANOVA and simply moving on to look at multiple comparisons. A traditional approach to ANOVA would say that if the three-way interaction between the variables in the ANOVA table was not statistical ($p < 0.05$), we should not explore comparisons of the levels of the variables any further. However, since we are looking for CIs and do not have any as yet, and since there are some authors (Wilcox, 2003, 2012b) who advocate ignoring omnibus results and simply moving on multiple comparisons, I feel justified in doing it.

Just for the three-way interaction, if we want to compare every possibility with every other, we will need to make 12 comparisons. In fact, there are 24 possible permutations of the data. We can calculate how many possible permutations there are by figuring out how many possibilities there are in our first choice (6, which is 2 levels of gender × 2 levels of music × 2 levels of pictures); then, having chosen our first variable, how many choices are left for the second slot (which equals 4: say we choose gender: then for the second slot we have 2 levels of music × 2 levels of pictures). Finally, in the last slot there is just one variable left, and since it only has 2 levels which will be compared to each other, there is only 1 possibility there, making for 6 × 4 × 1 = 24 possibilities. However, a comparison like Male/Music/Pictures: No Pictures is the same as Music/Male/Pictures: No Pictures, so although there are 24 possible permutations, we cut the possibilities in half because there will be no difference to the results in how we order the first two constituents. (In other words, Music/Male or Male/Music, it does not matter!)

I cannot find any way to make multiple comparisons of a three-way interaction in R, so it seems we will have to split up the data by some variable first and then look at pairwise comparisons among two variables. We will do this using the same glht( ) command from the multcomp package that we saw in Chapter 4.

Which variable shall we use to divide the data first? There is a package, phia (De Rosario-Martinez, 2015), post-hoc interaction analysis, which will give us a nice means plot before we start our analysis. Because the Obarow (2004) data has three variables, and we are not sure which one might yield anything interesting, it might be worth looking at a quick means plot of all of the two-way interactions between the three variables. The phia package has a very easy plot available that will easily take care of three variables, so follow along with me to install the package, load the package, create a linear statistical model with all three variables, and then create a multiple means plot.

```
install.packages("phia")
library(phia)
Obarow.Model1<-lm(gnsc1.1~gender*picturest1*musict1, data=obarowStory1)
obarow.mean<-interactionMeans(Obarow.Model1)
plot(obarow.mean) #by the way, adding multiple=F to this command
#would result in all of the means plots being printed separately and not in a grid
```

Figure 10.24 shows that while the interaction between gender and pictures looks very parallel, the interaction between gender and music, and between music and pictures, does not look parallel. Which one shows the possible largest interaction effects? The differences between the bars in plot 5 of Figure 10.24 (gender and music) look larger than the differences between pictures and music (in plot 6), so let us start the analysis by dividing the data up into those who were in the treatment with pictures vs. those in the treatment with no pictures and then looking at the two-way multiple comparison between gender and music.

First, let us divide the file up by the pictures variable:

```
attach(obarowStory1)
names(obarowStory1)
 [1] "gender" "grade" "rdglvl" "picturest1" "musict1" "treatment1" "pretest1" "gnsc1.1" "gnsc1.2"
levels(picturest1)
[1] "no pictures" "pictures"
O.nopics<-subset(obarowStory1, subset=picturest1=="no pictures")
O.pics<-subset(obarowStory1, subset=picturest1=="pictures")
str(O.nopics)
```

```
'data.frame':   30 obs. of  10 variables:
 $ gender     : Factor w/ 2 levels "male","female": 1 2 1 2 1 1 2 1 1 2 ...
 $ grade      : num  1 3 1 3 1 1 1 1 3 3 ...
 $ rdglvl     : num  1 3 3 2 3 2 3 3 2 2 ...
```

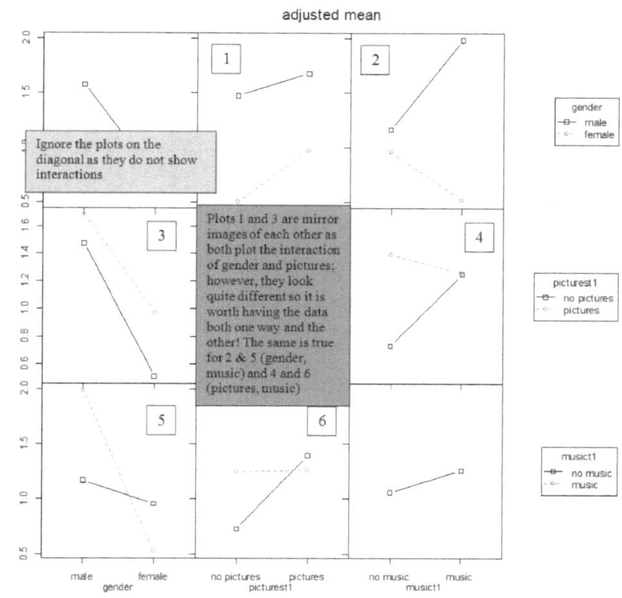

Figure 10.24 Means plot with Obarow's 3 variables using the phia library.

The **subset()** command divides up the data by just one level of a variable (like "no pictures"), but you will have to be precise and type the name of the level exactly as it is found in the file, which is why I first found out the names of the levels. A look at the structure of the new files (**str**) shows they contain data; specifically, we know there are N = 30 in the "no pictures" data set and N = 34 in the "pictures" data set.

Now that the data is divided this way, we can begin to make comparisons. The method of doing so in R, however, is not simple. The problem is that we need to create the correct coefficient matrix for testing the right contrasts. The code here follows Hothorn's (2014) method of how to analyze multiple comparisons for a two-way ANOVA. I will try to comment on the code as I give it to you here, but basically, you should just follow along and substitute your own data in where I have put the underlines, if you have two levels of each variable. (If you have more levels, see the online document "Two-Way Factorial ANOVA-R".) As you type in the code, copy it over to Notepad or a Word document; that way you can then easily change it and copy it back in later because we will be using the same code a number of times to call up the 12 contrasts we need to make.

detach(obarowStory1)	We will not use this data set anymore, so detach it.
library(multcomp)	If this package is not yet open, you must use it for the glht() command.
Tukey=contrMat(table(O.nopics$gender),"Tukey")	For the O.nopics file and order Gender, Music, create Tukey contrasts with your data.
K1=cbind(Tukey, matrix(0,nrow=nrow(Tukey), ncol=ncol(Tukey))) #You might want to type in the finished product (for example, >K1) to see what #you're making as you go!	Binds the Tukey matrix together with a matrix full of zeros that is the same dimension (row and column) as the Tukey matrix. Since there are two levels to gender, we need to have two 2 × 2 matrices; if you had three levels in gender, you would need three matrices bound together here. (See the online document "Two-Way Factorial ANOVA-R" for an example.)

<table>
<tr><td>rownames(K1)=paste(levels(O.nopics$musict1)[1], rownames(K1), sep=":")</td><td>The [1] here refers to the first level of the music variable; put the other variable in here, the one you did not use in the third line of the code (which was Gender).</td></tr>
<tr><td>K2=cbind(matrix(0,nrow=nrow(Tukey),ncol=ncol(Tukey)),Tukey)</td><td>This puts together one 2 × 2 matrix full of zeros first, then the Tukey matrix.</td></tr>
<tr><td>rownames(K2)=paste(levels(O.nopics$musict1)[2],rownames(K2),sep=":")</td><td>The [2] refers to the second level of the variable; use the same variable as for the rownames for K1; if you had a third level you would need to add in another matrix with [3] specified. (See online document for an example.)</td></tr>
<tr><td>K=rbind(K1, K2)</td><td>Make a matrix of these two contrast matrices.</td></tr>
<tr><td>colnames(K)=c(colnames(Tukey), colnames(Tukey))</td><td>Give the columns the names of your variable in the first line (for me, gender); here, they are repeated twice because there are two levels for gender, so we have put together two matrices that are 2 × 2, resulting in four columns in K. (Check and see!)</td></tr>
<tr><td>O.nopics$gm=with(O.nopics, interaction(gender,musict1))</td><td>Create a new variable (a factor) called gm which is derived as the interaction between gender and music (note comma between variables not period!).</td></tr>
<tr><td>cell=lm(gnsc1.1~gm-1, data=O.nopics)</td><td>Put the results of a linear model into the object cell; use your K matrix to specify which contrasts to use.</td></tr>
<tr><td>summary(glht(cell, linfct=K))

Simultaneous Tests for General Linear Hypotheses

Fit: lm(formula = gnsc1.1 ~ gm - 1, data = O.nopics)

Linear Hypotheses:
Estimate Std. Error t value Pr(>|t|)
no music:female - male == 0 -0.03571 0.84817 -0.042 0.9989
music:female - male == 0 -1.90000 0.89762 -2.117 0.0852 .

Signif. codes: 0 '***' 0.001 '**' 0.01 '*' 0.05 '.' 0.1 ' ' 1
(Adjusted p values reported -- single-step method)</td><td>This command will pull up the "old statistics" t- and p-values of the model; they are adjusted for multiple comparisons.</td></tr>
<tr><td>confint(glht(cell,linfct=K))

Simultaneous Confidence Intervals

Fit: lm(formula = gnsc1.1 ~ gm - 1, data = O.nopics)

Quantile = 2.3687
95% family-wise confidence level

Linear Hypotheses:
Estimate lwr upr
no music:female - male == 0 -0.03571 -2.04475 1.97332
music:female - male == 0 -1.90000 -4.02616 0.22616</td><td>This command will pull up the CIs of the difference between means of the comparisons; they are adjusted for multiple comparisons, although it does not say so.</td></tr>
</table>

The code above creates a contrast matrix based on Tukey's contrasts for gender for each level of music. So all of this work just got us 2 out of the 12 comparisons we want to make, if we want to test all the possible comparisons. What we can say from looking at the results is that the comparison between males and females with No Pictures and No Music has a mean difference of 0.04 points, with an adjusted 95% CI of [−2.04, 1.97]. This passes through zero and is strongly centered around zero and thus we would not expect any effect at all. On the other hand, the comparison between males and females for No Pictures and Music has a mean difference of 1.9 points, with an adjusted 95% CI of [−4.03, 0.22], which does go through zero but is not centered around zero, indicating that something interesting may be happening here, and that as the CI becomes more precise it might show an interesting effect. In fact, because the data have been adjusted for multiple comparisons, we might suspect that this CI would show a stronger effect if it were unadjusted. (And indeed it does, in the SPSS output, where I was able to call for CIs without any adjustment.)

Now we want to call up the comparisons for the condition of No Pictures where we compare the condition of Music vs. No Music for males and females. Just reverse the order of the variables gender and music in the previous code to get this contrast matrix for music for each level of gender. (Be sure to also change the name of this new interaction term you are making, which was called gm previously, for Gender-Music. I changed the new one to mg, for Music-Gender).

```
Tukey=contrMat(table(O.nopics$musict1),"Tukey") #this is letter "o"
K1=cbind(Tukey, matrix(0,nrow=nrow(Tukey), ncol=ncol(Tukey))) #this is number "ø"
rownames(K1)=paste(levels(O.nopics$gender)[1], rownames(K1), sep=":")
K2=cbind(matrix(0,nrow=nrow(Tukey),ncol=ncol(Tukey)),Tukey)
rownames(K2)=paste(levels(O.nopics$gender)[2],rownames(K2),sep=":")
K=rbind(K1, K2)
colnames(K)=c(colnames(Tukey), colnames(Tukey))
O.nopics$mg=with(O.nopics, interaction(musict1,gender)) #it's a comma between Music1 and gender
cell=lm(gnsc1.1~mg-1, data=O.nopics)
summary(glht(cell, linfct=K))
confint(glht(cell,linfct=K))
```

```
         Simultaneous Confidence Intervals

Fit: lm(formula = gnsc1.1 ~ mg - 1, data = O.nopics)

Quantile = 2.3687
95% family-wise confidence level


Linear Hypotheses:
                              Estimate lwr     upr
male:music - no music == 0     1.4500  -0.7630  3.6630
female:music - no music == 0 -0.4143  -2.3273  1.4987
```

The output here is the opposite of the output shown for the first set of code! Now we can say that the comparison between Music and No Music with No Pictures among males has a mean difference of 1.45 points, with an adjusted 95% CI of [−0.76, 3.66]. This passes through zero but is not as strongly centered around zero as some of our other comparisons. It is not an important effect but could be an interesting possibility for further research (and dovetails with the previous interesting possibility of a difference between males and females for No Pictures and No Music). On the other hand, the comparison between Music and No Music with No Pictures among females has a mean difference of 0.41 points, with an adjusted 95% CI of [−2.32, 1.50]. There does not seem to be any effect on learning for females whether music is played or not when there are no pictures.

By now I hope you see where this is going. We will have to keep manipulating the data to obtain all 12 comparisons we want. But how do we know we are doing the right comparisons? Even with three variables that only have two levels each, it gets fairly complicated, and it would probably help to write out all of the possible permutations of the data. I did this in Table 10.10. This table lays out all 24 possible permutations for the three-way interaction, but I have put permutations which are equal on the same row. For example, in row 1 the permutation No pics-Music-M:F is exactly the same comparison as Music-No pics-M:F, so we only need to test it once.

So far we have done four comparisons, corresponding to the permutations in rows 1, 2, 5 and 6 of Table 10.10. We can call up four more comparisons by simply substituting in the O.pics data file for the O.nopics file in the code above, giving the permutations in rows 3–4 and 7–8. So what we need for the last four permutations are those in rows 9–12. Divide up the original data file (remember, that was obarowStory1) by the Music variable like this:

```
attach(obarowStory1)
levels(musict1)
[1] "no music" "music"
O.nomusic <-subset(obarowStory1, subset=musict1=="no music")
O.music <-subset(obarowStory1, subset=musict1=="music")
str(O.nomusic) #check your new files to make sure there's something there!
detach(obarowStory1)
```

Table 10.10 Pairwise comparisons for a three-way interaction for a 2 × 2 × 2 ANOVA

1	No pics	Music	Male: Female	Music	No pics	Male: Female
2	No pics	No Music	Male: Female	No Music	No pics	Male: Female
3	Pics	Music	Male: Female	Music	Pics	Male: Female
4	Pics	No Music	Male: Female	No Music	Pics	Male: Female
5	No pics	Male	Music: No Music	Male	No pics	Music: No Music
6	No pics	Female	Music: No Music	Female	No pics	Music: No Music
7	Pics	Male	Music: No Music	Male	Pics	Music: No Music
8	Pics	Female	Music: No Music	Female	Pics	Music: No Music
9	No Music	Male	Pics: No Pics	Male	No Music	Pics: No Pics
10	No Music	Female	Pics: No Pics	Female	No Music	Pics: No Pics
11	Music	Male	Pics: No Pics	Male	Music	Pics: No Pics
12	Music	Female	Pics: No Pics	Female	Music	Pics: No Pics

What if you are using data with more levels than me and you have a lot more comparisons you want to make? Take a look at the online section "Two-Way Factorial ANOVA-R" for an example of a model with more than two levels, although it has fewer variables. By accident I discovered that if you put parentheses around the interactionMeans( ) command from the phia package, it will list all of the possible permutations of your variables. So I had a model with all of my variables in it:

```
Obarow.Model1<-lm(gnsc1.1~gender*picturest1*musict1, data=obarowStory1)
```

and the following command gave this output:

```
(obarow.mean<-interactionMeans(Obarow.Model1))
```

```
  gender  picturest1  musict1 adjusted mean
1   male no pictures no music     0.7500000
2 female no pictures no music     0.7142857
3   male    pictures no music     1.5833333
4 female    pictures no music     1.2000000
5   male no pictures    music     2.2000000
6 female no pictures    music     0.3000000
7   male    pictures    music     1.7777778
8 female    pictures    music     0.7500000
```

This is not a perfect way to get all of your permutations because actually we want to compare the two levels in the third slot, but it shows that for the situation where we compare Music/No Music in the third slot, we will need four contrasts. If you change the order of the variables in the model, you can get other permutations. This might be helpful for figuring out your permutations if you are having trouble getting started.

Now we can use the same syntax as used above (starting with the line that says Tukey=contrMat) to do the two-way comparisons that compare Pictures and Gender within the No Music and Music file. When all is said and done, we do not end up with any CIs that show a clear effect for any combination of the three variables, although the range of the CI for No Pictures/Music/Males: Females makes us think that with more precision we might find a very small effect. However, let us conclude that there are no statistical three-way interactions, and move on to the two-way interactions.

Of course, we already know how to do two-way interactions because we have been doing them, we just need to substitute in the undivided data file, obarowStory1, instead of the split data files, to look at the three two-way interactions Music/Gender, Pictures/Gender, Music/Pictures. First, let us look at the two-way interaction between Music and Gender. In the case of two-way interactions for these data, there are only four possibilities for testing (4 choices for the first slot, which is 2 levels of music × 2 levels of gender, and 1 choice for the second slot because it only has two levels which will be compared to each other, meaning 4 × 1 = 4 possibilities). Note that these possibilities for numbers of permutations would get exponentially larger as the number of levels in a variable increased. For a two-way interaction if both your variables had 3 levels, you would have 9 × 3 = 27 choices (9 choices for the first slot, which is 3 levels of A × 3 levels of B, and 3 choices of comparisons for the second slot, because comparing every level to every other level when you have 3 levels takes 3 comparisons).

It might be nice to look at an interaction plot of this data, and we have already opened the phia package necessary for this command, so I make a new model with just two variables and run the syntax to make the interaction plot:

```
Obarow.Model2<-lm(gnsc1.1~gender* musict1, data=obarowStory1)
obarow.mean2<-interactionMeans(Obarow.Model2)
plot(obarow.mean2)
```

I will not display the plot, but it shows that the interactions are not parallel, although the scale of the differences is small, so we may not find an effect:

```
Tukey=contrMat(table(obarowStory1$musict1),"Tukey")
K1=cbind(Tukey, matrix(0,nrow=nrow(Tukey), ncol=ncol(Tukey)))
rownames(K1)=paste(levels(obarowStory1$gender)[1], rownames(K1), sep=":")
K2=cbind(matrix(0,nrow=nrow(Tukey),ncol=ncol(Tukey)),Tukey)
rownames(K2)=paste(levels(obarowStory1$gender)[2],rownames(Tukey),sep=":")
K=rbind(K1, K2)
colnames(K)=c(colnames(Tukey), colnames(Tukey))
obarowStory1$mg=with(obarowStory1, interaction(musict1,gender))
cell=lm(gnsc1.1~mg-1, data= obarowStory1)
summary(glht(cell, linfct=K))
confint(glht(cell,linfct=K))
```

The CIs show no effect for the two-way interaction between Males and Music: No Music (95% CI [0.68, −0.52]), but there is a small effect for Females and Music: No Music (CI [−0.42, −1.69]). The difference between females when they have music or not could be just 0.42 points of difference in learning vocabulary words, or as large as 1.69 words, but even so this is very small and not far from zero. Checking descriptive statistics for the Music by Gender interaction (use the tapply( ) function seen earlier but only list two variables):

```
tapply(obarowStory1$gnsc1.1, list(gender=obarowStory1$gender,
musict1=obarowStory1$musict1), function(x) sum(!is.na(x))) #this command gives counts; use
#mean and sd for the other descriptives
```

We see that females scored lower when they heard music (M = 0.50, SD = 1.29) than when there was no music (M = 0.92, SD = 0.79). Notice that males scored more highly with music (M = 1.93, SD = 1.94) than without it (M = 1.25, SD = 1.62), but probably the larger amount of variance (reflected in the bigger SD) meant that the comparison for males did not show an effect. This is two of the four comparisons we need to do. To do the other two comparisons, exchange the place of musict1 and gender in the syntax.

Now, the results show that the comparison between males and females when there is no music has effect (95% CI [−1.58, 0.92]), but the comparison between males and females when there is music does show an effect (95% CI [−2.65, −0.21]). Again, like all of the effects we have found in these data, it is a small effect and the difference could be as small as only 0.21 points difference in learning vocabulary words. Using the descriptive statistics we see that when there was music, males scored higher (M = 1.93, SD = 1.94) than females (M = 0.50, SD = 1.29).

If we continue on in this fashion we can find CIs for the other two-way interactions, but there are no effects for any of the other comparisons. Now that we have found differences for one of the two-way interactions, however, we have no further need to look at the main effects (the effect of just Gender, for example). The main reason is that understanding any differences in main effects would not add any more to our understanding than the two-way interaction. In other words, we have found that there is some interaction with a small effect between gender and music, with males learning more vocabulary when music is present, and females seeming to do worse with music than without it. So, if we then looked at the comparison in scores just between females and males, that would not give any more insight into the situation because it would not be taking the effect of music into account. In fact, reporting that males scored higher than females in the gain score would obscure some information, such as that the comparison shows a difference only when music is present or not.

Now if, in your own data, you did not find anything interesting in the two-way interactions, you would want to move on to looking at main effects. To examine CIs for the differences between the levels of just one variable, you could refer back to Chapter 9 (if you have more than two levels) or to Chapter 8 (if you had only two levels).

Thus, in reporting on the results of this factorial ANOVA, because there is a real difference for one part of the two-way interactions, I would likely report on all 12 of the pairwise comparisons in the three two-way interactions, reporting the mean scores in each case, the mean difference between the groups and the 95% CIs of the mean difference between the groups. My conclusion for this data set would be that the interaction of music and gender produced a very small difference only in the context of music, with males performing better with music than without, but females performing worse with music than without.

What about the fact that we have carried out many comparisons? In the "old statistics" we used corrections like the Tukey's HSD test or Bonferroni correction to correct for the fact that having many comparisons might capitalize on the fact that just by chance some of our comparisons will be statistically significant. Cumming (2012) stated that the multiple comparison problem does not go away just because we are using estimation, but he noted that there is no well-established CI adjustment comparable to the Bonferroni correction. The package we used here, **multcomp**, did perform Tukey adjustments to our CIs, so we can report that some adjustments were made, although of course we did not test all of the comparisons at the same time so the adjustment did not take into account all of our comparisons.

Cumming (2012) does not think that multiple comparisons with CIs are a problem, because he would still prefer to rely on CIs rather than "calculating a 'corrected' criterion for evaluating a *p*-value when on replication *p* could easily be markedly different" (p. 422). However, he does think that if you have done a lot of comparisons, and noted any statistical results as "interesting possibility[ies] needing further investigation, rather than [being] established finding[s]" (p. 421), it is fine to explore your data and not worry too much about adjusting for multiple comparisons. Crawley (2007) suggested that if you have factors with large number of levels, meaning you will have many more comparisons to make than I made here, mixed-effect models that treat "the factors as random effects rather than fixed effects" (p. 483) might be a good idea. You can find mixed-effect models described online in the "RM-ANOVA the Mixed Effects Way" section, and in Cunnings and Finlayson (2015).

To conclude this rather long section, I have to admit that trying to use the estimation approach with CIs to look at the results of factorial ANOVA is a lengthy and complicated affair.

Performing a Traditional Three-Way Factorial Analysis Of Variance Using a Confidence Interval Approach in R (Advanced Topic)

1 To perform an omnibus ANOVA, in R Commander choose STATISTICS > MEANS > MULTI-WAY ANOVA. Choose your IVs under the "Factors" box. Choose a DV in the "Response Variable" box. Click on OK.

2 To use a "new statistics" estimation approach, ignore the omnibus ANOVA and look at multiple comparisons. Start with your highest interaction, such as one three-way interaction between three IVs. Figure out how many comparisons you will need to make. For a three-way interaction, the calculation is:

   Slot 1: Multiply the number of levels of all variables together (for example, 2 × 3 × 2 = 12).
   Slot 2: Multiply the number of levels of the two variables that are left together (for example, 2 × 3 = 6).
   Slot 3: Figure out how many permutations you can make of the two-way pairings of the levels in the last variable (for example, if a variable with two levels is left, there is only one possible pairing).
   Multiply the slots together and divide by 2, since the order of the first two slots is not important. For my example, this makes 12 × 6 × 1 = (272/2) = 36.

3 Create an equation that expresses the linear model of your data. (Copy it from the syntax you got from doing #1.)

```
Obarow.Model1<-lm(gnsc1.1~gender*picturest1*musict1, data=obarowStory1)
```

   Use the phia package and plot an interaction plot:

```
obarow.mean<-interactionMeans(Obarow.Model1)
plot(obarow.mean) #add multiple=F to this command to see plots one at a time (useful if you have a lot!)
```

4 Divide up the data so you can do comparisons between only two variables at a time. If you have three variables, divide the data into one level of the Slot 1 variable. Use the subset() command and make sure you write the names of the levels of your variable exactly:

```
O.nopics<-subset(obarowStory1, subset=picturest1=="no pictures")
```

5 Open the multcomp package and copy in the 11 lines of command given in this chapter to create a coefficient matrix that will test the relevant multiple comparisons. Keep this syntax handy so you can later substitute in different subsets of the data or different variables to test all of the multiple comparisons that you want.

6 Examine the CIs to see if they show any real effects of the comparisons.

7 Use the tapply() command to look at the descriptive statistics for the two-way comparisons:

```
tapply(obarowStory1$gnsc1.1, list(gender=obarowStory1$gender, musict1=obarowStory1$musict1), function(x) sum(!is.na(x))) #this command gives counts; use mean and sd for the other descriptive
```

8 Stop looking at lower-order comparisons if you find effects at the higher level. In other words, if you find important differences for a three-way comparison, do not bother to look at two-way comparisons. If you find real effects for a two-way comparison, do not bother to look at main effects (the levels of one variable). If you need to examine main effects, use techniques for one-way ANOVAs if there are more than two levels, or techniques for *t*-tests if there are only two levels.

Using an "old statistics" approach, focusing on the results of the traditional ANOVA test, with its stars and *p*-values, and then doing multiple comparisons only for the statistical interactions or main effects using R commands (which are far more automated than what I have shown you here if you just want the *p*-values), seems fairly attractive at this point! and may be the only realistic option if you have many variables or many levels of your variable.

10.5.4 Planned Comparisons in a Factorial Analysis of Variance

Chapter 9, Section 9.4.6–8, described how to do planned comparisons for one-way ANOVAs, and in fact we would need to do something akin to a one-way ANOVA to be able to do planned comparisons for a factorial model. The regular factorial analysis of the two-way ANOVA found in this section can be found in the online document "Two-Way Factorial ANOVA".

The data I will be using in this section are adapted from a data set called "ChickWeight" from the R statistical program built-in package. I call this data set WritingOneWay.sav and we will pretend that these data describe an experiment that investigated the role of L1 background and experimental Condition on scores on a writing sample.

The DV in this data set is the score on the writing assessment, which ranges from 35 to 373. (Pretend this is an aggregated score from four separate judges who each rated the writing samples on a 100-point score.) The IVs are L1 (four L1s: Arabic, Japanese, Russian and Spanish) and Condition. There were three conditions that students were asked to write their essays in: (1) "correctAll," which means they were told their teachers would correct all of their errors; (2) "correctTarget," which means the writers were told only specific targeted errors would be corrected; and (3) "noCorrect," in which nothing about correction was mentioned to the students.

As to the results of the factorial ANOVA, suffice it to say that the factorial ANOVA found a modest effect for the interaction between L1 and Condition ($F_{6, 566} = 7.31$, $p < 0.001$, partial eta-squared = 0.07). Remember that planned comparisons are done when we want to examine only certain questions in the data and not compare every group, but decide exactly which groups to examine before we start the analysis.

Let me briefly illustrate how planned comparisons for this data set might work. Let us say we did look at our data graphically (not shown here, but see online section "Performing a Two-Way Factorial ANOVA"), thought about which questions were most important to us, and decided that we had three main questions:

1 Did Spanish speakers perform differently in every correction condition?
2 Did every L1 group perform differently in the NoCorrect condition than in the CorrectTarget condition?
3 Were the Spanish speakers different from the Arabic and Japanese speakers combined in the CorrectAll condition?

If you think about the way we specified contrasts in Chapter 9, we needed for each component of the variable to contain either a number or a zero, and the numbers had to add up to zero. If we have just one group compared against another group, we would only need a +1 for one group and a −1 for the other group, and all of the other (in this case, 10 out of 12) groups had a zero.

So for question #1, we want to really make three comparisons:

1A. Spanish – Correct All vs. Spanish – Correct Target
1B. Spanish – Correct All vs. Spanish – No Correct
1C. Spanish – Correct Target vs. Spanish – No Correct

This contrast is easy to make by just putting a +1 for the first group, and a −1 for the second group. Table 10.11, rows 1A–1C, shows how this could be accomplished, with the row total adding up to zero. Table 10.11 assumes that every cell that does not contain a number will contain a zero, to more clearly show what is happening.

For question #2, we want to give a number to every group in the NoCorrect condition and compare it to every group in the CorrectTarget condition. In other words, we are combining these groups and then pitting them against each other. We will give each CorrectTarget condition a +1, and each NoCorrect condition a −1.

For question #3, we want to compare Spanish speakers to the Arabic and Japanese speakers combined (only in the CorrectAll condition), so we will give the Spanish speakers a 2, and the Arabic and Japanese speakers each a −1 (summing to make −2) to balance out the comparison.

Table 10.11 Planned Contrasts for Three Questions for the Writing Data Set

	Arabic/ CorAll	Arabic/ CorTar	Arabic/ NoCor	Jap/ CorAll	Jap/ CorTar	Jap/ NoCor	Span/ CorAll	Span/ CorTar	Span/ NoCor	Russ/ CorAll	Russ/ CorTar	Russ/ NoCor
1A							1	−1				
1B							1		−1			
1C								1	−1			
2		1	−1		1	−1		1	−1		1	−1
3	−1			−1			2					

Unfortunately, for SPSS the only thing we will be able to get out of the planned comparison will be *p*-values, not CIs. However, R can return CIs.

10.5.5 Performing Planned Comparisons in a Factorial Analysis of Variance for SPSS and R

For SPSS, using the data from the file WritingOneWay, open the one-way ANOVA (ANALYZE > MEANS > ONE-WAY ANOVA) and put the Score variable in the "Dependent List" box and the newly created variable Treatment in the "Factor" box. Click on the CONTRASTS button and then enter in the numbers for each question as listed in Table 10.11 along the row (adding in zeros where the cells are empty). You can run the analysis and receive *p*-values back for the contrasts.

For R, first import the SPSS file WritingOneWay.sav into R as writing1. Create an object that defines your contrasts:

```
contr<-rbind("Span_CorAll_vs_CorTar" = c(0,0,0,0,0,0,1,-1,0,0,0,0),
 "Span_CorAll_vs_NoCor" = c(0,0,0,0,0,0,1,0,-1,0,0,0),
"Span_CorTar_vs_NoCor" = c(0,0,0,0,0,0,0,1,-1,0,0,0),
"NoCorrect_CorrectTarget" = c(0,1,-1,0,1,-1,0,1,-1,0,1,-1),
"Spanish_Vs_ArabicJapanese_CorrectAll" = c(-1,0,0,-1,0,0,2,0,0,0,0,0))
```

Now call for a CI on the multiple comparisons that use the object you just created as the contrasts. (The glht() command is from the multcomp package, so open that package if it is not already open.)

```
fit<-aov(score~treatment, data=writing1)
plot(glht(fit,linfct=mcp(treatment=contr)))
confint(glht(fit,linfct=mcp(treatment=contr)))
```

```
Multiple Comparisons of Means: User-defined Contrasts

Fit: aov(formula = score ~ treatment, data = writing1)

Quantile = 2.5182
95% family-wise confidence level

Linear Hypotheses:
                                          Estimate  lwr       upr
Span_CorAll_vs_CorTar == 0                 -58.3167  -82.7134  -33.9199
Span_CorAll_vs_NoCor == 0                 -173.7067 -197.0344 -150.3789
Span_CorTar_vs_NoCor == 0                 -115.3900 -136.8179  -93.9621
NoCorrect_CorrectTarget == 0              -349.7142 -390.2145 -309.2140
Spanish_Vs_ArabicJapanese_CorrectAll == 0    4.0627  -39.2214   47.3469
```

Looking at the CIs we can get from R, we see there were differences between all of the Spanish groups at each of the three conditions, with the biggest difference being in the CorrectAll vs. NoCorrect conditions. (We know from the descriptive statistics that scores were higher when no corrections were made.) Here the estimate of the difference was 174 points on a 0–400 scale, which is a very large amount of difference! The CI is almost 50 points wide but is very far away from zero, so we are confident in the very large effect of this difference of condition.

The second question asked whether all the groups together performed differently in the NoCorrect condition than in the CorrectTarget condition. The answer is that they did. Now the effect looks quite large but we should actually remember that since we combined the scores of 4 groups, the maximum possible points here was not 400, but actually 400 × 4 = 1600. The effect is still large as the estimate of 350 points out of 1600 is considerable, and the CI is far away from zero, but in proportional terms the difference between the Spanish speakers' CorrectAll vs. NoCorrect still has a larger effect.

Finally, for the third question of whether the Spanish speakers are different from the Arabic and Japanese speakers combined on the CorrectAll condition, our CI shows that we cannot presume that there is any difference between these groups. The CI is centered around zero and the estimate of 4 points (out of a possible 400 × 2 = 800) is negligible.

If you would prefer to see *t*-values and *p*-values, you can use the **summary()** command to call for them. The results are similar to what you get from SPSS:

```
summary(glht(fit,linfct=mcp(treatment=contr)))
```

```
Linear Hypotheses:
                                         Estimate Std. Error t value Pr(>|t|)
Span_CorAll_vs_CorTar == 0                -58.317      9.688  -6.019   <1e-07 ***
Span_CorAll_vs_NoCor == 0                -173.707      9.264 -18.751   <1e-07 ***
Span_CorTar_vs_NoCor == 0                -115.390      8.509 -13.560   <1e-07 ***
NoCorrect_CorrectTarget == 0             -349.714     16.083 -21.744   <1e-07 ***
Spanish_Vs_ArabicJapanese_CorrectAll == 0   4.063     17.189   0.236    0.998
---
Signif. codes:  0 '***' 0.001 '**' 0.01 '*' 0.05 '.' 0.1 ' ' 1
(Adjusted p values reported -- single-step method)
```

Since the CIs gave us more information than *p*-values, I will not explain any more about how the questions were answered.

10.5.6 Effect Sizes for Factorial Analysis of Variance

As with one-way ANOVAs, one issue in reporting effect sizes for factorial ANOVAs is what exactly to report effect sizes on! When doing regression (in the form of ANOVA), one effect size to always report is the overall coefficient of determination (R^2) of the regression equation. Then one may decide whether to report on effect sizes for main effects (and interactions) or whether to report effect sizes for post-hoc tests or planned comparisons; R^2 effect sizes are automatically reported in SPSS and R output. Effect sizes for main effects and interactions are also printed in the SPSS output if you call for them. They are the partial eta-squared values, which are a percentage variance (PV) effect size for the omnibus *F*-test. This effect size can also easily be calculated using SS:

$$_{partial}\hat{\eta}^2 = \frac{SS_{effect}}{SS_{effect} + SS_{error}}$$

or df and *F*-values:

$$_{partial}\hat{\eta}^2 = \frac{df_{hyp}\,F}{df_{hyp}\,F + df_{error}}$$

I do want to note here that calculating effect sizes for factorial designs is a complicated subject (Olejnik & Algina, 2000). Grissom and Kim (2005) noted that one should be quite careful in comparing the relative effect sizes of different variables in their study. It often happens that one *F*-test might have more power, giving a higher PV, than another factor. Also, if one level of a factor represents one kind of treatment and another level represents a totally different type of treatment, it may be like apples and oranges to try to compare their effect sizes.

To calculate effect sizes for post-hoc tests or planned comparisons, use the same approach as was given for a one-way ANOVAs in Chapter 9 (Section 9.4.9) to calculate Cohen's *d*. If you are using CIs, effect sizes are not necessary but could be given in addition to the CIs.

10.5.7 Application Activities with Factorial Analysis of Variance

1 Obarow (2004) data. In the text I performed a factorial ANOVA on the gain score for Obarow's Treatment 1. Using the file Obarow.Story2.sav, first rearrange the data correctly as explained in Section 10.4.1. You will need to decide whether to select cases. You will need to change the TRTMNT2 variable into two different IVs, music and pictures. (Use the values for TRTMNT2 to help guide what you do.) Then calculate a gain score. Once you have configured the data to a form ready to perform an ANOVA, visually and numerically examine the data with graphics and comment on assumptions. Next, perform a traditional factorial ANOVA to find out what effect gender, music and pictures had on the gain score for the second treatment (story). If using R, replicate the kind of analysis that SPSS uses for this analysis. Last, try to do an analysis using 95% CIs. It is rather complicated but you can work similarly to how I showed how to do it for Story1 in the text.

2 Larson-Hall and Connell (2005). Use the LarsonHall.Forgotten.sav data. Use the SENTENCEACCENT variable to investigate whether the IVs of gender and (immersion) status could help explain variance in what kind of accent rating participants received. Be sure to examine graphics and comment on assumptions.

3 Dewaele and Pavlenko (2001–2003). Use the BEQ.Swear.sav file. Dewaele (2004a, 2004b, 2004c) explored the question of whether multilinguals' perceptions of the emotional force and frequency of swear words depended on a variety of other variables that were measured in the Web questionnaire. The question that asked about the emotional force of swearwords was a five-item Likert scale that asked "Do swear and taboo words in your different languages have the same emotional weight for you?" Use a factorial ANOVA to examine the effect of context of acquisition of the L2 (CONTEXTACQUISITIONSEC) and L1 dominance (whether L1 is dominant or not) on the emotional force of swearwords in the L2 (WEIGHT2). Be sure to examine graphics and comment on assumptions.

4 Open the Eysenck.Howell13.LongForm.sav data set. These data were fashioned in accordance with a study by Eysenck (1974); apparently Howell (2002) did not have the actual raw data, but instead fashioned the data so that the mean scores for each group would equal the mean scores that Eysenck (1974) gave. Howell gives this data in his chapter 13. Eysenck wanted to see whether age group (young = 18–30 years, old = 55–60 years) would interact with task condition in how well the participants could recall words from a word list. There were five conditions, four of which ascertained whether the participants would learn the words incidentally, but some tasks required more semantic processing than others. The tasks were letter counting, rhyming the words in the list, finding an adjective to modify the word in the list, forming an image of the word and control (intentionally trying to learn the word). Instead of an omnibus ANOVA, perform planned comparisons to answer these questions:

   1 Did the older group perform differently in each condition?
   2 Did the intentional learning group ("Intentional" in the Task variable) result in higher recall on the Score variable than any of the incidental conditions ("Counting," "Rhyming," "Adjective" and "Image") taken as a group for either the younger or older group?

10.5.8 Reporting the Results of a Factorial Analysis of Variance

The results of a factorial ANOVA should include information about the type of ANOVA you used, and by this I mean information about the regression equation that was used in your analysis.

Your reader should know whether you used a full factorial model (as many commercial statistical programs like SPSS do) or whether you searched for the **minimal adequate model**, see the online document "Finding a Minimal Model Using R". Reports of these two different types of analyses will be quite different. If you do a minimal adequate model you should report on the steps you took in the search for the minimal adequate model and report the change in deviance and possibly also the Akaike information criterion (AIC) scores for the models.

The pieces of information that you will want to report from a factorial ANOVA depend on whether you decide to include the omnibus *F*-test. In reporting the results from an omnibus test, include at least the df between groups (also called the hypothesis df), the df within groups (also called the error df or residuals), the *F*-value and the *p*-value. Some people like to report the entire ANOVA table, with SS and mean squares as well, but I prefer just to report the raw data so that people can recreate my analysis or, if the sample size is too large, tell people I would be happy to send them the raw data. If you do not want to do that, I still do not see any compelling reason to give SS or mean squares information, but you can report them if you wish. Results should also include information about how you checked regression assumptions of the data, along with descriptive statistics such as the *N*, means and SDs.

If you do not want to report on the omnibus test but instead report results of multiple comparisons of the groups you should start with means, SDs and counts for each group. A nice graphic that shows interaction terms as well as box plots would an excellent addition to your results. The type of comparison used (post-hoc or planned comparison) and method used for controlling the familywise error rate, if used at all (for example, Tukey, false discovery rate, etc.) should also be specified. The heart of the matter is the 95% CI for the mean difference between the tests. Depending on which way the comparison was made (for example, NP–PTP or PTP–NP), the mean difference will be negative or positive, so the negative sign does not really matter, unless of course the CI goes through zero. Tell your reader if you used robust measures such as means trimming or bootstrapping on your CIs. I do not see any reason to report *p*-values but doubtless some will feel compelled to. Visuals that graphically show the CIs may be welcome.

Here is an example of a report you might write for the Obarow (2004) data if you looked at the full model and wanted to include the omnibus test. I am using the results found in Section 10.5.1 using SPSS:

> A 2 × 2 × 2 full factorial ANOVA examining the effects of music, pictures and gender on the increase in participants' vocabulary size found a statistical effect for the main effect of gender only ($F_{1,56}$ = 4.35, p = 0.042, partial eta-squared = 0.07). None of the effect sizes for any other terms of the ANOVA were above partial eta-squared = 0.03. Males overall learned more vocabulary after hearing the story three times (M = 1.53, SD = 1.76, *n* = 34) than females did (M = 0.67, SD = 1.12, *n* = 30). The effect size shows that this factor accounted for R^2 = 15% of the variance in the data (adjusted R^2 = 4%), which is a small effect. None of the other main effects or interactions were found to be statistical. The data were not normally distributed, as there were outliers and non-symmetric distributions of data. Analysis of the ANOVA model did not find any marked problems with normality or heteroscedasticity.
>
> Pairwise comparisons of the three-way interaction between music, pictures and gender found the following results (Table 10.12). Mean differences between groups and 95% CIs are listed.
>
> A weak but possibly interesting three-way interaction was found in one CI for No Pictures – Music – Males vs. Females. Descriptive statistics showed that males performed better in this condition (*N* = 5, M = 2.20, SD = 1.79) than females did (*N* = 10, M = 0.30, SD = 1.49). Investigation of CIs for two-way interactions found . . .

Here is an example of a report you might write for the Obarow (2004) data if you searched for the minimal adequate model: see the online document "Finding a Minimal Model Using R"

Table 10.12 Confidence Intervals for Obarow (2004): Three-Way Interaction Using SPSS Output

			Mean difference	*95% CI*
No Music	Male	No Pictures: Pictures	0.83	[−2.22, 0.55]
No Music	Female	No Pictures: Pictures	0.49	[−2.26, 1.29]
Music	Male	No Pictures: Pictures	0.42	[−1.27, 2.12]
Music	Female	No Pictures: Pictures	0.45	[−1.89, 0.99]
No Pictures	Male	Music: No Music	1.45	[−3.18, 0.28]
No Pictures	Female	Music: No Music	0.41	[−1.08, 1.91]
Pictures	Male	Music: No Music	0.19	[−1.53, 1.14]
Pictures	Female	Music: No Music	0.45	[−1.28, 2.18]
No Pictures	No Music	Male: Female	0.04	[−1.54, 1.61]
No Pictures	Music	Male: Female	1.90	[0.24, 3.56]
Pictures	No Music	Male: Female	0.38	[−1.23, 2.00]
Pictures	Music	Male: Female	1.03	[−0.45, 2.50]

> I started with a full factorial model for the 2 Gender × 2 Music condition × 2 Picture condition ANOVA. A bootstrapped stepwise algorithm returned a minimal model that included the main effects of Gender and Music, plus the interaction of Gender and Music, with an AIC of 239.0. However, a model with only the main effect of Gender had a lower AIC of 237, and there was no statistical difference between models, so I retained the simpler model with only the main effect of Gender. This model was also statistically different from a null model. The final minimal linear model of gnsc1.1~gender had a $R^2 = 0.08$, adjusted $R^2 = 0.06$, and was statistical, $F_{1,62} = 5.29, p = 0.02$.

For the Writing data set (you can find this section online: "Two-Way Factorial ANOVA") I would report that I conducted a 4 (L1) × 3 (Condition) full factorial ANOVA which examined the effects of L1 (Arabic, Japanese, Spanish and Russian) and experimental conditions (CorrectAll, Correct Target and NoCorrect) to explain writing scores as evaluated by four judges on a 100-point scale. The interaction between L1 and Condition was statistical ($F_{6,566} = 7.31, p < 0.0005$). This model explained $R^2 = 69\%$ of the variance in writing scores. Because the interaction was statistical I examined multiple comparisons and the last figure in the online section "Two-Way Factorial ANOVA" shows the CIs graphically. Then I would put in the information about my basic conclusions that I already stated at the end of the analysis (find it online).

10.6 Summary

In this chapter, we extended the ANOVA concept to the situation when there were three IVs. (An analysis using two IVs with more levels can be found in the online section "Performing a Two-Way Factorial ANOVA"). This is the beginning of multivariate analysis, because having more than one IV means we were able to look not only for main effects of the variables but also for interaction between the IVs. With a factorial ANOVA we can begin to model more complex research designs that better mirror reality. However, I gave a warning that our brains can probably not understand more than a three-way interaction, so it is not a good idea to throw too many separate IVs into the mix. We also saw that in trying to examine CIs, having variables with large numbers of levels will make finding all of the possible combinations of comparisons a very laborious process. Planned comparisons could help constrain the number of combinations needed.

Just as with a one-way ANOVA, a statistical omnibus effect from an ANOVA is not going to tell us everything we want to know about the effects of the IVs, so it is necessary to conduct further comparisons or pairwise tests to do this. In both SPSS and R we examined ways to look at CIs for the comparisons of two variables at a time, but that was the limit. There was no way to examine comparisons of three variables at a time, so if an analysis included a statistical three-way interaction one would need to divide up the data by one variable first and then examine the pairwise comparisons between two variables at a time. With *p*-values there are ways to adjust for having multiple comparisons, but there is no established way to do this for CIs. However, we are trusting in Cumming (2012), who suggested that unadjusted CIs are still better than *p*-values. In R, the **multcomp** package does adjust CIs to compensate for multiple comparisons.

Although interaction plots (also called means plots) are handy for understanding your data and are easy to generate in SPSS and R, a plot with more data, such as the combination interaction plot–box plot graphic shown in this chapter is a good choice for displaying your data visually to readers.

This chapter also presented information on how to conduct robust factorial ANOVAs. In SPSS, bootstrapping is available and affects the CIs that can be found when you do multiple comparisons of groups. In R, bootstrapping, means trimming and comparisons with other estimates of location instead of the mean are available using Wilcox's **WRS** package. (See the online document section "Robust Methods of Performing Factorial ANOVA in R" for more information.)

An additional advanced section found online, called "Two-Way Factorial ANOVA-R" and the section "Minimal Model for a Factorial ANOVA" shows how to reduce your ANOVA from a full factorial ANOVA, where all main effects and interactions are automatically included, to a minimally adequate model where the only terms left in the equation are those that are statistical (or the main effects of interaction terms that are statistical). This approach could be used to help reduce quite complicated models to more manageable ones, where CIs could then be calculated.

Chapter 11

Looking for Group Differences When the Same People are Tested More than Once

Repeated-Measures Analysis of Variance with Wug Tests and Instruction on French Gender

> Although complex designs and state-of-the-art methods are sometimes necessary to address research questions effectively, simpler classical approaches often can provide elegant and sufficient answers to important questions. Do not choose an analytic method to impress your readers or deflect criticism. If the assumptions and strength of a simpler method are reasonable for your data and research problem, use it. Occam's razor applies to methods as well as to theories.
>
> Leland Wilkinson (1999, p. 598)

In this chapter, I will examine a statistical design called "repeated measures." This design is used when the same participants are measured more than once. The repeated measurement may be separated by time, as these situations are:

- pretest, posttest and delayed posttest scores;
- proficiency levels measured after one month, six months and one year living in the USA;
- past tense forms provided in conversation after 5 and 10 years of using the language.

All of these situations would require a repeated-measures design, because they test the same people more than once. Repeated-measures designs are also often found in our field when there is only one testing point in time, but you have related tests that you view as an independent variable (IV), such as scores separated by categories, as when you divide the scores of a test instrument into:

- noun and verb parts;
- phonemic distinctions;
- syntax and morphology components.

In general, research designs that incorporate repeated measures are quite desirable, as they increase the statistical power of a test. In fact, the more closely correlated the measures are, the higher the statistical power will be with fewer participants (Murphy & Myors, 2004). This is an important factor to consider in our field, where sample sizes are generally small (20 or fewer).

I will consider two studies in this chapter. The first is a study by Murphy (2004) in which second language users of English were tested to see whether they would perform differently in creating past tense regular and irregular verb morphology on nonce verbs. Lyster (2004) carried out the second study; he wanted to see whether there would be positive benefits to form-focused instruction on grammatical gender in French. He tested his participants at three different time periods.

Recent Examples of Repeated-Measures Analysis of Variance in the Second Language Acquisition Literature

Chrabaszcz and Gor (2014)

Chrabaszcz and Gor tested a difficult phonemic contrast in Russian, that of soft vs. hard consonants (i.e. /mat/ "stalemate" vs. /mat'/"mother") in an AX discrimination task. Their ultimate goal was to look at how this contrast would interact with other factors for understanding sentences, such as syntactic, semantic and morphological features, but the repeated-measures analysis of variance (ANOVA) I report on here looked at the influences of three IVs on how well the learners discriminated pairs of words. One factor was the type of contrast, and this concerned whether the pair of words the Russian learners heard contrasted because of soft vs. hard consonants in Russian, or control consonant contrasts, such as /sut/ "court" vs. /sup/ "soup," which were easy for American learners of Russian to hear. This contrast is a within-subjects (repeated) contrast, because there was more than one contrast, but all of the learners participated in listening to all of the contrasts. The second IV was vowel environment. The consonant pairs were either found after an /a/ "or an". /i/. This contrast was also a within-subjects (repeated) measures because participants heard words with both these vowel environments. The last IV was language group. Participants were either native speakers (NS) of Russian (N = 12) or American learners of Russian (N = 32). This variable was a between-subjects (not repeated) variable because all of the participants belonged either to one group or the other. The question investigated whether there was any effect for the interaction of consonant contrast, vowel environment and language group on listening scores, resulting in a 2 (contrast) × 2 (vowels) × 2 (language group) repeated-measures ANOVA (RM-ANOVA). Participants heard a sentence that they had to listen to for meaning and then saw two words on the screen. Half of the sentences had a word that was congruent and fitting with the meaning of the sentence while half had incongruent words. Participants had to decide which of the two words they saw on the computer screen was the word they heard. (They also had to answer a question about the meaning of the sentence later on.) The results showed that the interaction between consonant contrast and language group was statistical ($F_{1,174} = 22.32$, $p < 0.001$, $\eta^2 = 0.08$); the effect size of $\eta^2 = 0.08$ showed that it was a medium-size effect and the interaction explained about 8% of the variance when all other factors in the design were controlled. The main conclusion is that learners of Russian performed worse on the hard vs. soft contrast than on the control contrasts, while NS of Russian performed similarly on both types of contrasts.

Xiao and Wong (2014)

Xiao and Wong reported that Chinese language programs in the USA are increasing in number, and that among US immigrants who speak a language that is not English, Chinese is the second most common language. Chinese heritage language learners, therefore, have been increasing, and the authors gathered data from a total of 176 students of Chinese, 87 of which were enrolled in special heritage language classes at their universities. The students took a number of different Likert scale questionnaires, which for the purposes of a one-way RM-ANOVA were divided up into four skill-based anxiety questionnaires: speaking, writing, listening and reading. The research question was whether students scored differently on these four tests and if so, where differences lay. Traditionally, speaking is seen as the skill that most provokes foreign language anxiety, but the analysis here, done with a one-way RM-ANOVA using a division into the four different types of questionnaires, found a main effect for skill ($F_{2,214} = 14.69$, $p < 0.001$, partial η^2 = 0.15), and subsequent comparisons found that the activity that causes the most anxiety was writing, followed by reading.

Toth (2008)

Toth investigated the acquisition of the Spanish clitic *se* with both qualitative and quantitative measures. Quantitatively, he investigated an interactionist approach by looking at whether a "focus on form" with a teacher-led, whole-class approach (called teacher-led discourse, or TLD, n = 28) differed from small-group interactions among learners (called learner-led discourse, or LLD, n = 25), and whether those forms differed from a control group who received no focus on the grammatical form. The treatment lasted for seven class periods. A 3 (Treatment group) × 3 (Time of testing) RM-ANOVA was used to test development on a production task with sentences elicited by means of pictures, and a statistical interaction of Treatment group with Time was found ($F_{4,148} = 15.2$, $p < 0.001$, partial $\eta^2 = 0.29$). Separate one-way ANOVAs performed at each of the 3 Times found no differences between groups on the pretests, but differences in the immediate and delayed posttests (24 days after the end of instruction), with the experimental groups performing higher than the control group on both posttests, and some indications that TLD was better than LLD. Qualitatively, looking at discourse transcripts from learners' interactions on a task and teacher-led group interaction on a task, Toth (2008) concluded that the TLD "appeared to have yielded a more consistent focus on the object of instruction than the LLD learners' discussion of L2 forms, which embraced a broader gamut of structures" (p. 265) and this may have been helpful in scaffolding the learners more ably to understand the grammatical form.

Xu, Chang, and Perfetti (2014)

Xu, Chang, and Perfetti noted that learning to understand the meaning of and pronounce Chinese characters is a very big undertaking for students who are learning Chinese. Their study thus focused on whether learning characters that share radicals (the grouped condition) would help facilitate later recall of their sound, meaning and form. There were two levels of students: first-year Chinese students, who were beginners ($N = 48$) and second-year Chinese students, who were considered intermediate learners ($N = 40$). Approximately half of the learners in each level were assigned to learn characters in the grouped condition while the others were assigned to the distributed condition. The learners took a pretest, had four learning lessons for four consecutive days, a posttest on the fifth day and a delayed posttest two weeks after the first learning session. The learning sessions and tests were conducted by computer. In the tests, participants had to write the pinyin (pronunciation) and meaning for any of the 48 characters they had learned in their sessions. For the first-year students, a 2 (groups) × 3 (testing time) RM-ANOVA on pronunciation (writing the pinyin for the character) found a statistical interaction between group and testing time ($F_{2,92} = 5.23$, $p < 0.01$, partial $\eta^2 = 0.10$). This meant that both groups did not perform in the same way at all three testing times. Further analysis found that those learning the characters in the grouped condition had an advantage in the immediate posttest, but it did not last for the delayed posttest. An identical analysis for the meaning of the characters found the same results. This was a statistical interaction ($F_{2,92} = 6.50$, $p < 0.01$, partial $\eta^2 = 0.12$) with the participants in the grouped condition performing better on the immediate but not the delayed posttest.

11.1 Understanding Repeated-Measures Analysis of Variance Designs

The main reason why a repeated-measures ANOVA is a more powerful test than a factorial ANOVA is because it can take individual variation into account. Remember that in factorial ANOVA, we have an error term into which we sweep all of the variance that we cannot explain. A lot of this variance is due to the fact that people are just different, and so may respond differently. A repeated-measures design is able to factor out some of the variation that occurs within individuals because it looks at the same individuals with at least two different measures.

Figure 11.1 shows that the variation in any ANOVA can be divided into variation *between* groups, such as teaching method, and variation *within* groups, such as individual variation. With a factorial ANOVA, we account only for between-group variation. However, with repeated-measures ANOVA (RM-ANOVA), we can also account for some of the within-group variation. This reduces the amount of error and thus increases power. Notice that we still have an error term, but it should be reduced because we can factor out some of the individual variation.

Howell (2002, p. 480) reinforces this idea when he says: "To put it succinctly, subjects differ. When subjects are observed only once, these subject differences contribute to the error term. When subjects

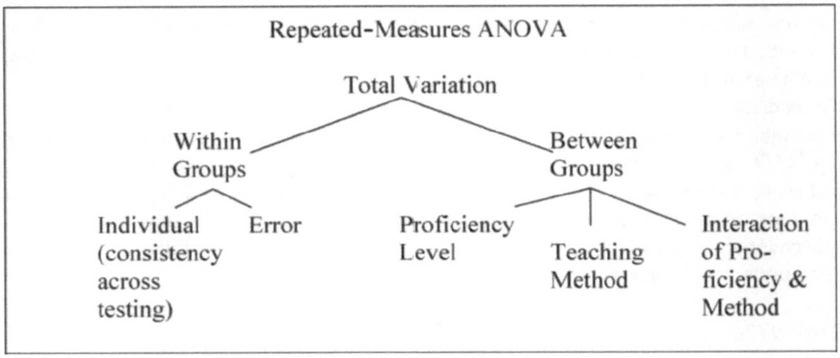

Figure 11.1 Visualizing how variance is partitioned in an ANOVA.

are observed repeatedly, we can obtain an estimate of the degree of subject differences and partial these differences out of the error term."

Like an ANOVA design, a repeated-measures design has one dependent variable (DV) and at least one categorical IV. The difference with a RM-ANOVA is that one or more of the IVs must be a within-groups factor. A within-groups independent variable must make a division that includes at least two scores for each participant, because:

- the person took a pretest and a posttest;
- the same individual took one test that was divided into parts, such as semantic and syntactic categories of sentence types, phonemic categories or pragmatic conditions;
- the person took the same test after receiving three different teaching treatments (i.e. the person participated in every condition of an experiment that involved multiple conditions), such as a person who might take a test after an implicit treatment and then again after an explicit treatment.

Tip: If it is a within-groups variable, then each participant will be included in *all* of the levels of the variable! For example, in a pretest/posttest design the same person will have both a pretest and a posttest score. In a design where the data are split into groups such as phonemic contrasts, the same person would have data for all of the phonemic contrasts.

In language acquisition data, it is very common that there will also be a between-groups independent variable. This variable will differentiate between groups, measuring things like:

- experimental group assignment;
- teaching method received;
- condition performed under;
- proficiency level;
- gender.

Tip: If it is a between-groups variable, then each participant can be in only *one* of the levels of the variable! For example, if a person receives instruction in only one teaching method, this is a between-groups IV because their scores are only found in one level of the Teaching Method variable. However, if the person received instruction in the three different teaching methods and scores were recorded after each type of instruction, this would be a within-groups variable since the same person's scores were in all levels of the variable.

Repeated-measures ANOVAs that measure *both* a between-groups and within-groups score are sometimes called **mixed between/within** ANOVAs. This is because they have both a between-subjects and a within-subjects variable. These are the types of RM-ANOVAs that will be highlighted in this chapter. Repeated-measures ANOVAs may, like factorial ANOVAs, be called one-way, two-way or higher depending on how many IVs are included.

11.1.1 Repeated-Measures Analysis of Variance Design of the Murphy (2004) Study

Murphy (2004) is an example of a repeated-measures study that results from splitting the items in one testing instrument into different categories. This is a 2 × 2 × 3 repeated-measures design. These numbers refer to the number of levels in each of the three IVs, which are Status, Verb Type and Similarity.

Murphy administered a 30-item "Wug" test to participants, meaning that each of the words was a nonce (nonsense) word. (The test was first used by Jean Berko Gleason in 1958.) Each participant had to provide an ending for each unknown verb they heard, such as *cleef* or *spling*. There was only one testing instrument, but Murphy hypothesized that non-native English speakers would perform like adult NS and treat the regular verbs differently from the irregular verbs. In fact, not only was Murphy interested in splitting the data into regular/irregular categories, but she had also engineered the verb sets so that the verbs showed three differing levels of similarity to real English verbs. This means that Murphy essentially divided the 30 points from the test into six categories. Note that Murphy, had she wanted to, could have said she had one within-groups IV with six levels (regular prototypical, regular intermediate, etc.), instead of looking at two IVs. If she had done this, however, she would not have been able to see whether similarity interacted with verb type (regular/irregular). The design of Murphy's study is shown in Figure 11.2.

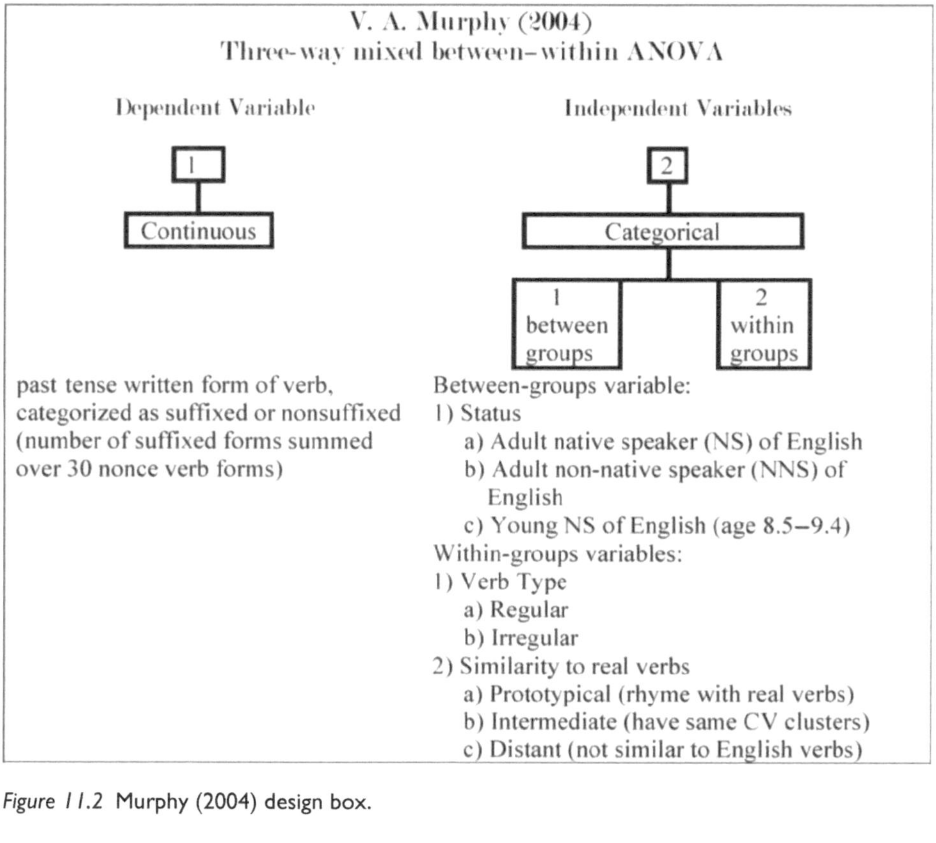

Figure 11.2 Murphy (2004) design box.

11.1.2 Repeated-Measures Analysis of Variance Design of the Lyster (2004) Study

The second study I will examine in this chapter, carried out by Lyster (2004), is an example of a study that gets its repeated measures from testing done over different time periods. This is a 3 × 4 repeated-measures design. These numbers refer to the number of levels in each of the two IVs, which are Time of Testing and Treatment Group.

Lyster gave the French learners in the study a pretest and then an experimental treatment followed by an immediate and delayed (eight weeks later) posttest. He also administered four different tests designed to measure learners' ability to manipulate French grammar correctly. Two were written tests, and these were a binary choice test (circle the correct article) and a completion test (assign gender to nouns in text and also write a recipe). The other two tests were oral and these were an object identification task (student says, "It is a raft") and a picture description task. Lyster conducted four separate RM-ANOVAs, one on each task, and I will mainly consider his written completion task in the chapter. The design of Lyster's study is shown in Figure 11.3.

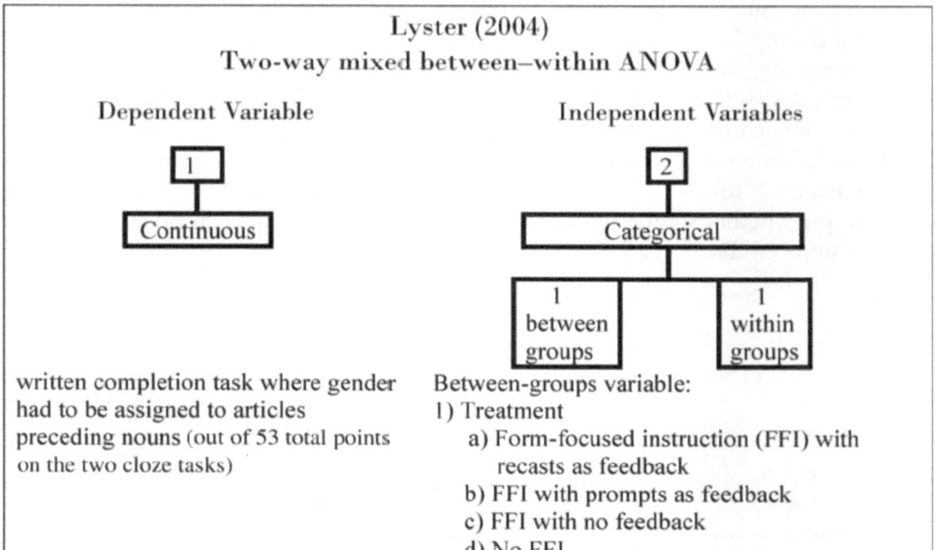

Figure 11.3 Lyster (2004) design box.

Note that, instead of a RM-ANOVA, Lyster could have performed two separate one-way ANOVAs (with Treatment as the only IV) on the gain scores from pretest to immediate posttest and from pretest to delayed posttest. This might make sense if there had been only one posttest, but even in that case, since repeated measures increase the power of a study, it is a good idea to choose a repeated-measures design.

11.1.3 Application Activity: Identifying Between-Groups and Within-Groups Variables to Decide between Repeated-Measures and Factorial Analysis of Variance Designs

In deciding whether you need a RM-ANOVA or just a factorial ANOVA, you need to be able to identify variables as between-groups or within-groups. This activity will give you practice doing this.

Read the following descriptions of actual linguistic experiments. Assume that all of the information given will be analyzed with one statistical test (although this may not have been the case in the real study). Label the DVs and IVs. Decide if each IV is between-groups or within-groups. Decide if you would use a repeated-measures or factorial ANOVA to analyze the experiment. (You will have to use a RM-ANOVA if any variables are within-groups.)

1 Schön et al. (2008) (This study description has been altered slightly for this exercise.) Schön et al. wanted to see whether singing may contribute to language acquisition. Eleven syllables were associated with a tone. There were three conditions and participants in condition 1 heard the syllables spoken; condition 2 heard the syllables sung but matched to the same tone for each syllable (so a C = gy, D = my, etc.); and condition 3 heard the syllables sung but each syllable could be used on any tone. Participants from two language backgrounds (English, French) were also tested. Participants were tested after hearing the continuous stream of syllables for seven minutes. The test presented them with two strings and asked which one was a "word" from the nonsense language, and scores were calculated from their correct answers.

			Status of IV
Dependent variable:			
Independent variable(s):	1	No. of levels	Within-group Between-group
	2	No. of levels	Within-group Between-group
	3	No. of levels	Within-group Between-group
For this research design, use:	RM-ANOVA		Factorial ANOVA

2 Erdener and Burnham (2005). Erdener and Burnham examined the effects of first and second language orthography as well as audiovisual stimuli on how accurately participants could produce non-words orally. The first language of the participants was either Australian English or Turkish. The participants heard or saw non-words in both Spanish and Irish in each of four conditions: (1) they heard the word pronounced (Aud-only); (2) they saw a videoclip of the lower part of a face producing the word and simultaneously heard the word (AV); (3) along with the videoclip, an orthographic representation of the non-word appeared on the video screen (AVorth); (4) they heard the word pronounced and saw the orthographic representation (Aud-orth). Participants had to repeat the non-words, and their responses were audiotaped and analyzed for accuracy. Erdener and Burnham predicted that orthographic information would enhance accuracy. They also expected to see an interaction between first and target languages. Specifically, speakers of a transparent orthography (Turkish) should perform more accurately with a similarly transparent orthography (Spanish) than with a more opaque orthography (Irish), but English speakers would not differ in their responses to the two orthographies as much.

			Status of IV
Dependent variable:			
Independent variable(s):	1	No. of levels	Within-group Between-group
	2	No. of levels	Within-group Between-group
	3	No. of levels	Within-group Between-group
For this research design, use:	RM-ANOVA		Factorial ANOVA

3 Larson-Hall (2004). In this study, I examined how accurately Japanese learners of Russian could perceive differences on 16 phonemic contrasts, such as [s] vs. [ʃ]. The students were from three

proficiency levels. There were five items in each category of phonemic contrast, and students were scored on whether they perceived the contrast correctly or not.

			Status of IV
Dependent variable:			
Independent variable (s):	1	No. of levels	Within-group Between-group
	2	No. of levels	Within-group Between-group
	3	No. of levels	Within-group Between-group
For this research design, use:	RM-ANOVA		Factorial ANOVA

4 Bitchener, Young, and Cameron (2005). English learners from a variety of L1 backgrounds living in New Zealand produced four writing assignments. After the first assignment students received one of three treatments with corrective feedback on their work. Students then produced three more writing assignments, and at each time students' errors were calculated as a percentage of correct use for three areas of linguistic error: prepositions, past simple tense and definite article. An accuracy performance score was calculated. The question investigated how type of corrective feedback would affect accuracy over time and whether different types of errors would be affected in different ways.

			Status of IV
Dependent variable:			
Independent variable (s):	1	No. of levels	Within-group Between-group
	2	No. of levels	Within-group Between-group
	3	No. of levels	Within-group Between-group
For this research design, use:	RM-ANOVA		Factorial ANOVA

5 Ellis, Loewen, and Erlam (2006). Students learning English in New Zealand were placed into three groups that differed according to whether they would receive explicit or implicit error correction or no error correction at all (a control group). Students' ability to form the past tense correctly was elicited on three types of tasks, including an oral imitation task, grammaticality judgment task and test of metalinguistic knowledge. Students took a pretest and then were given an immediate and delayed posttest. Accuracy scores on the three tasks were examined to see whether teaching method and type of task affected how well participants could score at the different testing times.

			Status of IV
Dependent variable:			
Independent variable (s):	1	No. of levels	Within-group Between-group
	2	No. of levels	Within-group Between-group
	3	No. of levels	Within-group Between-group
For this research design, use:	RM-ANOVA		Factorial ANOVA

6 Flege, Schirru, and MacKay (2003). This study examined four groups of Italian–English bilinguals depending on the age they began using English (young or old) and their amount of Italian use (high or low). These two ideas (age and use of language) were considered separate variables. The participants produced words, and NS of English judged the accuracy of the Italian–English bilinguals' vowel production.

			Status of IV
Dependent variable:			
Independent variable (s):	1	No. of levels	Within-group Between-group
	2	No. of levels	Within-group Between-group
	3	No. of levels	Within-group Between-group
For this research design, use:		RM-ANOVA	Factorial ANOVA

7 Chrabaszcz and Gor (2014). This study was explained at the beginning of the chapter. Another analysis made looked at the effect of the three different pairs of soft vs. hard consonants that were used in the study, /l-l^j/, /t-t^j/ and /f-f^j/, to see if there was any difference in how well participants could discriminate soft and hard consonants depending on the consonant used. Remember that there was a native Russian language group and an American learners of Russian group for language group. Participants listened to the pair of words and had to decide which member of the pair they heard.

			Status of IV
Dependent variable:			
Independent variable (s):	1	No. of levels	Within-group Between-group
	2	No. of levels	Within-group Between-group
	3	No. of levels	Within-group Between-group
For this research design, use:		RM-ANOVA	Factorial ANOVA

8 Xiao and Wong (2014). This study investigated anxiety in four different areas of language: speaking, writing, listening and reading. Participants, who were either L2 learners of Chinese or heritage language speakers, took Likert scale tests for all four different types of questionnaires. The research question was whether different language areas provoked different kinds of anxiety, and whether the anxiety was the same for L2 learners as well as for heritage language speakers.

			Status of IV
Dependent variable:			
Independent variable (s):	1	No. of levels	Within-group Between-group
	2	No. of levels	Within-group Between-group
	3	No. of levels	Within-group Between-group
For this research design, use:		RM-ANOVA	Factorial ANOVA

9 Ayoun and Salaberry (2008). Ayoun and Salaberry tested French learners of English to investigate whether they learned to use English past tense forms accurately over different lexical aspectual classes (namely: states, achievements, activities and accomplishments). Participants were tested with a cloze task where there were 59 verbs to be filled in; the necessary verbs came from all four lexical aspectual classes.

			Status of IV
Dependent variable:			
Independent variable (s):	1	No. of levels	Within-group Between-group
	2	No. of levels	Within-group Between-group
	3	No. of levels	Within-group Between-group
For this research design, use:		RM-ANOVA	Factorial ANOVA

11.2 Arranging the Data for a Repeated-Measures Analysis of Variance

If you are using a computer to do your statistics, for any statistical test your data must be arranged in the correct format for that software. In the case of the RM-ANOVA, SPSS and R have different requirements for the data. The following section explains how to make sure your data are in the correct format for the program and type of analysis you want.

11.2.1 Arranging the Data for Repeated-Measures Analysis of Variance in SPSS

For SPSS the data must be arranged so that the DV is split into as many parts as the product of the number of levels of repeated-measures IVs (variables where the same participants are measured more than once). In other words, if the analysis is a 2 (language) × 4 (condition) ANOVA where the condition is a within-group variable (repeated measure) while the language variable is a between-group variable (every participant belongs to only one level), the DV must be split up so that there are four columns of data, each column representing one level of the condition variable at a time.

This means that data for a RM-ANOVA must be arranged in the "wide" format. To understand how many columns of data you will need for the repeated-measures ANOVA, multiply the levels of the within-groups IVs together. For the Murphy (2004) data set, the IVs are verb type (regular or irregular), verb similarity (prototypical, intermediate or distant) and group affiliation (NS child, NS adult or NNS adult). The first IVs are within-groups. Multiplying the levels of the within-group IVs together, we get: 2 × 3 = 6. This means that the *DV* should be split into six groups. There will also have to be a separate column for every between-groups *IV*, so for Murphy's data there should be one column for group affiliation. Murphy's data, as shown in Figure 11.4, is already in the correct form for using a RM-ANOVA in SPSS and contains seven columns.

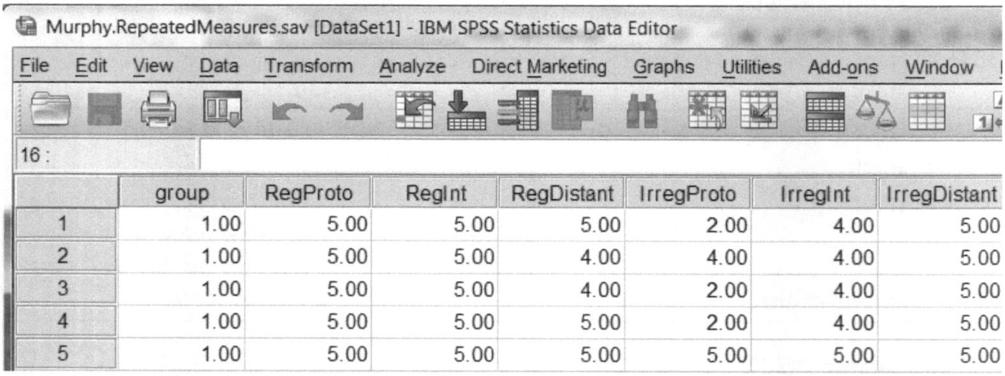

	group	RegProto	RegInt	RegDistant	IrregProto	IrregInt	IrregDistant
1	1.00	5.00	5.00	5.00	2.00	4.00	5.00
2	1.00	5.00	5.00	4.00	4.00	4.00	5.00
3	1.00	5.00	5.00	4.00	2.00	4.00	5.00
4	1.00	5.00	5.00	5.00	2.00	4.00	5.00
5	1.00	5.00	5.00	5.00	5.00	5.00	5.00

Figure 11.4 Murphy data arrangement in SPSS (wide form).

Arranging Data for RM-ANOVA Analysis

The data need to be in the "wide" form, where the number of rows equals the number of participants. There should be more than one column of within-group variable data. The number of columns should be the product of the number of levels of the within-group variables. For example, in the Murphy (2004) data the within-group variables are verb type (two levels) and similarity (three levels). There should thus be six columns of within-group variable data.

Lyster (2004) wanted to investigate how well learners of French could learn to use the correct gender of the article depending on whether form-focused instruction and different types of error correction were provided. Lyster did not view type of instruction and type of error correction as separate variables, but simply as one between-groups variable of treatment condition. This means Lyster needed one column containing indications of which condition people belonged to. The other IV was time, for the participants were tested at three different time periods. This is a within-groups IV with three levels, but it is the only IV, so the dependent data should be divided into three separate columns. Figure 11.5 shows that, for each of his tests, such as the binary choice test, there are indeed three columns with the dependent data measure divided into the time it was collected: PreBinary, Post1Binary and Post2Binary. Therefore, Lyster's data are already in the correct form to use in SPSS.

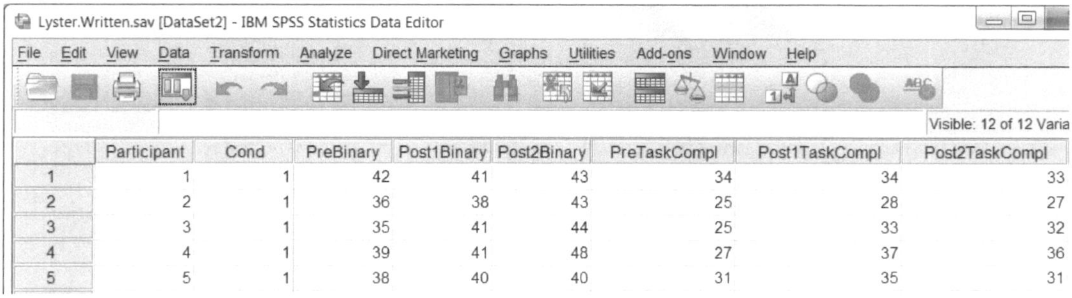

	Participant	Cond	PreBinary	Post1Binary	Post2Binary	PreTaskCompl	Post1TaskCompl	Post2TaskCompl
1	1	1	42	41	43	34	34	33
2	2	1	36	38	43	25	28	27
3	3	1	35	41	44	25	33	32
4	4	1	39	41	48	27	37	36
5	5	1	38	40	40	31	35	31

Figure 11.5 Lyster data arrangement in SPSS (wide form).

11.2.2 Changing from Wide Form to Long Form in SPSS

In some cases, such as, for mixed-model analysis, we will need to have our SPSS data in the "long" form, which means that all of the data for the response variable need to be in one column. There will then be index columns that specify the categorical distinctions for the IVs.

In Murphy's original data set, there were 60 participants with 6 recorded pieces of information each. (Participants' scores on the 30-item Wug test have been divided into categories depending on regular/irregular verb type and prototypical/intermediate/distant similarity to real verbs.) This means we will want one (60 × 6=) 360-item column along with four indexing columns: one for the participant themselves (since the participants' data will take up more than one row, we need to know which rows all belong to the same person), one for the between-group category the entry belongs to (NS adult, NS child or NNS adult) and two for the within-subject categories (one for verb type and one for verb similarity).

In SPSS, we can use the RESTRUCTURING WIZARD to help us transform our data. Call this amazing fellow forth with the menu choice DATA > RESTRUCTURE. For the opening window, you will see three choices. The top choice is the one for changing the wide form into the long form, so pick that one ("Restructure selected variables into cases"). Click on NEXT. Unless you have more than one DV, your choice for Step 2 of 7 will be the first choice, "One." You want to create just one DV that includes all of the measurements stacked on top of the others. Click on NEXT. On the next page, Step 3 of 7, we will have to slow down to think a bit (see Figure 11.6). Here we need to first decide how to create an index for the participants themselves. If you have a variable that already gives a number to each participant (and in the "wide" form you have the data for each participant on one row only), use that, but I do not, so I leave the default choice of "Use case number" and SPSS will automatically generate a participant index for me.

Next, we need to create our stacked column of scores. In the Murphy (2004) file, these are contained in the six columns that index Verb Type and Verb Similarity, so in the area titled "Variables to be Transposed" I type in the new column name "Score," throw all six of the score variables listed under "Variables in the Current File" into the "Variables to be Transposed" box, and finally move the Group

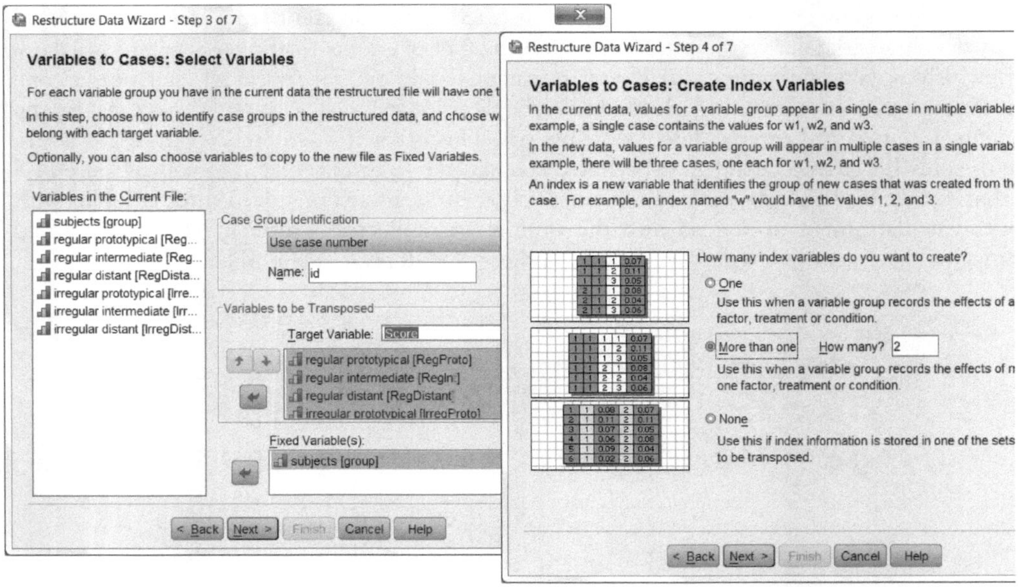

Figure 11.6 Restructure Wizard in SPSS (Steps 3 and 4).

variable to the "Fixed Variable(s)" file. Move any between-subjects variables (where the participants are separated and scores are not repeated) into this box. Click on NEXT. In Step 4 of 7 you have to decide how many indexing columns you need for your data. Previously, I stated that we needed two columns for the within-subject data—one for Verb Type and one for Verb Similarity. We need two, so we select the second choice, "More than one" and the number "2" is the default here (see again Figure 11.6). Click on NEXT.

In Step 5 of 7, you should give the two variables you have just created names. (You cannot have any spaces in the names.) I will call them VerbType and Similarity. It does not really matter what order you put them in, but you need to specify how many levels each one has (that part you should not mix up the order!). VerbType has two levels (Regular and Irregular) and Verb Similarity has three levels (Prototypical, Intermediate and Distant), so I type in those numbers of levels in the next box. SPSS tells you how many "combined levels" you need, which is the product of your levels here. I have 2 × 3 so six and that fits with what SPSS tells me on this page (see Figure 11.7). Click on NEXT. Basically, you do not need to do anything for the next two steps, so just click on NEXT and FINISH, and you will see your finished product (Figure 11.7). Additionally, there is a warning that says "Sets from the original data will still be in use in the restructured data. Open the Use Sets dialog in order to adjust the sets in use." I do not know what this means, but you will want to be sure to save the file under a different name from the one you started with, unless you want to totally replace the original file. (You do not here, because you will use both in this chapter.)

If you scroll down to the bottom of your new data file, you will see there are indeed 360 cases. You might want to hit the VARIABLE VIEW tab and make levels for your new VerbType and Similarity variables (the levels for Group were carried over from the original file), so you will remember what the 1, 2 and 3 mean. They should go in the order that we entered the variables in Step 3 of the RESTRUCTURE WIZARD (see Figure 11.6), so for VerbType 1 = Regular and 2 = Irregular. For Similarity, 1 = Prototypical, 2 = Intermediate and 3 = Distant.

For the Lyster (2004) data, I do not want to use all the data in this file, just the three columns of data that have "Compl" (for completion test) in them. There are 180 participants, so if I have three time periods to stack together, I should end up with 540 rows of data. This means I will want one

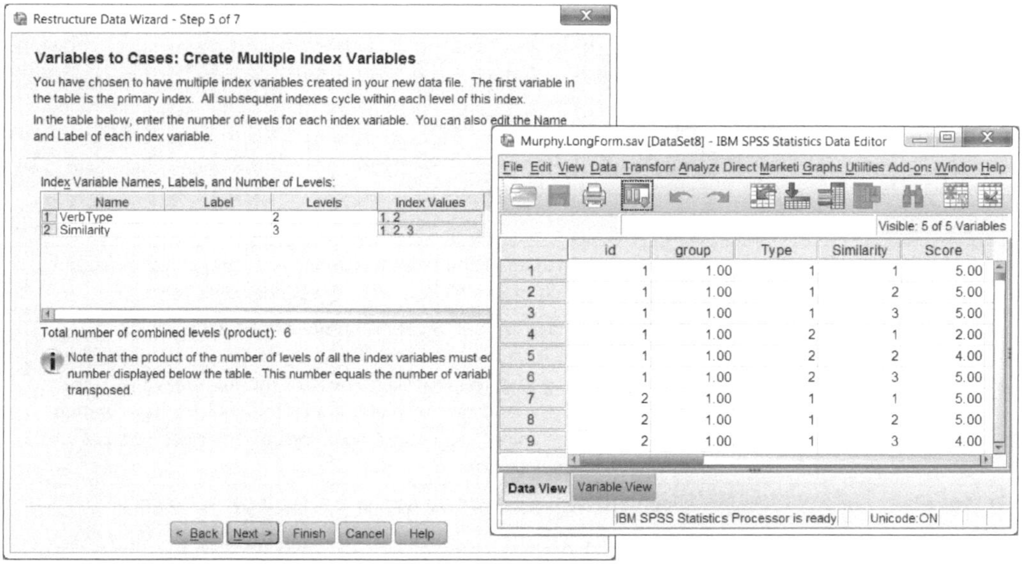

Figure 11.7 Restructure Wizard in SPSS (Step 5) and Murphy data in long form.

(180 × 3=) 540-item column along with three indexing columns: one for the participants themselves (since the participants' data will take up more than one row, we need to know which rows all belong to the same person), one for the between-group category of Condition the entry belongs to (FFIrecast, FFIprompt, FFI, Comparison) and one for the within-subject category of Testing Time (Pretest, Immediate Posttest and Delayed Posttest).

The only differences from the Murphy data are that in Step 3 there is already a Participant variable, so we will put that in the "Case Group Identification" area and choose the "Use selected variable choice" in the drop-down menu. Condition goes in the "Fixed Variable(s)" box, and I name the "Target Variable" Score and put in the three variables that have "Compl" in their name. In Step 5 I have a choice of using numbers for the levels, or the names of the three variables. This is the index that tells me which one of the three columns that I stacked the data refers to, so I decide to label it Time. I decide to use "Sequential Numbers" and go back later to the Variable View to give nicer value labels to the variable levels. SPSS tells me there are three levels in my Time variable, and indeed there are, so I am satisfied. I click on FINISH, check the data file, give the variable levels nicer names and save it under a different name.

11.2.3 Arranging the Data for a Repeated-Measures Analysis of Variance in R

Data for any type of linear modeling in R (whether regression, ANOVA or mixed-effects) needs to be arranged in "long" form, which means that all of the data for the response variable need to be in one column. There will then be index columns that specify the categorical distinctions for the IVs.

Murphy's (2004) original data set is arranged in the proper format to do a RM-ANOVA in SPSS (see Figure 11.4); therefore, it will need to be reconfigured for R. In the original data set there were 60 participants with 6 recorded pieces of information each. (Participants' scores on the 30-item Wug test were divided into categories depending on regular/irregular verb type and prototypical/intermediate/distant similarity to real verbs.) This means we will want one (60 × 6=) 360-item column along with four indexing columns: one for the participant themselves (since the participants' data will take up more than one row, we need to know which rows all belong to the same person), one for the between-group category the entry belongs to (NS adult, NS child or NNS adult), one for verb type and one for verb similarity.

There are a number of packages in R that help you reshape data, but I found the easiest to be the **reshape2** package (Wickham, 2007). Remember that you can install this package by typing install. packages("reshape2") in the R Console.

The following table will walk you through the steps in R for converting Murphy's (2004) data from a "wide" into a "long" form. (I will start with the imported SPSS file Murphy.RepeatedMeasures.sav that I called "murphy.wide" and convert it into murphy.long.)

names(murphy.wide) [1] "group" "regproto" "regint" "regdistant" "irregproto" [6] "irregint" "irregdistant"	Find out the names of the columns; group is a categorical variable specifying which of three categories the participants fit in.
murphy.wide<-cbind(murphy.wide, participant=factor(rep(c(1:60))))	We need to have an identification number for each participant, so we will add it to the data now. Because there are 60 rows, the rep( ) command says to create a column of the numbers 1–60, and the factor( ) command says to make it a factor, which I have named participant. The cbind() command combines the original data set with this new column of data.
library(reshape2)	Open the package; if you do not have it, get it by typing install. packages("reshape2").
fix(murphy.wide) names(murphy.wide) [1] "group" "reg_proto" "reg_int" "reg_distant" [5] "irreg_proto" "irreg_int" "irreg_distant" "participant"	To split up a variable, indicate how to split it by inserting an underscore between each part. Use the fix( ) command to open up the Data Editor (or go to R Commander and EDIT DATA SET). Underscore seems to work whereas a period did not for me. For a Mac, you'll have to change the name manually: murphy.wide$reg-proto<-murphy.wide$regproto.
murphy.long<-melt(murphy.wide, id.vars=c("group", "participant"), value.name="value")	The melt() command takes the data and stacks every column on top of itself, unless you specify it as an ID variable, as I did here with the IV group.The additional argument value.name gives a name to the newly stacked variable you create.

str(murphy.long)
'data.frame': 360 obs. of 4 variables:
$ group : Factor w/ 3 levels "NS children",..: 1 1 1
$ participant: Factor w/ 60 levels "1","2","3","4",..: 1
$ variable : Factor w/ 6 levels "reg_proto","reg_int",..
$ value : num 5 5 5 5 5 5 5 5 5 5 ...
	This command will tell you about the structure of the data frame. We have stacked 6 columns of 60 entries each, resulting in 360 observations in the long form (hooray, it worked!). We have a group factor, a column identifying the 60 participants (showing their data is repeated) and a column with the scores in it (value). But the column called variable has two different codings that we want split into different indexing columns, "Verb Type" and "Verb Similarity."

murphy.long<-cbind(murphy.long, colsplit(murphy.long$variable, "_", names=c("type", "similarity")))	The command colsplit() says to split up the column of variable based on the underscore split between names, and gives it the names "type" and "similarity." The cbind() command is used to add these columns to the murphy.long data frame.

str(murphy.long)
'data.frame': 360 obs. of 6 variables:
$ group : Factor w/ 3 levels "NS children",..: 1 1 1 1
$ participant: Factor w/ 60 levels "1","2","3","4",..: 1 2 3
$ variable : Factor w/ 6 levels "reg_proto","reg_int",..:
$ value : num 5 5 5 5 5 5 5 5 5 5 ...
$ type : Factor w/ 2 levels "irreg","reg": 2 2 2 2 2 2
$ similarity : Factor w/ 3 levels "distant","int",..: 3 3 3
murphy.long$variable <- NULL
	Verify the structure of the final result now. In addition to previously, we have a column identifying the group each person belongs to (group). We have a column for identifying the verb type (type) and the verb similarity (similarity). If these are not factors make them so: murphy.long$type<-factor(murphy.long$type). Last, we have a column with the scores in each case (value). Notice that variable is still here. We can remove that if we want, but we do not have to.

levels(murphy.long$type)=c("Irregular", "Regular") levels(murphy. long$similarity)=c("Distant", "Intermediate", "Prototypical")	A little cleanup to make variable level names more informative. Figure 11.8 shows the finished product. Be careful here to list the levels in the order shown in the str() command. Notice that although the verb similarity "proto" was first in order in the murphy.wide file, the verb similarity "distant" is first in order for the murphy.long file.

Tip: As always, it is crucial to type the command exactly in R to get the result you want. While I was testing out my syntax and trying to work from the wide form of the Murphy data set to the long form, I sometimes got error messages. In many cases, the error was that I had forgotten to type a quotation mark, or had forgotten the period in the middle of the file name (so I wrote murphylong instead of murphy.long). This tip is just to remind you that when you get error messages in R, the first thing to do is to check whether you have introduced a problem by typing something mistakenly. In some ways, it is best to copy and paste code when you are trying a new function out (that is what the R help files let you do, if you use the examples in them). In other ways, I find that typing out the code myself helps me understand better what I am doing. So just be aware that if you type things in yourself, you will probably make some mistakes, so check your code carefully before you go looking for other problems.

I also found a problem in this chapter where the example code for a command did not work! I was stumped for hours until I realized that I did not have an up-to-date version of the package. You can update your packages and avoid this problem by periodically using the menu choice PACKAGES > UPDATE PACKAGES.

murphy.long

	group	participant	value	type	similarity
17	NS children	17	5	reg	proto
18	NS children	18	5	reg	proto
19	NS children	19	5	reg	proto
20	NS children	20	5	reg	proto
21	NS adults	21	5	reg	proto
22	NS adults	22	5	reg	proto
23	NS adults	23	5	reg	proto
24	NS adults	24	4	reg	proto

Figure 11.8 Murphy data arrangement in R (long form).

To get the Lyster (2004) data into the long form, use this code after importing the Lyster.Written.sav file into R Commander as lyster.wide. I do not want to use all the data in this file, just the three columns of data that have "Compl" (for completion test) in them. There are 180 participants, so if I have three time periods to stack together, I should end up with 540 rows of data.

```
names(lyster.wide)
lyster.long<-melt(lyster.wide[c(1:2,6:8)], #use columns 1 & 2, then 6 through 8
id.vars=c("participant", "cond"), #identify the columns which are between-groups variables
value.name="compscore", #give a name to the stacked score from the 3 time periods
variable.name="time") #this specifies the time—pre, immediate post or delayed post
levels(lyster.long$time)=c("pre", "immediate post", "delayed post") #use this to clean up names if you like
str(lyster.long) #verify that there are 540 observations!
```

Figure 11.9 shows what the Lyster data look like after this shaping.

There are also commands in the reshape2 package that can change a data set from the long form to the wide form, but this is apparently trickier than wide to long. Actually, Wilcox and Schönbrodt (2014) command fac2list() from the WRS package does a good job putting long form data into the wide form, although the transformed data is not nicely labeled (but you could easily add your own labels). This command has been seen throughout the book and I refer interested readers to it.

lyster.long

	participant	cond	time	compscore
354	174	Comparison	immediate post	29
355	175	Comparison	immediate post	31
356	176	Comparison	immediate post	32
357	177	Comparison	immediate post	31
358	178	Comparison	immediate post	37
359	179	Comparison	immediate post	32
360	180	Comparison	immediate post	30
361	1	FFIrecast	delayed post	33
362	2	FFIrecast	delayed post	27
363	3	FFIrecast	delayed post	32

Figure 11.9 Lyster data arrangement in R (long form).

Converting Data from Wide Form to Long in R

The basic command used in this section was the melt( ) command from the reshape2 package. The basic syntax of this command is:

melt(data[c(1, 2:3)], id.vars=c("column name"), value.name="score")

where id.vars identifies by name any variables that are between-groups and value.name gives a name to the stacked DV. If your data are not specified, every column that contains numbers will be stacked up into one long column. To specify certain columns, just type in their position numbers after the "c".

Other problems, such as how to get two indexing columns if your original columns encode two different variables at the same time (like the Murphy data does) or how to change the names of levels after the melt() command (as in the Lyster data), or how to add a column to identify participants (as in the Murphy data) were covered in this section.

11.2.4 Application Activities for Changing Data from the Wide to the Long Form (Necessary for Use with the R Program Only)

Note: These files will be used in later application activities, so please save the files after you create them or save the code you used to manipulate the data! You can easily save in R Commander by choosing Data > Active Data Set > Export Active Data Set, choose "Comma" as your field separator, then click on OK. Navigate to wherever you want to save the file and give it a name. It will be saved as a comma-delimited .csv file, which will open up automatically in Excel.

1 Use the Lyster.Written.sav file and make a long form data file with the three binary choice variables (instead of the Completion task, which was used in the text). You will have four columns of data: one for the stacked score, one for the participant index (you will have to create this), one that specifies the Condition and one that gives the Testing Time.
2 Use the Cole (1927) data. The participants were in different teaching condition groups. (One focused on writing and the other on grammar translation.) They took three related tests at two different times. Combine the data from columns 1 through 7 into a "long" form data file. You will have five columns of data: one for the stacked score, one for the participant index (you will have to create this), one that specifies the Teaching Group, one for the type of measure (Vocab, Grammar or Reading) and one for the Testing Time (Time 1 or Time 2).
3 Use the Larson-Hall (2004) data. This data set gives results for how well Japanese students of Russian (and a control group of Russian NS) perceived 16 contrasts, with 5 items in each contrast. Since the contrasts are related, they are repeated measures, but as 16 makes for a huge set, create a

new data set in the long form for only 3 contrasts: R_L, SH_SHCH and PJ_P. You will have four columns of data: one for the stacked score, one for the participant index (you will have to create this), one that specifies the language level (Group) and one for the type of contrast (out of the three only that you will include).

4 Use the Erdener and Burnham (2005) data. Erdener and Burnham hypothesized that speakers of a transparent orthography (Turkish) should perform more accurately with a similarly transparent orthography (Spanish) than with a more opaque orthography (Irish), but the English speakers would not differ in their responses to the two orthographies as much. The scores in the data files are error scores, so a higher number means more errors. Combine the data from columns 2 through 9 into one stacked score variable. You will have five columns of data: one for the stacked score, one for the participant index (you will have to create this), one that specifies L1 (between-groups measure), one that specifies target language (Spanish or Irish) and one that specifies the condition (4 levels with auditory and visual information; you could split this further into two components, but the authors did not so we will not either).

5 Use the Toth (2008) data, using the file called Toth2008Prod.sav. This study was described at the beginning of the chapter. There are three times in different columns—pretest, posttest and delayed posttest. Put these into the "long" form. You will have three columns of data: one for the stacked score, one for the participant index (you will have to create this although there is a column with participant ID now, but you will need to replicate it two more times for the "long" form) and one column that specifies the testing time.

11.3 Visualizing Repeated-Measures Data

As data get more complicated, graphics continue to be important means of exploring and understanding your data before running any statistical tests. Section 11.3.1 shows the Murphy (2004) and Lyster (2004) data using the combination interaction plot and box plot graphic I demonstrated in Chapter 10, and further sections illustrate another nice graphic that is quite useful in understanding how individuals contribute to the group scores called a parallel interaction plot.

11.3.1 Exploring the Murphy (2004) and Lyster (2004) Data with the Combination Interaction Plot and Box Plot

Figure 11.10 shows this type of plot for the Murphy (2004) data. It was created in R using the HH package and the following code. (I set up the colors and line types using the lattice parameter settings as explained in Section 10.2.1.) Chapter 10 explains the code for this command if you want to understand it better. Note that for this command to work in R, you need to have changed the SPSS data into the long form by following the instructions in Section 11.2.2.

```
attach(murphy.long)
library(HH)
interaction2wt(value~type*similarity*group,
par.strip.text=list(cex=.6), main.in="Effects of Verb Type, Verb Similarity and Group on Verb
Formation", box.ratio=.3, rot=c(90,90),
factor.expressions=
c(type=expression("Verb Type"),
similarity=expression("Similarity"),
group=expression("Group")),
responselab.expression="Num.\nsuffixed\nout of\n5")
detach(murphy.long)
```

The means plot shows that all groups treated regular and irregular verbs differently, suffixing more regular than irregular verbs, and there do not appear to be any interactions. (The lines are fairly

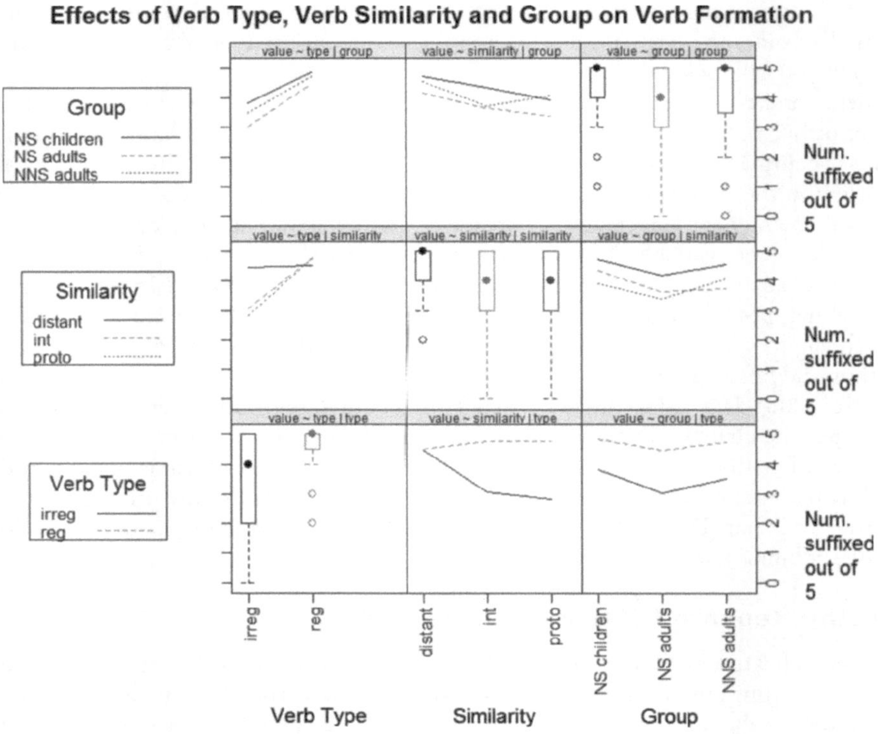

Figure 11.10 Murphy data combination interaction and box plot (using R command interaction2wt()).

parallel.) For irregular vs. regular verbs, NS children scored the highest, while NS adults scored the lowest. Keep in mind that the measurement is of the number of "-ed" suffixed forms, so a score toward minimum means fewer of the forms were suffixed while a score toward maximum means most of the forms were suffixed. The box plots for Verb Type show that both of these levels were heavily skewed toward higher scores, with a couple of outliers for regular verbs. Distributions are non-normal and clearly heteroscedastic.

There does appear to be some interaction between Similarity and Verb Type as the lines intersect. For regular verbs, verb similarity does not seem to matter much, while for irregular verbs prototypical verbs are suffixed the least and distant verbs are suffixed the most. The box plots for Similarity show that the only type of verb that had a more restricted range were the Distant verbs, which skewed toward high scores. Scores are not normally distributed, and Distant verbs had smaller variances than Intermediate or Prototypical verbs.

For the intersection of Group and Similarity, there is a little bit of crossing of lines. For Distant and Intermediate verbs, the same pattern of NS children scoring the highest and NS adults scoring the lowest that was seen earlier still holds, but on Prototypical verbs, NNS adults act similarly to the NS children instead of intermediate to the NS children and adults' behavior. Box plots for Group show no group has a normally distributed distribution, and variances are larger for the NS adults than the other two groups.

Figure 11.11 shows the same plot for the Lyster (2004) data. I will not give you the entire code for the figure as it is almost identical in everything except the variable names to the code for Figure 11.10, but here is the main command once you have the HH package open:

```
interaction2wt(lyster.long$compscore~ lyster.long$cond* lyster.long$time)
```

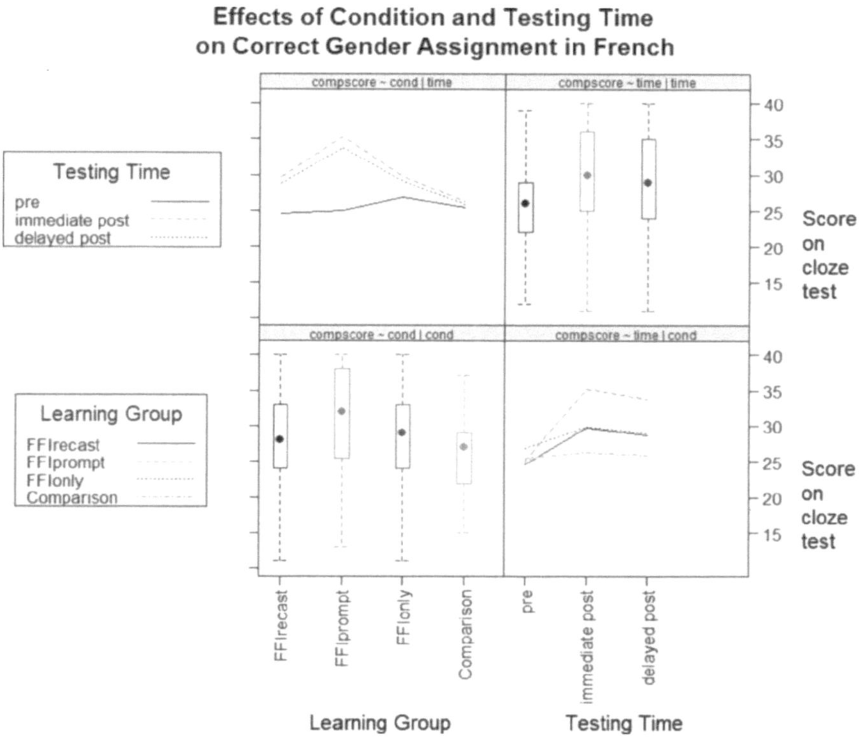

Figure 11.11 Lyster data combination interaction and box plot (using R command interaction2wt()).

There does seem to be an interaction of condition and time, as the lines are not all parallel whether you look at Condition:Time or Time:Condition. The box plots for Testing Time show that scores improved from pretest to posttest, although the range of the box plots is quite large in all conditions and nearly the same even though the median score is higher for the posttests. The box plots for Condition also show large ranges but with median scores higher for the FFI conditions than the control group, and highest scores for the FFIprompt condition. Some of the box plots show a little skewness but there are no outliers. Variances seem somewhat unequal for both Condition and Time.

11.3.2 Parallel Coordinate Plots

A very nice graphic that takes the place of the means plot and contains many more points of data is the parallel coordinate plot (sometimes called a profile plot). Adamson and Bunting (2005) suggested that a profile plot can help viewers get a general impression of the trends of individuals that go into a means plot. I especially like it because it is a data-accountable graphic (Larson-Hall, in preparation) that lets the viewer see both individual performance and group trends. An example of a profile plot for the Lyster (2004) data is shown in Figure 11.12. This shows the performance of individuals in the four different conditions over the three times participants were tested (pretest, immediate posttest and delayed posttest) on the written completion task.

The graphic shows a line representing each individual, and separate panels are given for the participants within each treatment group. Considering that the higher in the panel a score is the better it is, an upward orientation in a line indicates that the learner has improved on their ability to use French gender correctly for this task. We see a very strong trend toward learning for the FFIprompt

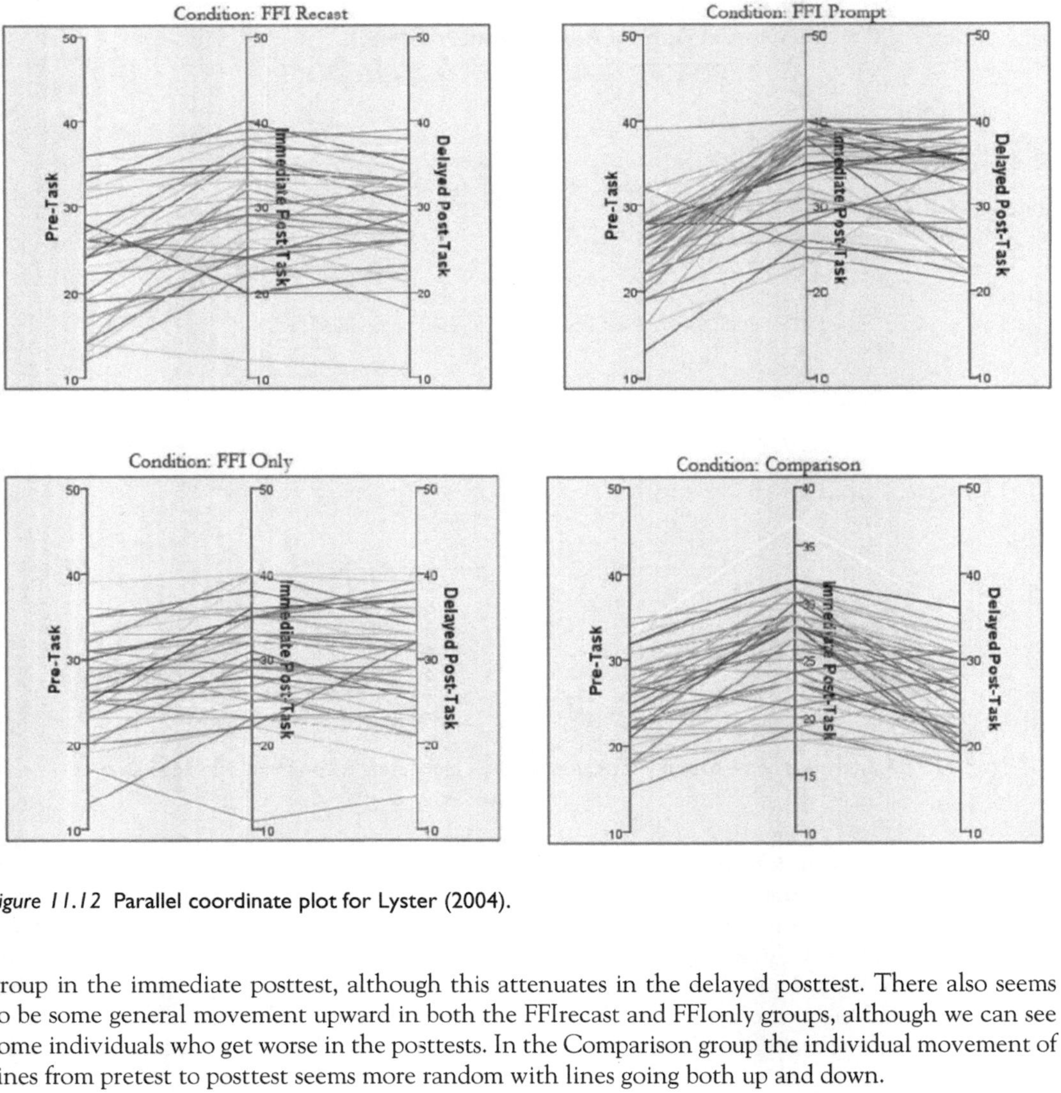

Figure 11.12 Parallel coordinate plot for Lyster (2004).

group in the immediate posttest, although this attenuates in the delayed posttest. There also seems to be some general movement upward in both the FFIrecast and FFIonly groups, although we can see some individuals who get worse in the posttests. In the Comparison group the individual movement of lines from pretest to posttest seems more random with lines going both up and down.

11.3.3 Creating a Parallel Coordinate Plot in SPSS

Figure 11.12 was created in SPSS and can be called for by following the menu sequence Graphs > Graphboard Template Chooser. When the Template Chooser opens, click on the three variables in the Lyster file: PreTaskCompl, Post1TaskCompl and Post2TaskCompl. (Do this by holding down the Ctrl button while clicking with the mouse.) You will see that SPSS recommends a number of types of plots for this type of data (Figure 11.13). Choose the graph labeled "Parallel."

Actually, since SPSS does not provide a way to split this by groups, you will find that you have just one big plot here with lots of lines instead of the ones I showed in Figure 11.12. To get plots that look like Figure 11.12, you will need to split the file by Condition (Data > Split File) and then run the graphic. After I got the four separate plots, I altered them to put more informative names on the axes and to make sure all of the axes had the same minimum and maximum point so they could

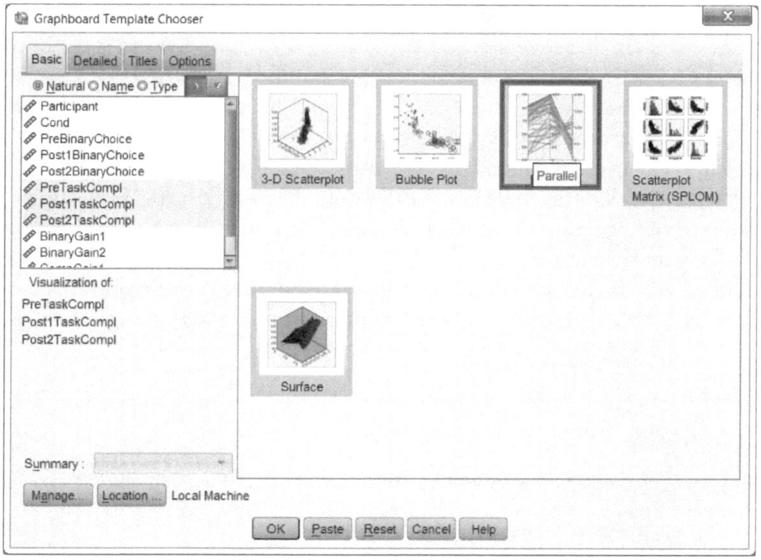

Figure 11.13 The Graphboard Template Chooser in SPSS.

be compared. To copy what I did, double-click on the graph in your output. The GRAPHBOARD EDITOR will start up. If you click twice, slowly, on the title, it will become horizontal and you can delete it and type in your own title. (Figure 11.14 illustrates this—the title in blue is ready for input.) Also note that, at the bottom of the GRAPHBOARD EDITOR, there is tab called SCALE. If you click on one of the vertical axes, a group of tabs will appear below the graph. Here you can set the "Min" and "Max" values for your axes, which I set to a minimum of 10 and a maximum of 50.

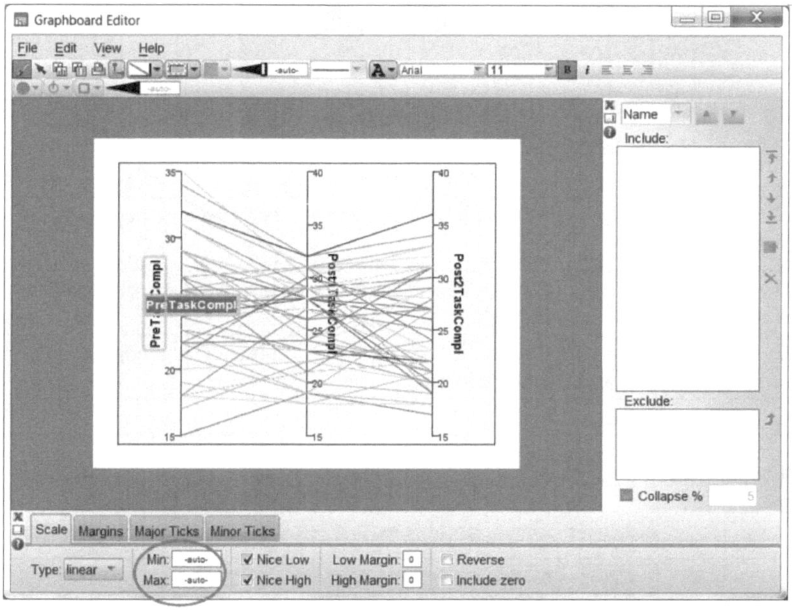

Figure 11.14 The Graphboard Editor in SPSS.

This menu choice makes it considerably easier to make a parallel coordinate plot in SPSS than it was in the first edition of this book, when I explained how to use the syntax to make it. (That syntax is now outdated and does not work in SPSS version 22.0.) This is a nice improvement. However, I was also hoping to reverse the axes of this plot, as I prefer this graph turned the other way, but I could not find anything in the GRAPHBOARD EDITOR that would let me do that. Note that the GRAPHBOARD EDITOR is different from the CHART EDITOR, which is the dialog box that pops up when you double-click a graph obtained through the GRAPHS > LEGACY DIALOGS menu (and which has a button that looks like this  that reverses axes). A quick search on the Web shows that some people have been having trouble getting the GRAPHBOARD EDITOR to work, so more development may be in the works for it in the future.

One more note about Figure 11.12 is that I took my four separate parallel coordinate plots, copied them into Microsoft Paint, added a title to identify which condition they came from and then pasted this into one figure.

Creating Parallel Coordinate Plots in SPSS

1 If you have a between-groups variable that you would like separate plots for, split the file by that variable first (DATA > SPLIT FILE).
2 Go to GRAPHS > GRAPHBOARD TEMPLATE CHOOSER.
3 When the Template Chooser opens, click on two or more variables and in the recommended graphs you will see a choice labeled "Parallel." Choose that.
4 If you wanted to change your labels, double-click on the graph in your output. The GRAPHBOARD EDITOR will appear and you can slowly double-click on your labels to retype them. You can also change a number of other parameters, such as the minimum and maximum points.

11.3.4 Creating a Parallel Coordinate Plot in R

The syntax for creating a parallel plot in R is quite simple, but the data need to be in the wide form. I imported the Lyster.Written.sav file, which is already in wide form, as lyster.wide and used the following two lines of code to get a figure similar to Figure 11.12:

```
library(lattice)
parallelplot(~lyster.wide[6:8] | lyster.wide$cond, data=lyster.wide)
```

parallelplot (x, . . .)	Command for parallel coordinate plot; x should be a data frame or matrix, as the lyster data set is.
(~lyster.wide[6:8]	The name of the matrix is lyster.wide and the brackets enclose the three columns of the matrix that should be used.
| lyster.wide$cond	The vertical line (found by using the SHIFT key plus \) precedes the conditioning variable, in this case, the condition (cond).
data=lyster.wide	Specifies the data set.

Here are some further arguments you could add to change features of the parallel coordinate plot:

horizontal.axis=F	Changes orientation of lines.
lwd=1.5	Increases or decreases line width.
ylab="Accuracy" xlab="Accuracy"	Add labels to the x- or y-axes.
main="Written Completion Task"	Overall title.

scales=list(cex=1)	Sets the size of the font used in the labels of variables (here, points in time).
scales=list(x=list(rot=90))	Rotates x-axis labels by 90 degrees.
colors and types of lines	If you wanted to change these, see Tip 1 in Section 10.2.1 and you can do it the same way.
varnames=c("Pretest", "Immediate\n Posttest", "Delayed\n Posttest")	Changes the names of variables that denote points in time here.
between=list(x=0.5, y=0.5)	Controls the amount of space between your boxes.

It is also possible to easily split the output with another variable. For example, in the data from the previous chapter by Obarow (2004), a parallel coordinate plot could be done showing the change from the pretest to the immediate posttest to the delayed posttest according to each of the four conditions. (We can do this because Obarow tested over more than one time period, thus providing the data for a repeated-measures study, even though we ignored the variable of time in the last chapter on factorial ANOVA.) However, that study also found a statistical difference for gender, so we could include this variable to split each of the four conditions (see Figure 11.15). The code I used for this is:

```
parallelplot(~obarowStory1[7:9]|obarowStory1$treatment1*obarowStory1$gender,
lwd=2.0, varnames=c("Pretest", "Immediate\n Posttest", "Delayed\n Posttest"),
main="Obarow Story 1 Vocabulary Scores")
```

The syntax for adding more than one IV is to just connect it using the asterisk ('*').

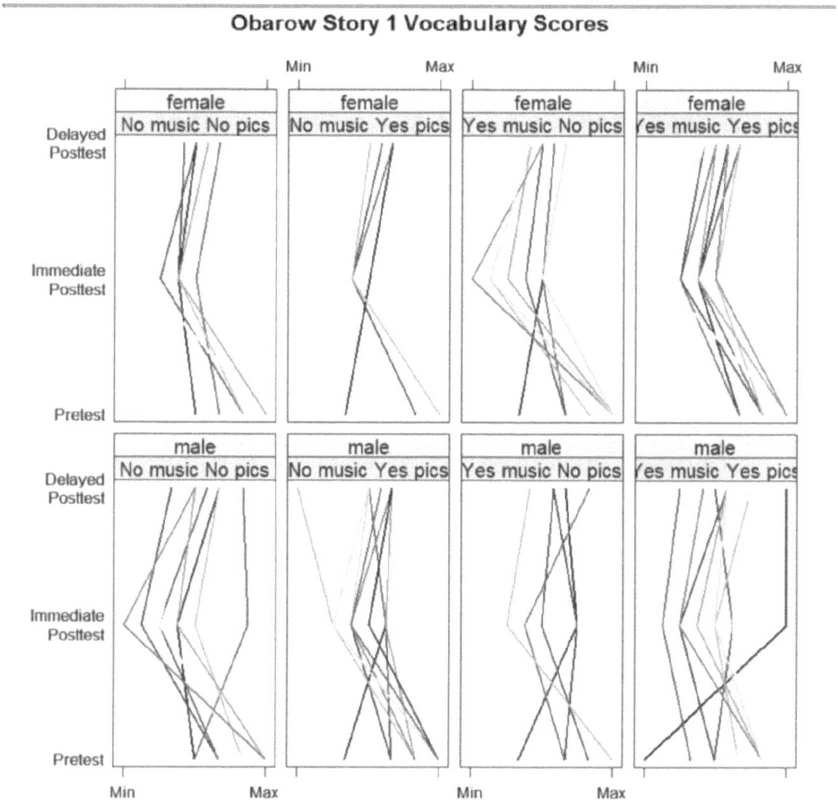

Figure 11.15 Parallel coordinate plot for Obarow Story 1.

You can extend the parallel coordinate plot to plot three variables, but in this case R will print two different pages of R graphics, split by the last variable in your list. For example, the command:

```
parallelplot(~obarowStory1[7:9]|obarowStory1$obarowStory1$picturest1*obarowStory1$musict1*
obarowStory1$gender)
```

will give one page of graphics with just males split by pictures and music, and another page of graphics with just the females split by pictures and music. (Try it!)

Creating Parallel Coordinate Plots in R

The basic command in R is:

```
library(lattice)
parallelplot(~lyster[6:8] | lyster$cond) OR
parallelplot(~obarowStory1[7:9]|obarow Story1$treatment1*obarow Story1$gender)
```

where the data need to be in a data frame or matrix so that columns can be selected for the first argument of the command.

11.3.5 Application Activities with Parallel Coordinate Plots

1 Murphy (2004) data. Create a parallel coordinate plot for the Murphy.RepeatedMeasures.sav file, but just for the three variables for regular verbs. Describe the trends you can see in the parallel coordinate plot. Why are there only a couple of lines for each group? Try splitting the file as well if you are using SPSS.
2 Lyster (2004) data. Create a parallel coordinate plot for a different task in the Lyster data set (Lyster.Written), that of the written binary task. Use the three variables that have "binary" in their name. Make four different plots for each of the different conditions. Describe what the plots show for each of the four groups.
3 Use the Ayoun and Salaberry (2008) data set. Create a parallel coordinate plot for the different lexical aspectual classes. Describe the trends you see.
4 Use the Cole (1927) data. Create parallel coordinate plots that show the interaction of Testing Time, Language Measure and Teaching Group. Describe the trends you see.
5 Use the Toth (2008) production data. Create parallel coordinate plots that show the three Testing Times. Make different plots for the three groups. Describe what the plots show for each of the three groups.

11.4 Repeated-Measures Analysis of Variance Assumptions

For the RM-ANOVA, besides the two familiar assumptions of normality of data and homogeneity of variances for both data and residuals, there is an additional assumption called **sphericity**. Sphericity is not a simple concept, but very simply it measures whether differences between the variances of a single participant's data are equal, so it is like our homogeneity of variances assumptions for the same person when we have repeated measures. Your output will have a place to do a formal check of this assumption, and we can also eyeball the assumption by looking for **compound symmetry** in the covariance matrix. (I will show you what that looks like later on in the chapter.) Explanations of how to test the assumptions and what to do if assumptions are not met are found in Table 11.1.

11.4.1 Exploring Model Assumptions

Let us examine both of our featured data sets to see if they adhere to the assumptions of normality and homogeneity of variances. For the Murphy (2004) data, from Figure 11.8 we have already seen that the

Table 11.1 Assumptions for RM-ANOVA

Meeting repeated-measures ANOVA assumptions		
1 Normal distribution of data (looking at the data according to groups)	Required?	Yes
	How to test assumption?	Examine box plots; plot normal curve over histogram; use Q-Q plots (see Chapter 3).
	What if assumption not met?	Use a robust RM-ANOVA with trimmed means or bootstrap procedures; transform data and reexamine.
2 Equal variances (looking at the data according to groups)	Required?	Yes
	How to test assumption?	Examine side-by-side box plots; look at summary statistics for variance (see Chapter 3); examine spread versus level plot (called for in ANOVA).
	What if assumption not met?	Use a robust RM-ANOVA with trimmed means or bootstrap procedures; try transformation with a log function and reexamine.
3 Sphericity	Required?	Yes
	How to test assumption?	(1) Use Mauchly's test of sphericity to formally measure sphericity. (Box is too conservative, according to Howell, 2002, but Mauchly's test is not very robust.); (2) Howell (2002) also asserts that sphericity is not a big concern for between-subject terms if there is homogeneity of variances.
	What if assumption not met?	(1) Use a mixed model if sphericity does not hold (Howell, 2002; Landau & Everitt, 2002); (2) Use a correction (either the Greenhouse–Geisser or Huynh–Feldt) for the test of overall main effects and the interactions (Howell, 2002). (Howell actually recommends using these corrections even if sphericity is met according to Mauchly's test.); (3) Test within-subject effects by using separate RM-ANOVAs for each level of a group (Howell, 2002), but to control for increased type I errors (increasing the effective alpha level) decide beforehand the important questions to look for and use the separate RM-ANOVAs to answer those questions only. (Remember, you do not have to report everything you discover!)
4 Normal distribution of residuals	Required?	Yes
	How to test assumption?	Call for residuals and examine a histogram of their distribution.
	What if assumption not met?	Use a robust RM-ANOVA with trimmed means or bootstrap procedures; transform data and reexamine.
5 Equal variances of residuals	Required?	Yes
	How to test assumption?	Examine scatterplot of predicted values versus studentized residuals. Should see random horizontal scatter and no patterns of data.
	What if assumption not met?	Use a robust RM-ANOVA with trimmed means or bootstrap procedures; transform data and reexamine.

data are not normally distributed, nor are variances homoscedastic. We will proceed with this analysis, noting that our data do not meet the requirements for normality or homogeneity of variances. We will examine the assumption of sphericity in the main output of the RM-ANOVA.

Looking at the Murphy (2004) data numerically in Table 11.2, there is fairly wide variation in each variable (comparing down the columns) as to standard deviation (SD) (which, squared, equals the variance). For example, for the regular intermediate verbs, there are only five points possible but the SDs vary from 0.2 to 0.9. This confirms what we saw visually, which is that the groups are quite different from each other in how much variance they had.

Table 11.2 Numerical Summary of the Murphy (2004) Data

Group	N	*Regular Prototypical*	*Regular Intermediate*	*Regular Distant*	*Irregular Prototypical*	*Irregular Intermediate*	*Irregular Distant*
NS children	20	5.0 (.0)	5.0 (.2)	4.6 (.6)	2.9 (1.2)	3.8 (.9)	4.9 (.4)
NS adults	20	4.5 (.7)	4.6 (.9)	4.3 (.9)	2.3 (.9)	2.7 (1.1)	4.1 (1.0)
NNS adults	20	4.8 (.5)	4.8 (.4)	4.7 (.5)	3.4 (1.1)	2.7 (1.6)	4.5 (.8)

For the Lyster (2004) data we should look at the pretest, immediate posttest and delayed posttest divided by the four conditions. From Figure 11.11 we have already seen that the data are not normally distributed, nor are variances completely homoscedastic.

Numerically, Table 11.3 shows the sample size, mean scores and SDs for the task completion (cloze) test from the Lyster (2004) study. In studying these with respect to the homogeneity of variances assumption, there is some variation especially in the pretest, where the smallest SD is 4.7 and the largest is 6.8, almost two points of difference.

Table 11.3 Numerical Summary of the Lyster (2004) Data

Group	*Pretest*			*Immediate posttest*			*Delayed posttest*		
	N	*Mean*	*sd*	N	*Mean*	*sd*	N	*Mean*	*sd*
FFI Recast	38	24.6	6.8	38	29.7	6.4	38	28.8	6.0
FFI Prompt	49	25.0	4.7	49	35.3	5.0	49	33.8	5.8
FFI only	42	26.9	5.4	42	29.8	6.3	42	29.1	6.2
Comparison	51	25.5	4.9	51	26.3	4.3	51	25.9	5.1

To summarize, both data sets violate assumptions of normality and homogeneity of variances. We will proceed cautiously with our analysis, keeping in mind that we may be losing power by not being able to exactly satisfy assumptions, and we will also look at robust analyses.

11.5 Performing a Repeated-Measures Analysis of Variance with the Least-Squares Approach

There are two basic research designs in the field of second language research that might call for a RM-ANOVA: either data is collected from the same people at different time periods (longitudinal data, as in the Lyster study, or data obtained after participants undergo different conditions of a treatment) or data is collected from the same people at one time but divided up into categories where each person has more than one score (such as the regular versus irregular verbs in the Murphy study). Both of these situations will be illustrated in this section.

In both SPSS and R, we have a choice when we perform a repeated-measures analysis. We can use an ANOVA approach that will result in the same types of results for testing the statistical significance of interactions and main effects that we have seen in Chapter 10 for one-way and factorial ANOVA. This is an approach where we partition the overall variation into variation between subjects and variation within subjects. For this analysis to work correctly, we have the assumption of sphericity which we can test, and if it is violated we have several options for remedying it (see Table 11.1).

One of the options, which does not require sphericity, is to use a multivariate analysis of variance (MANOVA). However, this type of analysis is usually used when you have more than one DV that you want to test simultaneously, not when you only have one DV, as in this chapter. Howell (2002) stated that it is more common now to have an analysis with **mixed models** instead of MANOVA, and you can find this analysis in the supplemental online materials. This type of approach is also called multilevel modeling or hierarchical modeling. A mixed-models analysis relies on a different type of technique, one which is called restricted maximum likelihood (REML) instead of the least-squares approach that was used in the ANOVA analyses up to now and which I discussed in a little detail in Chapter 3, Section 3.1.1. Howell (2002) stated that one great advantage to the mixed-model approach, besides not having to assume sphericity, is that it deals much more easily with missing data, which is common in a design where participants have multiple points of data. In case you are wondering, a maximum likelihood approach is one that takes the mean and variance estimated from the sample and uses an estimation method that maximizes the probability of the observed data under some defined distribution such as a Gaussian (normal) distribution. Restricted maximum likelihood is a refinement of maximum likelihood that produces unbiased estimates of variance and covariance parameters. (You can see the use of both in the online section on mixed-effects models.)

One thing to notice in this chapter is that I will not talk about how to use a "new" statistics type of approach to RM-ANOVA, but instead rely on *p*-values. This is because the "new" statistics approach needs to look at simple comparisons, and as such, does not use the more complicated approach of looking at interactions between multileveled variables that the RM-ANOVA does. Cumming (2012) responded to the criticism that the "new" statistics cannot do this type of analysis by pointing out that many times such complicated research designs are really more complicated than the author actually wanted, and can be difficult to interpret. If you want to use the "new" statistics approach, you can always simplify your design and go back to comparing repeated-measures data with only two levels compared at a time (as was shown in Chapter 8 for paired *t*-tests).

11.5.1 Least-Squares Repeated-Measures Analysis of Variance in SPSS

To get started, I will use the Murphy.RepeatedMeasures.sav file. From the SPSS menu bar, choose ANALYZE > GENERAL LINEAR MODEL > REPEATED MEASURES. The first box to appear is shown on the left panel of Figure 11.16. This box asks you to define your within-subject IVs. For the Murphy (2004) analysis there are two within-subject IVs, which I will call VERBTYPE (with two levels) and SIMILARITY (with three levels). In the line labeled "Within-Subject Factor Name" type your first within-subject IV and the number of levels it has; then click on the ADD button. The right panel of Figure 11.16 shows what the dialog box looks like after clicking on the ADD button. I go ahead and define the second IV, click on ADD and, when I am done and both IVs are in the box, I click on DEFINE.

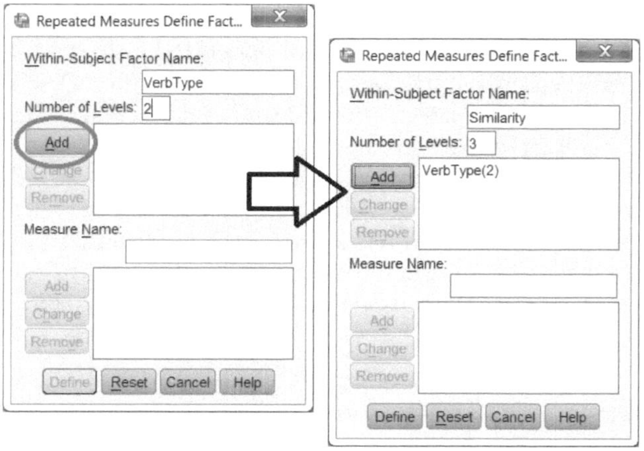

Figure 11.16 Defining within-subject factors in RM-ANOVA in SPSS.

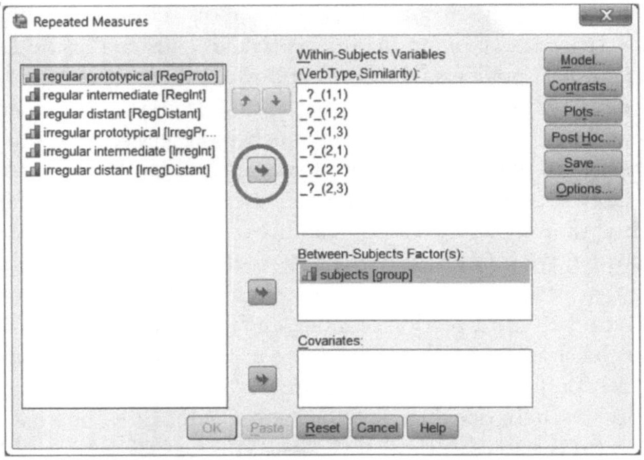

Figure 11.17 **The Repeated Measures dialog box for the Murphy (2004) data.**

Again, notice that you are only defining *within-subject* variables in the first dialog box. After you click on DEFINE, the REPEATED MEASURES box in Figure 11.17 appears. At first, you will see question marks asking you to define your variables. For example, (1,1) asks for the data corresponding to level 1 of VERBTYPE and level 1 of SIMILARITY. (Notice that these variables are listed in this order above the box.) Since the data are already in the correct format, it is an easy step to move all six variables over to the "Within-Subjects Variables" box. Move the between-subjects variable (GROUP for this data set) to the correct box, too.

As with every other SPSS procedure, we will also be interested in changing a few settings before continuing with the analysis. Along the side of the REPEATED MEASURES box we will open up the MODEL, PLOTS, POST HOC, SAVE and OPTIONS buttons.

In the MODEL button you can change to a Type II sum of squares (SS) analysis if you agree with me that it makes more sense than a Type III SS (See Section 10.4.4 for an explanation.) In the PLOTS button you can call for some interaction plots. (Choose a few configurations to see which works the best.) The POST HOC button can only be used to test for differences in the between-subjects variable, so if that variable has more than two levels choose a post-hoc test. Howell (2002) has recommended the Games–Howell test, which has separate covariance matrices. This post-hoc is used when equal variances are not assumed, and we saw for the Murphy (2004) data that variances are not equal, so that is a safe option. Also open the SAVE button and tick "Unstandardized" under Residuals and "Cook's Distance" under Diagnostics. Lastly, open the OPTIONS button and tick the boxes for "Descriptive statistics," "Estimates of effect size," "Residual SSCP matrix," "Spread vs. Level plot" and "Residual plot." Then click on the OK button on your REPEATED MEASURES dialog box.

For the Lyster (2004) data (Lyster.Written.sav), when we open the REPEATED MEASURES dialog box we are confronted with the question of what our within-subject variable should be called. We know that we have measurements on the task completion test at three different times, so we will call the variable TIME, and it has three levels. Then, when we need to define the RM-ANOVA, we will just put the three measurements in the "Within-Subjects Variables" box as shown in Figure 11.18.

11.5.2 Repeated-Measures Analysis of Variance Output

The first two pieces of output outline how your within-subject and between-subject variables are set up and are shown for the Murphy (2004) data in Table 11.4.

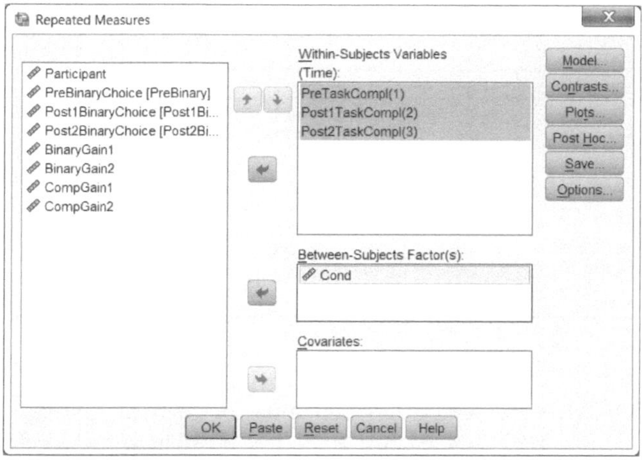

Figure 11.18 The Repeated Measures dialog box for the Lyster (2004) data.

Table 11.4 The First Two Boxes of Output from the RM-ANOVA in SPSS (Murphy, 2004, data)

Within-Subjects Factors

Measure: MEASURE_1

VerbType	Similarity	Dependent Variable
1	1	RegProto
	2	RegInt
	3	RegDistant
2	1	IrregProto
	2	IrregInt
	3	IrregDistant

Between-Subjects Factors

		Value Label	N
subjects	1.00	NS children	20
	2.00	NS adults	20
	3.00	NNS adults	20

We see that the first verb type is regular verbs, with the three levels of similarity, and the second verb type is irregular verbs. We also see there are 20 participants in each (between-subjects) group. The next piece of output is descriptive statistics for each group within the six verb factor levels. Remember that, the closer the score is to 5, the more often the group put an "-ed" ending on the verb. You should find some way to give your reader your descriptive statistics, whether in a table or in prose, as you report your results (such as those I created in Table 11.2). Note that it is not a good idea to simply cut and paste the output table into your report, as the results can be consolidated much better in a different kind of table. Table 11.5 shows just the beginning of this very long table in the SPSS output.

Skipping over "Barlett's Test of Sphericity," the next part of the output is labeled "Multivariate Tests" and is shown in Table 11.6. This output is actually a multivariate ANOVA (MANOVA) procedure, which is used when you have more than one DV. SPSS gives these results because a MANOVA test does not require sphericity. Some researchers note that you can use the MANOVA results whenever sphericity does not hold (Landau & Everitt, 2004), while Tabachnick and Fidell (2001) have given detailed advice about how to do so for those who want more information. However,

Table 11.5 Descriptive Statistics from the RM-ANOVA Output

Descriptive Statistics

	subjects	Mean	Std. Deviation	N
regular prototypical	NS children	5.0000	.00000	20
	NS adults	4.5000	.68825	20
	NNS adults	4.8000	.52315	20
	Total	4.7667	.53256	60
regular intermediate	NS children	4.9500	.22361	20
	NS adults	4.6000	.88258	20
	NNS adults	4.7500	.44426	20
	Total	4.7667	.59280	60

Howell (2002) suggested that a MANOVA is considerably more complicated than an ANOVA and does not have as much power, especially for small sample sizes. Since it is possible to use correction factors for a RM-ANOVA or perform separate RM-ANOVAs for within-subjects simple effects or use a mixed-model, I will skip the multivariate (MANOVA) tests section of the printout. Thus, you should be aware that the "Multivariate Tests" table *does not contain the results you are looking for*! I have actually not included any information about conducting a MANOVA in this book because it is so rarely used in our field. Those who claim to have used it have almost always actually used MANOVA results from a RM-ANOVA printout. (I can tell because they have only one DV, and a MANOVA is used where there are multiple DVs.)

The next section of the printout is Mauchly's test of sphericity. Just as with most formal tests of statistical assumptions, this test suffers from not being very robust or powerful or not for a specific

Table 11.6 Multivariate Tests Output from the RM-ANOVA—Warning, Do Not Use!

Multivariate Tests[d]

Effect		Value	F	Hypothesis df	Error df	Sig.	Partial Eta Squared	Noncent. Parameter	Observed Power[a]
verbtype	Pillai's Trace	.804	233.239[b]	1.000	57.000	.000	.804	233.239	1.000
	Wilks' Lambda	.196	233.239[b]	1.000	57.000	.000	.804	233.239	1.000
	Hotelling's Trace	4.092	233.239[b]	1.000	57.000	.000	.804	233.239	1.000
	Roy's Largest Root	4.092	233.239[b]	1.000	57.000	.000	.804	233.239	1.000
verbtype * group	Pillai's Trace	.072	2.200[b]	2.000	57.000	.120	.072	4.399	.431
	Wilks' Lambda	.928	2.200[b]	2.000	57.000	.120	.072	4.399	.431
	Hotelling's Trace	.077	2.200[b]	2.000	57.000	.120	.072	4.399	.431
	Roy's Largest Root	.077	2.200[b]	2.000	57.000	.120	.072	4.399	.431
similarity	Pillai's Trace	.561	35.775[b]	2.000	56.000	.000	.561	71.551	1.000
	Wilks' Lambda	.439	35.775[b]	2.000	56.000	.000	.561	71.551	1.000
	Hotelling's Trace	1.278	35.775[b]	2.000	56.000	.000	.561	71.551	1.000
	Roy's Largest Root	1.278	35.775[b]	2.000	56.000	.000	.561	71.551	1.000
similarity * group	Pillai's Trace	.227	3.640	4.000	114.000	.008	.113	14.562	.866
	Wilks' Lambda	.774	3.830[b]	4.000	112.000	.006	.120	15.322	.884
	Hotelling's Trace	.292	4.013	4.000	110.000	.004	.127	16.054	.899
	Roy's Largest Root	.290	8.276[c]	2.000	57.000	.001	.225	16.552	.953
verbtype * similarity	Pillai's Trace	.708	67.920[b]	2.000	56.000	.000	.708	135.840	1.000
	Wilks' Lambda	.292	67.920[b]	2.000	56.000	.000	.708	135.840	1.000
	Hotelling's Trace	2.426	67.920[b]	2.000	56.000	.000	.708	135.840	1.000
	Roy's Largest Root	2.426	67.920[b]	2.000	56.000	.000	.708	135.840	1.000
verbtype * similarity * group	Pillai's Trace	.179	2.808	4.000	114.000	.029	.090	11.232	.752
	Wilks' Lambda	.821	2.909[b]	4.000	112.000	.025	.094	11.635	.769
	Hotelling's Trace	.219	3.005	4.000	110.000	.021	.098	12.019	.784
	Roy's Largest Root	.218	6.223[c]	2.000	57.000	.004	.179	12.447	.878

a. Computed using alpha = .05

b. Exact statistic

c. The statistic is an upper bound on F that yields a lower bound on the significance level.

d. Design: Intercept+group
Within Subjects Design: verbtype+similarity+verbtype*similarity

case, but it is impossible to tell whether it has sufficient power or not (Wilcox, 2012a, 2012b), so we will look at the results but not put too much faith in them. In Table 11.7, you should notice that, for Murphy's data, the within-subject VERBTYPE variable has only two levels, so the test for sphericity cannot be applied. The requirement for sphericity only applies when there are more than two comparisons to make in a variable or interaction term, so a variable with only two levels cannot be tested for sphericity (and does not need to follow it). According to Mauchly's test for Murphy's data, there is no problem with sphericity for SIMILARITY (the Sig. column shows that the *p*-value is *greater* than $p = 0.05$, meaning the assumption that sphericity holds should not be rejected), nor for the interaction of VERBTYPE and SIMILARITY (again, because $p > 0.05$). We will examine another method for assessing sphericity later on in this chapter.

Table 11.7 Mauchly's and Barlett's Test of Sphericity Output from the RM-ANOVA

Mauchly's Test of Sphericity[b]

Measure: MEASURE_1

					Epsilon[a]		
Within Subjects Effect	Mauchly's W	Approx. Chi-Square	df	Sig.	Greenhouse-Geisser	Huynh-Feldt	Lower-bound
verbtype	1.000	.000	0	.	1.000	1.000	1.000
similarity	.988	.661	2	.719	.988	1.000	.500
verbtype * similarity	.991	.506	2	.776	.991	1.000	.500

We come now to the main table that we want to look at, which is titled "Tests of Within-Subjects Effects," shown in Tables 11.8, 11.9 and 11.10. Notice that the table is conceptually ordered by rows of three, and I will display these groups separately.

The first three rows, shown in Table 11.8, deal with the within-subjects variable of VERBTYPE. The first row shows simple main effects for verb type; the second row shows the interaction between VERBTYPE and GROUP; the third row shows the error for VERBTYPE. Remember, one of the features of repeated measures is that, instead of using the same error term as the denominator for every entry in the ANOVA table, a RM-ANOVA is able to use different (appropriate) error terms as denominators and thus factor out subject differences.

Table 11.8 Tests of Within-Subjects Effects from the RM-ANOVA, Rows 1–3

Tests of Within-Subjects Effects

Measure: MEASURE_1

Source		Type II Sum of Squares	df	Mean Square	F	Sig.	Partial Eta Squared	Noncent. Parameter	Observed Power[a]
VerbType	Sphericity Assumed	138.136	1	138.136	233.239	.000	.804	233.239	1.000
	Greenhouse-Geisser	138.136	1.000	138.136	233.239	.000	.804	233.239	1.000
	Huynh-Feldt	138.136	1.000	138.136	233.239	.000	.804	233.239	1.000
	Lower-bound	138.136	1.000	138.136	233.239	.000	.804	233.239	1.000
VerbType * group	Sphericity Assumed	2.606	2	1.303	2.200	.120	.072	4.399	.431
	Greenhouse-Geisser	2.606	2.000	1.303	2.200	.120	.072	4.399	.431
	Huynh-Feldt	2.606	2.000	1.303	2.200	.120	.072	4.399	.431
	Lower-bound	2.606	2.000	1.303	2.200	.120	.072	4.399	.431
Error(VerbType)	Sphericity Assumed	33.758	57	.592					
	Greenhouse-Geisser	33.758	57.000	.592					
	Huynh-Feldt	33.758	57.000	.592					
	Lower-bound	33.758	57.000	.592					

Rows 4–6, shown in Table 11.9, deal with the within-subjects variable of SIMILARITY. The first row shows simple main effects for similarity of verbs; the second row shows the interaction between SIMILARITY and GROUP; the third row shows the error for SIMILARITY.

Table 11.9 Tests of Within-Subjects Effects from the RM-ANOVA, Rows 4–6

Tests of Within-Subjects Effects

Measure:MEASURE_1

Source		Type II Sum of Squares	df	Mean Square	F	Sig.	Partial Eta Squared	Noncent. Parameter	Observed Power[a]
Similarity	Sphericity Assumed	32.372	2	16.186	38.216	.000	.401	76.433	1.000
	Greenhouse-Geisser	32.372	1.977	16.376	38.216	.000	.401	75.546	1.000
	Huynh-Feldt	32.372	2.000	16.186	38.216	.000	.401	76.433	1.000
	Lower-bound	32.372	1.000	32.372	38.216	.000	.401	38.216	1.000
Similarity * group	Sphericity Assumed	6.678	4	1.669	3.942	.005	.122	15.767	.894
	Greenhouse-Geisser	6.678	3.954	1.689	3.942	.005	.122	15.584	.891
	Huynh-Feldt	6.678	4.000	1.669	3.942	.005	.122	15.767	.894
	Lower-bound	6.678	2.000	3.339	3.942	.025	.122	7.883	.686
Error(Similarity)	Sphericity Assumed	48.283	114	.424					
	Greenhouse-Geisser	48.283	112.678	.429					
	Huynh-Feldt	48.283	114.000	.424					
	Lower-bound	48.283	57.000	.847					

The last three rows, shown in Table 11.10, deal with the interaction between the two within-subjects variables. The first row shows the interaction between VerbType and Similarity. The second row shows the three-way interaction between VerbType, Similarity and Group. The third row shows the error term for the interaction.

Table 11.10 Tests of Within-Subjects Effects from the RM-ANOVA, Rows 7–9

Tests of Within-Subjects Effects

Measure:MEASURE_1

Source		Type II Sum of Squares	df	Mean Square	F	Sig.	Partial Eta Squared	Noncent. Parameter	Observed Power[a]
VerbType * Similarity	Sphericity Assumed	62.539	2	31.269	62.630	.000	.524	125.261	1.000
	Greenhouse-Geisser	62.539	1.982	31.551	62.630	.000	.524	124.143	1.000
	Huynh-Feldt	62.539	2.000	31.269	62.630	.000	.524	125.261	1.000
	Lower-bound	62.539	1.000	62.539	62.630	.000	.524	62.630	1.000
VerbType * Similarity * group	Sphericity Assumed	6.544	4	1.636	3.277	.014	.103	13.108	.823
	Greenhouse-Geisser	6.544	3.964	1.651	3.277	.014	.103	12.991	.820
	Huynh-Feldt	6.544	4.000	1.636	3.277	.014	.103	13.108	.823
	Lower-bound	6.544	2.000	3.272	3.277	.045	.103	6.554	.600
Error(VerbType*Similarity)	Sphericity Assumed	56.917	114	.499					
	Greenhouse-Geisser	56.917	112.983	.504					
	Huynh-Feldt	56.917	114.000	.499					
	Lower-bound	56.917	57.000	.999					

In trying to interpret this table, I would advise researchers to look first at the largest interactions and then work backwards, since main effects for single variables may not retain their importance in the face of the interactions. The largest interaction is the three-way interaction between verb type, similarity of verb and participants. The p-value, found in the column labeled "Sig.," shows that this interaction is statistical ($p = 0.014$). What this means is that participants from the different groups performed differently on regular and irregular verbs, and they also performed differently on at least one of the types of similarities of verbs. In other words, the groups did not all perform in a parallel manner on both types of verbs and all three types of verb similarities. The partial η^2 effect size (which we have seen previously in conjunction with ANOVAs) shows that the three-way interaction accounts for about 10% of the variance in scores on this test. This is a medium effect size. Additionally, the power analysis shows that this interaction had sufficient power (over 80%) to find statistical differences in the interaction. (Although Cumming, 2012, has provided good arguments about why post-hoc power is essentially meaningless as it is computed from the obtained effect size.) We will want to note a couple more pieces of information about this interaction, which are the F-value and the degrees of freedom (df).

The value of the F statistic and the df will often depend on which of the four choices we use (Sphericity assumed, or the Greenhouse–Geisser, Huynh–Feldt or Lower-bound corrections). The **Greenhouse–Geisser correction** is more conservative than the **Huynh–Feldt correction**. In the case of Murphy's (2004) data, there are basically no differences in the *F*-value for any of these choices, but there are differences in df. Because Mauchly's test for sphericity had a *p*-value above 0.05, we might use the "Sphericity assumed" line, but Howell (2002) advocates always using a correction whatever the results of Mauchly's test. I would therefore report, say for the three-way interaction, that it was statistical using the Greenhouse–Geisser correction ($F_{3.96, 112.98} = 3.28$, $p = 0.014$, partial $\eta^2 = 0.10$).

The process of understanding the output is the same for other interactions and main effects, although, as we will see in Section 11.6 where we analyze this data further, you may not want to report every effect.

The next table is "Tests of Within-Subjects Contrasts," and we will ignore this table. The following table is the "Tests of Between-Subjects Effects" and is shown in Table 11.11. The output shows that there was a statistical effect for group ($p = 0.006$, partial $\eta^2 = 0.17$), but, since we already know that the three-way interaction that involved group is statistical, we may not really care too much about this particular result.

Table 11.11 **Tests of Between-Subjects Effects from the RM-ANOVA Output**

Tests of Between-Subjects Effects

Measure: MEASURE_1

Transformed Variable: Average

Source	Type III Sum of Squares	df	Mean Square	F	Sig.	Partial Eta Squared	Noncent. Parameter	Observed Power[a]
Intercept	5945.469	1	5945.469	3132.328	.000	.982	3132.328	1.000
group	21.506	2	10.753	5.665	.006	.166	11.330	.844
Error	108.192	57	1.898					

a. Computed using alpha = .05

The next part of the output is called the "Residual SSCP Matrix," shown in Table 11.12. I called for this piece of output to show you the matrix that can be examined for the requirements of sphericity. This matrix is called the **SS and cross-products (SSCP) matrix**. This table contains three rows, but I am examining only the middle row that says "Covariance."

The numbers above the diagonal line in Table 11.12 are the variances within each treatment. (the SS of the intersection of each treatment with itself). To show compound symmetry and satisfy sphericity, these numbers along the diagonal should all be rather similar. However, the largest number (1.476) is almost six times larger than the smallest number (0.249), meaning these variances are not similar. The other part of the matrix involves the off-diagonal elements, which are the covariances or cross-products of two variables (and are mirrored in the table, so that you only need to look at either the top or the bottom half). These covariances should also be more or less equal, although they do not need to be of the same magnitude as the variances. Here there is even more disparity, as the largest number (0.652) is 18 times larger than the smallest (0.035). Thus, even though the formal sphericity test (Mauchly's) did not show any problems with sphericity, examination of the covariance matrix shows that there is disparity. We would be well advised to use one of the correction factors.

Table 11.12 **Residual SSCP Matrix to Test Sphericity from the RM-ANOVA Output**

		regular prototypical	regular intermediate	regular distant	irregular prototypical	irregular intermediate	irregular distant
Covariance	regular prototypical	.249	.035	.168	.112	.225	.216
	regular intermediate	.035	.342	.075	.193	.173	.219
	regular distant	.168	.075	.448	.183	.346	.292
	irregular prototypical	.112	.193	.183	1.216	.652	.160
	irregular intermediate	.225	.173	.346	.652	1.476	.478
	irregular distant	.216	.219	.292	.160	.478	.604

The next part of the output (not shown) is labeled "Post Hoc Tests." The previous "Tests of Between-Subjects Effects" concerned the same main effect of the between-groups IV, "Group," that this "Post Hoc Tests" concerns, but here we see separate levels being compared (and we see confidence levels here, too!). Thus, we will still not be too concerned about these results since there was an interaction between Group, Verb Type and Similarity that supersedes the main effect. From this table labeled "Multiple Comparisons" and using the Games–Howell post-hoc test, we see that NNS adults perform more like NS children than NS adults (since there is a statistical difference between NS children and NS adults, but not between NS children and NNS children). Again, however, we may not be particularly interested in this in light of the interaction. Keep in mind that the post-hoc tests are only done for between-group variables. If, for the Murphy (2004) data, you had found no interaction and one statistical simple main effect, such as similarity, you would still not know whether the comparisons among the three levels of similarity were all statistical, because the post-hoc would not address that comparison.

I will explore the specific conclusions that we can draw from the output for the Murphy (2004) data, how to understand interactions and how to get further comparisons for the within-group variables if you need them in the following sections of the chapter.

After this part of the output, the spread vs. level plots are shown (not shown here). Remember that these test for the assumption of homogeneity of variances in the data. For this data set, there are so few points (just three in each plot) that it is hard to tell whether there are any patterns at all. The residual plots are also divided up according to the six categories of verbs. Here we will examine the Std. Residual vs. Predicted table. These look fairly random. To examine the assumption of normality of residuals, look to the columns appended to the end of your data set called RES_1 through RES_6 (one for each of the verb types). These can be examined for normality by looking at histograms. One wonders whether anyone ever goes through all of the work to do this though! The assumptions become very complicated once we move to RM-ANOVA, and there is not much recourse if we violate the assumptions. So we soldier on.

Finally, the last part of the output will be means plots if you called for them, and studying these can help you understand the trends in your data, although for publication I recommend you move over to R and get a combination interaction plot and box plot like I had in Figure 11.10. If possible, I would rather include a parallel coordinate plot than a means plot, as it lets the reader see all of the data visually but is still able to capture patterns within groups. However, for the Murphy (2004) data the parallel coordinate plot is not very informative and the means plot may be much more helpful for understanding interactions.

Turning to the Lyster output, Mauchly's test of sphericity was statistical (Sig. = 0.000). The null hypothesis (H_0) of Mauchly's test is that the variances that are tested are equal, so if the p-value is *below* 0.05 we reject H_0 and accept the alternative hypothesis that the variances are not equal. We know that Mauchly's test is unreliable, having too little power when group sizes are small and being overconservative when group sizes are large, so we take these results with a grain of salt, and we were planning to apply a correction factor anyway.

Table 11.13 shows the test of between-subject effects for the Lyster data, which only had two IVs (so the three rows shown in Table 11.13 are all of the output). Here again the interaction between the two IVs of time and condition is statistical using the Huynh–Feldt correction ($F_{5.5,265.8} = 21.1$, $p < 0.0005$, partial $\eta^2 = 0.3$). The effect size is quite large. Because the interaction is statistical, we are not really interested in the main effect of Condition, the between-groups IV tested in the "Tests of Between-Subjects Effects" and "Post Hoc Tests" sections. Looking at the "Residual SSCP Matrix", (not shown) here we see that the numbers along the diagonal for the Covariance row are not very different from each other (29, 29 and 23), and the numbers above or below the diagonal are also similar (17, 16, 23). These numbers are much more similar to each other than the numbers for the Murphy data were, even though Mauchly's test told us that the Lyster data violated sphericity while the Murphy data did not. The numbers in the SSCP matrix seem to be telling the opposite story, which is that the Murphy data violate sphericity while the Lyster data do not. This is a failing of the formal test, and a reason to always use a correction as advocated by Howell (2002).

Table 11.13 Tests of Within-Subjects Effects from the RM-ANOVA for Lyster (2004)

Tests of Within-Subjects Effects

Measure:MEASURE_1

Source		Type II Sum of Squares	df	Mean Square	F	Sig.	Partial Eta Squared	Noncent. Parameter	Observed Power[a]
Time	Sphericity Assumed	2338.026	2	1169.013	100.759	.000	.364	201.517	1.000
	Greenhouse-Geisser	2338.026	1.791	1305.233	100.759	.000	.364	180.486	1.000
	Huynh-Feldt	2338.026	1.839	1271.123	100.759	.000	.364	185.329	1.000
	Lower-bound	2338.026	1.000	2338.026	100.759	.000	.364	100.759	1.000
Time * Cond	Sphericity Assumed	1466.697	6	244.449	21.069	.000	.264	126.416	1.000
	Greenhouse-Geisser	1466.697	5.374	272.934	21.069	.000	.264	113.223	1.000
	Huynh-Feldt	1466.697	5.518	265.801	21.069	.000	.264	116.261	1.000
	Lower-bound	1466.697	3.000	488.899	21.069	.000	.264	63.208	1.000
Error(Time)	Sphericity Assumed	4083.944	352	11.602					
	Greenhouse-Geisser	4083.944	315.264	12.954					
	Huynh-Feldt	4083.944	323.724	12.616					
	Lower-bound	4083.944	176.000	23.204					

a. Computed using alpha = .05

Performing a Repeated-Measures Analysis of Variance Using SPSS

1 Make sure data are in the correct "wide" format, with as many columns as needed. (The number of columns will be equal to the product of the number of levels of the within-group variables.)
2 ANALYZE > GENERAL LINEAR MODEL > REPEATED MEASURES.
3 With the first box open, enter your own descriptive names of within-subject variables into the factor name box and put in number of levels. Click on ADD after each variable, and click on DEFINE when done.
4 Move within-subject variable(s) to the large box labeled "Within-Subjects Variables" and move the between-subject variable(s) to the "Between-Subjects Factors" box.
5 Change the SS to type II in the MODEL button. Open the PLOTS button and create some interaction plots, useful for discerning trends. Open the POST HOC button if your between-subjects variable has more than two levels, and call for post-hoc tests using the Games–Howell method. Click on the SAVE button and tick "Cook's Distance" and "Unstandardized." Click on the OPTIONS button and tick "Descriptive statistics," "Estimates of Effect Size," "Residual SSCP Matrix," "Spread vs. Level Plot" and "Residual Plot."

I will explore the specific conclusions that we can draw from the output for the Lyster (2004) data, how to understand interactions and how to get further comparisons for the within-group variables if you need them in the following sections.

11.5.3 Least-Squares Repeated-Measures Analysis of Variance in R

There are actually a number of ways to perform a least-squares, RM-ANOVA in R. It turns out it is probably better to do a mixed-effects model if you have repeated values (and you can see how I do that in the online section "Performing a RM-ANOVA the Mixed-Effects Way"), but if you want output that most closely resembles the kind of output you get from SPSS when doing a RM-ANOVA, this section will show you how to get that by using the **ez** package (Lawrence, 2013) (which is a wrapper of the **Anova{car}** function). Please install and open this package:

```
install.packages("ez")
library(ez)
```

The command to use, **ezANOVA()**, will need the long form of the data. For the Murphy (2004) data, remember that we have two within-group IVs (**type**, **similarity**) and one between-group variable (**group**), and for the long form these are in the data file **murphy.long**. Here is the command I would use:

```
murphyModel1<-ezANOVA(data=murphy.long, dv=.(value), wid=.(participant),
within=.(type,similarity), between=.(group))
```

The syntax is pretty transparent, if somewhat different from what we have seen up until now. Just put the names of the variables into the correct parentheses. The term "dv" is for the dependent or response variable, the term "wid" is the variable that lists which participant the data came from, the term "within" is for within-group variables and the term "between" is for the between-group variables. If your variables are not factors, you do not have to worry; this command will convert any variables you list in the "within" and "between" arguments into factors.

The command defaults to the Type II SS model (see Section 10.4.4 for more information about which type you might want) but you could change it with the argument type=3. For these data it will not make any difference since the numbers in each group are the same. There is also a default argument that detailed=FALSE, which you can set to TRUE. It actually does not make much difference in the output, as the only difference I see is that it lists the intercept.

Another useful tool in the ez package is the descriptive statistics with all of the data divided up three ways (since we have three IVs). Use the ezStats( ) command with the same arguments as the ezANOVA() command:

```
(murphyStats<-ezStats(data=murphy.long, dv=.(value), wid=.(participant),
within=.(type,similarity), between=.(group)))
```

If you run this command (which you will automatically if you put the parentheses around it as I have written it) you will get the kind of descriptive statistics that you would need to compile a table like that seen in Table 11.2. Note that besides *N*, the mean and the SD, there is one more statistic that is labeled FLSD (Fisher's Least Significant Difference). This statistic can be ignored for the analysis we are using. (It is used to create confidence intervals (CIs) when making comparisons of two mean scores.)

I do not see that the ez package has any way of returning diagnostic plots or data regarding any assumptions other than sphericity, so at least when using this package, you will have to live without those.

Let us now call for a printout of the RM-ANOVA data:

```
print(murphyModel1)
```

There are three main parts to the printout which I will discuss in turn. The first part, shown in Table 11.14, tests the interactions and main effects of the ANOVA. Notice that the lines are numbered, but we are missing line 1. Line 1 lists the intercept, and can be called for by setting the argument detailed=TRUE, but since the intercept line simply tests the hypothesis that the grand mean is different from zero, it is rarely of interest to us so I do not see any reason to call for it.

I advise researchers to look first at the largest interactions and then work backwards, since main effects for single variables may not retain their importance in the face of the interactions. The largest interaction is the three-way interaction between type of verb, similarity of verb and participants,

Table 11.14 ezANOVA Interaction and Main Effect Tests for Murphy (2004)

```
$ANOVA
                   Effect DFn DFd          F            p p<.05        ges
2                   group   2  57   5.665023 5.701635e-03     * 0.08004880
3                    type   1  57 233.238953 8.350065e-22     * 0.35852865
5              similarity   2 114  38.216431 1.987415e-13     * 0.11581270
4              group:type   2  57   2.199704 1.201584e-01       0.01043242
6        group:similarity   4 114   3.941664 4.923864e-03     * 0.02630830
7         type:similarity   2 114  62.630454 4.445156e-19     * 0.20194102
8 group:type:similarity   4 114   3.277013 1.390538e-02     * 0.02579656
```

found on the line labeled "8." The *p*-value, found in the column under "p" shows that this interaction is statistical ($p = 0.0139$). The stars in the column under "$p < 0.05$" quickly let us see that most of the terms of the model are statistical, but when you report your results, do include the actual *p*-value and do not just say "p < 0.05."

The column labeled "ges" gives an effect size, a generalized η^2 measure, which is a more recent proportion of variance effect size proposed by Olejnik and Algina (2000) and discussed in Bakeman (2005) specifically for repeated-measures. Generalized η^2 is meant to be an effect size that provides a comparable estimate when designs are repeated measures (have within-group variation) or simply between groups (like the one-way ANOVAs or factorial designs seen in Chapter 10). Generalized η^2 (also written as η^2_G) differs from η^2 and partial η^2 (η^2_p) in its denominator. According to Bakeman (2005), while η^2 includes all the component sums of squares in its denominator and η^2_p includes only some of them, η^2_G includes only some of the component sums of squares but generally more than partial η^2 because it includes variability from individual differences as well as from factors manipulated in the study. Generalized η^2 is easily calculable from the printout that gives SS, but formulas vary based on the study design (see Bakeman, 2005, table 3 for a summary for repeated-measures designs), so I will not list formulas here. As with any effect size, the meaning of the statistic can only be understood in context, and we see that although the three-way interaction is statistical, it does not account for a large proportion of the variance in the model, only about 3% (the "ges" for the three-way interaction). The interaction of type and similarity, for example, accounts for a much larger proportion of what is going on, at 20%.

The meaning of a three-way interaction is that participants from the different groups performed differently on regular and irregular verbs, and they also performed differently on at least one of the types of similarities of verbs. In other words, the groups did not all perform in a parallel manner on both types of verbs and all three types of verb similarities.

Looking at the last part of the output, Mauchly's test for sphericity is given. Just as with most formal tests of statistical assumptions, this test suffers from not being very robust or powerful, but it is impossible to tell whether it has sufficient power or not for a specific case (Wilcox, 2012a, 2012b), so we will look at the results but not put too much faith in them. In Table 11.15 you should notice that Mauchly's test is applied to several different components of the ANOVA model, but not all. Specifically, the test is only applied to within-subject variables, so it is not calculated for GROUP, which is a between-subject variable and does not have repeated measures. The variable TYPE is a within-subject variable, but it has only two levels, so the test for sphericity cannot be applied. The requirement for sphericity only applies when there are more than two comparisons to make in a variable or interaction term, so a variable with only two levels cannot be tested for sphericity (and does not need to follow it).

According to Mauchly's test for Murphy's data, there is no problem with sphericity for SIMILARITY (the "p" column shows that the *p*-value is *greater* than $p = 0.05$, meaning the assumption that sphericity holds should not be rejected), nor for the interaction of GROUP and SIMILARITY (again, because $p > 0.05$), or the interaction between TYPE and SIMILARITY or the three-way interaction.

Although the formal test indicates no problem with a violation of sphericity, Howell (2002) has advocated always using a correction whatever the results of Mauchly's test. The next part of the output gives the terms for the ANOVA corrected for violations of sphericity (Table 11.16).

GGe is the Greenhouse–Geisser value (epsilon), p[GG] is the *p*-value after using the Greenhouse–Geisser correction, HFe is the Huynh–Feldt value (epsilon), and p[HF] is the *p*-value after using the

Table 11.15 ezANOVA Tests for Sphericity for Murphy (2004)

```
$`Mauchly's Test for Sphericity`
                  Effect         W         p p<.05
5             similarity 0.9882646 0.7185387
6       group:similarity 0.9882646 0.7185387
7        type:similarity 0.9909980 0.7763153
8 group:type:similarity 0.9909980 0.7763153
```

Table 11.16 ezANOVA Correction Factors for Murphy (2004)

```
$`Sphericity Corrections`
                   Effect       GGe        p[GG] p[GG]<.05      HFe        p[HF] p[HF]<.05
5              similarity 0.9884007 2.671667e-13         * 1.023700 1.987415e-13         *
6        group:similarity 0.9884007 5.109354e-03         * 1.023700 4.923864e-03         *
7         type:similarity 0.9910783 6.253682e-19         * 1.026622 4.445156e-19         *
8 group:type:similarity 0.9910783 1.419445e-02         * 1.026622 1.390538e-02         *
```

Huynh–Feldt correction. The Greenhouse–Geisser correction is more conservative than the Huynh–Feldt correction, so Abdi (2010) has recommended the Huynh–Feldt as the best correction to use. However, the maximum value of epsilon is supposed to be 1, since "epsilon represents the extent to which the correlations [matrices] are similar to each other" (Huynh, 1978, p. 169), so I don't understand why the Huynh–Feldt correction since it is actually *above* 1. Therefore, to use a correction factor, let us use the Greenhouse–Geisser correction to illustrate how the process works.

If you were to report the results of the statistical three-way interaction without any correction, you would say that "the three-way interaction between Group, Verb Type and Verb Similarity was statistical, $F_{4,114} = 3.28$, $p = 0.01$, $\eta_G^2 = 0.03$." To report the correction, multiply the Huynh–Feldt epsilon by the df and round the number to the nearest integer (Abdi, 2010). Thus, we would now report that "the three-way interaction between Group, Verb Type and Verb Similarity was statistical, $F_{4,113} = 3.28$, $p = 0.01$, $\eta_G^2 = 0.03$" because $4 \times 0.9910783 = 3.96$, rounded to 4, and $114 \times 0.9910783 = 112.98$, rounded to 113. We should use the corrected *p*-value, but in this case there is no difference in the value from the uncorrected *p*-value. The Huynh–Feldt correction in principle works the same way: multiply the epsilon value by your df (both df, the first of which is the df for the time or condition, and the second of which is the df of the error) and round to the nearest integer, and then substitute in the corrected *p*-value. The correction affects the df (not the *F*-value), which results in a more accurate *p*-value. In this case it did not change the results at all, but there are some situations when it could.

I will explore the specific conclusions that we can draw from the output for the Murphy (2004) data, how to understand interactions and how to get further comparisons for the within-group variables if you need them in the following sections.

Turning to the Lyster output, I would set up the ezANOVA command as follows (using the lyster.long file that we created earlier in the chapter and looking only at the completion task for now):

```
lysterModel1<-ezANOVA(data=lyster.long, dv=.(compscore), wid=.(participant),
within=.(time), between=.(cond))
```

```
Warning: Converting "participant" to factor for ANOVA.
Warning: Data is unbalanced (unequal N per group). Make sure you
specified a well-considered value for the type argument to ezANOVA().
```

```
print(lysterModel1)
```

Before I show you the printout, let me discuss the two warnings underneath the model. The first warning tells us that the column of participants we created was not a factor, but **ezANOVA** kindly changed it into a factor for us. It also warns us that the design of the ANOVA is unbalanced, meaning there are different numbers of participants in each group. For the Murphy (2004) data, the design was balanced and so we did not get this warning. When there are unequal numbers of participants in a design, it is said to be non-orthogonal, and the computation of the various parts of the ANOVA become more complicated and there will be differences in the outcome due to your choice of the method of calculating the SS. But as pointed out in Section 10.4.4, this will only affect the calculation of main effects, not interactions. In that section I sided with researchers who say that Type II SS are to be preferred, and not (what is in SPSS the default) Type III SS, so please read that section for more information. The **ezANOVA( )** command uses type II as the default, but gives a warning to readers that they may want to consider which type they would like to call. I advocate using type II and thus will keep the default here. If you wanted to change to Type III, simply add the argument **type=3** to the command.

Now, here is the output from the earlier command:

```
$ANOVA
      Effect DFn DFd          F            p p<.05        ges
2       cond   3 176  11.17092 9.537292e-07     * 0.12484455
3       time   2 352 100.75862 2.514354e-35     * 0.12556213
4  cond:time   6 352  21.06939 3.987235e-21     * 0.08263479

$`Mauchly's Test for Sphericity`
      Effect         W            p p<.05
3       time 0.8834746 1.958753e-05     *
4  cond:time 0.8834746 1.958753e-05     *

$`Sphericity Corrections`
      Effect       GGe        p[GG] p[GG]<.05       HFe        p[HF] p[HF]<.05
3       time 0.8956357 6.265292e-32         * 0.9042458 3.285934e-32         *
4  cond:time 0.8956357 3.633670e-19         * 0.9042458 2.503726e-19         *
```

Our first glance at the effects shows that the interaction between Condition and Time is statistical, as are the main effects. The generalized effect size says that the interaction accounts for 8% of the variance in scores, which is respectable but does not seem very large. Moving to the next part of the output, we see that Mauchly's test of sphericity is statistical because the *p*-value is less than 0.05. (In fact, it is quite small.) The H_0 of Mauchly's test is that the variances that are tested are equal, so if the *p*-value is *below* 0.05 we reject H_0 and accept the alternative hypothesis that the variances are not equal. We know that Mauchly's test is unreliable, having too little power when group sizes are small and being overconservative when group sizes are large, so we take these results with a grain of salt, and we were planning to apply a correction factor anyway. Note that there is no test of sphericity for Condition, because it is a between-groups factor. Choosing the more powerful Huynh–Feldt correction factor of epsilon = 0.9042458 and multiplying this by the df for the interaction ($df_{between} = 6$, $df_{error/residuals} = 352$), we would report that "the interaction between Condition and Testing Time was statistical, $F_{5,318} = 21.1$, $p < 0.001$, $\eta^2_G = 0.08$." Because the *p*-value is so small ($2.5e^{-19}$, which equals 0.00000000000000000025), we will not report it exactly, but this is the correction *p*-value, not the original *p*-value of the interaction, which was $3.98e^{-21}$.

For specific conclusions that we can draw from the output for the Lyster (2004) data, how to understand interactions, and how to get further comparisons for the within-group variables if you need them, see the three online sections "Least-Squares Repeated-Measures ANOVA in R using aov( )," "Robust Methods of Performing One-Way RM-ANOVA in R" and "Robust Methods of Performing RM-ANOVA with Between-Group Independent Variables in R".

Performing a Repeated-Measures Analysis of Variance Using the ezANOVA( ) Command in R

1 Make sure your data are in the correct "long" format, with all of the response (dependent) variable data in one long column, a column marking data as to which participant it came from, the within-group IV(s) and any between-group IVs.

2 Open the ez package: library(ez) (If you need to download the package: install.packages("ez").)

Put the names of your data set into the parentheses for each appropriate part of the command:

```
murphyModel1<-ezANOVA (data=murphy.long, #give your model a name (murphyModel1) and
#then put in name of data (murphy.long)
dv=.(value), #your response/dependent variable name
wid=.(participant), #your participant index, telling which participant produced the data
within=.(type,similarity), #your within-group variables
between=.(group))) #your between-group variables
print(murphyModel1)
```

3. To get descriptive statistics, repeat the same format as above, the only difference being you use the command name ezStats:

```
(murphyStats<-ezStats(data=murphy.long, dv=.(value), wid=.(participant),
within=.(type,similarity), between=.(group))) #extra parentheses will print it automatically
```

11.5.4 Application Activities with Least-Squares, Repeated-Measures Analysis of Variance

Note that I do not ask you to look at the data visually in any of these activities. I do think it is a good idea and you should do it, but the answers have just become so long and complicated already that I do not outline how to do it here again. If you have been working through the book you have seen it in every previous chapter and should be familiar with how to do it.

1 Conduct a RM-ANOVA with the Lyster (2004) data on the binary test. (Use Lyster.Written.sav; if you are using R, use the file you created in Section 11.2.4 with the "long" form of the binary choice data.) You are testing the question of whether correction Condition affected how participants performed on the binary choice task, and whether that performance differed according to the time they were tested, and whether there is any interaction between Condition and testing Time. Describe the results of the RM-ANOVA by first talking about the results of interactions and then, if the interactions are not statistical, talking about the results of the main effects. If you can, talk about whether the assumption of sphericity has been upheld, and whether the residuals are normally distributed and have equal variances.
2 Use the Cole (1927) data. (Use Cole.sav; if you are using R, use the file you created in Section 11.2.4 with the "long" form of the binary choice data.) These are data that tested whether students studying French would benefit more from a teaching approach using free composition vs. another that focused on translation. (All of the students were male high school students.) The students took three types of language measures (Vocab, Grammar or Reading) twice, once in the middle of the semester and once at the end of the semester (four months apart). Test whether teaching approach made any difference to their scores, whether their performance improved over time, and whether they performed better on any of the three types of language measures. Use a RM-ANOVA to see if there are any interactions between teaching approach, testing time and language measure. Describe the results of the RM-ANOVA by first talking about the results of interactions and then, if the interactions are not statistical, talking about the results of the main effects. If you can, talk about whether the assumption of sphericity has been upheld, and whether the residuals are normally distributed and have equal variances.
3 Conduct a RM-ANOVA with the Larson-Hall (2004) data. (Use LarsonHall2004.sav; if you are using R, use the file you created in Section 11.2.4 with the "long" form of just three of the phonemic contrasts). You are testing the question of whether participants performed similarly regardless of the type of phonemic contrast (only test the three contrasts R_L, SH_SHCH, and PJ_P) and regardless of which language proficiency level they were in, and whether there was any interaction between contrast and language proficiency level. Describe the results of the RM-ANOVA by first talking about the results of the interactions and then, if the interactions are not statistical, talking about the results of the main effects. If you can, talk about whether the assumption of sphericity has been upheld, and whether the residuals are normally distributed and have equal variances.
4 Use the Erdener and Burnham (2005) data. (Use Erdener&Burnham2005.sav; if you are using R, use the file you created in Section 11.2.4 with the "long" form of the data.) The RM-ANOVA will answer the question of whether participants performed similarly regardless of L1 and the target language, and whether performance was similar regardless of whether they received information auditorily or visually, and whether there was any interaction among L1, target language and condition that information was received in. Describe the results of the RM-ANOVA by first talking about the results of the interactions and then, if the interactions are not statistical, talking about the results of the main effects. If you can, talk about whether the assumption of sphericity has been upheld, and whether the residuals are normally distributed and have equal variances.
5 Use the Toth (2008) data from his production task. (Use Toth2008Prod.sav; if you are using R, use the file you created in Section 11.2.4 with the "long" form of the data.) The RM-ANOVA will answer the question of whether the groups performed in the same way at all three time periods. Run the RM-ANOVA and see if you can get the results reported at the beginning of the

chapter for this data set. Describe the results of the RM-ANOVA by first talking about the results of the interactions and then, if the interactions are not statistical, talking about the results of the main effects. If you can, talk about whether the assumption of sphericity has been upheld, and whether the residuals are normally distributed and have equal variances.

11.6 Furthering a Repeated-Measures Analysis by Exploring Simple Interaction Effects and Simple Main Effects

After conducting a RM-ANOVA, it will most likely be necessary to do further investigation to explore simple interaction effects or simple main effects to find out where the differences between levels of our variables lie. There are a number of techniques we can use to do this, and they will be illustrated as I further investigate the Murphy (2004) data set. Further exploration of the Lyster (2004) data set will be left as an application activity.

11.6.1 Exploring Simple Interaction Effects and Simple Main Effects in the Murphy (2004) Data (SPSS and R)

For the Murphy (2004) data set, we found a statistical three-way interaction between verb type, verb similarity and group. We want to understand where the differences lie, so we will need to break down the three-way interaction into different components, called simple interaction effects. We conduct simple interaction effects when we look at the interaction of two factors at one level of a third factor. For example, we can look at the interaction of verb similarity and group at one level of verb type ("regular") only, and then look at the interaction of similarity and group at the other level of verb type ("irregular").

At first it can be very confusing to think about what an interaction between three variables means (and this is why many authors recommend not using *more* than three variables, because you could end up with mind-blowing four-way or five-way interactions!). This is where the means plot can conceptually make understanding easier.

We previously saw means plots (also called profile or interaction plots) in 10.2.1, but Figure 11.19 shows means plots broken down the way that we intend to do our analysis—at different levels of the VERBTYPE variable.

SPSS lets you call for these plots from the PLOT button in the RM-ANOVA dialog box by putting GROUP in the "Horizontal Axis" box, SIMILARITY in the "Separate Lines" box and VERBTYPE in the "Separate Plots" box. (The plots in Figure 11.19 are from SPSS, although I have edited the plots and changed the look of the line using the CHART EDITOR that appears when you click twice on the plot in the output.) By the way, it is hard to make a means plot directly from menu choices in SPSS when your data is in the "wide" format, so if you do not have a plot like this in your RM-ANOVA output, I recommend just running the analysis again and calling for it.

In R, call for plots exactly like these by following these steps:

mreg<-murphy.long[1:180,] mirreg<-murphy.long[181:360,]	Use the "long" form of the Murphy data and split it up into two separate files, one for Regular verbs (mreg) and one for Irregular verbs (mirreg).
names(mreg) str(mreg)	Commands if you need to look at the names of the variables or the structure of the data file.
interaction.plot(mreg$group, mreg$similarity, mreg$value, type=c("b"), xlab="Group", ylab="Mean score", trace.label="Verb Similarity")	The interaction.plot( ) command needs to have the following order of variables: (1) factor that forms the x-axis, a categorical variable (mreg$group); (2) factor that will call for separate lines, a categorical variable (mreg$similarity); (3) response variable that the data are found in, a numerical variable (mreg$value). The type=c("b") argument labels the lines with numbers at each point.

You could also replicate the graphs in Figure 11.19 by first splitting your data as shown earlier, then in R Commander make mreg your active data set, and then pick GRAPHS > PLOT OF MEANS and choose group and similarity as your "Factors" and value as your "Response variable." The OPTIONS tab lets you pick whether you want error bars, and which type, and also how to label axes and the graph. This plot uses the command plotMeans() and will look slightly different from the interaction.plot() command. By the way, since I do not think simple means plots are the best graphic to include in your published reports and because many people misunderstand how to interpret error bars on such graphics (Cumming & Finch, 2005), I have not worried about how to help you see error bars in the interaction.plot() command. I think it is best to just use these graphics to help you understand your data, but not to publish them in this form.

The plot for regular verbs on the left panel of Figure 11.19 shows that the number of suffixed forms for type of verb similarity depends on both group membership and verb similarity. Native-speaking adults suffix regular verbs less than NS children and NNS adults, but verbs that are distant (very non-prototypical) receive less suffixing than the intermediate or prototypical verbs. For the irregular verbs on the right panel of Figure 11.19 we see even more striking differences between group membership and verb similarity. Here, the NNS adults clearly suffix more prototypical irregular verbs than intermediate verbs, while it is the opposite for NS adults and children. This shows the interaction between group and similarity. Comparing across the regular and irregular verb plots in Figure 11.19, we also see the interaction between verb type. For regular verbs, distant verbs are suffixed the least by all groups, but, for irregular verbs, distant verbs are suffixed the most by all groups.

What we would like to know now is which comparisons are statistical. For example, is the difference between verb similarities statistical for all three groups of participants? Is the difference between verb regularity statistical across all three similarities of verbs? Some of these questions we can answer based on data already contained in the output, but some we will have to do some extra work to request.

Howell (2002) noted that researchers should not feel compelled to report every statistical effect that they find, feeling they must do so for the sake of completeness. In addition, Kline (2004) observed that non-statistical effects may be at least as interesting as, if not more interesting than, statistical effects. One important point to consider is the effect size. If a certain comparison has an effect size that is noteworthy but the comparison is not statistical, this may be due to insufficient power (probably owing to a small group size), and further testing with larger groups would probably uncover a statistical relationship. If we can get to comparisons involving only two means at a time, CIs can also show us the magnitude of the differences between groups. If this information could further hypotheses, then it should probably be reported.

What should get reported? Results that are pertinent to the theoretical hypotheses and address the issues the researcher wants to illuminate are the right choice. A report full of statistics can be

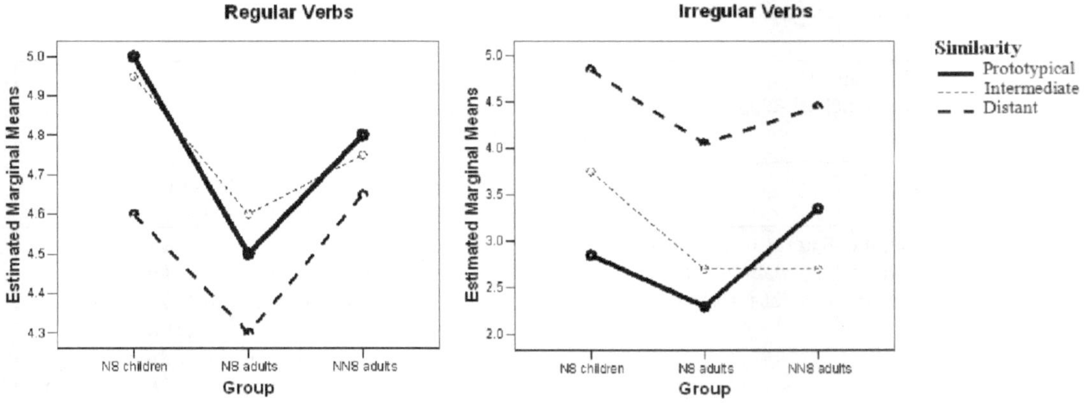

Figure 11.19 Three-way interactions between Verb Type, Similarity and Group for the Murphy (2004) data.

mind-numbing for readers (I confess to a few of these kinds of articles myself! Please forgive me), so choose only the information that is vital.

For the Murphy (2004) data, let us look at the hypotheses Murphy formulated and, knowing that there is a statistical three-way interaction, decide which further comparisons to look at. Murphy's hypotheses were:

1 All groups will add more "-ed" forms to regular verbs than irregular verbs.
2 Similarity should play a role on irregular verbs but not regular verbs.
3 Group differences in amount of suffixed forms should only be seen in the irregular verbs, not the regular ones.
4 No previous research looked at these three groups, so it is unclear which groups will pattern together.

For hypothesis 1 (All groups will add more "-ed" forms to regular verbs than irregular verbs) we could first look at descriptive statistics of the score of each group for regular verbs vs. irregular verbs. Table 11.2 gave descriptive statistics for the Murphy (2004) data, but the data are not in the right form to answer the question of how regular and irregular verbs pattern together, since they are further split by similarity. To get our answer, we want to compare all of the data with regular verbs to the data from irregular verbs. We will need to manipulate our data so all of the regular verbs are in one column and all of the irregular verbs are in another column.

In SPSS this can be done by using TRANSFORM > COMPUTE VARIABLE and creating two new variables, one adding together all three regular verb columns and the other adding all three irregular verb columns. (You could just add the numbers together so each of these columns will have a maximum score of 15 points, or you could divide by 3 to keep to a uniform score of 5.) I called my two new columns of data REGULARS and IRREGULARS and added the three columns together and divided by three. Then separate these new variables by group membership (GROUP) using the DATA > SPLIT FILE command and call for descriptive statistics (ANALYZE > DESCRIPTIVE STATISTICS > DESCRIPTIVES).

We are going to do the same thing in R that we did in SPSS. Start with the wide form of the data from murphy.wide, and create a new column by adding together the three different types of irregular verbs and dividing by three:

```
murphy.wide$Irregulars <- (with(murphy.wide, irreg_distant+ irreg_int+ irreg_proto))/3
murphy.wide$Regulars <- (with(murphy.wide, reg_distant+ reg_int+ reg_proto))/3
```

Now use tapply() to ask for the mean score:

```
tapply(murphy.wide$Irregulars, list(Group=murphy.wide$group), mean) #sd also
#use function(x) sum(!is.na(x)) for counts and make sure there are 20 in each group
```

The descriptive statistics show in every case that regulars were suffixed more than irregulars. The mean scores were: NS children: reg.V = 4.9 (0.2), irreg.V = 3.8 (0.6); NS adults: reg.V = 4.5 (0.6), irreg.V = 3.0 (0.8); NNS adults: reg.V = 4.7 (0.4), irreg.V = 3.5 (1.0).

We saw in the earlier sections that there is a statistical difference with a very strong effect size for "verb type" using the Huynh–Feldt correction and SPSS results ($F_{1,57} = 233.2$, $p < 0.0005$, $\eta^2_p = 0.80$), but no interaction between verb Type and Group ($F_{2,57} = 2.2$, $p = 0.12$, $\eta^2_p = 0.07$). Since there were only two levels for verb type and we know that verb type is statistical and from the lack of interaction know that all the groups performed similarly, no further analysis is necessary to state that regular verbs received statistically more "-ed" forms than irregulars, and that all of the participant groups followed this pattern.

For hypothesis 2 (Similarity should play a role on irregular verbs but not regular verbs) we would want to see an interaction between similarity and verb type. In the main analyses (Sections 11.5.2 and

11.5.3), the interaction was indeed statistical, with a large effect size, using the Huynh–Feldt correction and SPSS results ($F_{2,114} = 62.6, p < 0.0005, \eta^2_p = 0.52$). We need to know more about this interaction so we want to look at simple main effects. Remember that simple main effects are the effects of one factor at just one level of the other factor.

For SPSS, to look at the comparisons we really want, we can use the technique mentioned in Section 10.5.1, where we call for the syntax to analyze the marginal means of type*similarity. To do this in the Repeated Measures box, click on the PASTE button to get to the syntax, but you will have to remember what the syntax is. If you want to generate the syntax first, as we did in Section 10.5.1, you will have to go back and run a factorial ANOVA to get it (but do not trust the results of that since you have repeated measures). Here is the syntax for the Murphy (2004) data:

```
/EMMEANS = TABLES(type*similarity)COMPARE(type)
/EMMEANS = TABLES(type*similarity)COMPARE(similarity)
```

In R we can use the pairwise.t.test() command to look at post-hoc comparisons with the interaction. I do not want to perform post-hoc tests comparing the regular verbs to irregular ones, however, so I will use the data sets we generated earlier that only have regular verbs or irregular verbs in them. The pairwise.t.test() command is different from the paired samples *t*-test discussed in Chapter 8, which used the t.test() command that R Commander uses, and which could return CIs. The pairwise.t.test() call only returns *p*-values, although we are happy they can be adjusted for multiple comparisons:

```
pairwise.t.test(mreg$value, mreg$type:mreg$similarity, p.adjust.method="fdr")
```

To get the results for the irregular verbs, just use the mirreg data file and repeat what I did.

SPSS produces the most complete results, so please examine them in Table 11.17. To know what the numbers in the output in Table 11.17 refer to, we will need to look back at the first piece of output in the SPSS file, and there we see that type 1 is regular verbs, and type 2 is irregular. Similarity 1 is prototypical, 2 is intermediate and 3 is distant. We can look at CIs here, and see that for regular verbs,

Table 11.17 Pairwise Results between Verb Type and Similarity in the Murphy (2004) Data (SPSS)

Pairwise Comparisons

Measure: MEASURE_1

type	(I) similarity	(J) similarity	Mean Difference (I-J)	Std. Error	Sig.[b]	95% Confidence Interval for Difference[b] Lower Bound	Upper Bound
1	1	2	.000	.093	1.000	-.187	.187
		3	.250*	.078	.002	.095	.405
	2	1	.000	.093	1.000	-.187	.187
		3	.250*	.103	.019	.043	.457
	3	1	-.250*	.078	.002	-.405	-.095
		2	-.250*	.103	.019	-.457	-.043
2	1	2	-.217	.152	.160	-.521	.088
		3	-1.617*	.158	.000	-1.933	-1.300
	2	1	.217	.152	.160	-.088	.521
		3	-1.400*	.137	.000	-1.674	-1.126
	3	1	1.617*	.158	.000	1.300	1.933
		2	1.400*	.137	.000	1.126	1.674

Based on estimated marginal means

*. The mean difference is significant at the .05 level.

b. Adjustment for multiple comparisons: Least Significant Difference (equivalent to no adjustments).

prototypical and intermediate verbs are suffixed similarly (mean difference = 0.0, 95% CI [−1.87, 1.87]), but prototypical verbs are differently suffixed from distant verbs (mean difference = 0.25, 95% CI [0.1, 0.41]) and intermediate verbs are differently suffixed from distant verbs (mean difference = 0.25, 95% CI [0.04, 0.46]). We can see from the CIs that we are not too confident about the actual amount of difference because in both cases the CIs are wide, and that it could be quite a small difference (just 1/10 of a point for prototypical vs. distant and 4/100 of a point for intermediate vs. distant). A look at the summary statistics in Table 11.2 shows us that regular prototypical and regular intermediate verbs are more suffixed than distant verbs.

This contradicts the hypothesis that similarity plays no role for regular verbs.

For irregular verbs (verbtype 2), the pairwise comparisons show that prototypical and intermediate verbs are suffixed similarly (mean difference = 0.22, 95% CI [−0.52, 0.09]), but prototypical verbs are differently suffixed from distant verbs (mean difference = 1.62, 95% CI [1.30, 1.93]) and intermediate verbs are differently suffixed from distant verbs (mean difference = 1.40, 95% CI [1.13, 1.67]). A look at the summary statistics in Table 11.2 shows that irregular distant verbs are prefixed more than prototypical or distant verbs.

Although the broad outlines of the pairwise comparisons are the same for regular and irregular verbs, we do see why we have a three-way interaction because what is going on with the irregular verbs is stronger than what is happening with the regular verbs. With the regular verbs the CIs were broad and close to zero even if they did not go through it, but with the irregular verbs, for the differences between prototypical and distant verbs and also the differences between intermediate and distant verbs, the CIs are still broad (about half a point) but much further away from zero, with at least one point of difference in both cases.

I would conclude that hypothesis 2 has a good possibility of being correct. That is, there seems to be a qualitative difference in the size of the effects when we compare verb similarities in the irregular verbs to the regular verbs. Even though at first blush, and only looking at *p*-values, one would conclude that hypothesis 2 is incorrect and that different levels of similarity cause different effects in regular verbs as well as irregular verbs, examining the CIs here would lead me to argue that there is not very strong evidence for real effects between regular verbs even though they are statistical. In her paper, Murphy (2004) pointed out that the effects for regular and irregular verbs run in opposite directions; participants suffix least for distant similarity when verbs are regular, but suffix most for distant similarity when verbs are irregular. (Look back to the means plot in Figure 11.19 to confirm this visually.)

Hypothesis 3 (Group differences in amount of suffixed forms should only be seen in the irregular verbs, not the regular ones) posited that the groups would suffix differently on the irregular verbs but not on the regular verbs. In other words, there should be an interaction between verb type and group, but there is none, according to SPSS and using the Huynh–Feldt correction ($F_{2,57} = 2.2$, $p = 0.12$, $\eta^2_p = 0.07$, power = 0.43). We could stop there, but we could also run further post-hoc analyses on the data. For this question, we do not care about differences between the three levels of similarities of verbs, and are in fact collapsing our data over similarities to just look at the effect of group for regular verbs, and separately for irregular verbs.

To do this for SPSS, basically we can run the RM-ANOVA analysis again but only put in regular verbs (so there would only be one IV of similarity). We would run it again with just the irregular verbs too. Howell (2002) actually recommends this procedure for testing the levels of the within-subjects effects. He worries that sphericity adjustments may not be adequate with the original repeated-measures ANOVA, so running the repeated-measures ANOVA again with within-groups variables separated will result in a more appropriate error term. Post-hoc tests will then tell us whether the groups performed differently on the regular verbs (in the first run) and on the irregular verbs (in the second run). Thus, you should run the RM-ANOVA as explained in Section 11.5.2 but in your first dialog box only put in the variable of similarity with three levels, and then in the main Repeated Measures box only move the three columns with regular verbs to the "Within-Subjects Variables" box. Also put the Group variable in the "Between-Subjects Factor(s)" box. Click on the Post-Hoc button, move Group to the right under "Post Hoc Tests for," and choose the Games–Howell post-hoc test. Repeat with the three columns of irregular verbs.

Why not use a one-way ANOVA? After all, we are simply testing for differences in one variable, that of Group. Actually, this would be fine conceptually, but the data in SPSS is in the "wide" form and is not set up to run in a one-way ANOVA. It is easier to simply run the RM-ANOVA as explained earlier.

In R, use the **mreg** and **mirreg** data files that only have data from either the regular or irregular verbs in them. We can look at the main effect of **group** or not, and perform post-hoc comparisons between **group** levels. Since **group** has only three levels, we can do this by running a one-way ANOVA in R Commander and choosing to return pairwise comparisons of means. (DATA > STATISTICS > ONE-WAY ANALYSIS OF VARIANCE; pick **group** for "Groups" and **value** for "Response Variable"; tick "Pairwise comparison of means.) This method will return comparisons that also have CIs.

For regular verbs, I found that the variable of GROUP was statistical, according to SPSS output ($F_{2,57}$ = 4.36, p = 0.017). Post-hoc CIs showed that children are statistically different from NS adults (mean difference = 0.38, 95% CI [0.04, 0.73]), but children are not different from NNS adults (mean difference = 0.12, 95% CI [−0.13, 0.36]). Native- and non-native-speaking adults are not statistically different from one another (mean difference = 0.27, 95% CI [−0.11, 0.65]). This means the only statistical difference is between NS children and NS adults, but the closeness of the lower limit of the CI here (0.04) means that we could also argue that there is essentially no difference for any of the groups for the regular verbs.

Tip: Sometimes logic doesn't work with multiple comparisons! For example, you may at times find that statistically Group A is different from Group B, and Group B is different from Group C, but statistically Group A is not different from Group C. As Howell (2002) points out, logically this seems impossible. If A ≠ B and B ≠ C,then logically A ≠ C. However, logic is not statistics and sometimes there is not enough power to find a difference which logically should be there. Howell says sometimes we just have to live with uncertainty!

For irregular verbs, I found that the variable of GROUP was statistical, according to the SPSS output ($F_{2,57}$ = 04.97, p = 0.01). Post-hoc CIs showed that children are statistically different from NS adults (mean difference = 0.80, 95% CI [0.25, 1.35]), but children are not different from NNS adults (mean difference = 0.32, 95% CI [−0.32, 0.96]). Native- and non-native-speaking adults are not statistically different from one another (mean difference = 0.48, 95% CI [−0.20, 1.16]). This means the only statistical difference is between NS children and NS adults, and the lower limit of the CI is larger and further away from zero for irregular verbs (0.25) than it was for regular verbs (0.04).

Just as they did for hypothesis 2, I think the value of the CIs would help argue that hypothesis 3 is also a good possibility, since there is a more solid difference between children and NS adults in the irregular verbs than there is in the regular verbs.

Note that running a couple more tests beyond the original RM-ANOVA to answer a hypothesis (such as I just did for hypothesis 3) does not mean that you need to adjust p-values for everything because you have run too many tests. Howell (2002) has only two cautions in such cases. One is that you should not try to include every result from the tests. Just get the results you need and do not look at the rest. The second caution is that, if you are going to use *many* more results from such additional testing, then you should adjust the familywise error rate. However, in this case where only a couple of results were investigated (in fact, we did not look at the results of every single comparison included in the "Tests of Within-Subjects Effects"), there is no need to adjust the error rate.

Hypothesis 4 was concerned about which groups would pattern together since previous research had not been done on these three groups in this context. Since we know that the three-way interaction was statistical, we know the answer to the question of how the group pattern depends on whether the verbs are regular or irregular, and also on the similarity of the verbs. The results surveyed in hypothesis 3 are a little problematic in making any clear conclusions about grouping, since NS children could be said to group with NNS adults (since they are not different from them), but then NNS adults group with NS adults too (since they are not different from them either!), so then logically (as noted in the previous tip) it seems like no one is really different from anyone else. We could then divide the data into groups of verbs that pattern similarly (Prototypical, Intermediate and Distant) and look at the effect of group on them, repeating the process of what we did for hypothesis 3, but breaking the data down into three different groups of verb similarity. Doing this results in something very similar to what happened in hypothesis 3 for the Prototypical verbs and the Distant verbs—strictly speaking, the comparison between NS children and NS adults was statistical, but the effect was very small, with the lower limit of the CI being almost negligible (0.03 for Prototypical verbs, 0.04 for Distant verbs). Only for the Intermediate verbs were there modest differences between NS children and NS adults (mean = 0.70, CI [0.22, 1.18]), and in that case there was also a possibly very small effect for the difference between NS children and NNS adults, with a lower limit of 0.05. So, in several cases there was a weak patterning of NS children being different from NS adults but my conclusion would be that overall there were no clear patterns of groupings.

Evolving statistics: If you were comparing this second edition with the first edition of the book, you would see that I reached the opposite conclusions on hypotheses 2 and 3 in the first edition. Why do I now conclude that (hypothesis 2) verb similarity plays a role in irregular verbs but not regular verbs, and that (hypothesis 3) group differences in the amount of suffixed forms is seen in the irregular verbs but not the regular ones? The short answer is the "new statistics" way of looking at the world. In the first edition, I advocated using CIs and they were included, but I still trusted in a black-and-white view of the world where if the CI ran through zero the difference was not statistical, while if it did not run through zero, the difference was statistical. The "new statistics" tells us that making these kinds of categorical decisions without looking at the actual precision (width) and upper and lower limit of the CI will cause us to miss important information. Looking at these characteristics, I saw a difference in effects between the regular and irregular verbs in hypotheses 2 and 3, and thus concluded that there was evidence to support the hypotheses.

11.6.2 Reporting the Results of a Repeated-Measures Analysis of Variance

When you do a RM-ANOVA you will get a lot of results! As noted several times in the text, please do not feel obligated to report *all* the statistics that are returned to you by any procedure. As Howell (2002, p .451) said, it is "not good practice to test everything in sight just because it is possible to do so." What will be important to report are results that address the questions you have asked. You should definitely report that you have run a RM-ANOVA, because this is only one of a number of possible analyses that could be run on the data. You may have run additional analyses, such as one-way RM-ANOVAs or one-way ANOVAs to try to ascertain the effects of an interaction, and the fact that you did these should also be reported.

You should report on the results of preliminary examination of the data for satisfying the assumptions of a RM-ANOVA, and also include the results of tests for sphericity. If your data do not meet the assumptions of homoscedasticity and normality of distribution, this fact should definitely be reported, but does not mean your results are invalid. It is not true that an ANOVA is necessarily robust to these deviations from assumptions (in fact, it most likely is not, given what Wilcox, 2001, reported), but any statistical results you report are likely to be accurate. Deviations away from normality and homoscedasticity are likely to result in a loss of power to find statistical results (Larson-Hall & Herrington, 2009; Wilcox, 2001).

When you report the result of one term in a RM-ANOVA model, you should include the df between groups, the df for the error (also called residuals), the *F*-value, the exact *p*-value and an effect size. Several examples of this were given for the Murphy (2004) data in Section 11.6.1. It is not necessary to report the results of every component of the model, however. It is not the case that you should only report on components that are statistical. What you report should depend on what you are interested in, and whether higher-order interactions mean that you are not very interested in main effects.

When doing more complicated analyses in this chapter, we have seen that it has been impossible to maintain a "new statistics" approach if we want to report on the results of complex interactions. Yet, Section 11.6.1 showed that most complex interactions get broken down into smaller parts in the end to answer researchers' questions, and in these cases, you should bring in CIs as they will result in more accurate and nuanced information about your results.

Here is how I would report my findings for the Murphy (2004) data set.

> To test the following four hypotheses, I ran a 3 Group × 2 Verb Type × 3 Verb Similarity RM-ANOVA on the response variable of verb prefixation. Twenty participants in each group created the past tense of nonce verbs that differed in whether they resembled regular or irregular verb types in English, and in how similar they were to real English verbs (Prototypical, Intermediate or Distant). Examination of descriptive statistics (Table 11.2) and graphics (Figure 11.10) showed that the data were neither normally distributed nor had equal variances. Mauchly's test of sphericity was not statistical ($p > 0.05$), but examination of the residual SSCP matrix showed deviations from sphericity, so a correction factor was used. No important deviations from normality and homogeneity of variances for the residuals were discovered.
>
> The three-way interaction between group, verb type and similarity was statistical and is reported using the Greenhouse–Geisser correction ($F_{4,113} = 3.28$, $p = 0.014$, $\eta^2_p = 0.10$). The effect size shows that this interaction accounts for a fairly small amount of the variance in the model. Because the interaction was statistical, I decided to undertake further investigation of the phenomenon by looking at the answers to my four hypotheses.
>
> Hypothesis 1: All groups will add more "-ed" forms to regular verbs than irregular verbs. Descriptive statistics show that this is true (see a chart, which I would insert). By logic, because the two-way interaction of Type and Group from the RM-ANOVA was not statistical ($F_{2,57} = 2.2$, $p = 0.12$, $\eta^2_p = 0.07$), but the main effect for Type was statistical with a very strong effect size ($F_{1,57} = 233.2$, $p < 0.0005$, $\eta^2_p = 0.80$), I will assume that all of the groups performed the same way on the regular verbs, and all of the groups performed the same way on the irregular verbs. Since there are only two levels of verb Types and descriptive statistics show that the level of "-ed" suffixing was higher in regular verbs, I conclude that hypothesis 1 is upheld.
>
> Hypothesis 2: Similarity should play a role on irregular verbs but not regular verbs. To test this hypothesis, I split the data into regular and irregular verbs, and looked at pairwise comparisons between the levels of the Similarity variable. Summary statistics show that regular prototypical and regular intermediate verbs are more suffixed than distant verbs, and 95% CIs on the mean differences between verb Similarity show that no important differences can be found between the three levels:
>
> **Regular verbs**
> Prototypical vs. Intermediate verbs: mean difference = 0.0, 95% CI [–1.87, 1.87]
> Prototypical vs. Distant verbs: mean difference = 0.25, 95% CI [0.1, 0.41]
> Intermediate vs. Distant verbs: mean difference = 0.25, 95% CI [0.04, 0.46]
>
> Summary statistics show that irregular distant verbs are prefixed more than prototypical or distant verbs; 95% CIs on the mean differences between verb Similarity for irregular verbs show that some substantial differences can be found between some groups:
>
> **Irregular verbs**
> Prototypical vs. Intermediate verbs: mean difference = 0.22, 95% CI [–0.52, 0.09]
> Prototypical vs. Distant verbs: mean difference = 1.62, 95% CI [1.30, 1.93]
> Intermediate vs. Distant verbs: mean difference = 1.40, 95% CI [1.13, 1.67]
> The conclusion is that hypothesis 2 is upheld.

Hypothesis 3: Group differences in amount of suffixed forms should only be seen in the irregular verbs, not the regular ones. A 3 Similarity × 3 Group RM-ANOVA was run separately on the regular and irregular verbs. For the regular verbs, the main effect of Group was statistical ($F_{2,57}$ = 4.36, p = 0.017). Summary statistics show that for regular verbs, NS children had the highest level of suffixation (4.9) followed by NNS adults (4.7) and then NS adults (4.5). Further post-hoc comparisons on the Group variable found a negligible difference between NS children and NS adults, which for all practical purposes I will assume does not exist.

Regular verbs
NS children vs. NS adults: mean difference = 0.38, 95% CI [0.04, 0.73]
NS children vs. NNS adults: mean difference = 0.12, 95% CI [–0.13, 0.36]
NS adults vs. NNS adults: mean difference = 0.27, 95% CI [–0.11, 0.65]

For irregular verbs, the effect of Group was statistical ($F_{2,57}$ = 4.97, p = 0.01). Summary statistics show that although prefixation levels overall were lower, for irregular verbs the same order as regular verbs held: NS children had the highest level of suffixation (3.8) followed by NNS adults (3.5) and then NS adults (3.0). Further post-hoc comparisons showed a stronger effect among irregular verbs for a difference between NS children and NS adults, but not any other groups:

Irregular verbs
NS children vs. NS adults: mean difference = 0.80, 95% CI [0.25, 1.35]
NS children vs. NNS adults: mean difference = 0.32, 95% CI [–0.32, 0.96]
NS adults vs. NNS adults: mean difference = 0.48, 95% CI [–0.20, 1.16]
Although the effect was not strong, there appears to be some validity to the claim of hypothesis 3.

Hypothesis 4: No previous research looked at these three groups, so it is unclear which groups will pattern together. The short answer is that since there is little strong evidence that any groups are different from each other, no clear overall patterns emerge as to patterning of groups and they are mostly similar to each other in almost every condition. The more detailed answer is that since the three-way interaction was statistical, the answer to the question of how the groups pattern depends on whether the verbs are regular or irregular, and also on the similarity of the verbs. As for patterning with verb type, hypothesis 3 showed differences between NS children with NS adults on irregular verbs, which should mean that NS children pattern with NNS adults (since they are not different from them), but NS adults can also be said to pattern with NNS adults (since they also not different from them). Therefore, no clear pattern emerges. An examination of CIs between groups for each of the three different types of verb similarities using pairwise comparisons showed differences between NS children with NS adults on intermediate verbs only, so again, there does not seem to be any clear patterning between groups.

11.6.3 Application Activities with Further Exploration of Repeated-Measures Analysis of Variance Using Simple Interaction Effects and Simple Main Effects

1 Section 11.6.1 explored the results of the RM-ANOVA with Murphy's (2004) data. Using Lyster's (2004) data on the task completion test and starting from the omnibus RM-ANOVA results (as shown in Sections 11.5.2 for SPSS and 11.5.3 for R; use the lyster.long data file created in Section 11.2.3), answer Lyster's research questions for this particular task (which I have paraphrased):

   a Will FFI help students to assign French grammar more accurately? (In other words, are all three groups that received FFI better than the control group?)
   b Is FFI more effective with feedback (i.e. FFIrecast and FFIprompt) than without (FFI only)?
   c Which type of feedback is more effective in FFI—recasts or prompts?

You can see that you will need to use planned comparisons to answer questions #1 and #2 since you want to combine some of the conditions together and compare them against other conditions. For question #3 you can use simple main effects to look at the comparison between just two levels. However, you cannot test these types of contrasts using the repeated-measures data at the same time. So you will need to create a new variable that is the gain score between the pre-task and the immediate post-task. (You could also make one between the pre-task and the delayed post-task, but for simplicity's sake, let us not!). Then you will be able to run a one-way ANOVA using planned comparisons (see Sections 9.4.7 and 9.4.8, then subsequent appropriate sections for information about running planned comparisons). Try to use CIs to answer the questions; also calculate effect sizes.

2 In Section 11.5.4 you conducted an omnibus RM-ANOVA with Lyster's (2004) data on the binary test. Answer the same three research questions asked for the completion test in exercise #1 for these data. Try to use CIs to answer the questions; also calculate effect sizes.
3 In Section 11.5.4 you conducted an omnibus RM-ANOVA with Cole's (1927) data that tested whether students studying French would benefit more from a teaching approach using free composition vs. another that focused on translation (all of the students were male high school students), and whether there were any interactions between teaching approach, testing time and language measure. Cole (1927) was published before doing statistical work of the kind you are doing now was common, so no actual statistical tests were performed, but the research question was whether the free composition method would be better than the grammar translation method. You could answer that generally from the RM-ANOVA, but answer it for each of the separate language measures in this analysis, performing simple interaction effects for each language measure. I also love the humble last sentence of this article, and it should be a caution to all researchers: "It must be borne in mind, however, that in all cases the number of students was extremely small [15 students per group], and the methods of testing limited, so that the results are more in the nature of a tendency than a proved conclusion" (Cole, 1927, p. 206). Try to use CIs to answer the questions; also calculate effect sizes.
4 In Section 11.5.4 you conducted an omnibus RM-ANOVA with the Larson-Hall (2004) data to examine the question of whether Japanese students of Russian were able to perceive three different phonemic contrasts equally well depending on the contrast and their language proficiency level. Because there were three levels for contrast and four for language proficiency level, simple interaction effects are needed to answer the question of which contrasts were most difficult and which proficiency levels performed differently. Try to use CIs to answer the questions.
5 In Section 11.5.4 you conducted an omnibus RM-ANOVA with the Erdener and Burnham (2005) data to test whether L1 orthography and presentation medium (audio, visual) affected how well participants could read a target language. Test the following research questions:

   1 Do all of the participants perform better in conditions with visual information?
   2 How does L1 interact with TL on scores? (Remember what is recorded are error scores, so the lower the better.)

   To answer #1, use planned comparisons to compare the two conditions with video in them to the two other conditions without video. For #2, like exercise #3, there are only two levels of each variable so although you can use a RM-ANOVA for SPSS, you will need to use a *t*-test to examine this question in R. Try to use CIs to answer the questions.
6 In Section 11.5.4 you conducted an omnibus RM-ANOVA with the Toth (2008) data to test whether the different groups developed in their ability to use Spanish *se* equally well at all Testing times. Test the question of how the groups differed at the immediate posttest. You will need to examine simple main effects on the immediate posttest. Try to use CIs to answer the questions; also calculate effect sizes.

11.7 Summary

The RM-ANOVA test is the one you will want to use when you test the same people more than once (and have more than just two mean scores, in which case you would just use a paired samples *t*-test).

There are two distinct types of situations in the field of second language research when RM-ANOVAs are necessary. One situation is when you test the same people more than once, as in the Lyster (2004) study when participants were tested at three different times. The other situation is when you test the same people just once, but you divide your test up into different parts that you see as an IV, such as phonemic contrast distinctions or types of verbs, as we saw for the Murphy (2004) data.

One thing that makes RM-ANOVA somewhat confusing is that your data must be arranged differently than the way they would be for a factorial ANOVA. The RM-ANOVA analysis in SPSS needs data to be arranged in the "wide" format, where the number of rows is equal to the total number of participants, and scores for IVs are split into different columns. In R the data are in the "long" form, but there must be a column that lists which participant the data came from, as the same participant will contribute to more than one row for the "long" form of the data in a RM-ANOVA.

The output of a RM-ANOVA is voluminous and returns a large number of tests. I have emphasized in this chapter that you do not need to report all of the statistics that are found in the output; be selective and report only on the tests that will answer your research questions. In some cases, additional analyses, such as one-way ANOVAs or pairwise comparisons may have to be used to answer all your questions, and previous chapters provide information about those simpler types of tests.

The assumptions for a RM-ANOVA test are similar to those of other parametric tests we have seen (normality, homogeneity of variances), but also include the assumption of sphericity. We have seen in the chapter that most real data sets will violate one or all of these assumptions! Correction factors are available in the output if sphericity is violated, and I advised you to always use the correction factor whether or not the formal test for sphericity is violated. Violation of assumptions means that you may not have the power to find differences that may actually exist, and many researchers have recommended using mixed-effect models to examine repeated-measures data instead.

Mixed-effects models are similar to the RM-ANOVA in that their syntax looks like a regression (which is, after all, what an ANOVA is) for the fixed terms of the model, but they also add in a random part of the model that lets intercepts or slopes vary between groups. For reasons of space, a mixed-effect model analysis of these data is not included here, but you can see this analysis online in the "Performing an RM-ANOVA the Mixed-Effects Way" section. Because such models need to be constructed in a variety of ways and the best model found through looking at the results of tests of fit, syntax (instead of a menu-driven system) is the best way to approach these models, and this is why I have only shown how to perform mixed-effects models in R (as there is no advantage to using SPSS). These types of models have several advantages over the RM-ANOVA, primarily in that they do not assume sphericity, can include both continuous and categorical factors, and deal better with missing data. However, for simpler models with few groups, the mixed-effects model may not provide much improvement over the classical RM-ANOVA analysis.

Appendix A
Doing Things in R

This appendix is not an exhaustive list of all the things that R can do, but rather a list of some common steps you may want to take gathered in one convenient place, and a place to throw a few miscellaneous ideas about R that did not fit neatly anywhere in the book.

Getting Started

I am Looking at the R Console. What Next?

The very first thing to do is to get R Commander going so you will have a menu-driven graphical user interface (GUI) to help you. To get R Commander, in R Console pull down the PACKAGES menu and click on "Install packages." The first long, skinny window that will pop up is labeled "CRAN mirror." You need to choose a CRAN mirror site before you can download packages. Choose any site, but preferably one near your geographic location. Click on OK, and then another long, skinny window will pop up. Scroll down to the "Rs" and double click on "Rcmdr." Once it has finished installing, type this (exactly!) in the R Console window:

```
library(Rcmdr)
```

The R Commander GUI will open.

Getting Data into R

I think the easiest way to do this is to use R Commander. Open R Commander (type library(Rcmdr) into the R Console) to get R Commander to open. In R Commander, choose DATA from the menu, then IMPORT DATA. If you have a SPSS (.sav) file, choose the FROM SPSS DATA SET option. The only thing I change in the dialog box that pops up is the name of the data set.

If you have a ".txt file," use the FROM TEXT FILE, CLIPBOARD OR URL choice. This is a little trickier and you will have to know whether your numbers are separated by white spaces, commas, tabs or something else. If a file is ".csv," this means it is comma-delimited, so tick the COMMAS button under "Field Separator." You might have to experiment with this to get the correct format of your imported file. Once you click on OK, R Commander lets you browse your computer to find the file.

With R Console, if the file you want is in the R/bin folder, just type:

```
lafrance<-read.csv("lafrance.csv")
```

The first lafrance is necessary to put the .csv file into an object named "lafrance" that is in the workspace. If you only do the read.csv("lafrance.csv") command, it will print out the file on the R Console but you cannot manipulate the object.

Finding Out the Names of a Data Set

```
names(lafrance)
```

Looking at a Data Set

If you want to see what your data file looks like, press the "View data set" button on the R Commander window. This shows you the active file (lh2004 in this case):

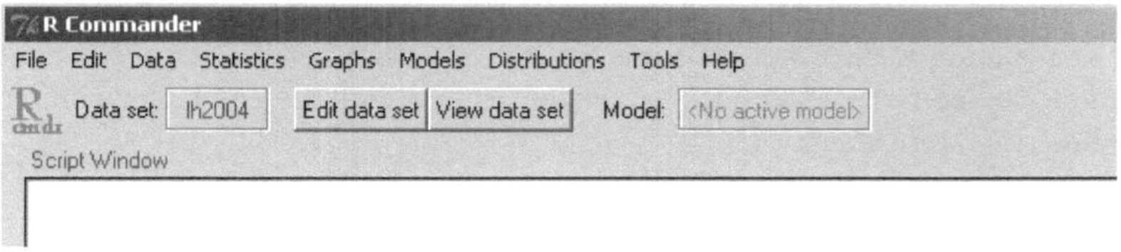

Making R Work for You in the Long Run

Make it a habit to collect all the R commands and analyses that you do in some type of separate file, whether a Word document, Tinn-R (an ASCII file editor intended to be better than Microsoft Notepad, and found at nbcgib.uesc.br/lec/software/editores/tinn-r/en) or R's own. The ".Rhistory" file can be opened with Notepad and contains a collection of the commands you made during your session. You can make comments on what you did (preceded by a # so that R will ignore them if you run the commands again) to help you remember your analyses years later.

Getting Help!

How to Pull Up Specific Help Files

Let us say you want to understand the "lmRob" function better, so you pull up the Help file for it (and you have already opened the **robust** library). You can pull up this Help file in the following ways:

```
help("lmRob") #use of quotes optional here
?lmRob
```

In the R Console: HELP > RFUNCTIONS (TEXT), then type in lmRob.

How to Find Help When You are Not Sure What You Want

Suppose you want to make a histogram but you are not sure how to do it in R. You have tried **histogram(my.data)** but that does not work, so you can type the following to find out more about how to make histograms:

```
help.search("histogram")
```

R will come up with a list of relevant topics. It says "Type 'help(FOO, package=PKG)' to inspect entry 'FOO(PKG) TITLE'." What this means is that if you see the list that help.search brings up (something like this):

```
R Information
File  Edit

hist.data.frame(Hmisc)
                           Histograms for Variables in a Data Frame
histbackback(Hmisc)        Back to Back Histograms
scat1d(Hmisc)              One-Dimensional Scatter Diagram, Spike
                           Histogram, or Density
dpih(KernSmooth)           Select a Histogram Bin Width
histogram(lattice)         Histograms and Kernel Density Plots
```

then you can type the following into R to get more information about the first entry:

```
help(hist.data.frame, package=Hmisc)
```

Notice that FOO is just shorthand for the function name.

You can also try the **apropos** command, which is a partial name search and looks for commands relevant to the topic you put in parentheses:

```
apropos("hist", ignore.case=False)
```

A number of possibilities will appear.

How to Understand R Help Files

There are eight basic parts to help files: Description, Usage, Arguments, Details, Value, References, See Also and Examples. I often find it easiest to start with the examples. You can type:

example(crPlot)

and if there are example files, they will run on R and show you what the function does. This is especially helpful if graphics are involved. To find out more about what **crPlot** is and how it works, type one of these equivalent commands:

help(crPlot)
?crPlot

The following window will appear:

crPlots {car} R D

Component+Residual (Partial Residual) Plots

Description

These functions construct component+residual plots (also called partial-residual plots) for linear and generalize models.

Usage

```
crPlots(model, terms = ~., layout = NULL, ask, main,
    ...)

crp(...)

crPlot(model, ...)

## S3 method for class 'lm'
crPlot(model, variable,
  id.method = list(abs(residuals(model, type="pearson")), "x"),
  labels,
  id.n = if(id.method[1]=="identify") Inf else 0,
  id.cex=1, id.col=palette()[1],
  order=1, line=TRUE, smoother=loessLine,
        smoother.args=list(), smooth, span,
  col=palette()[1], col.lines=palette()[-1],
  xlab, ylab, pch=1, lwd=2, grid=TRUE, ...)
```

Arguments

model	model object produced by `lm` or `glm`.
terms	A one-sided formula that specifies a subset of the predictors. (

We see that **crPlot** is part of the **car** library (a very useful library). The Description section tells us that these plots are component+residual plots. The Usage section shows you exactly what arguments can be used in the function. For the **crPlot** function, there are several different usages. The first is:

crPlot(model, terms=~., layout=NULL, main . . .)

This is the most general syntax of the function. It tells us that we will need to put a model in the first argument position. The next argument is the terms that contain the predictors, as in a regression. Other arguments include one called "ask" for class "Im". You can find out more about what these arguments are in the Arguments and Details sections. The default settings for these arguments are also given here. For example, in the "S3" method, the third argument, the default for order will be "1". Do not give up if you cannot understand the Usage section right away, because there is more information later in the help document! The other variations in the Usage section tell us that this plot might also be called **crp**. Its usage with **lm** and **glm** models gives additional arguments that a user might be interested in setting. So they are all the same command, but different variations of it for different situations.

The Details section also often has some useful details that the author does not have any other place to put. For example, for **crPlot**, it is noted that the model cannot contain interactions. This is an important piece of information. References are self-explanatory. The See Also has clickable terms that can lead you to related functions that will help you figure out how to use the function.

The Arguments section can help clarify the syntax. For example, Arguments tells us that the model in the first argument position needs to be a regression object created with either lm or glm.

If you type:

example (crPlot)

You will see the following graph:

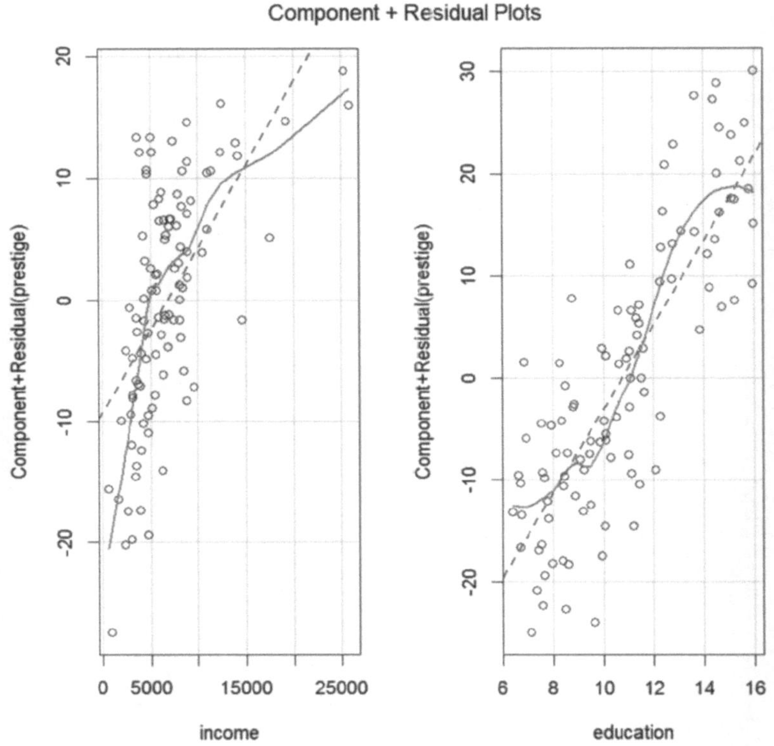

As you become more familiar with the R Help pages they will make more sense and become more helpful!

Finding Out the Arguments that are Needed for a Command

```
args(lm)
function (formula, data, subset, weights, na.action, method = "qr",
   model = TRUE, x = FALSE, y = FALSE, qr = TRUE, singular.ok = TRUE,
   contrasts = NULL, offset, ...)
```

When You Want More Information about a Certain Package

Let us say you want to do robust regression and you have noted that robustbase is a package that does robust regression. There are a couple of ways to get more information about this package:

```
help.start()
```

In R Console: Help > HTML Help

Find the Packages hyperlink. Many packages have links here so that you can hyperlink from one function to another within the package. However, not all packages are found here. For example, say I want to know more about the prettyR package. Another thing to try is vignettes:

```
vignette(all=T)
vignette("grid") #for a vignette from a specific package
```

I still cannot find anything about prettyR so I go to this website: www.cran.r-project.org

Click on "Packages" on the left-hand side bar. This has PDF documents from many packages that can be quite helpful, and it has one about prettyR.

Helpful Online Articles or Sites that Explain More about R

- On the R website (www.r-project.org), under Documentation, go to Manuals and you will find An Introduction to R.
- An Introduction to the R Statistical Computing Environment by John Fox can be found at http://socserv.socsci.mcmaster.ca/jfox/Courses/R-course/index.html
- Tom Short's R reference card, organizing R syntax by function and giving short explanations in a compact format can be found at http://cran.r-project.org/doc/contrib/Short-refcard.pdf
- A short online tutorial about using R for psychological research can be found at www.personality-project.org/r/r.guide.html
- Notes on the Use of R For Psychology Experiments and Questionnaires can be found at www.psych.upenn.edu/~baron/rpsych/rpsych.html

A general resource can be found on the R home page; under Documentation, click on Other, then click on the link to "contributed documentation" where you will find many articles.

Getting Help Online

If you are having a problem, the R Help archives usually have some answers. You can also post a question to r-help@lists.R-project.org. However, before posting you must be sure to research your question by searching the archives and reading the posting guide, which can be found by clicking on Mailing Lists and reading the information there.

To search for answers in the R Help archives, go to the R website (www.r-project.org) and click on Search. I usually go to Baron's R site, which is the first hyperlink on the page. Insert your term and browse away.

When you post a question, the posting guide does ask you to state what version of R you are using. You can get this information by typing:

```
sessionInfo()
```

This tells you what version of R you are using, what packages are attached, and what versions those packages are

Types of Data

Understanding the Types of Data in R

If you import an SPSS file into R, it will be a "data frame." A data frame is a collection of columns and rows of data, and the data can be numeric (made up of numbers) or character (a "string" in SPSS, or in other words, words that have no numerical value). It only has two dimensions, that of rows and columns. All of the columns must have the same length. Most of the data you will work with in this book are in data frames, and you can think of it as a traditional table. Here is an example of a data frame:

```
  condition cloze    time
1 FFIrecast    34 Pretest
2 FFIrecast    25 Pretest
3 FFIrecast    25 Pretest
4 FFIrecast    27 Pretest
5 FFIrecast    31 Pretest
6 FFIrecast    26 Pretest
```

A "matrix" is similar to a data frame but all the columns must be of the same format, that is, either numeric or character. Like a data frame, a matrix has only two dimensions (row and column) and all columns must be of the same length. Here is an example of what happened when I turned the data frame above into a matrix:

```
  condition    cloze time
1 "FFIrecast" "34"  "Pretest"
2 "FFIrecast" "25"  "Pretest"
3 "FFIrecast" "25"  "Pretest"
4 "FFIrecast" "27"  "Pretest"
5 "FFIrecast" "31"  "Pretest"
6 "FFIrecast" "26"  "Pretest"
```

You can see that all the cells are now surrounded by quotation marks, meaning they are characters. A look at the structure of this matrix reveals indeed that all the variables are now regarded as character, meaning they do not have any numerical meaning.

A vector is just one line of data that might represent one column of a data frame or matrix. It can be composed of numeric, character or logical entries:

```
a=c(3,6,7,10,3) #numeric
b=c("Type A", "Type A", "Type B", "Type C") #character
c=c(TRUE, TRUE, FALSE, FALSE, FALSE, TRUE) #logical
```

If you take one column from a data frame, this is also a vector:

```
lh2004$group
[1] 1 1 1 1 1 1 1 1 1 1 1 2 2 2 2 2 2 2 2 2 2 2 2 2 3 3 3 3 3 3 3 3 3 3 4 4
[36] 4 4 4 4 4 4
```

A list is a collection of vectors that do not all need to be the same length. The elements of the list can be of different types as well. For example, we can create a list that holds all of the vectors presented earlier:

```
my.list=as.list(c(a,b,c))

> my.list
[[1]]    [[2]]    [[3]]    [[4]]     [[5]]
[1] "3"  [1] "6"  [1] "7"  [1] "10"  [1] "3"

[[6]]           [[7]]           [[8]]           [[9]]
[1] "Type A"    [1] "Type A"    [1] "Type B"    [1] "Type C"

[[10]]        [[11]]        [[12]]         [[13]]
[1] "TRUE"    [1] "TRUE"    [1] "FALSE"    [1] "FALSE"
```

Each entry is referenced by its position in the list. For example, the 13th member of the list can be referenced by:

```
my.list[[13]]
[1] "FALSE"
```

An array is a similar to a data frame, but it can have more than two dimensions. The array for the "Titanic" data, found in the vcd library, is an array.

```
> Titanic
, , Age = Child, Survived = No

      Sex
Class  Male Female
  1st     0      0
  2nd     0      0
  3rd    35     17
  Crew    0      0

, , Age = Adult, Survived = No

      Sex
Class  Male Female
  1st   118      4
  2nd   154     13
  3rd   387     89
  Crew  670      3
```

This data set has four dimensions, which can be ascertained by their dimension names:

```
> dimnames(Titanic)
$Class
[1] "1st"  "2nd"  "3rd"  "Crew"

$Sex
[1] "Male"   "Female"

$Age
[1] "Child" "Adult"

$Survived
[1] "No"  "Yes"
```

A factor is a vector that R considers a categorical variable and it contains two parts—a vector of integers as well as a vector of character strings that characterize those integers. Here I have created a factor called "category":

```
category=c(rep("A", 10), rep("B", 15))
category=factor(category)
category
 [1] A A A A A A A A A A B B B B B B B B B B B B B B B
Levels: A B
summary(category)
 A  B
10 15
```

In the summary, R knows that this is a factor and so it counts up the As and Bs separately. If we had not made "category" into a factor and performed a summary, it would simply count up 25 character entries.

Changing Data from One Type to Another

There are many commands to change data types (use methods(is) for a complete list), but essentially there are only a few that are likely to be useful. One is when you want to change your data from separate vectors to a data frame, like this:

```
collect=as.data.frame(results, group, type)
```

Another may be when you want to change a data frame into a matrix:

```
collect.matrix=as.matrix(collect)
```

Another common task is changing a non-factor into a factor:

```
murphyLong$verbtype=as.factor(murphyLong$verbtype)
```

Remember, you can check the class of your data by typing:

```
class(collect.matrix)
```

Manipulating Data

This is my collection, but there are other very nice places to search on the Web if you cannot find the R code to do what you want when it comes to manipulating your data. One I have found useful is www.cookbook-r.com/Manipulating_data/ (Cookbook for R).

Finding Out What Class Your Data Is

```
class(lafrance)
[1] "data.frame"
```

Possible classes include "data.frame," "matrix," "array," "vector," "table" and "list." For more information about what the different types of data classes mean, see the "Types of Data" section. If you use class on a vector, it will tell you whether it is numeric or character:

```
class(lyster$cloze)
[1] "numeric"
```

Finding Out the Size of Your Data

```
dim(lyster)
[1] 540  4
```

This specifies that the data frame has 540 rows and 4 columns.

Finding Out How Many Rows in One Column of Data

```
length(murphy$REGULARV)
[1]  60
```

Finding Out about the Structure of Your Data

The str command will give you a wealth of information about your data:

```
str(Forbes2000) #data found in HSAUR library
```

```
'data.frame': 2000 obs. of 8 variables:
$ rank      : int 1 2 3 4 5 6 7 8 9 10
$ name      : chr "Citigroup" "General Electric" "American Intl Group"
$ country   : Factor w/ 61 levels "Africa","Australia",..: 60 60 60 60 56 60 56 28
$ category  : Factor w/ 27 levels "Aerospace & defense",..: 2 6 16 19 19 2 2 8 9
$ sales     : num 94.7 134.2 76.7 222.9 232.6
$ profits   : num 17.85 15.59 6.46 20.96 10.27
$ assets    : num 1264 627 648 167 178
$ marketvalue: num 255 329 195 277 174
```

The first line tells us what class of object it is and also that there are eight variables.

The next eight lines tell us about each of the variables, whether they are character (chr; for the Forbes2000 data, these are not factors because none of the strings is repeated; they are all different companies), factors (and how many levels in each factor; you get a factor if you import with character strings) and num (just plain numbers).

Looking at Just a Few Rows of Your Data

```
head(murphy) #lists the first few rows
murphy[1:15,] #lists the first 15 rows
murphy[sort(sample(60,5)),] #samples 5 rows from the 60 possible
```

Attaching and Detaching Data

You can find out which data sets are already attached by typing:

```
search()
```

If any data sets are attached, they will be listed. If more than one data set is attached, the last one attached is in the highest position and will take precedence if they have any names that are the same.

Attach a data set by typing:

```
attach(lyster)
```

One good reason to attach data is so that you can perform subsequent commands using just the names of the variables inside the attached data set instead of having to always append the name of the data set. In other words, if you have not attached the data, to calculate the mean of the "cloze" variable inside the lyster data set, you will need to type:

```
mean(lyster$cloze)
```

On the other hand, if you have attached the data set, you can just type:

```
mean(cloze)
```

Note that if you modify something in the data when they are attached, then changes will not be seen until you detach and reattach the data. To detach the data:

```
detach(lyster)
```

or just:

```
detach()
```

which detaches the most recently attached data set (the one highest up in the search path list).

Picking Out Certain Rows or Columns

With a data frame or matrix, there are a number of syntax equivalents you can use to pick out a certain column:

```
lyster[,3]
lyster[[3]]
lyster$time
```

To pick out a row:

```
lyster[15,]
```

Finding Out Which Objects are in Your Active Desktop

This command lists all active objects, which are data sets and user-defined functions:

```
ls()
```

Finding Out Which Data Sets are in a Package or Library

```
data(package="languageR")
```

This command causes a separate window with a list of the data sets to appear. To find out more about the data sets, in the R Console choose HELP > HTML HELP and when a new window pops up, choose "Packages." Choose your package (such as "languageR"), click on hyperlink, then navigate to the name of the data set to find out more about it. To find out about all available data sets, type:

```
data(package=.packages(all.available=TRUE))
```

Remove an Object from Your Active Desktop

Assume you have created an object that you now want to get rid of:

```
rm(meanFun)
```

You can remove *all* active objects this way, just make sure that is really what you want to do!

```
rm(list = ls())
```

Remove Specific Points from an Analysis

To remove just one point:

```
model2=lm(growth[-7]~tannin[-7]) #removes row 7 in these 2 variables
```

To remove more than one point from an analysis:

```
model3=lm(growth[-c(1,7)]~tannin[-c(1,7)]) #removes row 1 and 7 in these 2 variables
```

Remove All Missing Data from a Data Frame or Matrix

There are three ways you could take care of data that is not available (NA), i.e. missing data:

```
newlh=na.omit(lh) OR . . .
newlh=na.exclude(lh)
```

The omit function will filter the NAs whereas exclude will delete them. The following command also works by asking R to include any entries in which the logical answer to the question of whether there are NAs (is.na) is FALSE (! indicates a logical negation).

```
newlh=newlh[!is.na(lh)]
```

Order Factors of a Categorical Variable

First, find out if your variable is a factor:

```
is.factor(beq$CATDOMIN)
[1] TRUE
```

If it is not, you can easily make it so:

```
beq$CATDOMIN=as.factor(beq$CATDOMIN)
```

Next, check to see if it is already ordered:

```
is.ordered(beq$CATDOMIN)
[1] FALSE
```

You will need to know the exact names of the levels:

```
levels(beq$CATDOMIN)
[1] "YES"    "NO"    "YESPLUS"
```

Now you are ready to order the levels to your own preference:

```
beq$CATDOMIN=ordered(beq$CATDOMIN,levels=c("YES", "YESPLUS", "NO"))
```

If your factors came without names, you can set those in this command too:

```
group=ordered(group,levels=c("2", "3", "1"), labels=c("NS adults", "NNS adults", "NS children"))
```

Recode Factors of a Categorical Variable into Different Factors

First, find out if your variable is a factor:

```
is.factor(beq$FIRSTLAN)
[1] TRUE
```

You will need to know the exact names of the levels:

```
levels(beq$FIRSTLAN)
[1] "  " "Afrikaans"  "Albanian" "Arabic"
[5] "Armenian" "Basque" "Bengali" "Boobe"
```

(There are 108 levels! We want to consolidate.)

Now you can begin to form groups:

```
levels(beq$FIRSTLAN)[c(57,93,78,79,80)]="Italic" #the numbers are row numbers
levels(beqmore$FIRSTLAN)[c(27,24,25,26,40,41,42,43,44)]="Germanic"
etc.
```

The plyr library has a nice command that lets us recode intuitively, but it only works if the variable is already a factor:

```
library(plyr) #if needed, install.packages("plyr")
new.obarow$musict1<-revalue(new.obarow$trtmnt1, c("No music No pics"="no music",
"No music Yes pics"="no music", "Yes music No pics"="music", "Yes music Yes pics"="music"))
```

Rename Factor Levels

```
names(ChickWeight)
[1] "weight" "Time"  "Chick"  "Diet"
levels(ChickWeight$Diet)
[1] "1" "2" "3" "4"
levels(ChickWeight$Diet)<-c("Grass", "Feed", "Weeds", "Fruit")
levels(ChickWeight$Diet)
[1] "Grass" "Feed"  "Weeds" "Fruit"
```

Extract One Column from a Matrix and Make a New Variable

```
data=lyster[,'cloze']
data=lyster$cloze #both of these commands are equivalent
```

Convert Numeric Variable to Character Variable (Change a Variable into a Factor)

When your splitting variable is characterized as "character," it will be listed when you click on the "Plot by groups" button in R Commander. If this does not work (and sometimes it seems not to), you can fix it by using the R Console. Just make sure the data set is not attached (detach()) before you run the following code:

```
lyster$condition=factor(lyster$condition)
is.factor(lyster$condition)
[1] TRUE
```

Convert an Array into a Condensed Table

```
library(vcd)
(STD=structable(~Sex+Class+Age,data=Titanic[,,2:1,]))
```

Replace Certain Cells in a Matrix with Something Else

Here I am thinking of a situation where you might import a data set that had a "99" everywhere that data were not entered. To use this data set correctly in R you will need to have NAs in those places. If we assume that m1 is a matrix or vector (this will not work with a data frame), you can use the following command:

```
m1[m1==99]=NA
```

Creating a Vector of Data

This will just put data into one variable:

```
data<-c( 22, 23, . . . )
```

Putting Vectors of Data Together into a Data Frame

```
my.data.frame=data.frame(rt=data, subj=factor(subject), drug=factor(treatment))
```

Note that if "treatment" were already a factor, there would be no need to specify it as such in the data frame.

Adding Columns to a Data Frame

```
new.data.frame<-cbind.data.frame(participant=1:20, my.data.frame)
```

Name the Columns of a Matrix or Data Frame

```
dimnames(Ela.mul)[[2]]=
c("subj", "gp", "d11", "d12", "d13", "d21", "d22", "d23")
```

Here the [[2]] refers to the column names so this is generalizable to any matrix or data frame.

```
Ela.mul
  subj gp d11 d12 d13 d21 d22 d23
1    1  1  19  22  28  16  26  22
2    2  1  11  19  30  12  18  28
```

Subset a Data Frame (Choosing Columns)

You can pick out the columns by their names (this data is in the HSAUR library):

```
Forbes3=Forbes2000[1:3, c("name", "sales", "profits", "assets")]
```

or by their column number:

```
Forbes3=Forbes2000[1:3, c(2,5,6,7)]
```

Note that this subset also chooses only the first three rows. To choose all of the rows, leave the space before the comma blank:

```
Forbes3=Forbes2000[,c(2,5,6,7)]
```

This way of "subsetting" puts the columns into the order that you designate.

You can also subset according to logical criteria. The following command chooses only the rows where assets are more than 1000 (billion):

```
Forbes2000[Forbes2000$assets > 1000, c("name", "sales", "profits", "assets")]
```

Subsetting a Data Frame (Choosing Groups)

To subset in R Commander, go to DATA > ACTIVE DATA SET > SUBSET ACTIVE DATA SET. You will need to know the exact column name of the factor that divides groups, and the exact way each group is specified in that column to put into the "Subset expression" box. The R syntax is:

```
lh2004.beg <- subset(lh2004, subset=LEVEL=="Beginner")
```

Note that a double equal sign (==) should be used after the index column name (LEVEL) and quotation marks should be around the name of the group (in this case, Beginner). This syntax includes all columns in the data set. To fix your independent variable so that it reflects the correct levels, use this command:

```
lh2004.beg$LEVEL <- factor(lh2004.beg$LEVEL)
```

Check your levels:

```
levels(lh2004.beg$LEVEL)
```

If you want to exclude just one level of a group, use the "!=" syntax:

```
lh2004.NOTbeg <- subset(lh2004, subset=LEVEL!="Beginner")
```

This keeps every level except for Beginner.

If you wanted to choose two different variables to subset on, you need to use the "&" function:

```
lh2004.beg&5 <- subset(lh2004, subset=level=="Beginner" & zh_sh==5)
```

You can also use the "|" operator to make an "or" subset with two different variables:

```
lh2004.begOR5 <- subset(lh2004, subset=level=="Beginner" | zh_sh==5)
```

The "select" argument lets you choose only certain columns to subset:

```
lh2004.beg <- subset(lh2004, subset=LEVEL=="Beginner", select=c(PJ_P,R_L,SH_SHCH))
```

Subset a Data Frame When there are Missing Data

First, create a new variable composed of only rows that do not have NAs:

```
library(HSAUR)
na_profits=!is.na(Forbes2000$profits)
```

```
table(na_profits)
Forbes2000[na_profits, c("name", "sales", "profits", "assets")]
```

Subset a Data Frame to Remove Only One Row while Doing Regression

```
model2=update(model1,subset=(tannin !=6)
```

The exclamation point means "not" that point, so this specifies to remove row 6 of the tannin data set for the updated model.

Order Data in a Data Frame

Say we want an index with sales in the order from largest to smallest:

```
order_sales=order(Forbes2000$sales) #in HSAUR library
```

Now we want to link the company name up with the ordered sales. First, rename the column:

```
companies=Forbes2000$name
```

Now order the companies according to their sales:

```
companies[order_sales]
```

Finally, use the ordered sales as the rows and then choose the columns you want to see:

```
Forbes2000[order_sales, c("name", "sales", "profits", "assets")]
```

Change the Order of Rows or Columns in a Data Frame

```
data(Animals,package="MASS")
brain<-Animals[c(1:24,26:25,27:28),]
```

This takes rows 1–24, then row 26, then row 25, then 27–28 and all of the columns since there is a blank after the comma. To change the order of columns, just specify numbers *after* the comma:

```
names(lh2004)
 [1] "LEVEL"  "ZH_SH"  "ZH_Z"   "L_LJ"   "R_L"    "SH_S"   "SH_SHCH"
 [8] "TS_T"   "TS_S"   "TS_CH"  "PJ_P"   "PJ_BJ"  "MJ_M"   "F_V"
[15] "F_X"    "F_FJ"   "R_RJ"
lh2004.2=lh2004[,c(5,7,11,2:4,6,8:10,12:16)]
names(lh2004.2)
 [1] „R_L"    „SH_SHCH" „PJ_P"  „ZH_SH"  „ZH_Z"   „L_LJ"   „SH_S"
 [8] "TS_T"   "TS_S"   "TS_CH"  "PJ_BJ"  "MJ_M"   "F_V"    "F_X"
[15] "F_FJ"
```

Name or Rename Levels of a Variable

```
levels(dataset$gender)
[1] "1" "2"
levels(dataset$gender)=c("female", "male")
levels(gender)
[1] "female" "male"
```

Creating a Factor

The following creates a factor with four numbers, each repeated the number of times specified inside the "c" to create a vector of length 41:

```
TYPE=factor(rep(1:4, c(11,12,10,8)))
```

The following code creates a factor where the numbers 1 through 3 are repeated 20 times each, then cycled through again to create a vector of length 120. A factor can also be created with the gl function ("generate levels"). The following syntax creates the same results as the previous rep command:

```
group=rep(rep(1:3, c(20,20,20)), 2)
```

In the following code, the first argument specifies how many different factors are needed, the second specifies how many times each should be repeated and the third argument specifies the total length. Note that this can work so long as each factor is repeated an equal number of times. What is nice about the gl function is that factor labels can be specified directly inside the command:

```
group=gl(4, 20, 120, labels=c("Quiet", "Medium", "Noisy", "Control")
```

Adding a Created Factor to the End of a Data Frame

Assume that TYPE is a created factor:

```
lh2003=cbind(lh2003,TYPE)
```

Changing the Ordering of Factor Levels Without Using the "Ordered" Command

First, find out the current order of factor levels in the murphy data set (Murphy.Repeated Measures.sav):

```
levels(murphy$group)
[1] "NS children" "NS adults"   "NNS adults"
summary(murphy$group)
NS children   NS adults  NNS adults
         20          20          20
```

Now, change the factor order so that NS adults are first, NNS adults are second and NS children are third:

```
murphy$group=factor(rep(rep(c(3,1,2),c(20,20,20))))
```

Relabel "group" with level labels in the order of the numbers—the actual order in the list has not changed, but R will interpret the first name as corresponding to #1 and so on:

```
levels(murphygroup)=c("NS adults", "NNS adults", "NS children")
```

Divide a Continuous Variable into Groups to Make Factors

This can be done in R Commander. Choose DATA > MANAGE VARIABLES IN ACTIVE DATA SET > BIN NUMERIC VARIABLE. The R command is:

```
ChickWeight$timecat = bin.var(ChickWeight$Time, bins=3, method='natural', labels=c('early','mid','older'))
```

This command divides the continuous variable into three partitions.

Sample Randomly from a List of Numbers

Suppose you want to generate a matrix that samples randomly from the numbers 1 through 5, which might represent a 5-point Likert scale. The following command will generate a 100-row (assume that is the number of respondents) and 10-column (assume that is the number of items they responded to) matrix:

```
v1=matrix(sample(c(1:5),size=1000,replace=T),ncol=10)
```

Obviously, you could change this to specify the numbers that would be sampled, the number of columns and the number of rows.

Creating Nicely Formatted Tables

```
library(Epi) #first install.packages ("Epi")
stat.table(group, list(count(),mean(value)),data=murphy.long) #use file created on p. 414
```

```
--------------------------------------
group            count() mean(value)
--------------------------------------
NS children          120        4.33
NS adults            120        3.74
NNS adults           120        4.12
--------------------------------------
```

Create a Table, Summarize Means Over Groups

The tapply function is quite useful in creating summary tables. The generic syntax is:

```
tapply(X, INDEX, FUNCTION)
```

where X could be thought of as a response variable, INDEX as the explanatory variable(s) and FUNCTION as any kind of summary function such as mean, median, standard deviation, length, etc.

```
tapply(murphy.long$value, list(murphy.long$type, murphy.long$similarity), mean)
```

```
       distant      int    proto
irreg 4.450000 3.050000 2.833333
reg   4.516667 4.766667 4.766667
```

Change All of the Names to Lower Case

```
names(airquality)<-tolower(names(airquality))
```

Graphics

Demonstration of Some Cool Graphics

```
demo(graphics)
```

Other Interesting Demonstration Files

```
demo(lm.glm)
```

Choose a Color that You Like

```
library(epitools)
colors.plot(TRUE) #choose colors then menu STOP > STOP LOCATOR
```

This command activates a locator and you click on the colors you like from the R Graphics device. The names of the colors you click on will now show up in the R Console.

Placing More than One Graphic in the Graphics Device

Use the parameter setting to specify the number of rows, then columns:

```
par(mfrow=c(2,3)) #two rows, 3 columns
```

Getting Things Out of R Into Other Programs

Round Numbers

This command rounds off the value of the first argument (a vector) to the specified number of places. This can be useful for cutting and pasting R output into a manuscript:

```
round(x, 2)
```

Getting Data Out of R

If you wanted to save a data set that you worked with in R, write.table(object1,"file1") is the command to use. However, it is much easier to do this by using R Commander, which gives you a variety of options and lets you choose the file you will save it at. In R Commander, choose DATA > ACTIVE DATA SET > EXPORT ACTIVE DATA SET. If you choose "spaces" as a field separator, your file will be a .txt file. If you choose "commas," you can append the .csv designation to the name of your file, which means it is a comma-delimited .csv file. A program like Excel can open either of these types of files, but there are fewer steps if the file is .csv than .txt.

Troubleshooting

Understanding Error Messages

Quite often error messages are cryptic. The first thing you should suspect is a typing error. Fox (2002b) suggested that if you get an error telling you "object not found," suspect a typing error or that you have forgotten to attach the object or the library that contains the object. Fox also suggested that the traceback command can provide some help, showing the steps of the command that were undertaken:

```
traceback()
```

Getting Out of a Function that Will Not Converge or Whose Syntax You have Typed Incorrectly

Click on the ESC button on your keyboard.

Resetting the Contrasts Option for Regression

This is the default contrast setting in R:

```
options(contrast=c("contr.treatment", "contr.poly")
```

Miscellaneous

Trimmed Means if there are Missing Data

To get the 20% trimmed means, it is necessary to use the na.rm=T argument (which removes NA entries), as the mean command will not work with missing data (NAs) in the data column:

```
mean(murphy.long$value,tr=.2,na.rm=T)
[1] 4.412037
```

Using the Equal Sign instead of the Arrow Combination

According to Verzani (2004; www.math.csi.cuny.edu/Statistics/R/simpleR) the arrow combination ("<-") had to be used as the assignment operator prior to R version 1.5.0. I often use the equal sign as it requires less typing.

Calculating the Standard Error of the Means

R does not have function for the standard error (SE) of the means, but it is easy to calculate because SE is just the square root of the variance, divided by the number of observations. The SE makes it easy to find the confidence interval for those means:

```
se<-function(x)
        {
        y<-x[!is.na(x)] #remove the missing values
        sqrt(var(as.vector(y))/length(y))
        }
```

Once you have defined your function, you can use it with **tapply** to get a table:

```
lyster.long$compscoreIND=list(lyster.long$cond, lyster.long$time), FUN=se)
```

```
tapply(lyster$condition,IND=list(lyster$group, lyster$sex), FUN=se) #use the lyster.long file
#created on p. 415
```

	pretaskcompl	post1taskcompl	post2taskcompl
FFIrecast	1.1109385	1.0315819	0.9712495
FFIprompt	0.6716374	0.7190319	0.8322428
FFIonly	0.8349246	0.9678548	0.9556926
Comparison	0.6792809	0.6057523	0.7194876

Suppress Stars that Show "Statistical Significance"

This can be placed in the **Rprofile** file of R's etc. subdirectory for permanent use, or can be used temporarily if simply entered into R Console in a session:

```
options(show.signif.stars=F)
```

Load a Data Set that is Already in R, so R Commander Can See It

```
data(ChickWeight)
```

Check Which Objects You have Attached and Packages You have Opened in Your Workspace

```
search()
```

Glossary

95% confidence interval A range for any parameter that specifies where the true parameter will be found in 95 cases out of 100 if the test were repeated that many times.

Alpha (α) In a regression equation, the alpha is the intercept. It is a constant number that is generated from doing the regression and it is the same for all individuals.

Alpha level (α-level) The point we choose for deciding whether a *p*-value is extreme or not. In the field of second language research, the alpha level is generally set at $\alpha = 0.05$.

Alternative hypothesis (H_a) A hypothesis that posits that there is a relationship between variables or that there is a difference between groups. It can be accepted if you can reject the null hypothesis.

ANOVA A model that includes at least one categorical independent variable. We are basically interested in seeing whether groups defined by the independent variable or variables performed differently on the dependent measure. The statistic returned by the ANOVA is an *F*-ratio.

Array An array is a collection of data; a one-dimensional array is a vector; a two-dimensional array is a matrix; arrays can be larger than two dimensions as well.

Assumptions When you use a statistical test there are certain assumptions that are made about your data. For parametric statistics these assumptions are that your data are normally distributed and if there are groups that they have equal variances (homogeneity). Data should also be independent, i.e. one person's score does not affect another person's score. For a correlation, there is an assumption that the relationship between the variables is linear. Checking your data numerically and graphically can help you determine if your data meet the assumptions of the test. If your data do not meet the assumptions of the test, then you will have less power to find the true results.

Assurance (Represented by the Greek letter gamma—γ) is the "probability expressed as a percentage, that our sample MOE is no greater than target MOE" (Cumming, 2012, p. 370).

Bar graph A graphic that divides data into results obtained by different groups. It is appropriately used for counts of data, but often poorly used to show mean scores by the height of the bar for different groups.

Beta (β) In multiple regression output, beta (β) is the standardized regression coefficient. Some people use standardized coefficients to compare the strength of the predictor variables, but I have instead recommended using the change in R^2. In addition, in a regression equation, beta is the slope. It is a number that is multiplied by the data (x) for each person. In a regression with more than one variable, there will be several betas, and these are called partial coefficients (because they only partially give the slope if considered singly).

Between-groups design A name for a research design where people are members of one and only one level of a group.

Between-groups independent variable See **Between-groups variable.**

Between-groups variable A variable that divides people into groups and each person is a member of one and only one level of a group. In other words, people participate in only one condition of the experiment for that variable.

Between-subjects variable See **Between-groups variable.**

Bias-corrected and accelerated bootstrap Developed by Efron in 1987, the bias-corrected and accelerated (BCa) bootstrap adjusts for the median not being equal to the mean.

Bimodal A distribution that has two or more highest points.

Bivariate correlation See **Correlation.**

Bonferroni correction An adjustment made to the alpha level whereby the alpha level is divided by the number of tests. This results in a new alpha level, and to be statistical a test must be below this level. This test is very conservative, especially when adjusting for a large number of tests.

Bootstrapping Procedure where values are randomly resampled from the original sample of data to form new samples.

Box plot A graph conceived by Tukey that uses a box to enclose the middle part of the data (the 25th to 75th percentile of the data). The box plot shows a median line and then whiskers drawn out from the box to the minimum and maximum points, unless those points lie beyond one and a half times the length of the box, in which case they are labeled as outliers. The box plot is the best graphic for examining the distribution of data when there are groups involved (much better than a bar graph).

Categorical variable A variable that is divided up into categories that have no inherent numerical value but are just named. An example would be first-language background. This is also called a nominal variable.

Chi-square test A non-parametric test that uses only nominal data for both the dependent and the independent variable. It tests whether there is a relationship between two variables. This test is not the only one that is based on the chi-square distribution (some of the non-parametric tests in Chapter 14 (online) are as well), but this test has become known as the chi-square test.

Cohen's *d* An effect size that measures the difference between two independent sample means. This is a group difference index of effect size. Cohen's *d* can start from zero and range as high as it needs to, although a $d = 1$, meaning the differences between groups are as large as one standard deviation, would generally be considered a large effect size.

Cohen's f^2 An effect size that measures differences between groups and is generally appropriate for multiple regression or ANOVA. This is a group index of effect size, but it is not used as frequently as Cohen's *d*. Cohen's f^2 can start from zero and range as high as it needs to. It measures differences between groups in terms of the number of standard deviations they differ by.

Compound symmetry A sum of squares and cross-products (SSCP) matrix has compound symmetry if the numbers on the diagonal (which are the sums of squares of the variable) are of similar size, and the numbers off the diagonal (cross-products of pairs of variables) are also of similar size (but they need not be the same size as the numbers on the diagonal).

Confidence interval The range of values around a statistic such as the mean that defines the range where the true population value of the statistic will be found on repeated testing of the research question, with 95% confidence.

Contingency table A table with two or more rows and two or more columns that examines the intersection of categorical variables such that all the events that could happen can be seen (all contingencies!). The numbers inside the grid represent counts. Such tables are commonly made when using a chi-square analysis on categorical (nominal) data.

Continuous variable A group of data measured with numbers that have a wide range of possible answers. A continuous variable is opposed to a categorical variable.

Cook's distance A diagnostic test in multiple regression that measures the influence of one case on the whole regression; values higher than 1 are cause for concern that there are influential outliers.

Coplot A conditioning plot is a graphic that we saw used to show complex relationships among three or four continuous variables.

Correlation A statistical test that measures the strength of a relationship between two variables, for example, between language learning aptitude and intelligence. The higher the correlation positively or negativelly, the stronger the relationship.

Covariate A variable that is entered into an ANOVA model and which the researcher includes not so much to examine its effect on the dependent variable but to subtract out its influence from the other independent variables. A covariate is indeed also an independent variable, and as such its statistical influence on the dependent variable can also be considered.

Cramer's *V* An effect size for a chi-square analysis that has only categorical variables. It is a variant of phi that is used when there are more than two rows or two columns in the contingency table.

Critical value The number above which the test statistic will be considered statistical for a given distribution and given degrees of freedom.

Cronbach's alpha (α) A measure of internal consistency, it is the ratio of variability attributable to subjects divided by the variability attributed to the intersection between subjects and items.

***d*-family of effect sizes** See **Group difference index**. The term was coined by Rosenthal (1994). This family of effect sizes measures how much groups vary in terms of standard deviations of difference.

Data To conduct a statistical analysis you need information, and this is your data. You obtain data by conducting some type of experiment or analysis. Statistical analysis can only be used with quantitative data, or data which can be measured (not all data can!). Data comes in different forms, and may be measured by different types of variables—categorical, ordinal, or interval.

Data Editor The first window that SPSS brings up when you open the program; it is the area that looks like a spreadsheet, where the data are entered.

Data frame This is a traditional table with columns and rows.

Data view One of the tabs in the Data Editor of SPSS. This is where you see the data arranged with columns representing variables and rows representing individual data observations (usually participants in second language research).

Degrees of freedom A number that is reported in conjunction with a statistic and specifies the number of components that are free to be chosen. Think of a bowl of 10 marbles—how much freedom is there to choose the first marble? There are 10 choices. For the second marble, there are only nine choices. By the 10th marble, there are no choices—you must pick the last marble. Therefore, $10 - 1 = 9$ degrees of freedom for choosing the order of the marbles in.

Dependent variable The variable that is of direct interest in the experiment, usually thought of as the "data" that is collected, the one which shows outcomes. This variable might be scores on a proficiency test, number of errors in a writing assignment, number of vocabulary words learned or number of words elicited in Spanish. Also called the **response variable** in a multiple regression.

Descriptive statistics Statistics such as the mean, median and standard deviation, which are calculated from the sample of people (or texts or test scores) who participated in the experiment.

df See **Degrees of Freedom**.

Dichotomous variable A variable with only two choices. By necessity, this will be an ordinal or categorical variable, not a continuous variable.

Directional test See **One-tailed test**.

Effect size An effect size measures how much effect can be attributed to the influence of an independent variable on a dependent variable, or to the relationship between variables. Effect sizes do not depend on sample size. Basically, effect sizes tell you how important your statistical result is (i.e. whether it is "statistically significant" or not). Measures include Cohen's *d*, partial eta-squared, Pearson's *r* and R^2.

Error sum of squares (SSE) The total of the sum of squares calculated separately for each group. This gives a measure of the variance calculated for each group separately (within each group). In SPSS, this number is found in the "Within" line of the ANOVA table.

Explanatory variables Another name for independent variables; I have used this term with multiple regression because these variables are trying to explain parts of the variance of the response variable. For example, you might measure language learning aptitude, motivation and level of anxiety to explain students' scores on a language proficiency test, such as the Test of English as a Foreign Language (TOEFL). The measurements for aptitude, motivation and anxiety will be your explanatory variables. You will try to explain differences in TOEFL scores through the differences in scores on aptitude, motivation and anxiety.

Factor Another name for an independent variable.

Factorial ANOVA A parametric test that has two or more independent variables and one dependent variable. It is used to test for interactions between the independent variables.

False discovery rate (FDR) A correction applied to *p*-values to control the familywise error rate, which has much more power to find differences than the too conservative Bonferroni correction. The FDR was devised by Benjamini and Hochberg (1995); p. 287 gives a simple command for calculating the FDR.

Familywise error rate (FWER) The amount of type I error that you allow to enter into your statistical calculations. If you run a large number of statistical tests all concerning the same research question then you need to think about controlling the FWER by using some type of correction. (Bonferroni is quite conservative, and I have recommended the FDR in this text.)

Fixed effects Fixed effects are those whose parameters are fixed and are the only ones we want to consider. Fixed effects have informative labels for factor levels, and the factor levels exhaust the possibilities. For fixed effects we are interested in the levels that are in our study and we do not want to generalize further. Examples of fixed effects are treatment type, gender, status as native speaker, child versus adult, L1 and target language (TL).

Frequency counts A count of how often a certain value occurs in a data set; counts of frequency data can be displayed visually in a histogram, stem and leaf plots or bar graphs.

Greenhouse–Geisser correction A correction that is used when data in a repeated-measures ANOVA do not satisfy the assumption of sphericity. Some authors (Howell, 2002) recommend always using a correction even if statistical tests indicate that your data do satisfy the assumption of sphericity. The Greenhouse–Geisser correction is more conservative than the Huynh–Feldt correction.

Group difference index A type of effect size that measures the difference between two independent sample means, and expresses how large the difference is in standard deviations. Cohen's *d*, for example, is a group difference index. This effect size may be larger than 1, although a $d = 1$ is generally considered a large effect. This is also called a *d*-family effect size.

Heteroscedasticity The condition when the variances of the groups in question are different; the opposite condition is homoscedasticity, which is a general assumption for all parametric statistical tests.

Hierarchical multiple regression See **Sequential multiple regression.**

Histogram A graphic that divides data up into partitions and, in the usual case, gives a frequency count of the number of scores contained in each partition (called a bin).

Homogeneity of regression slopes (assumption) An assumption for an analysis of covariance (ANCOVA) which says that the slopes of all of the groups on the cross between the dependent variable and the covariate should be similar. In other words, the relationship between the covariate and the dependent variable is constant across different treatment levels.

Homogeneity of variance (assumption) An assumption used by all (parametric/ inferential) statistical tests that, if there are groups, their variances should be the same (or their standard deviations, because the variance is just the square of the standard deviation). In a regression, it means the error variance around the regression line is the same for all values of the explanatory variables.

Homoscedasticity The condition of having homogeneity of variance.

Huynh–Feldt correction A correction that is used when data in a repeated-measures ANOVA do not satisfy the assumption of sphericity. Some authors (Howell, 2002) recommend always using a correction even if statistical tests indicate that your data do satisfy the assumption of sphericity. The Huynh–Feldt correction is more liberal (and thus more powerful) than the Greenhouse–Geisser correction.

Hypothesis A formal statement of what you expect to find when you conduct your experiment.

Independence (assumption) An assumption in many statistical tests (except for the ones that measure the same people on more than one experimental condition) that one person's scores will not affect another person's scores, or that the behavior of one person will not affect the behavior of another. Independence is required whether a test is parametric or non-parametric.

Independent samples *t*-test A parametric test that can tell you whether scores of two separate groups on one measure are statistically different from one another.

Independent variable The variable the researcher thinks will influence outcomes, often controlled by the researcher in experimental work. This variable might be group membership, first language background, gender or the number of times a person attends a chat group in a language. Independent variables are also called **explanatory variables.**

Inferential statistics Statistics that generalize to the population that a sample was randomly drawn from, meaning that the results of a statistical test may be generalized to a wider group of people (or texts or test scores) than just those who participated in the experiment.

Interaction When there is more than one independent variable (IV) in an ANOVA we may find that the effect of the IVs is different depending on how the IVs are combined. For example, looking at the IVs of age and L1 on reading ability in Chinese L2, if we find that being older when you start learning an L2 is difficult no matter whether you have L1 English or L1 Japanese, the IVs are parallel. However, if we find that being older is only more difficult if your L1 is English but not Japanese, then there is an interaction between the two variables.

Interquartile range (IQR) The 25th to 75th percentile of the data. This is another way of examining the central part of a distribution.

Inter-rater reliability Measures the extent to which all of the data (that came from judges who rated something) agree.

Interval scale A scale where all the points on the scale are equally distant from one another, for example, scores on a test where we assume that the difference between receiving a 71 and a 72 is the same as the difference in receiving a 41 versus a 42. An interval scale measures **continuous variables.**

Kendall rank correlation coefficient (Kendall's tau-b) A non-parametric test of correlation that is preferred with ordinal data.

Kolmogorov–Smirnov test A non-parametric test that examines a data set to assess its normality. I do not recommend using this test as your sole source of information about normality because when your data set is small it is not very sensitive to deviations from normality and when your data set is large it is too sensitive to deviations. I prefer visual judgment of normality, and tried to show that when data sets are small it may be impossible to accurately judge if the data come from a normal distribution or not.

Kruskal–Wallis test A non-parametric counterpart to the one-way ANOVA. It should be used when you have one independent variable with three or more levels and one dependent variable.

Kurtosis A concept that refers to the shape of a distribution curve, whether it is pointy or flat in the middle. If it is pointy with a small range of values (i.e. there are too many data points in the center of the distribution), it is called **leptokurtic**; if it is flat with a wide range of values (i.e. it is too flat at the peak of the normal curve), it is called **platykurtic.**

Least-squares principle This principle says that the line which best fits a collection of points is one where the sum of squares has been applied.

Leptokurtic A curve that has too many scores collected in the center of the distribution.

Level Used to define different groupings within a categorical (usually independent) variable. For example, if the categories are experimental groups and there are three of them, then there are three levels for the variable of group.

Levene's test A formal statistical test of the assumption of homogeneity of variances. The hypothesis is that variances are homogeneous, so that a *p*-value of less than 0.05 means we must reject the null hypothesis and accept the hypothesis that variances are heterogeneous. I do not recommend using this test as your sole source of information about homogeneity, as it suffers from too much sensitivity when data sets are large and not enough sensitivity (power) when data sets are small (Dalgaard, 2002; Wilcox, 2003).

Likert scale A scale often used in questionnaires that asks participants to rate some idea using a range of numbers, usually not more than 10. A typical Likert scale may have five points, where 1 = strongly agree, 2 = somewhat agree, 3 = neutral, 4 = somewhat disagree and 5 = strongly disagree. Most researchers treat this type of data as interval data, although strictly speaking it may not be.

Linearity An assumption in a correlation is that the relationship between two variables can best be described by a straight line, and this is the assumption of linearity. I have suggested that the best way to assess this assumption is visual comparison of a regression line against a Loess line.

Loess line A running-line smoother that follows the trend of the data. It is useful to compare a straight regression line with a Loess line to see whether the data are linear or not.

McNemar's test A non-parametric test that can be used when all variables contain categorical (nominal) data.

Mahalanobis distance A diagnostic for multiple regression that investigates influential outliers. Values that would be a cause for concern here depend on the sample size.

Main effect The effect of a variable, by itself, on the dependent variable. In an ANOVA analysis, this can be compared to an interaction effect, which is the effect that two variables together have on the dependent variable. It is also called a simple effect.

Mann–Whitney U test A non-parametric alternative to the independent samples *t*-test. It is used when you have an independent variable with just two groups and one dependent variable. It is essentially the same as the Wilcoxon rank-sum test.

Margin of error (MOE) The MOE is the estimate of variability around the standard error. It is a statistic expressing the amount of random sampling error in a survey's results.

Matched samples t-test See **Paired samples t-test.**

Matrix In R, a matrix is a type of data format where all of the data must be in the same format, either numeric (numbers) or character (categorical data).

Mean (X or M) The average of a group of numbers.

Median The point at which 50% of the scores are higher and 50% of the scores are lower.

Minimal adequate model. This type of regression model is one that starts with a maximal number of terms or variables, and then through testing, the terms are whittled down to only statistical terms, or statistical interactions and their supporting main effects. (So if the interaction of Time × Group is statistical, one needs to keep the main effect of Group and Time both.)

Mixed between/within ANOVA Another name for a **repeated-measures ANOVA**; an ANOVA that has both a between-groups independent variable (such as group membership, gender, L1) and a within-groups independent variable (such as pretest and posttest scores, scores on both a semantic and a syntactic section of a related test or scores from each of the experimental groups).

Mixed models A type of analysis that uses a more sophisticated measure of difference between points and the mean than the least-squares principle (namely, it uses restricted maximum likelihood) and is less biased than the RM-ANOVA procedure, does not need to satisfy the assumption of sphericity, and deals with missing data better than the RM-ANOVA.

Mode The most frequently occurring score in the data set.

Multicollinearity A situation that is examined in regression and looks at the amount of correlation that exists among explanatory variables. If there is multicollinearity it means that the variables are too closely related and thus should not be entered into a regression because they explain the same part of the variance.

Multiple imputation A technique which fills in values that are missing in your data by analyzing the other values, predicting the value of the missing data, and adding randomness to the data. If your missing data do not have a clear pattern (missing at random), it is a better choice for dealing with missing data than pairwise or listwise deletion.

Multiple regression A test used when you have two or more continuous variables and one is the response variable (dependent variable) and one or more are explanatory variables (independent variables). The point of a multiple regression is to find out how much of the variance in scores the explanatory variables explain or predict future performance on the response variable.

Multivariate analysis of variance (MANOVA) This is used when you want to examine the effects of more than one related dependent variable at a time. It is not a common procedure in second language research, so I have not demonstrated it in this book.

Negatively skewed A distribution where the majority of the cases are found in the upper end of the scale and the tail is long to the left side of the distribution.

Nominal scale A scale that does not really measure at all but labels groups or things as belonging to one class or another, for example, experimental group or L1 classification. A nominal scale measures a **categorical variable.**

Non-orthogonal data. Data that is not complete, that is missing values, is said to be non-orthogonal.

Non-parametric statistics Statistics that do not depend on the data having a normal distribution, but which still impose assumptions on data distribution, such as the requirement that variances be equal across groups. Examples are the Mann–Whitney U test and the Kruskal–Wallis one-way ANOVA. Many robust statistics used in this book are also non-parametric.

Normal distribution A distribution of data where the probability curve follows a bell-shaped distribution. Normal distributions are symmetric around their mean. The requirement for a normal distribution is exact; the data must come from this particular distribution. However, verifying this fact with small sample sizes is usually impossible.

Null hypothesis A hypothesis that there is no relationship among variables or that there will be no difference between groups or variables. It is represented by "H_0" and can be tested statistically. Often this is not the real hypothesis that researchers want to test, but they set it up so that it will be easy to find data to refute it. (For example, "There is no relationship between smoking and the incidence of lung cancer".) If the *p*-value is below 0.05, we may reject the null hypothesis.

Null hypothesis significance testing (NHST) An approach to testing statistics that features a null hypothesis and estimation of the conditional probability of the data with statistical tests. It focuses on *p*-values as the important criterion to use to determine whether the null hypothesis can be rejected or not. It also provides an alternative hypothesis that can be accepted if the null hypothesis is rejected. For an excellent and readable critique of problems with NHST, see Kline (2004) as well as Cumming (2012).

Odds ratio An alternative to an effect size, an odds ratio tells you how likely one event is in comparison with another event. This type of summary number is sometimes recommended as being more intuitively understandable than an effect size. People have heard of odds ratios such as "You are ten times more likely to die by age 50 if you smoke than if you don't."

Omnibus test In an ANOVA, an omnibus test reveals whether a given factor can be considered statistical or not. If there are more than two levels within this variable, the omnibus test cannot reveal which levels are statistically different from each other. This will need to be ascertained through a post-hoc test.

One-tailed test Returns a probability that the sample statistic could be as extreme as or larger than only either the positive or negative value of the statistic. In other words, it uses only one side of the distribution to test the hypothesis. One-tailed tests should be used with caution and mostly if there has been previous research showing the direction of influence, but they can give you more power to find differences.

One-way ANOVA A parametric test that has one dependent variable (such as score on a test) and one independent variable (such as experimental group). It is usually used when there are three or more levels in the independent variable, but can be used when there are only two (in which case a *t*-test could also be used). The one-way ANOVA asks whether groups differ in their performance on the dependent variable.

Operationalize Take an abstract idea and make it measurable.

Ordinal scale A scale that measures a property in relation to others (ranking), but where the steps between the measurements may not be equal, for example, measures of language anxiety or amount of language usage.

Orthogonal data These are data that are complete and not missing any values for any of the participants (or rows).

Outlier A point or points which do not fit with the rest of the data trends. Means can be substantially skewed (biased) by outliers, while medians are not.

Paired samples t-test A parametric test that can tell you whether the scores of two groups where the same people were tested twice are statistically different from one another.

Pairwise comparisons These are comparisons between only two mean scores and, as such, are really the same as post-hoc tests.

Parameter The value of a sampling statistic (such as a mean) or a test statistic (such as an r) in the population, not just in the particular sample taken.

Parametric statistics Also known as inferential statistics, parametric statistics rely on data fulfilling stringent assumptions of having a normal distribution, having equal variances between groups, having interval-scale (continuous) data and being independent.

Partial coefficient This is the beta (β) in a regression equation with more than one explanatory variable. The output of a regression equation will give you the value of each beta, and these are multiplied by the score of the person on each variable to obtain the slope for that particular variable.

Partial correlation A type of correlation where three variables are involved. This type of correlation is used when you want to get rid of the influence of the third variable.

Pearson's correlation The technical name for a correlation test that is parametric and inferential; correlation formally tests for a covariance in scores between two interval-level variables. This test asks whether there is a relationship between two variables.

Percentage variance (PV) effect size An effect size that measures how much of the variance of the dependent variable the variable in question explains. For example, the age that a person begins learning a second language has been found to explain about 50% of their ultimate proficiency in many language areas. This 50% is a PV effect size. This number can go only from 0 to 1 (or 0 to 100 if expressed in a percentage).

Phi (ϕ) An effect size that can be calculated for a chi-square (all nominal variables) statistical test where both variables have only two levels (they are dichotomous).

Planned comparisons A planned comparison can be used instead of an omnibus test and post-hoc tests in an ANOVA. Planned comparisons are usually used in order to retain more power to find statistical differences. Post-hoc comparisons will test all possible pairs, but, if the researcher is not interested in all pairs, using planned comparisons will help preserve more of the 5% alpha level that gets diluted with more comparisons in post-hoc tests. For example, if a test has an IV of L1 background and you have four levels—L1 French, L1 German, L1 Turkish, and L1 Dutch—you may decide beforehand you do not want to test all of these levels against each other. Instead, what you are really interested in is the comparison between L1 Turkish and all the other L1s together. In this way, you end up doing only one comparison, and you reserve more power (more of the p-value) to find real differences rather than splitting the p-value by conducting six separate tests to see if all of the L1 groups are different from each other. Planned comparisons may also be used by researchers interested in a comparison different from simple pairs, such as A and B versus C.

Platykurtic See **Kurtosis.**

Point-biserial correlation (r_{pb}) A correlation between one dichotomous variable (only two possible choices) and a continuous variable. This test asks whether there is a relationship between variables.

Population The wider group of people (or texts or test scores) that you would like your experiment to say something about. Most of the time authors do not state what their particular population is, and you must infer it. In the second language research field an intended population may be all English as a second language (ESL) learners in a particular country, but this may be overreaching if only a few ESL learners at one particular university are tested!

Positively skewed A distribution where the majority of the cases are found in the lower end of the scale and the tail is long to the right side of the distribution.

Post-hoc test So-called because it is performed after an omnibus test in an ANOVA, it finds a statistical difference between levels of a variable. The post-hoc test performs paired tests between groups or levels to find out which levels are statistically different from one another. The post-hoc test will perform all permutations of paired comparisons, so if there are three levels there will be three comparisons (AB, AC, BC), if there are four levels there will be six comparisons (AB, AC, AD, BC, BD, CD), and so on.

Power The probability of detecting a statistical result when there are in fact differences between groups or relationships between variables. You may think of power in terms of looking through a microscope—if it has sufficient power to see the details, you will be able to see the true situation, but if the power is too low you will not be able to find out any useful information. It is suggested that a power of 0.80 is a good level to try for.

Precision Precision in the "new statistics" is similar to power in the "old statistics". Precision refer to the length of one arm of the confidence interval, which is the MOE (margin of error). We can calculate how many participants are needed in a study design by determining a target precision level.

***p*-value** The probability that we would find a statistic as large as the one we found if the null hypothesis were true.

Quantile-Quantile plot (Q-Q plot) A graphic that plots the quantiles of the data under consideration against the quantiles of the normal distribution.

Quantitative approach An approach to collecting and analyzing data that focuses on collecting measurements that can be represented by numbers. This approach asserts that there is one objective, verifiable truth. This type of research is often thought to be reliable because it can be replicated.

***r*-family of effect sizes** See **Relationship index.** The term was coined by Rosenthal (1994); this family of effect sizes measures how much the independent and dependent variables vary together.

Random effects Random effects are those effects where we want to generalize beyond the parameters that constitute the variable. Random effects do not have informative factor levels, and the factor levels do not exhaust the possibilities. We want to generalize beyond the levels in our study if we have a random effect. A "subject" term is clearly a random effect, because we want to generalize the results of our study beyond those particular individuals who took the test. Other examples of random effects are the particular words or sentences used in a study, the classroom or the school test. Note that the difference between fixed and random factors is *not* the same as between-subject and within-subject factors.

Randomize The process of randomly collecting data from a sample that adequately represents the population you intend to test. Testing intact classes would not be random selection of participants for an experiment. Getting a list of all volunteers for a study and then randomly selecting a smaller number of the volunteers would be a good way to randomize data, but perhaps not a very realistic method in the field of second language research!

Random variables See **Random effects.**

Range A single number that shows the distance between the minimum and maximum points. For example, if the maximum score on a test was 199 and the minimum was 76, the range would be 123. Ranges can be greatly affected by outliers.

Ratio scale A scale where all the points on the scale are equally distant from one another and there is a true zero point that signifies a lack of that quality. Age is a good example of a ratio scale.

Regression See **Multiple regression.**

Regression coefficient In a multiple regression, the regression coefficient is the number that is put in front of the variable to create the regression equation, like this: TOEFL score = 29.2 + 10.1*Hours of study + 12.6*MLAT score. In this example, the 10.1 and the 12.6 are regression coefficients. Regression coefficients are reported in a standardized (beta or β) and unstandardized (B) form. I recommended not using the standardized regression coefficients to compare the strength of the variables; instead, use the change in R^2.

Regression line A line drawn on a scatterplot that is the best fit to the data. When the regression line slopes up, this indicates a positive correlation; sloping down indicates a negative correlation. A horizontal line indicates no relationship at all between the variables.

Regression model An equation that models the relationship between two or more variables by means of a regression equation, e.g. TOEFL score = constant + hours of study + MLAT score.

R Graphics Device This is the window that pops up and displays graphs when you call for them in R Commander or the R Console.

Reject the null hypothesis If your *p*-value is sufficiently large, this means the probability of finding a statistic as large as or larger than was found, given that the null hypothesis is true, is over the acceptable limit (usually set at 0.05). In this case, you can reject the null hypothesis.

Relationship index A type of effect size that measures how much an independent and dependent variable vary together or, in other words, the amount of covariation in the two variables. Pearson's *r* statistic, for example, is a relationship index. When squared, this type of effect size is also called a percentage variance effect size because it is interpreted as how much of the variance in one variable is explained by the other variable. This effect size ranges from 0 to 1 for both the non-squared and squared versions of the effect size, although how large the effect size is, is interpreted differently depending on whether it is a squared or a non-squared measurement. This is also called the ***r*-family of effect sizes.**

Reliability DeVellis (2005) defines it as the "proportion of variability in a measure ascribed to the true score" (p. 317). Mackey and Gass (2005) define consistency in a test instrument as being a reliable test; in other words, a person would receive the same score if they took the test again. A study should report the reliability of any test instruments used in the study, but reliability is only a valid construct in the sense of the reliability of a test with a certain sample of test takers. Thus, you should not report the reliability of a test given by someone else in lieu of your own reliability statistics.

Repeated-measures ANOVA An ANOVA that has a within-groups independent variable (such as pretest and posttest scores, scores on both a semantic and a syntactic section of a related test, or scores from each of the experimental groups). If there is only one within-group variable with just two levels, then this would be a paired samples *t*-test.

Research question A question you have that has motivated you to conduct your research. The research question does not need to be posed as a formal hypothesis; it can just be a common-sense formulation of the question that you hold.

Residual In a regression equation, this is the part that cannot be explained by any of the posited explanatory variables. It is also called the error. Obviously, we want to minimize this number. The smaller this number is, the larger the percentage of variance that is explained by the explanatory variables.

Response variable Another name for dependent variable. In a regression, this is the variable you are trying to predict. For example, you might measure language learning aptitude, motivation and level of anxiety to explain students' scores on a language proficiency test, such as the TOEFL. The TOEFL score would be the response variable. You will try to explain differences in TOEFL scores through differences in the other variables you have measured.

Robust statistics Statistics that do not depend on the data having a normal distribution or, in fact, any certain type of distribution.

Sample The actual people (or texts or test scores) who participate in the experiment. They will hopefully be representative of the population you would like to test.

Sample size (*N*) The number of participants in a study. This is often represented by the letter *N*, upper or lower case.

Sampling distribution The probability distribution of data obtained from repeated samples of the population. For example, if you test a large number of samples from a population and calculate their mean score on a test, their scores will form a distribution that can be examined to discover the probability of receiving that particular score. This distribution is called the sampling distribution.

Sampling error Variation in scores that cannot be attributed to any factors that we have tested. The term "error" makes it sound as though there has been a mistake, but really error is the part of the score that we cannot explain.

Sampling statistic A number that measures something about the sample that has been collected. Examples are the mean and standard deviation of the scores of a sample.

Scatterplot A graphic which plots two interval-level variables against each other; this is an excellent graph for displaying a large amount of information and for showing relationships among variables.

Sequential multiple regression A type of multiple regression where the explanatory variables (also known as independent variables) are entered into the equation in steps. The model counts all areas of overlap of the explanatory variable with the response variable (the dependent variable) so that the order in which variables are entered into the model can often make a difference as to whether they will be found to be statistical predictors. The researcher tells the computer what order variables should be entered in. See **Hierarchical multiple regression.**

Significance level See **Alpha level.**

Simple effects After a more complicated ANOVA, one can examine the effects of one factor (with a number of levels) at just one level of the other factor and this is called a simple effect. There are no interactions involved.

Simple interaction effects After a more complicated ANOVA, we can break down the interaction to examine simple interaction effects when we look at the interaction of two factors at one level of a third factor. So we are still examining an interaction, but only at one level of a third factor.

Skewness A concept that refers to the shape of a distribution curve, whether it is symmetric around its mean or not. If it is not symmetric it is called skewed. A distribution can be positively skewed (i.e. the bulk of the data are toward the lower end of the scale so the tail is in a positive direction) or negatively skewed (i.e. the bulk of the data are toward the upper end of the scale so the tail is in a negative direction).

Spearman's rank order correlation A non-parametric version of Pearson's product-moment correlation. It tests for the possibility of a relationship between two interval-scale variables.

Sphericity An assumption for ANCOVA analyses. Sphericity refers to compound symmetry in the variance–covariance matrix, and measures whether the differences between the variances of an individual participant's data are equal.

SPSS Viewer The window that contains SPSS output, including graphs, tables and statistical tests.

SSCP matrix A matrix that contains the sum of squares for a variable on the diagonal and the cross-products between pairs of variables in the off-diagonal places. We used the SSCP in an ANCOVA analysis to numerically examine the assumption of sphericity. If sphericity holds, all of the numbers on the diagonal will be of similar magnitude, as will all of the numbers off the diagonal.

Standard deviation (usually abbreviated as *s*, s.d. or SD) A measure of how tightly or how loosely data are clustered around the mean. The variance is equal to the standard deviation squared.

Standard error of the mean (SEM) The standard deviation of the sampling distribution of the mean. The SEM is an estimate of the variability in the mean that you would get if you repeated the same experiment several times over and looked at the distribution of the mean. Thus, smaller SEMs are much to be preferred over larger ones!

Standard multiple regression A type of regression technique where only the areas of unique overlap of the explanatory with the response variable are counted. In other words, there is no order effect for the order in which variables are entered.

Statistic A number that is reported from a statistical test and is associated with a mathematical symbol such as χ^2, r, t or F. This number results from calculations mostly involving the mean and standard deviation of the variables involved.

Statistical regression See **Stepwise regression.**

Statistical result (statistically significant result) When the outcome of a statistical test is such that the null hypothesis can be rejected, this is commonly known as a "statistically significant result." Kline (2004) recommended that we return the word "significant" to its common meaning of "important" and instead call such a result a "statistical" one.

Stem and leaf plots A graphic that divides up the data like a histogram but uses the actual data itself as the way of binning the data (the last number of the score is tallied as a count).

Stepwise regression A type of multiple regression where the explanatory variables (also known as independent variables) are entered into the equation in steps. The model counts all areas of overlap of the explanatory variable with the response variable (the dependent variable) so that the order in which variables are entered into the model can often make a difference as to whether they will be found to be statistical predictors. This type of regression, however, leaves the decision of which variables to enter first up to the computer, and for that reason is not recommended. See **Statistical regression.**

String variable SPSS labels any variable that contains letters as a string variable. A string variable is counted as a categorical variable and can participate in a statistical test as one.

Sum of squares The number obtained from the procedure of subtracting each point from the average of all the points and then squaring the number, summing over all the points treated this way, and taking the square root of the entire sum. This procedure minimizes the distance from a line to any number of points.

Symmetric distribution One in which both halves of the curve around the midpoint are mirror images of one another.

Syntax Editor In SPSS, this is a window where commands will run based on written input instead of using the menu system; we used this when we wanted to obtain post-hoc tests for the interaction of two variables in ANOVAs. It could also be useful (faster than the menu system) if you wanted to replicate the same procedure a number of times. From SPSS version 16.0, the syntax for each procedure you do is printed to the output window.

t-distribution A probability distribution that is used to calculate the probability of two mean scores being statistically different from one another.

Test statistic A statistic for which we know the frequency with which different values occur. This statistic is used to test the null hypothesis. For parametric tests, the statistics we have seen in this book are F for ANOVA, r for Pearson's correlation and t for t-tests. For non-parametric tests we have seen χ^2, U, w and Z.

Three-dimensional (3-D) graph This type of graphic can be rotated in space to show three dimensions of the data, thus allowing for better understanding of complex relationships among several continuous variables.

Total sum of squares (SST) The sum of squares for all participants in a study, no matter what group they belong to. This gives a measure of the variance from a mean score for all groups taken together. In SPSS, this number is found in the "Total" line of the ANOVA table.

Transform data (transformation) A mathematical procedure performed on the distribution of a variable to try to make it more normally distributed using functions such as the square root or a logarithmic function.

Tree models Graphics which show relationships and divisions among variables with different branches where certain factors have more influence on the outcome of the response variable. Tree models are useful for thinking about what factors to include in a regression.

t-test A parametric test that is used when you have one independent variable with only two levels and one dependent variable. You want to know if the two groups are different from each other.

Two-tailed test Use this test when you want to know the probability that the sample statistic could be as extreme as or larger than both the positive and the negative value of the statistic. In other words, it adds together the probabilities that a statistic that extreme would be found on both the left and the right tail of the distribution.

Two-way ANOVA A parametric test that has exactly two independent variables and one dependent variable. This is also called a factorial ANOVA.

Type I error Occurs when the real situation is that there are no differences between groups (or no relationship between variables) but the researcher mistakenly concludes that there are differences (or a relationship). This has been called an error of being "overeager."

Type II error Occurs when the real situation is that there are differences between groups (or relationships between variables) but the researcher mistakenly concludes that there are no differences (or no relationships). This has been called an error of being "overly cautious."

Variable A collection of data that all belong to the same sort, such as a test score, a participant ID or an experimental group label.

Variable view One of the tabs in the Data Editor of SPSS. This is where you see the data arranged with rows representing the variables. Columns let you define things like how many decimals to display and what numbers for a categorical variable refer to.

Variance The variance is a measure of the amount of variability around a mean. Formally, it is the average squared distance from the mean to any point. The variance is the square of the standard deviation.

Vector A vector is basically a column of data if you think of the data set up in a spreadsheet.

Wilcoxon rank-sum test A non-parametric test alternative to the independent samples t-test that is used when you have one independent variable with two levels and one dependent variable. It is functionally the same as the Mann–Whitney U test.

Wilcoxon signed-ranks test A non-parametric test alternative to the paired samples t-test that is used when you have two mean scores that are related, by being either from the same group at different times or from the same group taking two different tests.

Within-groups variable A variable that is repeated among the participants. If your participants have taken more than one set of scores, they have essentially repeated scores. This type of data must be treated with a repeated-measures ANOVA *unless* you have only two mean scores, in which case you use a paired samples t-test.

z-score A standardized expression of a variable's values. The z-score expresses how many standard deviations each score is away from the mean. This new distribution has a mean of 0 and a standard deviation of 1.

Bibliography

Abdi, H. (2010). The Greenhouse–Geisser correction. In N. J. Salkind (Ed.), *Encyclopedia of research design* (pp. 544–548). Thousand Oaks, CA: Sage.

Abrahamsson, N. (2012). Age of onset and nativelike L2 ultimate attainment of morphosyntactic and phonetic intuition. *Studies in Second Language Acquisition*, *34*(2), 187–214.

Abrahamsson, N., & Hyltenstam, K. (2009). Age of onset and nativelikeness in a second language: Listener perception versus linguistic scrutiny. *Language Learning*, *59*(2), 249–306.

Adamson, G., & Bunting, B. (2005). Some statistical and graphical strategies for exploring the effect of interventions in health research. In J. M. P. Gilbert (Ed.), *A handbook of research methods for clinical and health psychology* (pp. 279–294). New York: Oxford University Press.

Adler, J. (2010). *R in a nutshell*. Sebastopol, CA: O'Reilly.

Albirini, A., & Benmamoun, E. (2014). Concatenative and nonconcatenative plural formation in L1, L2, and heritage speakers of Arabic. *The Modern Language Journal*, 98(3), 854–871.

Algina, J., Keselman, H. J., & Penfield, R. D. (2005). An alternative to Cohen's standardized mean difference effect size: A robust parameter and confidence interval in the two independent groups case. *Psychological Methods*, *10*(3), 317–328.

Allison, P. D. (2002). *Missing data*. Thousand Oaks, CA: Sage Publications.

American College of Physicians (2001). Primer on statistical significance and *p* values. *Effective Clinical Practice*, 4(4), 183–184.

American Psychological Association (2009). *Publication manual of the American Psychological Association* (6th ed.). Washington, DC: American Psychological Association.

Anscombe, F. J. (1973). Graphs in statistical analysis. *The American Statistician*, *27*(1), 17–21.

Aragon, T. J. (2012). epitools: Epidemiology Tools. R package version 0.5-7 [Software]. Retrieved from http://CRAN.R-project.org/package=epitools

Ayoun, D. (2014). The acquisition of future temporality by L2 French learners. *Journal of French Language Studies*, *24*(2), 181–202.

Ayoun, D., & Salaberry, M. R. (2008). Acquisition of English tense aspect morphology by advanced French instructed learners. *Language Learning*, *58*(3), 555–595.

Baayen, R. H. (2008). *Analyzing linguistic data: A practical introduction to statistics using R*. Cambridge: Cambridge University Press.

Baayen, R. H., Davidson, D. J., & Bates, D. M. (2008). Mixed-effects modeling with crossed random effects for subjects and items. *Journal of Memory and Language*, *59*(4), 390–412.

Bakeman, R. (2005). Recommended effect size statistics for repeated measures designs. *Behavior Research Methods*, *37*(3), 379–384.

Baker, W., & Trofimovich, P. (2006). Perceptual paths to accurate production of L2 vowels: The role of individual differences. *International Review of Applied Linguistics in Language Teaching (IRAL)*, *44*(3), 231–250.

Baron, J., & Li, Y. (2003). *Notes on the use of R for psychology experiments and questionnaires* Retrieved from www.psych.upenn.edu/~baron/rpsych/rpsych.html

Bates, D., Mächler, M., Bolker, B. M., & Walker, S. C. (2014). Fitting linear mixed-effects models using lme4. *Journal of Statistical Software*. Retrieved from http://arxiv.org/pdf/1406.5823v1.pdf

Beattie, G., Webster, K., & Ross, J. (2010). The fixation and processing of the iconic gestures that accompany talk. *Journal of Language and Social Psychology, 29*(2), 194–213.

Benjamini, Y., & Hochberg, Y. (1995). Controlling the false discovery rate: A practical and powerful approach to multiple testing. *Journal of the Royal Statistical Society, Series B, 57*(1), 289–300.

Berko Gleason, J. (1958). The child's learning of English morphology. *Word, 14*, 150–177.

Bialystok, E., Craik, F. I., Klein, R., & Viswanathan, M. (2004). Bilingualism, aging, and cognitive control: Evidence from the Simon task. *Psychology and Aging, 19*(2), 290–303.

Bitchener, J., Young, S., & Cameron, D. (2005). The effect of different types of corrective feedback on ESL student writing. *Journal of Second Language Writing, 14*(3), 191–205.

Blackwelder, W. (1982). "Proving the null hypothesis" in clinical trials. *Controlled Clinical Trials, 3*(4), 345–353.

Bliese, P. (2013). Multilevel modeling in R (2.5): A brief introduction to R, the multilevel package and the nmle package [Software]. Retrieved from http://cran.r-project.org/doc/contrib/Bliese_Multilevel.pdf

Boers, F., Eyckmans, J., Kappel, J., Stengers, H., & Demecheleer, M. (2006). Formulaic sequences and perceived oral proficiency: Putting a lexical approach to the test. *Language Teaching Research, 10*(3), 245–261.

Brace, N., Kemp, R., & Snelgar, R. (2003). *SPSS for psychologists: A guide to data analysis using SPSS for Windows*. Mahwah, NJ: Lawrence Erlbaum Associates.

Breaugh, J. A. (2003). Effect size estimation: Factors to consider and mistakes to avoid. *Journal of Management, 29*(1), 79–97.

Byrnes, H. (2013). Notes from the editor. *The Modern Language Journal, 97*(4), 825–827.

Canty, A. J. (2002). Resampling methods in R: The boot package. *R News, 2/3*, 2–7. Retrieved from www.r-project.org/doc/Rnews/Rnews_2002-3.pdf

Canty, A., Davison, A. C., & Hinkley, D. V. (2015). boot: Bootstrap Functions [Software]. Retrieved from http://cran.r-project.org/web/packages/boot/

Carpenter, J., & Bithell, J. (2000). Bootstrap confidence intervals: when, which, what? A practical guide for medical statisticians. *Statistics in Medicine, 19*(9), 1141–1164.

Carver, R. P. (1978). The case against statistical significance testing. *Harvard Educational Review, 48*(3), 378–399.

Chapelle, C. A., & Duff, P. A. (2003). Some guidelines for conducting quantitative and qualitative research in TESOL. *TESOL Quarterly, 37*(1), 157–178.

Chatfield, C. (1985). The initial examination of data. *Journal of the Royal Statistical Society, Series A, 148*(3), 214–253.

Cherciov, M. (2013). Investigating the impact of attitude on first language attrition and second language acquisition from a Dynamic Systems Theory perspective. *International Journal of Bilingualism, 17*(6), 716–733.

Chernick, M. R. (2007). *Bootstrap methods: A guide for practitioners and researchers*. Hoboken: John Wiley & Sons.

Chrabaszcz, A., & Gor, K. (2014). Context effects in the processing of phonolexical ambiguity in L2. *Language Learning, 64*(3), 415–455.

Clark, M. (2014a). ANCOVA (Class notes). Retrieved from www.unt.edu/rss/class/mike/6810/ANCOVA.pdf

Clark, M. (2014b). Equivalence Testing (PowerPoint slides). Retrieved from www.unt.edu/rss/class/mike/5700/Equivalence%20testing.ppt

Clark-Carter, D. (2005). The importance of considering effect size and statistical power in research. In J. Miles & P. Gilbert (Eds.), *A handbook of research methods for clinical and health psychology* (pp. 185–192). New York: Oxford University Press.

Clay, R. (2009). Set your data free: Efforts to share research materials gain ground within psychology. *Monitor on Psychology, 40*(5), 28.

Cohen, J. (1962). The statistical power of abnormal-social psychological research: a review. *Journal of Abnormal and Social Psychology, 65*(3), 145–153.

Cohen, J. (1988). *Statistical power analysis for the behavioral sciences*. Hillsdale, NJ: L. Erlbaum Associates.

Cohen, J. (1992). A power primer. *Psychological Bulletin, 112*(1), 155–159.

Cohen, J., Cohen, P., West, S. G., & Aiken, L. S. (2003). *Applied multiple regression/correlation analysis for the behavioral sciences*. New York, NY: Routledge.

Cole, R. D. (1927). Free composition vs. translation into the foreign language in developing ability to write a foreign language. *The Modern Language Journal, 11*(4), 200–206.

Crawley, M. J. (2002). *Statistical computing: An introduction to data analysis using S-PLUS*. New York: Wiley.

Crawley, M. J. (2005). *Statistics: An introduction using R*. Chichester, West Sussex, England: J. Wiley.

Crawley, M. J. (2007). *The R book*. Hoboken, NJ: Wiley.

Crawley, M. J. (2012). *The R book* (2nd ed.). Hoboken, NJ: Wiley.

Cumming, G. (2008). Replication and *p* intervals: *p* values predict the future only vaguely, but confidence intervals do much better. *Perspectives on Psychological Science*, *3*(4), 286–300.

Cumming, G. (2012). *Understanding the new statistics: effect sizes, confidence intervals, and meta-analysis*. New York: Routledge.

Cumming, G., & Finch, S. (2005). Inference by eye: confidence intervals and how to read pictures of data. *American Psychologist*, *60*(2), 170–180.

Cunnings, I. (2012). An overview of mixed-effects statistical models for second language researchers. *Second Language Research*, *28*(3), 369–382.

Cunnings, I., & Finlayson, I. (2015). Mixed effects modeling and longitudinal data analysis. In L. Plonsky (Ed.), *Advancing quantitative methods in second language research*. New York, NY: Routledge.

Cuza, A., & Frank, J. (2015). On the role of experience and age-related effects: Evidence from the Spanish CP. *Second Language Research*, *31*(1), 3–28.

Dahl, T. I., & Ludvigsen, S. (2014). How I see what you're saying: The role of gestures in native and foreign language listening comprehension. *The Modern Language Journal*, *98*(3), 813–833.

Dahlen, K., & Caldwell-Harris, C. (2013). Rehearsal and aptitude in foreign vocabulary learning. *The Modern Language Journal*, *97*(4), 902–916.

Dalgaard, P. (2002). *Introductory statistics with R*. New York: Springer.

Davison, A. C., & Kuonen, D. (2003). An introduction to the bootstrap with applications in R. *Statistical Computing & Statistical Graphic Newsletter*, *13*(1), 6–11. Retrieved from www.statoo.com/en/publications/bootstrap_scgn_v131.pdf

De Rosario-Martinez, H. (2015). phia: Post-Hoc Interaction Analysis. Retrieved from http://CRAN.R-project.org/package=phia

DeKeyser, R. M. (2000). The robustness of critical period effects in second language acquisition. *Studies in Second Language Acquisition*, *22*(4), 499–533.

DeKeyser, R., & Larson-Hall, J. (2005). What does the critical period really mean? . In J. F. Kroll & A. M. B. de Groot (Eds.), *Handbook of bilingualism: Psycholinguistic approaches* (pp. 88–108). New York, NY: Oxford University Press.

Dethorne, L., Johnson, B., & Loeb, J. (2005). A closer look at MLU: what does it really measure? *Clinical Linguistics and Phonetics*, *19*(8), 635–648.

DeVellis, R. F. (2005). Inter-rater reliability. In K. Kempf-Leonard (Ed.), *Encyclopedia of social measurement* (pp. 317–322). San Diego, CA: Academic.

Dewaele, J.-M. (2004a). Blistering barnacles! What language do multilinguals swear in?! *Sociolinguistic Studies*, *5*(1), 83–105.

Dewaele, J.-M. (2004b). The emotional force of swearwords and taboo words in the speech of multilinguals. *Journal of Multilingual and Multicultural Development*, *25*(2/3), 204–222.

Dewaele, J.-M. (2004c). Perceived language dominance and language preference for emotional speech: The implications for attrition research. In M. S. Schmid, B. Köpke, M. Keijzer, & L. Weilemar (Eds.), *First language attrition: Interdisciplinary perspectives on methodological issues* (pp. 81–104). Amsterdam/Philadelphia: John Benjamins.

Dewaele, J.-M. (2013). The link between foreign language classroom anxiety and psychoticism, extraversion, and neuroticism among adult bi- and multilinguals. *Modern Language Journal*, *97*(3), 670–684.

Dewaele, J.-M., & Pavlenko, A. (2001–2003). Webquestionnaire: Bilingualism and Emotions. Retrieved from www.academia.edu/2134800/Web_questionnaire_bilingualism_and_emotions

Dewey, D. P. (2004). A comparison of reading development by learners of Japanese in intensive domestic immersion and study abroad contexts. *Studies in Second Language Acquisition*, *26*, 303–327.

Dixon, J. J. (2012). *Timelines for English language acquisition: A study of the rates of second language acquisition among Hispanic English language learners including exceptionalities* (Doctoral dissertation) Available from ProQuest Dissertations & Theses database. (UMI No. 3492862)

Dromey, C., Silveira, J., & Sandor, P. (2005). Recognition of affective prosody by speakers of English as a first or foreign language. *Speech Communication*, *47*(3), 351–359.

Efron, B., & Tibshirani, R. J. (1993). *An introduction to the bootstrap*. New York, NY: Chapman & Hall.

Ellis, R. (2000). Editor's statement. *Language Learning*, *50*(3), xi–xiii.

Ellis, R., Heimbach, R., Tanaka, Y., & Yamazaki, A. (1999). Modified input and the acquisition of word meanings by children and adults. In R. Ellis (Ed.), *Learning a second language through interaction* (pp. 63–113). Amsterdam; Philadelphia: John Benjamins Publishing Company.

Ellis, R., Loewen, S., & Erlam, R. (2006). Implicit and explicit corrective feedback and the acquisition of L2 grammar. *Studies in Second Language Acquisition*, *28*(2), 339–368.

Ellis, R., & Yuan, F. (2004). The effects of planning on fluency, complexity, and accuracy in second language narrative writing. *Studies in Second Language Acquisition*, *26*(1), 59–84.

Erceg-Hurn, D. M., & Mirosevich, V. M. (2008). Modern robust statistical methods: An easy way to maximize the accuracy and power of your research. *American Psychologist*, *63*(7), 591–601.

Erdener, V. D., & Burnham, D. K. (2005). The role of audiovisual speech and orthographic information in non-native speech production. *Language Learning*, *55*(2), 191–228.

Everitt, B., & Dunn, G. (2001). *Applied multivariate data analysis* (2nd ed.). New York: Oxford University Press.

Eysenck, M. W. (1974). Age differences in incidental learning. *Developmental Psychology*, *10*(6), 936–941.

Faul, F., Erdfelder, E., Lang, A. G., & Buchner, A. (2007). G*Power 3: A flexible statistical power analysis program for the social, behavioral, and biomedical sciences. *Behavior Research Methods*, *39*(2), 175–191.

Faulkner, C., Fidler, F., & Cumming, G. (2008). The value of RCT evidence depends on the quality of statistical analysis. *Behavior Research and Therapy*, *46*(2), 270–281.

Field, A. P. (2005). *Discovering statistics using SPSS* (2nd ed.). London: Sage.

Field, A., Miles, J., & Field, Z. (2012). *Discovering statistics using R*. London: Sage.

Filzmoser, P., & Gschwandtner, M. (2015). mvoutlier: Multivariate outlier detection based on robust methods. R package version 2.0.6 [Software]. Retrieved from http://CRAN.R-project.org/package=mvoutlier

Flege, J. E., Schirru, C., & MacKay, I. R. A. (2003). Interaction between the native and second language phonetic subsystems. *Speech Communication*, *40*(4), 467–491.

Flege, J. E., Yeni-Komshian, G., & Liu, S. (1999). Age constraints on second-language acquisition. *Journal of Memory and Language*, *41*(1), 78–104.

Fordyce, K. (2014). The differential effects of explicit and implicit instruction on EFL learners' use of epistemic stance. *Applied Linguistics*, *35*(1), 6–28.

Foster, P., Bolibaugh, C., & Kotula, A. (2014). Knowledge of nativelike selections in a L2. *Studies in Second Language Acquisition*, *36*(1), 101–132.

Fox, J. (1997). *Applied regression analysis, linear models, and related models*. Thousand Oaks, CA: Sage Publications.

Fox, J. (2002a). Linear mixed models. Appendix to An R and S-PLUS companion to applied regression. Retrieved from http://cran.r-project.org/doc/contrib/Fox-Companion/appendix-mixed-models.pdf

Fox, J. (2002b). *An R and S-PLUS companion to applied regression*. Thousand Oaks, CA: Sage Publications.

Fox, J. (2003). Effect displays in R for generalised linear models. *Journal of Statistical Software*, 8(15), 1–27. Retrieved from www.jstatsoft.org/v08/i15/

Fox, J. (2005). The R Commander: A basic statistics graphical interface to R. *Journal of Statistical Software*, *14*(9), 1–42. Retrieved from www.jstatsoft.org/v14/i09/paper

Fox, J., Friendly, M., & Monette, G. (2014). heplots: Visualizing hypothesis tests in multivariate linear models. R package version 1.0-12 [Software]. Retrieved from http://CRAN.R-project.org/package=heplots

French, L. M., & O'Brien, I. (2008). Phonological memory and children's second language grammar learning. *Applied Psycholinguistics*, *29*(3), 463–487.

Friendly, M. (2010). HE plots for repeated measures designs. *Journal of Statistical Software*, *37*(4), 1–40.

Galwey, N. W. (2006). *Introduction to mixed modelling: Beyond regression and analysis of variance*. Chichester: Wiley.

Geeslin, K. L., & Guijarro-Fuentes, P. (2006). Second language acquisition of variable structure in Spanish by Portuguese speakers. *Language Learning*, *56*(1), 53–107.

Gelman, A., & Hill, J. (2007). *Data analysis using regression and multilevel/hierarchical models*. New York: Cambridge University Press.

Gerlanc, D., & Kirby, K. (2013). bootES: Bootstrap effect sizes. R package version 1.01 [Software]. Retrieved from http://CRAN.R-project.org/package=bootES

Gigerenzer, G., & Murray, D. J. (1987). *Cognition as intuitive statistics*. Hillsdale, NJ: Erlbaum Associates.

Glass, G. V. (1976). Primary, secondary, and meta-analysis of research. *Educational Researcher*, *5*(10), 3–8.

Granena, G. (2012). *Age differences and cognitive aptitudes for implicit and explicit learning in ultimate second language attainment* (Doctoral dissertation). University of Maryland, College Park, College Park, MD. Available from ProQuest Dissertations & Theses database. (UMI No. 3517774)

Grissom, R. J., & Kim, J. J. (2005). *Effect sizes for research: A broad practical approach*. Mahwah, NJ: Lawrence Erlbaum Associates.

Grömping, U. (2006). Relative importance for linear regression in R: The package relaimpo. *Journal of Statistical Software*, *17*(1), 1–27. Retrieved from www.jstatsoft.org/v17/i01/paper

Gross, J., & Ligges, U. (2015). nortest: Tests for Normality. R package version 1.0-3 [Software]. Retrieved from http://CRAN.R-project.org/package=nortest

Gurzynski-Weiss, L., & Baralt, M. (2014). Exploring learner perception and use of task-based interactional feedback in FTF and CMC modes. *Studies in Second Language Acquisition*, *36*(1), 1–37.

Harlow, L. L., Mulaik, S. A., & Steiger, J. H. (1997). *What if there were no significance tests?* Mahwah, NJ: Lawrence Erlbaum Associates.

Harrell, F. E. J., & Dupont, C. (2014). Hmisc: Harrell Miscellaneous. R package version 3.14-5 [Software]. Retrieved from http://CRAN.R-project.org/package=Hmisc

Hatch, E., & Lazaraton, A. (1991). *The research manual: Design and statistics for applied linguistics*. New York, NY: Newbury House Publishers.

Hedges, L. V. (1981). Distributional theory for Glass's estimator of effect size and related estimators. *Journal of Educational Statistics*, *6*(2), 107–128.

Heiberger, R. M. (2015). HH: Statistical analysis and data display: Heiberger and Holland. R package version 3.1-5. [Software]. Retrieved from http://CRAN.R-project.org/package=HH

Heiberger, R. M., & Holland, B. (2004). *Statistical analysis and data display: An intermediate course with examples in S-PLUS, R, and SAS*. New York: Springer.

Herrington, R. (2001). An introduction to robust measures of location using GNU S-PLUS. Retrieved from www.unt.edu/benchmarks/archives/2001/july01/rss.htm

Herrington, R. (2002). Controlling the false discovery rate in multiple hypothesis testing. Retrieved from www.unt.edu/benchmarks/archives/2002/april02/rss.htm

Hirata, Y. (2004). Computer assisted pronunciation training for native English speakers learning Japanese pitch and durational contrasts. *Computer Assisted Language Learning*, *17*(3–4), 357–376.

Hoenig, J. M., & Heisey, D. M. (2001). The abuse of power: The pervasive fallacy of power calculations for data analysis. *The American Statistician*, *55*(1), 19–24.

Honaker, J., King, G., & Blackwell, M. (2011). Amelia II: A Program for Missing Data. *Journal of Statistical Software*, *45*(7), 1–47.

Hothorn, T. (2014). Additional multcomp examples. Retrieved from https://dssm.unipa.it/CRAN/web/packages/multcomp/vignettes/multcomp-examples.pdf (August 18, 2004 version).

Hothorn, T., Bretz, F., & Westfall, P. (2008). Simultaneous inference in general parametric models. *Biometrical Journal (Biometrische Zeitschrift)*, *50*(3), 346–363.

Howell, D. C. (2002). *Statistical methods for psychology* (5th ed.). Pacific Grove, CA: Duxbury/Thomson Learning.

Howell, D. C. (2007). *Statistical methods for psychology* (6th ed.). Belmont, CA: Thomson Wadsworth.

Howell, D. C. (2010). *Statistical methods for psychology* (7th ed.). Belmont, CA: Thomson Wadsworth.

Howell, D. C. (2012). Treatment of missing data: Part 1. Retrieved from www.uvm.edu/~dhowell/StatPages/More_Stuff/Missing_Data/Missing.html

Huang, B. H. (2014). The effect of age on second language grammar and speech production. *Journal of Psycholinguistic Research*, *43*(4), 397–420.

Huber, P. J. (1981). *Robust statistics*. New York: Wiley.

Huberty, C. J. (2002). A history of effect size indices. *Educational and Psychological Measurement*, *62*(2), 227–240.

Huynh, H. (1978). Some approximate tests for repeated measurement designs. *Psychometrika*, *43*(2), 161–175.

Inagaki, S., & Long, M. (1999). Implicit negative feedback. In K. Kanno (Ed.), *The acquisition of Japanese as a second language* (pp. 9–30). Amsterdam; Philadelphia: John Benjamins Publishers.

Insightful Corporation (2002). S-PLUS 6 Robust Library—User's Guide Version 1.0. Retrieved from https://r-forge.r-project.org/scm/viewvc.php/*checkout*/pkg/robust/Robust.pdf?root=robust

Jensen, E. D., &Vinther, T. (2003). Exact repetition as input enhancement in second language acquisition. *Language Learning*, *53*(3), 373–428.

Jiang, N., Novokshanova, E., Masuda, K., & Wang, X. (2011). Morphological congruency and the acquisition of L2 morphemes. *Language Learning*, *61*(3), 940–967.

Johnson, J. S., & Newport, E. L. (1989). Critical period effects in second language learning: the influence of maturational state on the acquisition of English as a second language. *Cognitive Psychology*, *21*(1), 60–99.

Juffs, A. (2005). The influence of first language on the processing of wh-movement in English as a second language. *Second Language Research*, *21*(2), 121–151.

Jurečková, J., & Picek, J. (2006). *Robust statistical methods with R*. Boca Raton, FL: Chapman & Hall/CRC.

Kabacoff, R. (2011). *R in action: Data analysis and graphics with R*. Shelter Island, NY: Manning.

Kang, S.-Y. (2012). *Individual differences in language acquisition: Personality traits and language learning strategies of Korean university students studying English as a foreign language*. (Doctoral dissertation). Available from ProQuest Dissertations & Theses database. (UMI No. 3507501)

Kim, J. (2013). *Developing conceptual understanding of sarcasm in a second language through concept-based instruction.* (Unpublished doctoral dissertation), Pennsylvania State University, State College, PA.

Kirby, K. N., & Gerlanc, D. (2013). BootES: An R package for bootstrap confidence intervals on effect sizes. *Behavior Research Methods, 45*(4), 905–927.

Kirk, R. E. (2003). The importance of effect magnitude. In S. F. Davis (Ed.), *Handbook of research methods in experimental psychology* (pp. 83–105). Malden, MA: Blackwell Publishing.

Kline, R. B. (2004). *Beyond significance testing: Reforming data analysis methods in behavioral research.* Washington, DC: American Psychological Association.

Kondo-Brown, K. (2006). How do English L1 learners of advanced Japanese infer unknown "Kanji" words in authentic texts? *Language Learning, 56*(1), 109–153.

Konis, K. (2007). Questions about interpreting lmRob output. Retrieved from https://stat.ethz.ch/pipermail/r-sig-robust/2007/000170.html

LaFlair, G. T., Egbert, J., & Plonsky, L. (forthcoming). A practical guide to bootstrapping descriptive statistics, correlations, *t* tests, and ANOVAs. In L. Plonsky (Ed.), *Advancing quantitative methods in second language research.* New York: Routledge.

Lafrance, A., & Gottardo, A. (2005). A longitudinal study of phonological processing skills and reading in bilingual children. *Applied Psycholinguistics, 26*(4), 559–578.

Landau, S., & Everitt, B. (2004). *Handbook of statistical analysis using SPSS.* Boca Raton, FL: Chapman & Hall/CRC.

Langsrud, Ø. (2003). ANOVA for unbalanced data: Use type II instead of type III sums of squares. *Statistics and Computing, 13*(2), 163–167.

Larkin, J. H., & Simon, H. A. (1987). Why a diagram is (sometimes) worth ten thousand words. *Cognitive Science, 11*(1), 65–100.

Larson-Hall, J. (2004). Predicting perceptual success with segments: A test of Japanese speakers of Russian. *Second Language Research, 20*(1), 33–76.

Larson-Hall, J. (2006). What does more time buy you? Another look at the effects of long-term residence on production accuracy of English /r/ and /l/ by Japanese speakers. *Language and Speech, 49*(4), 521–548.

Larson-Hall, J. (2008). Weighing the benefits of studying a foreign language at a younger starting age in a minimal input situation. *Second Language Research, 24*(1), 35–63.

Larson-Hall, J. (2013). *Why seeing visually equals thinking statistically. Language Learning Rountable.* Paper presented at the Improving Quantitative Reasoning in L2 Res, Georgetown University.

Larson-Hall, J. (in preparation). *Graphics and data accountability in L2 acquisition research.*

Larson-Hall, J., & Connell, S. (2005). *Evidence for a critical period: Remnants from forgotten languages.* Paper presented at the Second Language Research Forum, Teachers College, Columbia University, New York.

Larson-Hall, J., & Herrington, R. (2009). Improving data analysis in second language acquisition by utilizing modern developments in applied statistics. *Applied Linguistics, 31*(3), 368–390.

Larson-Hall, J., & Plonsky, L. (2015). Reporting and interpreting quantitative research findings: What gets reported and recommendations for the field. *Language Learning, 65*(suppl.1), 127–159.

Lawrence, M. A. (2013). ez: Easy analysis and visualization of factorial experiments. R package version 4.2-2 [Software]. Retrieved from http://CRAN.R-project.org/package=ez

Lee, J. H., & Macaro, E. (2013). Investigating age in the use of L1 or English-only instruction: Vocabulary acquisition by Korean EFL learners. *The Modern Language Journal, 97*(4), 887–901.

Leow, R. P. (1997). Attention, awareness and foreign language behavior. *Language Learning, 47*(3), 467–506.

Leow, R. P., & Morgan-Short, K. (2004). To think aloud or not to think aloud: The issue of reactivity in SLA research methodology. *Studies in Second Language Acquisition, 26*(1), 35–57.

Letts, C., Edwards, S., Sinka, I., Schaefer, B., & Gibbons, W. (2013). Socio-economic status and language acquisition: Children's performance on the new Reynell Developmental Language Scales. *International Journal of Language & Communication Disorders, 48*(2), 131–143.

Little, R. J. A., & Rubin, D. B. (1987). *Statistical analysis with missing data.* New York: Wiley.

Little, T. M. (1981). Interpretation and presentation of results. *HortScience, 16*(5), 637–640.

lqs Help (2015, April 17). Resistant regression. Retrieved from https://stat.ethz.ch/R-manual/R-devel/library/MASS/html/lqs.html

Lyster, R. (2004). Differential effects of prompts and recasts in form-focused instruction. *Studies in Second Language Acquisition, 26*(3), 399–432.

Macaro, E., & Masterman, L. (2006). Does intensive explicit grammar instruction make all the difference? *Language Teaching Research, 10*(3), 297–327.

Mackey, A. (2006). Feedback, noticing and instructed second language learning. *Applied Linguistics, 27*(3), 405–430.

Mackey, A., & Gass, S. (2005). *Second language research: Methodology and design*. Mahwah, NJ: Lawrence Erlbaum.

Mackey, A., & Silver, R. E. (2005). Interactional tasks and English L2 learning by immigrant children in Singapore. *System, 33*(2), 239–260.

Manly, B. F. J. (1997). *Randomization, bootstrap and Monte Carlo methods in biology*. London: Chapman and Hall.

Maronna, R. A., Martin, R. D., & Yohai, V. J. (2006). *Robust statistics: Theory and methods*. Chichester, England: J. Wiley.

Maxwell, S. E. (2004). The persistence of underpowered studies in psychological research: Causes, consequences, and remedies. *Psychological Methods*, 9(2), 147–163.

Maxwell, S. E., & Delaney, H. D. (2004). *Designing experiments and analyzing data: A model comparison perspective* (2nd ed.). Mahwah, NJ: Lawrence Erlbaum Associates.

Maxwell, S. E., Kelley, K., & Rausch, J. R. (2008). Sample-size planning for statistical power and accuracy in parameter estimation. *Annual Review of Psychology*, 59, 537–563.

McDonald, J. L. (2000). Grammaticality judgments in a second language: Influences of age of acquisition and native language. *Applied Psycholinguistics, 21*(3), 395–423.

McGuire, M. (2009). *Formulaic sequences in English conversation: Improving spoken fluency in non-native speakers*. (Master's dissertation). Available from ProQuest Dissertations & Theses database. (UMI No. 327681)

McKnight, P. E., McKnight, K. M., Sidani, S., & Figueredo, A. J. (2007). *Missing data: A gentle introduction*. New York: Guildford Press.

Medina, S. L. (1991). *The effect of a musical medium on the vocabulary acquisition of limited English speakers*. (Doctoral dissertation). Available from ProQuest Dissertations & Theses database. (UMI No. DP25424)

Meehl, P. E. (1978). Theoretical risks and tabular asterisks: Sir Karl, Sir Ronald, and the slow progress of soft psychology. *Journal of Consulting and Clinical Psychology*, 46(4), 806–834.

Meyer, D., Zeileis, A., & Hornik, K. (2006). The Strucplot Framework: Visualizing multi-way contingency tables with vcd. *Journal of Statistical Software, 17*(3), 1–48. Retrieved from www.jstatsoft.org/v17/i03/

Meyer, D., Zeileis, A., & Hornik, K. (2015). Package 'vcd' [Software]. Retrieved from http://cran.r-project.org/web/packages/vcd/vcd.pdf

Miles, J., & Shevlin, M. (2001). *Applying regression and correlation: A guide for students and researchers*. London: Sage Publications.

Mizuno, N. (1998). *The impact of study abroad experience on American college students who studied in Japan* (Doctoral dissertation). Available from ProQuest Dissertations & Theses database. (UMI No. 9902846)

Morris, S. B., & DeShon, R. P. (2002). Combining effect size estimates in meta-analysis with repeated measures and independent-groups designs. *Psychological Methods, 7*(1), 105–125.

Moyer, A. (1999). Ultimate attainment in L2 phonology: The critical factors of age, motivation, and instruction. *Studies in Second Language Acquisition, 21*(1), 81–108.

Mu, G. M. (2014). Heritage language learning for Chinese Australians: The role of habitus. *Journal of Multilingual and Multicultural Development, 35*(5), 497–510.

Muenchen, R. A. (2008). *R for SAS and SPSS users*. New York: Springer.

Muñoz, C., & Llanes, A. (2014). Study abroad and changes in degree of foreign accent in children and adults. *The Modern Language Journal*, 98(1), 432–449.

Munro, M. J., & Derwing, T. M. (2006). The functional load principle in ESL pronunciation instruction: An exploratory study. *System, 34*, 520–531.

Munro, M. J., Derwing, T. M., & Morton, S. L. (2006). The mutual intelligibility of L2 speech. *Studies in Second Language Acquisition*, 28(1), 111–131.

Murphy, K. R., & Myors, B. (2004). *Statistical power analysis* (2nd ed.). Mahwah, NJ: Lawrence Erlbaum Associates.

Murphy, V. A. (2004). Dissociable systems in second language inflectional morphology. *Studies in Second Language Acquisition*, 26(3), 433–459.

Murrell, P. (2006). *R Graphics*. Boca Raton, FL: Chapman & Hall/CRC.

Nelder, J. A. (1985). Discussion of Dr Chatfield's paper. *Journal of the Royal Statistical Society, Series A, 148*(Part 3), 238.

Nelder, J. A. (1994). The statistics of linear models: Back to basics. *Statistics and Computing*, 4(4), 221–234.

Nelder, J. A., & Lane, P. W. (1995). The computer analysis of factorial experiments: In memoriam—Frank Yates. *The American Statistician*, 49(4), 382–385.

Obarow, S. E. H. (2004). *The impact of music on the vocabulary acquisition of kindergarten and first grade students*. (Ed. Dissertation). Available from ProQuest Dissertations & Theses database. (UMI No. 3120733)

Olejnik, S., & Algina, J. (2000). Measures of effect size for comparative studies: Application, interpretations, and limitations. *Contemporary Educational Psychology*, 25(3), 241–286.

Oswald, F. L., & Plonsky, L. (2010). Meta-analysis in second language research: Choices and challenges. *Annual Review of Applied Linguistics*, *30*, 85–110.

Oyama, S. (1976). A sensitive period for the acquisition of a nonnative phonological system. *Journal of Psycholinguistic Research*, *5*(3), 261–283.

Paavola, L., Kunnari, S., & Moilanen, I. (2005). Maternal responsiveness and infant intentional communication: Implications for the early communicative and linguistic development. *Child: Care, Health and Development*, *31*(6), 727–735.

Pandey, A. (2000). TOEFL to the test: Are monodialectal AAL-speakers similar to ESL students? *World Englishes*, *19*(1), 89–106.

Patkowski, M. S. (1980). The sensitive period for the acquisition of syntax in a second language. *Language Learning*, *30*(2), 449–468.

Pearson, B. Z., Fernandez, S. C., Lewedeg, V., & Oller, D. K. (1997). The relation of input factors to lexical learning by bilingual infants. *Applied Psycholinguistics*, *18*(1), 41–58.

Peters, E., Hulstijn, J. H., Sercu, L., & Lutjeharms, M. (2009). Learning L2 German vocabulary through reading: The effect of three enhancement techniques compared. *Language Learning*, *59*(1), 113–151.

Pierce, C. A., Block, R. A., & Aguinis, H. (2004). Cautionary note on reporting eta-squared values from multifactor ANOVA designs. *Educational and Psychological Measurement*, *64*(6), 916–924.

Pinheiro, J., Bates, D., DebRoy, S., Sarkar, D., et al. (2015). nlme: Linear and nonlinear mixed effects models. R package version 3.1-120 [Software]. Retrieved from http://CRAN.R-project.org/package=nlme

Pinheiro, J. C., & Bates, D. M. (2000). *Mixed-effects models in S and S-PLUS*. New York: Springer.

Pison, G., Van Aelst, S., & Willems, G. (2002). Small sample correlations for LTS and MCD. *Metrika*, *55*(1–2), 111–123.

Plakans, L., & Gebril, A. (2013). Using multiple texts in an integrated writing assessment: Source text use as a predictor of score. *Journal of Second Language Writing*, *22*(3), 217–230.

Plomin, R. (1999). Genetics and general cognitive ability. *Nature*, *402*(6761 Suppl), C25–C29.

Plonsky, L. (2013). Study quality in SLA: an assessment of designs, analyses, and reporting practices in quantitative L2 research. *Studies in Second Language Acquisition*, *35*(4), 655–687.

Plonsky, L., Egbert, J., & Laflair, G. T. (2014). Bootstrapping in applied linguistics: Assessing its potential using shared data. *Applied Linguistics*. doi: 10.1093/applin/amu001.

Plonsky, L., & Oswald, F. L. (2014). How big is "big"? Interpreting effect sizes in L2 research. *Language Learning*, *64*(4), 878–912.

Poehner, M. E., & Lantolf, J. P. (2013). Bringing the ZPD into the equation: Capturing L2 development during computerized dynamic assessment (C-DA). *Language Teaching Research*, *17*(3), 323–342.

Pohlert, T. (2015). PMCMR: Calculate Pairwise Multiple Comparisons of Mean Rank Sums [Software]. Retrieved from http://cran.r-project.org/web/packages/PMCMR/index.html

Polio, C., Fleck, C., & Leder, N. (1998). "If I only had more time:" ESL learners' changes in linguistic accuracy on essay revisions. *Journal of Second Language Writing*, *7*(1), 43–68.

Polio, C., & Gass, S. (1997). Replication and reporting: A commentary. *Studies in Second Language Acquisition*, *19*(4), 499–508.

Porte, G. K. (2002). *Appraising research in second language learning: A practical approach to critical analysis of quantitative research*. Philadelphia, PA: John Benjamins.

Porte, G. K. (2010). *Appraising research in second language learning: A practical approach to critical analysis of quantitative research* (2nd ed.). Philadelphia, PA: John Benjamins.

Porte, G. K. (2012). *Replication research in applied linguistics*. Cambridge: Cambridge University Press.

Preece, D. A. (1984). Biometry in the third world: science not ritual. *Biometrics*, *40*(2), 519–523.

Proctor, C. P., August, D., Carlo, M. S., & Snow, C. (2006). The intriguing role of Spanish language vocabulary knowledge in predicting English reading comprehension. *Journal of Educational Psychology*, 98(1), 159–169.

Quené, H., & van den Bergh, H. (2004). On multi-level modeling of data from repeated measures designs: A tutorial. *Speech Communication*, *43*(1–2), 103–121.

Quené, H., & van den Bergh, H. (2008). Examples of mixed-effects modeling with crossed random effects and with binomial data. *Journal of Memory and Language*, *59*(4), 413–425.

Raaijmakers, J. G. W., Schrijnemakers, J. M. C., & Gremmen, F. (1999). How to deal with "The language-as-fixed-effect fallacy": Common misconceptions and alternative solutions. *Journal of Memory and Language*, *41*(3), 416–426.

R Core Team (2013). R: A language and environment for statistical computing: Reference index. Retrieved from http://web.mit.edu/r_v3.0.1/fullrefman.pdf

Reali, F. (2014). Frequency affects object relative clause processing: Some evidence in favor of usage-based accounts. *Language Learning*, *64*(3), 685–714.

Revelle, W. (2005). Using R for psychological research: A simple guide to an elegant language. Retrieved from http://personality-project.org/r/r.guide.html

Revelle, W. (2015). psych: Procedures for psychological, psychometric, and personality research [Software]. Retrieved from http://cran.r-project.org/web/packages/psych/index.html

Ricci, V. (2005). Fitting distributions with R (release 0.4-21). Retrieved from http://cran.r-project.org/doc/contrib/Ricci-distributions-en.pdf

Rietveld, T., & van Hout, R. (2005). *Statistics in language research: Analysis of variance*. New York: Mouton de Gruyter.

Ripley, B. (2015). tree: Classification and regression trees [Software]. Retrieved from http://CRAN.R-project.org/package=tree

Rizopoulos, D. (2009). bootStepAIC: Bootstrap stepAIC. R package version 1.2-0 [Software]. Retrieved from http://CRAN.R-project.org/package=bootStepAIC

Robb, T., Ross, S., & Shortreed, I. (1986). Salience of feedback on error and its effect on EFL writing quality. *TESOL Quarterly*, *20*(1), 83–95.

Robinson, P. (2005). Cognitive abilities, chunk-strength, and frequency effects in implicit artificial grammar and incidental L2 learning: Replications of Reber, Walkenfeld, and Hernstadt (1991) and Knowlton and Squire (1996) and their relevance for SLA. *Studies in Second Language Acquisition*, *27*(2), 235–268.

Rodgers, D. M. (2011). The automatization of verbal morphology in instructed second language acquisition. *International Review of Applied Linguistics in Language Teaching (IRAL)*, *49*(4), 295–319.

Rosa, E., & O'Neill, M. D. (1999). Explicitness, intake, and the issue of awareness. *Studies in Second Language Acquisition*, *21*(4), 511–556.

Rosenthal, R. (1994). Parametric measures of effect size. In H. Cooper & L. V. Hedges (Eds.), *The handbook of research synthesis* (pp. 231–244). New York: Russell Sage Foundation.

Rosenthal, R., & DiMatteo, M. R. (2001). Meta-analysis: Recent developments in quantitative methods for literature reviews. *Annual Review of Psychology*, *52*(1), 59-82.

Rosnow, R. L., & Rosenthal, R. (1989). Statistical procedures and the justification of knowledge in psychological science. *American Psychologist*, *44*(10), 1276–1284.

Rousseeuw, P. J., & Leroy, A. M. (1987). *Robust regression and outlier detection*. New York: Wiley.

Russell, J., & Spada, N. (2006). The effectiveness of corrective feedback for the acquisition of L2 grammar: A meta-analysis of the research. In J. M. Norris & L. Ortega (Eds.), *Synthesizing research on language learning and teaching* (pp. 133–164). Amsterdam; Philadelphia, PA: John Benjamins Publishing Company.

Salsburg, D. S. (1985). The religion of statistics as practiced in medical journals. *The American Statistician*, *39*(3), 220–223.

Sanz, C., & Leow, R. P. (2011). *Implicit and explicit language learning: Conditions, processes, and knowledge in SLA and bilingualism*. Washington, DC: Georgetown University Press.

Sanz, C., & Morgan-Short, K. (2004). Positive evidence versus explicit rule presentation and explicit negative feedback: A computer-assisted study *Language Learning*, *54*(1), 35–78.

Sarkar, D. (2008). *Lattice: multivariate data visualization with R*. New York: Springer.

Sasaki, M. (2004). A multiple-data analysis of the 3.5-year development of EFL student writers. *Language Learning*, *54*(3), 525–582.

Savage, I. R. (1957). Nonparametric statistics. *Journal of the American Statistical Association*, *52*(279), 331–344.

Schauer, G. A. (2006). Pragmatic awareness in ESL and EFL contexts: Contrast and development. *Language Learning*, *56*(2), 269–318.

Schmid, M. S., Gilbers, S., & Nota, A. (2014). Ultimate attainment in late second language acquisition: Phonetic and grammatical challenges in advanced Dutch–English bilingualism. *Second Language Research*, *30*(2), 129–157.

Schön, D., Boyer, M., Moreno, S., Besson, M., Peretz, I., & Kolinsky, R. (2008). Songs as an aid for language acquisition. *Cognition*, *106*(2), 975–983.

Sedlmeier, P., & Gigerenzer, G. (1989). Do studies of statistical power have an effect on the power of studies? *Psychological Bulletin*, *105*(2), 309–316.

Shadish, W. R., Cook, T. D., & Campbell, D. T. (2002). *Experimental and quasi-experimental designs for generalized causal inference*. Boston, MA: Houghton Mifflin.

Sheskin, D. J. (2004). *Handbook of parametric and nonparametric statistical procedures* (3rd ed.). Boca Raton, FL: Chapman & Hall.

Smith, B. L., McGregor, K. K., & Demille, D. (2006). Phonological development in lexically precocious 2-year-olds. *Applied Psycholinguistics, 27*(3), 355–375.
Snow, G. (2013). TeachingDemos: Demonstrations for teaching and learning. R package version 2.9 [Software]. Retrieved from http://CRAN.R-project.org/package=TeachingDemos
Starkweather, J. (2010). Linear mixed effects modeling using R. Retrieved from www.unt.edu/rss/class/Jon/Benchmarks/LinearMixedModels_JDS_Dec2010.pdf
Staudte, R. G., & Sheather, S. J. (1990). *Robust estimation and testing*. New York: Wiley.
Stevens, J. P. (2002). *Applied multivariate statistics for the social sciences*. Mahwah, NJ: Lawrence Erlbaum Associates.
Streiner, D. L. (2003). Unicorns do exist: A tutorial on "proving" the null hypothesis. *Canadian Journal of Psychiatry, 48*(11), 756–761.
Tabachnick, B. G., & Fidell, L. S. (2001). *Using multivariate statistics* (4th ed.). Boston, MA: Allyn & Bacon.
Taguchi, N. (2007). Chunk learning and the development of spoken discourse in a Japanese as a foreign language classroom. *Language Teaching Research, 11*(4), 433–457.
Takimoto, M. (2006). The effects of explicit feedback on the development of pragmatic proficiency. *Language Teaching Research, 10*(4), 393–417.
Toth, P. D. (2006). Processing instruction and a role for output in second language acquisition. *Language Learning, 56*(2), 319–385.
Toth, P. D. (2008). Teacher- and learner-led discourse in task-based grammar instruction: Providing procedural assistance for L2 morphosyntactic development. *Language Learning, 58*(2), 237–283.
Trofimovich, P., & Baker, W. (2006). Learning second language suprasegmentals: Effect of L2 experience on prosody and fluency characteristics of L2 speech. *Studies in Second Language Acquisition, 28*(1), 1–30.
Tryon, W. W. (1998). The inscrutable null hypothesis. *American Psychologist, 53*(7), 796.
Tryon, W. W. (2001). Evaluating statistical difference, equivalence, and indeterminacy using inferential confidence intervals: An integrated alternative method of conducting null hypothesis statistical tests. *Psychological Methods, 6*(4), 371–386.
Tufte, E. R. (2003). *The cognitive style of PowerPoint: Pitching out corrupts within*. Cheshire, CT: Graphics Press.
Tukey, J. W. (1962). The future of data analysis. *The Annals of Mathematical Statistics, 33*(1), 1–67.
Tukey, J. W. (1975, 3–5 November). *Useable resistant/robust techniques of analysis*. Paper presented at the Proceedings of the First ERDA Symposium Los Alamos, New Mexico.
Tversky, A., & Kahneman, D. (1971). Belief in the law of small numbers. *Psychological Bulletin, 76*(2), 105–110.
van Buuren, S., & Groothuis-Oudshoorn, K. (2011). mice: Multivariate imputation by chained equations in R. *Journal of Statistical Software, 45*(3), 1–67.
van Compernolle, R. A. (2012). *Developing sociopragmatic capacity in a second language through concept-based instruction* (Doctoral dissertation). Pennsylvania State University, State College, PA. Available from ProQuest Dissertations & Theses database. (UMI No. 3674265)
Venables, W. N., & Ripley, B. D. (2002). *Modern applied statistics with S*. New York: Springer.
Venables, W. N., Smith, D. M., & R Development Core Team (2005). *An Introduction to R. Notes on R: A Programming Environment for Data Analysis and Graphics* Retrieved from www.american.edu/cas/hpc/upload/R_intro.pdf
Verzani, J. (2004). *Using R for introductory statistics*. Boca Raton, FL: Chapman & Hall/CRC.
Volker, M. A. (2006). Reporting effect size estimates in school psychology research. *Psychology in the Schools, 43*(6), 653–672.
Wang, Y. -J., Shang, H. -F., & Briody, P. (2013). Exploring the impact of using automated writing evaluation in English as a foreign language university students' writing. *Computer Assisted Language Learning, 26*(3).
Wartenburger, I., Heekeren, H. R., Abutalebi, J., Cappa, S. F., Villringer, A., & Perani, D. (2003). Early setting of grammatical processing in the bilingual brain. *Neuron, 37*(1), 159–170.
Wasserman, S., & Bockenholt, U. (1989). Bootstrapping: Applications to psychophysiology. *Psychophysiology, 26*(2), 208–221.
Weinberg, S. L., & Abramowitz, S. K. (2002). *Data analysis for the behavioral sciences using SPSS*. New York: Cambridge University Press.
Westfall, P. H., & Young, S. S. (1993). *Resampling-based multiple testing: Examples and methods for p-value adjustment*. New York: Wiley.
Wharton, G. (2000). Language learning strategy use of bilingual foreign language learners in Singapore. *Language Learning, 50*(2), 203–243.
White, L., Spada, N., Lightbown, P. M., & Ranta, L. (1991). Input enhancement and L2 question formation. *Applied Linguistics, 12*(4), 416–432.

Wickham, H. (2007). Reshaping data with the reshape package. *Journal of Statistical Software, 21*(12), 1–20. Retrieved from www.jstatsoft.org/v21/i12/paper

Wickham, H. (2009). *ggplot2: Elegant graphics for data analysis*. New York: Springer.

Wickham, H. (2011). The split-apply-combine strategy for data analysis. *Journal of Statistical Software, 40*(1), 1–29. Retrieved from www.jstatsoft.org/v40/i01/paper

Wilcox, R. R. (1992). Why can methods for comparing means have relatively low power, and what can you do to correct the problem? *Current Directions in Psychological Science, 1*(3), 101–105.

Wilcox, R. R. (1995). ANOVA: A paradigm for lower power and misleading measures of effect size? *Review of Educational Research, 65*(1), 51–77.

Wilcox, R. R. (1998). How many discoveries have been lost by ignoring modern statistical methods? *American Psychologist, 53*(3), 300–314.

Wilcox, R. R. (2001). *Fundamentals of modern statistical methods: Substantially improving power and accuracy*. New York: Springer.

Wilcox, R. R. (2003). *Applying contemporary statistical techniques*. San Diego, CA: Academic Press.

Wilcox, R. R. (2005). *Introduction to robust estimation and hypothesis testing*. Boston, MA: Elsevier/Academic Press.

Wilcox, R. R. (2012a). *Introduction to robust estimation and hypothesis testing* (3rd ed.). Boston, MA: Academic Press.

Wilcox, R. R. (2012b). *Modern statistics for the social and behavioral sciences: A practical introduction*. New York: CRC Press.

Wilcox, R. R., & Keselman, H. J. (2012). Modern regression methods that can substantially increase power and provide a more accurate understanding of associations. *European Journal of Personality, 26*(3), 165–174.

Wilcox, R. R., & Schönbrodt, F. D. (2014). The WRS package for robust statistics in R (version 0.24) [Software]. Retrieved from http://r-forge.r-project.org/projects/wrs/

Wilkinson, L. (1999). Statistical methods in psychological journals: Guidelines and explanations. *American Psychologist, 54*(8), 594–604.

Williams, J. N. (2005). Learning without awareness. *Studies in Second Language Acquisition, 27*(2), 269–304.

Winter, B. (2013). Linear models and linear mixed effects models in R with linguistic applications. Retrieved from http://arxiv.org/pdf/1308.5499.pdf

Wuertz, D., & R Metrics Core Team (2014). fBasics: Rmetrics—Markets and basic statistics. R package version 3011.87 [Software]. Retrieved from http://CRAN.R-project.org/package=fBasics

Xiao, Y., & Wong, K. F. (2014). Exploring heritage language anxiety: A study of Chinese heritage language learners. *The Modern Language Journal, 98*(2), 589–611.

Xu, Y., Chang, L.-Y., & Perfetti, C. A. (2014). The effect of radical-based grouping in character learning in Chinese as a foreign language. *The Modern Language Journal, 98*(3), 773–793.

Yates, K. (2003). *Teaching linguistic mimicry to improve second language pronunciation* (Master's dissertation). Available from ProQuest Dissertations & Theses database. (UMI No. 1415258)

Young, M. A. (1993). Supplementing tests of statistical significance: Variation accounted for. *Journal of Speech and Hearing Research, 36*(4), 644–656.

Zareva, A. (2005). Models of lexical knowledge assessment of second language learners of English at higher levels of language proficiency. *System, 33*(4), 547–562.

Author index

R commands

Subject index